Kenneth Turan and Joseph Papp

FREE FOR ALL

Kenneth Turan has been a film critic for the *Los Angeles Times* since 1991 and the director of the Los Angeles Times Book Prizes since 1993. He teaches nonfiction writing and film criticism at the University of Southern California and provides regular reviews for *Morning Edition* on National Public Radio.

Joseph Papp (1921–1991) was an American theatrical producer and director. Papp founded the New York Shakespeare Festival in 1954 with the aim of making Shakespeare's works accessible to the public.

FREE FOR ALL

FREE
FOR ALL

*Joe Papp, The Public,
and the Greatest
Theater Story Ever Told*

Kenneth Turan
and Joseph Papp

with the assistance of Gail Merrifield Papp

Anchor Books A Division of Random House, Inc.   New York

FIRST ANCHOR BOOKS EDITION, NOVEMBER 2010

Copyright © 2009 by The Estate of Joseph Papp and The New York Shakespeare Festival

All rights reserved. Published in the United States by Anchor Books,
a division of Random House, Inc., New York, and in Canada by
Random House of Canada Limited, Toronto. Originally published in hardcover in the
United States by Doubleday, a division of Random House, Inc., New York, in 2009.

Anchor Books and colophon are registered trademarks of Random House, Inc.

The Library of Congress has cataloged the Doubleday edition as follows:
Turan, Kenneth.
Free for all : Joe Papp, the public, and the greatest theater story ever told /
Kenneth Turan and Joseph Papp.—1st ed.
p. cm.
1. Papp, Joseph. 2. Theatrical producers and directors—United
States—Biography. 3. Joseph Papp Public Theater (New York, N.Y.)
4. Papp, Joseph—Friends and associates—Interviews. 5. Actors—
United States—Interviews. I. Papp, Joseph. II. Title.
PN2287.P23T87 2009
792.02'32092—dc22
[B] 2008050887

Anchor ISBN: 978-0-7679-3169-4

Author photograph © Patricia Williams
Title page photograph © Ken Reagan/Camera 5
Book design by Maria Carella

www.anchorbooks.com

Printed in the United States of America
10 9

To the three who believed—Gail, Kathy, B—

and to Joe,

olev ha'shalom, *who made it all happen.*

Contents

Contents

FREE for ALL

Introduction

More than twenty-three years ago, I signed a contract with producer Joseph Papp to work on a definitive oral history of the New York Shakespeare Festival/Public Theater, the most significant not-for-profit theater group in the country. Over the course of the next eighteen months, I interviewed more than one hundred and sixty people and turned nearly ten thousand pages of transcript into a roughly eleven-hundred-page manuscript. I considered it then, and still consider it today, the most significant and compelling work I've done in more than forty years of journalism. The story of why something with so much to recommend it would take so many years to appear is in some ways as dramatic and surprising as the book itself.

I came to this project because Joe Papp, in search of a collaborator, came to my agent, Kathy Robbins. Though theater was not my main passion, Kathy thought of me because, despite decades of difference in age, Joe and I shared a common background as first-generation Americans, both raised in Brooklyn by Yiddish-speaking immigrant parents.

Also, I had a feeling for collaboration and voice: in the years before and since, I've worked on books involving Patty Duke, Carol Matthau, Kareem Abdul-Jabbar, Sid Caesar, and Ava Gardner. More than that, as a journalist I knew that Joe's story was among the most significant of contemporary cultural narratives, a critical piece of American theatrical history, and I wanted to be part of telling it.

In his years with the Shakespeare Festival and the parallel Public Theater, Joe had made theater in America both accessible and essential. He'd produced landmark plays like *Hair, A Chorus Line, That Championship Season, The Normal Heart,* and *Short Eyes,* plays that people had to pay attention to because they transcended their moment in time.

Papp had been essential in starting the careers of actors like George C. Scott, Meryl Streep, Raul Julia, Kevin Kline, James Earl Jones, and Martin Sheen. He'd had towering disputes with everyone, from New York City's all-powerful bureaucrat Robert Moses to the very playwrights and actors he hired, but almost everyone ended up doing their best work for him. When he died the *New York Times*, noting the more than 350 plays he'd brought to the stage, called him "one of the most influential producers in the history of the American theater." He was larger than life just by being himself.

A story like this, filled with alive, articulate not to mention theatrical people, turned out to be especially suited to the oral-history format. There is a vividness and immediacy about direct speech, a sense of life about individuals speaking for themselves, that makes oral history the most intrinsically dramatic of narrative mediums. The people interviewed were, almost without exception, wonderful talkers and tellers of tales.

The weaving together of these various strands created a kaleidoscopic tapestry of memory that made a virtue of what sounds like a potential liability: every participant has their own story, their own truth, and everyone remembers the same situation in slightly different ways. But this *Rashômon* effect also means that when you put all these stories together, minor discrepancies fade and the joined voices provide a sense of the texture of reality, of what actually happened, which nothing else can. In a similar fashion, even though the severity of the illnesses that killed them prevented me from talking to Michael Bennett (*A Chorus Line*) and Miguel Piñero (*Short Eyes*), conversations with friends and collaborators brought them to life in a very real way.

Though New York is the center of the Shakespeare Festival's universe—the place, for instance, where Joe's right hand, Bernard Gersten, patiently led me through the twists and turns of his almost lifelong connection with the man—interviewing for the book led me across the country.

I have strong memories of listening to Tommy Lee Jones calmly dissecting what went wrong with *True West* while he meticulously brushed down a horse at his remote California ranch. I remember taking the train to Connecticut to spend long hours with David Rabe, and still appreciate the time and care he took to be thorough and thoughtful about his enormously complicated dealings with Joe, a relationship that was the most significant and intensely emotional of any the festival produced. And I am unlikely to forget flying to Scranton to interview Jason Miller, who took me straight from the airport to a raucous social club that seemed right out of *That Championship Season*. When I tentatively commented on the resemblance he grinned, shot me a look from his dark, intense eyes, and said, "Are you kidding? This *is* the play!"

Wherever they were, these people knew what a good story was and how to put it across. To hear Colleen Dewhurst talk about acting with George C. Scott for the first time; to hear Scott himself describe the *Richard III* that made his career (and tops my list of productions I wish I'd seen); to listen to Roscoe Lee Browne tell how Leontyne Price helped advise him about a career in acting; to discover that Bob Fosse, of all people, had been a shipmate and collaborator of Joe's during World War II; to hear how *The Pirates of Penzance* came together and how that benighted *True West* fell apart—this is to be present at the creation of theatrical history.

And then there was Joe himself, who both disliked taking time to talk about the past when he could be working on some future project and recognized his obligation to do so. The veteran, as he well knew, of innumerable battles and clashes of will ("If I were estranged from all the people I had arguments with," he told playwright Lawrence Kornfeld, "I'd have nobody to talk to"), he was reticent about nothing he'd been through, no matter how upsetting the memory, once he sat down to talk.

The only exception to that were stories about the difficult poverty of his childhood, which, along with the youthful radicalism it led to, was critical in informing the decisions he made, the kind of institution he was determined to build. After a Saturday-afternoon session in his Greenwich Village apartment talking about that painful period, Joe walked me to the door, looked at me, and said quietly, "I'm never talking about that again." He didn't just mean to me, he meant to anyone.

Working with Joe on a project of this scope, talking to all the people he'd written notes to asking for collaboration, was enormously exciting, but from time to time I also feared that, as had happened with others he'd worked closely with, a rift would develop between us. And once he read the manuscript, that is what happened, with a vengeance. Disturbed and troubled, Joe refused to allow the book to be published.

Even at this remove, I don't feel completely sure about how the factors involved in that decision combined in Joe's mind. In part, he was upset by some of the things the people he'd fallen out with said about him, but the reality is that what I'd handed in was an overlong and likely repetitive first draft, and with the usual tightening and fine-tuning that go into the editing process, much of that material would as a matter of course have not made it into the final draft.

Equally important, at least as I see it, was a horrible accident of bad timing. At roughly the same time as the manuscript was handed in, Joe discovered that his son Tony had contracted AIDS and that he himself had been diagnosed with the prostate cancer that was to kill him three years later.

Always mercurial in nature, Joe could not have been further from the measured state of mind that would have allowed for the kind of back and forth that many books go through before they are published. It must have seemed simpler and cleaner to him to simply say no, to cut his losses and move on.

Needless to say, this was devastating, not only because of the work put into the project but also because of how important I felt it was to tell this story and tell it in this form. The blow was so severe that I had difficulty talking about what transpired for weeks, months, even years after it happened. Though I was of course angry, I found that my anger was never directed at Joe. He was simply being the person I had discovered him to be during my research and interviews, and in my heart I could not fault him for that.

Finally, perhaps a dozen years after the fact, I sat down on the porch of a house on Vashon Island, Washington, and wrote a letter to Gail Merrifield Papp, Joe's widow and collaborator, and a woman whose clear vision and integrity I had always admired and respected. This project, I said, was too important to die. Was there not some way we could bring it back to life?

Gail thought perhaps there was, and what followed was a series of meetings that took place over years (my day job as film critic for the *Los*

Angeles Times was too consuming to allow for things to move faster), during which we discussed the manuscript and its future. More than any other factor, it was Gail's belief that brought the project back to life. I was so encouraged that, in a guesthouse on Kauai, I took a deep breath and reread what I'd written from front to back, something that had been too painful to do for all those years. The thoughts I had then led to more discussions with Gail and, finally, in 2006, to a month spent at the MacDowell Colony in New Hampshire where a new draft of the book was put together.

The isolation and total immersion of the MacDowell experience, the way the self-imposed seclusion encourages you to go deeper than you thought possible into your own work, was critical to getting a new perspective on the manuscript, to seeing it in several ways I hadn't before. I was in effect a new reader experiencing the book for the first time, trying to figure out what it was that all these people had been trying to tell me.

Reading *Free for All* so closely also felt, frankly, like entering King Tut's tomb, like being exposed to treasures of memory long hidden from sight, and that sense of the integrity of the past solidified my conviction that to add new interviews to what I'd already done would be ruinous. In a sense this book is a historical document, a snapshot of people's thoughts at a given moment in time, and splicing in a facile updating, inserting new ideas from a radically different era, felt fatally anachronistic.

With the difference in perspective that the passage of time and perhaps even an increased maturity provided, I felt more strongly what should have been obvious from the start: the most dramatic aspect of Joe's story is not whom he locked horns with but what he accomplished. All of his battles, all the clashes of will and temperament are here in their full glory—how could they not be, given his life—but what he achieved against truly impossible odds dwarfs everything else. While Joe was alive, there was a sense from the doubters that if he hadn't done what he did, someone else likely would have. Today, with no one since his death having come anywhere near his level of accomplishment, it's clearer than ever how singular his life's work has been.

My other change of perspective about *Free for All* is both more personal and more universal. Sitting in my tiny MacDowell cabin in the New Hampshire woods, I increasingly felt not the sense of personal aggrievement about this book that had been part of my life for too long but rather the weight of history, the powerful responsibility I had to the people who had talked to me at such length. All alone in the woods, I sometimes found myself literally in tears at the thought of the people, Joe first among them, who had been painfully honest about the most significant events of their lives and counted on me to relay their last testament to the world.

More than forty of the voices in this book—roughly one out of every four—have died in the two decades since I did the interviewing. No one else will be hearing their stories from their lips, and to read this book is to reenter as if by magic a moment in history ripe for rediscovery and amazement.

Backstory
1921-42

Joseph Papp at age fourteen
Courtesy of the New York Public Library

PHILLIP MARTEL   Joe was Peck's bad boy; from the start he was never around the house. He was always running, always in trouble with the school authorities about attendance and this and that. He was a leader, always full of vibrant ideas. You could see from the beginning there was something there, something special. "Let's go here, let's go there, let's form a club, let's try a trick on this guy." He was always in the forefront, and whoever was around him listened to him. Our sister was the one who was worried about keeping something on the table; I don't think the stuff of geniuses feeds on worrying about mundane things like bread and butter and milk. He was like a rebel with a cause, a lot of causes.

RHODA LIFSCHUTZ   Joe was always out doing something. He was never around. He was very restless. I knew he was reaching for something that was different. I just felt it. He needed challenges all the time. It was hard to know, really, what went on in his mind. Nobody knew what he really felt. He'd run off somewhere, it would get late, and I used to go crazy, running and looking for him, and never telling my mother because I didn't want her to worry. He was different. I worried all the time that something was going to happen to him, because he had the type of personality that wouldn't take any nonsense. I felt he would get into trouble. But we should all get into the same kind of trouble he got into.

Our mother, Yetta Miritch, came from Lithuania; our father, Shmuel Papirofsky, from Kielce, Poland. His father was a famous teacher, known in the town as Moshe Melamed. Except for one of my father's brothers, who lived in Israel, the whole family was gassed by the Nazis. My mother came to New York by boat when she was eleven, alone, an orphan, and a frightened child. She never talked about her past. She met my father in a park with rides in Brooklyn called Goldberg's Farm. Most of the marriages in those days were all arranged, people didn't even know each other. This was the real thing.

My mother was beautifully dressed, always conscious of her clothes. She was always cleaning—she'd clean instead of thinking of having something to eat. It was more important to keep the house clean. She was so immersed in problems, she wasn't that demonstrative. Maybe because she was an orphan and hadn't been given that, she couldn't give it herself. My father was much more emotional, and Joe was very close with him. My father always had an accent and he spoke Yiddish most of the time. My mother spoke beautiful English. You'd never know she wasn't born here.

JOSEPH PAPP My ancestral roots are in Eastern Europe, and I'm very conscious of that, conscious that I'm in the tradition of the Holocaust. I was born at home, in the Williamsburg section of Brooklyn, in 1921. Williamsburg was not what it is now, with a large Hasidic community. Our area was a mix of a lot of different ethnic groups, Italians in particular, and Jews were isolated there. You always felt that you were slightly embattled. You didn't have the emotional support and protection of other Jews in great numbers around you. I came from a certain kind of poverty level, which was really below that of most of New York's Jews. I've always felt that distinction, I've always felt slightly removed from, for instance, the world of Broadway and the Shuberts. I can talk to them, I'll walk with them, but, as Shylock would say, I won't eat with them.

My mother was a beautiful woman, very gracious with a great deal of her own kind of style. She was very poor, but she always had a kind of aristocracy about her. She was a determined woman, and her energy was amazing. My rhythm is like hers was, very rapid. I remember her going up and down five flights of stairs like a whiz with these grocery bags that weighed a ton, sometimes two. She played the role of a Jewish wife, which meant she took care of everything, made everything ready for the house and for the holidays. It was a very traditional relationship in that respect. Her hands, particularly in the bitter winters, would start to bleed because of the cold. They were extremely rough, but to me they felt as tender as the softest hands you can imagine, because they were a mother's hands.

My mother was not a typical Jewish mother; she didn't fit into that category. I didn't know what a Jewish mother was, except what I learned later on. She had a certain aloofness and a certain kind of elegance and pride. She was very conscious of her clothes; she was always impeccably clean, everything was starched and ironed and had to be beautiful, because when you're in poverty, you try and dress very well.

My mother spoke very, very little. Her main communication was nonverbal, but I would do anything to make her happy because she had kind of a sad look in her eye. She was always setting goals for me, even though they were not clearly expressed.

In the tenements where we lived, people would dry clothes on a rope hooked up to a pulley attached to a telephone pole. Once, I must have been about eleven, we moved into a fifth-floor apartment and the rope was worn out and had to be replaced. My mother said, "Well, how are we going to do this?" And I said I would take care of it.

I had to first climb that pole, which must have been fifty or sixty feet in the air and looked awfully precarious. After I got up to the top—and it looked like a thousand miles down—I had to attach some hardware, climb down, and then climb up again to make sure the rope was aligned correctly. She smiled at me when I did it, and I felt I was her knight in shining armor. If she wanted me to, I'd do anything for her.

In a funny way, my mother represents the unfulfilled aspect of myself: you keep striving because you never feel you've really accomplished something; you never feel that it's over. That has its advantages, it creates a drive, but it has the disadvantage that you'll never be satisfied. She was an enigma, and I identified very much with her. She was an orphan, and I in some way hooked into her sense of isolation, her feeling disconnected from the world. I feel alienated wherever I go; it's natural for me to feel that way.

My father was just the opposite. He gave me a strong connection because he was solidly of this earth. There was no enigma there, he was what he was: open, generous in love and spirit, and religious in the best sense of the word.

When he came here, my father was a trunk maker. He made a kind of trunk that was covered with tin, *blekh* in Yiddish. He worked in this small shop, no bigger than four telephone booths. Even when he was working full-time, which was rare, I don't think he ever made more than $30 a week, and that was considered amazing.

My father was what I would call a very personal, natural Jew. His religiosity is the strongest thing that stays with me today, because it was never ideological. His Jewishness, his relation to God, was as natural to him as eating and drinking. He never tried to push it on anybody, not even on the oldest son.

I would see him get up early in the morning, five or even four thirty sometimes, to daven, to pray. He told me that when he was about to be drafted into the Polish army—and they treated Jews like dogs there—he escaped and traveled through forests so he could get to a ship and come to America. On the way he used to daven in the forest, without any display, just like he did at home.

Most of the time my father would daven in a very poor storefront shul on our block and he would take me with him. It was very rustic and small, unlike some of the grander and much more beautiful synagogues that were several blocks away. Nothing was sentimentalized or cutesy here; these were serious working people who prayed every day. I used to feel very good there, being with my father as he was communicating with God.

If anything at all played a role in what I finally ended up doing—and a lot of it is pure accident—it would be music. Music to me is the source of all art: I don't see how anybody can call himself an artist without appreciating music. We were a singing family; my sisters, my brother, and myself would sit around in the evenings and make music.

In all that poverty, music was so important to my father. My parents bought a beautiful RCA Victor console record player. It cost $150 and it took a hundred years to pay the thing off. We had numbers of Yiddish records, but my father loved American songs as well. One time we found a haul of old 78 records. Someone had thrown them out, I couldn't understand why. They were all scratched up, but there was a great variety, and that's a key to my taste now. The singers we had ranged from the great Russian basso Chaliapin to Caruso to the Irish tenor John McCormack. My father loved it all, no one made a distinction between classical music and popular music, no one told me, "This is good, this is bad."

I began collecting records, a series you could get by mailing in coupons. They weren't made of the kind of flexible material they use now; they were very large, very rigid 78s. We had just played Schubert's "Unfinished" Symphony, I'd put it on a chair, and my father, not realizing what he was doing, sat right on the record and broke it. I was destroyed; just because it was the "Unfinished" Symphony didn't mean he had to finish it off! My father almost cried. I never saw a more grief-stricken look on a man's face. I felt so terrible about that. Finally, years later, I got another copy, but the look on his face, what it meant to him, always stuck in my mind.

When I was about twelve years old, this dapper little guy with a bristling mustache went through my neighborhood scouting for poor Jewish boys he could train to sing in a synagogue choir for the High Holidays. He came up to our apartment on the fifth floor, the family was there, and he said, "Will you sing something for me?" I had a lovely, high, soprano voice, and he seemed to be impressed. He said he'd teach me the songs, but I'd have to come every day after school for three months, and he lived way the hell up in the Bronx. But when he said to my father, "We'll pay him $35," everybody went, "Aaahh."

The shul I sang in was a gorgeous old Portuguese-Jewish synagogue on Ocean Parkway in Brooklyn. My father was poor; he'd never been in such an enormous, elaborate place. There was some dispute about whether to charge him to watch me sing because we didn't have the money for High Holidays tickets; a big fuss was made about that. They finally allowed him in, but he felt very nervous and out of place. I saw him sitting on one side kind of by himself. He was wearing his old prayer shawl, he didn't have any of his friends there, and I felt a little sorry.

PHILLIP MARTEL We had a lot of deprivations, if you look at it now. I remember a lot of times walking around for months with the soles of my shoes flapping. Joe, too. Fruit boxes for furniture. We never had birthday gifts or parties. Pictures? I think I had one picture taken until high school. We never had any kind of luxuries in life, but we were never starving. All our friends were poor, we didn't know any better, so what the heck? You just rolled with it. And I knew our parents were doing the best they could to keep us together and keep us fed.

JOSEPH PAPP You looked forward to certain holidays when you had nuts and special kinds of food. Food was very important to a poor family. Except for Friday night, when my mother would find the best chicken we could afford, it was very rare that we'd have a full meal. We were always hungry, there was always an edge of hunger, though when you're young, unless it's to the point of starvation, you're unconscious of it. We weren't bone poor, but there were times when we felt like there was nothing. One of the effects on me now is when I invite people over, the horn of plenty is a symbol at my table. I always want to have more than less. If you have three people, you get twelve bagels. And there should be plenty of cream cheese and lox.

I remember walking to school when the weather was bad and having to put cardboard in my shoes because the soles were gone. I'd get drenched, my socks were all wet, and one time, the teacher had to send me home. Yet I wasn't intimidated by poverty. And in terms of having it rough financially because I came out of a poor family, I don't think there've been any scars. Poverty with good family support doesn't have to be that destroying. In fact, it could make you stronger.

What I've always experienced more intensely than poverty, more intensely than anything, is anti-Semitism. I always feel it's just below the surface: scratch in some way and a lot of it will come out. I feel, "Don't get too comfortable. You're a Jew and your fortunes can change tomorrow." That makes me fight for things, for any aspect of minority rights, black, Hispanic, and so on. To me, intolerance is a greater threat than poverty.

We moved three or four times while I was growing up, often in the middle of the night because we owed a lot of rent and couldn't pay. Except for the last move, to Brownsville and our first steam heat when I was about fourteen, we stayed in cold-water flats in Williamsburg. They were mostly two-bedroom apartments, heated by a coal stove in the kitchen. We would buy a ton of coal at the beginning of winter and would have to hand-carry it up to the fifth floor, where the cheapest apartments were.

We lived for a while on Boerum Street, where I published a little one-page newspaper called "The Boerum Eavesdropper" or "Boerum Through a Keyhole." I'd seen all these movies starring Lee Tracy as a tough reporter and that was my first love. I cut out the letters P-R-E-S-S from headlines in the *Daily News*, pasted it on some cardboard, stuck it in my father's hat, and went around listening to things. When I had enough material, I'd borrow a typewriter from the guy next door, make copies with carbon paper, and hand them out on the street. I'd write items like, "Who is that shy lad and woman-hater now becoming a ladies' man? Not you, A.B." Sometimes I'd get into trouble, I wrote that Getta, an Italian girl, was on the roof with a Polack, and her father went after me. So I wore my Boy Scout hunting knife under my shirt, and ran an item saying, "Which newspaper editor is going around with a knife strapped around his chest?"

Wherever we lived, I spent most of my time in the street. I used to run away from time to time. When I was younger, I had to be careful where I ran, I couldn't go too far. I once got lost and I was only around the block. My older sister, Rhoda, was the one who used to run after me all the time and try to bring me back. I guess I wondered why my mother didn't bring me back—why was it always my sister? Running away was a risk, but it was exciting. I always wanted to be on my own, there was always a feeling that I wanted to be free of any kind of connection.

There was inevitably violence in the neighborhoods as I was growing up, and at one point I formed a kind of informal gang with three or four of my friends. Because I was always looking for something out of the ordinary, the first name I came up with was the Martyrs, but it ended up being changed to the Mustangs. Once we got into a fight with a group led by this guy called the Crutch. If you came anywhere near him, he would hit you with that thing and knock you down. You just wouldn't dare go up to him.

When I was about fourteen, the family moved to Brownsville because of a specific case of violence. There was an Irish guy named Whitey who lived in our building. He was a psychotic case who ended up in prison later on. The first time he saw me, he just hit me in the face, as hard as he could, and made my mouth bleed. I always remembered what the shock of that was like, what that did to me psychologically. Whitey would try and shake me down all the time because I was Jewish, and because he lived in the same building it was impossible to avoid him. My father couldn't deal with that. I remember him standing by helplessly one time while this guy was hitting me. My parents decided to move because they really felt Whitey would kill me.

. . .

When the Depression came, there was no work for my father—there was no work for anybody. He looked every day, but he could never find anything. During the winters, he would shovel snow for a dollar a day. We could hardly wait for it to begin falling; we'd get so happy because it meant work. To this day, when it begins to snow in New York I think of my father and feel happy.

We had a really tough time for a while, we had no income at all, and then we got on relief. Even though that was little enough, at least food would come into the house, and on certain holidays they'd bring in a big bag of groceries. What I didn't like were the investigators who used to come around all the time and really interrogate you. They wanted to know if my mother had any kind of diamond wedding or engagement ring. My father had a $1,000 life insurance policy that he'd managed to pay into for fifteen or twenty years: he had to cash it in for $150 in order to get on the rolls. You couldn't have anything of value, they wanted you to be absolutely destitute.

When we still couldn't pay the rent, the landlord told us we'd have to take care of the building. So I became the guy who took the garbage out, washed the stairs down, cleaned out the place, and in general did all the chores to compensate for the rent. I was a little kid when this started, but I'd try and make money myself. I did all kinds of jobs to help support the family. One of the first things I did was get hold of a pushcart and go to Wallabout Market and buy tomatoes. And I would push that cart for what seemed like a hundred miles, all the way to downtown Brooklyn, with a little scale and some bags. But I made a basic mistake, I let people squeeze before buying, and by the end of the day I could have made tomato soup out of what was left over.

After that pushcart failure, my father and I decided to sell peanuts in front of the Brooklyn Botanic Garden. We'd buy the nuts by the pound, roast them ourselves, pack them in little bags, and then push the cart five or six miles to get there. But we never made very much money because the cops would always chase us away. In all these ventures, most of the eating was done by the family at the end of the day.

Another job I tried on evenings and Sundays was working in a poultry market as a chicken-flicker. After the shochet, or ritual slaughterer, had slit the chicken's throat with a sharp razor and turned it upside down to let the blood drip out, they'd hand me that dangling chicken and I'd have to take it from there on. I would go to a table at the far end of the market and pluck the feathers off the chicken, a job which would really brutalize your hands. But the worst thing was that you were in chicken shit all the time. My shoes were heavily laden with it; you'd never get rid of the smell. But it was a job, and I was very happy to get it. It meant income for the family.

Almost as challenging was the time I spent shining shoes. Though I made myself a shoe box out of heavy wood I'd picked up off the street, an investment of several dollars was needed to buy various kinds of washes and polish, the white liquid for the "nickel extra" cream shine, and different kinds of rags. The line I used on the street was "Shine, buddy?"

My first day out, no customers. It began to drizzle and I was carrying this box that weighed a ton. Finally a woman in a dress shop said, "Gimme a shine." And she had these dainty little shoes—I'd never really seen anything like that before. I had this little round brush with a handle on it to apply the wash, and though I tried to do it carefully, boy, I got a big black blotch right on her stocking. And she says, "What's the matter with you? Don't you know what you're doing? Get the hell out of here!"

I picked up my box and ran outside. It was really raining now, and there I was, first day on the job, a failure on my first attempt. I felt so terrible I was crying. I went around the corner and I saw this black guy, the kind we used to call a "sport," and he wanted a shine. He had black-and-white shoes—black tip, white in the center—and I was very careful with them. But I was sobbing as I was working, and he asked me, "What's the matter?" I told him the story, and even though it was only a nickel a shine, he gave me a quarter. I was in seventh heaven. It felt so good to feel that money jingling in your pocket. I used to run my fingers through it to feel how good it felt.

Another street job I had was selling newspapers. In the middle of the day, an "Extra" would come out. They'd get a story and suddenly attack the streets, sending guys like me through the neighborhoods saying, "Wuxtree! Wuxtree! Read all about it! Manhattan Model Slain in Love Tryst!" It was a highly competitive job because there were always people who'd say, "What are you doing on this corner? Get the hell off my corner." There were always fights about where I was standing. But I would always sell out my newspapers. I never had extras at the end of the day.

My most interesting job, however, was working as a messenger for Postal Telegraph, Western Union's competition at the time. I wore a little uniform, blue with red piping, and a kind of hat with a black brim. To get the delivery job I had to come up with $12 for a balloon-tire bicycle. That was a big investment, and the whole family had to sit around the kitchen table and decide if it was worthwhile to come up with the money. I had that job for quite a while, and the way it ended was something out of Saroyan. It was Christmas Eve and I was working very late delivering in downtown Brooklyn. There were a lot of trolley-car tracks there, and everything was slightly frozen, glazed with ice and very slippery.

Suddenly, the bicycle's wheels turned out from under me. I went down and felt a tremendous pain in my knee and a cracking sound. I was told to see the company doctor, but a friend of mine advised me to get someone of my own. I went to a doctor who said, "Let me handle it." I couldn't work for a while, and suddenly these checks started coming in, like $5 a week. I thought, "I'm going to get this for a few weeks, and that'll be it." Well, I got the checks for almost a year. I was so nervous, I thought they had made a mistake and that somebody was going to ask me to give the money back. Some arrangement had clearly been made, but no one had told me anything about it. The checks did finally stop coming, but that knee bothered me for years and years and years.

. . .

I wasn't particularly intellectual as a kid, though I went to the library a lot. I loved reading books like Tom Swift and Dickens, as well as all kinds of comics and pulp magazines, anything that had an interesting story. But I didn't go for any kind of school assignments. There didn't seem to be any connection between the library and what I did at school.

Being in school often meant being in trouble. One time I did something wrong and the teacher came over and gave me a shot in the back of the neck with one of those huge rulers that weighed a ton. I grabbed her and her hair came off! She'd been wearing a wig and was as bald as she could be. She was horrified, and I yelled, "Don't you ever hit me again, goddamn it!" The whole class started laughing. As punishment, she locked me in the coat closet. Well, I went through everybody's pockets to see what I could find there. It was a mistake putting me there.

I don't know how it happened, but in the first grade I was selected to play Scrooge in a play version of *A Christmas Carol*. That turned out to be the leading part, the equivalent of Shylock or Richard III. I can still remember all the lines, not only my own but everyone else's. I didn't know from acting, but I learned those lines.

I was always enamored of the word. All language was interesting to me; I didn't know what the hell Gitche Gumee was in *Hiawatha*, but it sounded very good to me. Aside from Scrooge, I can also remember the texts of little poems, mostly about nature, that I memorized. Things like "Who has seen the wind? Neither you nor I. But when the trees bow down their heads, the wind is passing by." I just loved that little couplet. One of my favorite narrative poems was Robert Browning's "Incident of the French Camp." It was about a severely wounded young messenger bringing news to Napoleon. " 'I'm killed, Sire!' and . . . Smiling the boy fell dead." My favorite story was "The Little Match Girl," about a little girl who freezes to death in front of the window to a very comfortable home, she just dies of cold. I was so moved by that. On Christmas or holidays, when I'd look in from the outside and see people well dressed and having a good time, I used to feel that way myself. I wasn't freezing to death, exactly, but it was cold.

Though I wasn't involved much in school, I had some interesting teachers who had considerable influence on me. The first was Miss McKay, who called me "the poet laureate of Isaac Remsen Junior High" because I wrote poems like "Ode to a Skunk": "Hail to thee, O creature fair, striped charmer of the dale! I'd rather pet a mountain bear than stroke thy lovely tail." After she heard that, my wife Gail called me "striped charmer" for years.

Miss McKay was an English teacher who was in charge of dramatic presentations, and one year the play chosen was *Julius Caesar*. That was what first really got me interested in Shakespeare, though at the time I was truthfully more interested in the character of Mark Antony than in the play. I had to memorize some of his speeches, but I decided to learn the "Friends, Romans, countrymen" soliloquy on my own. When I had it down, I went to a place on Fourteenth Street filled with small booths where you could go and record something on a little metal disk. Background music was allowed and I picked Stravinsky's *Firebird Suite*. To be on a record was important to me; at that time to hear your own voice was a great thing.

I think what drew me to Shakespeare then is what I'm still attracted to now: it sounded good and it gave you something you could really chew on and learn. You can memorize Shakespeare much more easily than other plays because the speeches are constructed like music. There's a structure, a beat, a rhythm, a whole design, and after a while your ear becomes attuned to that and you can pick it up.

Maybe I wanted to be an actor, but I never thought of reciting Shakespeare as acting because I had no idea that this kind of thing was ever done on a stage. I really wasn't aware that there was even such a thing as theater, and though I was living in New York, I didn't know anything about the existence of Broadway. Later, when I was in high school, I went on a school trip and saw both John Gielgud and Leslie Howard in *Hamlet*. I had no particular standard, except for what I'd seen of acting in the movies, and I thought the language sounded funny, too elaborate and flowery. There seemed something phony about the way people spoke onstage, and I never liked that. I said to myself, "Why can't they speak in a normal way?" It was the written word that was more impressive to me.

I went to Eastern District High School in Brooklyn. To me high school was not about academics, it was a place where I met people and found out about life. I didn't study; I never cracked a book at home.

My best friend was Phillip Lerner, who was a poet and a scientist; fire engines were around his house all the time because of the things he'd blow up. I taught him how to ride a bike and how to play punchball and stickball, and he taught me all about free verse. I was the outgoing person—I was an activist, always doing things—while he was extremely intellectual, with a fine mind. We were two entirely different types, but we were the closest of friends.

Until I met Phil, my musical background had been the records we had at home, plus attending free concerts the Goldman Band gave in Prospect Park. But together we used to go to a music library up on Fifty-eighth Street, put on heavy earphones, and listen to recorded symphonies. Phil would say, "Hey, did you hear this? Tchaikovsky's Sixth. You've got to hear it!" We'd rediscover all the composers, starting with Beethoven, and later, Ravel and Stravinsky.

One night, I was standing in front of Carnegie Hall in my torn leather jacket when suddenly this black limousine pulled up and the guy inside said, "Hey, son, I have an extra ticket. You want to go in and see the concert?" I said, "Yeah!" It was one of those gala evenings, with everyone in evening clothes, and there I was, with a seat in the front house box, listening to Rudolph Serkin play Brahms's Piano Concerto. It was thrilling, but I was also embarrassed because I was not exactly dressed for the occasion.

The music factor continued to be very powerful in high school. I sang in the glee club and appeared in Gilbert and Sullivan operettas like *The Mikado*. At the same time, I joined the Dramatic Society, where I met the person who had the greatest influence on me any teacher's ever had. She was a very thin, coffee-colored woman who carried herself marvelously, always looked impeccable but not dressed up, and had a dignity that reminded me of my mother. Her name was Eulalie Spence, and many years later, while visiting a black history exhibition, I found out that she had been a rising young poet when she was seventeen or eighteen. But poetry didn't pay very well during the Depression and she had to teach.

Miss Spence spoke so well, I used to love to hear her talk. She began to direct me in plays, and she began to work on my speech and diction, bringing my Brooklyn accent to my attention. Other teachers would call me Joe, or, when they were angry, Mr. Papirofsky. She'd call me Joseph, and say things like, "Consonant endings, Joseph." She had that look in her eye that reminded me again a little bit of my mother, the look that said without words "There are goals for you." She worked very hard with me and I responded. I ended up president of the Dramatic Society, and when I graduated it said in the yearbook, "On the stage he's won renown and fame, all of Eastern has heard his name."

One of the kids I knew at Eastern was a girl who played the violin. She was very intellectual and I admired her because she spoke and dressed so well. She asked me to come to her home, and I can still remember feeling shabby there. I really didn't have any clothes, just the one suit I'd wear to school and a frayed sweater. They weren't exactly patched over but they were definitely threadbare, a lot of needlework had been done on them. And the mother spoke perfect English. She said, "Come in, how are you," that sort of thing. I knew my mother couldn't say that. I was too embarrassed, too ashamed to invite anybody to my house. Even though it was scrupulously clean, there was nothing comfortable about it. For a period of time, there weren't even any chairs, we sat on fruit boxes. Everything was so poor.

I had a similar experience when I was asked to visit one of my English teachers and his wife at home. My god, I was knocked out by seeing furniture and lamps. I said to myself, "People live like this?" Where I was raised, the only light was from a bare bulb in the ceiling. And except when the Sabbath candles were lit on Friday night, everything looked rather bleak. All I wanted out of life at the time was a good job so I could have a decent place to live.

. . .

When I was just a young guy, I was nothing politically, I didn't know what I was. My father was never involved in any politics at all, so there was nothing at home to draw from. But in the thirties, particularly in major cities like New York, there was a tremendous radicalization going on, and I was halfway through high school when I became aware of it. Phil Lerner was reading about Norman Thomas, and I became very interested in what he was doing. I'd also listen to the Communists and Socialists who were speaking in the streets, though they'd often confuse me because they both seemed to want Socialism. I thought, "Don't the Communists want Communism? If not, why do they have that name?"

The block I lived on was much more radical than my high school because it was right in the middle of the poorest neighborhood. This was a time when people who couldn't pay their rent had no protection; they were put right out on the street. Even in the dead of winter, you'd see all the family's household goods—pillows, mattresses, all kinds of tableware—piled right in front of the building. And the family would be standing next to them, sometimes with three or four or five children, all looking helpless, like after a fire.

There were several strong young guys on the block who were part of the Young Communist League—there was even a store right on the block that said that on the window. Though the word "Communist" was not as offensive then as it seems to be today, there was some antagonism to them in the community, but they were tolerated because it was such a poor neighborhood.

One of these fellows lived in my building, and he said to me, "Listen, we're forming a committee. We want to get a group of guys who are going to put this stuff back into the apartments of the people who've been evicted. You want to do something about it?" I said, "Well, okay, sure." And as soon as the deputies would leave, we'd take it all back. And if they came back again, we'd do exactly the same thing. And that was my first political act.

I began to talk to these guys, and what they were saying was quite interesting to me, particularly their talk about the masses, about poverty, about people who had a lot versus people who didn't have anything. I was attracted for the reason poor people always turn to the Left, strictly on the basis of economics. Plus, I was feeling at the time that the Socialists were talking a lot but not doing anything, and here was this group that wasn't afraid to take action. These guys were really involved, they were helping the community.

I attended some of their meetings, and they talked about what was happening in Soviet Russia, and things like the elimination of poverty and class distinctions sounded very good to me. Someone said, "You should read this book," and it was *The History of the Communist Party of the Soviet Union*. It was one of the longest, most boring books on record. I didn't know what the hell it was about and I could have never gotten through it. The same was true of *Das Kapital*. Extremely boring. I used to carry it around, I knew its importance, and I was familiar with certain basic tenets, but I never got through that book, either.

Those meetings, however, had other lures. There were some very pretty girls in there, plus there was a cultural element that was very exciting to me. I always had an appetite for things like that, and the YCL put me into contact with the very rich Russian experience. I became very interested in Eisenstein's work; I saw films like *Battleship Potemkin*. I would never have read Gorky, I would never have read Gogol, if I had not been interested in Soviet Russia. I read Michael Gold's *Jews Without Money*, an extremely radical book, as well as writers like Sean O'Casey, who considered himself a Communist. This was all a tremendous education for me. It intellectualized me more than anything I'd experienced before.

One night, we were on a corner near Pitkin Avenue where a small, handmade platform had been set up, and one of the guys said to me, "Look, why don't you get up there and talk tonight?" I was scared as hell. I said, "I don't know if I can. What'll I say?" "Just say what you feel about things." My heart was pounding away, but I got up there and started to talk.

I'd been a barker at Coney Island, so I had a little bit of experience with getting a crowd together, and people began to gather. "We should not be poor," I said. "There's so much wealth in this country, there's no reason why we should be poor." I added something about Soviet Russia and a couple of people in the back started booing me, saying, "Shut up! Get the hell off!" People were always saying, "Why don't you go back to Russia if you don't like it here?" Well, I liked it here, this was always my country and I felt very patriotic about it. But I frankly felt strongly about changing the system.

I ended up speaking for about ten minutes, and I was sweating when I finished. I was about sixteen years old and it was very challenging.

From then on, I became even more active. I'd go to demonstrations at Times Square, where we'd hide signs under our coats, and then at a certain moment, like 8:02 PM, we'd all whip them out in unison and start chanting. Police on horseback would chase us down; they'd try and get us on a side street so they could start slamming away. A lot of people would get their heads bloodied. It was a little scary, but we felt we were doing something.

I'd also do crazy things like go on the subways trying to raise money for the anti-Franco forces. There was a lot of resistance in some areas. The followers of Father Coughlin, who were violently anti-Semitic and very much pro-Franco, would try and break us up and often there were fights. Once on a subway, someone taunted me by saying, "Why don't you sing the national anthem?" I said, "I'll sing it if you can sing the second verse." I finished and the guy couldn't proceed, so I gave him the whole second verse as well. There was a stunning quiet after that, and I realized there was some value in memorizing things.

A lot of the guys I knew in the YCL went to Spain, and many of them didn't come back. I wanted to go myself, I was a little envious of those who did, but not being eighteen, I wasn't old enough to volunteer. My parents, of course, knew nothing about any of these hairsbreadth things that were going on. My father was still living his life the way he'd always lived it, going to shul every day, and I didn't want to bother him. Even if I would have gone to Spain, I wouldn't have told my parents ahead of time.

One of my strongest legacies from that period was the feeling that culture, by itself, was not significant. It had to be always doing something for the masses, for ordinary people, not just servicing an elite. When I got into doing Shakespeare, the whole idea was to give it to people in the parks so that there would be large numbers there who might be influenced. I don't believe in knowledge for its own sake. My first question always is: "What do you do with it? How can you turn it into something meaningful?"

Even today, I'm still pursuing the goal with which I started. I don't feel very good when I have just the people who can afford to pay inside my theaters. Whenever I feel the play I'm doing is not reaching out for a mass audience, or not saying something socially important, I feel I'm not doing anything.

. . .

After graduation from Eastern, I wanted desperately to go to Brooklyn College. I had good grades in some subjects, but there was no one either at school or at home to counsel me about academics, and when I ended up not finishing math and not doing well in science, it turned out I hadn't met the requirements to get in. Even if I had, for economic reasons I really had to go to work. I've always deeply regretted that. I was just beginning to get some sense of learning, and going to college would have meant a great deal to me.

Instead, since Phil Lerner went to college, I got his job at the laundry our teacher's father ran. The job was primarily to pick up dirty clothes and deliver bags full of clean stuff, which sometimes meant carrying them up four or five flights of stairs. In those days, though, a lot of highly trained, well-educated people had no suitable employment—they were running elevators and doing odd jobs. Delivering stuff all over the city, I got into conversations and picked up a hell of a lot, all of which seemed very romantic in a Thomas Wolfe kind of way.

One experience I had was with the woman at the laundry who did most of the ironing. She was a little bit off, she was always singing something from the 1812 Overture and saying, "Down the elevator shaft!" When a customer came into the shop, part of my job was to cover for this woman, to pretend I was engaging her in conversation. She'd say, "Down the elevator shaft!" and I'd respond, "Personally, I don't think the shaft is so interesting" or "I wouldn't go to that shaft anymore if I were you." It was all improvisation, part of my training as an actor, right?

I finally lost that job because I refused to work twelve hours, and went to work as a shipping clerk at Dinhofer Jewelry at 150 Lafayette, just down the street, ironically, from where the Public Theater is now. Julius Dinhofer was a very tough boss, terrible with his workers. I mean, if you dropped one of those little chipped diamonds we worked with, he'd have your nose on the floor for ten hours until you found the thing. Everybody was underpaid, and since this was a time when the world was really going hog wild, I decided that I would organize the place.

There was a union at the time called UOPWA, the United Office and Professional Workers of America, and they gave me the okay. I organized the office workers, had secret meetings, got everybody involved, but the union wanted me to stay on the inside so I could tell them what was going on. But after being on strike for three weeks, the union's man told me, "You're too good in there, you're doing too much work. You'd better come out, too."

So I went to Mr. Dinhofer and said, "I'm quitting. I'm going on strike with the rest of them." He started to attack me. He said, "I had great plans for you. You should be ashamed of yourself." And I said, "You're full of shit. The way you treat people is ridiculous. You're a Jew, you should represent something much higher, but you treat people so rotten, I'm the one who's ashamed. This country's fighting Hitler and we have a Hitler right here. I'm going to join up, and if I have to fight for people like you, it's a disgrace." I walked out, and soon after I joined the navy.

These were times when the world was starting to go up in flames, when life itself was so dramatic and so alive. It was an enormous moment in history, and it gave more meaning to everything. It was one of the few times when the needs of a political radical and the needs of a Jew were very much in tune with the nation's needs, and there was something very agreeable in for once swimming with the tide. I felt the country was at last fighting for something that was right, fighting a battle I could really be proud of. We were coming together, we were joining the mainstream, and to be a part of all that felt terrific.

2

The Navy and the Actors' Lab

1942–49

Papp (second
from left) and
navy buddies
Courtesy of the New
York Public Library

JOSEPH PAPP Because I was opposed to the military draft on principle,
I was determined to enlist. Even though, as someone who could just barely
swim, the navy had seemed questionable to me, a navy commander I met
told me that since I was articulate and could also type, I could come in as a
third-class petty officer, the equivalent of a sergeant.

That, in fact, is what happened, but not right away. Before they let me
enlist, I had to have my teeth fixed. One thing about being poor was that
there was no such thing as a filling when I was a kid, and my mouth was in
rotten shape. You waited until the tooth was finished and then you went to
a roughneck dentist who just yanked it out without Novocain. Also, the first
time I went off, after saying goodbye to everyone, there was some screwup

and I had to come back home that same night. I was so embarrassed, I hid. I didn't want anybody to see me.

The next day, the navy sent me to boot camp at Bainbridge, Maryland. My milieu up to then had been very small, very narrow, and I'd been in a lousy period in terms of my personal relationships. I'd married a girl from the neighborhood, had a daughter, and was soon to be divorced. Suddenly, my hair was cut and I was thrown in with all these strange guys. I felt peculiar, totally isolated from who I'd been at home. On the other hand, I had free medical attention, and for the first time in my life I was able to eat three squares a day. The state was taking care of everything; it was like living under Communism.

About four or five weeks into boot training, as much out of boredom as anything else, I'd get some guys together on Sundays and we'd kid around and put on little shows right there in the barracks. In my mind, this had nothing to do with theater. I thought plays were effete, plays were sissy. What I liked was vaudeville, skits, singing, and dancing.

An officer who'd been trying to start some kind of entertainment unit on the base heard about what I was doing. He asked if I would do some shows in the main theater and I said I'd try. I put together a variety show, with guys singing, guys tap-dancing, things like that, and I emceed it. It was a success, and when I completed my boot training, the navy asked me, "Do you want to do some more of this?" And I said, "Sure."

So I spent some time at Bainbridge putting on shows, I even brought entertainers like the Russian ballerina Alicia Markova down from New York. Then I was shipped out as a chief petty officer on a small aircraft carrier, one of those converted tankers we called Kaiser Coffins because they were slow-built at the Kaiser Shipyards. Our job was sending planes out to search for submarines, but there was a lot of in-between time, and the ship's chaplain, who'd read on my record what I'd done at Bainbridge, asked me to put together some shows on the ship's hangar deck. It was things like three guys putting mops on their heads and mimicking the Andrews Sisters, and once again I'd be the emcee.

I was transferred from that ship to Treasure Island in San Francisco, where I was supposed to be put on another carrier. The navy was trying at the time to start a unit of in-service entertainers that would play for the troops in various Pacific Islands. They really wanted an officer to be the head of it, but they couldn't find one. I don't know if it was luck or what, but they asked me as a chief petty officer whether I would put together such a group.

I began interviewing people. None of them had reputations of any kind; they were just young and talented. One of them was this very thin, Irish-looking kid, a dancer whose idol was Gene Kelly. His name was Bob Fosse and I took him on. Not that I was struck in particular by him—I didn't say, "Oh, this is Bob Fosse! Boy!" He was just a young kid, you know. But as the tour went on, as we played islands all the way to Japan, I became very friendly with him. Because I was a couple of years older than most of the guys, I was like a father to the group.

BOB FOSSE   I was a city kid. I'd been a professional dancer in Chicago since I was thirteen, playing all the cheap nightclubs. I enlisted in the navy when I was seventeen, right out of high school, and I was put into something called the Navy Entertainment Group. They would send us all through the South Pacific on tours with names like "T.S.," or "Tough Situation." One guy would sing Irish songs, somebody would sing hillbilly songs, there was a tap dancer and a guy who did impressions of James Cagney.

We played a different base on a different island every day, places like Hawaii, Guam, Chuuk, Okinawa, Wake, all the way through to Tokyo. The guys preferred the shows with girls in them, so we had two strikes against us there, but still we were very successful. We'd do sketches with a lot of inside jokes about the navy, like if an officer and a Wave got married, what would their life be like after the war. I played a girl in that skit—I was in drag with wigs and everything.

Usually an officer was sent with these troupes. Besides being in charge of all the travel arrangements, he was frequently the director. And he was someone who kept us all in our place; he was the only discipline we had. Joe was the only noncommissioned officer to be in charge of a group.

Joe seemed very quiet; he talked very little about himself personally. And he had a very mischievous sense of humor. There was another dancer in the troupe; his name, strangely enough, was Roland La Fosse, and whenever I'd complain about how corny his work was, Joe would get a little twinkle in his eye and say, "Well, why don't you tell him?" It was like he would get bored with all of us and wanted to see something happen.

Performing together, with the give and take of being onstage, we'd get into arguments about how something should be done. And Joe used to let those arguments go on with that same little twinkle in his eye. If we went too far or started to get physical, he would step in, as any good officer in charge of men should do. But up till then he would not only watch but also stimulate the situation a little bit. He really enjoyed two people arguing, he liked to watch that kind of combat. He didn't smile a lot, but those were the times he did.

Though in a lot of ways Joe was very enigmatic, he was just terrific with me, very supportive, I must say. He took on a kind of teacher role, talking to me for many, many hours about acting, the theater, music, and politics. He spent a lot of time talking about my future, whether he thought it would be in films or stage. And he seemed very open to ideas. I was into a sort of semi-fake-arty dance period: with twenty thousand sailors in the South Pacific looking at me I'd be dancing Ravel's *Boléro*. They'd rather see some hot number, but Joe was supportive about that, too. All his attitudes were terribly liberal, and all of it was new to me.

I remember him sitting outside for long hours, always reading, always with a book under his arm. He would read certain passages aloud to me; that seemed like such a nice thing. He also used to lend me books. Once he wanted me to read something by a psychologist named Karen Horney and then tell him what I thought about it. I sensed he was into a tremendous amount of self-improvement himself. He was really extraordinary with me, and I owe him a great deal.

PHILLIP MARTEL Right after the war, Joe was in charge of a show at the Brooklyn Navy Yard for some navy bigwigs. The final rehearsal was the day before, and all these guys were young sailors, anxious to get through with it and see the town. The show went on for about two, two and a half hours, and it looked pretty good to me. But after the whole thing was over, Joe, being the perfectionist he is, said, "All right, from the top." And that set off such a wave of "Oh no, Joe! Oh, jeez c'mon!" But even though it was late in the day, he brooked no reply, he made them run through the whole damn performance again. They had to stay another three hours before they got off. Even then you could sense that what he did, he wanted to do right. He was always a leader, and a leader likes to have what he says done. That goes with the territory.

JOSEPH PAPP I was so glad when the war was over and I was out of the navy. Because with all the positive things about it, you're still under a system that, though not exactly repressive, has many oppressive elements. For instance, because I was very socially conscious, I raised a fuss when I noticed that not only weren't there any black officers on our ship, there wasn't even a black chief petty officer. I was told in no uncertain terms to shut the hell up if I didn't want to end up in the brig. You couldn't say your piece, and that was lousy.

I was discharged from the navy in New York and I was in a state of marvelous euphoria. I had no job, I had no money, I had no skills, but Fascism had been defeated, a tremendous victory had been won for democracy, and the world would certainly now begin moving in the right direction. Then I thought of someone I'd known in the navy, a guy who lived in Hollywood and had done some screenplays, and I remembered he'd asked me to come out and visit him on the coast. And I said to myself, "Well, why not?"

I had no goal, no objective, no job, nothing. I also didn't have enough money to get on a plane, so I took a chance. I didn't have my military ID card anymore, but I still had my uniform. I snuck onto a marine base and got on this plane that went out to an air base in Bakersfield. When I landed, I saw these two marine guards coming toward me, and I thought it was all over. But they just said, "Hi'ya, chief," and I said, "How ya doin', fellas," and kept walking. If they'd stopped me, I had no identification, absolutely nothing. I was crazy, I guess.

I got in touch with my navy buddy and told him I had to do something. "Have you ever heard of the Actors' Lab?" he said. "They've got a very good school. You've got the GI Bill, the government will pay you something while you go to school, why don't you take advantage of it?" I said I was ready to try anything and I went down to the Actors' Lab that very day. And this is really where my journey begins. From that moment on was the serious beginning of my life in the theater.

MORRIS CARNOVSKY   If the Group hadn't existed, the whole nature of any conversation about Joe Papp would have been very much altered.

PHOEBE BRAND   It began with the Group Theatre. About thirty of us started the Group on the East Coast in 1931, and it was a very radical departure for the theater. American plays at the time were bedroom farces, drawing-room comedies, and star vehicles, all very shallow, and we wanted to do something to shake things up.

We decided to have a common method of approach, a common language for acting, and after the Moscow Art Theatre came over and showed us what good acting was, we worked with Lee Strasberg on speech and exercises in what came to be known as the Method. We didn't think of the type of plays we came to do as socially conscious, we thought of them as American. Harold Clurman, one of the founders, was very anxious that every play say that somewhere there was a way out. No depression, no hopelessness, a positive point of view. We were very lucky to get Clifford Odets, who became our playwright and with works like *Waiting for Lefty* and *Awake and Sing!* wrote from the point of view of the Group.

Eventually, the Group fell apart, as unfortunately most theater groups do. Roman Bohnen, we called him Bud, was the first to go to Hollywood. John Garfield went, as did Joe Bromberg, Morris and I, and several others. Bud started to gather together actors and he said, "We need something here in Hollywood. We've got to have a theater of some kind, and a school."

That was how the Actors' Laboratory began. It was different, in a way, from the Group because it didn't start out to be a theater. It was a gathering place, a workshop, somewhere for people to work on their craft, a kind of open arms out to Hollywood to come and partake. We did things you couldn't find anywhere else, like a lecture series on the history of the theater called "From the Birth of Dionysus to *Death of a Salesman*" that included staging and costuming a scene from each of the relevant plays.

We had a good acting school, and the studios often sent us their starlets and young actors to train. I remember a class I taught where I said, "Who knows who Hamlet is?" and there was only one who knew, Jean Peters, a lovely girl, one of the few who had a brain. And the place grew and grew in popularity, it became a center for actors from all over Hollywood.

They would come and sit in the alley and chat, people would meet people, it was a lovely place.

JOSEPH PAPP I went down to the Actors' Lab, which was a series of two or three small wooden buildings right behind Schwab's Drugstore on Sunset Boulevard, with rooms for classes plus a stage and an auditorium. It was a sunny, beautiful Southern California day. I was just out of the navy, it felt great to be free, and I felt as if I could do anything. Or do nothing and feel just as happy.

I saw a young woman sitting inside a small window, so I went over and said, "I want to try out to get into this school. How do you do it?" She asked if I was a veteran and then said, "You're just a little late. We've had all our auditions, five hundred people applied and we've selected twenty-five up to this point. In fact, we're just finishing up, we're having only two or three final callback auditions today."

I said, "Okay." It didn't matter to me. I felt, so? I sat down on a bench and struck up a conversation with a guy sitting there. He mentioned that he was taking a workshop with Charles Laughton. I said, "Charles Laughton?" because names of movie stars I knew. Later, I got to know both Laughton and Bertolt Brecht when Laughton appeared in Brecht's *Galileo* at the Lab. Brecht was mostly pinching women when I knew him—he seemed to be hot on ladies all the time. At that point, though, I didn't know Brecht from a hole in the ground.

While we're talking, the girl from the window called to me and said, "Could you help us out? This girl is doing a final audition and the guy she's supposed to do it with can't come. Could you read with her?" I'd had no experience in acting except for the little I'd done in high school—I really hadn't done much since I'd played Scrooge in the first grade—but I said, "Okay, I'll try it."

The girl showed me the play. It was *Desire Under the Elms*, by Eugene O'Neill. Never heard of it. I looked at it and it was all in this New Englandy kind of dialect. We went over the script a couple of times and then they told us they were ready in the theater. It was very dark inside, I couldn't see who was there, but I later learned that Phoebe Brand, who became my first acting teacher, was in the audience.

We got up onstage, read the scene, and started to walk out when someone said, "Just a minute." The girl turned around but they said, "No, thank you, miss, you can go. Mr. Papirofsky, why do you want to be in the theater?" I said, "I really don't know. I just got out of the navy. I have a GI Bill. I thought this would be a good school to go to." They asked me several more questions, I answered them as best I could, and then they went into a huddle.

What interested them about me? I can't see how my acting could have been any good, so I think they liked my philosophy, my social consciousness. When they asked me about the theater, I talked about the masses, about my ideas about democracy and socialism. It all connected with my experiences in the thirties, which probably reflected some of the ideas of the Group. They seemed to feel I was the kind of person they wanted in the school, because they broke the huddle and someone said, "Just a minute. Mr. Quinn would like to talk to you outside." And out of the darkness of the theater here comes Anthony Quinn.

ANTHONY QUINN The Actors' Lab was for me a wonderfully exhilarating period, one of the most creative of my life. But I had the responsibility of approving all those applying to be actors, and my god, it was a tough job. I mean, my god, there were about ten thousand—well, I'm exaggerating. But there must have been about three or four thousand applications, and we could only take a hundred, hundred and fifty. A lot of the kids were very dedicated, the "I'm dying to be an actor" type of thing. It was tough to weed them out.

Then I figured out a special questionnaire that served wonderfully, which really settled everything. What was it? I can't tell you. It's a secret. I still use it today, and the kids don't know how I come to the conclusion of who's an actor and who isn't. But there's something in the questions that makes me understand whether the person is or not.

Now, I didn't think Joe was an actor, but he did belong in the theater. We weren't only casting for actors; we were casting for directors, for everything that needed talent for the theater. What the Actors' Lab was looking for was content—that's what acting is all about, content, people who had something to say about the war, about life. What we wanted was dedication to the job of theater. Anybody that smelled of theater, we would encourage. And Joe was one of the people that I'm very proud to have backed.

JOSEPH PAPP Quinn and I went into this little, boxlike office which seemed to be put together with spit; there wasn't a solidly built building in the place. He said, "Sit down, I'm going to ask you a few questions. If you had to go onstage some night, and you got some bad news just before you went on, how would you act that night?"

"I'd probably feel terrible."

"What do you mean you'd feel terrible?"

"Well, if I got bad news, I'd feel bad about it."

All at once Quinn began to harangue me. "If you go on the stage, you're not supposed to feel bad about anything!" And I thought, "What the fuck is going on? Who is this guy to be giving me this bull?" Then, suddenly, he screamed, "Aaaaghghgh!" He got up, rolled up his pants, rubbed his leg, went outside, picked up some mud, and started rubbing that on his leg. He'd been stung by a bee in the middle of his harangue. We laugh about it now, but he wasn't laughing then.

At any rate, it turned out that the Lab wanted me, but the funds I was getting from the GI Bill were inadequate. I was paying alimony from my first marriage, I just didn't have any money. They asked me if I minded taking a job cleaning the place in the morning before classes, sweeping, mopping, and just brushing things up, and I said I'd be happy to. That was worth an extra $10 or $15 a week.

Though I didn't know it then, the Lab turned out to be the intellectual center for all of Hollywood. It was made up of two sections: a school and a theater. The theater included people like Laughton, Quinn, Vincent Price, John Garfield, Franchot Tone, almost everybody who'd been in the Group, the best actors in the country. Lee J. Cobb worked there. I admired him tremendously. He used to prepare like three or four hours before he went onstage.

Shelley Winters used to hang around. Her career didn't seem to be going anywhere, and then I remember her telling me, "Oh Joe, I have some wonderful news. I got a role in a picture called *A Double Life* with Ronald

Colman." Remember, I was a kid from Brooklyn who suddenly found himself plop in the middle of Hollywood. Seeing all these people I'd seen on the screen, people of great reputation, it was an exotic experience for me.

As a school, there was nothing comparable in terms of the level of its staff and the quality of the work—it was the finest school in the country. Since it was in Hollywood, some of the students had the idea that they would use it as a showcase to get into the movies, but the faculty were talking about people like Eleanora Duse and teaching deep, deep commitment to the real art of acting. Twentieth Century Fox sent five of their contract players there for training, including Marilyn Monroe, who was, no kidding, in my body-training class.

Another veteran I got to know was Audie Murphy. He was a sweet guy, gentle, sincere, with the nicest smile, and he wanted so badly to be a good actor. He took speech with me, a class taught by Margaret P. McLean, who wrote a definitive book on phonetics called *Good American Speech*. I was still talking like I came from Brooklyn and I became a challenge to Margaret P. McLean. I started out with the worst speech in the class, but I became interested in speaking well and became her best student. In fact, she made me responsible for Audie's speech; he had this Southern accent they wanted him to lose.

I also took a class on theater history, where I read a book by John Gassner called *Masters of the Drama*—from Aeschylus to O'Neill—that made me aware of something I'd not been aware of before: that the theater had a tradition. I'd had no idea, for instance, that Greek drama even existed. It was a revelation for me, everything was so new. I began to do a hell of a lot of reading.

After school, I'd teach what I'd learned about acting in downtown Los Angeles at a place called the California Labor School. Again, it was not enough to find myself studying acting and being amongst the "Hollywood bourgeois" with all their aims and goals; I always felt a strong societal obligation. The guy who headed this school was a fine man with a great deal of integrity. I named my first son, Michael, after him.

The class was made up of working people, and though most of them were really exhausted after a day's work in factories, once they became engaged in this sort of thing, they lost all their weariness. They were full of energy and excitement. It was a pleasure for me to meet these people because they were much more direct, they had no careers at stake.

I used to hang around with a few guys who were my buddies and one day we got hold of a phonograph record of Laurence Olivier's *Henry V*. There's a climactic speech in the final act that goes, "Once more unto the breach, dear friends, once more, or close the wall up with our English dead." It's a great speech, and it got us all riled up.

Near the end of it Henry says, "God for Harry, England, and St. George!" And the way Olivier did it was to elongate "England" and then rise to a shrill crescendo, hit a very high note, and sustain it with "St. George." That note seemed to last forever, and we started to get terribly excited. By the time he hit the top, we started to scream, we started to yell, and we ran out as a group right down Sunset Boulevard for about ten blocks, yelling at the top of our voices. Jimmy Anderson was a Southerner, he came from Alabama, and he had a whoop that really was the highest you'll ever hear, and he was running down the block and yelling, he didn't care. That was how intense our response was to Olivier, and to Shakespeare.

The tradition of the Group Theatre, however, was social realism, and there was a split at the Lab between those who wanted to do contemporary plays and those who wanted to do more classical things. The Method was like a new religion there, but I later came to reject a lot of that way of acting because it stood in the way of a certain kind of skill that was necessary in dealing with poetry and language. Acting Shakespeare required getting the emotion from the language rather than trying to shovel around in your own innards looking for parallels. The Method turned out some fine actors, but I'm telling you, poetry was not their strong point. I remember Leo Penn once telling me about a Shakespearean soliloquy, "If the goddamn fucking words weren't in the way, I could act the hell out of this."

My first acting teacher at the Lab was Phoebe Brand, and she directed me in a scene from *Romeo and Juliet* with this girl I liked a lot, which was why I couldn't play the scene too well. This girl and I were backstage, hugging each other and rehearsing the balcony scene—"Soft, what light through yonder window breaks"—and then we went on and suddenly all these people were there. I felt as if I didn't know which part of the experience was real. Was it what we were doing backstage, or was it when we went on the stage? My mouth was dry as could be, I felt awful, and the whole scene, which couldn't have lasted more than ten minutes, felt interminable. There was applause when it ended, but I went offstage, ran out the back of the theater, and just kept running. I didn't come back until very late that night. I felt I'd been so terrible, I was ashamed to show my face.

PHOEBE BRAND I cast Joe. He looked like a Romeo to me, very handsome. I don't know why he should have felt embarrassed about his performance, it wasn't too bad at all. A lot of people didn't think he was an actor, but I always liked what he did. I didn't think he was the greatest actor in the world, but he had something, a passion, a spirit. He was a very dramatic person and he loved acting, he loved theater.

I understand why Joe does Shakespeare, and why he does new plays that have meaning. It all comes from the Lab. Morris and I emphasized Shakespeare because Shakespeare is the answer to almost everything—his plays are eternal. The directors in the Group shied away from Shakespeare. Lee Strasberg would say, "You're never going to be able to do it. You're not ready. You have to be absolutely great or you can't touch Shakespeare." Well, the only way you can get good in Shakespeare is to do it, and that's what I admire Joe for. He just went in and did it.

BERNARD GERSTEN Joe and I have known each other for forty years. I went out to Los Angeles in 1948 and joined the Actors' Lab, where Joe and I became best friends.

Joe was brash and he was bright and he was intense. I didn't know he was Jewish, I thought of him as this nice Polish guy, Joe Papirofsky. He was a strong person, unquestionably opinionated, and highly political. We used to go out campaigning for Henry Wallace, going door to door on Sunday mornings.

As an actor, I remember Joe appearing in a thirties or forties agitprop play called *The Plant in the Sun*. It was another *Waiting for Lefty* about a group of workers in a paper-box factory organizing themselves and joining the union. And Joe played the key organizer, a character not unlike Joe in many respects, who was always quick to anger and fiery-tempered. At one point someone said to Joe's character, "You gotta apologize." And I can still hear in my head the reading Joe gave the reply. He said, totally eliminating the *a*, "'*Pologize?!* I don't 'pologize!"—a line that has burned in my memory ever since.

Joe and I were also the prime movers of a street fair at the Lab which operated under the title Exuberanza, and our little inside joke for all the years since has been to say it backward and call ourselves the Aznarebuxe. It's remained a slogan known only to Joe and me; under that banner we flew together and we played together.

JOSEPH PAPP Everything at the Lab was very exciting to me because it was all new and I was able to do everything that I liked. I was learning, I was working, I was doing something socially important, and I was having a good time. A lot of the people at the Lab made a picture now and then and were pretty well off compared to me, but then anybody was well off compared to me.

I don't know how I got the money for it, but I bought a secondhand car. It was a small English Nash, a blue convertible, and I used to drive really fast up and down the canyons with the top down. Bernie Gersten and I and another guy named Charlie Cooper became good friends quite early on. We could drink all night, be out at the Lab with our foils at five or six in the morning, stripped to the waist and fencing, then I'd clean the place up and we'd start classes.

Gradually a clash developed at the Lab between its two halves, the theater and the school. The students wanted to get on the stage, they wanted to mix with the professionals, but the professionals didn't want the students, they wanted to do their own productions. An unusual woman named Mary Tarcai was the head of the school, and I became her find, her pet, almost a cat's paw.

Because of my background, because I was an activist interested in theater, I was exactly what was wanted by these people. I became the symbol of what they believed in. And because of Mary Tarcai's influence, I was the first student to be put on the board. I had input on the choices of plays presented. They would ask me, "How do the students feel about this?"

I was always good at organizing things, and because of that I was then made managing director of the entire organization. Though Mary Tarcai had the power, I was responsible for the running of the theatrical operation, setting schedules, selling tickets. That ability to get people together and do things was a talent I always had. I never thought about having this kind of leadership thing about me, I just had it.

PHOEBE BRAND Even as a young student coming in, we turned a lot of the running of the place over to Joe. He was a born producer, he had those qualities even then. His passion all went into organization, that was his forte, and since none of us were very capable in that department, we handed him everything to take care of. He was a morale builder, he did his best to keep things steady and organized and happy. He was the only one who seemed to have any sense of what to do. If the Lab had gone on, he would have run the whole thing.

The Lab fell apart, however, because we began to be attacked as a left-wing organization. The dissension inside increased—it got to be very unpleasant. There would be pickets, and do you know one of the things they were picketing? We used to do animal characters in class, they were fun but also very useful at times. And one of the pickets had a sign reading, "I didn't come to the Actors' Lab to learn how to do Rin-Tin-Tin."

The gossip columnists would call and try to talk to me about the politics of the situation, and when I didn't want to talk to them, they called me "Clam Brand." Really ugly things were done. You marvel at a country that can do that to people. You can't run a place under that kind of dissension, and in 1950 the Lab broke up. It was a shame. It was a great organization.

JOSEPH PAPP The Lab closed for a variety of reasons. One was the entire political climate of the time. Attacks by the Tenney Committee and the House Un-American Activities Committee froze Hollywood into a great Frigidaire. The atmosphere was poisoned, everybody was terrified, it was the coldest place in the world.

I remember one man in particular, Roman Bohnen. He did not cooperate with the Tenney Committee, and I felt very proud of him. He'd been told by Elia Kazan that he wanted him to play the lead in a new play by Arthur Miller called *Death of a Salesman*, but then a few months later he read in *Variety* that Lee J. Cobb got the role. After that time he became very depressed.

Bohnen then appeared in a Dutch play at the Lab that featured a carnival-like atmosphere with people throwing confetti and balloons and the actor himself dressed quite festively. The play's first act ends in a wild frenzy. Bohnen's character is angry at his daughter, he's shouting and yelling.

I was in the house that night, and as the act came to a close, Bohnen was shouting as usual but his face was getting very red. And then, just before the curtain, he collapsed and the curtain came down. Everybody applauded—they thought it was part of the play. I ran backstage and there he was. By an extraordinary coincidence, it was a doctors' theater party, and three or four of them ran back with me and pronounced him dead. One doctor said he could see Bohnen having the stroke as it happened. Somehow, he was able to keep playing right until the curtain.

I recall that scene so vividly: Bohnen lying there amidst all this confetti, all the appurtenances and artifices of the theater. And all these actors, myself included, just standing around and starting to weep. You may say, "That's the way to go, onstage, at the end of an act," but he was a very unhappy man.

Aside from politics, what killed the Lab was the lack of strong leadership. Although there are some theaters that operate on this principle, democracy in the theater is ridiculous, I don't believe in it. Imagine you're in a military situation, the enemy is firing at you, and every time you want to do something you have to say, "Let's have a meeting." It may sound more democratic, but I'm telling you, it's destructive. Someone has to be in a position to make a decision.

Also, the Lab had an executive board made up of actors, which I came to recognize was its other major weakness. It taught me what a board is supposed to do for a not-for-profit organization with financial needs: its fundamental function has to be to raise funds for that organization. What you don't want to have is a board of performers who want to use the institution, who have a particular ax to grind.

By being in the midst of all this at the Lab, I got a great sense of how theaters work. I learned there has to be a single idea by which a theater operates, otherwise you go here, you go there, you don't know where you're going.

Some people think I do a lot of different things, but it all comes out of one basic concept, which is to try to reach the highest number of people, particularly those who ordinarily would not go to the theater, with quality work. You create an ambiance for theatrical creation, you spend whatever time is necessary to see things through, and you begin to become a magnet for writers and directors and actors.

On Broadway, they look for that one show that's going to make it. That's not a way to make a theater. What is it Brecht says? "If you search for happiness, happiness comes in last."

MORRIS CARNOVSKY The great discovery that Joe made at the Lab was guts. He found out that one had to have them, and could have them, even under adverse circumstances. And if you did, something would happen, people would accept and respect the charm of your boldness. So he demanded money and, by god, he got it. And he demanded a certain kind of play, accompanied by a certain kind of actor, and he got it. He was able to command.

3

Death of a Salesman, CBS, and Sean O'Casey

1950–52

Papp as stage manager
at CBS
Courtesy of the New York Public
Library

JOSEPH PAPP It was a sad thing when the Actors' Lab closed down. Both my wife and I had been working there, so we now had no income. I went out looking for any job I could find, and I ended up at a sheet-metal factory making fire doors. They weighed about five hundred pounds apiece, and to load these things, you had to be able to spin them. They had a lot of young Mexican guys working there, and I was older than most of them, close to thirty. I was still in fairly good shape, but not like them, so it was tough work.

I'd been working there for several months when I got a telephone call. It was a stage manager I knew who said he'd been trying to track me down. The national touring company of *Death of a Salesman* was playing in Los Angeles, and they wanted me to be the assistant stage manager as well as understudy both of Willy Loman's sons, Biff and Happy. I'd have to audition, and whoever was selected would also have to open the play in Pasadena within ten days as a two-week replacement for Darren McGavin, who was then playing Happy but had to leave to make a film.

I went down to the theater and there was a line of actors halfway around the block. It was all these Hollywood beach-boy types—big, handsome, bronzed guys. And me. I was called out of the line and the stage manager who'd telephoned met me inside. We sat down and he said, "Okay, you're going to be assistant stage manager."

"You mean I have the job? What about all those people out there?" I was startled; I thought I was going to have to read or something.

So there I was, and I didn't know a damn thing about anything. I hadn't acted professionally, ever, and I certainly hadn't stage-managed. There had never been that much equipment at the Lab, so I'd never become very good as far as anything technical was concerned. I had to call cues, and "curtain going up," and give actors their half-hour and five-minute calls. I was also responsible for calling lighting cues, and I didn't know a Leko lamp from a Fresnel. But I pretended that I knew a little bit, and this stage manager, who must have seen that I was a novice, took me under his wing, and things began working out.

The acting part proved more difficult. I had to get ready to go onstage in a major professional house, playing opposite Thomas Mitchell, the old movie actor, who was Willy Loman. I was very happy to play with him, but when I started to play with him, I wasn't so happy.

My first concern, however, was the script. I looked at the part and I worried, "Can I memorize all this?" I struggled and I struggled with those lines. I had one run-through, but I had to hold the script in my hand as if my life depended on it. And the night I had to go on, when the announcer said, "Ladies and gentlemen, for tonight's performance the role of Happy will be played by Joseph Papirofsky," the audience burst out laughing. I was dying backstage, I thought they were making fun of me. Then the announcer comes offstage and it turned out his fly was wide open.

I went on that night, and though I was nervous as a cat I remembered every line. The only problem I had was with Thomas Mitchell. I'd been taught, Stanislavsky and everything else, that when you act, you look at the person, but Thomas Mitchell would never do that—he'd always look past me when we had dialogue together. I got through that performance, but it was on sheer nerve alone.

On my second night, however, they should have given the audience their money back because I couldn't remember a single line. I was so bad, some of the actors broke up onstage. And Mitchell, who'd been drinking, was furious, as angry as can be. That was a nightmare, the worst night I'd ever had in the theater. It was a horrendous feeling, standing up there and not remembering anything. I finally managed to get through it, but I was drenched in sweat by the time it was over. I don't know how the audience felt.

After several more nights, I finally began to feel good in the part, but Thomas Mitchell was always a problem. He'd get into these altercations with another old-time actor who played the Lomans' next-door neighbor. This actor would get drunk and Mitchell would come off the stage with me and say, "Isn't it a disgrace? I mean, a man of the theater getting drunk. People should get their money back." And the next night *he* would be drunk. And this guy would say, "Disgraceful isn't it? The star of the show, not setting an example." And it would go on and on in this sort of way.

About halfway through the tour, I finally find out why I'd been hired. Everybody was treating me so courteously and so nicely, I couldn't understand it; I thought maybe it was my personality. I was talking to one of the stagehands and he said, "Hey Joe, how's your uncle Kermit?" I said I didn't know, but I realized that these people were under the impression that I was the nephew of the show's New York producer, Kermit Bloomgarden.

Much later on, I discovered that Burt Conway, an actor who'd been a very close friend of mine at the Lab and a member of the New York production of *Salesman*, had recommended me highly for the job, and since the order had come from the New York office, people got the notion that I was a relative of the producer. Well, I never disabused them of that idea, I didn't want to create a shock in the company.

The national tour played major cities like Salt Lake City, St. Paul, Chicago, Boston, and Washington, D.C. I was on the tour for six or seven months, understudying Biff and Happy and being assistant stage manager.

I didn't mind the time, however, because I'd met Peggy Bennion, the woman who'd be my next wife.

PEGGY BENNION PAPP   My parents were Mormon homesteaders in Utah, real pioneers. They cleared the land and made the desert bloom—literally. I became interested in the theater because my mother was always in love with it. One of the first public buildings the Mormons built was a theater, and my mother never got over the fact that as a child she had seen Maude Adams, the most popular actress of the American theater during the early 1900s, in *Peter Pan*. And, going back to the homestead in a wagon, she passed the spot where the train carrying the show had just wrecked and scattered the scenery all over the sagebrush. My mother ran through it all, touching the artificial treetops that were glittering in the moonlight. I never forgot that story.

I was always enamored of movie stars and Hollywood, and when I was eighteen, I hopped a Greyhound bus with three of my college sorority sisters and went to California to seek my fortune. I started writing for movie magazines. I was the youngest writer in Hollywood, and I sold an idea for a series called "I Had a Date With . . ." It was fulfilling a fantasy, very glamorous and lots of fun.

I went out with Rex Harrison and Peter Lawford, but the most interesting was Burt Lancaster because he didn't care about Hollywood. I remember talking about how I thought life was so exciting and so beautiful and, oh, wonderful, and he sat there and on a napkin he drew a picture of an old whore leaning out of a dilapidated building with a cigarette hanging from her mouth.

I wrote for movie magazines for three years. Then one day I woke up and looked at the covers. One of them said something like, "Why I Became a Blonde," by Linda Darnell, and I said to myself, "Is this what I want to give my life to?" So I decided I didn't want to write about actors, I wanted to be an actress.

I looked for work in both New York and L.A., and then in Los Angeles a friend called up and said, "Peggy, my girlfriend is leaving *Death of a Salesman*, get down there. It's a call girl, so dress the part." I read the play and I couldn't move out of my chair for two hours. I said, "This is the greatest play I've ever read. I want to be with that play."

So I put a lot of makeup on, padded myself, wore ankle-strap shoes and a tight-fitting dress. I was living in Hollywood, and it took an hour and a half to get by public transportation from there to the Biltmore Theatre, where Thomas Mitchell, the star, was auditioning people. And every night for two and a half weeks, the stage manager, Scott Jackson, and the assistant stage manager, who was Joe, would tell me, "Oh, Thomas Mitchell isn't here" or "Thomas Mitchell's not in the mood to hear you" or "He's too tired. Come back tomorrow night."

Finally my chance came. I said my lines, trying to act like a call girl, and Thomas Mitchell came up out of the black auditorium and said, "Honey, you have to know what this girl is the minute she walks onstage, and no matter what you do, you look like the girl next door." However, I did get the part, and I think it's because Joe and Scott were so impressed with my persistence and my desire that they were pulling for me. And that's where Joe and I met.

When I first saw Joe, he was wearing a sweater, and he looked so young, like a little kid, that I thought, "He couldn't work here, he must be somebody's son." It turned out he was supposed to understudy both Biff and Happy, and I'd watch him being rehearsed. He was wonderful as Happy, he got all the laughs, but as Biff, I'd never seen anything so funny in all my life. He's supposed to be this big football player, this hero, but not only didn't he have the build of a football player, he couldn't catch the ball if his life depended on it. They kept throwing the ball to him during rehearsal, and he kept dropping it, and I was sitting there laughing. Oh my god, it was like a comedy routine.

The thing that attracted me to Joe was that he had the answer to everything in the world. Anything you wanted to know, you went and asked Joe. He was extremely cocky, he presented himself as invincible, and at that time in my life, when I felt I didn't have any answers, or few, that was extremely appealing to me.

And Joe had other qualities. He was extremely charismatic and he had a brilliant mind—inquisitive, imaginative, and creative. He had a wonderful sense of humor, and he also was extremely energetic and very ambitious. I had gone out with other guys who had those qualities, but Joe had a quality that was different. He was extremely idealistic—politically, professionally, and socially—and that reminded me of my father and really attracted me to him.

My father, though a Mormon, was very liberal. He was Utah's secretary of state when Joe and I were first married, and later he ran for governor. Every boyfriend I ever went with would say to me, "Oh, Peggy, if only one day I could be like your father." He was real Americana, like a relic of the Old West. He had extraordinary integrity and honesty and belief in the Golden Rule. And Joe adored him. He said that he was the most wonderful man he had ever met, and the only man he had ever met that he trusted. He told some friends of ours, after we had separated and my father was dead, "Never a day goes by but what I don't think of Peggy's father and miss him."

The tour ended up in New York, and Joe and I got married. We were living on my unemployment insurance; Joe didn't have a job at all. We had enough money, I think $10, to buy one wedding ring, but we wanted a double-ring ceremony. We were walking down the street, wondering how we were going to get another $10 to buy the other ring, when we *found* one in the gutter. We just found one! We were walking down the street and Joe said, "What is that?" He saw something glittering and it was a wedding ring. Isn't that amazing? It really is like a metaphor for Joe's life.

JOSEPH PAPP When I came to New York, I'd never seen a New York production. I'd never been backstage in a Broadway house before. But Lee J. Cobb, who I knew from the Lab, was on at the Morosco—a theater I later tried to save from being torn down—and it was very thrilling for me to be there.

I was out of work, and acting was the only thing I knew, so I applied for acting jobs around New York. I never got any. To pursue acting, you really have to have a consummate desire to act. I never had that; I didn't have that kind of persuasiveness. I enjoyed acting, but to spend my life doing it was something else.

The first job I got was in Ulster County in upstate New York, working as a social director at a small hotel where a lot of Jewish people would come for the summer. While I was there, I met this very old woman, a marvelous old lady, very dignified, who was a member of the Daughters of the American Revolution and also one of the owners of the *Daily Worker*. I told her, "Gee, if I had a little bit of money, I could put on some one-act plays up here and we wouldn't have to have that schlocky Borscht Belt stuff we do all the time."

She agreed, and that was the first grant I got. It was very little money, but it was enough to get three or four actors up there, as well as Peggy and some friends. We called ourselves the Ulster County Players and we did things like Brecht's *The Jewish Wife* and Noël Coward's *Red Peppers*. I acted in all the plays, directed them all, built the scenery—I did everything.

PEGGY BENNION PAPP Joe was so busy doing everything, he would forget his lines. Every night, he would open his mouth, and nothing would come out, and I would start to laugh. And then he would forget the dance steps. That whole time was fun and really funny. That was his first venture in the theater.

JOSEPH PAPP Back in the city, I was desperate. I had no money and I just had to get a job. I'd thought about television before, but that was the last place in the world I'd wanted to go. In those early days, we in the theater had nothing but complete contempt for television. That was amateur night in Dixie as far as we were concerned; no self-respecting theater person would be caught dead in a television show.

But time went by, people were not getting other jobs, and CBS in particular was employing a lot of ex-theatrical stage managers in a job they at the time called floor manager. So I applied for that and in 1951 I was hired, first for what was known as per diem jobs, calling me when they needed someone. And even though I got the time mixed up, absolutely missed my very first show, and feared they were going to fire me, CBS eventually took me on a permanent basis.

I'd never worked at a television station before, but no one broke me in or anything like that. They gave me these earphones, they were called cans, attached to a little box, through which I'd get instructions from somebody else telling me what to do. "Put your cans on!" they would say. Whenever I have dreams where I feel as though I'm at the bottom of the ladder, I always end up carrying those damn cans.

I put them on and I heard so many people talking, I couldn't tell one voice from the other, I didn't know who the hell was talking to who. Then someone said, "Cue him."

"What?"

"Cue him! Cue him! Cue him!"

So I pointed my finger at somebody, and I learned that that's one of the main things a TV stage manager does. But I still had plenty to learn. One of the things I used to hear all the time was, "It's 41 to Tellecini. Tellecini, are you there? Rack up 46A." And I thought, "Jesus, wherever I go, there's this Italian guy Tellecini. He must be working night and day." It took me a long time to realize that it wasn't a person but a department, telecene, that was responsible for bringing up particular slides.

Once I got good at it, though—and I eventually became one of the top four or five guys—I enjoyed the job tremendously. On huge shows, I'd be responsible for the entire operation, including the changing of sets: you really stage-managed the whole thing. I'd have two or three hundred cues, and I wouldn't carry a book. I'd have to memorize them, because things would happen too fast to consult a book.

Also, I was able to meet a lot of important actors, and I had the influence to get some unemployed friends jobs in things like crowd scenes. And I became very active in the Radio and Television Directors Guild. I was on the negotiating committee that pushed through the name change in our jobs from floor manager to stage manager.

There was a recklessness in the early days of live television that I found very stimulating. We'd have huge cameras that these fantastic cameramen would hurtle across the floor, changing positions and focusing very rapidly. No one minded if the camera shot off the set or if things went askew, because the whole situation had a dynamic that was so vital.

CBS wanted to promote me up the ladder, first assistant director and then director, but I never had those ambitions. I didn't want to get stuck in a situation where I was always under the control of other people. In my theater I could choose my own plays and put them on; I couldn't do anything like that in television.

The first person I worked with was Ernie Kovacs. I was so new to this at the time, and he was so crazy, it was some combination. I came over onstage and introduced myself as the stage manager. He was puffing away on his cigar, running around, talking to people. I thought this was some kind of rehearsal, I wondered when the hell the show was going to start. Well, it had been on for fifteen minutes and I'd been in the camera's way—my picture had come up at least ten times, all without my knowing anything about it.

After that, I worked on everything from *I've Got a Secret* to Mike Wallace's first show, a friendly-friendly talk thing called *Mike and Buff*, to *Studio One*, *Omnibus*, and many David Susskind productions. I did a couple of Shakespeares, including, in 1953, a very interesting *King Lear* starring Orson Welles and directed by Andrew McCollough. Peter Brook was stage manager.

Brook was like a little firefly flitting around. Orson would say, "Peter—I'd like—" and it was always, "I'll be with you in a moment, Orson, I'll be with you in a moment." Brook would just sort of evade him, never let Orson come down on him. During the dress rehearsal, Orson did not make any strong effort to *play* the part and he was absolutely brilliant. I'd almost never seen a performance that good. But when he got on the air, he resorted to his old tricks, his kind of rolling voice, and he ended up being very pompous. He smoked great cigars, though, the best I ever got were from him and Ernie Kovacs.

Very early on in that job, my name got changed from Papirofsky to Papp. In the navy, people used to call me Pappy, and now, at CBS, because the space available to write down the names of stage managers on assignment sheets was very narrow, they squeezed my name into "J. Pap." I didn't like that—it sounded like mother's milk—so I added another *p* and then I thought "I'll start to use that name" and I changed it officially.

I sort of regret having done that and I tried to restore it at one point, but I thought it would be difficult for the children. Recently, the Brooklyn Botanic Garden put together a celebrity footpath with names of people born in that borough. My name was down there as Joseph Papp and I said I'd like to have Papirofsky instead. They said, "We've already made up the stone, it'll cost you $800," and I said I'd pay for it. I'm very proud of that name.

LAMAR CASELLI Joe and I were both working for CBS as stage managers in the early fifties. Our primary function was to run the stage and be the voice of the director up in the booth. It was a big job, and what made Joe good at it was that he was very calm, very cool. If something had to be done in an emergency situation, he'd do it. He always had the sense that the show must go on. If the stuff was hitting the fan, his attitude was, "Let's not all get hysterical here. Let's see what's going on and what we can do about it."

Joe was a very warm person, but he was pretty hard, too, and pretty goddamn stubborn. He was very independent, he knew what he wanted to do and he'd say what he thought. He knew the risks of certain things; he'd say his piece and take his lumps. Joe was his own man. He might dream up something, but he also figured out how to do it. He might not have steps one, two, three, and four all worked out, he might only have one and two, but he'd figure, "I'll get three somehow."

At the same time, Joe had a romantic, if you will, idea, a somewhat disingenuous notion, I thought, about the capability of most human beings to act in the common good. I felt that beyond a certain point, when it got a little too tough, the common good went out the window for most people. Joe, who was also much more political than I was, was more idealistic about that. He had a genuine interest in working people. He felt that they could participate and create a valid, living culture from the roots up, and that was his basic motivation. He wasn't interested in television; he wasn't interested in that particular job, even though he did it well. Television was the superficialities of life, and he wanted to get down to the basics.

Right from the time I knew him, Joe was very dedicated to establishing a repertory Shakespeare company that would be motivated from the ground up by involved people. He talked about Shakespeare all the time— he'd read all the plays, knew them by heart, backward, upside down, and so forth. He went into the history of other groups that had been successful in repertory, and he looked into every possible way to get public money to do this thing. He wouldn't just *say* anything, he'd *do* it. That's the thing I remember about Joe more than anything else.

DANIEL PETRIE I met Joe Papp when I directed a television version of *Body and Soul* for CBS, with Ben Gazzara in the John Garfield role and Franchot Tone as the fight promoter. Our floor managers were Kenny Utt and Joe, and they were the hottest shots in town. On big shows you oftentimes needed two, and it was always, "Can we get those two guys?" because if you had them, you had the first team. I had dozens of floor managers at that time, and I don't remember any of them; you could hypnotize me and maybe I could come up with some names. But Joe stood out, no question. He seemed always to have a great equanimity, to be undaunted. It was like being in good hands with Allstate. You were in good hands with Joe Papp.

There were a number of guys around at the time who had not made it in our business, and I never expected that they would because they didn't have any dream. But there were other guys who, when you'd stop and have a cup of coffee on the set, the conversation got around to something that was beyond the here and now. These were the young Turks, they wanted to go on. Arthur Penn was one of those guys, and Sidney Lumet, and Joe was in that echelon, you knew that he would do very well.

I never felt that I was Joe's boss. I always thought Joe and I were working together on a show. Neither he nor Kenny Utt were subservient-type employees. These guys didn't let you have any kind of feeling of obsequiousness. Joe had his job and I had mine. He was watching me in my performance, I was watching him in his, and you didn't give too many "attaboys." And so, when he started putting on Shakespeare and he asked me to direct, when I got that kind of approval from him, it made me feel good.

I don't know how widely he talked about it, but Joe did talk to me on several occasions about his dream of a free Shakespeare theater. But the dream was not "We'll have this great production, it'll be Stanislavsky or Artaud," it was never in those terms. The emphasis for Joe was political as opposed to artistic, to give something to the masses. It was always the audience, who would the audience be.

Joe had a feeling for ordinary people, and not in any kind of cloying or condescending way at all. He felt they were terrific people who life had cast in this kind of mold where they hadn't been able to go to schools. They'd had to get out and work, they didn't make a lot of money, and so on. But Shakespeare, the greatest dramatist of them all, would speak to these people. Even though they maybe wouldn't understand all those highfalutin' words, the people would enjoy that stuff. And since they couldn't afford good theater, he wanted to supply a place where ordinary people could go and experience it. Therefore, it was very important that the theater not have a fee or an admission price.

Shakespeare, I'm sure, had a symbolic meaning for Joe, in that it was high art and he felt that the lowly could be reached by it. So while the prevailing sentiment was that it was much too good for them, he was trying to say to the world, "It's not so at all. They're capable of supporting and appreciating it, and I'll prove it to you." Joe was absolutely messianic about that. It was a cause, a righteous one, and he really cared about it.

JAMES KIRKWOOD   I was on a soap opera on CBS in the fifties called *Valiant Lady.* I was son of Valiant Lady—sounds like a racehorse, doesn't it? "Son of Valiant Lady, coming into the stretch . . ." I was on it four years, which is enough to give you a concussion. And one of our floor managers was Joe Papp. I remember him always squatted down with the earphones, throwing us our cues. He seemed like a street fighter, tough and cocky with a lot of energy. And he used to make fun of our show. He'd say things like "You're not going to go out there and do *that*, are you?" Now, we had to get out there and treat it like it was deadly serious and good, and a couple of the actors, maybe even Valiant Lady herself, were annoyed that Joe made that much fun of what we had to do.

Then the show went off the air, thank god, because if it hadn't I would have stayed until they buried me. I went to California—I thought I was going to become a movie star—and I lost track of Joe. I came back to New York several years later, and I heard people talking about Joe Papp's Shakespeare in the Park. And I said, "Joe Papp! No . . . that can't be the same Joe Papp. This cocky little street fighter isn't going to be doing that." I'd always liked Joe, but if anyone had told me he was going to have anything to do with Shakespeare, it would have been a laugh, the two just seemed so disparate to me. When we started working on *A Chorus Line*, I used to say to him, "Hey, Joe, what about us and Valiant Lady?" And Joe would look at me almost like "Oh, yeah, um-hm, well, now—uh—"

JOSEPH PAPP Besides working at CBS, I taught classes and directed at places like Sanford Meisner's Neighborhood Playhouse. I tried to keep going one way or another. I'd always liked the Irish writers, Sean O'Casey in particular, and at the Actors' Lab I'd met people who knew and worked with him. His plays were so rich, filled with very colorful writing, and though from a political point of view he seemed to be in the same place I was, there was nothing in his plays that was overtly Marxist or ideological. So I began to write to him in Ireland, asking if I could put on some of his plays for nothing. He wrote me a no-nonsense letter. "I make my living by writing," he said. "I can't give you anything for nothing." But finally I convinced him to let me have, for a small royalty, three one-act plays, *Hall of Healing*, *Bedtime Story*, and *Time to Go*.

BERNARD GERSTEN I was working as a stage manager in New York when Joe called me and said, "Listen, there are these three great plays by Sean O'Casey. I want to produce them. Why don't we do it together?" The difference between Joe and me is, Joe is driven and I drive. Joe had to produce those plays, he had to, it was a necessity for him. To me, it was just Joe saying, "Let's do it," and me saying, "Sure." And that was our relationship, it was typified by countless things like that.

So Joe and me and Charlie Cooper, one of our Aznarebuxe from the Actors' Lab, and a new guy, Peter Lawrence, the four of us set out to produce. We had to raise, I don't know, maybe $5,000 or $10,000, which was a lot of money, and to this day I don't know where the hell we got it. We put the plays on at the Yugoslav-American Hall on Forty-first Street just west of Eighth Avenue. It's since been torn down to make way for the Port Authority Bus Terminal. And we got into considerable trouble with certain people because they thought the hall might be a hotbed of Titoists. We really didn't know if we could withstand being excoriated on those grounds; there were plenty of brushes for tarring with in those years.

JOSEPH PAPP The Yugoslav-American Hall was not the most attractive place. It was noisy, and these Yugoslavs were drinking every night and rousing it up. We used to hear them shouting and arguing in Serbo-Croatian. So we were working not under the best of circumstances.

Not only was I one of the producers, I directed two of the plays, and I did some unusual things with the casting. I used some members of the James Connolly Association, kind of a left-wing Irish organization headed by Big Tim Murphy. I don't know what their aim was; I hope they had a bad one. They were real Irishmen, though, very lively. They'd spend nights reading poetry and arguing with one another. They were anarchists, but their biggest violence was invariably verbal.

While the James Connolly people added a touch of reality, I also used black actors in some of the parts. I wasn't crazy—I made sure these people could play the roles. I didn't want someone with a Deep South accent playing an Irishman, but it wasn't a casual decision. The reason I selected these people was to give black actors a chance. My whole upbringing and background had brought me to that. Coming from one myself, I've always had a connection with minorities, a strong identification with people who were struggling, and I always felt it was my obligation to do as much as I could for them.

Here I was, producing and directing, and I was not really equipped. I had very little experience going in, and I was dealing with actors that had much more experience as actors than I had as a director. But I've always functioned better under those conditions. The actors gave me a lot and I was able to use what they had. Initially, I cast Lee Grant as the lead in *Bedtime Story*, but she had to leave the show because the man she was living with felt that this was an anti-woman play. Now if O'Casey was anything, he was hardly anti-woman, but she left the show. I had met Anne Jackson when her husband, Eli Wallach, had played Sancho Panza in a production of *I, Don Quixote* I stage-managed at CBS, and I hired her as a replacement.

LEE GRANT I had made an enormous kind of splash as an actress. I'd done *Detective Story*, first on Broadway and then on film, won the best actress award at the Cannes Film Festival, and was nominated for an Oscar. My visibility was very high at the time, and then the blacklist hit. When I couldn't work, I think it was a very natural thing for Joe to reach out, first of all, to a person who was young and blacklisted, and also because I had name value.

Joe wanted me to do an O'Casey play. It was a very charming kind of sex-romp comedy, and I was dying to do it. But my husband at that time objected. The blacklist had just hit us, and there were so many other priorities, like two little children that my husband had who were very tiny and needed to be taken care of.

I don't think Joe realized that his offer caused a real tug-of-war in my house, because the opportunity of doing O'Casey was terribly, overwhelmingly appealing to me. But it just did not fit in with the kind of stringent house requirements that I had at the time, so I had to pass that by.

ANNE JACKSON My play, *Bedtime Story*, was about a young woman who goes to bed with a man, and it's the reverse of what usually happens in those situations. Instead of the woman saying, "Oh, what did I do, why did this happen?" it's the man who starts lamenting his fate. Joe directed it as a very serious piece, and I thought, "Seems to me like it's farcical and funny," which, as it turned out, it was.

But in the old days Joe was a very serious young man, almost too serious and extremely conscientious. He was very handsome, and the world weighed heavily upon his shoulders. I don't think any of us thought that he was going to be the number-one man in theater. If anything, we thought he would be a bit of a maverick, a malcontent, and a stirrer-upper of things.

....

BROOKS ATKINSON,
"At the Theater," *New York Times*, May 8, 1952

Eighteen years having elapsed since a new O'Casey play was done in this town, a patron of the arts instinctively rises to attention when a new bill is announced. Some actors who admire the most invisible of our dramatists have put on three O'Casey one-act plays at Yugoslav-American Hall, 405 West Forty-first Street, where they opened last evening.

The plays were written a good many years ago, but they were not published until last autumn . . . These are three of his main themes and principles. But there is no way of evading the fact that the plays are inferior O'Casey. You would hardly suspect that the man who wrote them is also author of *Juno and the Paycock* and the most glorious autobiography written in our time, two volumes of which are yet to be published.

Although the actors and impresarios of the current bill have Mr. O'Casey's best interests at heart, they are not doing him any great service on the stage. To judge by the performances of the first two pieces, the acting is frantically inadequate. Neither the director of the first two plays nor the actors who are in them have any sense of genre style for Irish drama. If there were no Equity actors among them, you would assume that they were amateurs taking a fling at something for which they have little talent.

In short, the current enterprise leaves the O'Casey saga about where it stopped eighteen years ago, when *Within the Gates* made the author many friends and a number of enemies. Since then, he has written five or six full-length dramas, most of them presenting difficult problems of performance. They need to be staged and acted exclusively by geniuses, preferably nurtured on the old sod and saturated in Yeats and Synge.

• •

JOSEPH PAPP Brooks Atkinson came to see the show without being invited. He looked very distinguished, like he didn't belong in the hall; he certainly wasn't Serbo-Croatian. I died when I saw him there. We were in dress rehearsal, we weren't even ready. But he was a big supporter of O'Casey, and I have a feeling O'Casey, who would have dropped dead if he knew we used black actors in it, must have said to him, "Why don't you go and take a look at it? See if they've destroyed me or not."

The review came out the morning after we opened. A lot was riding on it—it was my first really professional undertaking, my first review—and I was devastated. It just cut my legs off, cut the ground out from under me. My reaction to things like that always surprises me, and this meant more to me than I'd thought it would. I don't allow myself to experience the way I really feel. If I did, it would be so powerful a feeling that it would not permit me to function properly, so I instinctively distance myself.

I read the review in the morning, and I began to walk around Central Park. It was a pleasant day, but the park wasn't very crowded, so I sat on a bench, listened to the birds twitter, and thought, "Maybe I should do something else." And then, "But what do I know?" My qualifications were nonexistent. I didn't know anything else; theater was something I thought I knew. But Atkinson was telling me I didn't know that, either. He was saying, "Who is this person who did this?"

I had made what I felt was such a strong effort. Everything I'd done had led up to those plays, everything was riding on them. What if they really were that bad? Having your name in the *Times*, being told you're not good, that you should get out of the theater—it was one of the lowest points in my life. But I didn't give up. What would I give up to? How do you give up? I don't know how. What do you do, drown yourself? The only way to give up is to commit suicide, and I'm not in that vein.

PEGGY BENNION PAPP Joe didn't know his ass from his elbow, so what did he do, he chose, of all things, some Sean O'Casey. It takes someone very experienced in English and Irish theater to pull that off. It was blasted by the critics, particularly Brooks Atkinson, who said something like Joe should get out of the theater.

We went and sat on a park bench, and Joe said, "Well, that's the end of my theatrical career. I'm no good, I have no talent, I'm a bomb, and I have to find another career. I'm not trained for anything else. Maybe I'll go back to school. I don't know what I'll do, but obviously I have no ability in this field." But Joe is like a ball that bounces back. Somehow or other, no matter how many times he slips and falls, he bounces back. That's another of the qualities that I admired in him.

4

Early Shakespeare:
The Emmanuel Presbyterian Church
1953-56

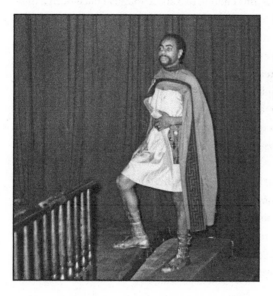

Roscoe Lee Browne in
Julius Caesar at the
Emmanuel Presbyterian
Church
© George E. Joseph

JOSEPH PAPP After the Actors' Lab, I was always trying to start a theater.
I was consumed by the idea. I never liked freelancing, the thought of one-
shots, of going from this to that to the other thing. The Lab taught me that
you need a place to go to every day, something you can build on. I wanted
to reconstitute a home, always, and I also had to be doing something that
was useful and important. I always saw theater as an important poetic and
political force. I never wanted to be in show business—that idea was anath-
ema to me.

My reputation at the time wasn't much. It was based on what I'd done with the Ulster County Players, plus the fact that I'd been on the road with *Death of a Salesman*. But somehow this amateur troupe called the Oval Players found me. The group was mostly made up of married people who lived in the Stuyvesant Town and Peter Cooper Village housing projects. They were putting on plays at the nearby Emmanuel Presbyterian Church, 729 East Sixth Street, between Avenues C and D, and when they asked me to direct something called *The Curious Savage* in 1951, I agreed.

I was taken to see this church, to a space that had once been a Sunday school. Though I was thinking of all kinds of plays, Shakespeare must have been foremost on my mind. It wasn't necessarily an immediate reaction, but as I used the space, the thought kept coming back to me, "Hey, this would make a great place to do Shakespeare." There was something quite lovely and simple about the architecture—there was even a little stairway that led to a balcony. Though the usable space was not like the Globe and its seats were crumbling, the feeling of the place as a whole—its age and its dimensions—reminded me of Shakespeare.

SYLVIA GASSELL It was like an amphitheater, the seats graded down to a slightly elevated floor, which was the playing area. There were windows in the back, high up, behind the audience. If one wanted to do a quick sketch, it was like one of Gordon Craig's very simple designs brought down to a small scale. Everything was wood, even the floor was wood, so when you spoke, the acoustics were simply wonderful.

JOSEPH PAPP As much as I liked that space, there was nothing I could do about it. This other group was there and I wasn't going to encroach on them in any way. Then one day in 1953 I heard that the Oval Players had disbanded, and I thought, "Here's an opportunity to get a place." I went down there and rang the little bell of the reverend's residence, which was right next to the church. A cheery-faced man answered the door, and I said, "Reverend Clarence Boyer? Do you have a moment?" And he was so polite, he said, "Oh, sure. What can I do for you?"

He took me into his office. It was so cluttered, there was almost no place to sit. With one of these big rolltop desks, the whole place, including Reverend Boyer, looked right out of Dickens. Cheerful, ruddy, big-bellied with a round, boyish face, he was a real Presbyterian, a very gentle and kind person, but quite strong in the way he functioned.

"Reverend Boyer," I said, "I want to start a Shakespeare workshop in your theater here. I want to put on plays by him and other Elizabethans."

"Aha!" His eyebrows went up and he said, "You realize that you'll have to pay for the heat. That'll be at least $10 a week."

"That's not bad," I said. I realized he wasn't even going to charge me any rent—he would let me use the auditorium as a community facility.

Then Boyer smiled at me and asked, "Do you think anybody will come?"

"I really don't know," I said. "We're going to try this, see if it's possible." I tried to give him some of my ideas, but I wasn't quite sure I knew myself. I just wanted to get some actors together and experiment with doing Shakespeare.

Why Shakespeare? In terms of theater, he is a master, there is no greater writer for the stage in the English language, and that happens to be a fact. You can't be an educated person unless you have more than a passing familiarity with the works of William Shakespeare.

I fell in love with this man and his work very early on, it opened up whole educational areas for me. I began to think about my life in larger terms. To me, he's the symbol of everything that's great on the stage—a marvelous, nourishing greatness. Everything else seems a diet of thin gruel: actors and audiences can't grow on that, they'll be undernourished.

And if you want to go further—and you don't have to, that's certainly enough—his plays give you an insight into the processes of life that is not available in as concentrated a form anywhere else. If you say you know the thirty-six plays of Shakespeare, you're saying a lot.

RALPH K. HOLMES Once Joe got the right to use the church down on Sixth Street, we got together a crew of like twenty-one stagehands, friends of ours, a fabulous crew who donated their time to pull this thing together. Some of them were working in television; they would come for four hours and go back to work. Or they'd show up in the morning for a couple of hours on a Saturday, leave to work a matinee, and return for a couple of hours in the evening.

Because we worked at CBS, we knew about a lot of theaters that had been turned into TV studios where there were just piles of old lighting equipment lying around that no one would buy or use. We knew a lot of this stuff was going to be thrown out; it was just sitting in a basement ready to be hauled away. We scrounged these things. We took a piece from here and a piece from there, and we put together a whole lighting system. There was a company called Meyer Harris that had the cheapest, oldest, crummiest theatrical lighting equipment in the world, and they wouldn't have bought what we scrounged.

We were also able to get enough drapes to make a surround and some carpeting so we could do the aisles and the stage floor. I got together a whole sound system, including speakers and amplifiers, which I donated. And if a network had gone into a theater and taken out ten or fifteen rows of seats to build a control room right in the middle of the orchestra pit, those seats would also be just in a junk heap down in the basement. So we transformed this whole space into a theater.

JOSEPH PAPP I tried to outfit the theater, to get some equipment. There was one guy named Leo Brody I hooked into, who had an army-navy surplus store right in that area. He had no experience in the theater, but he was very supportive; he put in a bit of money. But he became very upset when he wanted to be coproducer with me and I said no. I always instinctively protected that function; the fundamental idea was mine and I knew I was the best person to represent it. I don't think the organization would have survived if I had not done that.

One of our biggest problems were those crumbling benches. Then someone brought me an ad that said that the seats from the Windsor, an old twenties movie theater in the Bronx, were for sale.

I went up there and found a guy sitting and waiting for customers to show up. It looked like nobody was buying those damn things. I went up to him and said, "I'd like some of those chairs."

He looked at me and said, "Thirty-five dollars a chair."

I said, "I'll give you fifty cents," and he said, "Okay."

I asked him how to get the chairs out of there and he just said, "Well, you'll have to get them out," which was a lot easier said than done. The theater was pitch-dark, there was no electricity, and the chairs were connected in rows and bolted down into the concrete floor.

I called my friend Lamar Caselli and he came up with two hammers, a screwdriver, and a flashlight. We lay on our sides, with the flashlight on the floor next to us, trying to knock off those bolts. It took forever, hour after hour for days. I don't know how the hell we were able to do it. And then, because six of those heavy metal chairs together weighed an enormous amount, once the bolts were off, they'd all flop over and we could barely move them.

That was only step one. Then we had to get the seats down to the church. Around Sixth Street, I saw this beat-up truck. It looked like it had been around for hundreds of years. I asked the driver if I could rent it, and if he could bring some people with him. He agreed, but the guys he brought looked as though they'd rather fall asleep than work. We started to load the damn things on the truck, and sure enough these guys turned out to be useless. Lamar and I carried most of the stuff. I never did more lifting than I did in those days.

We finally got to the church, but because the seats were still in rows, we couldn't get them through the goddamn door. So we spent more hours trying to separate them, and we finally managed to bring them in two at a time. We had to stack them against a wall because we hadn't yet gotten around to taking out the crumbling benches.

Once that was done, the question was, "How are we going to bolt these seats down?" I wasn't a very experienced carpenter or anything like that, plus the flooring had been around for a long time, and the wood didn't look very steady to me. But I knew I would have to connect the seats from underneath the wood.

How would I get under the floor? I found a passageway, but the dust was so thick, I don't think anyone had been under there for a hundred years. To be able to work I would get a wet handkerchief, put it around my nose and mouth, lay on my back, and drill holes in the floor. First I tried to use heavy screws, but as soon as somebody sat down, the seats popped up.

Then I thought of toggle bolts, and I had to go under there again and bolt everything down, and even with that the seats leaned back a little bit when people used them.

I originally called the place the Elizabethan Theater Workshop because I didn't want to limit myself, but eventually I ended up with the Shakespearean Theater Workshop. In the meantime, I decided I'd put an ad in one of the show-business papers, basically saying, "I'm looking for actors." Some people I already knew came down, and their friends, but to my amazement the group started to grow, actors told other actors, there were little stirrings of interest from the outside in what I was doing.

There must have been a crying need for this, or else why were people coming down to this godforsaken place on East Sixth Street. There's a constant need for young people, who don't have a chance, to have a place to go. If I opened a place like that again on East Sixth Street, I'd get people coming the same way. It's not even breaking in—it's needing to act, needing to direct, needing to write music. The problem is, how do you maintain and sustain this, because once somebody is recognized, they'll leave. How do you get continuity in all of this—that's the job of it all.

MERLE DEBUSKEY I got a herald one day, announcing a series of scenes that were being done in a place called the Emmanuel Church, and across it Joe Papp had written, "Hey, can you help us get anything in the papers about this?"

I had had a lot of experience working in what became known as the off-Broadway movement, and I'd publicized the one-act plays by O'Casey that Joe had coproduced. So I went down to this church, which was way out of the orbit in those days, and I found a group of unknowns that Joe was responsible for gathering together. They were working toward being able to handle the language of Shakespeare. They were evolving, hopefully, a new American style toward the classics to replace what at that time was a rather mediocre mirror-image of the British theater. They had reached the point where they decided they would like people to see them, and the gist of this communiqué was: Could I do anything that might help them get an audience?

You have to understand that the circumstance of the late forties and early fifties was not the circumstance of the middle fifties or what followed.

Anything away from Broadway was considered amateur. An actor who had played Broadway would almost never go down away from Broadway. There was not an area known as off Broadway which could be described and which played a consistent part in the tableau of the theater. So to get anything into the papers was rather difficult. However, we did persevere and were able to get some small attention, though we got a lot more in publications like *The Compass* and *PM* than we did in the *Times*.

STUART VAUGHAN   I was understudying Cyril Ritchard in the Theatre Guild's Broadway production of *The Millionairess*, but that gets a little boring, so one looks around for other things to do that wouldn't mean quitting a paying job.

In *Show Business*, a little newspaper, I saw that something called the Shakespeare Workshop was having auditions for a nonpaying showcase production of *Romeo and Juliet*. I went down to this church on the Lower East Side and there was this nice-looking, black-haired, fast-talking-selling sort of fellow in charge. He also had this Actors Studio–cultivated "I don't believe you because you talk funny because you're not from New York" quality to him. The young Lee Strasberg had the same quality; a lot of these people half insulted everybody they met. I think it was kind of a left-wing thing to do.

The whole setup seemed somewhat spurious to me and fly-by-night. It was not pleasing even to a rather wet-behind-the-ears recent arrival out of Indiana, so I didn't come back.

SYLVIA GASSELL   I became a professional actress in 1952, when I appeared with Shirley Booth in *The Time of the Cuckoo*, the only hit I've ever been in on Broadway. As a result of that play, which was directed by Harold Clurman, I joined his acting class. It was a very exciting class for professional actors held after the curtain came down, and a handful of people who were not known at the time but were eventually going to become very prominent, like Colleen Dewhurst, were in it.

One night in 1954 Harold assigned me the role of the Nurse in a scene from *Romeo and Juliet*. Afterward, an actor in the class told me they were looking for someone to play the Nurse in some group over on the

Lower East Side, over in what they called Alphabet City, between Avenues C and D. I didn't know anything about it, no name that he'd mentioned meant anything to me, but I figured, "Why not?"

I called up Joe Papp, the name I'd been given. He told me to come down, and when I got there I discovered this perfectly beautiful theater in a church house, with a harmony and a spatial arrangement that was immediately attractive. And I discovered that several of the actors who were sitting around in a circle with me, though not top stars, were rather prominent in the theater, people like Alfred Ryder, Anthony Franciosa, and Olive Deering. I also realized that one of my co-students in Harold's class, Peggy Bennion, was Joe's wife. We had a funny exchange at one point.

"Oh, Sylvia, you're so much smarter than I," she said. "You married a director."

"But Peggy, you married a producer."

"Oh," she said at the time. "What does that mean?"

COLLEEN DEWHURST I got a call one day—it was over in my cold-water flat on West Fiftieth between Ninth and Tenth—from a man who said his name was Joe Papp. He said he wanted to start a small Shakespeare group, and that his wife, Peggy Bennion, who was in Harold Clurman's class with me, had suggested he call. Then he mentioned *Romeo and Juliet*, and that was my famous line: "Have you ever seen me?" He said no and I said, "Well, I couldn't have been Juliet when I was twelve." He said that it didn't matter, I should come down anyway.

Why did I go down there? I think probably I was delighted that someone had called. I was the kind of actress who lost apartments when I did summer stock and then took any job I could find when I came back. I would go anywhere there was work. I didn't care whether they paid or not, I just wanted to work. I thought someday some big mogul would call and say, "I have this wonderful play and the lead is just for you." This, of course, turned out to be the big phone call, but who was to know it? Certainly not Joe and I.

SYLVIA GASSELL We had several rehearsals with these people, mostly just reading *Romeo and Juliet*, and then the more prominent names seemed to disappear and drift off. They might have gotten job commitments, or they may have wanted to see things move faster than they were.

This was the production where they couldn't keep a Romeo—Joe went through like eight of them. The situation finally devolved, if that's the proper word, to just two of us, a girl named Bryarly Lee doing Juliet and myself doing the Nurse. Joe had already done a program of scenes called *An Evening with Shakespeare and Marlowe*, and though they were sweet, to my eyes they kept demonstrating that there was something amiss in the approach to the work.

By this point, early in 1955, when I knew that *Romeo and Juliet* was really dead, that nothing was going to move it now, I felt I knew Joe well enough to say, "Please let me bring my husband, Joel Friedman, into the situation." I told him Joel had an uncanny ability to communicate to American actors who had been trained, for want of a better word, in the internal method of theater, and bring them up to the technical demands of Shakespeare. He had an unusually close knowledge of the classic theater, Shakespeare in particular, and he was very much involved with dramatic criticism from the psychoanalytic point of view as well.

I think one of the secrets of Joe's ability to succeed as he has is that he's got a good nose for what might happen and he's willing to let people run with an idea. And that's what happened here. I told him why I thought Joel would be a profit to the theater, and he said, "All right, have him prepare a scene and then we'll talk after that." So I asked Colleen Dewhurst if she would do a scene from *Henry V*. It played, along with our one scene from *Romeo and Juliet*, in an evening called *Shakespeare's Women*. Well, the thing was no sooner over than Joe said, "Let's go out and talk immediately." We told him about us and he said, "Okay, we'll form a company."

JOEL FRIEDMAN   Joe appeared very open and very willing to try new things. Of course, at this point, he really didn't know where to turn. He was running out of actors. He'd had all these semi-celebrities down there and they'd disappeared. So he really didn't quite know what to do until he met me. But he was very willing to accept any ideas that either of us offered him.

The first thing I said was, "Let's do a whole play, not just scenes." I think he selected the first production, which was *Much Ado About Nothing*, and it was decided that he would bring down his people and we would bring down ours, no questions asked. Whoever was brought down, that would be it.

Colleen Dewhurst couldn't join this first company—she couldn't give her days because she was working as a telephone operator for SAG at the time—but she sent down her husband, James Vickery, plus J. D. Cannon. We came in with about fifteen actors. Everyone there seemed to be one of our people, except for a thin young man, about seventeen or eighteen. I assumed Joe had brought him, so even though we were disheartened because he had terrible speech, I cast him as Verges, one of the constables in *Much Ado*. And Joe came up to me later and said, "Why did you cast him?"

"He's your actor," I said. "We made an arrangement to give everybody a part."

"He's a neighborhood kid," Joe said. "He cleans the theater."

We were so delighted with his nerve; we didn't dream of taking the part away from him. Later, I gave him the part of William in *As You Like It*. He eventually changed his name to Joe Spinell and you've seen him in a thousand films, he plays hoods and maniacs and so on. He was a street kid, and it literally changed his life.

JOE SPINELL I started acting at the Madison Square Boys Club on the east side when I was nine years old. I appeared there with Raymond Duke, Patty Duke's brother, in *The Ransom of Red Chief*. I had come in twelfth in a citywide Shakespeare contest for high school students, doing Cassius based on Joseph Mankiewicz's *Julius Caesar*, which Marlon Brando was in, and my English teacher at Seward Park High School told me about Mr. Papp.

I was seventeen, I'd just graduated, and I met Mr. Papp. He was very nice. He told me I had this New York accent and whatever, but he said maybe he could put me in somewhere. The first order of business was to get the theater in shape. So Mr. Papp gave us some hammers and nails, and because I knew about things like that, I was nailing down these theater seats, wherever he was stealing them from. We were putting down rugs, and these lamps Ralph Holmes would be lugging in—I don't know whether they robbed those or not.

Mr. Papp never promised nothing. He said, "This is what it is." But I liked the idea of being with all these professionals, people like J. D. Cannon, James Vickery, Paul Stevens, Sylvia Gassell, and Joel Friedman, and I hoped that I would improve my speech. I worked there for three years. Whatever he needed me for, I would do. Why not? Nothing wrong with that. I didn't only work backstage, he also let me audition for little parts. I played the dumb guy in *Much Ado* and I played William in *As You Like It*. One time some people didn't show up and I had to play three little parts in one show.

"I don't know if I can remember all those lines," I said to Sylvia Gassell.

"You're a Catholic, aren't you?" she asked. "Well, say a prayer." And as I said my prayer, she kicked me onstage.

When we appeared in a play, we had our pictures posted outside. You saw all these black-and-white pictures of Paul Stevens and J. D. Cannon, very professional. I couldn't afford that, so I used my old high school graduation picture, which was tinted in brown, like I was Paul Muni from the old days. And that's what they used to call me: Sepia Joe. Which was all right with me.

The wonderful thing about Joseph Papp was that he was a visionary; he was going to sell Shakespeare, American style. For the most part, Americans really couldn't give two shits for Shakespeare because they couldn't understand it. Joseph Papp wanted to use American actors and bring it to people in a simplified manner. Regular people in the neighborhood started coming—my mother, my sister, my girlfriend from high school. And they were getting into it, they were digging it, which is the greatest tribute I can give to him, because it's like teaching someone from a foreign land, Borneo, who doesn't know the words of the Bard.

I changed my name when I did summer stock because they told me Joseph Spagnuolo, which is what it was, was too Italian. They told me I could keep my initials, though, so I looked in the phone book, saw Spinell Diamonds, and that's how I became Joe Spinell.

Sylvia Gassell once asked me what I wanted to be, and when I said, "I want to be a movie actor, make lots of movies one day," she laughed at me. But it happened. I was in *Rocky* and *The Godfather I* and *II*. But my proudest moment was when Mr. Papp gave me his penknife with the initials "J.P." To have a knife from someone you admired so much, it was really wonderful.

J. D. CANNON   I heard from a friend of mine, Colleen Dewhurst, that somebody was going to do Shakespeare on the Lower East Side, so I went down to see about it. I wasn't working as an actor at the time. I was a cashier in the Russian Tea Room on Fifty-seventh Street. I did summer stock, things like that, but the rest of the time it was scrounging around trying to get anything. The church was way the hell and gone over there, and the only reason I went at all was because I wasn't doing anything and it was a place to act, a place to learn.

I met Joe and it became obvious pretty soon that he was full of piss and vinegar, what with his commitment to this thing with no money at all. The first director was Joel Friedman. He had kind of a hysterical personality and some very strange ideas about how words should be pronounced in Shakespeare. Whenever he could find a word that had any kind of a sexual connotation, it was to be pronounced in such a way as to enlarge on that. Joel was a very hard worker and a dedicated guy, but the workshop was Joe's baby, there was no question about it.

The spirit of the company was very good because none of us had anything to lose. Nothing was at stake as far as our careers hanging in the balance and that made for very good rapport. It had to be good, because going way over there, working with little heat in the middle of the winter, Christ almighty, the circumstances were horrendous. We had a lot of people who came down and wouldn't have any part of it. No money was involved— it looked like such a loser proposition—they could see no redeeming qualities.

For myself, I kept at it because I was learning and I wasn't being offered anything else. By the time Joe started that whole thing, I'd gotten so discouraged I wasn't even making the rounds anymore. So it's really due to that that I've had any kind of career at all. The creative juices were flowing, I was involved in something I believed in, not just another paycheck, and I got to do parts that I would never have gotten to do in the commercial theater. That was probably the high point of my acting life.

God knows, though, I never thought it would become what it has, but it did because Joe remained a visionary, because of his commitment. He could be pretty roughshod with people, like: "There are only two ways of doing it, my way and my way." But you have to think that way if you're going to do what he's done. People who have done a lot less than Joe have made enemies, too, you know.

JOEL FRIEDMAN It was very fortuitous that we met Joe at just that time, because he was also passionate about Shakespeare. It was a very happy union of the three of us. We all had the same goal of trying to get the American actor to do Shakespeare because our generation was all Actors Studio influenced. In the fifties, if you didn't get into Actors Studio, you bought a gun. It was as simple as that. There was nowhere else to go, nothing else to do.

And as for training in the classics, Actors Studio was unbelievably deficient. These actors were all internally trained, so there was a reluctance on their part to deal with language. When you're doing Clifford Odets, when you're doing contemporary playwrights, everything is not expressed. In Shakespeare, everything is expressed. I'd try to get them to work on the line, to appreciate the music of the line, and this was all very strange to them.

The breakthrough happened with Paul Stevens. He had been going on in the usual way, hesitating and acting in pantomime for a half hour before he said the next line. Then one time he came on and he thought he was going to ridicule me. He started doing the lines musically and rhythmically and out and big. When it was over I said, "That's absolutely right! I know you're joshing me, I know you think you're putting me on, but that's the way to play it." And from then on, we had no problems. It was the first Shakespeare done by American actors of our generation that did not have that kind of kitchen-sink feeling about it.

Joe always had a sense of bringing theater to the people, this was always uppermost in his mind, and that's why the plays were free to the public. Because there was no money, I said to Joe, "Why don't we do black-and-white Shakespeare," that's what I remember calling it. Joe pointed out that we had no black actors in the company, and I said, "No, no, no, no. All the men have white shirts and black pants to wear, or if they don't they can borrow them."

Somewhere along the way it was discovered that in a loft on Fifth Avenue there were discarded, unworn bridal gowns from Lord and Taylor selling for $5 apiece. They were lace and satin and silk, absolutely beautiful. We dressed the women in these white ball gowns and things looked pretty stunning.

I told Joe, "Don't use any gels. We'll just use white light and make it very stark. And we'll hold the books. The actors will memorize the parts thoroughly, but holding the books will give the audience a kind of limited expectation as far as production elements are concerned." And that's how we did the very first production.

As far as dealing with the actors, theory, or the technical aspects of acting, Joe let me have my head. He produced and I directed, and I don't recall him ever wanting to preempt me in any way. He kept the organization running, he provided everything I as a director needed. All I had to do was worry about the aesthetic elements. And I could lean on him and depend upon him. It was a very affable relationship at the time.

PEGGY BENNION PAPP   It was a very exciting time because it was so new and so daring. Doing Shakespeare way down on the Lower East Side was certainly idealistic. The actors were totally unknown at the time, and the audiences were very small. Sometimes, if we had a snowstorm, there were more people onstage than in the seats. Who on earth would come to a place like that to watch a dinky company that nobody had ever heard of? Playing in wedding dresses? They certainly weren't working-class people, they were friends of the cast, word of mouth, and far-out groups. There are little intellectual pockets here in New York of people who go anyplace and do anything.

FLORENCE ANGLIN   We had to dress and rehearse in a gym, which was in back of the stage. A lot of the windows were broken, and in cold weather, because there was no heat in the building, we had to rehearse in winter coats and boots. It was really most inhumanly cold at times. Finally, Joe went out and got one of those little round kerosene heaters, which we put in a side room, because in the gym it wouldn't have given off enough heat to make a difference.

Because we worked in black-and-white, I remember going around to thrift shops looking for women's graduation robes to turn into some kind of costume. There wasn't money for anything else. Every once in a while Joe would give us some money for carfare. That was the only payment we saw.

I came into the workshop through Joel Friedman. I had never actually performed Shakespeare before, and I was glad to have the opportunity to do it. Joel had a very respectful regard for the language, and he made playing it very simple. He'd make the play a living thing rather than a museum piece. You had great confidence that he knew his Shakespeare—you just absolutely took his word for everything. Joe Papp left Joel alone, and I believe the experience was a learning process for Joe. If you put me on the stand I couldn't prove it, but it's my feeling that what Joe Papp knew about Shakespeare he learned from Joel Friedman.

SYLVIA GASSELL I think the whole group had the experience of a lifetime, but you must remember we were all working for no money. The day of off-off-Broadway, where not getting paid was the rule, did not exist then, and some of the company, like Paul Stevens, had achieved, if not fame, the status of a regular working actor. So it was a little hard to keep people going on the love of the theater.

Joe used to pass the hat after every performance, and Joel and I were a little snobby, we didn't like the idea. It made us look like we were street actors, and this was long before the day when street actors became the vogue. If you were a professional, you didn't pass the hat, and that upset us a good deal backstage. However, Joe was right and we were wrong.

After the 1955 season, Joe came up with the suggestion that he might be able to provide carfare, ten cents each way, when we assembled again. Then it turned out that he couldn't, and for a moment it seemed as though we would not continue because the actors had been rather strong about at least getting carfare. I remember Joel saying to Joe at one point, "Look, I'm not getting paid, so make sure my name is on all the advertisements. That will be my payment." And I think Joe learned that, once he was the one in control, he wanted his stamp to be on everything.

Joe also had the brainstorm of getting chartered as a tax-exempt organization by the University of the State of New York Education Department. It was probably the first indirect grant, a grant without money, that anybody got. It backfired for the professional actors in the company, because the very word "educational" made it seem like they were amateurs and led to patronizing mentions in reviews, like "This isn't really Broadway." But it gave the workshop cachet; it was an opening point for approaching people and for getting a grant.

BERNARD GERSTEN   Getting a charter for the Shakespeare Workshop, having a great idea and formalizing it that way, was critically important. What you have to appreciate is that in 1954 there were not the number of not-for-profit theaters that there are today. We take that whole universe for granted because they're now littered all over the landscape, but thirty-four years ago the idea that a theater might be organized for purposes other than making money was by no means commonplace.

JOSEPH PAPP   Getting a nonprofit charter, raising whatever little money we needed just to do what we were doing, outfitting the place, getting actors, getting directors, advertising, and so forth—all of this was going on simultaneously. It was quite a job, especially since I was still working for CBS. I operated partially out of our apartment, using the address as the theater's return address, and partially out of a little place I fixed up—a terrible location, there were rats around and so forth—at the church. It was all a mosaic of how you put a theater together.

Productions cost practically nothing; there were virtually no props except a few things we'd make ourselves. My sister-in-law worked at Lord and Taylor, and we found a way to get old wedding gowns for costumes for like $5 apiece. Whatever people had, they brought. The only cost of the productions, essentially, was carfare to rehearsals for those who couldn't afford it. And occasionally, I'd buy them a sandwich or two, but not very often. But even with budgets of just a few dollars there was absolutely no money. And because people weren't making a living, many nights a guy who had a leading part just wouldn't show up, and I had to go on and do the role. After each performance, I'd make a speech: "Ladies and gentlemen, you must realize that we have no funds whatsoever for this operation." We would collect maybe $10 if we were lucky. We sent letters to the shopkeepers in the area, but we didn't do too well with that. They considered us "those crazy people doing Shakespeare." I owed the printing guy down the block $23 and he wrote me saying, "Mr. Shakespeare, I know you're poetic and all that, but I need to keep my business afloat."

There were other problems as well. When we first started at the church and we thought about doing *Romeo and Juliet*, I had eight Romeos leave, one after the other. My first reaction was, "Oh, no." When you're losing your Romeo, it's not the most pleasant news to receive.

But I got past that because I had to. I always bounce back, and in fact, most of the time you come up with a better situation than you had before. You can call that luck or whatever, but that has always happened to me. It's not that things don't get me down. I'm affected very strongly, perhaps even more than other people, but I don't sustain it. If I dwelt on setbacks, I couldn't take the next step, and you have to take the next step.

When we finally did a full production of *Romeo and Juliet*, in December of 1955 with Sylvia Gassell as Juliet, as soon as she would say, "Romeo, wherefore art thou Romeo, deny thy father and refuse thy name," *clang-clang-clang-clang* would go the steam pipes. It would happen every night around the same time, and she accused me, she confronted me and said, "*You're* doing it."

In the summers, the theater would get terribly hot, but Hilmar Sallee, an extremely capable Southerner who just walked in off the street and became my right-hand person, figured out a solution. He was fearless, he'd climb up anything and was excellent with tools, and he got up on the roof with a hose and hosed everything down. That's how we kept the place cool.

Nobody in the company expected anything, everybody just gave. We provided the platform and minor sustenance; we'd quench somebody's thirst or satisfy some extraordinary hunger. But the greatest hunger and the greatest thirst was to do the work. We didn't see the situation as a hardship. It was an opportunity, and boy, it was exciting. Another group called the Shakespearites would come down and watch us.

"How do you do it?" they'd ask. "You don't pay people anything, right?"

"No, everybody works for nothing."

"What does it cost you to put on a play?"

"Maybe—well, $22, $25 sometimes."

And that's what it was. But people were young and enthusiastic, and that made all the difference.

I wanted to direct, and I did so with a production of *Cymbeline* in 1955 and Middleton's *The Changeling* in 1956, but I had to direct with one hand and keep the organization together with the other. I left the interior problems of artistic choices of a particular production to the director; if he felt like this was something he could do with this company now, why not? There was no way I'd ever have anything *to* direct unless the institution was strong.

I'd seen that with the example of the Actors' Lab. It was made clear to me then that a theater needs strong leadership. I think that's what's kept the damn thing alive; otherwise, it would have gone under. Without being the major talent of the company, I became the foundation, the mainstay. Everybody could leave, but I would stay on. That's the way it is. When people would leave me, I'd say, "Well, I'm still here."

The Friedmans and, later, Stuart Vaughan and his wife, Gladys, were all extremely important in building this theater. They laid a lot of the groundwork, and they can take as much credit as anybody for that. I learned a lot from their very American approach because they had a lot of experience with language, literature, and the stage, mostly from university backgrounds. I had to undergo a lot of training to know what to do, and I appreciate them now more than ever.

But in all cases, I made the choice. I have an instinct for getting the right people, and with both the Friedmans and the Vaughans I got the right people at the right time. I made it possible, and you can't call it luck because it's been a consistent thing—it's been true almost straight along the line.

But after a while, these people naturally wanted to have more of a say in how the operation was run. And I always felt no, I just won't do that. The running of the organization clearly has to be mine. While the directors were interested in directing Shakespeare, I was interested in a larger idea. I was interested in the social aspects of how you use Shakespeare. I was interested, so to speak, in Shakespeare for the masses.

JOEL FRIEDMAN   There was no disagreement with Joe and me at all. After two seasons I just upped and said, "There's no money and I'm tired of running around." And, of course, the big breakthrough came just when I left, that's when the gravy hit the fan. When Stuart Vaughan came in, the organization was there. It was not the Rock of Gibraltar, but we had done the pneumatic drilling. By then it was easier for directors to find a home and see a future in it, but when we were there we were all flying blind.

I didn't have the vision that Joe had at all. We had done *hundreds* of these types of things by that time. I didn't think this was something unique but just another one of these fly-by-night companies that I was passing through. I don't suppose we'll get the Nobel Prize for best judgment.

SYLVIA GASSELL   To me, Joe seemed to be a very complicated and complex man. There were things about him that would startle me. The word "no" meant nothing to him; it would daunt many another person, but he was not daunted. He could go through a lot of disappointment and a lot of negative things and still keep going.

Yet he was capable of very touching sentimentalities. For example, when we opened *Romeo and Juliet*, I didn't get a good review. God knows I knew that I was not the ideal casting for Juliet, but my pride was hurt. The bell rang unexpectedly and up came Joe with a huge box of roses. I was terribly touched by that, and yet if you would have asked, "Would you expect Joe to do that," I would have said, "No, never." I was very intrigued by that very sweet and generous gesture, by his concern for me and how I felt.

If Joe was a role and I was to play him, the characteristic I would pick would be that he gets hurt a lot and he doesn't show the hurt. Or he shows it in what, to other people, are incomprehensible actions. If someone has hurt him, he may not attack the person to his face; he may never see them again. Joe drops baggage, but almost all successful people in the theater have to do that. You want to keep moving with the tide. You can't have fifteen brilliant actresses and eighteen actors and have something for them season after season.

Joe gets a great deal of satisfaction from discovering talent. Then, when the discovered persons begin to assert themselves because they've achieved their own success, it's like a child suddenly saying to his father,

"Look, I'm grown up and I can disagree with you." I think at that point the pleasure diminishes. We who are not successful, we have to try and patch things up. We have to try to come to understandings with people we have disagreements with because we don't want to lose them. He doesn't have to. He has the world, so he doesn't have to dwell on anybody.

5

The East River Park Amphitheater
1956

The Taming of the Shrew
at the amphitheater
© George E. Joseph

JOSEPH PAPP I love this city, and I've always done a lot of walking, trying to see it all. North, west, east, south—I've taken every approach, explored all of the different parts, especially the Lower East Side. I used to walk through those streets all the time.

During one of my walks, in 1956, I stumbled on this place called the East River Park Amphitheater. It had been built in 1941, during the La Guardia administration, by the Works Progress Administration. It was in a park that runs along the East River, right across from the then-active Brooklyn Navy Yard: I'd see destroyers and flattops coming in, and often in the middle of performances you'd hear, "Now hear this, now hear this, Seaman First Class Perkins, report to the quarterdeck immediately."

Even though everything was concrete, the amphitheater was kind of an interesting space. The sixteen hundred seats were backless wooden benches and the stage was really a raised band shell, not suitable for any theatrical presentation. In fact, we ended up playing in front of the stage so we could be closer to the audience. There were poplar trees on both sides of the amphitheater; they used to sway beautifully at the slightest breeze, so when we built the Delacorte in Central Park I insisted poplars be planted around it. It was a very soothing location, although it was dangerous at night. There was a lot of violence in the neighborhood—there'd recently been a stabbing and so forth, and I was advised not to go in there because it was unsafe. At the time I had no thought of leaving the church, pardon the expression, but you take what you can get and when I saw this space I felt, "This is the place to go."

I went to the Arsenal in Central Park, the headquarters of the city's Department of Parks, to get permission to put on plays by Shakespeare that summer. Because they were already thinking of abandoning the place, I ended up with use of the facility. They'd raise this objection and that objection and then set up certain restrictions, but I'd try and get around the objections and not pay attention to the restrictions. And because they were not on the scene, there was only so much they could do about me. They'd tell us, "You can't dig into the concrete to put up poles for lighting." Well, I just dug into that concrete—it was the only way I could get those poles to stand up. If we had to, we'd hook them up in the rain; we'd take our lives in our hands because it was all live-wire stuff. It was a tremendous amount of work, but we got it going.

Working at CBS, I'd run across a couple of Telefunken microphones and speakers that were really terrific. The company was trying to establish itself in this country, so I thought, "Why don't I go to them and ask for some speakers in return for our announcing that they'd provided them?" I was very market conscious, I was working on all levels, and besides, I thought those Germans owed us something.

As we progressed, we kind of liberated stuff from CBS. It was very hard to get lights, you can't sneak those out of CBS, but we got some chairs and some cable now and then. And I'd have people bring me some lumber or I'd get some things built. Years later, when I was negotiating this $12 million contract with CBS, I told them, "You don't realize how helpful you've been to me in the past."

Since Joel Friedman had left, I needed a new director. Because I loved the language, I went to see a staging of one of Sean O'Casey's autobiographies, *I Knock at the Door*. I thought it was well directed, and I called the director, Stuart Vaughan, and asked if he was interested in working in the amphitheater. He said, "Yes, very much."

Both Stuart and Joel were very capable directors. I would never tell them how to direct then, and I still don't tell people how to direct today. The director is the person holding the show together, and I've made tough choices—fired actors who didn't deserve to be fired—because the director was having problems and if I fired him or her the show would fall apart. It's very rare that there's a contention between me and the director. Of course, if there is such an irresolvable contention, then the director goes.

STUART VAUGHAN   I was doing scenes with an actress named Carol Gustafson in a night class that Harold Clurman was teaching when I got my first New York directing job. It was an off-Broadway production of O'Casey's *I Knock at the Door*, and I wouldn't have had the chutzpah to write for myself the review Brooks Atkinson wrote in the *Times*. It was a glorious start for someone who preferred acting and had always half avoided directing. I'd felt hauled into directing, largely because I could organize things, get people going, and get it done.

Anyway, Carol Gustafson now said to me, "Come meet Joe Papp; he's down at this little church."

"I've met Joe Papp," I said.

"He wants to do outdoor Shakespeare and he needs a director. He saw your O'Casey thing and thought it was wonderful. O'Casey is his other love besides Shakespeare."

"Well," I said, "he gets full marks so far." Carol set up a meeting and this time we got on very well.

While the first meeting had seemed showbiz and fast talk, by now there was a project in view, there was something to be fervid about. The idea seemed well-timed and it interested me.

Joe suggested we walk over and look at the amphitheater. Here was this big, hundred-yard-long concrete oval with a band shell behind it, and he said, "What about *Julius Caesar* and what about *The Taming of the Shrew?*"

"Okay," I said. "It seems really exciting, and almost impossible, and therefore worth doing. But we've got to have costumes." I'd seen a couple of productions in the church and knew what they'd used. I'd always felt that the amount of spectacle is dictated by the space you're in, and while their solution was adequate for the intimate space of the church, now we had this broad space under an open sky to deal with. "Hell," I said, "it can't be *Quo Vadis,* but there's got to be something to see."

Where were the costumes going to come from? There was a little money the Papp family could put up, and there was a little bit of money the Vaughan family could put up. And there was this guy named Chester Doherty who had also been in Harold Clurman's class. His father owned a small costume house someplace on Broadway, and Chet was willing to loan us costumes for program credit and the unspoken assurance—nevertheless, an assurance—that he could play a part in the show. He was an adequate actor, and there was nothing wrong in doing this.

We had a lot of fun down there. It was exciting in that space, doing the impossible. We had some trouble at first with the neighborhood kids. They stood around and jeered at us from the top of the auditorium, and then they began to throw rocks down. We were rehearsing in the sun, about twenty strapping guys, and I said, "Let's just walk up and meet these kids." So we walked in a sort of company front and when we got close the kids said, "Hey, hey, it's all right, guys."

By the end of our four weeks' rehearsal, far from being difficult or unpleasant, these kids were helping move props. At first, when we would all say "Hail, Caesar! Hail, Caesar!" for the big Caesar entrance, they'd all stand up at the top and make a big "Hey Caesar" noise themselves, but that all stopped. They got genuinely interested; they began to think it was all fun.

JOSEPH PAPP My favorite memory is of a lovely little boy who must have been about seven years old. He was Hispanic, and he would come and watch rehearsals every day with a little smile playing on his face. He never said a word, so one day I put my arm around him and said, "How ya doin'?" He looked up at me and smiled and I realized he was deaf.

I found out he lived across the street with his old grandmother; this was the only place he had to play. His parents, god knows where they were. I began to call some doctors I knew to see if there was something they could do about his deafness. I didn't know very many people, but compared to him I was like Rockefeller.

Finally, there was some work done on his ears, paid for through some charitable organization, but one day he stopped showing up. I was told his grandmother died and he moved out. I've never forgotten him, watching these people doing Shakespeare every day and not hearing them. He was so sweet. He just sat there quietly, as though he were deeply involved in what was going on.

GLADYS VAUGHAN This was in the days of the gangs, you know, and there were young toughs around the neighborhood. They'd see these actors speaking these fantastic lines, using language they didn't understand, and they'd start screaming all sorts of unpleasant things at the fellas, like "Oh, you're a bunch of gays."

So we established a policy that the actors weren't to respond in any way; they would just ignore them. Then, suddenly, the toughs' whole attitude began to change. They saw this passion in people; they saw the vitality and the eagerness. They began to want to come in and watch rehearsals, and we were very thrilled. Then they wanted to help on the crew, and we thought it was just marvelous. We thought we had accomplished this extraordinary thing by affecting the young toughs of the neighborhood.

And some of them really would come and help. One day, unfortunately, we discovered that all the places underneath the stage where we had stored donated electrical cables and tools had been broken into. All of this stuff had been stolen by one of the fellas. We had been so thrilled and then suddenly we turned very cynical. The whole experience was full of all sorts of things like that. Things you laughed at, things you would be upset about, things you had to struggle with.

Julius Caesar was the first production, and I was responsible for doing costumes. I'd had a couple of courses in that when I was doing my graduate work, but I wasn't a costumer and we had nothing, literally nothing. We borrowed some clothes from a young man in the show whose father had a costume company. Then I went all through Orchard Street and spent my whole budget for the year on this very cheap, twenty-five-cents-a-yard ecru white sateen that was used to line draperies. I designed shapes for togas and tunics, and Joe got a woman he knew from CBS to sew them. And this inexpensive sateen, which wouldn't have withstood a lot of washing and a lot of touring, turned out to have a wonderful effect. It fell in all these tiny folds and drapes, the wind would blow it as the senators were walking around, it gave the sense that these were people wearing clothes, rather than actors wearing costumes. And it was because they were the cheapest fabric one could possibly find.

We would all bring our own things in. I eventually even brought my mother's old sewing machine from the twenties, one of the early electric portables. We were trying to build the sets ourselves, and Stuart once said to an actor, "Come on and help."

"What can I help with?" he said. "There aren't any hammers, there aren't any saws."

"Don't you have a saw at home?" Stuart said. "Don't you have a hammer? Don't you have anything we can use? Well, bring them! Bring your irons, bring your ironing boards, bring whatever you've got." The spirit of those days was incredible. It just felt like something really different and new.

ROSCOE LEE BROWNE Though I had previously taught literature at Lincoln University in Pennsylvania, in 1956 I was working for Schenley Import Corporation as a national sales representative. On one particular Friday, Schenley announced to us that our company was being merged into Schenley Industries and I was offered another enormous position, higher up. I said, "Wait, I have to think about it."

So on my way home, I thought about it, and I invited Leontyne Price and two other in-the-bosom close friends to dinner. The first course was strawberry soup, and Leontyne said, "Strawberry soup?"

"Yes, dear," I said. "It's going to open your palate."

Next came crabmeat imperial, and right in the middle of the crabmeat Leontyne said, suddenly, "I suspect this dinner."

"You mean you're not liking it?" I said.

"No, honey, there's some other reason going on here."

So I told them the whole story about Schenley and they said, "So what have you decided?"

"I've decided that tomorrow I shall become an actor." Though I'd done occasional amateur stuff when I was going to graduate school at Columbia, I didn't presume to think I would have a job. I just said, "Tomorrow, I shall become an actor."

I thought they would all be very happy, but they came at me like absolute witches. "One, you're not a kid," they said. "Two, you don't even know you're black. Three, it's difficult for everybody." And I can still hear Leontyne saying, "And they'll have you bearin' torches."

I'd never read a trade paper, but we went out in a spring rain to get them. The first one I looked at was *Variety*, and I couldn't even read the first page. It said "Boffo-box-wox-lox." I didn't know what those words were, and I pushed it aside. The second one seemed to be gossip and would not interest me, and I put it aside.

The third one was called *Show Business*. Now I tend not to remember page numbers, but on page 25 it said that people who wished to audition for an outdoor season of Shakespeare should meet Joseph Papp. It said you had to know one speech from *Julius Caesar* and be prepared to read from another play. It gave the location, and the date, which happened to be the next day. So I simply said to those ladies, "I'll just go down there and try."

A bunch of others came, as I, to audition. They were nervous wrecks because you had to read right in front of everybody else sitting there, which I didn't know was not the way you normally audition. Having run track, having been twice an American champion, used to running in front of thousands and thousands and thousands, it made no difference to me.

So I spoke a speech of Cassius, and Stuart Vaughan, the director, said, "It's very good, it's really very good." But he, in a very sweet sense of

Plutarch, knew there couldn't be a colored Cassius, and besides, they had already chosen Jack Cannon. But while he went off, having this colloquy with Plutarch in a corner, deciding what I could play, this rather nifty, rip-cord-muscled slim fellow with lots of black hair quite casually came down the aisle and I knew right away, this is the fellow.

"I'm Joe Papp," he said. "How long have you been an actor?"

"Twelve hours," I said. "But I have no intention of bearing any torches."

"No, no, no," he said, laughing. "You'll have words, you're good."

It was just that simple, and it was extraordinary. He asked Stuart something and Stuart came back and said, "You know, Mr. Browne could play a soothsayer, and then in the second half he could come back as Pindarus." And I was thinking, "Yes, that's exotic enough."

It was a wonderful production and a marvelous time for me. Joseph was as natural as rain, as approachable as your best friend, clear in his criticism of you, and absolutely splendidly wrathful about what was professional and what was not. But that he would become one of the lights of the American theater, one would not have known that.

ELSA RAVEN   I called and said, "Mr. Papirofsky, I'd like to volunteer my services as an actress for your free Shakespeare."

"Actresses I don't need," he said. "What else can you do."

"I run the New Dramatists Workshop and I work in production."

"Yeah, yeah, that sounds good. I need production help."

I went way the hell downtown to meet him. When he found out that not only was I available but that I worked for an organization that was also nonprofit, and that nobody was in our suite of offices through the summer, he worked it out with my boss to use our suite. We had limited use of the mimeograph machine, the phones, and the space. And Joe decided that I would be a good liaison between him and Stuart Vaughan, so I agreed to be the coordinator. Because I was the only full-time person in the office, it was a job that meant doing everything, *everything*.

The first thing I had to do was get staff. I put up notices at the various unions, and out-of-work actors would volunteer for things. The Majzlin twins were a couple of the first volunteers—their father was a doctor and a major theater supporter. They were fifteen or sixteen, with suntanned bodies and dark-golden, curly hair, and they were very popular with the neighborhood girls who used to hang on the fences and call to them.

I had friends doing everything. I had worked previously at one of the biggest public relations outfits in the world, and I got the head of the mailroom to be one of the supers, one of the people of Rome. Then I went to him and said, "We need two thousand programs a performance, can you help me out?" He talked to the head mimeograph operator, and I would type up the stencil for each week's program and they would run it off.

It went okay until the end of the summer when we had to account for all that paper. "Elsa, I'm having a problem," my friend said. "Some of the accounts that put out a lot of releases don't question anything. But, for instance, Freeport Sulphur, which only puts out one release a year, wants to know why they are suddenly being charged for four thousand sheets of mimeograph paper." There was nothing I could do. We couldn't afford the paper, but we worked it out and there was no real problem.

Joe had lovely contacts, and people would lend us props. He would say, "Go to such-and-such and speak to so-and-so," and I'd walk away with arms full of armor and swords. Cabbies wouldn't even stop for you with things like that, and we had no money, anyway, so I was riding around on the subways carrying everything. I'd plan to take the crosstown bus for the last two miles to the amphitheater, but if the buses were crowded, the drivers would shake their heads no, they wouldn't let me on with swords and armor, so I'd end up walking. I lost twenty-five pounds that summer, just walking and carrying props.

We were an unknown quantity, so when I would go with Joe to the Parks Department to ask for things like security people—because the Lower East Side was a frightening place at night; things got stolen from us every time you'd turn around—these men kept saying no. Joe always looked a lot younger than he was, and they thought here was this kid who wanted to put on free Shakespeare. Basically all they were giving us was the use of the space.

Meyer Berger, the columnist for the *New York Times*, had heard about what was going on, and he wrote this lovely piece about us. That reached a lot more people than we might have thought, because as we approached curtain time on opening night, people started coming. We turned away hundreds that first night. What was gratifying, and what Joe loved, was that a lot of the neighborhood people came, and they were at home. They would yell at each other, they'd bring their supper. Joe compared it to Shakespeare's time, when they sold oranges in the audience. We were a popular hit that very first night.

MERLE DEBUSKEY The community in that neighborhood was made up of people living in projects that were created back in the thirties by organizations like the ILGWU, as well as newer immigrants. We tried to inform people by flyers; we tried to involve community organizations, everything.

You had to cross over the FDR Drive to get to the amphitheater, and people would start wandering across a footbridge while the sun was still up to see this strange whatever it was. This was the first we saw of an attitude that characterized our audiences when we later went around the city with the mobile unit. It was summer. It was warm. It was unpleasant to stay in the house. This was an activity, obviously an entertainment. No one was being told what was good for them. It was free. And you could wander in— there was no impediment to your coming or to your leaving. You had nothing to lose. If you didn't like it, you could watch the boats go by. So people were kind of seduced into walking over there and taking a look, just because it was there.

Until the symbolic curtain went up, it sounded like the biblical speaking in tongues. You heard Spanish, Yiddish, Italian, Chinese, everything but Shakespearean English. The audience was very friendly. The people down there didn't read the *New York Times*. They never came in with the attitude: "So prove it, now show me." It was: "Okay, fellas, what's happenin'?"

And they appreciated it. People in there weren't sure what the hell it was they were going to see, with these people in strange garments talking in this funny way. But somehow these interpreters of Shakespeare managed to penetrate the audience. Even though they weren't sure of all the words, they gathered what was going on and they were held by it. As the sun began to sink and the light in the sky changed from dusk to darkness, with an occasional ship going by with red-and-green lights on its mast, it was quite beautiful and quite marvelous.

JOSEPH PAPP There were gates at the very top of the amphitheater, and though it was still light, there were hundreds of people outside waiting for the first performance. When the gates were opened, people rushed in pell-mell. Old people, young people, Jewish people, Hispanic people, a few black people—it was really the Lower East Side spilling into the theater, packing every seat. Word of mouth brought them. We had been rehearsing there for a month or more, and the whole neighborhood knew about us.

There were these huge projects right there, some of the earliest low-cost housing developments, built by the ILGWU and the Amalgamated Clothing Workers after terrible, terrible tenements had been torn down. A lot of elderly Jewish people came from those, and during the course of the play you'd hear all these comments similar to what used to go on in the Yiddish theater. They'd yell to Caesar, "Watch out, he's killing you!" and "Oh, it's a shame!" They would comment on it because they felt this was actually happening. You'd watch people, and they were really enjoying it.

When the play started, frankly, I was scared to death. I didn't have the faintest notion what to expect. Obviously, most of the people out there had never seen live actors before. They might stone us to death for all I knew.

Then came the great speech at the very beginning of the first act, where the tribune Marullus says, "You blocks, you stones, you worse than senseless things!" It's a very strong speech, kind of a crowd-pleaser, and toward the end of it, people started to cheer. It was really loud and it sounded like cheering anyplace—it could have been a baseball game, the kind you'd hear when someone gets a hit in the clutch. By the last lines, when Marullus says, "Fall upon your knees, pray to the gods to intermit the plague that needs must light on this ingratitude," I could tell that here was an audience that really identified. I never felt so relieved in my life.

Earlier that day, I had been walking down Grand Street. There was a Sherman cigar store there, and I really loved that tobacco smell. It was just before the opening, the sun was just about ready to go down, and I said, "I'll take *that* cigar." It was a Corona and it cost me thirty cents, which at the time made it a great luxury. But that night, it seemed the right thing to do. And, boy, was that a great cigar.

Putting on plays at the amphitheater was more expensive than at the church: *Julius Caesar* fully costumed cost almost $800. And that was with me doing the trumpet calls by cupping my hands together and making an appropriate noise offstage. I was having to use my own money, as I much as I had left over from what I needed to live on, which wasn't much.

So I was always trying to raise a little money here and there. I'd try and get $10 from somebody, $15 from somebody else. We had enough money to do *Caesar*, but I wanted to put on *The Taming of the Shrew* as well. Henry Hewes, a critic for *The Saturday Review* who'd liked the first play, connected me with a philanthropic group called ANTA, the American National Theatre and Academy.

I was always working, so I came to the ANTA meeting, which took place on Fifth Avenue, in dirty work clothes. They should have asked me to wipe my feet before I walked in there. Everyone was sitting around this table drinking coffee and I was told, "Look, you're ahead now, you've established yourself, why don't you sit back a little bit, give yourself a chance to reorganize and do something in a better style."

"No," I said. "I don't want to wait. Like one swallow, doing one play does not a spring make. We have to do two plays. We're geared to do it and we're going to do it. I want money, and I want it now, to put this play on." I pounded my fist on the table a lot. I said, "I've done the work, now you provide the money, it's your responsibility," and I ended up with $500, the amount I needed to proceed.

COLLEEN DEWHURST   I'd met Edward Everett Horton while doing stock in Kennebunkport, Maine. He asked me and my husband, James Vickery, to do a three-character play with him on tour. He had negotiated my salary, it was $100 or so a week, and I was so excited at getting so much money.

The tour had reached Ephrata, Pennsylvania, in the Amish country, when I got the call from Joseph.

"I'm doing *The Taming of the Shrew* and you're my Kate," he said.

"I'm on my way," I said.

"We can't pay you, you know that," he said. "For *Julius Caesar* we sent announcements to agents, newspapers, everything, but nobody has come. No critics, no nothing, but it's mobbed every night."

Why did I say yes? I'd like to say all the right things, but truthfully I had no idea where we were going with this whole thing. It just seemed exciting and natural. It was a sense of theater, a sense that this was the way you did things.

I had to get my release from Edward Everett Horton. He said, "You're going to work *outdoors*? For *nothing*? Oh, Colleen, Colleen."

We opened, and as Joseph said, the place was mobbed. It was someplace to go at night—people of *all* colors and races, sitting on those concrete banquettes with their kids. We also did matinees in the sunshine on the concrete. You were so *hot* and your head was spinning. By the time J. D. Cannon, who played Petruchio, and I had run around and knocked each other down, I could see three or four of him.

Usually when you play anything that's marked with what we think of as class, you have an audience that sits as if they were impaled to their seats. But this audience didn't act that way. One night they kept screaming at J.D., "She's coming! She's coming! Look out! *Look out!*"

Yet they understood the play perfectly, because when we got to the part where Kate submits and falls to her knees, all of a sudden this man yelled out from the back—but straight, not meaning to be funny—"Aw, give 'er a pillow!" And the whole audience went, "Give 'er! Give 'er!" It was so sweet.

One night, standing there giving the play's last speech, there was a lot of laughing and giggling. I thought, "Well, well, am I good tonight!" Suddenly I looked down and standing beside me was a little boy about four, and all he had on was a little jersey top that only went to here. When they realized I'd spotted him, the audience began to scream. He took my hand and I continued with the soliloquy. I will never forget that. That could only happen once in your lifetime.

The audience would come up to us afterward and their reaction was love without adoration, kind of "Gee, it was terrific, thank you for the party." No critic told them it was good or bad, they were just reacting of a summer night to what was happening. I realized that theater is not an elitist art; theater is for the people. I could have gone through a whole career not having had that kind of experience. I thought finally, "This must be the way Shakespeare really was."

ROSCOE LEE BROWNE Jack Cannon and Colleen were quintessential Petruchio and Katherine. Jack was quite handsome, with no frills to it. He was just a straight-on fellow, and the fact of his being handsome interested him not one bit at all. And as for Colleen, there were only two words for her in that piece, and they were: "Glory, hallelujah."

Colleen was uncommonly beautiful, and she tans deeply and incredibly. Standing there with those blue-green eyes coming out at you from this deep, deep, deep burnished color, and with that exquisite figure, she was absolutely Kate, without even being one bit tomboyish. If the Martians were to have arrived—and we all know that when they do, they'll come directly to me—and said, "Roscoe, show us man, show us woman," I would have pointed right at the two of them.

ARTHUR GELB I had joined the drama department a year or two before, and off Broadway was burgeoning. Brooks Atkinson was the first major critic to go off Broadway and to review everything, sitting on hard benches in un-air-conditioned rooms, down in stuffy cellars or four- or five-flight walk-ups to lofts. It was miserable from a physical point of view, but it was very exciting creatively.

Joe was part of the scene. He would come into the drama department every so often and urge us to review one of his plays. He came out of nowhere, as far as we were concerned, and started putting on free Shakespeare in these off-off-off-Broadway theaters. Joe was a very good salesman, he had an impeccable sense of timing and promotion, and he had managed to convince someone to give him the East River Amphitheater for the summer of 1956. But he had a shoestring operation, he lived on handouts, and by August things weren't going well for him.

Joe came to the office several times and urged me to come to see his show. As it happened Brooks Atkinson was away, and Louis Funke, the drama editor, was away, and I was in charge of the department. I told him Brooks would be back in another week or so, but he said, "No, I can't wait. We've run out of money and unless the *Times* recognizes what we're doing in the amphitheater, we will have to close. I'm not asking you for a good review or a bad review; obviously, you're not going to do me a favor in that regard. But please come and see the show. Write whatever you want about it, but please come and see it. It's a question of life or death for the company."

"I can't go," I said. "I'm doing a Sunday piece and I have a couple of daily pieces and I'm filling in for Brooks. I just can't take a night off and go."

"I'm going to camp here," he said. "I'm going to stay here until you decide to go."

I very politely said that that was nonsense, but he said, "No, I'm desperate."

"All right," I said. "Go away and I'll be there tonight and I'll take a look."

My wife and I were going to see some other Broadway production, but she was a good sport about it and we drove down to this East River Amphitheater. The show was *The Taming of the Shrew* and the star was Colleen Dewhurst. I didn't know who she was; I'd never seen her before. When we got there the skies looked threatening, and I said to Barbara, "Oh boy, I hope it doesn't rain. I'm certainly not going to come down again tomorrow night."

GLADYS VAUGHAN From the very beginning of the night Arthur Gelb was there, storm clouds were threatening heavily. I remember sitting in the audience just praying and hoping with all my might that those clouds would wait before they broke into a storm, until we got through the first major scene between Petruchio and Kate, because Jack Cannon was a very special kind of Petruchio, and he made that scene really come alive. Rather than the whiplashing man, he had a vulnerability to him. He'd kind of pull the audience in, in effect saying, "This is a rough situation and this is what my plan is. Now, what do you say about that? Do you think this'll work?" At any rate, we'd just finished that scene, I think it was at the tail end of it, when the skies opened, the water poured down, and everybody ran for cover.

ARTHUR GELB The show started, and it was just amazing to me. On came this fantastic woman, Colleen Dewhurst, but I was watching the audience as much as I watched the production. They ate it up, they roared with laughter, they enjoyed every second of it. Not since then have I seen an audience like that. I was really delighted that Joe had not only urged me to go but had in fact made it almost impossible for me not to go.

It started raining, and the audience did not leave. They remained glued to their seats until it came down pretty heavily. Then there was such a mood of disappointment that I realized that this was something very, very special. I was so moved I did something I never do. I grabbed my wife's hand and we went up onstage, where the actors were just standing there with the rain pouring down.

"Joe," I said, "you really have something here. I guess I'll have to come back and review it."

"We're going to close in a day or two," he said. "This really finishes us because we have no money. We're broke. That's the end of us."

So as I left I said to myself, "I'll go back and I'll review one act. I mean, what the hell?" Which, under the headline "Rained Out," is what I did. I also noted that unless $750 could be raised, the company would have to disband. "It seems a shame," I wrote, "that a project evidently bringing so much joy to so many people should be permitted to die aborning."

What happened now was amazing. I got a number of phone calls the next morning: "How can we help out?" The most important call came from Herman Levin. Then the famous, well-heeled producer of *My Fair Lady*, he'd grown up on the Lower East Side and he said the review brought a tear to his eye. He didn't know Joe Papp from a hole in the wall, but he could envision what was going on down there and he said, "Tell me, what does Joe Papp need?" I called Joe and he answered, "Just what I said. I need $750." And Levin sent the check immediately and saved the festival from closing.

When Brooks Atkinson got back from vacation he read my review and said, "Is it really—is it that good?" And I said, "Brooks, it's wonderful, you really have to go down and see it." He went right down, came back, and said to me, "It's just remarkable," and he wrote this rave review for his Sunday column.

Now Brooks Atkinson was a monument and to get the lead of his Sunday column was really a great achievement. A theater would do anything for it. There was no one writing about the theater with his integrity, his character, his critical acumen. When Atkinson gave you his blessing, a combination of his talent and the power of the *New York Times*, it was the most important applause that anyone in the theater could get.

For Joe Papp to get that much space, discussing his plans and how much money he needed, was very unusual. And once Brooks Atkinson recognized Joe's producing artistry, he did one article after another about him. He hardly ever gave a Papp production a bad notice.

JOSEPH PAPP My aim was to get Brooks Atkinson down. He was all-powerful at the time. I didn't want a second-stringer to come down; I wanted the most distinguished critic in New York to come down. Had we not done it, I don't know if I'd be here today talking about this thing.

I went up to the *Times* and said, "I'd like to speak to Brooks Atkinson."

"He's not in now."

"Well, I'll wait."

"He's not going to be here."

"Well, I'll wait."

Every five minutes, someone came out, looked at me, and reported, "The guy's still out there." I refused to leave. I sat there for hours, and finally in walked Brooks Atkinson, followed by a man I later learned was Robert Whitehead, the producer. I stopped him and said, "Mr. Atkinson, can I see you for a moment?"

He was an extremely distinguished-looking man, but very friendly. He said he wanted to converse with Mr. Whitehead first. After about fifteen or twenty minutes, he called me in. And everybody else in the department was looking out from the other doors, saying, "He's in there now! How the hell did he get in?"

"Look," I said, "I'm trying to start this theater. We're working very hard to do this well. You have to come see it. I need you there to see it."

I told him exactly what my goals were and he said, "All right. Will you pick me up at the Harvard Club at seven thirty?" And I said, "I'll be there."

The night in question came and the only vehicle I had was this big, old, dirty two-ton truck I'd been driving around—a very serviceable vehicle for carrying lots of heavy stuff but hardly appropriate for the Harvard Club. I went in wearing my work clothes—I didn't have any other clothes—and asked for Mr. Atkinson. He came out to the truck wearing this elegant suit and I said, "Okay, here we go," and started to drive this damn thing.

We were driving on the downtown side of the FDR Drive and the amphitheater was on the uptown side, and I always used to take a shortcut. I said, "Just hold on for a minute, Mr. Atkinson," and I jumped the divider to great screeching of tires all around. By the time we got to the amphitheater, Atkinson was breathing hard.

After the show, he was very nice, but he didn't say a word to me. I didn't know how the hell he felt. I drove him back, and this time I didn't have to jump the divider.

I was backstage the next day and I got a call from this sweet woman, Clara Rotter, who was Atkinson's personal secretary. "Don't tell anyone about it," she said, "but Brooks has written a wonderful piece, it's going to be his first Sunday column of the season."

And it was a wonderful piece, and that was the document I was able to use to really raise funds on a larger level. It was the most important thing you could have. It came from the most distinguished critic and it gave me a certain entrée into some of these places.

I'd studied foundations like you'd study the palm of your hand if you were a palmist. I went through books on them. I'd say, "Which people can help us to do this?" I became an expert on foundations. The first place I took Atkinson's column was the Doris Duke Foundation and they gave me $10,000. That was a *lotta* thousands of dollars, and it broke the ice. I still had no office, I was still working out of my home, but I was already planning for next season.

What I was trying to do was create a theater. That's an enormous undertaking. It's like creating a living thing that will express my ideas and my feelings, that will give me a place to go day in and day out, that will enable me to say that I have a career, I have a profession. I was profession-less and career-less, and I always felt a need, not in any crazy way but in the simplest way, to have some identification.

There were people who'd say to you, "What do you do?" And I never knew what to say. At one point I'd say, "I'm an actor," but I didn't feel like I was an actor. I said "I'm a director" for a while, but I didn't have experience to prove that. It was at this point, because I'd done it and I'd achieved something in the process, that I began to feel like I was a producer. I don't want to use the word "destiny," maybe it's more of a Buddhist idea, but there was something that said that that was the way I should go.

COLLEEN DEWHURST I'll never forget my first review. There was an old, old man who had a newsstand by the old Madison Square Garden on Eighth Avenue and Fiftieth Street who was very sweet and protective of me and I adored him. I remember picking up the *Times* there and going home and there was a review. I went, "Whoa! This is it! No more worries. I'm going to have a private bathroom, not one in the hall. I'm ready to roll. Going to get a big, big penthouse, have lots of lovers, and be very famous."

After that, it was just like a flip-flop at the amphitheater. Suddenly all these people mobbed in and there was never an empty area. I remember what my eye caught was white shirts. Your eyes would go up and what you were seeing was a shirt, a tie, a jacket on a hot night, and you said, "What has happened?"

After that review, I had all these calls from agents. It was my first experience with these gung-ho men, ready to send you to the Coast, all the things you'd heard about. I went instead with Jane Broder, who'd seen me before the reviews. She was very elderly by then, but she'd come and sat on the concrete with her sister before it was cushioned by the *Times*. She had great morality. We never signed anything in all the years I was with her, we never signed anything at all.

ELSA RAVEN Closing night of *Shrew*, Joe made a little speech to the audience. He said, "You know that in any theatrical production, what you see is the tip of the iceberg. Underneath are all the support people, the people who made the production possible. So we're going to bring the rest of the iceberg out." He called all the production staff and crew, and it was really funny. We were so piddly compared to this great big cast, there were like six or eight of us who were putting on this great big production.

Now that it was over, we still had to return so much borrowed equipment and props and draperies. We were this big hit, and here's Joe and I, alone at the amphitheater one night, loading his borrowed station wagon with all this incredibly heavy stuff. You had to laugh.

Joe was getting a lot of pressure from the House Un-American Activities Committee. They wanted to talk to him about people he had worked with in Hollywood years before. He just absolutely refused, and he knew it was getting to the point where just his refusal was going to get him cited for contempt.

He thought that might endanger the Shakespeare Festival, so he asked me that night to become associate producer so that I could take over as producer if necessary. My name was clean, and he would advise and counsel me. But I knew that I couldn't take the job in name only, that if I took it, I'd have to do it. Plus, I wanted to be an actress. Joe was very understanding when I turned it down.

COLLEEN DEWHURST   There are many people who, out of pride, you'd never call on a bad dark night, but Joseph you'd call. You'd figure it would be very short, he would have understood it all within a few sentences, you'd have your response, and he would hang up. When you're standing next to Joseph, you know that nothing, no person or organization, can intimidate him. They can do whatever they want, but they better not hurt anything he wants and believes in, because he will fight and fight and fight.

6

Shakespeare in Transition:
The Mobile Unit, Central Park,
and the Heckscher Theater

1957–59

Unpacking the mobile
unit in Central Park
© George E. Joseph

JOSEPH PAPP I always felt that we should travel. After all, Shakespeare did both: he had his own theater, and he also toured from time to time. True, he went to avoid the plague, but that notion was always there. I wanted to bring Shakespeare to the people, that was the whole idea. I had to reach the thousands of people who lived and died in their neighborhoods.

To do this we raised money from foundations—the New York Foundation, the Old Dominion Foundation, and others—a total of $35,000. The Astor Foundation had never given money to anything like this before, but the woman in charge, who was from Queens herself, said to me, "I'd be curious to see how the people in Queens react to Shakespeare." That's what got her interested.

In order to tour, we planned a wooden folding stage, to be mounted on the bed of a forty-five-foot platform trailer truck. I'd gotten estimates, and we were talking like $20,000, $30,000. But I knew this guy in Brooklyn who had a kind of body shop and he was going to give me a bargain. "I have some old trucks back here," he said. "I can fix one up for you for $3,000 or $4,000." I went crazy about trucks for a while. I kept watching the way he was putting this thing together; I could hardly wait.

Even when the truck was finished, the tires on it had been worn down quite a bit and the whole thing was never totally steady. It was a very rough, barely put-together piece of work; the hinges couldn't really support the weight that well. The truck looked like it had come out of Eastern Europe. When it would go around a corner it would list to one side to an extraordinary degree; you'd think it would never recover. You talk about two planks and passion, that was it, and even the planks were kind of worn through. We looked awfully strange going through the city streets, but for the money we couldn't go wrong.

I guess everything was hard at the beginning, but the most difficult thing was getting through the bureaucracy at the Department of Parks. I mean, who was I? Rules and regulations were all over the place. You couldn't do this, you couldn't do that, you couldn't do this.

Finally, I managed to reach Stanley Lowell, a deputy mayor, and a tour was approved. We began at the Belvedere Tower area of Central Park in Manhattan and then went on to War Memorial Park in Brooklyn, Kings Park in Queens, Clove Lakes Park in Staten Island, and Williamsbridge Oval Park—later changed to the Hunter College campus—in the Bronx.

STANLEY LOWELL   I was deputy mayor of New York under Robert F. Wagner, and I got a telephone call one day saying, "My name is Joseph Papp, and I was told that you'd be the best one for me to talk to, that you'd be sympathetic to my idea." I asked what it was about and he said, "I don't want to talk to you about it on the phone. I'd like to come in to see you."

He came in the next week and he told me, "My idea is to have free Shakespearean plays in Central Park."

"What do you mean, 'free'?"

"Nobody will pay."

"Why are you talking to me about it?"

"I've already gone to some of the commissioners and I'm not getting any cooperation, they're not telling me they're going to help." He had a long list of things he needed—a stage, chairs, lighting—so he was not talking only about the parks commissioner, he was talking about gas and electricity, the Public Events Department, a variety of areas.

"That sounds very exciting, I like the idea," I said. "Why don't you let me think about it. More important, let me talk to Mayor Wagner about it."

If you know Joe Papp, he immediately bridled. He thought I was sloughing him off, that I was telling him no in a nice way.

"Just a minute, Mr. Papp," I said. "I'm the deputy mayor; I'm not the mayor. Let me talk to the mayor about it. It won't take long. You call me up next week."

ROBERT F. WAGNER Stanley was deputy mayor, and he got ahold of me down at city hall and said that he'd been talking to this fellow, Joe Papp, who had approached him to try to help start Shakespeare in the park. And Joe Papp had said he wasn't going to charge any admission. And Stanley, of course, asked the next natural question when you're in government: "How much do you want from the city?" And Joe said, no, he would just like to be allowed to function and to get some cooperation, maybe help with some extra benches and getting lights. That surprised Stanley, and when he told me, it surprised me. So I said, "That sounds pretty good to me." A lot of people didn't think I was that interested in the arts, but I was, and I did a lot.

JOSEPH PAPP The first production we took around the city was *Romeo and Juliet*, starring Bryarly Lee. She was such a wonderful Juliet, so fine, so out of this world. She had this ethereal, wispy voice, and you felt that she was really in love. I've never seen a Juliet like her.

GLADYS VAUGHAN Bryarly Lee was a very lovely, fragile kind of Juliet, and the degree to which she was personally involved with the role was made especially evident at one performance.

It was very, very stormy that night, and right in the middle of the death scene, one of the torches fell over. Stephen Joyce, who played Romeo, was already lying there dead, and as Bryarly was just waking up in the bier, the torch caught her garment.

Well, Bryarly went right on with her speech. Stephen saw what was happening, and you could see that his entire body was saying, "I don't know what to do." His character was dead, he didn't really want to move, but at the same time, Bryarly was going to be burned up. And she would have, I think, if he hadn't gotten up and set the torch right.

By then, the whole audience was so sympathetic and so totally involved, that when he lay down and went back to being the dead Romeo, they broke out into this appreciative applause.

STUART VAUGHAN Bryarly was vague like a fox, awfully bright, *very* sensitive, and very successful in the role. One day, during a particularly chaotic rehearsal, I came onstage to make some adjustment and said to her, "What's that on your dress? It looks like blood."

"Oh, well," she said, "I guess it is blood."

"What's it doing there?"

"I wanted to see what the dagger felt like, so I stuck myself."

"You know how it feels now?"

"Yes, yes."

"Well, don't do it anymore." What else were you going to say?

ROSCOE LEE BROWNE These two kids were wonderful. They were everything they were supposed to be, they were the whole thing, they were it. You'll never see a Romeo and Juliet like these two kids were. I almost weep when I think about them, they were so exquisite.

This was the time of the gangs. They'd come to the performances, all pockmarked with acne and passion, with their jackets emblazoned, and not in Greek. But they became enthralled, and what we would hear was screaming on the order of: "*Don't do it, Romeo! Don't do it! She ain't dead! Oh, fuck! Don't do it! Fuck! Don't! Don't fuckin' do it! She ain't fuckin' dead!*"

It was extraordinary, that's what Shakespeare would wish for most. And most of the audience who heard "fuck" for the first time rather loved it, too.

JERRY STILLER I had been hired the year before to work with some great American actors doing Shakespeare at the American Shakespeare Festival at Stratford, Connecticut. It was a very tough season, because nobody knew what was going on. Jack Palance, the big movie name, was doing Jack Palance; Raymond Massey was Abraham Lincoln doing Brutus; Jack Klugman was Quincy as the First Citizen, talking the way he still talks. He had notes on every iambic syllable.

I thought I had hit the top when I got to Stratford. We actually were on *The Ed Sullivan Show*, on the same bill with Bill Haley and His Comets, so it was a historic event. We thought we were the height of everything. The only trouble was, it turned out to be one of the most depressing seasons Stratford ever had. The critics hated it, the audiences didn't understand what we were doing, and as an actor, after so much promise, there was nothing going on. So Anne Meara and I, who were already married, went back to being like a lot of people who were running around New York at the time, looking for whatever was going to happen to us.

Then I got a call from somebody named Joe Papp, because in those days he was manning the phones himself. "I heard you were very good up in Connecticut," he said. "We're going to tour the five boroughs and we'd love you to come down." I said to myself, "Look at this. One season I'm up there at Stratford and now I'm getting hired to go on a truck and play the parks."

I didn't know what to say, whether to accept this thing or not. Except I had heard about the work he was doing, that it was very exciting because he was using American actors the way that American actors should be used. So against my own conceit and the sense of ego that is so strong in me, I said, "Why not go down and do this thing?"

I got the role of Peter in *Romeo and Juliet*, and they expanded the role, they gave me things to do that I never dreamed I could do. There was, for instance, a moment I fell asleep onstage while standing up. At Stratford, the English director we had would never have permitted it. I was given such comedic freedom here, it was so new, the atmosphere was so open, and risk was part of the game.

Still, from the point of view of being in a career situation, I kept saying in my head, "What am I doing in Staten Island? What am I doing in the Bronx? Under the Brooklyn Bridge?" And the irony for me was that one of these parks was on a block I used to *live* on. "Look at this!" I said to myself. "What kind of a business is this? I've been trying to be an actor for I don't know how many years, and I'm four blocks from where I started. I haven't moved from one end of the park to the other."

But being outdoors was an electric feeling, different than anything you could ever experience. Even though you had to dress in the same men's room used by the people who were watching the show—you were putting on makeup, using the water, and guys were coming in and doing what they had to do.

The people in the audiences were so unjaded, they were so pure in their feelings about what they were seeing. And if they liked you, you were absolutely knocked out from their liking, because their minds were not cluttered with the way they thought it should be or could be. And as an actor, that made you do things you would not ordinarily do. If you were a comedian, you became more inventive. You wanted to please them, you had to relate, and that changed what you were doing and filled you with great joy.

Some people didn't even come for the show; they came to be around, to hang out. They sat, they talked, they brought their lunch, it was like in a cafeteria. It's not just you onstage, you don't get caught up in yourself here. There's life around you. If you have to talk louder, you talk louder.

When we did *Romeo and Juliet*, there were a lot of Hispanic kids up front one night, and they got so caught up in the excitement of this thing that when we got to the love scene, "Romeo, Romeo, wherefore art thou Romeo," one of the kids hollered out, "Give it to her, Romeo! Give it to her, man! Don't let her get away, man, don't let her get away!"

DAVID AMRAM We had to record the music for *Romeo and Juliet* on a home tape recorder, and at every performance the stage manager had to sit with the tape machine and turn it on and off just at the right cues. Sometimes, because we didn't have a really good tape machine, it would have a nervous collapse and go on fast-forward. It would produce this screaming, insane sound, like a bunch of crickets drowning underwater or avant-garde electronic music. Eventually the machine would slow down, they'd wind it backward, and try and find out where we were.

Joe was this tower of energy. After the shows were over, he would get out there and give a speech to the audience, and he was an amazing speaker. He would spellbind the audience. All of us that worked there would just be knocked out by his ability.

He would talk about how as a boy he had loved Shakespeare so much, how it gave him a whole picture of life outside of where he grew up in Brooklyn. It had let him know that there was something else out there that was much older, that was beautiful and universal. This was something he could really relate to from a spiritual and intellectual point of view, and it had given his whole life an extra shape and an extra meaning.

Then, at the end, he would pass the hat and collect money so that they could buy some paint for the little sets or give the people who were borrowing clothes and making up the costumes a chance to at least take them to the dry cleaner. Everything was done on just a shoestring.

JOSEPH PAPP   We rehearsed in Central Park, often staying as late as three in the morning. During our first dress rehearsal, we'd been in a hurry and had not waited to put safety railings up. Eulalie Noble, who played Lady Capulet, was up on a balcony, maybe eight or nine feet off the ground, and suddenly she stumbled and hit the stage with an awful smack and lay absolutely still. I thought, "We're finished."

The only other person watching the show was Dr. Majzlin, the father of the teenage twin boys who worked as crew. He walked up to the stage, looked down at Eulalie, and said, "Come on, get up."

Nothing.

"Come on, get up, get up, get up."

Nothing.

"Get up."

One eye opened. He reached out to her and she lifted her hand. She'd fallen flat, knocked the stuffing out of herself, and was so terrified that she was dead that she didn't want to move. She thought she'd broken every bone in her body, and she hadn't broken anything. The doctor helped her up and ten minutes later she was fine and we went on with the rehearsal.

Another night during *Romeo and Juliet* we were having dinner with Dr. Majzlin and his family in Brooklyn when suddenly the telephone rang. It was a Sunday, we weren't playing, and it had been raining all day.

"I think you better come out here," someone said.

"What happened?"

"You have to come and see. The towers have collapsed. It's really a mess."

We had two huge, forty-five-foot light towers at the park that we had put up and guyed ourselves. We thought we knew how to do it—we had some steel cable on each side—but obviously we weren't professionals. Across those towers we had placed pipes from which we'd suspended thirty or forty lights. It all had kind of an erector-set look to it.

I got back there as fast as I could. My heart was really pounding. I couldn't believe the scene. The towers had been torn loose from their moorings and they'd collapsed over about six rows of seats, maybe eighty or ninety seats. The metal chairs were bent totally out of shape; the wooden chairs were just splintered. All the lamps were smashed, there was glass all over the place, and the area looked like it had been hit by a cyclone. And the first thought that came to my mind was, "My god, what if this had happened during a performance."

There were about five of us there, it was still raining hard, but we had to clean up everything. We worked about four or five hours, getting rid of all the debris, and early the next morning we brought in a truck to take all that stuff out. We also brought in two new towers and had them guyed by professional people. That night, the show went on and nobody knew the difference. We've never told that story.

If the towers had collapsed during a performance, they would have killed a number of people and that would have been the end. Disaster. You never would have had Shakespeare in the Park. But God was on our side. Couldn't have done it without the Almighty. You need a lot of luck along the way, because anything can happen.

EDWIN SHERIN I started in the business as an actor for Joe Papp in 1957, his first year in Central Park. I was studying with John Houseman at the American Shakespeare Festival Theatre and Academy. We had been working on soliloquies, and when I auditioned I went in and did, "But, soft, what light from yonder window breaks." Poured my heart into it, all my passion and beauty and lyricism, and Stuart Vaughan told me, "Your sense of humor is terrific. I like the way you approach Romeo tongue in cheek." Anyway, that's where I met Joe.

My early recollections of Joe were of a guy with a strong need to develop the idea of doing the classics for nothing for the people of New York, a man who seemed to have a passion and the intellectual will to pull it all together. He was, in those early meetings, charismatic. There was no question that he was a special human being with a lot of power, and a sweetness, an open smile, very welcoming and loving.

But though he was quite supportive of Stuart, Joe always held the reins. There was never any question of who was boss, there was never any question of whose festival this was, even though in point of fact, Stuart contributed in the early stages as much if not more than Joe. Because what he was putting on that stage was aesthetically pleasing to critics and audiences, and that got the New York Shakespeare Festival off and running. Stuart was a martinet, but the fact is that Stuart had a staging genius, a sense of space and how to fill it excitingly.

From the very moment we started, from the very first preview, the obvious joy of the patrons was clear. They were more spontaneous in response, that I can understand. But they were also intellectually more with it. People followed material far more accurately than you would think, better than Broadway audiences. With many of them speaking English as a second language, I never understood how they got the jokes and understood the language. To this day I can't figure it.

As a theater, this was probably the most exciting I've ever participated in. This despite having open partitions for dressing rooms, which meant there were people watching us dress as we turned our bare asses to them. And despite Joe, when he directed *Twelfth Night* the following year, being not in any sense subtle. I had real acting problems. I thought my character was a cipher, I didn't know why the hell he did anything, and I remember one afternoon at rehearsal asking, "Joe, Joe, why do I come onstage? Why?" And he said, "Because I'm paying you, that's why."

Yet overall the experience was feverish, passionate. There was a kind of disease that took me into the theater, and it's called stagestruck. It has to do with getting up in front of people and having them say, through their applause, that you're wonderful. It's obsessive, like falling in love, you can feel it in the pit of your stomach.

Being in that company was the realization of all those fantasies about what the theater is. It was like, "Don't blink." In the years after, I did six Broadway shows and a hundred television shows and I directed many too many plays. I've never had that feeling again.

STUART VAUGHAN During one *Romeo and Juliet* dress rehearsal, which because of rain didn't start until midnight, the music cues were booming out across Central Park West through our Telefunken speakers and, naturally, agitating all the people in the fancy apartment buildings there.

The police came along, and they said, "Who are you? What is this? What are you doing here? This noise has got to stop." Joe was not there—he was doing double duty at this point, working for CBS and trying to do the show, so when he was not around he was either working dead on his feet or on his back—and I was the guy in charge.

"You want to take us in, you take us in," I said. "It'll be on the front page of the *Times* that you've interrupted our work and Shakespeare in the Park has been stopped because a lot of rich cats over in those apartment buildings are losing sleep. If that's the kind of publicity you want, you can have it. Otherwise, we'll get done as quietly as we can and as best we can, and we'll have a show that even you will be proud of. Now which way do you want to play it?" And they backed off.

We were filled with a kind of zeal in those days. It was very exciting to make something out of nothing and to know that we were doing it genuinely for the love of it. There was no producer getting fat, there wasn't the star getting paid too much for knowing too little, or any of those things. We knew our cause was just.

MERLE DEBUSKEY The first tour through the city parks was a marvelous adventure, more of an encounter than a planned presentation. Inherent in it was a sense that Shakespeare was for everybody and that one way to make certain that anybody would see it was to remove all the obstacles by bringing it to them and charging no admission. It was absolutely impossible to do, absolutely impossible, yet he did it.

At one point, during a period of time when street gangs were flourishing, we had a problem with security at a playground in Brooklyn. Joe and I went to this negotiation with the gang leaders and they said to us, "What are you doing around here? This ain't your property, who asked you in? Get your ass out."

"Are you kidding?" Joe said. "Look down the street. I don't know what you think about yourself, or where you come from, or how long you've been here, but I was *born* down there, and I was raised down there, so don't tell me I don't belong here. You're fulla shit."

That changed the tone of the situation considerably, and Joe enlisted their aid and made them responsible for our security and crowd control. We soon had them with us instead of against us, and that was fun.

JOSEPH PAPP When we did the mobile unit again, between 1964 and 1969, we'd make arrangements with the local community. We would have a truck or a van going around announcing the fact that we were having a show, but this time we just came in. The greatest thing about the mobile, though, was that the audience would almost invariably take care of the dissenters in the crowd. We had to close up a couple of times, but I've never had cops come into the theater area. I'd say to them, "You must stay outside."

From time to time people would throw a rock or something on the stage, or miss and hit a woman in the front row. I would get up and say, "Ladies and gentlemen, if another rock is thrown, we'll cancel the performance." And the audience would say, "No! No! No!" The great majority was always attentive, they demanded respect from everybody, they'd take responsibility for someone who was carrying on or misbehaving, and they handled some rough customers, too.

You have to give the actors a lot of credit for courage in situations like that. It was scary at times, but we never had any serious problems. They were getting tired, driving around from place to place with a very crude stage and makeshift dressing rooms, but there was no such thing as demoralization. You can't imagine the spirit of these people.

ANN KINGSBURY RESCH In 1965 I went up to Harlem with Bernie Gersten to see the mobile unit production of *Taming of the Shrew* at a school playground. Everyone there was black, and all the seats were absolutely filled. There were people hanging out of their apartment windows, people climbing up on the fence to watch. There was a mother nursing her baby right in front of us. It was really very different from what I'd experienced on Forty-fourth Street and Broadway.

I'd had a lot of training in Shakespeare both in college and at the Guildhall School of Music and Drama in London, but I'd never gotten the earthiness of some of those jokes until I saw that production. The laughter was just terrific; those people understood the jokes better than I did with my private-school background. I was just overwhelmed.

JAMES EARL JONES Sometimes, when we were in the Bronx, we'd walk from our trailers to the stage and kids would stop us and say, "Hey, you. Hey, you. You gonna be the clown tonight?" They weren't putting us down. They thought, What's show business but clowning? You're in costume, that must mean you're a clown.

When we'd get onstage, we'd get Coke bottles, usually paper clips and rubber bands thrown at us. We had to be careful of our eyes. Actors have told me of reaching out to shake so-called fans' hands and realizing that the fan had a razor blade in his hands. Just sort of random hostility. I figured it was because we were invading their turf. That meant we were subject to their rules and their behavior. If we'd invited them to our theater, it would have been a whole different kind of behavior.

MARTIN ARONSTEIN In the summer of 1957 I was working for my stepfather and going to summer school, making up a statistics course that I had no concept of how to pass. The touring production of *Romeo and Juliet* was playing in Kings Park in Queens, and I passed by there on my way from this summer course to my stepfather's shop. One day, just out of curiosity, I asked someone if they needed help.

"What do you do?"

"I've been working in lighting in college."

"See John Robertson. He's over there in that truck."

A Parks Department van was being used as an electric truck. I sort of called in and this very exhausted-looking, tousled head with bulging eyes came out and said, "Yeah, whaddaya want?"

I told him and he said, "Yeah, we can use help. Come around tomorrow morning."

"What time should I show up?"

"As early as your mother'll let'cha outta the house."

It was grueling work, setting up temporary scaffolding in various sites around the city, hanging the lights every single day, and, using city-owned civil-defense generators for power, plugging them into antiquated systems. And if it wasn't difficult enough to do alone in the hot, humid New York summer, it would be raining. Midway through the season, however, I didn't have the subway fare to get there anymore; it was just becoming impossible for me. So I was put on the payroll as Marty the Electrician for the magnificent sum of $10 a week.

JOSEPH PAPP After the last touring performance of *Romeo and Juliet*, we returned to Central Park and never left. The equipment was breaking down and so were the people, so I just squatted there and assumed it was all right. Anyway, nobody had the equipment to move that damn stage out of there; nobody was strong enough. We were there to stay.

DAVID BLACK In January of 1957 I'd gone with some friends to Rome to start the American Theater in Rome, and when that effort failed, we came back to the United States. In July of 1957, I was visiting with the head of the Equity Library Theater, and while I was talking to her, she got a call from Joe Papp.

He told her that after touring *Romeo and Juliet*, they literally just were exhausted, so they had gotten permission from the Parks Department to settle at the Belvedere Lake site where they had performed before.

"We really need someone to manage the whole audience and some of the house activity," Joe told her, "but I can't afford to do that." So he had gotten the Parks Department to hire someone for the summer as a temporary recreational assistant. And this woman said, "I happen to be sitting here with David Black, who's just gotten back from Rome. Let me ask him." She did, and I said, "Well, sure."

My job was to control the crowds. I think our seating capacity was somewhere between three and four hundred people, with folding chairs in front and then bleachers in the back. Because the plays became so popular, seating became a problem, and by the time the summer was over, the place looked like a concentration camp. I'd had to get snow fences and put them up to keep the audience from getting into certain areas, especially around the control truck and the lighting towers.

We tried to save a few seats in front each night for special guests and people who were contributing to Joe. With me standing at the rope and arguing with people who wanted to sit in that section, it became almost a knock-down, drag-out battle every night.

I was young, and I got into trouble a few times, upsetting people because I'd yell at them. Mostly I'd yell at smaller Jewish ladies who insisted on sitting in the front rows, and especially at the people who said, "Oh, well, I'm a personal friend of Mr. Papp's and he told me I could sit here." I hadn't yet learned all the nice things you have to do with people when you're dealing with nonprofit theater. It was a very challenging kind of summer.

JERRY STILLER After *Romeo and Juliet*, I said to Joe, "I don't think I can hang in here unless I get Anne into the next play." Joe understood the economics of life, and he hired Anne to play Julia in *Two Gentlemen of Verona*, while I was hired to play Launce, so now we had two salaries for the first time.

About eight or nine days before we were supposed to open, they couldn't find a dog to play the part of Crab, Launce's dog. At one point Ed Sherin, who was a friend of mine and just trying to help out, said, "Let me play the dog. I'd love to play the dog."

"No, no," I said. "We want a real dog, Ed."

So John Robertson, who was doing a lot of technical work, went down to the ASPCA and brought back a collie. All wrong. A beautiful dog, very frisky, with that kind of Irish setter–type thing, but all wrong. "This," I said to myself, "is not a Shakespearean mutt."

Everyone was saying to me, "Take the dog. Once he goes back to the pound, you know this dog is not gonna make it. You'll save a dog's life." I looked at the dog again, we tried to like each other. The dog licked me; I licked the dog. Nothing. I had great guilt, but I said, "What are we gonna do with this dog? This dog ain't right. It'll ruin the show."

Then came one of those things that just happens, serendipity, whatever you want to call it. We were rehearsing under the Brooklyn Bridge, and a dog walks up. Terribly emaciated, you could see the bones on the ribs, it looked like it might have once been a Dalmatian, white and gray and dirty. It had one eye that blinked constantly and that Myron Cohen hangdog look to it.

I looked at this dog and I knew immediately that this was the dog. "They're gonna break up," I said. "We'll fatten him up maybe a little bit so the people don't take pity on him, but they'll never stop laughing at this dog."

We brought it backstage, and I started to relate to the dog as an actor would. Not because I loved the dog but because I had to know him quick; we were going on soon. I said to Anne, "I'm going to have to *live* with this dog for eight days." I got a rubber inner tube, put a little blanket over it, and made a little bed for him right in front of our bed. Then I cleaned him and washed him and brought him in.

What happened was we would go to bed after rehearsals, and the dog would jump into bed with us. He'd separate us, and Anne said, "Get him outta here."

"I can't get him outta here," I said. "I've got to work with this dog. He's gonna be onstage with me, and I've got to somehow or other get related to this dog."

Now part of her was saying, "He's nuts, he's crazy, he's *meshuga*," and the other part said, "We're actors, he's right."

In addition to that, the dog wouldn't eat ordinary food. I could see why his ribs were like that; he didn't eat scraps or anything like that. So I started cooking him chicken necks. I'd spice them a little bit, smelled good. I fed him the chicken necks hoping that he would learn to love me, "love this guy," whatever.

The long and short of it was that we went onstage and when that audience saw that dog, you couldn't walk, you couldn't get the first line out. The people loved that dog because he paid no attention to anything I said. He wasn't distracted, he wasn't doing numbers, he wasn't doing anything. He just stood there, and every line was a laugh. I would take the dog home at night and people would say to me, "By that dog thou shalt be known." I loved this dog.

EDWIN SHERIN   Crab was an amazing animal, amazing, and Jerry was probably the only actor alive who could work with him. Here's a dog that was obviously not trained, it was found, but that dog *knew*, and it was Jerry's loving nature that invited Crab in. I think it was the most successful relationship between man and beast in the history of the theater. You would think that they had partnered and rehearsed for years, that they had a language, because as the dog did something, Jerry was always present. He was so involved in a given moment with Crab that the dog responded.

It wasn't that Jerry subverted the language; the language of the play somehow supported whatever those two were doing. For instance, Jerry would say, "When didst thou see me heave up my leg and make water against a gentlewoman's farthingale?" and the dog would look up at him and say, "I'm sorry, boss, but that's the way it was." Jerry would say, "Didst thou ever see me do such a trick?" and the dog would say, "Well, what can I do? I said I'm sorry."

Now those words obviously weren't spoken, but they were acted, you could perceive it. They fed each other, no question about it. I think they may have had the most successful two-actor relationship in the history of the United States theater. It was certainly the most honest and open and spontaneous.

JERRY STILLER   They had an article about the dog in *Theatre Arts Magazine*, he was on a CBS show called *Eye on New York*. They never talked about me. They talked completely about this dog. Once a guy came up to me at a party and he said, "I'm with Chock full o'Nuts, I'm president of the company, and because of the dog and you, I'm giving the Shakespeare Festival $25,000." I never felt so good in my life. I couldn't pay the rent that month, of course, but I went over, had another piece of pie, and said, "Gee, I feel good."

When the show was over, we had a dog in our life, and I didn't know what to do. I couldn't send the dog out on the street again—couldn't do it. I couldn't possibly give him to the ASPCA; they would probably kill him. "This dog is like a human being," I said. "He got laughs."

But if we were going to keep the dog, I had to get his eye fixed up. I couldn't look at this dog every morning with the eye blinking like that. He had to have an operation, which they said he might not survive because it turned out he had a heart condition, too.

"I'll take a chance with the heart," I said.

"The eye alone is going to cost you $500," they said.

"Five hundred dollars? I'm an actor, I'm broke, I'm not even working. I'm not doing anything."

"Okay, $50."

So Crab was fixed up for $50. He survived the heart thing and everything else. He lived with us for seven years after the play ended. And he was not an easy dog.

DAVID AMRAM This old dog became a sensation. *Romeo and Juliet* had gotten fantastic reviews, but *Two Gentlemen of Verona* got about the best reviews anything had in years. You've seen all these movies about people in Sardi's in their tails and tuxedos going out to get the newspapers and reading the reviews? Here were a bunch of people, all of whom had day jobs, coming out in the middle of the summer in street clothes or shorts and sandals, sitting in this funky little coffeehouse reading these reviews. Some people still had their makeup on because there wasn't enough room or time or sometimes not even enough stuff for them to take it off until they got home afterward. And we all flipped out. Now the crowds really started coming. It was free and it was fun. Suddenly the New York Shakespeare Festival was something that was really hot.

T. EDWARD HAMBLETON In 1953 Norris Houghton and I founded the Phoenix Theatre, which at the time was New York's only nonprofit subscription theater. In 1957, we were looking for a new artistic director, and Tyrone Guthrie was advising us. I told him, "There's a fellow named Stuart Vaughan who's been working for Joe Papp. How would it be to come and see his *Macbeth* with me tonight?"

We went to see *Macbeth*, the last production of the season, and it was one of those really hot, humid nights—you could almost cut the air with a knife, it was so wet. Thunder started as soon as we got there, and there were flashes of lightning when the witches appeared. When Macbeth made his entrance with "So foul and fair a day I have not seen," that brought a big reaction. It was really the most exciting first act of *Macbeth* I've ever seen. But by the end of the act, it started to come down in buckets and the production just ended at that point. Guthrie said, "This is certainly a novel beginning," and out of that evening came his feeling that Stuart would be our man.

EDWIN SHERIN Being out there in the weather during *Macbeth* was one of the most extraordinary things. The night Tyrone Guthrie came to see it, we got lightning, then thunder; you can imagine the witches saying "When shall we three meet again?" in that. It was stupendous for the actors, it was so enlivening. Oh, my god! It just lifted the sense of reality to a tumultuous level. It was like having an enormous mystical hand at work.

JERRY STILLER Colleen Dewhurst was Lady Macbeth. Every night, when she got to that "Out, out damn spot" speech, an airplane would go overhead. They tried to figure out a way to time it, to start the show later, but she'd get to that moment and it never failed. Then one night, here was this plane coming in again. She stopped and she looked up and she raised her fist and just hollered at the airplane, "Why can't you wait?" And the audience applauded at that moment. I'll never forget her taking the time to acknowledge the airplane, saying "How could you do this to me?" and then getting back in character again.

JOSEPH PAPP Up to this point, we were just playing during the summer. We'd had a certain amount of success, but we had no money. From the very beginning, my whole desire was to pay people salaries—later I changed it to a living wage! We were able to pay off-Broadway minimums of $35 a week, but that's all. And Stuart began to say, "We should certainly have some kind of winter company to have continuity."

If you develop a company, you don't have to start the search all over again and try to find new people every year. And in terms of fund-raising, you just can't come out and say you're a summer person. That made it even more important to have something year-round.

I'd done a lot of going around the city, looking for parks and playgrounds to play in, and now I began to look around for a suitable winter haven. And I stumbled across this place, I didn't know it existed, called the Children's Center on 104th Street and Fifth Avenue, where kids who came out of broken homes were kept for a while.

I walked into this place—I didn't know what brought me there—and saw this lovely little space called the Heckscher Theater. It was about 650 seats surrounded by marvelous murals of children's fairy tales by Willy Pogany. It hadn't been used for years—it was just there—and I thought, "Gee, this would be a good place for us to put on plays." This was a city building. It had a very important function, but I used everything I could and I must have been very effective, because I got use of the space.

I felt good in that theater because I established my first real office there in what had been a cloakroom. It was only about four feet wide and the hooks for the coats were still there. I shared it with Hilmar Sallee. We had to drag a lamp in there to get some light. But I was so delighted to have it because it was a great improvement over the place I had on East Sixth Street—at least the rats weren't coming through. There was no air, no windows, it was hot in there, but it was my office.

GLADYS VAUGHAN *Richard III* was the first play at the Heckscher and Stuart was looking for somebody to play Richard, which wasn't easy. You have to remember that at that time there weren't other theaters around, the scene wasn't just full of actors who had experience in Shakespeare.

We had a friend, an actress named Janice Halliday, who had come back from a stock company in Toledo, Ohio. "You have got to see this actor," she raved to us. "He is the most wonderful actor I have ever seen anywhere. We did a new play every week, and with everybody else you kind of guessed how they would play whatever role they were assigned. But with this man, George Scott, you never knew. You must get him in to see about *Richard III*, because I am telling you, he is *wonderful!*"

STUART VAUGHAN Janice Halliday said to me, "They're doing a reading of a play tonight with this wonderful actor I've been telling you about. You've got to go and see him." It was a play about the death of Marlowe, and George was playing one of the two spies who supposedly killed Marlowe in that tavern brawl. And, god, I was just knocked out with him. I went backstage and I said how great he was and could he come and read for us?

He did come in, but apparently he was hungover and it didn't work. He read badly and confusedly, yet it was kind of wonderful, there was something magnetic and powerful about him. We had him back a second time but an apprentice read with him, and she was trying to put on a show instead of letting him read, so that didn't work. So we had him back a third time, and that time it jelled.

In the meantime, we'd heard various other people who were better known, but they were dull or too classic, nobody else was right, and Joe and I finally just said, "Let's go with this guy." I didn't know, all during that production, that he was a drinker. There was never *any* problem of any sort with his discipline. I think he realized, "This is a chance a guy doesn't get very often. I'm ambitious, and I'm going to make it work for me."

GEORGE C. SCOTT I'd been an actor for some seven years, stock mostly, this and that, out in the provinces and sticks and Canada. This was my second or third trip to New York, and through fellow actors, general casting knowledge, barrooms, whatever, I heard about a production of *Richard III*. Although we didn't know each other, Stuart Vaughan had heard about me and I got an audition. I moseyed up there to 104th Street and Fifth Avenue and I read once. They called me back two or three days later, and I read very badly.

I was very upset about not doing well. I was a grown man, twenty-nine years old, I'd been kicking around at this a long time. I was unemployed as an actor. I wanted the part, *any* part, desperately. So I did something I'd never done before and I've never done since: I called Joe and asked for a third audition. I was terrified, really, no question about it. Joe was perfunctory, but he acquiesced. I wasn't even sure they remembered me, but he said, "Yes, by all means, come back again," and a date was made for the next day.

I had a couple of friends, Dick and Jean Shepherd, who lived down on St. Mark's Place. I used to hang out down there—I'd sleep in their garden, for Christ's sake. There was a very sweet friend of theirs, a girl who just happened to be hanging around the joint, and she said, "Would you like me to help you?"

"Gee," I said. "Would you? I want to work on two or three soliloquies."

And that child—I *cannot* remember her name to save my soul—stayed up with me all night long in the backyard, until dawn broke, rehearsing me over and over in these two or three soliloquies.

Of course I was dead on my feet, no sleep at all, and nerves and coffee and probably booze—I was a big drinker in those days—but I went back that day. I knew everything I wanted to do and I did it well, obviously, because I got the part. The money was nothing, $40 or $45 a week, but I was just ecstatic.

JOSEPH PAPP   I remember having to make a decision about George C. Scott. He was one of the actors that came in off the street, so to speak. He told us a little bit about his background: he hadn't studied anyplace, most of his experience had been watching movie actors. He had no reputation; we never knew he'd done anything else.

He didn't make a great impression at first. To his credit, Stuart liked him a lot, but I was a little dubious, and there was somebody else in contention. Believe me, it wasn't Laurence Olivier. It was somebody who we haven't heard from since, who I thought was a very good actor. Oh, I've made some blunders in my day. My first reaction is not always correct, but you only need a percentage.

· I didn't dislike George, it was just that I wasn't quite sure. I guess I didn't like his voice, it was very gravelly, and I wanted a better speaking voice. Everybody else was saying, "Oh, I don't know, he seems all right. He's interesting." He had another reading, which I thought was very good, and I finally decided, "Well, let's cast him."

DAVID AMRAM   That was George C. Scott's first role in New York doing any kind of part other than extra work or some teeny appearance way, way off Broadway. I went into the first rehearsal and I saw this guy in a T-shirt and khaki pants who looked like an ex-marine, which is what he was. He would start to be Richard III, and suddenly, right in front of you, with no costume, no makeup, no anything, he would change completely into this character. It was so terrific watching him that it wasn't even that hard to write that enormous amount of music—*Richard* had almost sixty minutes—for nothing.

STUART VAUGHAN   George was demonic as Richard. I've always thought that Richard was not just a little villain but a prince, Lucifer in a way. In the first part of the play, we're with him because he's more vital and alive than anybody else. We share in his delight as we watch him make fools of these people. And that's fine until he gets what he wants, and then we see the other side. We realize how empty he feels and how it all turns to ashes in his mouth.

George could do all of that. He had the lusty humor of it, the twinkle in the eye, and yet the hardness and the cruelty. He had supernatural, larger-than-life strength and power, so that the Lucifer/demonic prince thing happened as well. And Richard is such an actor, he's always pretending these things to people and he convinces them. He doesn't do "heh-heh-heh." He's sincere to Lady Anne; he makes her believe he's in love with her.

Then, at the end of the play, as it turns cold, George could do that, too, because he had that rage that he could let work for him. And just before the end, in the great dream scene in which Richard wakes up from the nightmare and is at his lowest, George was like a child, and you were sorry for him. Oh, that was harrowing, and it was pitiful. It was amazing.

JAMES EARL JONES   One of the most difficult scenes is the courtship of Richard and Lady Anne, and George's performance will always be used as an example of how it can be made real and scary at the same time. You always wonder: What does Richard really feel about her, what was the passage of chemistry between them? There is a moment when Richard says, "If you don't take me, I'll just kill myself." And George put the butt of his sword on the floor and leaned over the sword, and you knew he was going to do it. Every night, you knew he was going to fall on that sword. It was so scary.

GEORGE C. SCOTT   The Heckscher wasn't the most fashionable joint in the world, but considering the places I'd been working in, it wasn't too bad. And once I got rolling into rehearsals, I felt very confident, very strong. It's very seldom I've been that confident in a part. And I was a strong man in those days, physically, I was athletic and could bounce around the stage and do all that sword fighting and mace fighting and all that garbage.

We put on performances for schoolkids, and the first one, for junior high school students, was one of the most memorable times of my life. It was a matinee, and we were told, though I can't believe this is true, that the teachers abandoned the students in there and departed, all went out to get a beer or something.

Anyway, we were in there with these hundreds of wild, crazy kids. They didn't give a shit about Shakespeare or anything else. We could hear this roar backstage, and we said, "What the hell is that? Sounds like the Roman circus, throwing Christians to the lions." And when I walked out with the gimp and the twisted arm and the twisted leg and the hump and the bangs and the birthmark, the whole schmear, they thought that was the funniest goddamn thing they'd ever seen. They just *roared* with laughter.

Lester Rawlins, who had kind of stovepipe legs and shook a little bit, played Clarence. He shook a little more that day. He was very nervous because he had to come down the aisle through the audience to get up on the stage. I didn't think he was going to make it for a minute there, because *I* was scared, for Christ's sake.

But, by golly, once we got going, they started to pay a little attention. And at the end, when I was mobbed and killed, they booed. They thought that was unfair gang warfare. And so we all came off pretty well in that.

GLADYS VAUGHAN   George would walk right out, looking at the audience, and those kids would be yelling and screaming. They made the most unbelievable noise, and George would wait them out. And then he would have them right in his hand. It was incredible.

After he had wooed Lady Anne and she had sort of given in, George came down and sat on this platform that was built out into the audience and gave the "Was ever woman in this humour wooed?" speech. At the end, in this mood of incredible elation, he turned a backward somersault and ended up on his feet.

One day after the somersault he lost his wig. I don't know many actors who wouldn't be rather thrown by that, but George pulled out his sword, scooped up the wig on the tip of it, and twirled it as he said the line, "Shine out, fair sun, till I have bought a glass, That I may see my shadow as I pass."

People who saw that may have thought that that was an incredible, really bizarre choice, but they didn't know whether it had been planned or not. That was the sense of life that George brought to the play. After that performance, nobody has ever touched Richard III for me again.

GEORGE C. SCOTT   It laid there like a muskrat, right in front of me. I picked it up and talked to it, something like that. The audience loved that—they thought it was great. I was a little embarrassed, but it didn't seem to bother them. They thought it was terrific.

The whole performance was somewhat electrifying, apparently. I got my agent through that. I started to get a few jobs in television, that sort of thing, and it just went right on from there. It was breathtaking. I couldn't believe it. And I owe a lot of that to Joe Papp.

MERLE DEBUSKEY   I went over to the *Times*, got a copy of the review, and took it to a restaurant on Eighth Avenue that was a theater hangout. George, who was driving a truck for a living at that time, and Joe and Stuart and a couple of other actors gathered around and read this glowing review.

Now, I've been fortunate over the years to work on a lot of plays that George has been in, and the one thing in the world he doesn't want to hear about, good, bad, or indifferent, is a review. Keep it away, almost so it's a phobia. But I remember looking at George that day when this first review came in, and I remember the joy that suffused his being.

STUART VAUGHAN   The only problem George and I ever had came in the next production, when he did Jaques in *As You Like It*, and it was over a costume. We'd been playing Jaques as a drunk in rehearsals. He was bright and full of wisdom and all that, but there was that drunkard's concealed mischief and malevolence underneath it all.

It's the first dress rehearsal, and here comes the costume. It was open and disorderly. The makeup was kind of awful—George had smudges and dirt all over his face. Though the bottle had always been there, I had never thought that he would be slovenly.

"Are you going to look like that?" I said.

"I had planned to."

"But Jaques is a gentleman. He wouldn't be dirty. He wouldn't look like that."

"Well," George said, "I'm not going to play this part like some English fag!"

"George," I said, "you *couldn't* play this part like an English fag."

I could tell he was angry, but we made a compromise and that was the end of it.

GEORGE C. SCOTT   They call that character "melancholy Jaques" and this and that, but that's not the way I felt about him. I played him more sardonically and rather bitterly, not just melancholy. He was kind of pissed off at the world, and I had a lot of that in me at the time anyway. So I played him pretty hard until the "Seven Ages of Man" speech, and that changed the whole characterization. I'll never forget what Walter Kerr said: "I heard this damn speech for the first time in my life." That was a great critique.

DAVID AMRAM   By the time we did *As You Like It*, the house was full of actors. Everybody was coming to see this fantastic new actor—everybody said, "We've gotta see this guy Scott." I was working the night shift at the post office then, and I'd be late every night so that I could hear George say the "Seven Ages of Man" speech before I ran downtown.

JERRY STILLER   George used to love to play bridge downstairs before he'd go on. He'd hear his cue, put the cards down, go upstairs, do the "Seven Ages of Man," hear the applause, go downstairs, pick up the cards, and begin again from where he'd been playing. He made you feel like you were all wrong.

EDWIN SHERIN I played Octavius Caesar opposite George in *Antony and Cleopatra* at the Heckscher, and holy Jesus, there was only one way I could have been noticed on that stage and that was never to look at him. Because the moment I looked at George, I was sucked up in his vortex. Just, whoosh, gone. So I played the whole scene looking at the audience. You can imagine what that was like.

Colleen Dewhurst played Cleopatra, and they were very connected. They were hot. There was obviously a lot going on between them, and they were capable of bringing that private and public feeling together. They were two extremely passionate people, and when I say "extremely," I use the word advisedly.

George proved how powerful he was. He would do incredible things. As Antony he had to commit suicide by falling on his sword, and not only did it seem that the blade went in him, but his head hit the deck in such a resounding manner that you heard this "boom-oom-oomm" coming off the balcony.

It was that kind of physical abandon of the moment which marked his work. The things that would govern you and me—is this within the bounds of good taste, is this appropriate—never meant anything. It was one of the reasons his performing was so electric. You could not take your eyes off the man.

COLLEEN DEWHURST I had not seen George in *Richard III*. I was hostile then, hostile with Joe, rather antagonistic because I felt he would not give my then-husband, Jim Vickery, a chance. Everybody talked about him, but I wouldn't go.

I'd talked about doing Cleopatra, and I said, "But who's going to do Antony?" And Alice and J. D. Cannon took me to see *As You Like It*, and when George came out as Jaques she said, "This is your Antony." And I said, "Too short." And she was furious with me.

By the time we did *Antony and Cleopatra* together, we were a couple. There were several men I've really enjoyed playing with, but George is the best. As my agent said, "Well, dear, I think it's very good when you work with Mr. Scott, because if you roar, he can roar louder." And it was true.

I'd gotten very bored with the word "strong." I began to realize that every reviewer was calling me "strong, animal-like," et cetera. And when I worked with George those adjectives never appeared. With him you felt you could let out all the stops. You could go into the role, and you always knew he was standing there ready to catch any energy coming at him. You didn't have to feel at any time that you should hold back because of how you were going to look. It's marvelous to find an actor like that.

GEORGE C. SCOTT   We were doing *Antony and Cleopatra*, in which I was awful. I was unfit for the part, it just wasn't my cup of tea at all. It was too romantic for me. I was never a leading man or anything like that. Let's face it, Richard Burton I wasn't.

JOSEPH PAPP   Stuart Vaughan was offered a job at the Phoenix Theatre and he left in 1958. At the time, I'd been called before the House Un-American Activities Committee, and I told him, "Listen, I may go to jail. I don't know what's going to happen." I wanted him to take over. It was very little to give him, though, and he said, no, he was going to go to the Phoenix, where they'd offered him a big contract and he had an opportunity to direct other things.

You'll always find with a theater, even when something is in its kind of formative stage, a contention, a struggle for power that goes on, on some scale. It may not have been that literal, but someone would say, "I want to be able to decide this and decide that." And I would say, "No, I can't let you decide that." I wasn't just being obdurate; this was what my experience at the Actors' Lab had ingrained in me.

I was very supportive of these people. I didn't want my name on the posters at the beginning; I gave them all the credit. My whole thing was just to do it, make it happen. Certainly Stuart virtually had total artistic control. That's the best way to work: you don't impose your will on people if they're capable. If they're not, then you're in trouble. But I suppose with Stuart, at a certain point, he had his own kind of ambition and driving force, which is good. But I would never share the power.

STUART VAUGHAN   There was a conversation across from the Heck-scher in a nice little garden area of Central Park. I said, "Fill me in, what's going on?"

"You have a right to know, since you helped make this whole project possible," he said. "Yes, I was a card-carrying Communist. I was a member of the Party until Peggy and I got married, and she convinced me that it was stupid to belong any longer."

It's possible that an offer was being made in pain and veiled terms that I wasn't even prepared to hear, because I didn't think things were that bad. I could imagine taking the position that I had just taken on the job of artistic director at the Phoenix Theatre, that the Shakespeare Festival needed him, he must stay at the helm.

Joe and I really didn't part company; we oozed apart. He offered me a couple of things, and I was always busy, so it just kind of dwindled. There was never a blowup. It was never "I quit" or "You've got to go." The bloom was off the rose and my first wife then began to direct for Joe, and that was an atmosphere that I didn't want to be around. Also there was a friction of egos between me and Joe that made me uncomfortable, that I didn't need.

I always found Joe to be scrupulously honest about money and things, but he's not always been careful to give credit where credit is due. I think that's a form of blindness. There wouldn't have been a Shakespeare Festival without me, but he doesn't like to think of those things. I don't know why gratitude is so difficult in the theater. We all would like to be self-made; we'd all like not to have to attribute our origins to anybody.

When I first took the Phoenix job, the Shakespeare Festival was only functioning in the summertime. The Phoenix was winter work. I never thought of the two things as being mutually exclusive. But when Joe spoke of it one time he said, "You left us, we didn't leave you." Joe expects a loyalty in a form that no thinking person can give easily. It's a Mafia loyalty; it's the loyalty of the street. "Be loyal to me. Whatever I want, whatever I tell you to do, be loyal to me. Whatever I'm going for, be loyal to me."

Well, an artist can't abide that emotion. An artist is loyal to the art. He'll work shoulder to shoulder with the most arrogant bastards and sons of bitches, because who cares what they do in their private life? Who cares whether they're good people or bad people, as long as we're working with the art? Who cares about *any* loyalty, except the loyalty toward the goal?

I scare a lot of people, and I think maybe Joe scares people, too. I don't think we ever scared each other. I'm equally single-minded and equally strong. I was awfully glad to find somebody with like capabilities. I have not found them so since. We were in some measure competitive, like a couple of stags out in the field—there's that false masculine head-butting thing that I wish we'd all get rid of—but aside from that, we were in many ways a very good combination.

JOSEPH PAPP   I needed someone who would be a production manager. Bernie Gersten had been an excellent stage manager. We'd worked together on the O'Casey plays; he had a lot of experience. I tried to get him a couple of times, but he was too busy making money on Broadway and in television and everybody at the festival worked for nothing. By this time, though, he was finally available and I could offer him a real salary, so he came aboard and I was very pleased that he did.

Bernie was key in my life. We had a working relationship of the highest order, the longest relationship of that kind I've had with anybody in the organization. He was the executive that was closest to me, and he was an extremely capable man. In other words, I could leave the store and Bernie would be there. He had nothing to do with the artistic selection of things, that was where the line was drawn. But in all other things that I did, he was involved. He took a tremendous load off my shoulders in many ways. His contribution is incalculable. He owns a part of the festival.

BERNARD GERSTEN   I worked at the Stratford, Connecticut, American Shakespeare Festival through the summer of 1959, but I was not rehired. And then Joe said, as spring was coming up, "Why don't you come to work for the New York Shakespeare Festival?" I thought that was a pretty good idea and went to work for $125 a week. We had a very tiny office—a former checkroom at the Heckscher which had stairs running up above—that only had room for two desks, one for Joe and one for Hilmar Sallee. So what Joe did was pull out the old-fashioned letter-writing board of his desk, and that little board became my desk.

The job at first was production manager, which meant organizing and being responsible to the producer for the entire process of producing three plays in Central Park on a very, very slight budget. I've always had a very distinct memory of the budget for that first season in 1960: it was $125,000.

There were always two aspects to the relationship between Joe and me. The one which was tremendously positive was the extent to which Joe understood that I was not competitive with him, that I wasn't threatening him, that I was there as a support force. That recognition was a pervasive one, and it certainly governed during all of the years that we worked together. There were certain lines in *King Lear* I always felt characterized my behavior. Lear says to Kent, "What would you of me, sir?" And Kent says, "I would serve you, sir." And I thought that fit. I was in Joe's service; that was always my image.

The other aspect was that Joe, being by nature impatient and restless, would at times become very irritated and angry with me for some failure on my part to satisfy him, to please him, and then we would have fights. So perhaps there were a number of precursors to what was the ultimate separation between Joe and me, but I never thought of them that way.

7

HUAC and Robert Moses
1958-59

Papp and attorney
Ephraim London at
the HUAC hearings
© Bettmann/Corbis

I am not now a member of the Communist Party . . . I just think it is wrong
to deny anybody employment because of their political beliefs.

Joseph Papp, testimony before the House Un-American
Activities Committee, June 19, 1958

As to Papp, he was and is an irresponsible Commie who doesn't keep his
word or obey the rules and—again, anticlimax—he has no dough to pay the
actors or run the show decently and therefore surreptitiously passes the hat
like a damned mendicant.

Parks Commissioner Robert Moses, letter to Howard
Lindsay, August 10, 1959

JOSEPH PAPP The House Un-American Activities Committee hearings had already begun when I began to be pursued by two FBI men. They would meet me as I was leaving work at CBS, say "We're from the FBI," and start to walk down the street with me. I kept walking.

"We'd like to talk to you about some of the people that you knew in California." They were more nervous than I was—they were shaking, actually.

"I have nothing to say to you."

"Well, it would be to your advantage—"

"Listen, I have nothing to say to you. If you want to do something official, do it officially. Otherwise, I have nothing to say to you."

So they'd leave and I'd go in the subway. A couple of weeks later, there they were again, starting what became a routine of trying to break me down. Meeting me in front of CBS was part of that—making me wonder whether I'd lose my job, whether they had already informed CBS that I was going to be called to testify.

"I think you'd better cooperate, if you know what's good for you," they said the last time they met me.

"Are you threatening me?"

"I'm just telling you what you should pay attention to."

A few days before I was called, there was an offer to go to Washington to appear at a closed hearing and not be subjected to an open proceeding. I turned it down, even though I knew it meant I would be subpoenaed. I was not going to engage in naming names. I saw people that I knew starting to repudiate everything they ever stood for. They found all kinds of rationales, excuses for naming people, for holding on to their goddamn jobs. And I found that disgusting. I was very disappointed in that kind of behavior.

Some of the most radical people would say, "I was young and I really didn't believe in it. I didn't know any better." I was young, too, but I always knew better. I was very clear why I was doing certain things. I have deep-rooted convictions which I've had all my life. I'm not saying it's good or bad, but it happens to be me. It comes out of my background, and I would never deny that one bit. On the contrary, I'm very proud of it, I think it's made me capable of doing what I'm doing now, doing a service to the community, to people.

I was gritting my teeth, waiting to get a subpoena. The worst that could happen to me, if I was held in contempt, would be to spend a year in jail. And, psychologically, I was prepared for that. The terrible thing was that people were afraid to talk to you. Everybody looked at you as though you were something to be avoided. You became persona non grata.

I thought that as a result, whether I went to jail or was just publicly disgraced, the Shakespeare Festival would be destroyed. I felt that none of the big organizations would give us any money—they'd be afraid and all that business. The festival was getting someplace. As far as I was concerned, it was my life, and I felt that this would end it.

PEGGY BENNION PAPP   That was a terrible time. It was so frightening because we didn't know how we were going to live. Everybody was worried about it, everybody. People who had not been as left-wing as he were blacklisted. The FBI used to come to our door all the time and try to get Joe to inform. When he went to work, a lot of people wouldn't speak to him, or they'd come over and say, "Take my name out of your address book and never speak to me again. I don't know you." He nearly blacked out one night from the anxiety. But he always lived on the edge of crises, there was always brinksmanship, he would always take an enormous chance that was far beyond his present capacity, and somehow or other, he'd gear himself up to that leap.

It was his beliefs that supported him and saw him through. When he went to testify, I said to him, "Oh, Joe, I am so scared." And he said, "Peggy, I can't be scared for myself. I'm too worried about what this means for the whole country and whole world, the terrible meaning it has for a lot of other people." Oh, those were the kinds of statements he made that I admired.

MERLE DEBUSKEY   When Joe got a subpoena he called me. And I picked up the phone and called a marvelous man whose name was Ephraim London and who was very big in civil liberties.

"Eph," I said to him, "there's no money in this."

And he just very simply said, "Is he a decent fellow?"

"He is an especially decent, loving, significant guy."

"Well, fine, tell him to call me and come in."

Obviously, Joe was not going to be a cooperative witness. He understood what it was all about, and he wasn't going to demean himself for any momentary relief of the burden of being a decent, honorable person. And we evolved a whole program of how to parry the thrust of this guy being some kind of menace.

We compiled an enormous amount of material that by now had been printed about the Shakespeare Festival, including the cover story of a publication called *Amerika*, in which the State Department used him as the foremost example to demonstrate to Russia what America is and what it can do. By the end of it, a couple of committee guys walked up to Joe and congratulated him.

JOSEPH PAPP I was not aggressive before the committee; the circumstances were very intimidating. You can't understand, unless you were part of it, how grim those times were. You saw no future after testifying; you didn't see any light at the end of any tunnel. You didn't even see the tunnel, for that matter. Even if you took what might be seen as a heroic position, it was hardly something that you ran around bragging about. You just knew that your situation was terrible.

On the other hand, on the day I testified I felt very high, very emotional. It's a romantic notion, but for some reason when you get up there, you think that these people who are questioning you will understand your patriotism. You look for some sort of comprehension, but, of course, it isn't there. These people were simply insistent on getting what they wanted for their purposes.

But still I tried. I presented them with a copy of *Amerika*, a magazine published by the State Department and sent to Russia, where our work was depicted as representative of free democratic culture. It was just a piece of showmanship, but it was important to say that what I was doing was important. The guy was trying to find out if we were saying something subversive with Shakespeare. It was so dumb.

My position was that I'd answer any question about myself, but I wasn't going to answer any questions about anybody else. Ephraim London suggested to his clients in that position that they take the Fifth Amendment.

"It's up to you," he said, "but once you begin to answer things, they'll force you to answer everything, and you're going to have to start mentioning names."

"No, no, no," I said. "I won't do anything like that." Even though most of the people I knew in California had already been called before the committee, I wasn't going to use that as an excuse to name them. That would have been succumbing to them, and I was determined not to do that.

That particular position was purely a position of pride. To me, being a stool pigeon, informing on somebody else, was the lowest form of life. I knew that people who are put under pressure to save their necks will historically name other people. But, first of all, nobody was torturing me. It was just a matter of prison, possibly. But, I figured, that's not the worst thing in the world. At least they pay for your room and board.

I testified in the morning, and then I left to do a news show at CBS that same evening. I was on the subway and I saw all around me the afternoon newspapers—the *Journal American* and the *World-Telegram*—with my picture on them. There I was, and all these people were reading these big huge headlines about me, the "I've Got a Secret" Man, refusing to name names.

I walked into the studio, and the stagehands, my best friends, wanted to know what my position was. "I took the Fifth Amendment," I said, "because if I went further, I would have to tell them everything about other people, and I could not do that." They were all very good about it, except one embittered guy who said, "Oh, you Communist," and walked away. Another guy, a lighting designer I'd spent hours helping, came over to me. He was shaking.

"You didn't mention m-m-my name, did you?" he said.

"Why the fuck should I mention your name," I said. "You're nothing."

I was about to start my show when I got a call saying that Don Darcey, the head of the stage manager's department, wanted to see me. I did the show first, and then I went up to his office, where Don looked awfully uncomfortable.

"Joe," he said, "I'm going to have to lay you off."

"What do you mean? Why?"

"Well," he said, his eyes shifting a little bit, "you know we're a little overstaffed."

"Come on, Don. What are you handing me here?"

He looked at me and said very quietly, "There was a meeting about your testimony. William Paley was very upset."

"So what?"

"We've got too many people here. We're trying to cut back."

"Come *on*."

"That's what it is. I have to do it."

"I don't accept that."

"What do you mean?"

"I'm telling you, I find this totally unacceptable. I'm a member of the Radio and Television Directors Guild, and I'm going to take this up with the union."

DAVID AMRAM   I'm certain a lot of people were jealous of Joe because they read his name mentioned favorably by Brooks Atkinson in the *New York Times*. And in a certain sense that jealousy had something to do with terrorizing the CBS Corporation into thinking that in his powerful position as stage manager—moving props around and telling actors it was time for them to make their entrance—Joe was somehow going to overthrow the government of the United States and turn it into Soviet America.

EDWIN SHERIN   When he lost his job, that was the only time that I ever saw Joe really shaken—when he felt that that was going to impact negatively on the Shakespeare Festival, that he would lose whatever small funding he was getting as well as the permission of the city because his name was now besmirched. "They might just be able to get away with it," he said. "They might just be able to get away with it and knock me off." He was really shaken.

JOSEPH PAPP   Now you wouldn't exactly call the Radio and Television Directors Guild a fighting union. I tried for weeks to get them to have a board meeting to discuss this issue, but they were very reluctant to get into it. Meanwhile, I was out of a job, I had no income, and I had a child and a family to support.

One of the directors I'd worked with at CBS, Robert Mulligan, got a job on Broadway directing *Comes a Day*, starring Judith Anderson and George C. Scott, and he hired me as stage manager. One night, I was so distracted by all the things that were bothering me that while Judith Anderson was onstage alone giving a speech, I said, "Okay, hit the curtain." And, oh god, it was the wrong cue, she was only halfway through the speech. She sounded like she was struggling, strangling, but the guy kept bringing down this curtain. Boy, was she furious.

Finally, I got the board of directors to meet, and after going through a very complicated polling of the membership, they agreed to challenge the firing. That led to arbitration, and in November of 1958, CBS was ordered to reinstate me with $1,500 back pay. CBS had contended that my dismissal had nothing to do with my pleading the Fifth Amendment but had come about because I had concealed my association with the California Labor School. But the arbitrator ruled that CBS knew of that association for years, and since it had never confronted me about it, "it does not follow that six and a half years later it might rely on these omissions to justify a dismissal."

That was a major victory, I was feeling great, but when I came to CBS, I found they were assigning me to minimum tasks, saying people had not asked for me when I knew they had. I could tell they were starting to jerk me around, and I began to think, "Why am I hanging around this damn organization?" So I quit and devoted myself full-time to the Shakespeare Festival.

Still, winning was most gratifying, and not just because I felt I'd made a point. It restored a faith I had in this democratic system, confirmed my feeling that you could still get satisfaction in this country. From the very beginning, I've always believed in the justice of the United States, when we're at our best.

MERLE DEBUSKEY Joe became the first blacklisted person to be fired and then rehired, and even though most people today hardly remember it, that was very significant. His case was a kind of cause célèbre in the world of television and theater. I mean, the blacklist was a pretty heavy hitter. It had knocked a lot of big boys right out of the box, buried them, and here was Joe, not a major figure, coming out triumphant.

The festival was not yet a truly significant element in the conscious-ness of New York, but it was ascending, and as Joe became someone of more substance, became more notable, that became part of the atmo-sphere which allowed this thing to grow.

. . .

STANLEY LOWELL First of all, you have to know Robert Moses. Robert Moses was a fixture in government. He had about four or five different gov-ernment jobs, including parks commissioner and being the guy who ran the planning commission.

When Robert Wagner was elected mayor, about a dozen leaders of civic organizations came to visit him. They didn't think he should reappoint Moses to all the jobs he held, but when the mayor suggested each organi-zation pass a resolution stating that this is what they wanted, they all said, "Oh, we can't do that. We might get in trouble ourselves if we propose to do that to Bob Moses."

When they left, Wagner said to me, "Very interesting. They don't have to run for office, but they want me to do this. They want to tell me in secrecy and they're not prepared to support me publicly." That demon-strates just how powerful Robert Moses was.

JOSEPH PAPP Before the mess started, I rarely even thought of Robert Moses in relation to the parks. I dealt on a borough level, and he seemed outside the whole thing. If I thought of him at all, it was as a powerful, dic-tatorial person who smashed a lot of things, whose excuse for tearing up the city to put up new highways and housing projects was: "If you want to make an omelet, you have to break some eggs."

Robert Moses, though, was also a very cultured man, an expert in O'Casey, and we understood that he was, in his own way, kind of fond of us. In fact, in October of 1957, he wrote a piece in the *Herald Tribune* saying he was "tremendously interested" in our company. "They have been a con-spicuous and widely heralded success," he wrote, "but they haven't got enough money to reopen next year, so we are setting about to raise funds to support them." And as late as January of 1959 he wrote me a letter saying, "We will be very happy to cooperate with you as we have in the past."

ROBERT MOSES LETTER TO JOSEPH PAPP, MARCH 18, 1959

I have your letter of March 11 in which you ask that we permit you this summer to operate your New York Shakespeare Festival in Central Park, as you have in the past, on a free admission basis.

I regret that we cannot do this. First, there is no control in the area you have been using and a considerable park acreage is being damaged by your operation. We must have fencing for control if your operation is to continue.

Second, there are no sanitary or dressing facilities for your actors and others employed in your productions and no electric current is available for lighting. We were forced to run a portable generator at the site during your operating season. Adequate sanitary and dressing facilities must be supplied if you are to continue in Central Park.

Third, the area used by your audience needs seats and paving. We cannot permit your audiences to continue to use lawn areas in Central Park as theater seating areas. We can't maintain grass and serious erosion problems will soon face us unless the area is paved.

The cost of the work the City must do if your Shakespeare in Central Park is to continue is between $100,000 and $150,000. If your performances are worthwhile, people will pay a reasonable charge to see them.

The concession agreement we have offered you will, if you have even moderate success, return about $10,000 annually to the City which will help to amortize the cost of necessary improvements and pay in part at least the cost of City help assigned to control and service your operation.

Unless therefore you are prepared to agree to charge admission and to enter into a regular concession agreement with the Department of Parks, we cannot give you a permit to operate in the City Park system in 1959.

JOSEPH PAPP That letter was a shock to me. I thought I had the support of this man, and then this came out of the blue. It was a complete turn-around, like getting hit in the kishkes.

Now, I had believed in free seats for a long time. Ever since my days watching the Goldman Band, my basic philosophy was making theatrical entertainment accessible to the audience regardless of their ability to pay.

A year earlier, in response to a column by Walter Kerr suggesting I charge admission, I wrote back outlining my aims. "The only practical means of insuring the permanence of our theater is to tie it in with civic responsibility. The public library, an institution for enlightenment and entertainment, is a case in point . . . I know that if I had had to pay for books at the Williamsburg Public Library, it is doubtful that I would have read the plays of Shakespeare."

At that time in my life, I lived or died by that principle—it wasn't subject to some kind of interpretation. But people didn't accept it at face value, they were always asking me, "Why are you really doing this?" I'd get so mad at that. I felt something cynical in it.

I wasn't stupid. I could tell that the people who gave money responded to the fact that it was free, and not having to get involved with the unions was also a factor. But over and above that, my "art," if you want to put it in quotes, was this idea, this feeling of accessibility. It was my life.

But then came this letter from Robert Moses. I didn't know how to deal with it. I never felt intimidated; I just felt kind of helpless. He was the big shot and a powerful man, so powerful that I felt I couldn't win. I didn't feel like David versus Goliath—David had the Lord on his side—I just felt like I was the smaller figure in this battle with not the kind of power to really combat it efficiently.

For that reason, I initially didn't want an outside battle. In fact, I wrote him one letter saying I had "no interest whatsoever in provoking a public outcry." Moses wore so many hats, he was the head of so many things, he'd survived so many battles, I didn't know how I could beat him.

Moses's first assistant, officially the Parks Department's executive officer, was a man named Stuart Constable. He was a blustery person with a kind of British army officer's mustache. I would have cast him as the Constable in *The Pirates of Penzance*. I didn't like him at all. I could see he was anti-Semitic, anti-Communist, anti-everything; he was one of those red-faced fanatical people, and he became the prime advocate of getting us out.

Then I heard that an unsigned letter was being circulated about me, making allegations that I was a Communist and so forth. It seemed to come from a disappointed actor who had some kind of personal gripe. But the fact that Moses was doing something underhanded ended up working against him. A man so powerful, why did he have to do that? It was unbecoming to someone of such authority.

There was a lot of reaction; people felt it was underhanded and despicable. Even Mayor Wagner criticized him about it, and the *New York Post* ran an editorial headlined "The Park—and the Gutter," saying "No man with any claim to decency" would use such a letter. It was dismaying, but I wasn't as outraged as other people. My whole concern was: How does that affect our case? Were we going to get that theater back or not? That was what was on my mind.

ARTHUR GELB Moses was, in those days, a man of enormous power and influence. I can't think of anyone like him in city government today. And here was Joe, taking him on. Moses at first didn't take Joe seriously, and then something about Joe offended him. He decided he didn't like Joe's attitude or what he stood for and he decided to keep Joe out of the park.

I got a big kick out of the contretemps, because I had an instinctive feeling that Joe was going to win this battle. He had the people on his side, and Moses underestimated his fortitude. Joe was a street kid, a fighter. He never took no for an answer. He had the most energy of anyone I've ever seen in the theater. He did it by sheer force and dynamism. He was unflappable, unstoppable, that was his very nature.

ROBERT WHITEHEAD As a very active theater person, I was asked if I would join a meeting to discuss Shakespeare in Central Park. Most of the other people there were civilians: city officials and people important in business, the kind you see sitting on daises. I came as an innocent, but there came a point when I realized that what the meeting was really about was how they might get a replacement for Joe Papp. It was very subtle, but I also realized that this was born out of their uneasy feeling about Joe Papp's particular kind of politics.

Suddenly I said, "I cannot believe what I'm hearing around this table. I'm absolutely stunned that you're on the point of asking me who could take on this job other than Joe Papp. I'll tell you right off, if you want to ruin it, you'll get someone other than Joe Papp. Because you've got to have someone who's as crazy as Joe Papp, who's as relentless in his pursuit as Joe Papp, who is a genuine nut like Joe Papp. The theater will not come off if you get somebody who's going to be suitable to your political point of view and the level of respectability you want it to have."

I was stunned they were even considering this. Theaters like that don't happen because you get someone who's going to be pleasing to you. They happen out of a kind of vital, vigorous craziness which I knew Joe Papp had. I realized I was suddenly in the hands of people who knew nothing about the problems of the theater, so I was very clear and definite in expressing my feelings. And I found, much to my surprise, I'd spoken with enough fervor to quell the meeting. My statement brought the discussion to an end.

EDITORIAL, *New York Post*, MAY 6, 1959
My name is Robert Moses, I'm Commissioner of Parks;
On the subject of free Shakespeare I have a few remarks:
If the people of this city want this theater on my grass,
They'll have to pay two bucks a head to get a Moses pass.
Now it is clearly logical that those who disagree
Are probably subversive or at least a threat to me.
That's why I took it on myself to McCarthyize Joe Papp;
Who questions my sagacity gets purged right off the map.

MERLE DEBUSKEY It became a media event. This though Joe was not very well connected, either with people with lots of money or people who were in powerful positions in the city, or even influential in his own profession.

But when we reached the point where the annual to-do in the park was apparently not going to happen, it was as if all of a sudden spring had happened without spring training. Things seemed to be out of joint. Somebody was attacking this thing that had no reason to be attacked. How could you object to this because it was free and suggest that admission be charged? One round after another was covered by the media—even the conservative press was up in arms about it—and Moses was getting very frustrated and playing into our hands.

Every time something happened, when an elementary Catholic school in deepest, darkest Brooklyn put their pennies and nickels together to help support this thing, we used it, we fully exploited it in the media. It became Little Joe Papp and Big Robert Moses, and all the Shakespeare

Festival had on its side was its absolutely untarnished purity of purpose, and with that it fenced off all kinds of weaponry. I think in its own way that tortured the shit out of Moses. He was a colossus in this state, and deservedly so, not even Mayor Wagner would take issue with him, and all of a sudden, he was being confronted by this little ragamuffin.

JOSEPH PAPP I began to challenge this, I got into a fighting mode, and I'm good at that when I get started. I could not accept that this was the be-all and end-all, that this was going to be the end of the Shakespeare Festival. Even though we had no money and were in a lousy financial position, I said, "I'm going to save this thing from going under."

I accused Moses of discriminating against us while not charging baseball players, zoo-goers, and concert audiences. I talked about the mothers who forced him to change his mind a couple of years earlier about turning a Central Park play area into a parking lot and said he hadn't been the same since he was hit in the head by a baby carriage. It was never a clever thing, though. I didn't think, "Well, god, if we win this, this will be terrific." I just wanted to survive.

Thousands of people had already seen the plays in the parks, so there was a lot of consciousness about us. When Moses said he was trying to save the grass, a lot of people came to the fore and began to send him big packs of grass seed. I didn't initiate anything like that, it was simply done. The public really began to move, and the newspapers sort of picked up on it. Not much else was happening in the world, and I began to get front-page attention.

All during this time, not only didn't I ever meet with Moses face-to-face; I never even talked to him on the phone. I tried to make contact from time to time, but he was not reachable. We always communicated by mail. Imagine, the boss of all these programs, all the things he had to do, and the thing that was getting him more than anything else was me.

At one point, I finally got Stuart Constable to consent to a meeting. He must have believed those things about Communists carrying bombs, because he had four cops waiting outside his door. He made some accusations. I got up and said, "Now, listen . . ." And he said, "*Police!*" He claimed later I was going to hit him, but I would never do a thing like that. And they led me out of the damn place and threw me out. I said to myself, "What the hell is happening here?"

I was a little disappointed in Mayor Wagner. I thought he personally had more power than he used, but, on the other hand, this guy Moses was there year after year, while mayors disappeared.

There was a meeting between the two of them held, ironically, at the Players, which is a club for actors that was established by Edwin Booth. You'd think that something coming out of those surroundings would be favorable to a theater, but the mayor came out and said, "I'm sorry. I have to give up either my commissioner or Papp, and it has to be Papp." I didn't see that coming. I didn't see anything coming. Whatever happened happened, and then I would react to it.

The only initiative I really took was trying to get this into the courts. I went to John Wharton, a partner in this big law firm, and I said, "I can't let this go by. Can you represent us?"

"We do so much pro bono work," he said. "I really can't get involved anymore. Anyway, if we got involved, there are going to be some Communist charges. We'd have to open that whole thing up."

"Open it up," I said.

"Well, if you don't mind, then."

"No, I don't mind. Open it up. Anything."

So he reluctantly said he'd help us. He assigned a young litigating attorney, Sam Silverman, a shrewd, smart lawyer with a great deal of integrity, to help us. He was no schlepp, and I admired him a lot.

SAMUEL J. SILVERMAN I felt I had a respectable case and that we might have a fair chance of winning. There's a doctrine of law that says an administrative agency must not be arbitrary and capricious, must have some basic reason related to its functions for what it does.

I felt it was none of the business of the commissioner of parks to insist on a charge, that that was no part of his function. He was there to protect the people of the city and to protect the parks. He was not there to produce theater or tell anyone how they should do it. He could say, "We've got too little park space" or "That's not a proper park function," but what he was saying was, "This is fine for the park, but I want you to charge money." At that point, it would be none of his business, and I thought that the court might well interfere.

We lost at the supreme court at special term. The judge, a nice man, decided against us on June 2, 1959, saying that it wasn't up to the court to run the parks. You're always disheartened by losing, but I didn't think it was hopeless. I thought that we ought to have a fair shot on appeal. At first, it didn't occur to Joe that we could appeal or that we had any hope. He was rather pleased and surprised when he found out.

JOSEPH PAPP There were days, I'm telling you, when there was no movement whatsoever, and it looked terrible. Then, after losing in the lower court, it looked as though we were going to write it off. With the mayor coming out and saying what he said, where do we turn to? I didn't know about a higher court at that time, that there was such a thing as an appellate court that even handled things of this kind. Those days were very dismal, we were just wallowing around. I thought it was the end of it.

JUDGE J. MCNALLY, APPELLATE DIVISION
IN THE MATTER OF SHAKESPEARE WORKSHOP, APPELLANT,
AGAINST ROBERT MOSES, AS COMMISSIONER OF PARKS
OF THE CITY OF NEW YORK, RESPONDENT
JUNE 17, 1959

In no aspect of the case do we perceive a rational basis for the respondent's insistence upon an admission charge contrary to the wishes, policy and purposes of the petitioner. Nor do we see any connection between the power and duty of the respondent to preserve the parks and their functions and the requirement of a minimum admission charge . . .

No useful park purpose is served by the requirement that petitioner make an admission charge and retain 90% thereof when petitioner desires no part of it. Such a requirement incident to the issuance of a park permit is clearly arbitrary, capricious and unreasonable. When, as here, it is apparent that the sole substantial ground for the denial of the permit is arbitrary, capricious and unreasonable, the determination should and must be vacated and set aside.

COLLEEN DEWHURST There was a moment when I picked up the *New York Times* and saw that Joe had literally beat the government. I was stunned. He had no name, no political push, nothing. We had all been saying, "Come on, you can't win that." That's why I laugh now, when someone says, "Well, of course, Joe Papp will get into it and he'll have his way." And I say, "No, that's not why he'll have his way. There was a day when there was no way he could have it." I know a lot of people who have power, but he's probably the only person I know who has real power, because he had it before he had the trimmings.

ROBERT MONTGOMERY We were absolutely astounded when we won. We just couldn't believe it. We couldn't believe it. And Sam Silverman was like a kid on his birthday. He was running all over the place, he was so happy.

SAMUEL J. SILVERMAN I rather expected that if we won, there would be some kind of attempt to appeal, but the corporation counsel, Charles H. Tenney, who appeared for the city and was a close friend of Mayor Wagner's, never tried to appeal to the court of appeals.

The decision came down just before the summer recess, there may not have been time to go to the court of appeals, but they could have asked for a stay until the fall. It would not have been terribly hard for them to get one, and they didn't do that, either. And very soon after the appellate decision, it became clear that not only were they not going to oppose it anymore but they started to help on the financing and so on.

I think Wagner, for whatever reason, didn't have his heart in fighting this. He may have agreed with both our legal and our philosophical positions and felt "What business is it of the commissioner of parks to insist on an admission fee if the park's not going to be hurt?" Secondly, he may have felt that charging fees if the people who were running it were willing to foot the bill was a rather unpopular position to be in. If we can have free Shakespeare for people, why not?

DAVID AMRAM Joe said to me one time, "You know, I really don't dislike the man." And I was amazed, because Robert Moses was so intent on throwing the Shakespeare Festival out of the park. "He really has convictions and he believes in what he's doing," he said. "I think he's very brave to stick to what he believes, because as a politician he must realize how unpopular this makes him." I realized that though this man was trying to destroy everything that Joe had helped to create, he still admired Moses because he was so cantankerous and so convinced that he was right that he wouldn't back down.

BERNARD GERSTEN Moses believed that Joe was a Communist, and he had no hesitation in using that material in a calumnious way. But on the other hand he was a pragmatist, a doer, a consummate politician, and I'm sure he did 180-degree turns in his life whenever it was appropriate.

I don't mean to sentimentalize or romanticize Moses, but I suspect that somebody who is that powerful, who'd had his own way as often as Moses did, must have a secret regard for those who defeat them. Probably somewhere deep down in his heart, he admired Joe.

ROBERT MOSES, FROM *Enter Joseph Papp*, BY STUART W. LITTLE

Cultural people, by nature, training, and predilection, are intolerant people, even arrogant people. They honestly believe their objective is very important. They're very self-assertive. Perhaps they have to be to succeed. Yes, I'm self-assertive myself. You have to be to get anything done.

Papp is no more offensive than most of these people, and he's a hell of a lot more able. They all go in for assertion to a great extent, but they don't have the same problem we do—the duty to the people, the public job, the oath of office. They just have an idea, and that's different.

JOSEPH PAPP Even though we'd won, the court couldn't enforce its decision—they could only urge Moses to reconsider. And not only did he accept it, he just turned around and became supportive. He was allowed to impose "reasonable conditions" to compensate the city for any expenses, and though he could have set the amount impossibly high, he asked for $20,000.

Even that was difficult. Suddenly there's $20,000 to be raised. It's already mid-June and we're losing time. I didn't know what the hell to do.

The next morning I got two phone calls. Edward Bernays, the head of a public relations firm, said, "I'll give you $10,000 toward this thing."

The other call was from Mrs. Florence Anspacher, a woman I'd never heard of before. She said she'd like to meet me and an appointment was made at a tearoom. I was in old clothes as usual and she turned out to be a very wealthy, elegant woman in her late sixties or seventies, silver-haired with transparent skin and a classic Jewish profile.

"I'm very curious," she said. "I've never given a penny to anything in my life, but I think there's something interesting in this, about the grass and all that. I'd like to give you some money toward the amount you have to raise."

She gave me $10,000 and that was the beginning of a long friendship, culminating in the naming of the first and largest theater in the Public Theater after her and her husband.

ELDON ELDER Joe had held everybody on hold as long as he could, and then we had sort of disbanded. It looked like Moses had really won the day and there wasn't going to be a season. I'd given up hope and gone to L.A. to visit some friends and sort of case the joint.

Then came the court decision, and about seven thirty in the morning I got a call from Joe, very low-key and matter-of-fact, no big hooray or anything. "We're going to go ahead with one play, *Julius Caesar*, and Stuart's going to direct it. I don't know if it's worth it for you to come back to design it," knowing full well that if he put it that way, well, I was going to be on the next plane. And I think I was on a plane that afternoon.

JOSEPH PAPP Someone said, "What play?" And I said, "Let's do *Julius Caesar*." That was a calculated choice because it was about power. But I was still nervous. After all that fuss it could turn out to be a lousy production—the play could fall on its face.

Well, I went out there on opening night, the place was packed, every seat was taken. I said, "Ladies and gentlemen—" and I couldn't get any further than that. A roar, a *roar*. I mean, you never heard such a sound in your life. I just stood there and let it wash over me. That was the most amazing experience, to hear a couple of thousand people just yell at you. They felt it was their triumph, that the people had won. What a feeling that was.

As for Robert Moses, he always perplexed me somewhat. But I had a kind of respect for him, and later on, as I saw him slowly wither and become more withdrawn, as all his authority began to wane and he slowly became just an embittered man, I had the feeling you get when you watch a tall tree topple. It's a terrible thing to see a man of great success, who's achieved monumental work, end this way.

I only met him one time. I was going into city hall and I saw this man, all bent over, coming out. He looked at me, I looked at him, and then he turned away. His face was already drawn in from age and disappointment, and I always feel bad about seeing that happen, about seeing somebody crumble who "once the world held in awe."

SOLILOQUY:

Charles Durning

In 1962 I was appearing in *Two by Saroyan* off Broadway. It was a big hit in which we made $45 a month and had to go over the roof of another building and then through a window to get to our dressing room. Joe came to see the play and left a message for me at the box office: "Call J. Papp, N.Y. Shakes. Fest." I didn't know who Joe Papp was, or what "N.Y. Shakes. Fest." even meant, so I asked some of the people backstage, and they went bananas. They said, "My god, you must do this."

So I called him and he said, "Do you know *Julius Caesar?*" And me, always ready with that idiot wit that cost me many a job, said, "Not personally." There was a silence on the other end, like he thought maybe he'd made a mistake. Finally he said, "Look, I want you to read *Julius Caesar.* I want you to come in and do Cassius."

I started reading and I loved it. I thought, "My god, this is one of the best parts I've ever had." Even in those days, I didn't have a "lean and hungry look," but I just kept reading. I went over Cassius's big speeches five or six times.

I showed up at the Heckscher the next day, and Joe said, "All right, get up there and read Casca." "Casca?" I said to myself. "Cassius or Casca?" I said to Joe. He said, "Casca." I was too ashamed to tell him that I thought he had meant Cassius, so I got up and read Casca cold.

I stumbled around that for about ten minutes and finally Joe called me down off the stage. He never looked at me, he looked straight ahead at the stage. He took this long drag on this cigar, blew out the smoke, and said, "How dare you come here and read Shakespeare cold. If I hadn't seen your work, I wouldn't think you could do it at all. But we need to cast this part. We go into rehearsal in two days, so you get the role. Otherwise, I'd be trying to get someone else." I didn't tell him that story for about ten years.

Working for Joe opened up the gates of heaven for me. I never knew words like that existed, but I ended up doing more than a dozen Shakespeare plays. I once talked to Albert Finney and we realized I'd done more Shakespeare than he had.

I had been a nightclub entertainer, a hoofer and a ballroom dancer and a burlesque clown. I got kicked out of drama school because I had no talent, but Joe saw something that was rough and raw and he polished it.

If a show I was in closed, I would call Joe and say, "I'm out of a job." And he'd say, "No, you're not. Show up here Monday." He was always like my crutch and my mentor and, even though we're contemporaries, my surrogate father.

One time I was something like six months behind in my rent and almost destitute. I couldn't get any more money from Household Finance, the bank didn't even want to hear from me. I had two children at the time, with another on the way, and literally, there was no food on the table. So in desperation I went to Joe and I said, "Joe, I need some money."

"How much do you want?"

"I'd like to have $700."

"I didn't ask you how much you liked," he said. "How much do you need?"

"I need $1,400." And he gave it to me. He told me I was the only actor he ever gave money to.

"I want to thank you very much."

"Don't worry. I'll get it back," he said. "Because you're going to be working here until you can pay me."

As a producer and director, Joe was real tough, but always fair. He was a disciplinarian. If you fucked up, you were called on the carpet, but then he forgot about it. There's various ways of giving a beating, and he can beat you with that tongue. I mean he can really lash you.

I said to him once, "Joe, I'd like to be in *Troil-ee-us and Cress-eeda*." And he said, "First learn how to pronounce it." Another time, he said, "There's nine hundred choices you could have made, Charlie, and you picked the wrong one." When he says that in front of the company, it can be devastating.

Another time in the park we were rehearsing one of those plays where you wear very elaborate costumes: when they get wet they're three times their weight, they'll knock you down. Joe is sitting out in the audience and it's raining and raining and raining. And I said to him, "Joe, it's raining." And Joe said—and it was completely dry in the area where he was—"*I'll* let you know when it's raining."

In those days I felt very secure about how to handle myself. I had boxed a little bit, I was doing judo before anybody knew it existed in this country. So I used to walk Joe out of the park at night, and anytime there was an argument or a confrontation, I would go with him.

One time at the Public Theater an actor had given somebody some abuse onstage, the director had fired him and Joe stood behind the director. So we heard that this guy was heading for Joe's office, threatening to kill him. I was standing by the door, wanting to come in, but Joe said, "Get out of the office and send him in."

"Joe," I said, "this guy's got a knife."

"Send him in."

The guy walks in and Joe says, "What's this idea you want to stab me?"

The guy went, "Uh—uh—" And Joe said, "Don't give me that 'uh—uh—' Do you want to stab me or don't you want to stab me?"

"Jesus Christ," I said to myself. "It's bad enough he asked the guy in, now he's gotta provoke him."

"No," the guy said. "I'm not going to stab you."

"You can't make those kinds of threats, that frightens people, that's why you don't have the role," Joe said. "You cannot do things like that in the theater. You're either going to be a street fighter or you're going to be an actor. What are you going to be?"

"I want to be an actor," the guy says. So Joe talked him out of it. He went out being Joe's best friend. But he didn't get the job back, either.

If a man can love a man as a brother, I love Joe. And I consider him a dear friend, and a man of incredible integrity. But he has complications on top of complications in him; he has the same dark sides we all have. Joe has blinders on, and once in a while people resent that. It's because he's experimenting all the time. He's always looking for something new. Just when you think he's going in one direction, he's ready to change horses. And that can hurt people.

I said to Joe once, "How do you know who your friends are?" He said, "When you're in deep trouble, and your back is to the wall, when you look to your left and your right, who do you want alongside of you?" And I said, "Boy, it cuts it down considerably." He said, "Right away."

8

Shakespeare in the Park:
The Delacorte Theater

Papp at the
Delacorte Theater
construction site
© George E. Joseph

One: The Opening

JOSEPH PAPP   From the very beginning, I didn't want a permanent theater in Central Park. I was hesitant. I didn't feel anybody was doing me any
favors by offering to build me one. What I wanted to have was the mobile
unit. I always felt, "Get in and get out, fast. Own your own thing. Don't
come under the regulations of the Parks Department." With a theater,
you're under the auspices of whatever parks commissioner happens to
come into office, usually a favorite of the mayor, and many times an incom-
petent. I didn't want that at all.

   Also, believe it or not, I felt we shouldn't create another structure in
the park. Frankly, I'm a purist about that—I don't like anything being built

there. I felt, "Just come in, and when you're finished, pack up your stuff and go and let the park go back to nature for that period of time." And in fact all the seats in the Delacorte are not welded but just bolted together. You could take the theater apart and put it together again if you wanted to.

One thing I have avoided is having any kind of lease with the city. Once you sign an agreement, suddenly there are all sorts of rules and regulations which you become a party to. The city says, "Don't you realize this jeopardizes you?" And I say, "Whenever you feel you can put me out, put me out." There's more than you-just-try-it defiance in that attitude. I feel that as long as I'm socially useful and doing work that is creditable, I will be there. When I can no longer support my being there, then I feel they should get me out, if they can. Once I'm not doing anything worthwhile, history will take care of me.

But in August of 1959, just a few months after he lost the court decision, Robert Moses did a turnaround and asked the New York City Planning Commission for $250,000 to construct a permanent theater in the park. "Moses proposes? Everybody goeses." And I realized there would be a value in having certain facilities. Not having dressing rooms, for instance, was lousy for the actors. And I decided, "Well, it's better than not having one." But I was still very leery.

The Board of Estimate ended up budgeting only $225,000 for the project, and the lowest bid for the theater was a little over $370,000. We decided we'd have to raise that additional money privately, and that's when George Delacorte, someone I never knew existed, came into the picture.

BERNARD GERSTEN The story as we heard it was that one day Newbold Morris, the new parks commissioner, having learned only the day before that the theater the Parks Department had designed had come in $150,000 over the lowest bid, went for a walk with his friend George Delacorte, president of Dell Publishing. And Newbold was very disappointed. He would either have to submit the theater to redesign in an attempt to get it within the budgetary constraint or try to get a new budget line passed, all of which was a burden. He was stuck.

George Delacorte had recently given the mechanical clock at the

Children's Zoo. It was one of a series of gifts he had made in Central Park, and he was very, very happy with it. They were walking and talking and he said to Newbold something like, "Listen, I'm really happy about the park gift and the way it worked out. Is there anything else you need?"

Newbold said, somewhat jokingly, "Well, George, you'll never believe this, but I'm short $150,000 to build the Shakespeare Theater."

And George, who could see the site of the theater from where he lived on Fifth Avenue, said, "I think that free Shakespeare in Central Park is okay, and I'll give you the $150,000."

It was a very generous gift, and though the legend may be that George bought that as a name gift, that's not true. George did not trade off that money with a view that it would be called the Delacorte Theater. We were all surprised, and George was surprised, on the night of the dedication of the Free Shakespeare Theater, as it was called, when Newbold Morris said, "And I name it the Delacorte Theater."

GEORGE DELACORTE   I had lunch with Newbold. I'd known him for a good many years, and he suggested that I do some little thing that was so picayune that I just brushed it aside. I said, "I'd like to do something more important than that." And then he suggested Joe Papp and the theater in Central Park, and I liked the idea. After all, I was terribly interested in the park. I've lived all my life on the park, I walk through the park, I've even been mugged in the park.

JOSEPH PAPP   The Delacorte Theater opened on June 18, 1962, with *The Merchant of Venice*. I selected it because I just thought George C. Scott would be a brilliant Shylock; many times you start from that point of view. I never thought of the play as anti-Semitic. I was totally unaware that there'd even be an objection. And there wasn't until it was going to be done on television.

But once WCBS announced it would be broadcast in New York City, the New York Board of Rabbis protested, saying Shakespeare had perpetrated "a distortion and defamation of our people and our faith" and calling Shylock "an amalgam of vindictiveness, cruelty and avarice." They didn't mind it being done in the park; they felt the people who'd come to see the play there were cultured people. They'd never been to London; they didn't know there are cultured anti-Semites.

A lot of these rabbis, incidentally, came from very wealthy temples, and I still had my old feelings, which I could not get rid of, about that. They met with me several times. They said, "How come you, a Jewish person, could do this?" And I said, "Listen, I wasn't raised the same way you people were raised." I gave them all my resentments about poor Jews not being able to get into fancy synagogues. They started to put pressure on the mayor, but he really held firm. He said, "I'm not going to interfere with this play."

I was director of that play, along with Gladys Vaughan, so I had a lot at stake in it personally. George C. Scott was like a biblical patriarch, like a wrathful god, and I encouraged that. "You never turn the other cheek," I said. "When you get to the point where your daughter leaves you, you want one thing: revenge. You want to hurt these people that have hurt you. Don't soft sell it, go all the way. People will understand about that anger." As Kent says in *Lear*, "Anger has a privilege."

BERNARD GERSTEN Given an opportunity to cause a furor, Joe doesn't have to think about it, he does it automatically. There were only thirty-three other plays that he might have chosen that wouldn't have brought on the wrath of the Jews of New York. But Joe's automatic perversity was to pick *The Merchant of Venice*.

The weather had been awful in the weeks before the opening performance, there was lots and lots of rain, and one of the things the Sicilian Road and Asphalt Company, the subcontractor for the paving, had to do was to pave the walkways around the theater with asphalt. And they said, "We can't put the asphalt down because the mud is too soft. We've got to wait until the ground drains." And the mud was there and the mud was there, and we said, "The opening night's coming! The opening night's coming! When are you going to put the asphalt down?"

Finally, in the two days prior to the opening, they got the asphalt down. In fact the last of it was being put down and rolled an hour before the first performance, which was a benefit, and the audience began to arrive in their fancy clothes while the asphalt was still hot.

The style for women that year was stiletto heels, and immediately as they hit the asphalt that had been laid down minutes before, down they went—those heels went right into it. Men with normal shoes could walk, the asphalt would just kind of bubble and writhe, so the men were walking around lifting the women out of their shoes, then pulling the shoes up after them. It's so vivid to me, I can't tell you.

GEORGE C. SCOTT   Joe called me up and said, "How would you like to do Shylock?" And I said, "I don't know anything about it."

I'd read the play in high school or something, one of those horrible sessions where you're forced to read *Macbeth* and hate everything in it. But I reread it and I thought, "Jesus, what a wonderful part." Being a WASP, I had no ethnic interest in playing Shylock. I had no rapport with him as a human being. I wasn't particularly interested in money, except for feeding my child or keeping my wife from starving to death. But I said, "I'm gonna take a crack at it if you really want me," and he said, "Yeah."

I played Shylock as though he were dead right. And that he was screwed. Everybody piled on him, gang-fucked him, and that was that. And I didn't like it, so I played it one hundred percent on his side. It was easy for me to do that way, whether I had any ethnic connection or not. Didn't make any difference. And I played him so heartbroken when his daughter Jessica leaves with a Christian. Mother of God, what a blast that must have been to the old-timer. I was just *rent* when that happened. He was never a whole man to me after that. A damned interesting character, *damned* interesting. I account that some of my best work.

JAMES EARL JONES   Stanley Kubrick wanted to use George in his film *Dr. Strangelove*, and he came to see George's *Merchant of Venice* performance one night. In that B-52 bomber, he wanted the all-American representation—the Texan, the black guy, the Irish kid, the Jewish kid—he wanted the whole thing. I was playing the Prince of Morocco and Kubrick said, "I'll take the black one, too."

Two: Directing and Gladys Vaughan

JOSEPH PAPP   Stuart Vaughan was the big shot in his marriage with Gladys, but she was always so bright. After they separated, and after he left me and I was left holding the bag, so to speak, alone, she was really excellent. She was my right hand and she urged me to direct, she became insistent. "You're such a good director," she said, "you should do that more." She was very supportive and helpful. I learned a lot from her. And I returned the favor by having her direct as well.

I was always producing. I couldn't help that; in order for me to direct, I had to produce. But I get a great kick out of directing, working with a good actor, conceptualizing the play and getting to the heart of it. Directing is something I look forward to, like when you're in love and you're working hard and you think, "Hey, tonight I'm going to see the girl that I love." It makes you feel good about being alive, a pleasurable little secret you have all the time that keeps you going. Like love on the run, you never get enough, but it's still there, waiting for you.

DAVID AMRAM   Gladys Vaughan was one of my favorite directors, and one of the actors' favorite directors, gracious and exceptionally considerate. She was so sensitive, she would just sit there sometimes and stare up at the clouds for two or three minutes and say, "I'm thinking!" Then she would give you a big smile or hug, just make you feel good. Her husband, Stuart, was the most organized director I've ever worked with. Gladys, interestingly enough, had a whole different approach. She had a plan, but she tried to let each person discover what they could do and create within the context of that plan. She didn't have any axes to grind. She just loved the theater.

GLADYS VAUGHAN   I had been so close to Stuart, I was really in on so much, but since this was really before women's liberation, if I had ideas he'd say, "Now, Gladys, don't say this is your idea, because . . ." At the end of that marriage, I felt that I could be contributing in turn, so I worked with Joe. I think I helped talk Joe into doing his first show in the park. I had the feeling that Joe really had yearned in a way to be the creative artist, and I said I would do my best to help, I would be his assistant. I was kind of shy at that point—I disappeared into being a little mouse.

I came in to take notes on the production of *Twelfth Night* and Joe said afterward, "Everybody has given me notes about how they would do the production. Your notes are so helpful to me because you have sensed what I wanted to do, and your notes always address what isn't quite working about the way I'm wanting to do it." I think that meant a lot to him, and he felt that I ought to be able to direct my own show.

In 1964, Joe wanted Ossie Davis to play Othello, and Ossie Davis turned it down. James Earl Jones had been with us enough that we should have given him a chance, I felt it was only fair, but Joe didn't think he was up to it. There was a shyness in Jimmy at that time, he'd look down a lot, but I thought he really had a tremendous ability and gift, so I said, "I'll work with him." I really had a fight with Joe about it, but then he conceded.

We worked, all of us in the cast, practically every day for five hours a day for three or four months. I felt that to do really exciting work with Shakespeare, you needed more time than we usually had. It's because there is such a richness of idea in the language, and by having time to let that seep into your guts and into your spirit, the actor becomes one with that. Taking that period of time contributed a lot to *Othello* being a strong play.

JAMES EARL JONES There are a lot of wonderful directors I've seen do great things, but the directors that I've found that I could work with I list on one hand, and Gladys was one of them. She had a wisdom that I think was lacking in male directors of her generation when she took on the task of directing *Othello*, which was the best *Othello* I've ever been involved with, before and after.

She had a great sense of what passion was about. She never settled for emotion; she said, "Let's elevate it to passion." Especially out of doors, emotion can often be indulgent on the stage and never reach the audience. If you're crying, no one can see that past a few feet. She wanted that emotion elevated so that it would affect your voice and your body, so that it would project and also be of a size fitting to Shakespeare.

Modern audiences would want to laugh at an Othello who couldn't say, "So she's screwing somebody else. I'll just get a divorce and find somebody else to marry." That sentiment and that moral issue are viewed as anti-quated today.

Gladys, being a woman, was convinced that Desdemona, even though she had a lot less to do than Othello and Iago, was the third pillar of that play. If she wasn't cast as strongly and wasn't as well conceived by the direc-tor, the play could never work, you wouldn't know what the conflict is about.

Why is this man going mad and why is that other man, who's already mad, conspiring with him to kill a lot of people over somebody spreading their legs? Men have been so busy being afraid of sentiments, they push that aspect out of their hearts and out of their minds. Some plays shouldn't be directed by people who don't have feelings.

ANN KINGSBURY RESCH Gladys Vaughan's purity of interpretation, keeping to the value of the play, not introducing gimmicks or angles but sticking to Shakespeare, had very powerful results, and I will never under-stand why her talents weren't used more at the festival. She knew how to elicit the best from actors without being dictatorial. She had a gift for find-ing out where actors were coming from psychologically, and for removing protective barriers by gentle coaxing and analysis and questioning, until they gave the performance that was true to them and to the play.

DAVID BLACK As the festival was growing, and Joe was becoming a celebrity, the barriers started going up. I mean, they didn't want Bernie, they didn't want me, everybody wanted him, and he began to sort of sift out what he would deal with and what he wouldn't deal with. And in his rela-tionships with people, he would allow them to get only so close. Most peo-ple who achieve a kind of fame close the doors to personal involvement; you could just be torn asunder with demands and needs if you let people get too close to you.

I remember the case of Gladys Vaughan. She was, for a time, a mem-ber of the inner circle, and the expectation, I think, was that this wasn't going to end, that she had the in with him, and that she was going to be able to continue to direct. Not even knowingly, I think she started making demands, and what was happening in his mind was that he no longer wanted to deal with her. People were demanding too much of him and he just couldn't fulfill it.

GLADYS VAUGHAN I was always getting into a bind with Joe because I was feeling principles. At the time he said, "I can get most people over a barrel. I can get them to do something that I want, by offering them this or that. But you, you're exasperating. Because if you believe in something, if you feel it should be done a certain way, there's no *way* I can get you over a barrel. You'll just walk." Years later I ran into him once, and he said, "You were so creative and so talented, but you were such a pain in the ass."

Three: Freedman and Company

GERALD FREEDMAN In the late fifties I wrote to Joe Papp after I saw *As You Like It* at the Heckscher. I thought it was very poor, except for George C. Scott, and I wrote something like: "I would love to direct Shakespeare and I think I could do a better job." And Joe invited me to come and talk with him.

He had this little office under the stairs, it wasn't half as big as my hall. He talked, as I remember, quite extravagantly, "And you'll do this, and you'll do that," as if I was working for him, and we had just met. I came away very exhilarated, and then I didn't hear anything for a couple of years. In 1960, though, I got a call and he said, "Would you like to do *The Taming of the Shrew* in Central Park?"

I'd worked in Hollywood as Jerome Robbins's assistant director on *Bells Are Ringing*, *West Side Story*, and *Gypsy*, directing the book and serving as liaison with other elements of the production. I'd also been up at Harvard, directing the Hasty Pudding shows. I was introduced to a costume designer named Theoni Aldredge there, and I brought Theoni to Joe. Through a mutual friend, I met scenic designer Ming Cho Lee, and I sent Ming to Joe. Both became major forces in the festival, and to tell you the truth, I used to think of them as my team because of our work before we got into the festival.

Over the next several years, the style of Shakespeare that we did in the park really changed the way Shakespeare is perceived and performed in this country. We combined the Method and the word. We used the personality of the actor, the inner life of the actor, to invigorate the language. When there was a compromise to be made between an actor who had some balls and an actor who had technique, we'd go for the actor who had balls. I don't think we did it because it suited the park, but it did suit the park because playing outdoors to an audience that represented all areas of the city demanded energy and invigoration.

Joe was the best producer I ever worked for. We had one of the great artistic teams in the world: Ming Cho Lee and myself and Theoni Aldredge and Marty Aronstein did very important and beautiful theater. Joe has a reputation for taking over productions—the stories are terrible—but he would leave me absolutely alone. He would come in on a first technical, have a wonderful eye, and give me very practical, good observations that were invariably along lines I was progressing on and that I could accomplish before we opened.

Joe very much created a family feeling, and we loved being part of that family, and then there came a time when it seemed no longer to be a family. You were giving of your spirit, and you just expected to always be there.

MING CHO LEE We talked the same language, we seemed to understand each other, and we enjoyed working with each other. We didn't need long, long talks. We'd have one talk and things would come out. I had a feeling at that time that we were breaking new ground, not only for ourselves, for the New York Shakespeare Festival, but in terms of the American theater. We were doing things that were not normally done. It was very strong, very gutsy. We felt that we were on a mission. There was a company spirit. It was a real high.

THEONI ALDREDGE I met Gerald Freedman doing the Hasty Pudding shows at Harvard, and he said, "You have to come with Joe." So he made an appointment with me, and I went, and it was instant love, first sight, both ways. There was something in that man, something that you could look at him and say, "I'll hitch my wagon here. I want to be part of that." There was no "I'll think about it" from him, there was never a moment of that. He had such enthusiasm that it just took you with him.

He combined for me everything that a total man has. There was a father somewhere—he was supportive, loving. The care of a lover, almost, like "I have to protect you." And the patience, the unending patience of a good teacher. And he let you grow, he never imposed. He was there to help you, push you, but he let you make your own mistakes so you learned.

Joe gave me a home in the theater, which was unheard of at the time. Every year, he's never forgotten my birthday. He always sends flowers and a card. "To the first lady of the Shakespeare Festival." Your husband forgets more often than Joe. How can you not love him?

Four: Actors and Acting in the Park

RICHARD BENJAMIN In 1960 I had just graduated from Northwestern, and our acting teacher, Alvina Krause, called Jerry Freedman for me. We met in New York, I got into the company, and that put me into three plays: *Henry V*, *Measure for Measure*, and *The Taming of the Shrew*.

My very first professional job was carrying a bow and arrow in *Henry V*: when Henry says, "Once more unto the breach, dear friends," I was dear friends, along with a lot of other people. I wanted to carry a spear, so I could say that my first thing was a spear-carrier, but a bow and arrow was what it was.

I got $10 a week for *Henry V* and *Measure*, and $15 for *Shrew*. I had one line and you got another five if you had a line. Here I'd just gone to school, and my folks had been very understanding of everything I was doing, paying tuition, and now I'd gotten my first theater job. My father asked me, "Well, does it pay?" And I said, "It pays $10 a week." I had a hard time saying that.

They say there are no small parts, just small actors, but that's not true. There are small parts. You look around you and you want more, you always want more. You dream of playing a lead, I mean you dream about it all the time. So I tried to talk to Joe as much as possible, to make myself known to him, to come out of the group. This is what actors do all the time—they're performing and they're auditioning.

Joe was always on his way somewhere, and I'd try and have a disguised conversation so he wouldn't suspect what I really wanted, which was his attention. I would say things like, "Gosh, I think the costumes are great for *Measure*, don't you?" He could have turned to me and said, "How could *you* know *what* they are," but he didn't. He was always attentive, but formidable. We'd have a kind of conversation, but not long enough for me. I think he may have spotted what I was doing.

MICHAEL MORIARTY In 1962, during my senior year at Dartmouth, I applied for a Fulbright scholarship to study acting abroad. New York wasn't in the forefront of my mind. I was going to go to London and do serious theater. Joe was on the Fulbright board, and his first remark to me was, "Why do you want to go to London? They won't teach you anything over there."

I got the Fulbright, but I also auditioned for the part of Octavius in *Antony and Cleopatra* in the park that summer, and I got it. I felt like a bonus baby, the ballplayers who come out of college and go right into the pros. There I was, onstage with Colleen Dewhurst. No farm leagues, nothing.

I had difficulties in England, I had some real hard times, and I decided I didn't want to act. So I went back to Detroit and sold tires for a year. Then my father, who didn't want a son who sold tires, said, "The only thing you ought to do now is act, so go back to New York."

The first person I called was Joe Papp. I still was very, very shaky, I was in very bad shape, but he got me a job for the summer. Of all the things I remember about Joe, the key is he understands the artist completely. He will nurture artists, more through the bad times than the good because the good are the easy times. Joe just kind of puts them on their feet and then shoves them out in the street, saying, "I think you can fly now."

In 1973–74, I became very successful. Big success. I was on Broadway, I won a Tony Award. I was on television, I won an Emmy Award. I was in *Bang the Drum Slowly* and I should have won the Cy Young Award. Six months before, I'd been slipping dimes off tables as a waiter, and suddenly I'm a big shmoo, every headwaiter in town knows me by my first name, and I've never met any of them. What was going to be my next move?

Then Joe called me and I did *Richard III*. When one of his babies becomes successful, he's on the phone. "Meryl! It's Joe! I'm coming to pick up my IOUs, kid!" You can't blame him, that's the business. And that funded, off-Broadway artistic milieu is the only environment I've worked in without any kind of problems. Going back to working with Joe is like going home. It's my roots.

LEE GRANT *Electra* is an outpouring, like an opera, with demands on you physically and emotionally. When I got the part in 1964, I embarked on a whole series of lessons—not just vocal lessons, it was stamina. The blacklisting years had left an enormous need to act, to do an important role, and there were so many things written in between the lines in *Electra* that paralleled my own injustices. I trained for about two months, and I think it was probably the best work, the most important work, that I did in my life.

One time it was raining, my jersey dress was soaking wet, and during the one moment when I could turn my back to the audience, I said to Olympia Dukakis, who played my sister, "Get me out of here! Tell Bernie Gersten to stop the show. It's pouring rain!" And I turned around to face the audience, and there was this sea of people with newspapers over their heads, sitting there in the rain. *Nobody* had left. I was so stunned and moved. I got the lesson of my life out of that. I had no idea that the audience's motivation and need could have been as strong as mine. I had no concept of that before. I had underestimated them.

Next season I was to do *Love's Labours Lost*, but a week or ten days before I was supposed to open, my agent said, "Don't scream at me, don't yell, but I signed your name to a year's contract on *Peyton Place*."

"I can't leave the theater in the park. I can't leave Joe."

"There is no work here. You have a daughter to support. You have to save yourself. You have got to take this job."

And it was absolutely right. I didn't know where the next penny was coming from, I didn't know how I was going to get through the winter, but I was terribly afraid of telling Joe. I was terrified. When I told him, he got very reserved. He didn't yell at me, he just cut me off.

When I went to California, I wrote Joe, and I kept writing the whole year. And when I'd come back to New York, I would go up and apologize. He had given me the part of a lifetime, there's no question about it, and I left him in the lurch. There were many, many times when I thought, if I had stayed there, if I had developed myself along the lines that I was doing with Joe, as an actress I would have been much better.

When I came back to New York a few years ago, I came back having made the decision to establish myself as a director, and the highest thing on my list was to work with Joe again. I directed Václav Havel's *A Private View* for him in 1983, and I don't think I've ever been happier.

MARTIN SHEEN   When Joe hired me for *Romeo and Juliet* in 1968, I had never read the play. Well, you see *West Side Story*, you figure you know *Romeo and Juliet*. About the second day of rehearsal, I heard a magnificent speech by Mercutio and I was awed by it. I couldn't let it go. After the rehearsal, I went after Joe. I said, "Don't get me wrong, I'm so grateful for your giving me the part of Romeo, but let's face it, I'm not Romeo. I'm Mercutio. I can play that role. I'd be terrific, a great Mercutio."

"I know that, Martin," he said. "That's why you must play Romeo."

And Romeo is the worst part ever written in Shakespeare, because everyone knows your lines and he's an awful, self-pitying brat. My reviews were just devastating. I played with great energy, but I didn't play well. And I got slaughtered. There was a second-string drama critic for the *New York Times* who said, "Now we know what James Cagney would have been like playing Romeo." I was decimated. Decimated. And my wife was elated. "How dare you be upset about this," she said. "Don't you think James Cagney is a great actor?"

Joe wanted the fight with Tybalt to be more of a murder than a fight. He wanted Romeo to brutalize him. I'm upstage on opening night, charging downward with this big kick, and Tom Aldredge, who played Tybalt, starts backing up. And until my foot hit the surface of the stage, I didn't realize that the heel had come off my shoe and had gone over his head into the audience. The nails in my shoe were sticking out and had stuck in the stage. I had to wrench them out and I lost all my timing. I just became a hysterical actor onstage, trying to do the business and get off. I damn near slayed poor Tommy in fact that night.

COLLEEN DEWHURST   Joe called me one day in 1972 and said, "Now honey, you always wanted to play all of Shakespeare's women. We're going to do *Hamlet*. Want to do Gertrude?"

"I've got the kids," I said. "I don't know whether I should."

We hung up and five minutes later he called back and said, "If I told you that Jimmy Jones was playing the King, what would you say?"

"I'm going downstairs to read it."

What I found out later was that he'd said to Jimmy, "If told you Colleen Dewhurst was playing Gertrude, would you do it?"

I had trouble with my crown at the previews, and I was getting angrier and angrier. The crown slipped one more time over my eyes, and I said to this little girl dresser, a very nervous one, "Dear, come with me."

I went to the lakefront, took off the crown, and just threw it. "Just think, darling," I said, "we're never going to have to worry about this thing again." And she kept going, "Oh dear, oh dear." The apocryphal story I still hear is, "I wish I'd been there the night you took off the whole queen costume and threw it in the lake." And I go, "I did *not* take off the whole costume. *I only took off the hat.*"

GERALD FREEDMAN   Jimmy went to new lengths, I thought, in *Hamlet*, and it took tremendous patience on my part to let him do that. I had no idea, half the time, what was going on in the early parts of rehearsal. I'm very permissive in that. I feel that's the time for the actor to explore.

I think Jimmy was trying to discover how words were invented. He would break up the most obvious word, like "hospitality." He'd say, "hoss-pit— hos-pit-tal—" There was no scene being played, it was about Jimmy discovering language, or maybe "How do these words fit into my mouth?" But what came out of it was thrilling. Whatever Jimmy needed to do in terms of making that language his own, he did.

JAMES EARL JONES   That was the first chance I'd ever had to be comfortable enough in a role and with my fellow acting partners that I could finally drop that thing American actors get caught up in of trying to sound Oxonian. I said, "The hell with it. I'll speak as good English as I can, and the rest of my energy I'll use to enjoy playing this role. If the character wants to fart or scratch his ass, he's gonna fart and scratch his ass." Since I'm not raised in the tradition that says kings don't have assholes, I have no obligation to play them that way.

SAM WATERSTON   When we were doing *Hamlet* in the park in 1975, with John Lithgow playing Laertes, he tripped as he was jumping into the grave in the fight scene and he creamed his knee. An ambulance came, and once we were certain John was all right, I was sitting in the auditorium with Joe and I heard him say, "Well, you can't make a *Hamlet* without breaking some legs."

Five: The Audience and the Atmosphere

JOSEPH PAPP   We used to have lines for tickets that would go through the park, from the West Side to the East Side, and then go down Fifth Avenue for about fifteen blocks. Those were extraordinary lines. People would wait six, seven, eight hours. Some of the shows were so popular, people were there early in the morning, eight o'clock. They'd wait twelve hours.

I loved the lines, but I'm telling you, the people on them didn't like them much. It was just too much to ask people to do. Plus, we had to start dealing with the social problem of people getting off work at a certain time and not being able to get on line. Older people couldn't wait on lines, either. People from out of town who didn't have anything to do, they could wait on line.

We tried lots of systems. We tried to be as democratic as we could be, make the opportunity more available. We have a ticket system now, so people are at least assured of a seat, and each seat is numbered. Before, people used to rush in like animals. They were so wild, they'd jump over each other. I didn't like that. It wasn't civilized. It was worse than the subway.

SANTO LOQUASTO The park is this unique anachronism. It's difficult, but it has its own satisfactions. It's hot, it's horrible, in an unnatural space, it's full of problems, the weather being the least of it. It's wet for the first play, and then mosquitoes and sweaty and unbelievably hot for the second one. But there you are, doing summer stock, it's free, it's Shakespeare. It's just great that it's there.

CHRISTOPHER WALKEN The wonderful thing about the park would be those terrific moments when you're in the middle of a soliloquy and a dog walks across the stage, or some guy on his way to the bathroom just takes a shortcut.

We used to have to wear these Vega mikes, and maybe they weren't of the highest quality. Every time two actors would come together in a love scene, the mikes would start to wail and scream. In the middle of Shakespeare, they'd pick up a police squad-car radio. If somebody put a quarter in the Coke machine downstairs, the transaction would come right over the mike. Everything seemed to be connected electronically.

LINDA HUNT It feels big because that huge canvas that hangs over your head is vast and endless. I remember a wonderful night in one of Hamlet's sort of mock-mad scenes with Polonius. He speaks about dogs howling, and in fact, the dogs of Central Park were all standing in back of the theater, howling at the edge of the pond. Nights like that when natural wonders suddenly occur are memorable always in the park.

KATHLEEN WIDDOES The audience at the Delacorte was the loveliest thing because there was such a sense of togetherness. The people thought that they owned it; they thought it belonged to them. It was quite beautiful that way. The really wonderful thing was when it rained. After the first thunderstorm had stopped, you would step out into this absolutely moist, dripping, fragrant night, just open and clean, everything would be so alive and so vibrant, and you'd pick up again where you left off.

WILFORD LEACH It's the greatest audience anywhere. Never had a bad experience out there. I've never had an audience that wasn't terrific. They are the most intelligent, alive, supportive audience imaginable. During rehearsals you sit in that boiling sun, and you say, "God, I'll never do this again. I'm dying. I'm going to get sick." You throw up because it's so hot and so horrible. You finally get to the evenings, and the moon comes up, and that audience comes in, and you say, "Boy, it's worth it. It's really worth it."

KEVIN KLINE   It's its own world, neither Broadway nor off Broadway. There's no commercial sort of pressure. It's an oasis in the middle of this mad city. Because it's free, I always knew the audience was getting their money's worth.

When we were doing *The Pirates of Penzance*, we'd get into character of these ruffian, madcap pirates, and the stage manager would come back and stick his head in the dressing room and say, "It's places." And we'd say, "Fuck you! We'll come out when we're ready. They didn't pay any money, they can wait." We'd do it as a running joke, but it was based on a real thing.

Because it's free on every level, you can fail, in a sense. Once people know you, once you achieve a certain degree of success, there's always a fear of failure. In the park, you can do real work instead of having to do something that's successful, that's commercial, that will run. Critics have panned productions there, and the audiences still come. You're immune, in a way, to all the ugly parts of the business. It's just show without the business, and it's fun.

Six: *The Wars of the Roses*, 1970

JOSEPH PAPP   We were planning to do *The Wars of the Roses* as three separate plays over the course of the summer: the three parts of *Henry VI*, which were made into two plays, plus *Richard III*. We were in dire financial straits, however, desperate for money. I felt we had to dramatize our plight in some way, and I said, "Let's do the entire series in one dusk-to-dawn marathon."

Even though I hadn't worked with him for a while, I went to Stuart Vaughan to direct this because he was a marvelous organizer and had a good knowledge of the plays. I'm very practical. I never hold a grudge. I've always come back to people because I recognize their worth.

THEONI ALDREDGE Just the logistics alone, who belongs to what part, sixty-five actors all changing costume ten to twelve times to become the various armies, it was a marathon night. And the director insisted that all the armor be done realistically.

"What's realistically?" I said.

"You don't put zippers, you don't put Velcro, and you don't put hooks and eyes. You put straps and buckles."

"Sir," I said, "it will take twenty minutes for all thirty-six pieces of armor for these kids to get in and out of these garments." I said "sir" to be Little Miss Evil.

I could have insisted, I could have done it my way and he would have never known the difference, but I said, "Okay, you want to try that game?"

Comes dress rehearsal, we come to a screeching halt.

"Where is everybody?"

"They're unbuckling their buckles."

I know it will take twenty minutes. Joe is sitting very quietly in the back. He never interferes. But this director started, he went on the loudspeaker and said, "These clothes hang like an albatross around the neck." And I said, "Wait a minute."

I went to Joe and I said, "Humor me." So Joe very quietly went to this man and said, "Don't push it. She draws blood." He was so adorable. He had to support his choice of director, and he had to support this girl who had been with him for a while. So he played the psychiatrist. He played the mentor. He played the doctor. Unending patience. I would have shot people by then.

KEVIN KLINE My first job in New York was carrying a spear and a banner and any other prop that needed carrying in *The Wars of the Roses*. Jim Keach and I were Tressel and Berkley, the two lords in attendance with Lady Anne in the wooing scene in *Richard III*, so we decided we would be Tressel and Berkley in the three parts of *Henry VI* leading up to it. Even though we were just soldiers, we called each other that throughout.

When Joe came out and announced to the cast we were doing it as a marathon, he started doing the St. Crispin's Day speech, "We few, we happy few . . ." He was this guy with a cigar who rallied the troops, came and said inspiring words. We were going to have to use resources we'd never called on before. Could we stay standing upright all night? Who knew if we could do it? Joe was sort of like Henry V. He'd go from camp to camp. There'd be a little touch of Joe in the night, always.

When I stood by for Raul Julia in *Threepenny Opera* in 1976, I'd always be reintroduced to him and he'd say, "Nice to meet you." And I wanted to say, "Hey, I was Lord Tressel. You don't remember me? I was the fifth guy from the right, don't you remember?"

GAIL MERRIFIELD PAPP It was a great night, a corker. I loved being outdoors under a blanket with a bottle of wine. There were clouds of pot and a lot of eating going on. People brought dinners like they were going away for a week. Then it was 3 AM and people were passing brandy in Dixie cups down whole rows. Though it was a hell of a production, I remember it primarily as a human event. It was really just terribly moving.

CHARLES DURNING I played Jack Cade, the rebel in *The Wars of the Roses*. In my last scene, I'm in a garden, defending myself, dressed in a skirt and sandals. I thought we had the fight all choreographed. I was defending my thigh, and he went to the head and split my head open. I fell to the floor and couldn't do my death speech, which was more infuriating than anything else.

There was a pretty big gash on my head, and since the guy who did it to me was no longer onstage either, he took me to Roosevelt Hospital. We went into the emergency room and there's a guy who's been shot, another guy who's been stabbed in the stomach, and a third guy that had part of his arm torn off by a dog. We walk in, both dressed in skirts—miniskirts, in fact—and sandals and holding hands, and they're all looking at us kind of strangely. As a matter of fact, the guy that had his arm torn got up and moved about two seats away.

Finally one of the interns came out and said, "Where is the guy who got mugged in Central Park with a two-handed sword?"

"I didn't get mugged with a two-handed sword. I'm in a play there."

"You're in a play?"

"Yeah, we're doing Shakespeare in the Park."

"Shakespeare? In Central Park?" He'd never heard of it.

JOSEPH PAPP   I got awfully tired as the night went on, but you'd hear these gorgeous things going on, and the continuity of actors going from one play into another made the thing so vivid. And there was never an empty seat in that house. Some people would leave and others would come in and replace them. They kept feeding it all night long.

The night before, I'd called Jerry Ragni and James Rado from *Hair*, which was playing on Broadway at the time, and asked, "Can you bring some of the people over? Maybe sing in the morning, when we get to the morning." I had no idea when we'd end up. And at the very moment when the audience was applauding loudly and hilariously at the end of the play, and dawn broke out all over the stage, suddenly all these people from *Hair* came on the stage and began to sing "Let the Sun Shine In." It was so gorgeous, we hugged and kissed. You couldn't have planned anything like that.

But the most surprising thing was to pick up the *New York Times* the next day and see a story and a photo on the front page with the headline, "All-Night Shakespeare Enthralls 3,000." That amazed me. I thought they would do a story, but I had no idea it would be given that kind of coverage. And I suddenly realized, "Yes, it was extraordinary." I felt so much strength in that evening. I felt that Shakespeare was powerful. I don't remember if it brought in any money or not, but it certainly made it clear that we were there to stay.

9

The Public Theater

1966

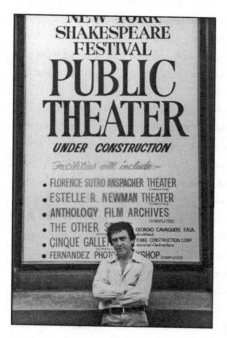

Papp at the Public
Courtesy of the New York Public Library

JOSEPH PAPP   I wanted to be doing contemporary plays, that was the major thing I was concerned with. I'd done only Shakespeare for so long, I felt the whole notion that you can do Shakespeare alone didn't work for actors or directors. In order to make Shakespeare alive, you have to be in the contemporary theater—each aspect enriches the other. So I needed a permanent home that would be a theater for new plays.

BERNARD GERSTEN   The materialization of the need for a full-time building had been growing since 1964, when Burt Martinson, the chairman of the board of the festival, took us on a trip to Europe. Seeing groups like the Berliner Ensemble and the Royal Shakespeare Company, plus the theaters we saw in Poland and Czechoslovakia, accelerated a latent desire in Joe to operate in a theater that was more sophisticated and could operate all year round.

Also, to understand the transition to this you have to understand Joe's restlessness. I once wanted to make a periodic table of Joe's restlessness cycles. One could almost track them; they're irregular, but they're rhythmic. Joe was not content the way some other theater operators are. More than anybody else, he does not get totally satisfied just by doing what he's doing. Joe periodically needs diversion. Joe cannot be in just one thing. Joe needs a radical shift, he needs change.

So we began looking for a building. We looked at a wonderful church on Spring Street and Seventh Avenue that subsequently burned down. We looked at the Friends Meeting House on Twentieth Street. There were a number of possibilities. One Monday, Hilmar Sallee came in with the Sunday *New York Times* real estate section, which on the front page had a photograph of this abandoned building, the windows boarded up, and the headline said something like "HIAS Building Up for Sale." There it was in all its vastness: 54,000 square feet, a grand-looking abandoned building.

The building, which had been the original Astor Library, the first free public library in the city of New York when it opened in 1854, had been purchased by the Hebrew Immigrant Aid Society in 1920. HIAS was a Jewish social welfare organization which dealt with waves of immigration from Europe, and its building was of special interest to me. My father, years and years before, had driven us by there and said, "When I came to this country, I went through that building, I was processed through there."

JOSEPH PAPP   I'd passed this enormous place a couple of times, but I'd never thought much about it. Certainly this was big and fancy compared to the church, but it was in a very dark, off-the-beaten-path neighborhood, with a lot of violence and robberies going on. It wasn't what it is today, but you start in neighborhoods like that. You always have to be in a place where most people don't want to go—that's where you get the buildings. If you want to start in a nice neighborhood, forget it.

Then we heard the building was for sale, and on a terrible rainy day we inspected the inside. Everything was dark and dreary, the building looked very old and ill-kept. It reminded me of a police station. Downstairs, where the Susan Stein Shiva Theater is, had been a synagogue, a shul. On the floor we found prayer shawls, prayer books, pictures of the officers of the congregation. Even after we'd been there for two years, old people would come around on Yom Kippur and say, "Where is the shul?"

The whole place had been partitioned both into small office spaces and into tiny cubicles with cots and mattresses on the floor where whole families had lived—there were even little rooms that had been put aside with bassinets for children. The entire building was littered with old pictures and file cards, thousands of them, lists of people who had applied to come over, all kinds of things lying around abandoned for forty years. With all the damp and disarray and leaking ceilings, it was very, very sad. It looked like there had been a pogrom in the place.

But, on the other hand, if you looked carefully you could barely see the outline of this gorgeous domed glass ceiling. The interior was quite beautiful, it was possible to see some of the past glories of that building. The problem was it had been so neglected, so covered over with junk and partitions and everything else, that its qualities were not immediately obvious.

BERNARD GERSTEN   There was a very short, feisty Jewish guy, Arthur Abraham, who was the caretaker of the HIAS building. He was the only person living in this huge building. He must have been seventy-five at the time. When we got there he said, "Vat d'you vant?" He didn't think that a bunch of guys from the theater were likely customers. When we bought the building, Joe kept him on.

JOSEPH PAPP   I walked in the building and he said, "I guess I'm out now, huh?"

"No, you're not," I said. "I bought the building, and you come with it."

That's the way it started, a tremendous friendship. He held off a guy who tried to hold up the box office—pushed the gun out of his hand. He put out a fire with his bare hands that would have burned the place down. He was really an amazing old man.

He was a little guy, about five foot five, raised in Europe. He'd been a featherweight boxer in his day, knew every opera under the sun, knew every racehorse on the track, knew every gambler in the district. He reminded me of one of those tough Jews that would come from Odessa, but he had marvelous taste.

"What do you think of the show?" I'd ask.

"Vell," he'd say, "the second act needs a little verk."

I went into his room one time, and there were pictures of me all over his walls. He would do anything for me. I became like his father. When he died, myself and six or seven others, we carried him. We put him in the earth, we shoveled the earth over him, we didn't let anybody touch him. He was just an amazing guy.

AUGUST HECKSCHER As President Kennedy's adviser on the arts, I had been particularly interested in repertory theaters, and I got to know Joe in those days. He got hold of me and we went through the building which was to become the Public Theater.

It was the most incredibly gloomy experience, because the weather was bitter cold and foul. And yet Joe was so absolutely transformed by the excitement of going through this place. He would point to what would seem to me like an impenetrable maze of small rooms and say, "And *this* will be a theater here." Then he'd grab me by the arm and take me into another part of the damp, dark, frigid building and say, "And here we'll have a café."

MING CHO LEE Bernie and I said, "My god! This guy has to be crazy. What is he going to do with all that room?" We were thinking that the summer, the Shakespeare Festival in the Delacorte, was still the main event, and that the involvement during the winter was just for continuity. I never expected that the continuity was going to be the leading force.

Joe and all of us would be showing people the building, it would be the dead of winter, and it would be colder inside than it was outside, terribly cold. It was unbelievable. But, nevertheless, Joe was right, and all of us were wrong.

BERNARD GERSTEN   The building had not closed, but a deposit had been made and it was under contract to a developer, Lithos Properties, Inc., who intended to tear it down. However, the city's Landmarks Preservation Commission, which was very young at that time, was interested in the possibility of declaring it a landmark. And Joe, with his quick eye, learned that data.

The commission said, "If you're interested in buying it, we will declare it a landmark." Joe said, "I'm interested," and that designation discouraged the developer because he now would have to fight to have his right to tear it down.

JOSEPH PAPP   I thought, "This guy's going to tear this building down. The first thing I better do is get to the city." I'd read that the Landmarks Preservation Commission had been formed, but they had not, at this point, designated any building in New York.

I was getting very hip with the city—I'd begun to understand the bureaucracy a little better—so I went to them and they got the paperwork very fast and they designated the building. But they said, "This doesn't save the building. The man has six months in which he can do this and do that." So though the commission claims credit for this, they really don't deserve it. I told them that in that six months, I'd get to work on it.

It took me a while to find out who this man was who had bought the building. I called him "Mr. Big" and I began to track him down. He kept sending me messages that if I wanted the building I'd have to pay, oh, extraordinary sums of money. I said, "I have to meet with him," but the people around him kept preventing that—they'd always send me to somebody else. This guy was so elusive, I thought he might be a gangster of some sort.

Finally, I found out that his daughter had been a contributor to the festival. Through her and some other people, finally the day arrived when I was able to come into the same room with this guy. He was a cigar-smoking real estate guy with a small office, not extravagant.

"Well," he says. "What can I do for you?"

"Mr. Big"—whatever his name was—"I want that building that you bought."

"What do you mean, you want that building?"

"I want the building. This is the building we're going to make into a theater and we're going to serve the people of this city. You have to realize that this building is going to stay. It's already been landmarked, and you don't want to start fighting the landmark thing. This city has been very nice to you. You've made a good living here. You've become rich as a result of this city. Why don't you just give us the building?"

"You must be crazy. I'm a businessman, Mr. Papp. I'm a businessman and I do this for money. I have over $50,000 involved in this already."

"Why don't we do this: I'll give you the $50,000 and you can contribute that to the festival."

"I can't do things like that. If I want to make contributions, I'll make them where I want to make them."

I argued with him for about an hour. I told him about his daughter supporting the festival, I talked about his being Jewish and the meaning of the HIAS building, but mostly it was about his citizenship. I went through a long spiel, it was very passionate. I was very angry at him. I felt very strongly that this was being done for the people. "Look," I said, "you should be doing something for the city after all it's done for you. It would be a disgrace if this building was torn down and we could not use it for this purpose."

He blinked his eyes at that, because all he knew was business, business, business. There was great resistance on his part to this, but he finally acceded and we had the building. I was not going to leave that place without that building, I'll tell you that. You get that determination.

THEONI ALDREDGE We owed so much money, we didn't know who was going to end up in jail. But Joe kept saying, "Don't worry about it. They never put somebody in jail that owes that much money because they want their money back." Your education was total with that man. It wasn't just costumes, you found out about how the world is run.

JOSEPH PAPP My whole idea was to create one 850-seat theater. I had plans drawn up to gut the building. I still have them, they cost $35,000.

But those plans took so long to come together that my taste became accustomed to the interior and I began to like it.

We'd start scraping away. We took down some of the partitions, and I said, "Gee, what a beautiful room. It would be a shame to lose that." I always liked old buildings, and I became fascinated with the history and tradition of this place.

One day I said, "I'm not going to do this. I'm going to create smaller theaters." We started with the second floor, once the fifty-foot-high skylit main reading room, and with money from Mrs. Florence Anspacher, my friend from the Robert Moses days who'd also donated $250,000 to the festival to make the purchase of the building possible, we began to construct what is now the 299-seat Anspacher Theater.

BERNARD GERSTEN We all fell in love with the building. My training is, once you agree to do something, you don't say "Oh, it's a piece of shit" or "This building was a terrible idea." You do it with a full heart. So once we'd said yes, the building became a great and wondrous adventure.

What could be better for people in the theater than to have the opportunity of building theaters, one by one, finding the money to raise them, putting on plays in them, and simultaneously trying to make the whole thing float? It was thrilling. After all, all we'd had up until that time was the big outdoor theater where all you could do was Shakespeare, and the mobile theater, where people threw rocks at you. So the prospect of having a theater where it didn't rain in and where they didn't throw rocks at you was a really terrific improvement.

PEGGY BENNION PAPP That was a very exciting time, but also a very difficult one because Joe had taken on an enormous responsibility. God, it seemed at times like it was going to be a white elephant. Many times he would feel totally overwhelmed, be very anxious and very desperate about whether or not he could pull it off, whatever it was he was attempting. For a long time, the Public Theater was nip and tuck. All the tremendous problems he encountered, tremendous renovations that had to be done, and it all took a lot of money. Oh, what a struggle. But it was also exciting. I think that was really the beginning of his dream.

BERNARD GERSTEN Joe's personality and character are symbolized in part by a total merging of himself with his theater. Just the time when we were going into the Public Theater was, though I didn't realize it, a period of extraordinary anxiety for Joe. He was having trouble, and the trouble had manifested itself for a while as something like palpitations. Joe thought it was his heart.

One day we went for lunch on Eighth Street with Jerry Freedman, who was our artistic director. Joe, on the way, said he wasn't feeling too well, so when we sat down, I said, "Joe, do you want to have a drink?"

"Yeah, maybe some brandy."

"Okay," I said, "I'll have brandy with you," because I'm a friendly guy. We got the waiter and right after we ordered Joe said, "I'm fainting. I'm going to faint. I think I'm going to die." And then Joe started to cave in in his chair, and suddenly he kind of slid to the floor and was stretched out.

Jerry ran to the maître d' to call for an ambulance. Everybody in the restaurant got very apprehensive, as people do when someone collapses, and Joe said, "I'm dying, I'm dying," and then something about his children. The ambulance came, they took him to Lenox Hill Hospital where he stayed for a series of tests for about a week, and they couldn't find anything wrong with him.

I think that it was anxiety. What I learned was very vivid and instructive: that Joe's identification with the theater was so total that threats to the theater—and the theater was threatened at that point, where would the money come from, could we go on?—became, psychologically or emotionally, threats to his life.

JOSEPH PAPP I move first and pull the money in afterward. I mean, if I'd waited until I had everything, nothing would happen. That's a risky way to live, but that's the way I work.

We didn't have enough money to finish anything, but I figured, "If we don't have four theaters, we'll do one. And as soon as we get enough money, we'll do another." That's the way we built the four theaters in the Public. I never say, "I have an idea, give me a grant." I say, "I've just done this, now give me a grant."

Everything you do, if you want to make any changes, is an enormous thing, impossible, but it becomes manageable once you start to deal with it. You have a sense of the end, but you can't operate from that point of view: you think of this one thing that has to be done right now. It's like cutting a hole into the side of a mountain. You have to start with just a few strokes, but at least you see something happening, a few shards are loosened.

But, I tell you, that starting is painful. I hate it. It's like the effort we had to put in putting up those enormous dimmer boards in the amphitheater. You come up against a lot of resistance, both physical and psychological, and you must go past the most extreme thing that you feel you can do.

Everything says to you "Don't do it, don't do it," but you can't back away. You want to follow the line of least resistance, that's only human, but something doesn't let you do that, and you grind it out. You do it, you do it, you do it, and you get to see that almost everything is doable, one way or another. It's the most painful, the most undesirable choice to make, but if you don't do that, you won't have a chance, nothing will budge.

10

Hair
1967

A scene from *Hair*
© Martha Swope

A kind of free-form, plotless "Oh, What a Happy Hippiedom," *Hair* ignites the key images and issues of the lost-and-found generation—youth vs. age, sex, love, the draft, race, drugs, Vietnam—into a vivid uproar that has more wit, feeling and musicality than anything since *West Side Story* . . . Twenty-one fresh faces and limber bodies have made the Public Theater the most exciting theatrical prospect New York has seen in years.

Jack Kroll, *Newsweek*, November 13, 1967

JOSEPH PAPP The basic question was, how was I going to operate that theater? That baffled me. I was insistent on doing new plays, but I'd never put on a play that had not been produced before. I asked myself, "What do you put on in a theater like that?" And I didn't know what to answer.

At first I felt I'd better not make this transition too severe by going directly from Shakespeare into an American contemporary play. Maybe I should get a popular, modern English play to begin with, keep things literary. I came across something called *Sergeant Musgrave's Dance*, a strange, interesting play where the language was very rich, and I said, "That's the first play I'm going to do." I optioned the piece, made a deal with the agent, I was ready to go.

At that time, I was teaching in the Theater Department up at Yale, and I was returning to the city one night on the train from New Haven. Suddenly I saw an actor I knew, Gerome Ragni, who'd been up at Yale in a play called *Viet Rock*. He was a friend of another actor, James Rado, who'd played some small parts in our Shakespeare plays. "Oh God," I thought, "he's going to start talking to me, and I just want to read."

He came over and sat down next to me. He was a chipper guy, always laughing, and a gen-u-ine hippie. It was not put-on with him, not bourgeois, he was really wild. I asked him what he was doing, and he said, "Jimmy and I are working on a play."

"Really? What is it."

"It's a musical. I have some pages right here. Would you like to see them?"

I said all right, and right then and there he showed me six or seven pages, a lot of words handwritten on some yellow paper. There were lyrics to some of the songs, including one called "Hair" and a few scenes. I wasn't quite sure whether I liked it or not, here and there the lyrics were smart and in other places they seemed absolutely silly, but he said he was still working on it. There wasn't any special interest on my part, but when someone says, "I want to show you some more," I don't say no.

To tell the truth, I was a little bit in conflict about opening with an English play. And one little scene he'd shown me, about a guy going off to war, had been intriguing. I always want to do something that comes out of the times we're living in, and all around us at the theater, in what was being called the East Village, were all the hippies. It was no bullshit, you'd go out the door and there they all were.

Also, Ragni was very persistent; he followed up in just a few days with more pages. He brought Jimmy Rado in, and when they started telling me more about what they were writing, I said, "Jeez, this sounds kind of interesting."

JAMES RADO We weren't these freaked-out hippies; we were actors who were very much involved in theater and had been writing all our lives. I'd done a lot of material for revues and had always wanted to do a book musical, but I never did till I met Jerry in a musical against capital punishment we were both cast in called *Hang Down Your Head and Die*. I saw some of his writing, he saw some of mine, and when we saw what was happening in the streets, we just decided to write a show about it.

GEROME RAGNI The script of *Hair* was typed and mimeographed like a regular script. It wasn't like little napkins and pieces of paper. The story that got out that we had written this on bags and like that, that was a joke. We had been working on it close to three years before Joe saw it. We thought it was antiwar, about the protest in Vietnam, but Joe said, "I like it. This is about the alienation of youth."

GAIL MERRIFIELD PAPP Joe brought this in, threw it on my desk, and said, "What do you think of this?" And I thought, "*Hair*? That's a title? God, what a strange title. What the hell is that, a play about hair?" I mean, I had no idea. I read it, but there was as yet no music, no composer, and I didn't know quite what to make of it.

DAVID BLACK I read it and I thought, "He's absolutely out of his mind. This thing has no substance. It's just going to be the biggest bomb, and we are going to be the laughingstock of the theater world." But when I saw the production Jerry Freedman directed, I thought, "This is not the work that I read, this is not the work that initially attracted Joe's attention." Then I really began to realize things about Joe: his intuitive sense about people, about playwrights, about work, and about the timing of things.

GERALD FREEDMAN Joe and Bernie had come to me with plans for the Public Theater and said, "We want you to be part of it," so I became artistic director. Quite frankly, Joe wasn't as knowledgeable about musicals as I was; this was my area of expertise. So when Joe was enthusiastic about *Hair*, and when Jimmy and Jerry played their tunes from it, he said to me, "What do you think?" I was very excited by the property, but their music was awful, it was dreadful, it was just terrible. I said, "I think you need a composer."

GALT MACDERMOT I wasn't into theater. I was a piano player, and I made a living, such as it was, making demo records. I always was a jazz fan, and I knew a jazz writer and publisher named Nat Shapiro who at the time was a producer. I kept bugging Nat, saying "I want to do a show," because I didn't know what else to do.

Jerry and Jim were still hustling *Hair*—they were going and seeing everybody—and when they met Nat, he put us together. When they came to me they said, "We've got a producer, Joe Papp. If we can get a score, he'll do it." Even though I wasn't into the theater world, when they said, "We have a producer," that sounded good.

Jerry and Jim were really into this hippie culture. They used to drag me down to the East Village. They'd say, "You've got to see how these people live or you won't be able to write this kind of music." They'd take me to Tompkins Square. There used to be a whole lot of hippies and druggies and everything there—it was quite a lively spot. But everybody thought I was a narc because I was wearing a tie and a white shirt. It was a little embarrassing.

JOSEPH PAPP They'd already contacted a composer, Galt MacDermot. Galt was certainly not a hippie by any means. He came in looking very proper and correct, like he'd just come out of a bank. He sat down at the piano and played the "Age of Aquarius" theme, and I was amazed that a guy who looked so square was playing this marvelous rock music. I loved the sound of the melody, but the stuff was half finished. "Why don't you write some more songs," I said, "and we'll see what we can do."

I'd called Bernie and a couple of other people in to listen, and when

Jimmy and Jerry and Galt left I said, "I'm not going to do that English play. I'm going to do a rock musical."

"A *what?*"

"A tribal rock musical."

"What is that kinda shit? You're outta your mind."

Everybody was against it, it was unheard of at the time, but I felt I was taking a tremendously positive chance. I was intrigued by it, it seemed extremely provocative, and it was about something that was going on. "Why the hell should I be doing an English play to begin with?" I said. "We should be doing American plays, that's the way to start a theater." And I didn't have to figure this out, this was brought in, it was thrust upon me, so to speak.

BERNARD GERSTEN I remember the sound of Galt's right foot pounding out the rhythms of *Hair* as Jerry and Jim were singing it, and I thought, "That's going to be our opening show? Impossible!" To think that the Shakespeare Festival would do a rock musical as the very first play it produced in a contemporary mode was about as great a stretch as one might have imagined.

It doesn't make any sense. If you thought about it objectively, you'd think of something that was serious and thoughtful and respectable. But a tribal love-rock musical? Gimme a break.

MARTIN SHEEN Joe'd call me intermittently for things and one day he said, "Do you sing, Martin?"

"Oh god. Not in public, Joe."

"Well, you never know. Come on down, because I've got this wonderful show called *Hair*, and I want you to audition for me."

So I came down and auditioned with Galt MacDermot. The songs were sensational. It was a free, open, powerful musical. My god, when you heard the first chords of "This is the dawning of the Age of Aquarius," Christ almighty, you got chills. I knew what it was going to be, can you imagine, but I kept pleading, "I can't sing."

I went home and I read the script sitting at the supper table that very night. My wife, Jan, said, "What is that you're reading?"

"I'm reading what is going to be the biggest hit ever. But can you picture me singing?"

"Well, I can't, but maybe you can pull it off somehow." But I didn't get the part. I would have been so delighted to have done *Hair*. That would have been something that would have changed my life.

SHELLEY PLIMPTON I was working as a hostess in a club called the Night Owl on West Fourth Street. Jerry and Jim had come in because through the window they had seen a band that had very long hair and they wanted to talk to them about doing their new play. As they were leaving, Jimmy said, "Wait. That girl. She's got something!"

So they came back in and they asked me if I could sing and I said no. Or dance, and I said no. Or act, and I said no. They were these long-haired basement types, you know what I mean. Basement art was going on, I could tell. So I said, no, no, no.

I was into the rock-and-roll scene then. I didn't know too much about what was going on in the theater. When you're in grade school and the teacher treats you badly, you say, "Someday I'm going to be a big famous actress, and then I'm going to say, at the Academy Awards ceremony, 'Despite this particular teacher's abuse of me, I went ahead and made it anyway.'" But that was it for acting.

Then they said, "Come and audition for us at the New York Shakespeare Festival." That sounded pretty uptown to me. That sounded like it wasn't really in a basement or a garret. I'd never sung in public in my life. When I sang for Jim and Jerry and Joe Papp it was the first time in my life. I sang "With a Little Help from My Friends" and a Donovan song, "Catch the Wind." Anyway, they liked me, I guess. They seemed to like me. It just happened.

MING CHO LEE My experience was very curious on *Hair*. In fact, it was an unbelievable experience. It was about two or three weeks before the rehearsal and I have never seen a script. "If I don't have a script," I said, "how do I start designing?"

"It's nothing like the usual musical," Jerry Freedman would say. "It doesn't really have a story. In fact, it doesn't really have a script."

"Let me read the lyrics. I mean, just something. We've got to talk, because if we don't talk, you'll have no set."

"Oh, even that doesn't matter."

So, finally, they gave me the script, which made no sense. I got to the page with the song "Hair," and it has one word, "hair, hair, hair, hair, hair," all the way down, I flipped the page and it was again "hair, hair, hair." And I said, "What kind of a thing is this?"

My assistant was from Tulane University, trained as an architect, a very formal-looking person. He was clean-shaven, came to work in a tie, but as he kept attending rehearsals, day after day, trying to find out what was happening, he slowly turned into a hippie. He grew a beard, then his hair got real long. Suddenly he's wearing a poncho and glasses where you look at him and see your own face, then he starts burning incense and stopped taking baths. Finally, we had to say, "Stop!" It just became total chaos.

MARTIN ARONSTEIN   You opened up this script and it was one of the most extraordinarily misshapen, totally unfocused, weird pieces of writing I've ever seen. Totally impractical, absolutely no story line. And in my opinion, Jerry Freedman shaped that piece, pulled the essence out, very much created *Hair* as much as Rado, Ragni, or Galt MacDermot. I'll never believe anything otherwise, because I was there, I saw it.

GERALD FREEDMAN   I had the responsibility of opening the Public Theater, of directing the first play, and I was worried about opening with a musical. I was damn scared, because I didn't think Joe knew how difficult it was to do a musical. I knew how to put one on, and nobody else I was working with did.

A lot of this material was really on loose-leaf stuff, it really wasn't together. I put it in a sequence; I made a shape for it. These guys had written this very talented thing that we all loved, and they had worked in the theater as actors. But, remember, this was the sixties and they had no sense of form. I said, "Will you guys please go to Central Park and leave me alone." And I took scissors and paste, and pasted together scenes, and I said, "This is what we're gonna do."

Ragni and Rado were very difficult to get along with. I say "difficult," they were extremely self-destructive. I was trying to create some kind of cohesive whole and every other minute they'd bring in some new fragment or they would say, "You gotta use this person." They'd change something every day—often very disruptive things. They wanted to take out "Good Morning, Starshine," and I made them keep that in.

The cast was a lot of undisciplined young kids. They were stoned most of the time and they thought that was cool. I remember slamming one kid, Paul Jabara, against the wall, and saying, "If you come in here high again, you're out on your ass." The guy's now a big record producer. I was trying to create a disciplined show, spontaneous but disciplined, and I couldn't cope with it.

THEONI ALDREDGE *Fairly* chaotic? It was *total* chaos. The kids, a lot of them, were nonprofessional actors, people who looked like what they were supposed to look like, and they all arrived with flowers. And I never trust that. No, I am peculiar. And I don't trust when people say, "I'll give it another three weeks and see how these people develop." When you're taken from the street and all of a sudden you're given a salary, how do you behave when you have a couple of pennies in your pocket?

After a while, everybody got a bit more secure in what they were doing, so it wasn't all this innocence. You got the normal fights. People learned phrases like "You upstaged me" or "You stepped on my line." I don't remember it as being a very happy experience.

SHELLEY PLIMPTON It was fun. I remember having fun every day, that's all I remember. During the rehearsal period, Jill O'Hara and I used to leave together and we would be walking down the street literally singing "Good Morning, Starshine," or whatever it was, because we were so happy. It was such a new, great thing, and we were so excited.

It was my first job. I didn't have any kind of performance pressure at all. I wanted to be good, but it didn't mean anything like my career. I was just a little thing in there, just one piece of fluff in a major mattress. There were negative things going on, but they didn't seem to affect me, they didn't seem to touch what I was doing at all. At that time in my life, it was like youth and springtime and falling in love and parental approval all in one. It represented the purest joy in the world. I don't think one gets all of that at once very often.

GALT MACDERMOT There was a conflict between the writers' and Freedman's concept of direction. The whole idea of *Hair* was freedom, and Freedman's not that kind of director at all. He's very, very organized, and I think he did some things that the guys didn't want done. But I think the show really needed that at the time, because the book was kind of spread out, and he reorganized it quite extensively. But that kind of thing is a stress between people and there was a lot of stress in that sense.

These guys tried to make a lot of changes. Jerry Ragni had this thing of interpolating stuff into the show all the time. He'd hear a tune and he'd want to put it in the show, and that started to get a little hard to take. It was never anything but trying to make it better, but you don't want to be always changing things. They never stopped thinking about this show, twenty-four hours a day, and you had to be on the same energy level as them, or it could worry you.

GERALD FREEDMAN To open the Public Theater on time, I elicited the help of Anna Sokolow, a choreographer, to stage some of the musical numbers. But she got appendicitis and I went ahead and staged everything. Then Anna came in. She's a very strong personality, and she had other ideas. The guys [Ragni and Rado] began to polarize us and turn toward her, and this began to exacerbate our situation.

Also, Jimmy Rado wanted to play the role of Claude and was constantly undercutting the people in the show, which I thought was very, very destructive. I once forbade them to even come to rehearsal, it got so destructive.

It came to the point where I felt, for the good of the theater, I should withdraw from the show. And Joe accepted my withdrawal, which hurt me deeply. Although I felt this is what I should do, I felt he would back me up. I don't think Joe should ever have let me go.

JAMES RADO Anna Sokolow really contributed a lot to the feel and mood of the piece. Her style was experimental and very wild, lots of crazy staging techniques: instead of people dancing in or walking in, she'd have them flying in on top of the arms of people. We thought it would end up perfect, but she and Gerald Freedman did not get along, so Gerald walked out of the production and Anna took over the directing. I couldn't believe that doing this one show, all of a sudden we had so much turmoil backstage.

Then, after the first preview, Joe fired Anna and rehired Jerry. We were in quite a bit of conflict over that—we were quite upset. Jerry Freedman had put some wonderful, beautiful things in, but we liked the idea of bringing a modern-dance element into the musical theater. So there were two directors with different ideas who were working on the show. One had to go, and she was the one.

GERALD FREEDMAN I went down to Washington and within a few days I got a call from Joe and a telegram saying, "Please come back." I took a look at the show and it was a shambles. What had happened in a week was unbelievable. They had changed so many things. They had fired the kid who played Claude, and Jimmy had taken the role. It was ghastly.

I made certain conditions before coming back. The kid had to be in the show, Jimmy couldn't do it, this and that had to go out of the show. Anna and I obviously could not work together, I had to have complete control. And Joe set down the law and that's the way it was.

We were opening two nights from then. The first night we played with my first act and their second act. The next night both acts were the way I had left the show, and then we opened. It was a big success.

JOSEPH PAPP Although Jerry Freedman was an excellent director, there were some very strong-willed people around, and he, by nature, is much more gentle. He could be tough—I've seen him in various situations where his nose got white—but there he was on the defensive a great deal. He had a lot of pressure from people who were hard-bitten and forcing him into certain compromises.

An issue arose over the choreographer, Anna Sokolow, who is a powerful woman with a great reputation. They were in contention all the time, and it ended up with him leaving. I tried to handle that as best as I could. It was a difficult thing for me because I liked Jerry very much, but it came down to that.

Ragni and Rado said Anna Sokolow could direct it, but it turned out she couldn't. The show was falling apart. Then the two guys said they would be able to direct it, but I realized none of them could direct it. I had to get Jerry Freedman back.

You see, I was kind of new to all of this. I'd never really had to deal with live authors before; it was a whole different ball game. I realized I had to put my foot down, I had to let them know who was boss, because they were creating chaos. I liked both of them, I never felt they were obnoxious, but they became very, very difficult. They were trying to take the wheel all the time, to take over command of the show, and since the thing was being created on the spot, since this was not a finished piece of work, that got kind of overwhelming.

What I did was use whatever clout I had as producer. I always have in my hands the right not to do a show, and I made it clear to them that I would do that if necessary. At that point, the show was already picking up a lot of interest, there was no way I was going to drop it, but they didn't know that. When I put my foot down, I think they were relieved.

GEROME RAGNI Joe said to us, "This is it or this show is going to close. Take your choice." We wanted the show to go on, so we said okay.

Joe was always strong, he seemed to keep it together and get what he wanted. I remember a couple of times we'd come in with complaints and he would not even listen, he'd just say, "So. Leave. Do the show. Stop analyzing it. Let Gerald Freedman direct."

One time we wrote a big, two-page letter to Joe on the nature and spirit of *Hair*, talking about what the spirit and character of Claude should be like. We left it on his desk and like an hour later someone came in and said, "Jim Rado? Jerry Ragni?"

"Yes."

And he handed us ripped pieces of paper. Joe had torn the letter to shreds.

JOSEPH PAPP *Hair* was a terrific popular success. For a show to open a new theater, if God had come and taken me by the hand and said, "I have a great miracle I want to show you," it would have been this. I guess I could have run it all the time, but I'd set up this policy of doing several shows a season, with new plays every six or eight weeks. I had other shows planned, including a *Hamlet* I was going to direct myself, and I didn't want to change that.

If I had known then what I know now, I would have run the show. I wouldn't have done my *Hamlet*, I would have waited. It was kind of dumb, because we had a success on our hands. I might have stayed with *Hair* and never done anything else, might have made us millions and millions of dollars. The thing was, I was young, this was all new to me, an entirely different world. In the nonprofit theater, I'd never dealt with that kind of success. I mean, you can't have a Shakespearean "hit." I really didn't know what a hit was.

BERNARD GERSTEN The show had a scheduled eight-week run, but the word about *Hair* had begun to spread, people really loved it, and it seemed too good to close. Since a production of *Hamlet* was coming in, we were looking for money with which to move the show.

There were two possibilities: moving it to the Cheetah, which was a disco on Broadway, or moving to the Henry Miller, a small theater on Forty-third Street. Our considered judgment was that we shouldn't move a show that had played in the semi-round on a thrust stage and try and make it conform to the demands of a proscenium stage, so the Cheetah seemed a better idea.

The chairman of our board, Burt Martinson, said, "I'll give you $50,000 to move it"—that was what we needed. And we said, "No, Burt, you can't give us $50,000 to move it, we don't feel we have the right to divert money that you might give us for our not-for-profit work to a speculative move to a Broadway theater. We have to get money that somebody otherwise would not give us." That was the doctrine of the time, and it was good doctrine.

GAIL MERRIFIELD PAPP At that time Michael Butler came onto the scene through a most extraordinary kind of phone call. It's one call I remember because it was so odd.

"My name is Michael Butler," he said.

"Yes, sir," I said.

"Well, I just want to tell you . . ."

"Yes?"

"Well, I really . . ."

"Yes?"

"I just wanted to tell you that . . ."

"Yes?"

"Well, you know, I saw *Hair*."

"Yes?"

"Well, I just wanted to let you all know that . . ."

"Yes?"

"Well," he said finally, "I liked the show, I really liked it."

"Thank you very much, sir," I said. I didn't know who this man was, I had no idea. "I'll certainly tell Mr. Papp you made this call in an effort to let us know that."

"I'd like to talk about it," he said. And I thought, "Oh my god."

He didn't demand to speak to Joe, he didn't tell me what he wanted, he just went on about the show in this dreamy way. Finally, he said he was very interested in what its future was, and I began to think, "I don't know who he is, but maybe Joe would like to talk about its future." Joe said okay, and Michael came in.

BERNARD GERSTEN One day we got a postcard from a guy who wrote, "Dear Mr. Papp, I saw your poster for *Hair* and was intrigued with it. I saw the show and fell in love with it. Could I get a poster? I will, of course, pay for whatever charges there are. Signed, Michael Butler." This was written on a very heavy, whipped-cream type of card from Tiffany's or better, embossed "Oak Brook, Illinois" in red enamel.

"Look at this," Joe said. "What do you make of this?"

"That," I said, "looks like a very wealthy person. It smells like money, it feels like money, and it sounds like money. Why don't we call him up?" And Joe called him and said, "Mr. Butler, we'll send you a poster, but what's your interest in *Hair*?"

That was the beginning of our friendship with Michael Butler. That's what led to his coming to town, visiting with us, and saying, "Yes, I'll give you the money." And we made a deal for Michael to coproduce, to move our first show to the Cheetah. And it failed there. It was the wrong place and the wrong style. It was just a mistake.

JOSEPH PAPP   Michael Butler was a guy who had first seen the poster, then the show, and then came to me and initiated the move uptown. And I, like a damn fool, thought, "I don't want to put it on Broadway; it doesn't belong on Broadway."

I was a purist then. I had great contempt for Broadway. I felt it was just a commercial marketplace that had nothing to do with art. I also had a social notion that *Hair* should be amongst young people. So I developed this concept of moving to the Cheetah, the idea that the audience would come to see the show first and then dance afterward. I felt there was no compromise there, but it turned out to be a dismal failure.

What I failed to understand was that *Hair* was really a white man's show, and that the mostly blacks and Hispanics who came to dance at the Cheetah were not interested in the show, they just showed up afterward to dance. So we essentially had no audience because very few people came to the Cheetah from the outside. Then Michael asked me if I would be interested in selling him the rights, and, not knowing very much about rights, I said, "Yes."

MING CHO LEE   We had the feeling, "We'll show you, Broadway, we're doing better things here." Joe was busy directing *Hamlet*, Jerry was interested in doing *Ergo* by Jakov Lind—plays that were worth doing—and in no way were we going to give that up for anything that had commercial value.

Meanwhile, *Hair* was a difficult show to keep up. If you're not careful, if it's not under firm control, it can get very campy in the worst sense of the word. Nobody was paying any attention to it, there was no supervision from the Shakespeare Festival, and it was going from bad to worse at the Cheetah.

When Michael Butler did not get any response to his saying, "You better come and deal with this," when all we had to do was send a technical director or a stage manager, he said, "To hell with you, if you're not interested, I'll just do it over again." And when *Hair* became a huge hit all over the world, we got almost nothing out of it, even though most people felt that Jerry's production actually was a better one. Losing *Hair* was horrible on a short-term basis, but it was a lesson Joe and Bernie learned very well. They never made that mistake again.

BERNARD GERSTEN   Michael, who really believed in *Hair* and loved it and became a flower child and a hippie instantly, Michael was the only person in the whole universe of the theater who was foolish enough to think that a play that had closed on Broadway might be reopened some four or five months later in a new version with a new director. That's what he did, and that resulted in the successful *Hair*.

If we had moved our version to the Henry Miller, *Hair* might have come to a different end or it might have come to the same end. Plays making it or not making it have to do with a kind of launching process, very much like launching payloads in rockets, and I don't know whether *Hair* could have gone to launch without the frontal nudity that the new production added. Our production didn't have that gimmick, the capper that captured the imagination of the New York theater, so it might not have gone to launch anyway.

And the royalty rate of one-half of one percent of the gross which we retained resulted in revenue for the theater of $1.5 to $2 million over the next four or five years, a very important source of subsidy for us. So Joe and I never regretted *Hair*. Everything we did had a logic of its own.

GERALD FREEDMAN   We had this exhilarating production of *Hair* that surprised everybody, set them on their ear, and Joe didn't capitalize on it. He was thrilled that it was good for the theater, but he was intent on doing his production, which was *Hamlet*. He admired my shows, but he did not exploit them. He exploited his shows.

And that's where I think things began to turn. After the success of *Hair*, something happened in terms of play choices. There began to be one eye on "Will this get to Broadway?" or "Will this be picked up?" I won't say it was immediate, but it was really soon after. And there wasn't the same freedom of choice that there had been.

I remember when we first walked into what is now the Anspacher Theater and he said, "This is your theater, Jerry." This is my theater? That's his way, and I took it personally. When we disagreed on a particular project, I remember crying at the lunch table when he said, "Maybe we should separate for a while." I had accepted the role of son, and I had helped build this thing. How could I be kicked out? It really was like growing up and leaving home, but I didn't want to leave home in that way.

MING CHO LEE Joe suddenly changed direction. He began to think completely on different terms about what his Public Theater should be. He changed direction when none of us knew he was changing direction.

He started having new playwrights, which was very important. But these new playwrights would like to work with directors that they grew up with, not Jerry Freedman, and Jerry was suddenly in the background. And the directors would like to work with designers they grew up with, therefore it's not me, even though I'm the principal designer. Suddenly, some of us are isolated in the park; the Delacorte becomes just something to do for the summer. Instead of having continuity, the whole thing of becoming a year-round theater actually created fragmentation.

DAVID MITCHELL Joe relied on Ming a great deal in terms of the way things should look, and in the early years that was very beneficial to the festival—it was a tremendous jump in terms of the quality of the productions. But with Joe there was always that restless desire for some kind of change, and he finally felt that he had had too much of a particular kind of style. There was a break with Ming and Ming's style, and he began looking for other designers. Joe has his enthusiasms and then loses interest, and either by benign neglect or whatever, certain people and certain ways of doing theater come and go.

11

The Naked Hamlet

1967

Martin Sheen as Hamlet
© George E. Joseph

The action takes place on what appears to be a bare stage, with the technical paraphernalia—steel poles and ladders and platforms and a spiral staircase—on view. At the opening, soldiers with flashlights rush in and beam their lights at the audience. The King and Queen are discovered asleep in a double bed, with Hamlet asleep in a coffin at the foot. They turn, sliding the blanket off him. He sits up, dangles his legs over the side, and starts his "O, that this too, too solid flesh" soliloquy, ending up, after a dirty look at his mother, with "Frailty, thy name is woman." The Queen wears a nightgown at first, and later changes into a short cocktail dress. The King wears a military uniform, as does Hamlet when he's not wearing underpants or a white suit with a black armband or a rubbish collector's outfit. The ghost is in long underwear a great deal of the time. Most of the words are Shakespeare's, and many of them are from *Hamlet*, but the speeches are broken up and scattered all over the play, as the actors are scattered all over the house.

Edith Oliver, *The New Yorker*, January 6, 1968

. . . .

JOSEPH PAPP   I don't like the word "favorite," but there's no question that *Hamlet* is a play I'm partial to. I've done it more than any other play. I was teaching at Yale at that time. We used to sit around a table at a bar around the corner and drink beer, that was the class. I said to the students, "I want to work on the first scene of *Hamlet*, the first sixteen lines, for the entire semester."

I was trying to create the psychological climate that justified the first line of the play. How do you start a play in the middle? How do you start something in the middle of life? That was the challenge. A man named Ted Cornell was my best student, very smart. He was the only one that seemed to understand what I was really trying to do.

TED CORNELL   Joe came up one or two days a week to teach directing and was immediately a figure of fascination to me. I had not spent considerable amounts of time in New York City, and I was struck by the fact that Joe was urban and argumentative and feisty—sort of a Fiorello La Guardia–type figure.

He arranged and brought up with him a group of professional actors for us to work with. One of Joe's insights into directing was that, as opposed to working on one scene for a while and then moving on to another scene from another play, you have to work on deeper strains in a work which only emerge over a long period of time. But given the constraints of time, and so that we could make use of the resources we had, he assigned the class the task of cutting *Hamlet* so that it could be done in forty-five minutes by six actors.

The concept that I used was to smash the play and use the shards of it, reassemble those shards in a way that captured some of the dramatic action. My version was selected for use by the class, and although I don't think it was enormously successful there, he invited me to come to New York and continue working on it at the Shakespeare Festival.

The version Joe directed was all done in one act, about ninety minutes long, with only twelve people in the cast. What had been done was to select eight to ten major sequences in the piece and then to cluster about them fragments from elsewhere in the play in a way that did, in fact, present a coherent story. I, in fact, wrote about a fourteen-line section to get us over one hump, and nobody noticed it.

The actors were encouraged, as they went along, to burlesque in certain ways, to pun off of the Shakespearean text. A very elaborate series of vaudevilles, such as Laertes delivering his farewell to Ophelia by the lifting of the lid of a garbage can, evolved over the six-week rehearsal period and had its own coherent life side by side with the text. It was all for low humor, and yet the significant emotional moments, and hopefully also the philosophical content, emerged.

The idea was that *Hamlet* had become so encrusted with so many interpretations, which lay like a thick varnish over it, that in order to give a person new to the script, or indeed a person very familiar with it, a new look at it, it was necessary to crack it.

What we had learned over the past fifty or sixty years about multiple points of view on the same object, whether through cubist painting or Stravinsky's music or relativity theory, all suggested that it was possible to shatter something and see it more clearly than when it was all of a piece. It made you go in and take another look at it, lose your assumption that *Hamlet* is an unchanging monument and instead make it something that is available, something that can be lived with.

JOSEPH PAPP This idea, which ended up being known both as "The Naked Hamlet" and "Hamlet as a Happening," was to do a kind of contemporary *Hamlet*, to really break the text apart. I was living in a funny time, this was the sixties, and I was going through a lot of things that were emotional as well as intellectual. My father had just died, and I know there's a strong connection between my father's death and doing *Hamlet*. The need to do that play was very, very strong upon me. There were a lot of secrets in it that I wanted to find out, and the breaking up of *Hamlet* seemed to me a way of revealing the play.

I felt absolutely free. Directing the whole work was like being in the most ecstatic kind of state because one creative thing after another would happen. I had Hamlet as a peanut vendor walking up and down the aisles. A lot of vaudeville I'd seen when I was a kid came into play here. I had Polonius standing there with a balloon, for instance, and when he died the balloon just left his hands and flew up to the ceiling. We'd never be able to get them down, the balloons stayed up there for days. It was just an extraordinary experience.

I felt Hamlet drove everybody crazy, that he was responsible for the deaths of all these people by driving everybody nuts. There was one fight in the play that was so real it was hard to know they were just pretending. Martin Sheen, who was Hamlet, got angry at Ralph Waite, who was Claudius, and said, "What the fuck are you doing? What the hell's going on here?"

"It was a mistake," Ralph said.

"Goddamn, I'm sick of it," Martin said, and they started to fight. It was so violent—real punches were thrown, they knocked things over—that it looked like the actors, not the characters, were fighting. The emotions were so real, you could not tell that this was not true. For that moment, and for three or four minutes after, the audience was absolutely stunned. It brought them up to a higher level of tension and it heightened the play.

A few days before opening, Ralph Waite came to me and said, "Joe, you're a great guy, I love you, but I don't think you know what the hell you're doing."

"What do you mean?"

"Man, we're going to open in three days and you haven't even staged the whole second act."

"Oh, is that what's bothering you? Okay, I'll stage it."

And in two hours I staged the entire second act, from beginning to end. It was always in my mind what I had to do. In the whole play, I operated totally from instinct, without any sort of cocksure, premeditated knowledge. I let the things happen as they came. It was the most gorgeous way to work, particularly having Martin Sheen there as Hamlet.

Martin was so unfamiliar with Shakespeare—it was all new to him. He didn't know how the play ended, he didn't know whether Hamlet died or not, until he read it. He'd sit in a corner and laugh when he was reading the text, his demeanor was extraordinary. He was so untarnished, so totally open, and he'd look at me wide-eyed with these beautiful, penetrating blue eyes. Every time I talked to him, he'd look at me with awe, and then he'd burst into laughter. But he was absolutely beautiful in this thing. He was like a flower that began to bloom, to bud.

MARTIN SHEEN I had first met Joe early in 1962, auditioning for a production of *Macbeth* that was going to tour the public schools. Joe was very encouraging and I was very intimidated. He was a master of the pun—I dubbed him the Great Pun Broker—and the puns were often on great literature, so I never got them. I auditioned with a speech from *Hamlet*; little did I realize that one day I would play Hamlet for him.

After that, Joe kind of kept me in mind, and occasionally I would hear from him. Meanwhile, things got bad for me. I had one baby, my wife was pregnant, we were living in the Bronx because it was so much cheaper than Manhattan, and we got evicted.

I moved us to a very cheap apartment in Staten Island, and I took a job at the Bay Street Car Wash washing cars. I was working there under my real name, Ramon Estevez, and because I was very embarrassed about being an actor, I didn't tell anyone I had this second name I used as a stage name.

One day, the manager of the car wash said to me, "Are you by any chance an actor?"

"Yeah."

"Do you use another name?"

"Yeah."

"Would you know a guy named Joe Papp?"

"Sure, yeah."

"Well, he's wanting you to call him."

It turned out Joe'd been calling me at the car wash but no one knew who I was. I got back to him and he hired me to play Scarus, a young lieutenant in the production of *Antony and Cleopatra* with Colleen Dewhurst that summer at the Delacorte. But I got a call to do an episode of a TV series that was shot in New York called *The Nurses*. So I left *Antony and Cleopatra*, I never opened. He was really mad at me and I didn't speak to him again. I felt very badly, I felt like I had offended Joe, but I needed the money.

As a result of my audition for *Hair*, Joe called me some two months later and asked if I would do *Hamlet*. "Of course," I said, "but I have to confess, Joe, I've never read the play." He said he wanted to kick it around and see if it stood up. He wanted to take the five pillars of the play, the five major monologues, and reconstruct the play on those pillars and see how it stood or fell. And that's what we did. We shook the piss out of it.

Joe was very right in choosing me because he could mold me and push me in any direction. I had no preconceived notion of how *Hamlet* should be done, how it should be presented, or how I should present myself in it. Whatever he said, fine, I tried.

I didn't know how to pronounce a lot of the words, honest to god, I could not, and he was hopelessly patient with me. I'd have to stop in the middle of something and say, "What's a bodkin?" The other actors were all schooled, many of them had gone to college, or at least read Shakespeare and knew. They would laugh among themselves, thinking, "Jesus, this Sheen. Where is this dummy coming from?" People would just wring their hands, throw up their eyes to heaven, while Joe had to explain to me what something was about.

I felt like an idiot, but I had to do this. You'd make an absolute ass of yourself and feel awful about it, and Joe'd say, "No, no, that's the way to go. It's okay to feel awful, it's quite all right. Challenge yourself. Dare to fail, because you'll never succeed on any level if you're not willing to fail to the worst degree. So make an ass of yourself. Fine."

Yet it was the most extraordinary thing, the most fun I ever had in my life doing anything, before or since. Couldn't wait to get to the theater, hated to go home, laughed and enjoyed every single minute on the stage.

During the rehearsals, something would happen. You'd be eating a sandwich and Joe would say, "Play a scene while you're eating the sandwich." And why not? I love to play golf, and one day I was swinging a broomstick like a golf club, rehearsing the lines, and Joe said, "Let's do it, let's do the scene that way." Anything was allowed to happen, and it did happen. It was the time of my life, the time of my life.

JOSEPH PAPP Martin Sheen has a Spanish father, so he had an impeccable Hispanic accent. Wearing a leather jacket, looking like a young Puerto Rican from New York, he did the "To be or not to be" soliloquy in an Hispanic accent, and that turned out to be the most extraordinary thing. All those words that we take for granted suddenly coming from a young kid on the street—they took on a tremendous meaning.

> . . . To die, to sleep
> No more; and by a sleep to say we end
> The heart-ache and the thousand natural shocks
> That flesh is heir to . . .
>
> For who would bear the whips and scorns of time,
> The oppressor's wrong, the proud man's contumely,
> The pangs of despised love, the law's delay,
> The insolence of office, and the spurns
> That patient merit of the unworthy takes . . .

The audience, which had started out laughing when he said "To be or not to be" with that accent, was suddenly quiet. Then, not only did it get quiet, you started to hear sobbing in the audience. People started to cry. Most amazing. He liberated those lines so people could listen to them freshly. And that had been my idea behind the entire production in the first place.

MARTIN SHEEN People were laughing uproariously and suddenly they were listening, some of them for the first time—feeling for the first time—to things that had been in the literature for four hundred years. Powerful stuff.

You began to see who was suffering the whips and scorns of time. It was the Puerto Rican in the community, who did all the dirty work behind the scenes and took all the blame and didn't get any credit. Building, suffering humanity. They were the latest immigrants and their cry was being heard through the great master, Shakespeare. Their words, their emotions, their accent was now coming through that great fire that fuels and never consumes the great literary works that belong to everybody.

TED CORNELL Marty Sheen was terrific. He was Joe's image of an energetic Hamlet, where energy and street smarts were not inimical to the ability to speak poetically and think politically and artistically. And Marty brought to it, in addition to his original insight and energies and comic ability, exactly that it was not something that he stood in awe of.

It was one of the most successful relationships that I saw Joe have with an actor, because Marty, like Joe, was always willing to throw away previous choices. One of the things that can be frustrating to an actor about Joe as a director is that he will just constantly change what he wants. And that didn't bother Marty at all.

In fact, the rehearsal process consisted basically of going through the play four times over a period of six weeks, doing it entirely differently each time, and keeping track of what those changes were. People were going, "Wait a second, what are we doing here?" Marty had no trouble with that whatsoever. He was not threatened by it. In fact, he thrived on it.

APRIL SHAWHAN One day it was decided that Hamlet would throw popcorn at Ophelia through the whole first scene, and that made me very upset. I just thought it was terrible, it was like being pummeled. So I walked out of rehearsal. Without saying anything, I left and went home.

Then I thought, "I'm not pleased with this scene, but I really don't want to leave this." So I went back the next day and Joe didn't say "What happened?" or anything, no one said anything, it was like it hadn't happened. The popcorn stayed in, but we worked on the scene, and it got better. You never knew what was going to happen in rehearsals, and that certainly was because of him.

CLIVE BARNES It was truncated, it was modernized. It was, to my mind, a mess. Joe was obviously very, very keen on this production, he took it very seriously indeed. We appeared on a TV program to talk about *Hamlet*, and Joe, all the way through, sat on a stool eating an apple, which completely upstaged me. As W. C. Fields might have said, never appear on television with dogs, children, or men eating apples.

JOSEPH PAPP   It became a controversy with the *New York Times* and Clive Barnes. I remember I threw peanuts at him on a television show. When I read the reviews after the play came out, I was devastated. Barnes hated it, he called it "a Hamlet for philistines." Walter Kerr said it was "exactly like the shows idiot children used to put on in their basements." It was mercilessly attacked. Said it was rotten, said it was lousy Shakespeare, everything you could say.

I had put everything I had in that play, and I was absolutely depressed. Finally, some of the later reviews began to extol the work as something totally reflective of the sixties, and boy, that cheered me up, because I thought it was a complete failure. I never really knew if it was successful or not. I never thought in those terms. I didn't approach the play that way.

At that time I had no problem confronting any critic. When Walter Kerr panned another of my shows, I wrote him, "Please stay away. Keep out. I don't want you here. You are incapable of judging and evaluating new works." Everybody's afraid to talk back to the critics because they'll get you the next time. I don't give a damn about the next time. The present is the most important thing.

Listen, when I get reviews, criticism of certain things in my shows, I know more than most critics what's wrong with it. For every criticism they have, I can give two. But I try to judge the entire work and say, "Isn't it an interesting evening in the theater?" That's the most important thing, because you can always very easily pick a production apart, particularly where it's far-out.

GERALD FREEDMAN   I was stimulated and frustrated. Stimulated because there were so many wonderful things, and frustrated because he hadn't really pulled it together with some coherent point of view. But Joe turned *Hamlet* into a major triumph for the theater because of the discussion that arose out of it. If they didn't like it and if they were critical of it and from his point of view didn't understand it, he wasn't going to take it lying down. So he entered into public debate over *Hamlet* and turned it absolutely around. From a disaster into a triumph, absolutely. Public relations triumph.

12

No Place to Be Somebody
1969

A scene from *No Place to Be Somebody*
© Friedman-Abeles

Here is a black panther of a play. *No Place to Be Somebody* stalks the off-Broadway stage as if it were an urban jungle, snarling and clawing with uninhibited fury at the contemporary fabric of black-white and black-black relationships.

The milieu is virtually the message, and playwright Charles Gordone knows it like the black of his hand . . . "Johnny's Bar" is no oasis for gentle day-dreamers. It is a foxhole of the color war—full of venomous nightmares, thwarted aspirations and trigger-quick tempers, a place where the napalm of hurt has seared each man's skin.

This hell away from hell is run by Johnny Williams (Nathan George), a black pimp who is as cold and dangerous as a switch blade. His whores saunter in and out between tricks, and the white one loves him. Johnny wants to challenge the Mafia, which is crimping his style, by assembling a "Black Mafia" to rule his own turf. An ex-con father figure who has gone straight (Walter Jones) warns Johnny that he has contracted "charley fever"—that is, trying to beat the white man at his own game. The fever inevitably proves fatal, and finally the stage is as loaded with corpses as the bloodiest Elizabethan tragedy.

Time, May 16, 1969

The play holds the interest, but what is really rewarding is the vigor of the writing and language. Witty, salty and convincing, the dialogue brings Johnny's West Village bar to vivid life, and Mr. Gordone can create characters.

Johnny . . . emerges as someone completely credible, and so does Gabe Gabriel, the narrator and link-man of the story. Gabe [Ron O'Neal] is the nearly white actor and playwright who finds himself becoming blacker than black in his search for identity. But he is also the spokesman for black moderation, and together with a white barman who eventually realizes that he will achieve nothing by making himself into a pretend-black out of guilt, the only hopeful aspect of a play full of bleak action.

Clive Barnes, *New York Times*, May 5, 1969

ROSCOE LEE BROWNE In 1961, Charles joined the off-Broadway company of Genet's *The Blacks* that I was in. It was quite a group, and quite an extraordinary evening: Maya Angelou, James Earl Jones, Godfrey Cambridge, Raymond St. Jacques, Lou Gossett, Cicely Tyson. Charles was always an absolute delectable. I adored him, but everybody did. His persona was street, absolutely urban. Marvelous humor, zinging wit that made him laugh before you did, and truly, fiercely loyal as a friend. You would have thought, "If Charles is with me, it's more than the whole world against me." One would have said, because of the period, this is a fierce black nationalist, but he was not quite so chauvinistic as that. He did think of most white people as crackers, but his view was a worldview.

Charles used to bring me his writing, and I'd say, "Why do you bring me these little dirty yellow pages?"

"Roscoe, read it, goddamn it, read it!"

"What is this, Charles?" I think I was the only one who called him Charles, the world called him Chuck.

"It's a fucking poem."

"These are not poems. There's some wit here, but these are not poems."

"I didn't mean they're some poems. They're fucking speeches is what they are. They're speeches."

"But Charles, how are they connected?"

"You'll fucking see." He was never really angry at me. He'd just look at me and say, "Roscoe, you be careful. I'm writing a play."

CHARLES GORDONE   I was working in Genet's *The Blacks* during the early part of the civil rights movement. Going to the theater every night, I began to listen more closely to Genet's words. I saw the genius in a lot of the things that he was saying, and I couldn't understand that here was a white man, and a Frenchman, who in many ways was bringing up the similarities and the identification that he had with black people.

I wanted to say something, but I didn't know how. I had had some idea to write, but didn't know when. All of a sudden it occurred to me that I better get down to the typewriter and begin. I had my days free, so I sat down at the typewriter and began to write *No Place*. During that time, between 1961 and 1967, other than taking acting and directorial jobs here and there, I was pretty consistently on the typewriter with that play.

It's a play that very definitely has to do with my own personal identity and the quest for it. It all came from my own experience in the Village. I came to New York in 1952 from Los Angeles, and I worked as a waiter and part-time bartender for a black Puerto Rican at his bar called Johnny Romero's on Minetta Lane, almost on the corner of Sixth Avenue. He was a real hood, but a hood with class, and he was the only black man to own a bar. A corporation really owned it, his wife and some other people, but he ran the bar.

I became interested in his character, which was very close to the other side of me. I originally came from the Midwest, from a fundamentalist religious background, and was brought up with all the straight-and-narrow values of the white middle class. All of which he knew nothing about. But the way he handled himself and moved in the society, what he drew from, were all the things I admired but at the same time detested.

He brought out things in me that I would have liked to have done to thumb my nose at society but would never have the guts to do because of my background. So in *No Place* I used his character and then my own straight side as two alter egos to go to battle. I never considered this play to be a black play. I just happened to be a person of color.

WALTER JONES I knew Chuck Gordone from acting and from just living on the Lower East Side in the sixties when he was trying to get his play on. He'd been trying to get it on for seven years. In 1967, we did a showcase version at the Sheridan Square Playhouse, and we'd rehearse in an old hotel on Eighty-sixth Street and Central Park West they were renovating into co-op apartments.

Chuck had been evicted from his house, mainly because he'd spent all his money trying to do showcases of the script. The hotel construction manager knew Chuck and said, "Hey, come and live in the lobby and sort of be the watchman. There's no heating system here, but you can stay for nothing until you get it together."

So Chuck was living in the lobby of this old hotel with his wife and little daughter and no heat while they were doing construction up above—we could hear the jackhammers while we were trying to rehearse. It was really kind of tragic in a sense, but we could see where Chuck was. He was really totally wrapped up into getting his play on, whether he was going to have to live on the street or what.

After the showcase, producers thought it was too long and maybe a little controversial. They didn't want to deal with it, so Chuck went up to Woodstock to do some rewrites. The Public Theater was just getting off the ground then, and I was working there with Ted Cornell on *The Mummer's Play* by Edgar White. I asked Chuck to allow me to show *No Place* to Joe, and he said, "Well, go ahead, but I don't think Joe's gonna like it. I've had it around seven years, I've shown it to everybody, nobody's gonna like it, blah-blah-blah." He had sort of lost a little faith in it.

I gave it to Joe, and Joe looked at it, and about a week later he said, "Hey, look, Walter, it's written in dialect, I really can't read it." I showed some of it to Ted, and Ted could understand the language a little better than Joe, and he said, "This is good. Let's get some actors together and we'll read it for Joe."

So we pulled some actors together, some of them from the Edgar White play, and we read it. Joe could hear the richness of the language and halfway through he got very excited and said, "Yeah, yeah, yeah! I wanna do it!" Right there on the spot he said he wanted to do it. I called Gordone up in Woodstock and he just didn't want to believe it.

"Hey, don't fool me," he said. "Stop jerking me off. I don't want to come down to New York, I'm up in the country. If he's not going to do it, I don't want to be wasting my time."

"Come on down, man."

So he came down and met Ted and everybody, and Joe said that he would like Ted to direct it, and so we got it off.

TED CORNELL Instead of touring "The Naked Hamlet," we'd put it on for the schools in what had been the shul space in the HIAS building, and money from the Board of Education went into building a set of bleachers and installing a very rudimentary lighting system. It's now the Susan Stein Shiva Theater, but then we called it the Other Stage, and I picked, with Joe's consent and active participation, a season of six plays to do down there in line with a small grant Joe had from the Rockefeller Foundation to deal experimentally with new scripts.

At that time, workshops were not a commonplace, and this was, in a way, the beginning of institutional theater. It began very modestly: we would have fifteen, twenty people in the audience. The sixth play that we did there, the last play of the first season, was *No Place to Be Somebody*.

It was brought in by an actor named Walter Jones, who thought it was like the best play he had ever read, something entirely new and different. It was in a mimeographed version, which was very difficult to read. Every sentence was all in capital letters with an exclamation point at the end. And I thought it was just incredible, I couldn't believe it.

It was a play that was both naturalistic and had a high degree of poetic intensity to it. It was poetry from beginning to end. It can seem like a soap opera in places, and it isn't until you see it played with a life-and-death commitment that you realize that the emotions can be sustained, that in fact these people are *that* upset. This play has the characteristic, as do many of Shakespeare's plays, that its people have a dramatic image of themselves, which they act out. You see these people trying to play a role and not always making it.

Joe didn't think a lot of the play when he read it. In fact, I think he only read the first act. It was very hard to read, this mimeographed text must have been the twelve-thousandth copy. But he trusted me, I had the job of looking at these things. He had a lot of other things to think about at the time. But when Joe saw it, he really got to like it.

I've heard complaints from people working with Joe that he is invasive and keeps a very close eye on the production, that he'll come in and see it and go, "I don't like this," and insist on some major change. But always in my experience, he has not come to rehearsals, or very, very rarely. In this case, he saw it, saw what the audience thought of it—with guns going off and people yelling at each other, it was a very electric sensation in that little tiny theater—and made a dramatic decision to offer it for review as a major production.

We'd only had about three and a half weeks of rehearsal, but about half of the people that we used had been in it before, which is one of the reasons we were able to get it done so quickly. But Joe just opened it and took an enormous chance. Because if the thing had not had really good reviews, I think he would have had trouble putting together the next season.

JOSEPH PAPP I didn't want to start doing this production. I didn't have the money for it. I hadn't planned it. But it seemed to have a lot of potential and it played much better than it read. It's a melodrama, so when you get good actors making it real, boy, it's really amazing how well it worked.

Joseph Papp, older sister
Rhoda, and their parents,
Yetta and Samuel
Courtesy of the New York Public Library

PAPIROFSKY, JOSEPH
Class President, President of
Dramatic Society, Assembly Per-
formances, Justice of Student
Court, Semi-Annuals, Debating
Society, "Eastern" Staff, Inter-
grade Basketball, "Gold and
White" Staff, Operetta.
On the stage he has won re-
nown and fame,
All Eastern is familiar with his
name.

Papp's senior yearbook page
from Eastern District High School
in Brooklyn
Courtesy of the New York Public Library

Papp in his Navy uniform
Courtesy of the New York Public Library

Papp with Eulalie Spence, "the person who had the greatest influence on me any teacher ever had"
Courtesy of the New York Public Library

Papp in Los Angeles with Actors' Lab classmates
Courtesy of the New York Public Library

Papp (second from left) as a member of the *I've Got a Secret* team
Courtesy of the New York Public Library

Peggy Bennion Papp and costars William Major and Sylvia Gassell in the
Emmanuel Presbyterian Church production of *As You Like It*
© Ottomar

Julius Caesar at the East River Amphitheater
© George E. Joseph

Colleen Dewhurst and J. D. Cannon in *The Taming of the Shrew* at the East River Amphitheater
© George E. Joseph

WALL ST. COMPLETE — FINAL PRICES

Journal American
AN AMERICAN PAPER FOR THE AMERICAN PEOPLE

No. 25,635—DAILY   THURSDAY, JUNE 19, 1958   10 Cents

7TH SPORTS RACING ★★★★★★
SPORTS COMPLETE

'Voice of America' Broadcaster Takes 5th at Probe

Our Festival Queen

Bares Aid To Goldfine In SEC Case

WASHINGTON, June 19 (AP)—Sen. Frederick G. Payne (R.-Me.) said today he arranged in early 1956 for an attorney for Bernard Goldfine to obtain information from the Securities and Exchange Commission.

He said the information was about a case involving one of Goldfine's companies.

See Brinks Loot Linked To Burke Pal's Slaying

Gangster John Michael Earle, 39, fatally shot yesterday in a W. 97th st. cafeteria, may have been "rubbed out" in an underworld feud over split-up of the million dollar loot in the Brink's Boston holdup.

JOSEPH PAPP
A Balky Witness

The producer of the TV show "I've Got a Secret," who also has made tape recordings for "Voice of America" broadcasts, declined to say today whether he had ever been a Communist Party member.

LATEST NEWS

Report Molotov Ousted as Envoy
WARSAW, June 19 (UPI)—Polish sources reported today that former Soviet Foreign Minister V. M. Molotov has been replaced as Ambassador to Outer Mongolia and is under surveillance in Moscow.

Senate Retains Auto Excise Tax
WASHINGTON, June 19 (AP)—The Senate today rejected a proposal to repeal the 10 per cent excise tax on passenger cars and to halve the 10 per cent levy on trucks and buses.

Report Coast Marine Strike Settled

Red Paper Warns Against Lebanon Aid
MOSCOW, June 19 (UPI)—The newspaper Soviet Russia today warned these planning intervention in Lebanon.

SAME NAME SIMPLIFIED

Ike Reports Upswing Sign

BASEBALL SCORES

Acrobatic Bandits Rob Teller at Bank

Stocks Slump On Tax Action

BELMONT PARK RESULTS

ON THE INSIDE

THE WEATHER — CLEAR

Papp's HUAC testimony was the banner headline in the June 19, 1958,
New York Journal American
Courtesy of the New York Public Library

J. D. Cannon and
Colleen Dewhurst with
neighborhood children,
1956
© George E. Joseph

George C. Scott in *As You
Like It* at the Heckscher
Theater, 1958
Courtesy of the New York
Public Library

Antony and Cleopatra
costars George C. Scott and
Colleen Dewhurst, 1959
© Marjorie Collins

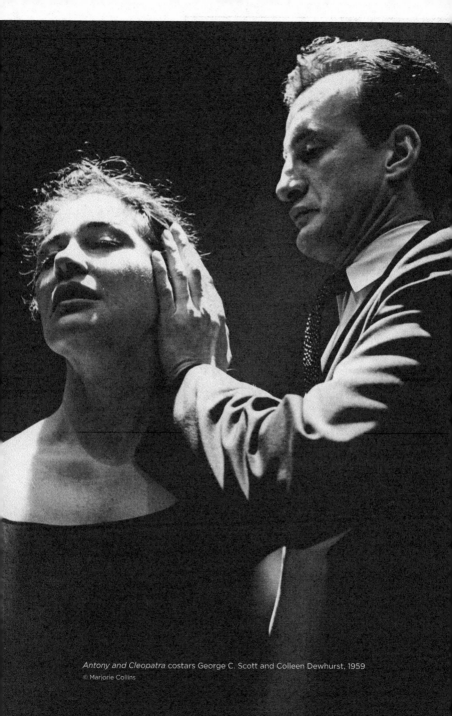

Antony and Cleopatra costars George C. Scott and Colleen Dewhurst, 1959
© Marjorie Collins

Loading the mobile theater
© George E. Joseph

An enthusiastic mobile theater
audience
© Friedman-Abeles

Robert Moses at his most imperial
© Alfred Eisenstaedt/Time & Life Pictures/Getty

The lines formed early for Shakespeare at the Delacorte
© Edward F. D'Arms

(Below) The Delacorte Theater with its Manhattan backdrop
© George E. Joseph

(Below, left) Papp at the Delacorte construction site
Courtesy of the New York Public Library

(Below, right) Papp in front of the Delacorte, 1964
© Dan McCoy

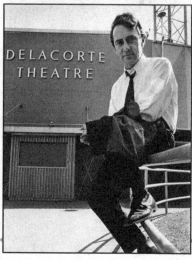

Façade of the Public Theater
© Martha Swope

A scene from *Hair*
© George E. Joseph

Hair's James Rado and Gerome Ragni
© UPI/Corbis

Charles Gordone, winner of the Pulitzer
Prize for *No Place to Be Somebody*
© Friedman-Abeles

(Top and right) Scenes from *No Place
to Be Somebody*
© Friedman-Abeles

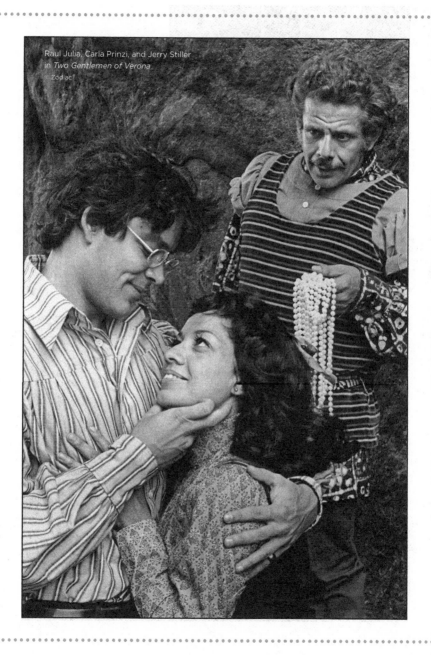

Raul Julia, Carla Prinzi, and Jerry Stiller
in *Two Gentlemen of Verona*.
© Zodiac

David Hooks and Gretchen Corbett
in *The Wars of the Roses*, 1970
© Friedman-Abeles

Donald Madden (foreground) in
The Wars of the Roses, 1970
© Friedman-Abeles

Anne Jackson and Tom Aldredge reflected in Cliff De Young's sunglasses in the CBS-TV production of *Sticks and Bones*
© CBS Photo Archive

Cliff De Young and Hector Elias in *Sticks and Bones*
© Friedman-Abeles

I met the author, quite a distinctive individual who looked half Indian and half black. Even for that time he was outrageous. Plus I felt good having black actors in my theater in numbers. I always feel good when the theater is well represented in terms of any kind of minority group. I feel that I'm doing my work, that I'm part of the city and doing something that's important for the community.

There were so many plays at the time that were "get whitey" plays; arguing that particular point of view was the fashion then for black writers. We did more black plays from black writers than anybody. They could and did show white racism, but I wasn't going to stand there being attacked because I'm white.

I never did any of LeRoi Jones's plays, although they were very good plays, because I felt they were too much just attacking whites for being white. There were too many liberals that just loved being in that position, too many people going around mea culpa-ing all over the place, wanting to hear themselves being attacked, and I didn't care for that too much.

But Gordone's play was more evenhanded, more universal. It showed black people being just as good or as bad as white people, and that was not fashionable, not acceptable in those times. It was such a relief to find a play that said, "Black is not necessarily beautiful, and white is not just terrible."

It was a big play, Shakespearean, almost, in its sprawling nature, with beautifully rich characters and wonderful acting roles. It was pure melodrama, but coming at that time, as a play about black people that didn't put the blame for all their problems on white people, that was quite interesting to me.

TED CORNELL Chuck Gordone was a person for whom I had enormous respect as somebody who was out there on his own as an artist. He was a denizen of off Broadway who was not making a living, the kind of bandit you had to be in order to keep it going. Incredibly high energy, just manic energy. Extremely verbal, extremely argumentative and confrontational.

Chuck did not want to write about an acceptable version of blacks. He always said that he wrote about "niggers," and when he wrote about that aspect of black life, it was condemned by black intellectuals as being a sellout. Clayton Riley wrote a piece in the *Times* called "O, Blacks, Are We

Damned Forever?" Chuck portrayed an underclass on its own terms and didn't try to pretend that it was not an underclass. He acknowledged its separateness and its inability to find a place for itself.

I think Chuck originally brought the play in just to have a place to do it, and he basically wanted me to leave it alone. He didn't want anybody else to direct it, let alone a twenty-four-year-old white man.

I grew up in an all-white neighborhood in a suburb of Boston, and although I had an enormous sense of not being as experienced as the people in the play, it didn't seem to me that there were things in there I didn't recognize. In apparently privileged situations, there can be enormous senses of oppression on an individual basis, and that was how I saw my life. So I thought, presumptuously, but nonetheless apparently accurately, that there were things about it that I understood. And also, I knew enough to draw on what the actors thought, as well as what the playwright had.

Chuck constantly insisted, and quite rightly, that the play always be confrontational, hence always the capital letters, always the exclamation points. He was all the time saying in rehearsals, "Do your thing, do the shit and get on off of there." I kept trying to work out what was going on around that impatience, and it would get too maudlin, and so we'd slam it back together again at an intense level. And that dialectic made for an extraordinarily live event.

I think another thing that made that production a success was that I insisted on the casting of Ron O'Neal for the Gabe part. It was a blindness in Chuck not to understand what his game was, what his strengths were. He saw him as effeminate, and tended to cast people who were weak in that role. He saw that role as losing to Johnny, and I insisted that it be played by somebody who was a match for Johnny.

There were any number of conflicts on that level, and the rehearsals were very much an argumentation about the play, which then translated into the arguments that were in the play. One of the things which I still say to casts came up at that time: "The energy that you're putting into this argument has to be at *least* as great as the energy you're putting into the play."

People tend to get energetic about the arguments and then go onstage and be very calm about talking about life and death. There was always the demand that that degree of commitment and energy be part of what was on the stage as well, so that those two things were the same thing.

CHARLES GORDONE   I liked Joe immediately. Joe's for Joe, he's surely going to win out somehow, but I don't have any bad words for him. He always dealt with me horse-to-horse. He was a very determined man, didn't let anything get in his way, and I identified with that immediately. He wasn't one of those straight, John-loves-Mary type of producers. He was just starting out and looking to do a different kind of theater, looking to take a chance. I was poor as hell, and he gave me $100 and I said, "Hell, let him go ahead and do it. I mean, nobody else wants it." The $100 he gave me for the play was $100 well spent.

Ted and I got along well, but I thought he was like a dummy. He was a nice kid and he was fresh out of Yale, you see, and he didn't know *what* to do with these people. And they came to him with knowledge *of* the play, because they had done it in showcase and had followed me during those years. We just took that cast and shoved it right in there. So what could he direct? I would talk to him about some of the deeper meanings in the play, but I had more frustration than he did. Because here I was, trying to direct the play through him. It was a terrible experience for me.

He didn't know anything about guns. He didn't know anything about these kinds of people. I thought it was really stupid, but Joe is one of these fellows that is as good as his word, and he'd given this fellow his word, so there was nothing to do. But I had to be there.

Joe said, "You ought to be there with him," because these people were like maniacs. You see, the play brings out certain things in people, and there were times when people would get into it in rehearsals, and he wouldn't know how to handle that. I knew the guts of the actors, and of course I knew the guts of the characters in the play, and I would push them no end. And the tension, sometimes you could cut it with a knife. I've directed some two or three hundred plays, but I've never had the kind of excitement and energy and creative tension that went on through that period of rehearsal.

WALTER JONES Chuck was so close to *No Place*—it was his baby that he'd created for seven years—he didn't want to let it go. During rehearsal, Chuck was always around, bothering the actors and messing with them, looking like he was really trying to stop the production from going on. He would give his opinions—you knew he was there. When he was sensible, a lot of the actors got a lot from him, he was very profound. But he would just go sometimes.

One night he came in and smacked this girl. He would take a lot of his anxieties out on the female actors, the girls who were playing the prostitutes.

One day he came in with this little two-shot derringer. He waved it at people, saying, "I'll shoot you! I'll shoot you!" He didn't put it in anybody's face, but he had it up there. He just wanted everybody to see that "I'm a gangster." He had these guys with him that he must have met someplace up in Harlem that looked like gangsters. You'd say, "Where did Chuck find this one?" He was really a show, man. Chuck was a show.

He was doing everything he could to keep Nathan George, who played Johnny, and Ron O'Neal at each other's throats, fighting each other. He was trying to get them to really hate each other because that's the way the roles were written. These guys were telling him, "We don't need that, Chuck," but I don't think they liked each other anyway. There was a lot of jealousy there, and Chuck had the insight to see that and he kept it brewing.

Even after the show was running and it was hitting and everybody felt secure, Chuck kept bugging Nathan and Ron. One time, the stage manager had just given the five-minute call, and Nathan looked through the dressing-room door and here comes Chuck running in. "Oh shit," he said, "not before I first go on." Chuck went up to him and began to say, "Nathan, I want you to . . . ," and before he could get it out, Nathan just smacked him. It was instinctive. One lick, man, and he fell, out cold for three minutes, he was on the floor. So they picked him up and took him out and he never really came back to the dressing room to mess with anybody.

All this craziness going on, man, and Joe would never come around. He would come by the door, peep in, and then go on. He would leave. It was like, "Don't come to me. As soon as you show up, I'm going to run back upstairs." He understood what was going on, but he saw that he had a good play, that he had some good actors in it, and he didn't feel that Chuck would be destructive enough to stop the play. Chuck would amuse Joe. Joe would look at him and say, "Let me see how far he's going to go this time." I really think Joe, deep down, got a kick out of watching.

Right up until maybe the day before we opened, Chuck was giving actors little notes and cutting their lines and adding another line. Finally, the actors and Ted were starting to get a little paranoid about it. They said, "Hey, Chuck, man, the work is *finished*. Stop rewriting these little things right up to the last minute." So he did, but he was still on people's throats right up until the opening.

The critics were very good and it hit everybody by surprise. Chuck never believed they were going to like us. He had this "They don't understand the damn thing, they're not going to understand it" attitude. I was surprised. I thought they would probably say, "Hey, this is a militant play. The man is yellin' and shoutin' and screamin'." But, no, the front-line critics focused right on what Chuck had there in the script, that he was dealing with human behavior and human relationships, which superseded the black-white thing. They were keen enough to see that, hey, there's a piece of heart here.

During the main run, when we moved to the Anspacher Theater, Chuck would be up in the balcony, on the floor, listening, line by line. We could hear him up there, grunting, "Move it along there, move it on, move it on." I mean, he would be up there mumblin' and grumblin'. One night I dropped a line; I got in the middle and I just went blank. And he threw me the cue from the balcony, and I said, "Oh, yeah." I don't know if people thought he was a prompter or what.

CHARLES GORDONE I was out of my skull at the time. At one point, a new stage manager was hired, and he changed something that I didn't know about, and I went up to him and raised hell about it. He said, "Bernie Gersten told me to do this," and I came down on Bernie about it. So I'm asleep in bed and Joe gives me a call and says, "Look here, Bernie's my right-hand man. The way you carried on and spoke to him, I'll yank this play tonight." And he does it as if he's saying, "Would you mind passing me the spinach?"

Around that time they asked me to play the sea captain in *Twelfth Night* in Central Park. I was always showing up late. I was being rough with the boy that I was playing with. I was really down because I didn't get a chance to direct *No Place*, so I hit the bottle pretty heavy. And Joe fired me because I was always late. He just took me upstage and said, "Look, man, I can't use you anymore in this." And the play was going on at the time.

That was a big blow, because I had never in my whole career been fired from an acting job. And then when I heard he'd fired Al Pacino, too, I didn't feel so bad. I told Al, "I guess I joined your club. You don't ever get too big for your britches with Joe. You can be replaced by two small boys and a singing commercial."

JOSEPH PAPP   Chuck came in to me and he said, "I have something that's going to make you very proud."

"What is it?"

"I'm going to get the Pulitzer Prize."

I was stunned. I felt so good. I thought, "Gee, that's remarkable." I remembered the Pulitzer Prize from when I was a kid and interested in becoming a journalist; it was always an important, high-class sort of award. And I also felt good that a black dramatist had won it for the first time in history for something that was in my theater. I felt very proud of him.

WALTER JONES   Once Chuck got the Pulitzer, it really took him overboard. He went out, man, his mind went on another plane. All of a sudden he became a spokesman for the black race, this Malcolm X character saying, "I'll tell you about where the black race has been." He began to do a lot of interviews, he became accessible to everybody.

He took on all these other responsibilities that he really didn't need, and he got away from writing. He started to travel and lecture. He became an entertainer and he didn't write that next play. It did a lot of good, but it did a lot of harm to him as a writer, a lot of harm. He hasn't really completed a play since then.

CHARLES GORDONE   Everybody knew before I did. It's strange, I didn't feel anything. It's only a year or so after you've won it that it begins to sink in. And once it begins to sink in, you begin to get very paranoid. You wonder if you can ever write like that again—can you go back to feeling like you felt when you were writing it?

And, of course, everything I put on paper smacked of *No Place*. And I said, "This is not it. I can't go back and co-opt myself." It's like writing a hit song and then going back and trying to write another hit song. You think of some of the same melody and some of the same phrasings, words, whatever—I couldn't do that.

So I made several furtive attempts to write for other people. I wrote for Hollywood, I wrote some articles, I did a one-man recital at Carnegie Hall, I lectured around, I talked about the play all over the place, but every time I sat down to the typewriter, it all sounded like *No Place*. I never stayed off the typewriter, but I couldn't write like I used to. It was a terrible experience, and I went through that for almost twenty years.

JOSEPH PAPP During the sixties and early seventies, at the beginning of black revolutionary consciousness, we were right in the middle of it. Since I was involved in producing black and Hispanic plays, I ran up against some inflamed passions. I've had more knives pointed at me than you can imagine.

Since I was the leading theater producing plays for black writers, there was competitiveness and jealousy, plus I was expected to solve everyone's problems. One guy in particular, he'd started a theater in Brooklyn, he claimed I had stolen James Earl Jones from him, which was ridiculous. And this guy said he was going to get me.

One time about ten twenty or so in the evening, Bernie Gersten and I were coming out of the Russian Tea Room and here is this guy. He'd just come from Brooklyn, where there'd been a big riot, blood was pouring down the side of his face, and he grabbed me and put me up against the door of Carnegie Hall. "Son a bitch," he said, "I'm gonna kill you," and he started to press on my throat. And thank god, at that precise moment, the concert let out from Carnegie Hall, people began to come out, and he sort of walked away. I couldn't breathe. I thought he was going to kill me.

Another situation was with an actor I'd befriended. He'd been in one or two of my plays. He brought me a play he'd written and said, "I want to do this in your theater." I read it and said, "No, I don't like this play." And he said, "You're gonna do this play." I said no. He said he wanted to show me how good it was and I agreed to attend a performance to be put on for me by a group called the Matches.

I came in, I sat down, and they locked the doors. I was the only one in the theater, and it was a very violent play. They had guys with guns, characters yelling, "You white son of a bitch!" Bang! Bang! Blank shots going off, guns pointed at me. I was quaking in my boots. I didn't know when the bullet was going to be real. Comes to the end, I'm unharmed, and I said, "I'm not going to do this play."

There was a big meeting in my office, and I just said, "This is still America, and you can't force me to do a play I don't want to do." The playwright was furious. He said, "We're going to burn this fucking place down." There were threats that came in every day, on paper, signed the Matches, but nothing was ever burned.

The funniest threat I ever received was first thing one morning when I went to the men's room at the Public and saw seven white cocks. Each one had a little sign around its neck, saying "We're going to kill Joe Papp."

They were beautiful birds, must have cost a lot of money, and my first thought was, "Jesus, what do we do with all these cocks? They should go to the prop shop or something." I was going to pass on it, but Gail made inquiries to the police department and their experts said that seven cocks had a mystical meaning and that this was indeed a death threat. I was more concerned with how the hell they got those damn things into that room.

13

The Happiness Cage
1970

Martin Sheen and
Dennis Reardon
Courtesy of Dennis Reardon

The Happiness Cage concerns an experiment to control our brainwaves electrically, and induce schematic, prefabricated happiness in human beings whose natural right it is to be individualized, and fractious and, when appropriate, unhappy. The Army is, obviously, very interested in the application of this leveling of the mental landscape to efficient soldiering, and the experiments are conducted under the auspices of a general in a veterans' hospital by a zealous neurosurgeon, Dr. Freytag. Opposing this cerebral regimentation is a lowly ex-GI, Reese, in the hospital with a broken arm. An intellectual without family, slightly paranoid, usually less than effectual in times of crisis, Reese is intelligent and courageous in his stand against mechanized and electrified philanthropy. Reese is an entirely believable contemporary hero, whose heroism is thrust upon him rather like a strait jacket . . .

Reardon not only writes totally assured dialogue—succulent, pointed, literate without being literary, and finding the rock-bottom poetry even in inarticulateness—he can also, best of all, make a philosophical debate catch fire on stage, as in the shattering, dialectical showdown between Dr. Freytag and Reese. Playwriting that can do that has everything and will travel . . . The production is the best Joseph Papp's Public Theater has given us since its inception with the original, non-O'Horganized *Hair*.

John Simon, *New York* magazine, October 14, 1970

DENNIS REARDON   I was on Okinawa during Vietnam. While I was in the service, I finished a script I'd been working on off and on for about four years. It was a heavily researched play. I did a lot of work on experiments in this field dating back to 1955. I went on leave to Japan, and I shipped the play off to my agent, Audrey Wood, who was also Tennessee Williams's agent at the time.

When I came back, there was a letter waiting for me, saying that she had sold it to a guy named Joe Papp. I'd never heard of the man in my life. She said something about "he did Shakespeare in the park," as if that was supposed to explicate the whole situation for me. I was from the Midwest, Kansas, Iowa, I didn't know anything about theater, except how to write plays. I had no conception at all of who he was.

Anyway, my immediate reaction was not that I'd sold a play, but "Can this guy get me out of the army early? Is there some way that I can maneuver this around so that he can get me out of this goddamn place?" So I proposed it to my agent, and Joe sent me a letter saying, "We want to begin rehearsals on January 15, and we will not do this play if Mr. Reardon is unavailable for rehearsals."

So I gleefully took this letter to a couple of colonels in the building I was working in, the power center for the island. I knew there was a regulation which had, from Revolutionary times on, permitted farm boys to go home in time to plant crops. It was called "early release for seasonal employment" and it was still on the books. I went to these colonels and I said, "Jeez, guys, you know, here it is, this is a New York producer, and he says he's not gonna do this thing if I'm not back there in time for it."

And one colonel looked at the other colonel and said, "Well, Joe, I don't know—didn't we just let some son of a bitch go last week so he could get back in time for fishin' season off the Florida coast?"

"Yeah, I recollect we did that."

"Well, I don't see how he's no different than that guy was."

So Joe got me out of the army seventy days early. It may not sound like much, but it's two and a half months of getting up at four in the morning and running in combats on concrete for several miles, and I was real indebted to him.

JOSEPH PAPP The whole topic of *The Happiness Cage* was of great interest, you couldn't believe it was going on, and I was always conscious that things like this should be revealed. But it wasn't just the topic. Essentially I was fascinated by the power of this writer. Dennis always reminded me of Strindberg a little bit, in terms of the pain.

I love writers who put their bodies on the line, because that's the way I work. Boy, can I feel that. Dennis is one of those writers. He never tells a lie. It's all truth—painful, dug out of his bowels. He was one of the most powerful writers we had, outside of David Rabe. I thought Dennis had power that was extraordinary.

DENNIS REARDON I got out of the army on December 31, 1969, New Year's Eve, and ten days later I was in New York City. I was so disoriented. I'd never set foot in New York before. I was scared of the subways; everything looked like a slum to me. I still had short hair and I was saluting everything that moved.

Joe had a desk the size of the state of Montana and there were placards all over the walls, but I still didn't know enough to be in awe or even to be impressed by him. And Joe had not acquired the kind of nimbus which was eventually to surround him. He struck me as the stereotypical, prototypical, archetypical producer. I mean, everything I had ever imagined a producer to be, he was.

He was sitting there with this big stogie, this big fucking cigar, and he's saying, "Read your play and really loved it. Have a cigar." And he hands me this thing, about a yard and a half long.

I understood you were supposed to bite one end off and it was supposed to work, but I didn't know which one. I picked an end to bite, and it got all into my teeth and tongue. He's talking away and all I'm thinking is, "I got tobacco all inside my mouth here. It tastes like hell." And in the first five minutes of my conversation with the great man, I had to stop and say, "Uh—excuse me, I gotta go find a restroom."

I'm wandering around the theater, looking for a place to spit this tobacco out of my mouth. I found a restroom with an open window in it and I remember vividly tossing this goddamn stogie about four stories down into a snowbank and going on back and finishing my conversation with him.

I have very little recollection of what materially transpired. All I know is, he was giving me names of actors that he had hired, none of whom meant jack *shit* to me. It turned out they were the biggest names in the business, but I thought, "This is routine, this is how things work."

Nothing surprised me, nothing amazed me, and nothing really embarrassed me. I was in a state of absolute blessed naïveté in January of 1970. I was unimpressed by everything, including myself. So he was telling me, "Yeah, I got Marty Sheen lined up, and Charles Durning, and a wonderful guy named Ronny Cox," and I'm thinking, "Jesus, he went ahead and cast this without even asking me?"

I was such a novice at this—I had literally never even heard a play of mine read out loud before. Suddenly I'm sitting around a table with guys like Marty Sheen and Charlie Durning and they're reading my words. Well, it's a staggering moment for a playwright. It's very hard to describe. You feel immensely flattered, you feel somewhat odd, you feel a little as if you're in a dream. I had not thought of myself as a playwright up till then.

TOM ALDREDGE Another director who had directed a lot of plays was assigned to it, but he had some personal feelings about the play, he couldn't approach it. Somehow, my name came up, and they let me read it. Oh, I just fell in love with it. It was antiauthority, anti-army, antigovernment, and it was also the loner against the world, which is what Joe is.

We started out doing it as just a workshop production, with Marty Sheen as Reese. I had been in *Indians* on Broadway with a bit player called Ronny Cox. He was terrified of acting, but I knew that he could be wonderful. I showed him the part of Miles, another hospitalized soldier, and he said, "Oh, it's too big. I've never played that big a role. I can't play it." I said, "Yes, you can."

I gave Charlie Durning his big break, because Joe had always cast Charlie as the Shakespearean fool. I knew Charlie better; we had become very close friends acting together in those years. I knew the rage that was in him. I knew Charlie shouldn't be playing fools. So I cast him in this terrifying role as the orderly.

CHARLES DURNING I had a scene with Marty Sheen where I was supposed to attack him. I hit him with a chair, and I hit him with a table, but I was completely under control. Because I'd had some war experiences, and sometimes you revert, Marty thought I was gone, he thought I was a little bonkers. He asked me under his breath during a couple of performances, "Are you all right?"

During one rehearsal, Joe had to move back about five rows from the first row, it was too brutal. He said to me, "I would love to see you lose your temper one time," and I said, "No, you don't want to see that, Joe."

When a movie of the play was made, people would tell Ronny Cox that the scene when the orderly goes berserk was frightening.

"You still watched it, though, didn't you?" Ronny said.

"Yeah."

"When Charlie Durning played it, you couldn't watch it."

JOSEPH PAPP Charlie scared me in that play. With all that jollity and joviality, there is tremendous rage in him. I'm sure he was an excellent soldier. I'm sure he didn't hesitate to kill anybody, because he had that in him. And this play brought that out; it generated that kind of feeling. When Charlie was ferocious, he was acting to the uttermost; he put his whole self into it. He played a sadistic, fearful person, and I couldn't bear to watch him.

DENNIS REARDON We opened in February as a workshop production in the Other Stage, and it was in many ways the best production the play received. The major crisis in January was, "Do we invite critics or do we pull this thing back and go for the full shot in the fall?" And the decision was made that it was working very well and it should be given a big-shot production.

In fact, it opened the Newman Theater, we inaugurated that. By that time, I was like Mr. Big Shot, "I've been through this before, I know what it's all about," giving advice to all these tinhorns like David Rabe and Robert Montgomery who were coming in and taking a look around. I'd tell them where it was all at.

GAIL MERRIFIELD PAPP The Newman is kind of a flagship theater, and to open it with a play of this sort was an interesting choice by Joe, certainly a problematic choice for a lot of people. Theatergoers who liked to go out and have a pleasant evening at this new, very lovely looking theater with the nice exposed brick were not going to be terribly, terribly happy with this choice. It was a different kind of play entirely.

MARTIN SHEEN Joe asked me to come and do the part when they had a full-fledged production with paying customers, but I didn't do that. I couldn't afford it. I'd left my babies and my wife in California, we'd just moved out there the previous year, maybe two. I was struggling there, and I couldn't divide myself that much.

DENNIS REARDON We were like two and a half weeks into rehearsal when Joe called us in and said he wanted to fire the leading man. Tom and I were just real reluctant to take that drastic a step. Joe is very used to hiring and firing, but we were thinking, "What does it do to the rest of the company? It's a very disruptive decision. Let's take the gamble that he's going to come across in the next week and a half." Tom and I got together and said, "Let's make a commitment." So we overruled Joe.

And I'll be goddamned if Joe wasn't right. We should have fired him. We absolutely should have fired him, and we lacked the chutzpah, the balls to do it. And it cost the show a lot. It threw it out of whack. For all his pleasant, amicable qualities, he was overwhelmed by these actors. He became subordinate to characters that should have been subordinate. Ronny Cox walked away with the show by miles. Charlie Durning got great notices. In fact, I really launched their film careers. They just ran away with the show.

Nevertheless, the show got reviews that I subsequently realized playwrights kill for, which I was too stupid to realize at the time. I mean, I couldn't even enjoy them. I thought, "What's this Clive Barnes says in paragraph seven, what is this modifier, this qualifying phrase here?" *God*, you look back on it and you think, "How could I have been so stupid as to not at least seize the moment?" But you don't know what the moment is until it's past.

That was not the last time in my life that I've been wrong and Joe's been right. That's why I'm now real, real hesitant to overrule him at any time. He can come in with the most cockamamie idea, and you've got to give it some consideration. He can be absolutely dead wrong or be dead right, and you never know which it's going to be.

It's sort of like going to the Delphic Oracle and hearing something get spewed out and trying to make sense of it in terms of the context of your own life and situation. You have to read everything he says with the full knowledge that he can be making a very insightful remark.

JASON MILLER Tom Aldredge hired me to understudy Lou Stadlen in *The Happiness Cage*. And Lou, who's a sweet, sweet man, said to me one day, "You want to go on for me? If you really want to go on for me, you want some people to come and see it, I'll let you know the day. I'll get sick and you go ahead on." Oh, he was a prince.

And A. J. Antoon, who didn't know me, happened to be there the performance I went on. He came back and said, "I was really impressed by the performance. I'm doing a thing called *Subject to Fits* by Robert Montgomery. Could you come and read for us?" I said, "Certainly," and about three weeks later I read and I got the role of Rogozhin. And that began my friendship with A.J. that led to *That Championship Season*.

14

Fund-raising, Fiscal Crisis, and the Buyback

Bernard Gersten and Papp watching a parade in front of the Public
Courtesy of the New York Public Library

One: Raising Cain

GERALD SCHOENFELD   Joe came to Princeton in 1974 for the first American Congress of Theater. When it was his turn to speak, he got up and said, "You know what the theater's all about?" Everybody leaned forward. "Money, money, money, money, money." That, of course, brought the house down. This is a business, a tough business, and if you don't operate as a business, then you can't survive.

ROBERT MONTGOMERY   Joe's the greatest money-raiser in New York. He is *superb* at that, there's nobody like him. You always knew somehow or other that the son of a bitch was going to do it, and he did. He has drive, energy, and conviction. He's never done anything that he wasn't convinced was the right thing, and by god he's going to persuade whoever else he has to persuade. And they believe him. People just have total confidence in Joe, and rightly so. They know he'll spend their money well, and that he'll accomplish something for it.

CLIVE BARNES   In terms of funding, Joe knows exactly where to go, where to move to, and who to move with. He is *very* adroit in this way—it's a sixth sense he has. I admire him enormously for it because, unhappily, one of the main things that the arts entrepreneur has to do in the modern world is to get the money in. Unless he gets the money in, whatever taste he exhibits isn't going to be very much use.

Joe has always understood the necessity of expansion—not the desirability of expansion but the actual necessity. He's always had a very clear idea that an arts organization is a living organism, and it's either growing, developing, and maturing or it's falling, decaying. The curve is either going up or it's going down.

He's always had this wonderful ability to think big—he realized that it's easier in many respects to raise $5 million than to raise $1 million—and this, I think, made him a very attractive funding prospect. He always had the courage of his convictions. Sometimes he had the courage of other people's convictions as well.

MICHAEL MORIARTY   Joe knows up front there's no way theater, like opera or ballet, can exist as a commercial venture. He's not going to play the game that you can turn a buck. He can turn a buck with success, but the kinds of things he wants to do have to be funded. And his social conscience has a great way of inflicting guilt on wealthy people. I think he really has a talent at that.

I've been at some of those benefit parties where sponsors and benefactors are around, and he certainly doesn't move humbly through them. He moves as a peer. I don't sense any disdain on his part, or superiority, but I don't sense that he is on his knee, like a poor painter into the Medici thing, "Oh, thank you, thank you." The gift to inspire the artists to work for nothing and the rich to give away all their money, there's a genius involved there.

PEGGY BENNION PAPP Material things are the last things in the world that he cares about. Every time there was a board meeting, and the board wanted to raise his salary, for many years Joe would say, even though he had two children, "Thank you, but no. I'm not going to take that money because I need it for the theater." And I would back him up. I would say, "I agree with you, that's good, we don't need the money." Although we did.

He had a profound belief that what he was doing was important, and he was a marvelous fund-raiser because of that. Rather than thanking people, he wasn't above insulting them and making them embarrassed that they hadn't given more. This was something that was so important, this was for everybody, why should he be grateful to them for giving him money? I remember him turning to someone who had given him a $10,000 check and saying, "You ought to be ashamed of yourself for giving me so little." That was always his attitude.

Yet he hated fund-raising. He used to say to me, "Oh, god, Peggy, I can't do that anymore. I just can't go out and do that again." But he had to. He hated begging, pleading, and he hated a lot of the people he had to beg from. It was humiliating and demeaning. He'd felt very demeaned in his childhood, and he never got over it.

CLIVE BARNES Joe asked me to help him do some fund-raising with Rebecca Harkness. Rebecca was a very, very, very rich woman. She poured a fortune—and when I say a fortune, I mean something in the region of $20 million—into dance over her career. And really got absolutely nothing out of it. She was well meaning, I suppose, but very, very arrogant with surprisingly little taste.

Joe, of course, noticed Rebecca Harkness, his antennae went up, and he rushed to handle it. We also had a relationship, Joe and myself. At that time we were fairly buddy-buddy and close, and because I knew Rebecca, Joe asked me to come and help him with fund-raising.

Rebecca was living at the Westbury Hotel, and we were summoned to this huge duplex apartment she had there, with masses of staff. We were kept waiting, which was very disturbing to Joe. As the minutes count up, he goes into overdrive and gets very, very tense.

Eventually she came, sweating from a ballet class she had been taking and drinking a diet cola. She asked if we'd like something to drink, and for some reason Joe said, "Brandy." I remember she produced some Courvoisier, which Joe sniffed and complained that it wasn't Rémy Martin. "Now," I thought, "this is really getting the whole thing off onto a good level."

We spent, I suppose, about three hours with her and, to my amazement, Joe was very, very aggressive. This was the first time I'd really seen him at work with a funding prospect, almost a funding quarry, and he went at it with such energy. He started to insult her, started telling her that she owed the Public Theater money, that she owed this and owed that, that her ballet company was no good, that she was wasting her money, et cetera, et cetera.

I, too, got in on the act and started to insult her. We were both drinking masses of brandy; the fact is that we finished the lot off. In a matter of about two and a half hours, we finished off what had been this unopened bottle. By the end we were almost screaming abuse at this woman, who took it rather meekly.

When we got outside, it must have been five o'clock on a rather gray, chilly afternoon. Joe looked at me, and I looked at him, and we kind of giggled in a certain kind of tipsy pleasure.

"Well," he said, "we really told her, didn't we?"

"Yeah, we really told her. We *really* told her. But do you think it did any good?"

"Oh yes. No doubt, no doubt. We'll get a fortune out of this. I'm not looking for a million. I'm looking for big, big bucks."

"Oh."

Of course, the outcome was that he never got a penny from her. As far as I know, he never heard a word from her again. But that was Joe, that was his mixture of technique and aggression.

JOSEPH PAPP This is the only institution of this scale in the city of New York that was started from the bottom by a poor boy and worked its way up. All the other major, established institutions were started by big money. This began from ground zero. There's nothing comparable.

Everybody, particularly newspaper reporters in the beginning, would look at me very strangely. "Come on, now," they said. "Why are you doing this? *Why* are you doing this?" I got those kinds of questions and I said, "I'm doing it because I love it." I was consumed by an idea. They thought I had something in mind, something that went to my own opportunistic advantage.

When I started the festival, I didn't take any money. In fact, for five or six years, I contributed my own salary because people were working for nothing. Even after I left my job at CBS, I still felt very funny about taking any money. I was raising money on the so-called Socialist line, asking people to sacrifice, to contribute money without expecting anything back in return, and if I'm getting money, I'd find it difficult to ask other people to do something for nothing, or just to do something for a low wage.

Even now, anything that I do on the outside, fees and everything else, goes to the Shakespeare Festival. If someone gave me $50 million now, I would not pass it on to my children. I would build some cultural institutions. I don't want anybody to ever possibly make the accusation that I have done something for money.

I met with a guy from the Mellon Foundation once and he was resisting. "Wait a second," I said. "Let's understand each other. You need me. You can't exist without me. I make foundations possible. You have to spend your money. It's so decreed by law. I'm giving you the opportunity to put money into something that's very important." I never felt I was doing anybody a favor, and they weren't doing me a favor, either. It was quid pro quo all the time.

Two: Herta Danis and LuEsther T. Mertz

HERTA DANIS I was a fund-raiser—that's what I did for a living. My husband was an accountant who took care of a number of theater people, and one night I did a little party for one of his clients. She called a couple of months later and said, "Listen, I just had lunch with a very interesting fellow who is having trouble raising money for his theater project. His name is Joe Papp. He's stuck up in this Heckscher Foundation building on Fifth Avenue and a-hundred-and-something street, there's no room for him anywhere. Do me a favor. Go talk to him. Have lunch with him. Just talk to him, that's all."

We made a date and I went up to his so-called office, which was the box office of the theater. That was the only space he had. His bookkeeper, David Black, was behind the curtain on the stage—that was his space. It was crazy. But Joe didn't care, that was not important to him. He would have stayed there forever because it was rent-free.

I spoke with him for at least an hour or two, and he was a very enchanting young man, a tremendous personality. He engaged you all the time. And he would look at you and say such outrageous things.

"Tell me something about your relationship with the community," I said. "You fight with everybody, you fight with Moses—"

"Everybody likes me."

I didn't laugh, I just didn't believe him, that's all. "Anything you want, I'll get you," he said. "You want the Queen of England? I'll ask her." And he would have, he had that kind of chutzpah. Without it, he never would have gotten where he did, there's no question about that.

After a few weeks of being up at the Heckscher, I said, "Joe, we can't stay here. There is no way we can work from 104th Street. Nobody's going to come up here. And if they came up, where would I put them to sit down? I want an office in the Fifties, in the Sixties, anyplace downtown."

"How the hell can we afford that?"

"Someone has to put up the money. Let's go see Burt Martinson," who was the chairman of the board of directors.

"Crummy is fine," I told him, "I don't care. It doesn't have to be fancy. Just let it be in midtown, where people will come to the office." Burt thought that was a wonderful idea, so we found space in a crummy hotel called the Great Northern on Fifty-seventh Street.

I went to see George Delacorte. I have told Joe many times that he got away with murder with the Delacorte being named for him. It didn't cost him very much to get that little plum, so he owed him. I came with a yellow pad—I never did anything without my yellow pad.

"Mrs. Danis," he said. "What can I do for you?"

"There isn't a lot you can do for me, Mr. Delacorte, but there's a lot you can do for the festival."

"Like what?"

"Like raise some money."

"Raise money? I've never raised money for anything."

"That's wonderful."

"What's wonderful about it?"

"Because I'm sure you give money to everybody in town, and if you've never asked them before, this is the moment, and it's great."

Joe was good at fund-raising because his whole heart was in this project, and when your heart is in a project, and you talk about it, you're good at it. If you don't like it, you're not good at it.

Yet Joe hated to do fund-raising. He *hated* it. He loathed it. And I couldn't do it for him, without him. They don't want to see me. They don't want to hear from me. I'm nobody. They wanted to hear from Joe Papp. I couldn't get this through his head—that he was the one that had to be there, he was the one who had to speak, not me. If I said, "You have to come to this meeting, you have to make this appeal," he'd say, "Are you out of your mind? That's what I've got you for." And I'd say, "No, you haven't."

There was a time he wouldn't put on a tuxedo for anything. That was too bourgeois. Once he arrived at a fund-raising function at a private club with dirty boots.

"You can't go to a meeting with shoes like that," I said.

"What's the matter with them?"

"They're dirty."

He thought I had some nerve to tell him that, but I did anyway. I always told him. He tried to brush off some of the dirt, but after that he came with clean shoes. You want to be a character, that's fine, but you can carry that too far. So be a character, wear dirty shoes on the weekends, but not at a meeting, that's all.

When we finally bought the Public Theater, it was a mess. You never saw such a mess like that place was. In the middle of all this, I said, "We should have a party here," and we did. We called it "Saved from the Wreckers Ball" and it was wonderful.

In the course of making up an invitation list, I put in a lot of names who were not contributors because you never know what will attract people. It was a $500 ticket, and one lady responded with a check for $2,500 for five. I was very pleased to see that money come in from her, and the night of the party I said to Burt Martinson, "When this lady comes in, I will introduce you, and please take her hand and be nice, because there's a lot of money there." It was LuEsther Mertz.

The first time I saw her after that was at a committee meeting, and I said, "Joe, get over there and talk to LuEsther." And, lo and behold, he and Bernie got invited to a party at LuEsther's house. Joe showed me this thing and said, "Who the hell wants to go to all this crappy stuff?"

"You go," I said. "It's important. *Go.*"

He went and it turned out to be very important in his life. LuEsther is just a very nice lady, and very generous, and crazy for Joe. The festival suddenly became like a child to her, it gave her a life she didn't have before. When we had a crisis, I said, "Call LuEsther first." She was at the top of the list.

LUESTHER T. MERTZ I'd heard about Joe before I met him. It was the David and Goliath story—the little guy who was giving plays with a truck in the park versus the great Robert Moses who said, "You can't do it unless you charge." And Joe defied him and did it anyway, said he was never going to charge, and that's really when some of the moneyed people in town began to get interested. That gave him the first lift.

My daughter and her husband were looking for a small theater to get interested in, and I went with them to a party in the Anspacher for the opening of the Public Theater. It was delightful. Joe called me and in a friendly manner said, "What did you think of our establishment?" He asked if I'd like to make a contribution, and I said yes, I would, and I did.

This wasn't an enormous one, but it evidently was a little more than he expected. Somewhere along the line, he asked me to come on the board, and I said, "What can *I* do on the board? I don't have any talents. And I won't go on a board just to be a name."

I wasn't very sophisticated then about what happens when you're on the board. I visualized that they rolled up their sleeves and did secretarial work and stuff. I said to Herta Danis, "I don't see how I can be useful." And she said, "Look, just go on it and you'll find out later that you are useful in one way or another." So I believed her and I did, and I've been on it ever since.

Joe kept saying, "I'm going to name a theater after you."

"No, you're not."

"Yes, I am."

"No, you're *not*, now. I'm not going to have it." This went on for a couple of years and one day he said he was turning one of the upstairs halls into another theater and it was going to be named after me.

"Absolutely not," I said.

"Well, I'm going to do it anyway."

Joe wouldn't really do that if it came down to it and we had a squabble over it, but I finally gave in because he was so determined about it. I said, "I will make a deal with you: you can use my first name." It's called LuEsther Hall and I said, "They'll all be saying, 'Who is that LuEsther Hall?' " That way, strangers don't know who I am, and that suits me fine. I'm low-key. I don't like publicity.

Let's face it, Joe has to have the limelight, but he fills it adequately and pleasantly. He does fight with some people, but a great many people are completely devoted to him. And I'm one, and I don't think I'm silly about it. I know his faults, but he'll always be my dear Joe.

Three: The City Politic

PEGGY BENNION PAPP Joe lived on the brink of crisis: he needed a million dollars, otherwise the Shakespeare Festival would be gone forever. That was the theme song of my life: "If I don't get a million dollars tomorrow, Peggy, it's over. It's gone forever. Forever! I've explored every source that's available. This is the end. This is the real end."

One year he walked into the mayor's office—Wagner, I guess—and said, "I've got to have a million dollars."

"Oh, Joe," the mayor said. "I don't have enough money for schools, I don't have enough money for subways, I don't have enough money to run the city. Where am I going to get a million dollars?"

"I'll show you."

And he made out a budget. He said, "You can take from here, you can take from here, you can take from here and here," and he walked out with a million dollars.

But that kind of drive, I tell you, oh, Jesus, what a price you pay. For a lot of us, success is very important, but we feel that we won't literally die if we don't succeed, we'll do something else. With Joe, it's a life-or-death issue. Physically, he would have died, and that's what gave him that tremendous force to be able to take over the Actors' Lab and to be able to walk into the mayor's office and say, "I'll show you how."

LEE GRANT   There was supposed to be some kind of little do at the mayor's office around the time of *Electra*, and I remember walking down the hall and hearing Joe's voice haranguing this group of people. It was the mayor and a couple of other people, and Joe's shouting at them, just letting them have it about the problems of the theater and what they had to do. It was not a supplication at all; it was a real attack, dressing them down. And it just astonished me.

JOSEPH PAPP   Whenever I used to ask for money, they'd always raise the question: "The city has only $50,000 and there are kids starving to death and you're putting on Shakespeare. What's more important? What would you do?"

"Oh, shut up with that, already," I'd say. "That's a ridiculous question. In the first place, the city has more than $50,000. And, certainly, the city wastes millions and millions of dollars on things that are not important. In the general scale of things, certainly it's important to take care of basic necessities, to take care of the ill and the homeless, to feed children. But part of the spiritual life of the city is its art, its plays, so you are creating a false distinction."

I always used to say that Shakespeare should be as important as garbage collection, and I liked having a line on the budget that was close to things that were necessities to the city. When we were down at the amphitheater, the different activities were listed on a wall, and Shakespeare was there along with things like basketball and sewing. We were not set out in any special way but part of a structure, and that's the way I loved it. That's what I think art should be: part of the city, part of everyday life.

AUGUST HECKSCHER The city gave, and I suppose it still does give, very considerable amounts to Joe Papp. He always complained loudly, of course, that we were giving him a totally insufficient amount. He would say, in public, "They've cut my budget!" And I used to be furious at him. I said, "Joe, we didn't cut your budget. We just didn't give you the increase which you asked for." He would say, "Well, I won't do that again," but he would. Couldn't help it.

He used to get quite angry at John Lindsay. John would sort of shake him up and say, "Joe, everybody else pays for things. You're coming to the city and begging. You're always claiming that we don't give you enough money, so why don't you charge a fifty-cent admission fee or something?"

Joe would get absolutely enraged, he would say, "Look, John, you pose as somebody who is a great supporter of the arts, but when it comes down to the crunch, you just don't want to give me or give the arts the money that's really needed." And I have sort of discovered, working for John Kennedy and for Lindsay and for Nelson Rockefeller, the more a political figure is dedicated to the arts and is recognized as being supportive of the arts, the less money he actually gives. He has the constituency already.

JOHN LINDSAY You've got one thing you want to talk to Joe about, and the next thing you know, he's pushing three other things on you that you didn't have any intention of getting involved in. He does have his own agenda; nothing wrong with that. I like people who get things done, providing they stay within the rules. He's not an Ollie North type; he's not going to be a buccaneer. He's very insistent, but that doesn't mean that he likes you less or respects you less if you said, "Tough, Joe. Go smoke somewheres else."

Joe Papp is such a loner; he operates under his own steam. He's probably less of a team player than a lot of other people you'll find, but those other people get less done. Joe's a doer.

Four: The Buyback, 1970–71

JOSEPH PAPP We always owed money, there was never a period of time when we didn't feel we owed somebody. But in 1970, we were desperate for money. We just had no income—we were going down. I went to the city and said, "You have to bail us out some way, it's your responsibility."

"Why doesn't the city buy the Public Theater building from you?" someone in the comptroller's office suggested. The city would in effect be giving us money so we could survive and pay off our debts and would then let us use the building.

"Why not?" I said. "That's okay with me." I had no choice.

AUGUST HECKSCHER In those years, much more than today, there was a great difference between the relative plenty of capital funds, which were raised by bonds, and the scarcity of current spending or tax funds. When we came to the end of what we felt we could do for Joe with tax money, when we found we couldn't meet the annual commitment that we would like to make for the running expenses of the theater, this idea grew up—because borrowing was very, very easy via these bonds—of buying the theater from Joe and leasing it back to him.

JOSEPH PAPP Mayor Lindsay requested that the city acquire the Public Theater, but in June of 1970, the city council turned him down. Lindsay was genial, but I don't think he was an advocate. On the surface, you would think that under the Lindsay administration, you'd have the greatest support for the arts, but I don't think that was true at all. I'd rather deal with a conservative than a liberal anytime. When Wagner was mayor, he was not an ex-actor, he didn't pretend that he loved culture. I had no problems with that. He didn't have artistic opinions, artistic judgments. He just said, "This is good for the people."

But when the Lindsay administration came in, they were like the yuppies of their time. I was already in there, more established, and they wanted to show they were the leading cultural figures in the city. I was always in competition. Not that I wanted to be in competition; I just happened to be in competition. So though the emotional support from John seemed to be positive, the actual support was not so great.

Night after the city council turned us down, the Yorke Construction Corporation threatened to impose what was called a mechanics lien and take over the building unless a bill of more than $400,000 for work done on the Newman Theater was paid.

We were dying, you know, this was a direct threat to our survival. That's when we put on the all-night *Wars of the Roses* to dramatize our plight, and right after that Mayor Lindsay promised to ask the Board of Estimate for $5.1 million: $2.6 million to buy back the building and $2.5 million to pay for completing its restoration.

GAIL MERRIFIELD PAPP It's like living in Jerusalem: you live in the problem; you never solve it. We had disaster scenarios that we used to joke about, one of which was that we would rent out every space in the whole building to whoever would pay us. Then Joe and myself and Bernie Gersten and Arthur Abraham, the old HIAS caretaker, and his dog, this small band of people would retreat to a basement corner and try to recover our resources from this headquarters in exile. It was a humorous scenario, but in my heart, I sort of believed it. It seemed, in fact, to be looming before us. I thought, "Things could get that bad, and this would be the way to go."

BERNARD GERSTEN The mechanics lien was something that we caused to take place. The mechanics lien was a charade. We really owed the Yorke Construction Corporation the money, but we always had very, very positive relations with them, and Victor Goldberg, the president, never meant to act under the rights he had under the mechanics lien.

We needed to have the pressure on us of somebody threatening to usurp the building, so we worked the strategy through to make it manifest that if we were not able to find succor, the building might indeed be sold out from under us. And it did dramatize and heighten the need to get the city into the act.

The original plan was to make the buyback price $5.1 million, which was the actual cost of the alterations to date and the amount it would take to complete the building. That was voted down at the Board of Estimate in December of 1970. So we said, "Let's go back and see if we can get the actual cost of the building to date," and that was $2.6 million. Our plan was to pay off the mortgage, pay off our mechanics lien and the rest of our debts, and retain $1.6 million to keep us going.

On March 11, 1971, we appeared again before the Board of Estimate. These are the action guys, the power group that votes the budget. It was a very hectic and furious day at the board having to do with, as so often it did, public housing in Queens, and the Queens homeowners were out in force.

We knew our issue would come up at the end of the day, by which time the presidents of the five boroughs and the other board members would be exhausted. Any politicking that we had done before was almost irrelevant in the face of the drama and dynamic of that kind of day. There were mobs there, there was shouting, it was very passionate.

Joe was the final speaker, and he made the argument about what the value of the Public Theater was and what the history of the Shakespeare Festival had been in the life of New York City. Joe had gotten a few sentences into his statement when the Queens borough president, Sidney Leviss, interrupted in a manner that was not unfamiliar to us.

The customary way in which the outlying boroughs expressed their antagonism to the mayor, or their hostility to any particular order of business, was by appealing to borough chauvinism, which Leviss did by saying, "What does this do for the people of Queens?"

This was fairly routine, and we had a traditional answer, because we had the mobile theater and the mobile theater indeed did go to the boroughs. But Joe, who, needless to say, was tense, as we all were, and always had a low ignition point anyway, said, "I've done plenty for the Borough of Queens. I don't have to take this shit from you!"

Leviss asked him to apologize, and Joe did all over again the line reading I remembered from *The Plant in the Sun* at the Actors' Lab. *"'Pologize?!"* he said. "I don't have to take this shit." And he turned on his heel and walked out the door. And the Board of Estimate, which was falling asleep because they were exhausted from the day, suddenly saw the sparks of controversy flying, and they came alive.

JOSEPH PAPP I was just getting tired of the whole business. They were setting up all sorts of conditions and saying that they wanted representatives from Queens and from the Bronx to determine this and determine that. That's one thing I cannot tolerate, when someone tries to tell me how to run the organization. When people begin to talk about having committee votes on these things, I don't like that kind of situation, that's the Soviet system and theaters don't operate that way.

GAIL MERRIFIELD PAPP   I was astonished to see him blowing his stack, talking this way to the Board of Estimate people and then stalking out. I couldn't believe he was really going through with it. "My god!" I thought. "That's amazing. Everything is hopelessly lost now." And then Bernie came in and took up the conciliatory role.

The old one-two punch, you know. It was uncalculated on Joe's part. He had no idea Bernie was going to rise and come forward; it was not part of his plan at all. He did it out of the way he felt. He knows the kind of loss involved, and he's willing to take it. Strange as it seems, that's really where it's at.

BERNARD GERSTEN   There was nobody doing anything, so I said, "I should really do something. After all, I'm Joe's subaltern, I'm his second-in-command." So I walked up to the microphone and I made nice. I don't know what the hell I said, but whatever it was, I did it for about fifteen or twenty minutes. Two of the board members led me down a garden path of questions, to which all the answers flowed like honey. I do talk well, sometimes, and that was one of the days.

I was very responsive to questions and apologized for Joe without apologizing too much, explained Joe without explaining too much. Joe had been the bad cop and I was the good cop; Joe woke them up and then I cleaned up. The board voted to defer action for two weeks, but we knew we had it that day. That was a wonderful day for me and the festival. And on March 25 the board voted unanimously to buy the Public for $2.6 million and lease it back for $1 a year.

JOSEPH PAPP   Now, I can walk out of someplace and know damn well that the issue is not over. I've done it several times, when I've felt that to say any more is just to lose. Even though the anger is real, the upsetness is real, everything else is real, it is a conscious choice I make.

I have a duality of situation. It serves a function. By walking out and leaving that guy from Queens there, that left the problem with him. Nobody convinced anybody of anything. The situation would have come up again, and we would have had to deal with it then.

The possibility always exists that you can lose, but I didn't think so. This is too important an institution to go down. Whether Bernie Gersten had been there or not, I don't think it would have made any difference. I know Bernie says he straightened it all out, but with all due respect, it was my act that made that possible.

MERLE DEBUSKEY We trooped down to the Municipal Building, an ill-maintained rabbit warren of offices where the walls were bureaucratic green and peeling and the furniture was old, to collect our check for $2.6 million. The clerk who was responsible for transacting the conclusion was an elderly man, small and skinny with a couple of teeth missing, who had an eyeshade and an old, gray office jacket with worn cuffs at the bottom of the sleeves.

In the middle of this, while we're signing documents and passing them back and forth, Joe, quite out of any context, sang with great aplomb an expansive selection from the *haftorah* from his bar mitzvah, word for word. It was to the great delight of Bernie and myself and the clerk, who knew what it was, and to the utter consternation of everybody else in the room and people who looked in as they went down the corridor and thought, "What the hell is going on in there?" I don't know how often people get bar mitzvahed in the Municipal Building.

"Okay," the clerk said when the signing was finished, "that'll be a couple of hundred dollars (or whatever the sum was) for the tax stamps." And Joe, with great dispatch, turned to David Black, who was the general manager and said, "Write out a check." David hesitated and started to write, at which point our banker leaned over to Joe and said, "You can't cover that check." Here we were down to collect $2.6 million and we didn't have enough money in the bank to cover the tax stamps.

15

Two Gentlemen of Verona

1971

Clifton Davis and Jonelle Allen
© Zodiac

Irreverence is occasionally a virtue much to be admired. The New York Shakespeare Festival Public Theater is currently doing Shakespeare a power of good and turning Central Park into a place of celebration with its new production of *The Two Gentlemen of Verona*. It is jeu d'esprit, a bardic spree, a midsummer night's jest, a merriment of lovers, a gallimaufry of styles and a gas. It takes off.

For years Joseph Papp, Bernard Gersten and all who have sailed with them have done gloriously right by Shakespeare. Now they have done gloriously wrong. They are presenting this tedious little play by Shakespeare and they have transformed it into a totally endearing New York pop musical. I adored it ...

Two friends fall in love with two women—but so differently. The romantic, the ardent Proteus, proves the cheat and the fraud, while the less fancified lover, Valentine, proves truer to his course ...

The piece looks a little thrown together, like a random basketful of cherries. But what it has, apart from much of the gutsiness of Mr. Guare and Mr. MacDermot, is this great feeling for the city of New York, especially its black and Puerto Rican elements. Its lovely Julia wails in Spanish at the drop of a heart throb, and black is very beautifully beautiful ...

The four lovers, Jonelle Allen, Carla Pinza, Clifton Davis and Raul Julia, could not have been better. All four swept the play with all its silliness into a summer night of bliss. They all seemed to be having such a very good and popcorn time of it. They were natural, unaffected and Shakespearean.

Clive Barnes, *New York Times*, July 29, 1971

· ·

MEL SHAPIRO Joe called one morning and asked if I wanted to direct *Two Gents* in the park. I said yes, then I turned to my wife and said, "What have I gotten myself into?"

I reread the play and thought it was a total dog. I went to see Joe and he said, "Oh, I forgot to tell you. After the park, it's going on the mobile theater unit that tours the boroughs." Right out of my mouth I said, "I think it should be done as a musical," because I couldn't imagine shoving this middle-brow Shakespeare rubbish down ghetto kids' throats.

He said, "Oh yeah, a musical. That means you'll add some songs." In my mind, I was going to just turn it into a musical. He asked me who I wanted to work with and I said John Guare, who I'd just done *The House of Blue Leaves* with, and Joe suggested Galt MacDermot, who'd just done *Hair*.

JOHN GUARE This was a summer of great racial tension and violence in the air, and Mel was afraid that if we brought this play about courtly sentiments and reflections on love around the five boroughs, there would just be machine guns out. Also, because it would be done on the mobile, it had to be one ninety-minute span.

Mel and I had been doing a lot of work together, and he asked me to just look at the script and tighten it, find a solid structure and protect what was valuable in it. Since it would be done on the street, and sometimes people get put off by hearing just Shakespeare on the street, we had this idea that the songs would function as kind of subtitles. You would be aware of the meaning, you would understand what the text was saying, and the poetry wouldn't get in the way. The idea was to really make it bold and simple, without reducing it in any way.

Joe gave us the go-ahead, and we did the show just among ourselves. The best thing about it was, we were entrusted. Joe left us alone in the park. This show was given to the people whose idea it was. We knew it would be exuberant. We went into rehearsal with maybe ten songs, and we ended up with a lot more, thirty-two. We'd just find moments, a lot of things were written right on the spot. We were outside and it was just so reckless, we would try anything.

One day Raul Julia would do a Harry Belafonte imitation, and the next day I'd say, "We have to have a Harry Belafonte number for Raul, and it'll be 'Calla Lily Lady.'" I would call Galt up and leave lyrics on his service, mail them to him, or drop them off. Songs were written, thrown away, and put back. Mel created a wonderful moonstruck atmosphere, and bit by bit we assembled it.

MEL SHAPIRO   I had seen a photograph in the *New York Times* of a silhouette on the side of a ten-story brick edifice in Chicago, almost trompe l'oeil, of a black person dancing, and that to me became the metaphor for the show. It was all about life in the city, about leaving the country to go to the city. I am very improvisational, and Galt is very improvisational, and so is Guare. We're three people who like to do things on the spot. And once the cast got our number, they all went with it.

We had whites and blacks and Puerto Ricans, everybody kissing one another and falling in love with one another and getting in bed together. It was crossing the color barriers, an interracial love-in, you might say, and very outrageous at the time. But it wasn't until after we'd had a reading that we realized what we had done in the casting. It was an accident.

Joe kept saying, "Are you going to keep the essence of Shakespeare?" And that was a very good note, a Rand McNally road map. What we did was keep the essence of Shakespeare, in the sense that it wasn't the play but the idea of the play. What we did was substitute, find metaphors. It was a real collaboration, a sensational time.

JONELLE ALLEN It was a Thursday morning, and my mother woke me up, because I was living at home, and she said, "Joseph Papp on the phone."

"What?"

"Joseph Papp on the phone."

I said hello and he said, "Hi, Silvia." And I said, "It's Jonelle." He said, "No, now you're Silvia," and that's how I found out I had the part.

The chemistry between the cast was absolutely incredible. The balmy summer nights, the idea of the love and fun and frolic in the play, the moon coming up over the Delacorte—it was magic, that's the only way I can describe it. Myself, Raul Julia, Clifton Davis, Carla Pinza, Jose Perez, Jerry Stiller, Alix Elias—it was a melting pot up there on the stage. The roles were so tailor-made for us; we brought a lot to it. Everybody was lusting after each other onstage, and offstage we were together all the time. We were like family, even more than family.

RAUL JULIA In the mid-sixties, I just wanted to work in the theater, but there was nothing happening. I had tried other jobs, selling subscriptions to magazines, teaching Spanish, but I wasn't happy.

Though I had done a few things for the Public, I didn't know Joe very well. Yet with his experimenting, his willingness to take risks with material that was not safe or commercial, he'd made the Public the ideal place for me. I could have worked there all my life. So for me to call him at that time was like a devout Catholic who wanted to work in the Vatican calling the pope. I didn't even know if he remembered me or not. It was very hard, very scary.

After pacing up and down my apartment for a long time, I gathered up the courage and I dialed the phone. His secretary answered, and I said, "I'd like to speak to Joe Papp."

"Who's calling?"

"Raul Julia."

"One moment, please."

"I can't believe it," I said to myself. "Is he really going to answer the phone?"

All of a sudden, I heard, "Hi, Raul. How are you?" I said, "Mr. Papp, the reason I'm calling is that I haven't worked in a while and I'm really going crazy. I tried other jobs, but I just want to work in the theater. I don't care what kind of job—I'll clean toilets or the floor or anything." And sort of joking around I said, "I'm ready to kill myself if I don't get a job in the theater."

He said, "Well, don't kill yourself yet, because you're gonna make a mess all over the rug. I'll give you a call in ten or fifteen minutes." He hung up and I was shaking. I couldn't believe I'd made the call, that I had actually gotten to him, and that he remembered me and was so gracious. He called back and said, "Have you ever been a house manager?" I said, "No, but I'll be the best house manager you've ever had." And he said, "Okay, come over."

Two Gentlemen of Verona came about a few years later because I had worked with Mel Shapiro in a previous musical. I think it was Joe who called me up. He said, "Do you want to do Proteus?" He didn't tell me anything about the production. I don't think he knew it himself. Nobody knew. This production came out of rehearsals.

We started reading the play, and Galt would write the music as we went along, and John Guare would write the script as we went along, eliminating some Shakespeare and putting in some of our own stuff. Mel Shapiro was very open and let the actors improvise a lot and do their own thing, and whatever we did, they would put down. John would come in the next day with some new lines and Galt would come in with a new song, and we kept doing that until we opened.

It was such a mixture, the music and Shakespeare combined with modern stuff and the actors' different styles, we didn't know what we had. We really didn't know until we put it in front of an audience. And from the very first preview, everybody went crazy for it, it was huge raves.

JERRY STILLER The Shakespeare Festival called and said, "Come back and do the same role you did the first time." But the difference was, the first time I did *Two Gentlemen*, Launce was the comic relief. Now it was the main characters who were funny: when Raul opened his mouth and started speaking verse and it came out Hispanic, like Desi Arnaz, the audience fell down laughing.

When I came out to do the stuff with the dog, I found myself totally astonished that no one laughed. So instead of going back to a role I thought I could do, to the triumph that I'd had—with a different dog, of course—I found myself suddenly standing there and not getting the laughs.

"Gee," I said, "I guess life has changed, times have changed." At one point, I was so quirked out by all of this stuff that I said to Mel Shapiro, "This ain't working out. You might as well get somebody to play this part who can get some laughs, because it's not going to happen for me."

"No, no," he said. "Give it a little more time."

"But playing the part straight doesn't make any sense at all. It's like eating white bread in a pastrami sandwich. It doesn't work."

"Well, have you any suggestions?"

"It's supposed to take place in Italy. Wouldn't it be funny if I came out and did these lines like Chico Marx?"

"Well, give it a try."

I actually had the gall to come out and try it that way. It was terrible. It was the worst. It was like somebody injected me with dumb serum. The first preview was within two days, and I really wished they would fire me, but Joe wouldn't fire me in a situation like that. He had sentimental feelings about the part, and the show was going well anyway, even if I didn't do anything.

On the day of the first preview, I went home after the rehearsal break, I was totally wiped out. I fell asleep, and I woke up in my sleep, in that cosmic moment where your mind is conscious before you awaken, and I said, "I've figured out how to do this play. I've got to do it like a Jewish guy, even if I don't do an accent, and the lines should be done as if I were doing the four questions at a seder."

I went down to the Delacorte and I did it that way, I found the character that night in front of the first preview audience. Suddenly, the character caught on. It amazed me that I survived that show.

BERNARD GERSTEN *Two Gentlemen of Verona* erupted, like a fungus. There it suddenly was, full blown. It had an improvisational quality to it, a spontaneity, an originality that was very much in the spirit of the theater of the time. It was flair with discipline, almost, and it burst on the audience like a rocket. It was accessible Shakespeare, as successful a musical version of a Shakespeare work as has ever been.

Rarely did anything engender the audience response that *Two Gents* did, and understandably. It was rock music, it was summer, and it was wonderfully performed. So it had this extraordinary success in Central Park, and then we put it on the mobile, and to the extent that anything could be imagined to be better than it was in Central Park, it seemed better.

And somewhere along the line, we didn't say "Let's take it to Broadway," we said, "It's going by itself. It just wants to go to Broadway, so who can stop it?" Various producers came and said, "Yes, we'll help you with this." Joe and I talked to each other, and we said, "What do we need them for? What are they going to do?" The play was already produced, that was the point. The producers knew the mumbo jumbo of Broadway, but we could make up the mumbo jumbo.

Since we couldn't come up with any reason why we shouldn't produce it, the next question was how to capitalize, how to finance it. We allowed that something like $250,000 was needed to move to Broadway. We talked about three possibilities to get money: from members of the board who would invest in it and take profit, from members who would give us the profit back, or to get a record company that was interested in album rights to invest.

Then, and I've never done this before or since, I sat upright in bed one night and I thought, "If we could get somebody to contribute the money to us, specifically earmarked to move the show to Broadway, while they took their tax deduction as a contribution to a not-for-profit theater, we then would not be beholden to anybody. We would own it one hundred percent."

I told Joe about this and he said, "Yeah, but who would give us $250,000?"

"There's only one person. Maybe LuEsther Mertz."

"Okay. Let's call LuEsther and we'll arrange lunch with her."

At lunch, we told her that we meant to take the show to Broadway, and that these were the circumstances under which we could do it. We could get the money from this source and they would get fifty percent of the profit, or we could get it from that source, and they would get fifty percent of the profit. Or, "If somebody were to give us the money as a tax-deductible contribution, then we would own one hundred percent of the show."

"Well, how much is that?"

"Two hundred and fifty thousand dollars."

"Why don't we get ten members of the board each to give $25,000?"

And we said, very gently, "We don't have ten people on the board who can give $25,000."

"Do you mean you want me to give the entire $250,000?"

"Yes, LuEsther, if you could, that would really be wonderful."

"Well, let me think about it." At least she didn't say no.

A day or two later we got a note from her saying, "I've thought about it, and I think that would be a wonderful idea if we were the first not-for-profit theater to move a show to Broadway and to own a hundred percent of it." And that set the pattern that is still being practiced by the Shakespeare Festival. Nobody else has ever been able to do that.

The Shakespeare Festival moved almost every one of its shows with the money of LuEsther. She did it for *Two Gents*, she did it for *That Championship Season*, she did it for *A Chorus Line*. It is amazing. That was my invention, and that was a great invention. LuEsther, that was God's work. And her spirit is also God's work.

LUESTHER T. MERTZ This wonderful, wonderful play was such a hit and every producer in town was on our necks, lots of people were ready to buy into it. Joe said, "Come on down, you and Bernie and I will go to lunch."

We were sitting around conferring about this. We said, "Are we going to have to give it up? What shall we do?" I thought, "Should I go around and canvass the board, get them all to buy a piece? Or shall I buy it all, or what?" And then I thought the smartest thing of all to do—and I didn't realize then how smart it was—was to give them the money and they would bring it to Broadway, and then there'd be no tax for me to pay.

They really were my own ideas, although Bernie says that it was his idea. "Well, Bernie," I say, "if it was, we both thought of it at the same time, because I have no consciousness of anyone else suggesting this." We may have both thought of the same thing, but definitely it was my idea.

JONELLE ALLEN When we took it indoors to the St. James Theatre, I had this wonderful dresser who'd worked for Katharine Hepburn and all sorts of people, she was really a Broadway-show dresser. After the first preview I said to her, "Oh, I think I should get something for my dressing room," and she looked at me and said, "Why don't you just wait, honey? Because I don't think this show is gonna go anywhere." But in the eleventh hour, it pulled itself together.

JOSEPH PAPP Mel, John, and Galt created a show there in the park. I made my comments and so forth, I encouraged them, but I wasn't very active in the collaboration. My participation was mainly as a producer. When we made the move to Broadway, then I became extremely active.

The biggest mistake we made was through John Guare's influence, and I have to share the blame for it, even though I had my own reluctance. We replaced Carla Pinza, who's hated me ever since, as Julia, because her voice wasn't good enough. And I replaced her with La Lupe, this kind of Cuban bombshell that John Guare favored. "You must see her, Joe. You absolutely *must* see her!" he'd say, with all that overwhelming enthusiasm he brings to things. I saw her, and I had my doubts, but John said, "She's terrific," this and that, and we engaged her. Mistake number one.

Mistake number two, the choreographer we engaged. Mistake number three, we had to replace Jerry Stiller, who was going into something else. Mistake number four, Mel Shapiro should never have directed a Broadway show. Mistake number five, John Guare should never try his hand at directing, because he became a part of that.

The only one who was impervious to it all and just sailed through the whole thing was Raul. He is the most single-minded person. The storm was brewing around him, things were falling on their face, and he didn't even comment. He was not involved.

We reached the first preview and the show was not getting together. We had a full house, and forty-five minutes into the show, half the audience left. The next night, almost two-thirds of the audience left. My friend Mel Shapiro was paralyzed. Paralyzed. He couldn't move. God knows what was going on in his head. He tried to do this, tried to direct something, but he couldn't do anything. And John Guare was ranting.

So, finally, I said, "Okay, I'm going to make a few changes." I just had to use the ax and take chances. I got another choreographer. I began to push the director to move, to get into it. I fired the Cuban bombshell, even though I had to pay her $2,000 a week for a *year*, and replaced her with Diana Davila, a marvelous young woman who had played Juliet for us in a Spanish translation of *Romeo and Juliet*. I figured if the show was successful, paying this woman wouldn't matter, and if we failed, we wouldn't have to pay her anything.

Because we were playing every night while these changes were happening, it took about ten days for things to get livelier. The first night we got rid of that woman, only half the audience left. A few days later, as the thing went on, a third of the audience left. And after the first night when nobody got up and left, I said, "Okay, we're in business."

I remember those ten days. It was horrible. We were on the verge of absolute disaster. Had that failed, *Sticks and Bones* would not have been able to run on Broadway and we would never have gotten those Tony Awards. The changes I made changed the whole complexion of the show. You may get another opinion about this, but I really feel I turned the show around.

JOHN GUARE I've read a number of times that Joe had closed the show down. I've read all different versions of events, that Joe had fixed the show, had taken it over. I revere Joe, but that has no truth in reality. It was a show that Mel and I did; if Joe helped us, I would give him all the credit in the world.

I had seen La Lupe, an astonishing performer, a combination of Edith

Piaf, Judy Garland, Diana Ross, Barbra Streisand, the greatest star in Latin America but unknown in our world. And so I thought, "Wouldn't it be amazing to have somebody like this in our play?" And it seemed to be in the spirit of the Public Theater. I went to Joe and I just said, "We have to have her."

We had the illusion that she could learn to speak enough English to get through the text. It just didn't work out. It was a great lesson. Diana Davila, who replaced her, had come to audition for the show originally and had come a week late. I've heard of people being an hour late, but she came a week late, apologizing.

It was real hit-or-miss, trying to get the show to begin. The first twenty minutes of the show were a nightmare. We went through a lot of trouble. The hardest part was rewriting it for inside. We tried and tried and tried to find the rule for the way the audience should take this play. It was different when you were outside: the full moon is there, you've brought a picnic, you've done half the work.

One day in rehearsal, I said to Jose Perez, "Just come out and say, '*Two Gentlemen of Verona*, a play by William Shakespeare,' and hit your head." And that night, the audience knew where they were, they knew they were seeing a play by Shakespeare that was to be spoken by this Hispanic man who hits his head. The rules of the play were set up in that second, suddenly it clicked into place, and we had created indoors what was in the park outdoors.

MEL SHAPIRO   We had a couple of months before the end of the mobile tour and the start on Broadway, and we improved it to death. We always had trouble with the first twenty minutes of the show, and by the time we opened to previews, we had trouble with the first fifty minutes of the show. It was like subtraction by addition. Six hundred people walked out during the first preview.

There was a little knock on my door at five in the morning. I knew it was John, because we were really sinking. John came in, eventually my wife got up and went to work, the boys went to school, and we were sitting and sitting, trying to solve this problem. Finally, we both said at once, "The problem with the first twenty minutes is that it's about—what is it about? What is it about?" And we said together, "It's about Julia falling in love."

Once we understood that, we focused on that event. We cut away the extraneous stuff and we pulled out an old song that we had cut. Galt went down in the pit and played it himself on the piano because there was no chart for it. And that night, which was the last preview, we got a standing ovation. We bumped into David Merrick in Shubert Alley on the day of the opening, and he said, "It's the first time I have ever heard word of mouth on Broadway change from negative to positive."

I can understand Joe. There's something of the street fighter, but it's also getting out of the shtetl, getting out of the ghetto. Even when you get out of it, you don't know you're out, you still have that drive.

What sets Joe apart is that not only does he want to get out of the shtetl but once he's out, he's in search of his own identity. He's a character in search of himself, and he's working it out in the most creative way. We're his therapy, you know. We're what he does to get himself better.

BERNARD GERSTEN By bringing *Two Gentlemen of Verona* to Broadway, the Shakespeare Festival began a movement that has become tremendously important for the theater. What we began in 1971 is now very much taken for granted, which is that a certain number of plays and musicals on Broadway spring from not-for-profit sources. It signaled a change in the theater: suddenly the not-for-profit theaters that were growing in sophistication and capability began to feed Broadway.

The idea that the institutional theater was pure and Broadway was corrupt was silly. You can be corrupt at anything, and you can be pure in anything, and in all likelihood, everybody's a little bit in between. So we had no qualms. We didn't think that we would be besmirched by going to Broadway with *Two Gentlemen of Verona*. We thought it would be rather a lark, and it proved to be a lark, and we went for all the larks we could find.

MING CHO LEE I felt that in the long term the fact that *Two Gents* was commercially successful and Joe retained control was not healthy. It became a way of sustaining the Public Theater; it informed a certain amount of subsequent artistic and theatrical policy.

You could see a desire every other year to do something that was totally commercial. It diluted, in a way, the mission that I think was initially part of the Public Theater and the New York Shakespeare Festival. They do good work, they do exciting work, but is there a guiding thing saying, "This is what we do"? You can't articulate that anymore. *Two Gents* was a transition point that changed the direction of the Public Theater.

MERLE DEBUSKEY   As successful as Joe was, as successful as anyone might be in his arena, you're at best triple-A; you're not in the National or American League. Your power base is potentially limited, you ain't gonna play in the World Series and receive the attendant attention that comes from that.

And if you're running a not-for-profit theater, the more respected you are, the stronger your position in public recognition is, the more you're identified with doing marvelous things, the better off you are, and the more likely it is that you will achieve the financing for your annual budget. And Broadway was also a chance to make some money for the festival and for the playwright. So when an opportunity came, Joe was in there.

Two Gentlemen became very successful, and there was no embarrassment in stepping up before the cameras on network television and receiving the Best Musical Tony Award before I don't know how many millions of people—the first of the Tony winners the festival started to accumulate. That changed the tenor of the ball game. We now had a guy who could hit a home run as well as bunt a single.

Two Gentlemen was Joe's first taste of what Broadway was, and the power of Broadway. It catapulted the festival into fame, and it was very providential. If you had a show that seemed to be commercially viable, from now on the thing to do was to move it. If one felt keenly about the work and wanted it to have wider exposure because of its significance, you'd take it to Broadway.

16

David Rabe, Act I:
The Basic Training of Pavlo Hummel
and *Sticks and Bones*
1971–72

David Selby and
Cliff De Young in
Sticks and Bones
© Friedman-Abeles

The Basic Training of Pavlo Hummel, a first play by David Rabe, directed by Jeff Bleckner, is an astonishing accomplishment. Mr. Rabe, with Mr. Bleckner's help, has succeeded in bringing alive on the stage of the Newman Theater (at the Public) an Army squad in training camp and later in Vietnam. So prodigal is the play in characterizations, military details, ideas and theatrical ideas, dramatic scenes, emotion, tragedy and humor, and so on key is its ring of truth, that it makes everything else I've seen on the subject seem skimpy and slightly false. So much has been tried off Broadway to get at the horror of war, but this time here it is. Mr. Rabe, who teaches at Villanova, is himself a veteran of Vietnam. His play, done as a flashback, is harrowing, all right, but it is not depressing. The action opens with the killing—by hand grenade in a Vietnamese bordello—of one Pavlo Hummel, pfc., white, a volunteer, and the illegitimate son of a crazy mother and an unknown father. He is a scrappy, boastful, funny, rebellious, and difficult liar and petty thief, so distraught and eroded by depression that after a fight in the barracks he tries to commit suicide by sniffing glue and downing a hundred aspirin. He is, in short, a remarkably complex character in that he is never allowed by the playwright to become Everyman (and he is given a remarkable performance by William Atherton).

Edith Oliver, *The New Yorker*, May 29, 1971

DAVID RABE I was in the army for two years, in Vietnam for a year. I was in a hospital unit at Long Bihn, near Ben Wah, maybe twenty miles outside of Saigon. Ten years later, it had become a sort of megalopolis, but when we got there it was very primitive: we put up our tents and stuff in fields and set up the hospital.

Pavlo Hummel was the first full-length play I started in the period after I came back from the army. I completed a draft of it, and then I wrote a draft for *Sticks and Bones*, which was called *Bones* at that time, and I also was working on some fragments of things that would eventually turn into *The Orphan* and *Streamers*.

Someone told me to talk to a director named Jeff Bleckner. They said, "This is maybe somebody that could do your play." I was working for the *New Haven Register* and I went up to do a story on the Williamstown Theatre, where he was directing a production of *Rosencrantz and Guildenstern Are Dead* with Sam Waterston. I was trying desperately to figure out how to make contact with this guy, but I couldn't do it. It was dusk, they were outside painting some sort of backdrop, and I sat in my car with my wife for a long time and thought about walking over, but I couldn't bring myself to do it. I never did do it.

I started submitting them to any number of places, all the regional theaters. I submitted both plays to the Public Theater—I felt a kinship there—but both were rejected. At some point, after going around the cycle, out of irrationality I submitted them again.

At the same time, though, at the O'Neill Center, the play had been put in the hands of a director named Mel Shapiro. He was thinking about doing it, and when he asked me where he should go to try and get it on, I said, "Try the Public."

It was just a feeling I had that if anybody was going to respond to my plays, Joe was the place. Mel told me that when he went in to meet with Joe, he had another copy on his desk. He hadn't decided to do it, but he had been sort of intrigued by it.

JOSEPH PAPP My first response to David's plays was never terrific. It's the way he writes, so enigmatic and so complex. When I read *Pavlo Hummel* for the first time, I didn't really fully understand the play. I thought Pavlo was a German–Puerto Rican—I didn't know where the hell the name came from. I didn't say immediately that this was a great play. Strange play, with some brilliant scenes, but I thought, "See, it has a lot of problems." It lay on my desk for a while. I wasn't quite sure what to do with it, but it was intriguing. And Mel Shapiro kept saying he was a very good writer.

I continually plead a certain amount of ignorance, up to today, about certain things that are new. It's very hard to adjust to a new artist. Sometimes my perception is very good, but sometimes it isn't. Someone will say, "This is very good," and I'll say, "What do you see in this thing?"

But once I got into one of David's works, it stuck to me like the most important thing in my life. I became so connected with his plays that I felt that I would protect them from anything. I'd say my connection with David was the strongest connection I've had with a writer in the theater's history. And I think he's the greatest writer we've produced. His talent is yet to be recognized.

GAIL MERRIFIELD PAPP There was, at that time, a very strong connection between David and Joe. Very, very unusual, strong connection—unusual in its intensity and perhaps in some ways in its unspoken character.

It was problematic at the outset, because what I saw in David was somebody who was like a volcano who was not erupting yet. And I felt that the world was in a state of uncertain health until that happened.

Joe had expectations of David that required loyalty, devotion, gratitude, honor—all the virtues of ancient chivalry. Joe does expect that of himself and wanted to have it reciprocated in kind from certain individuals he felt very strongly about.

None of David's plays were easy to direct, I have to tell you that. You don't know what the hell the play is at the outset, they were very inscrutable as to what exactly they were. David writes in a complex fashion. It's a deep probe and exploration. He also has very strong ideas about what he feels about his writing, and he's very protective of it. He's a very, very smart individual, but he's also extraordinarily resistant when it comes to the literal text of what he's written.

JEFF BLECKNER I first met Joe when I was a second-year student in the Yale Drama School and he was brought up from New York to teach. He had this great love for Shakespeare, which didn't make any sense. He didn't seem like a man that would like Shakespeare. He seemed like such a street guy, yet very urbane. He was very perceptive about the talent of the people he was dealing with, and he was always making very pungent, barbed remarks.

One of the things those of us in the second year had to do was direct a half-hour show, like a one-act, for the class at large, upon which your "reputation"—and I use that word very much in quotes—was staked. The shows were very competitive. Whether you were supposedly a good director or not depended on how these were received through the general population.

My half-hour play was up early in the year, and it was very well received. I was instantly hot, a second-year golden child, and Joe took notice of me. Then, it must have been just two weeks later, another director did a production and it was fabulous. Joe sat next to me while it was being presented, and as the lights went up, he leaned over and said, "Well, how does it feel to be a has-been?" He laughed, and I laughed, and I've never forgotten it. That comment probably had more to do with my education at Yale, in terms of dealing with the realities of the world I was headed into, than anything else. I mean, my life has documented that remark ever since.

A year or so later, I was just struggling along, trying to get started somehow, when Ed Cannan, an actor friend of David's who ended up playing a very small part in *Pavlo*, gave me two of David Rabe's one-act plays along with *Pavlo*. I loved the one-acts, then someone told me that there was a director already attached to *Pavlo* and I stopped reading it. Then I got a call one day from Joe Papp saying, "I would like you to read a play. If you like it, I want you to meet this writer, and if you guys get along, I think I'd like you to come over here and do it." The play comes over, and it's *Pavlo*.

So I met with David and he had great reservations about the fact that I had not been in military service. Finally, Joe said to him, "Look, if you want to do the play, this guy'll do the play, he likes the play." The way he is, he probably forced him a little bit.

We started to cast it. First we offered it to Al Pacino, but he didn't take it because he got a job in a movie called *The Godfather*. Then we decided to cast Billy Atherton, who was in a production of *The House of Blue Leaves* that Mel Shapiro had directed, so it's all very interwoven. The play started as a workshop and then graduated to a regular show in the Newman Theater as Joe got more and more excited about it.

JOSEPH PAPP When I saw David for the first time, I liked him immediately. He was tall, a very nice-looking guy, an ex–football player who carried himself well. He had very fair skin, his mouth was a little weak, but he had a good head and kind of blond hair. I remember him so well because I had to look into his face for years, and look into his soul sometimes.

There was something about him that was very pure, and I began to associate him with the play. I got to like his play better when I got to talk to him. That's always been my experience: when I get to know the writer, then I realize what's being said. It helps me. The only person I haven't had this association with is Shakespeare, and I doubt we'd have any problems, though he would probably drive a hard bargain for royalties.

David was very much inside of himself, but quite passionate about the things he believed in. He had a very interesting mind: on the one hand, extremely articulate, and on the other hand, difficult to follow sometimes. He was extremely serious about everything, profoundly thoughtful. He would examine things in minute detail, and he had an inexorable logic about things, to a fault. He found it very difficult to express his feelings, he would hold back a lot of anger—"Held Back in Anger," you could call it.

It was difficult for David to alter things. They came out really strongly shaped, of a piece, and it was very hard to move them. He was extremely protective about his work, and very uncertain about how to make the next move. He moved with extreme caution, to such a degree that sometimes he was in midair, he just didn't seem to be moving at all.

He'd been in Vietnam and evidently was amazingly transformed by that experience. He'd brought it home with him, it was all over his face. Yet I later began to believe that somehow he always had Vietnam in him, this sense of violence, even before he went there. I don't mean mindless violence, but rage at some injustice.

He had this bright, modern mind that was dipped, seemingly, into some primordial past, that went back to something very angry, savage, ritualistic, even weird at times. The contradiction between this young all-American-type guy and all these darker thoughts was very impressive to me. I took him all in all, with all these things. It's like a good friend or a child or a brother or sister, you have to accept them totally.

Pavlo Hummel was a strange figure—you never understand him. I learned about enigma then. David Rabe taught me, through my experience with him, that an enigma is closer to life than any kind of explained thing. I thought you had to understand who this person was, I thought you had to understand everything, but I learned that good writing never spells it out in detail.

The spin of David's mind was never to make that person clear. He changed me, he turned me around. I began to feel equally concerned about those who joined up or were drafted as about those who were not. The character of Pavlo was extremely real but surreal at the same time. Everything was in a fever yet it was firmly planted, because he was living on some heightened plane of reality at the same time as he was down deep in the dirt.

David was very, very careful as to who would do his play, and I suggested this young director, Jeff Bleckner, a student of mine at Yale. I'd worked with him before, and because there were things that had to be done with the play, I felt I would be active in this relationship. Jeff was kind of insecure, he depended on me a lot. I wanted him to get out on his own, and that was hard for him to do at the time.

Those guys did the job, but coming down to the wire, I saw that some of the problems of the play were not being solved, and I began to come into it. They would get so intellectual about it, and I said what I always feel: that nothing's set in stone; the only way to do it is to try it. There were some scenes we had to move around and juxtapose, we took some of the material of the first act and put it in the second act. David said what I did was very important; he felt I saved the play.

BERNARD GERSTEN   David became tremendously important as a playwright and as a troubled surrogate son to Joe. The work with David was full of turmoil—the turmoil was endless. There was a characteristic line which Joe used. He would see a dress rehearsal or a run-through and he'd say, "I know exactly what we have to do." I always marveled at that idea, because I always thought, "I don't have the vaguest notion of what to do." I always hoped that somehow the director and the author, who were there at rehearsal, somehow they would know exactly what to do. But Joe, as a man of action, needed to know exactly what to do to make all well.

Joe would turn things upside down, put the second act where the first act was, take this out and put that in, he would cut and paste and go off on a thesis, and the next day he would say, "No, that didn't work, but I know exactly what's wrong with it." And to the dismay, sometimes, of playwrights and directors, upon whom Joe would bring great pressure to bear, he would do that endlessly.

THEONI ALDREDGE   We were sitting around the theater one night and I said, "Let Joe watch it," because Joe never interferes until you ask him to come in or he sees a dress rehearsal. There was a trunk in the scene, they were all sitting around it and on it, and Joe said, "Get rid of the trunk." And all of a sudden, the scene worked, the scene moved. "Get rid of the trunk." Could you punch him?

WILLIAM ATHERTON   I will always be grateful to Joe for *Pavlo Hummel*, because it would never have been done any other way. I founded my whole career on that play. Joe Papp is a genius as a producer. Joe came down the last three days, saw what was wrong, and fixed it. When you're in the last three days of something, the smallest thing is big; the smallest thing can have a huge effect. Instead of playing the scene this way, you're playing it that way. Oh! Then everything comes together. It's the tiniest thing, the last-minute eye.

The second act was always difficult, and Joe changed the staging, which made the second act work. The first act was done using a modicum of furniture, while the second act got much more esoteric. You had different furniture for different scenes, all of which was shuttled on and off.

Joe got rid of all that. He kept with a basic formula of just very simple furniture. When you went from one place on the stage to another, the furniture that was moved was the basic training furniture. So when I went back to my mother's house, she was sitting on an army cot. The last-minute eye is what Joe had, and that's what he did with it.

DAVID RABE   Joe was the boss; he was this guy who ran the place, no question that he was running it. The thing that was unexpected was that he was a producer who had the kind of brains that he had. His artistic intelligence was very strong, that was always impressive to me. And I guess I was a little bamboozled by the knowledge of Shakespeare and the love of Shakespeare he had. You'd be talking about a play and he'd just throw lines out at you from Shakespeare. It made me feel that I was in good hands.

But also, I was very wary of him. I was wary of anybody who was going to work on my play. I was very concentrated and protective, and I knew this was my first big opportunity. I was sort of waiting, watching every step he made to see, "When is he going to try and fuck this up on me?"

Jeff Bleckner was tremendously strong with creating the physical production of the play, the physical life. There were scenes of marching and basic training in the play, and I used the marching to get from some scenes, one to another, but Jeff devised a way that you flowed from one scene to the next on the basis of marching throughout the entire play.

Joe'd come in to listen. He wouldn't actually start hearing it until it was played by actors auditioning, which is a tricky thing for a producer because you've got to be able to read it. We were struggling with the play at one point—it was working and not working at the same time—and Joe came in. He threw some ideas out about scrambling the structure. There was some suspicion. I did confront him—I wasn't easy about these changes—but he said, "Well, let's just try it for a night or two." And so we did. About half the ideas were wonderful, and the other half were not so good, but what we kept really did make a big difference.

There was a dressing sequence in the second act where Pavlo goes from civilian clothes to his dress uniform, trying to get himself together, after being completely drunk, to be shipped out to Vietnam. Joe suggested moving it to become the end of act one, when Pavlo was rising up out of having taken a hundred aspirins in a suicide attempt. It was ninety-nine percent the same dialogue, but it became very theatrical and almost exclusively metaphorical, and it gave the first act a tremendously solid and theatrical ending.

Joe made a substantial contribution to the structure of the play by forcing us to face these things and rewrite and restructure at a very late moment. And that was where I guess I swung over on Joe and began to more accept what he had to say about the plays.

JEFF BLECKNER   We got to just about where we were ready to preview before we showed it to Joe in a dress rehearsal. He came back after we got through the first act and said, "This show is fabulous." He was very, very excited, very, very happy. About ten minutes into the second act, Joe came back up to where I was sitting and told me, "We're in big trouble." Talk about being a has-been. It happened from the first act to the second.

Afterward, he let the cast go and said, "I want to talk to you and David." We went up to his office—he would always give you a drink when you'd go up there—and then he sat us down and said that while the first act was terrific, had great flow and movement, the second act was slow and turgid, didn't seem to belong in the same play as the first act, and David better get at his fucking typewriter and go to work on rewriting his play.

There was a typewriter sitting there, and I thought David wanted to pick it up and throw it at him. I had absolutely no idea what to do. I'd done some very good work as a student at Yale, I'd done a couple of original things, but this was the first time I'd done a play of this scope and I was really out of my element in terms of fixing a play in previews.

Finally, in the midst of all these things he was saying, some of which were quite startling and confusing to us, he said, "Well, I don't give a shit what you do. Take the fucking play and rip it apart. Take every scene and just smash it, fracture it, throw this in there and take that terrible scene where Pavlo goes to his mother and put it in the first act."

"How can we put it in the first act," I said. "In the first act he's in basic training, and that scene with his mother is in his house with all different sets."

"I don't know. Just stick it in the first act. You figure out a way to do it."

We came in the next day. We really didn't know what we were doing. We moved some scenes around, we took the scene where Pavlo talks to his mother and put it in the first act. And, because the barracks set was already onstage for the first act, I just staged that scene in the barracks. As I was doing that all of a sudden I went to myself, "We don't need any furniture in the second act. We could stage the whole show in the basic-training set."

So I threw out all this furniture that had been in the second act and it was tremendously liberating. What it did to me and David was let us look at the play less as a naturalistic narrative in which you had to go progressively and allowed us to treat it as if we were editing a film: "Let's take this scene, move it over here, cut it in half, finish it over there."

We literally fragmentized the second act of the play. We had Pavlo run through the pieces like stations of the cross, and we tied it together with the whole notion of basic training, so it became more than just basic training, it became life education. Joe came over and was thrilled. We opened and the *New York Times* was the only bad review we got.

WILLIAM ATHERTON   See, Joe never took it from anybody. He always had that persona of "I don't care." I was sitting in his office the night after *Hummel* opened. Jeez, I was twenty-three years old, I thought I was this hotshot; I'm sitting there and feeling all kind of terrific. Joe's on the phone to Clive Barnes, who gave us what I thought was a fabulous review in the *New York Times*, and he said, "Clive? What is this shit?"

And I went, "Oh, god! No!" I saw my whole career evaporating.

"I don't like this, Clive," he said. "I think you've got to rewrite this for the radio."

And Clive did it. If Joe went to bat for something, even if a person didn't entirely agree with him, they felt there was something they might have missed.

JEFF BLECKNER   I was in Joe's office the morning after the play opened, and he got on the phone and called Clive Barnes. He told Clive he was a jerk, he didn't understand the American theater, wouldn't know a good play if it came and hit him on the head. He told Clive he wished there was some way he could keep him out of the theater, that he was a jerk and didn't deserve to be on the *New York Times.* And then he read him Martin Gottfried's review that had been published that morning in *Women's Wear Daily.* He read Clive Barnes another guy's review over the phone! This, to me, was Joe Papp.

"This is what the play is about, Clive. Martin understood it. You don't. You just don't. You didn't get it."

Lap dissolve. The *New York Times* has a radio station in New York, WQXR. And Clive Barnes went on WQXR a day or two later, and re-reviewed *Pavlo* with a positive review. We then reprinted portions of Clive's WQXR review in all the ads, and *Pavlo* went on to become *Pavlo.*

That was the beginning of my career, and the beginning of David's career. The place Joe holds in my life is he's the man who started my career. Later, he also almost ended it, but I don't know what would have happened in my life if I'd never met Joe Papp.

I was about twenty-seven years old, which is a key point in my relationship with Joe. Twenty-seven was like a perfect age for Joe. Once I started spending time at the Public Theater, I remember feeling about Joe the way I felt about my father. A little bit in awe of him, a little frightened of him, very respectful of him. The Public was home. If I wasn't there, where would I be? Joe was very loving, in a fatherly sort of way, and seemed to care about us all. And even though I knew he wasn't, I thought he was very, very tall.

Later I went through some bad times with Joe, didn't see him for many years, and came back one day just to say hello after I had become somewhat successful as a television director. And all I could think of was how short he was. Like when I went back to my old neighborhood in Brooklyn and everything was so small. It was exactly the same feeling. Tall is how I remembered him. And he seemed like he could do anything.

DAVID MITCHELL One of the final decisions in terms of the props was what we were going to do for the coffin Pavlo is placed in at the end of the play. The army was not allowing us to use any of theirs, so we went back into *Life* magazine and got pictures of those aluminum caskets that they unloaded from planes.

We couldn't get one from the people that made it, so we had to fabricate one of our own out of wood. That was going to be very expensive. In those days $400 or $500 was a big thing for a prop, so finally Jeff went into Joe's office and threw it down on his desk and said, "This is what we have to have."

When it arrived backstage, just before we opened, it was like a bomb—it was so real, such a familiar image. It was one of the most important and powerful props that I can remember ever working on.

The scene was played with Bill Atherton in it, closed, and we thought we could get him right out. But it was almost like a memorial service, the casket was downstage center in a spot, and people would not leave the auditorium. They just stood and looked. And poor Bill was in there. We had to do a little life support for him, drilling holes in the casket's back. But he did it every night, and it was really a powerful, theatrical moment.

WILLIAM ATHERTON Joe's never liked people leaving him. When I wanted to leave *Hummel* after five and a half months, because I had a job in this movie because I really did have to eat, he physically threw me up against the wall. And I was saying, "Joe! I gotta make some money! I can't eat! I'm banging my head on the floor every night and I'm in pain!" Oh, yeah, he was pissed. He doesn't like people using him in that way. I worked there again after that, because I think he felt I didn't use him. I mean, I gave it a college try.

BERNARD GERSTEN Institutional theaters succeed to the extent that they identify their own playwrights, the playwrights who give them a voice.

Certainly, if you look at theater historically, Chekhov distinguished the Moscow Art Theatre, the essence of the Comédie-Française was Molière, the essence of the Globe was Shakespeare. Any theater that sees itself as part of a literary tradition wants a playwright more than it wants anything else, and that was a quest that the Public Theater was on from the first moment.

An actor is a sometime thing, but a playwright is forever. And David Rabe represented the acquisition of such a playwright for a socially oriented theater. He was not a playwright of manners; he was a playwright of the issues of the day. So, in that sense, David Rabe was well met by the Shakespeare Festival.

MERLE DEBUSKEY When I ran into David, I thought, "My god, we have an Arthur Miller of the seventies." I thought he was a person concerned, as Miller was concerned, with his day, and would write about his day in a fashion not many people were writing. We were all thrilled. Joe had himself a real playwright that he thought was the most significant playwright of our time. So he took David on as a surrogate son, and maybe David accepted him as a surrogate father.

JOSEPH PAPP On opening night I gave David a letter that said that regardless of the critical response to *Pavlo*, he'd always have a home in my theater. That is more or less my policy with most writers: you have to let people know that you're not interested in them only when you feel the show is good.

I was willing to recognize that writers have ups and downs, and I tried to adhere to that, particularly with David. I did all of his plays, whether they were good or not, whether I felt they were ready or not. I let him do the things he wanted to do. There wasn't a play of his I didn't do, regardless. These doors were always open to him. I was as loyal to him as one could possibly be.

DAVID RABE Joe said he wanted me to know that any play that I wrote he would want to do. It seemed like a really wonderful moment—and it was. I thought, "Wow, this is heaven. What else can you ask for? This is it. I'm going to be able to have my plays done in New York whenever I want." But there's a lot of unspoken baggage that came with that offer, the contract wasn't that simple, there's things that came along with it that weren't known or brought up at that particular moment in time.

Once you get tied into an institution, what you don't realize in the beginning is that your work is never going to be seen on its own but always as part of Joe's policy of this or policy of that. In other words, it's not just the play, it's now the example of Joe Papp's new play policy. And Joe didn't say, "And if you try to do a play anywhere else, that will piss me off." He didn't say a lot of things that were also emotionally part of the deal, things I couldn't know and maybe even he didn't know.

....

T. E. Kalem, *Time*, November 22, 1971

The bloody war in Vietnam actively festers in the imagination of one of the more promising young U.S. playwrights, David Rabe. In his drama of last season, *The Basic Training of Pavlo Hummel*, the taste of blood and the apprehension of imminent death gave the evening an elastic tension. His offering last week, *Sticks and Bones*, presented at Joseph Papp's Public Theater, might be a sequel to *Pavlo Hummel*. The hero has returned from Vietnam not dead but blind, a walking corpse in some perpetual nightmare of the soul. There is blood again, but it is a kind of insane red laughter gurgling in the throat.

....

Martin Gottfried, *Women's Wear Daily*, November 8, 1971

The play presents American life as a fraud created and perpetuated by the family situation comedy of television. Its characters are the Nelsons. Ozzie watches football games on television; Harriet fixes breakfast; Rick plays the guitar, and then there is David. David has returned home blind from Vietnam.

Sticks and Bones presents the contrast in reality awareness between David and his family. He has confronted a war in all its grotesque horror. He has learned the nature of love from a Vietnamese girl. Aware of the America to which he must return, he leaves the girl behind . . . But the girl is with him anyway, silently, wherever he is, watching and implying her comment . . .

His parents, his brother, refuse to accept any other reality but that of the television series. They do not want to hear of war, of yellow people, of blindness. But the catalytic presence of their embittered and merciless son forces them, one at a time, to confront life itself. First it is the father, plunged into a self-confrontation while family life continues blithely around him in semi-cartoon superficiality. Then the mother is drawn into the black yaw of truth, while Rick is still bouncing in and out, looking for fudge, taking pictures and singing his songs.

Finally, Rick himself steps into the ring and when he does he can only demand David's suicide. Otherwise the game cannot continue and life would have to be real—something none of them can face.

CLIFF DE YOUNG I came to New York in 1969, did a lot of off-Broadway things, and then I did *Hair* for a long time on Broadway. I wanted to be an actor, but I got hung up with all the hippie-dippies over at *Hair*, auditioned about five times for Tom O'Horgan for *Jesus Christ Superstar*, wasn't cast, and got very depressed and all of that. Then someone told me that *Sticks* was going down at the Public, and I thought, "This is the kind of thing that I wanted to be doing anyway."

The question was, could I just walk in off the street and get a part in a David Rabe play? I met Jeff Bleckner, read for him, and got the part of Rick. And I said, "Wow, this is amazing, you can just walk in here and because you're good enough, you can get into this hot play."

Every once in a while, Joe would come up and put his arm around you and go, "Cliff, you're a great guy, you'll always be working here. If you have any problems, please let me know." You get there, and you get your father figure. That's Joe, and he plays it, with the hand on the chin and the slap in the face and the arm around. So I'm in love now—I'm in love with Joe and I'm in love with the work.

I'm right off the boat, I don't know shit about Shinola, and I'm looking at these people going, "When are they going to find out that I don't know anything? When will I be discovered as the true wetback that I am?"

There's a question of tone in *Sticks* that we were searching for, trying to find. "What is it? Is it a comedy? Is it surrealism? Is it this-ism? Is it thatism?" We were just doing realism at first, saying the lines straightaway, even though there were these kinds of dream sequences and stuff.

It was maybe the third week of rehearsal, there was a scene I had as Ricky with Tom Aldredge, the father. I'm watching TV and I'm eating fudge and I'm going "Hi, Mom" and "Hi, Dad" and all this Americana bullshit that was the essence of the play, and Ozzie says, "Well, I got hit with an egg today." This is the start of Ozzie's disillusion. "I'm walking down the street, it's the same street I've walked down all these times, and somebody just rode by, hit me with an egg."

We played the scene pretty straight a couple of times. It's kind of laying there on the floor, we're wondering what the fuck to do with it, and then we try it again. And Tom Aldredge walks in the door as a person I've never seen before. He walks in like a wounded bird. I'm sitting on one end of the couch and he goes over and perches on the other end and goes into this horrible, birdlike, saliva-dripping, masklike thing.

In the meantime, I'm going "What the fuck is going on?" I look at Jeff Bleckner and he goes, "Yeah, go with it, man!" I'm convinced that I'm with an actor who's insane, and I'm just going to react as one would react to an insane person. I have my milk, I give him a little, I kind of wipe the spittle off his mouth, and everything is getting kind of weird.

Whatever it was, whatever he did there, that scene kicked something into gear, that brought *Sticks* into a place that we didn't know about before. The guy walks in the door, he perches like a weird vulture, and you go, "Okay, now we have to take action, because Dad's in trouble."

The minute that Dad got into that condition, as soon as he got hit with an egg and became this strange apparition because of David's coming back and trying to bring the war home to the Nelson family, we realize that we have to get together and save Dad, and the only way to do that is to get rid of David, and that's what the play is all about.

In a way, it was a memorable moment, but in another way it's gotten me in trouble since because I'm always trying to recapture it in everything I've done from then on. I've tried off-the-wall shit like that in different rehearsals and that maybe works one in five. The other four, people think you're crazy.

TOM ALDREDGE   I was awfully proud of that piece, particularly for the time we did it in. But it was a very difficult piece of work; there was no style to do this play in that I was familiar with. We had to invent it, and I don't think we satisfied David. It was hard to read him at that time. He was not very communicative, and you couldn't tell whether he approved or disapproved. When we floundered—and if you flounder in a piece like that, you really flounder—we would look to David for support, and it was the wrong place to look.

The audiences hated it and loved it. We had the most vocal audience you ever heard in your life. It was sort of Brechtian in the sense that it was not easy to watch but David made you watch it. He put startling things on the stage to wake up the audience.

"Listen to this; it's not going to be easy."

"Stop hitting me!"

"No, no, I want you to pay attention. Are you paying attention now?"

"Yes, I am."

"No, you're not."

And David kept slapping the audience. It wasn't easy to take, but he had a desperate message to tell, and it wasn't his purpose to make it easy. The message was the awful things we had done and our refusal to accept the fact that we had done them: it was over there somewhere, with gooks, with aliens, it didn't matter what we did to them. What David was trying to say was, it does matter.

That's what the kid in the play was trying to say: "I did these things and I smell badly. Don't you smell me? Smell me."

"No, I don't."

"Yes, you do. Smell me."

It was a difficult thing, and people revolted against it. "I don't need this shit. I know we're doing badly, but don't make me pay money to come see it. I don't want to know tonight."

JEFF BLECKNER   It was great to work with David, but David was a very complicated man. And though we had another very good collaborative experience on *Sticks and Bones*, it was very different working on that than it was on *Pavlo*. He had gone from teaching at Villanova and being very insecure about his talent to being told he was the next Eugene O'Neill, the second coming of the American theater.

And as his fame increased and his self-confidence rose, in instances where he might have been wrong, or I might have thought he was wrong, or we disagreed, it became very, very difficult. As David got more successful, it became more difficult for me to work with him; as he got more secure about his own strength, he became less collaborative and more dogmatic about what his visions were.

DAVID RABE It's a very odd play—it's ferocious when it works—and I've always felt that the tone was never quite achieved, though I don't know, given the political climate of the time, which it both suffered and benefited from, that it could have been achieved. The dark humor of it was very hard to get everyone to understand or to even be willing to play.

Part and parcel of the whole production struggle was not to show the transitions. If the characters were in a state of distress and someone popped in the door, the play wanted them to turn and instantly, without a transition, just go into some giddy, happy welcome. And that was hard for the actors.

The political frame of reference of everyone was such that they wanted to make clear that they knew that this was a horrible event. If you don't fight it, it's not very hard. You're not doing *Long Day's Journey into Night*, and you're not doing a total farce. You're doing something that goes from one to the other, that says, "These are two sides of the same event." If you fight it, you get into some middle ground and you're not going to end up with anything. We got maybe seventy or eighty percent.

People wanted the play to be about the returning vet, and in fact the central character in the play is the father, not the son. It was very hard to focus the play in that way, very hard to make that clear even to the actors in it, or even to the actor playing the father. He is, in the conventional dramaturgical sense, the central character. He's there when the play starts, he's there when it's over, he's the one that tries to really run the ship, he's the one that goes through the most changes. The son is a close second, but in a funny way. If you really follow the play, he's less sympathetic than the father.

JEFF BLECKNER   When *Sticks* opened off Broadway, Joe drove us up to the *New York Times* to get the review. When we got there, there was a police line, guys all around, and a body lying there with a tarpaulin over it. We had a rave review in the *Times'* late city edition, and by the time I came back to the car with the paper, I'd found out what had happened.

Some guy had parked his car in front of one of the bays where the *Times* delivery trucks were loaded, and one of the truck drivers was giving the guy shit, telling him to get out of the way because he wanted to get his truck out. They got into an argument, this guy shot and killed the truck driver, and the other drivers went on a wildcat strike because they felt they were being left out there unprotected. So though we had this rave review in the *Times*, the late city edition never hit the street. But once Joe figured this out, he actually got the *Times* to reprint the review in the next day's paper, so it worked out all right.

GAIL MERRIFIELD PAPP   It is hard and strange to remember those days. Nobody who came back from Vietnam, no matter how many medals they could display, was considered a persona grata. A lot of guys just didn't talk about it. If they had the medals they hid them. They pretended they'd never been there.

If you came back, you should be well-adjusted and not have memories. If you survived it, you should not even be bothered that much by having been maimed or hurt in any way by the experience. You should come home, and if your family was a conventional, loving family, you should just fit in.

Now, David was not writing this, and I really remember how much of an outcast that made a person. A different point of view was just not acceptable. Nobody wanted to hear it, nobody wanted to know about it.

So moving to Broadway was certainly a bold move on Joe's part, a real gamble, there's no question about it. He did it because he felt it had to be said. There was a tremendous kind of inner censorship and repression going on in the country, and he felt it had to be brought into the open. Not only was he willing to take a loss; he moved it with the idea that he *would* take a loss on it.

JOSEPH PAPP   When it came to moving *Sticks and Bones* to Broadway, I don't know what was in my mind. It was really a tough play to get across. It would hardly make an average audience respond with any kind of glee or happiness or acceptance. You're kind of damn stupid to bring that play to Broadway.

At the same time, I felt it was an important play and I wanted more people to see it. It certainly wasn't a moneymaker, but like most of David's plays, it addressed the time we were living in and that's why I felt good doing it.

I didn't particularly care for Broadway at that time in my life, but having it in that setting made the play more important. It lost $10,000 a week on Broadway, and since we were making roughly that on *Two Gents*, I would just take that money and keep *Sticks and Bones* running.

DAVID RABE   To have two of my plays running downtown, that was really thrilling and a high. I wanted to just let them run as long as they could off Broadway, that would have been what I would have been comfortable with and done on my own. I thought I had accomplished enough. I'd have never come up with the idea of taking that play to Broadway. I'm very daring or outgoing or adventurous in the writing, but I've found I'm not great at wanting to plow ahead. I'm a little too cautious.

I came back from Iowa and found that Joe wanted to go to Broadway. This thing was in operation and further along than I had anticipated it would be, which was perplexing, and I had some reluctance about it. I feared it wasn't correct for this material. I felt it was unlikely that a play like this could really succeed on Broadway, and there was also just a general wariness about how fast things were happening.

I don't want to call it a tactic, but I got into a kind of exchange that can frequently happen with Joe. It was clear that he wanted to do it, the whole facility of the Public Theater was mobilized to begin to do this, and then he called me and said that he didn't want to do it if I didn't want to do it. And I said, "Whoa, no, I want to do it," so off we went.

That really wasn't a bad decision. I would never say that it was. But you can look at the move to Broadway in two ways: you benefit from it, and you get maimed from it. It won a Tony and it was a success in a sense. It was very meaningful to my career and it's remembered as a more unqualified success than it actually was. On the other hand, it really had to struggle to run up there. And when we went up there and made that struggle, I was beginning to feel like there was no time to write. When we moved to Broadway, I began to feel the burden of it all.

CLIFF DE YOUNG People would get up and very loudly stomp out of the theater on Broadway, making all the noise they could. We had a couple of what they called colloquies after some matinees. People would say, "There are two sides to the war in Vietnam, you're just saying it's all against. Why can't you give the other view?"

Being a young actor, very hot and ready to kick ass, I would stand up and rail that "The artist doesn't have to do equal time. He's not a network television show, you schmuck!" I'd start yelling, they'd start yelling at me, they'd kick me off the stage, and I couldn't go to those things anymore.

Elizabeth Wilson, who played Harriet, had a friend, George C. Scott, who was one of my favorite actors. He was coming to a performance and Liz and myself and David Selby, who played David, were going to go to dinner with George C. Scott. "Fucking hell, man. Okay! Now we're on Broadway, now we're cooking, we're with George C. Scott, we're hobnobbing with Hollywood big shots."

Right at the end of the play, I come down and talk to David. I say, "You should really kill yourself, and here's the razor." And I hear this, "*Fuck this shit! Aw! Fuck—fuck this shit! Fucking shit!*" This person is walking very loudly all the way out of the theater.

After the show, I went, "Gee, Liz, that was weird. I hope George C. Scott didn't get pissed off because of this guy."

"That was him," she said.

Needless to say, we didn't have dinner with George C. Scott. But that reaction meant to me that we were cooking. For or against, we were getting them and they were pissed. Their reactions were so extreme, they would wait for you at the stage door to try and have some kind of discussion, and I'd say, "God, I'm just an actor."

GEORGE C. SCOTT I didn't like it at all, I suppose because I'd spent four years in the Marine Corps and it didn't jibe with my philosophy. I'd been curious about Vietnam. I couldn't make up my mind either way, so in 1965 I'd gotten myself accredited as a journalist and went. I wasn't pro the war, but I was extremely pro those Americans involved therein, and, of course, they got shit on.

It's in vogue now to say what great oppressed people these soldiers were, but this is fifteen years later we're talking about. I was for them when it wasn't popular to be for them, so I remember very well coming back and being appalled at the treatment these people suffered.

GAIL MERRIFIELD PAPP Both *Two Gentlemen of Verona* and *Sticks and Bones* won Tonys that year, it was a double whammy, one of the best moments ever. Here we were the newcomers, invaders of the Broadway establishment. I thought it was a foregone conclusion that we would be shut out, but we swept it with the Best Musical and the Best Play and, oh god, talk about excitement. I really didn't think it could happen. I still don't know why it happened. It was astonishing.

JOSEPH PAPP I was so emotionally involved with David and his work and my desire for him to succeed that even though we had just won the Tony for Best Musical for *Two Gentlemen of Verona*, which is supposed to be *the* big thing, what really moved me to my very core was when *Sticks and Bones* won for Best Play. When I collected the award as producer of the show, I was weeping, it made me feel so good and so proud.

JOHN GUARE I have this feeling of Joe as a Polaroid picture on that Tony evening in 1972, when *Two Gents* and *Sticks and Bones* both won, and Joe, having been the outsider all his life, suddenly became the insider. That was astonishing, to see the change.

John Ford Noonan

My name is John Ford Noonan and I did half a dozen plays with Joe over a period of five or six years. It started with a play called *Older Women* that I showed to Mel Shapiro, who gave it to Joe. He called Illinois at three o'clock in the morning and said, "This is Joe. I want to do it. We're gonna cast the play Monday." I said, "Who the fuck?" I thought it was Billy Devane, an old friend of Joe's who was always goofin' on me.

We rushed into it, and that sort of set the tone for everything we did, which was a lot of love, full of feeling, but none of the productions were ever very good. We were always doing the wrong thing with the plays. I became like the great gym fighter who kept pulling muscles before the Madison Square Garden main events. We never commercially or even artistically made it really sing.

I'm like a hurricane, you know what I mean? I used to be a terrific basketball player and a boxer. Those are the kind of things I do well, but I have trouble sitting down. And Joe catches my disease—I give it to him and he gives it to me—we make each other worse. David Rabe, who's a guy I really love, he's slow and reflective and moody. I think him and Joe mix better.

At the same time, I really feel close to Joe as a person. If he called me up and said, "Someone's bothering me," I'd come down and hurt him. If he asked me to produce a play, I'd try to go as slow as I could, because we might get crazy again. It's like two guys who get drunk in a bar and cause trouble. I have a similar relationship with Christopher Walken. We go out at noon and we have a few beers and the next thing you know, they're asking us to be quiet. We feed each other's mania. And to be really fulfilled, you've got to have people around you who maximize your strengths and minimize your weaknesses.

I have an unfinished play called *Shakespeare's Agent*, which is about Joe when he's locked in his office and won't come out. One of his playwrights is trying to commit suicide in the bathroom, and the only person Joe can talk to is this big bust of Shakespeare. His son's calling him and his daughter's calling him and his wives are calling him and the president's calling. Everyone's making him crazy, and he wants to be left alone and just talk to Shakespeare.

He says, "My dream in life would be if I could just find one undiscovered play of yours and market it. If I could just uncover one in some suitcase somewhere." Maybe Shakespeare will come in the room, I don't know, but that's the impulse.

Joe wants to be accepted. He has the same problem I have. I just got a rejection from some hunky-bunk theater in New Jersey of a play I love. I want to go over there and rip the theater up and throw it in the street, right? I want to be accepted.

At the same time, I refuse to be accepted on any terms but my own, so that's my dilemma. Joe has that same division. He wants to tell the truth, and yet he wants acceptance from a bunch of people who wouldn't know the truth if it hit them.

You know what's great about Joe? That there was somebody in power who you truly believed cared about what you were going to write next. If you asked him now, I know it matters to him what I'm writing, or that I still am writing, or that the plays are doing well, or that I'm affecting something somewhere. It's like if your father can't come to the Little League game, at least you know he hopes you play your best.

At the same time, when I walk up to the Public now there's a certain attitude. I'm treated like a garbage collector who broke the union line twelve years ago and isn't allowed back. It's like you meet a girl that makes you so hot you can't keep it in your pants. And a week later she says, "That's it." That's Joe. He gets you so excited, so up in the clouds, like an athlete in the locker room saying, "We're gonna kick ass," and then you're down by twenty at halftime. You're both an inspired pregame player and a guy that got his ass kicked.

There's a Mafia term called "in the alley." It's a guy you can count on if it gets heavy. If someone attacks you, he'll defend you. If someone hits you with a bat, he'll pick up the bat and hit them. That's the way Joe is. He commands incredible loyalty, and he does inspire you. Once he connects with you, it doesn't matter to him what you write. He might not like it at all, but he will stand behind you.

17

That Championship Season
1972

Charles Durning and Walter McGinn
© Friedman-Abeles

Wow! Here at last is the perfect Broadway play of the season, perfectly acted and perfectly staged. There is only one minor thing wrong with it. It happens not to be on Broadway. The play is Jason Miller's *That Championship Season* and it opened last night at the handsome Newman Theater in Joseph Papp's New York Shakespeare Festival Public Theater complex. It is gorgeous and triumphant . . .

Five men meet in a house somewhere in the Lackawanna Valley. Four of them were part of the team that won the Pennsylvania High School Basketball Championship in 1952. The fifth was, and seemingly still is, their Coach. It is his house, and every year they get together to relive their past glory.

One of them is the Mayor of the town, a small Allegheny township of

54,000 souls, more or less. Another is the town's chief industrialist and polluter, a made-good businessman who specializes in strip-coal mining, women and fast cars. The third is a local high school principal, and supporter of the Mayor. The last is the teacher's brother, a visiting alcoholic from the Coast.

For a long night's journey into day they talk and fight. They bare themselves and their beliefs and their towns. They are funny, obscene and tragic. They are lost people. The Mayor is a middle-aged buffoon with a beaten face. But these are all beaten people, living in the past. That basketball success was their finest hour. And that, it turns out, was a fraud . . .

I remember Mr. Miller's first play so well that I never expected to be seeing his second. But this is a quite different matter. Here the playwright is dealing with a world he knows and understands, and he treats it with a wary mixture of love and disdain . . .

Clive Barnes, *New York Times,* May 3, 1972

JASON MILLER   I was an actor but I had written a play called *Nobody Hears a Broken Drum,* which was about the Irish miners' revolt in Pennsylvania against the oppressiveness of the basically English mine owners. It was done off Broadway, where Clive Barnes objected to its anti-English tone.

It was not a success, and I went to Fort Worth, Texas, to do a stint in *The Odd Couple* in summer theater. I had all my afternoons off, and I mean, in Fort Worth in 1969, what are you gonna do? Not a lot was happening. So I sat there for four or five hours a day—I was there for eight weeks—and I finished *Championship Season.*

My first play had twenty characters, which even then was kind of prohibitive in terms of money. I wanted something of mine done. I realized that I couldn't do the Sistine Chapel, and I decided to bring the scope down a bit. The new play ended up with one room and five men.

Without sounding mystical, it didn't start out as a reunion, it wasn't prefabricated in my mind. I just heard two guys talking in a room, and one guy said, "Scotch and water on the rocks?"—one of the opening lines in the play—and from there I just kind of sat back and listened and it began to evolve itself into what it was, what it became. I rewrote it three times, but the script that Joe did was the first draft.

The show was over; we were leaving on a Monday morning. I'd finished the play a week before, I had 153 yellow legal pages and I had them in a leather writing book. The actors were all going back to New York; we were all helping each other to pack in two cars. I was in the lead car headed for the airport with three or four other actors, four or five were in the car behind us.

For some reason, even today I can't understand why, there was something I wanted to put in the play, some flash thought came into my mind, and I looked for the play. I thought it was beside me, and when I couldn't find it, I said, "Would you stop the car?" I went in the back, I looked in my bags, and I could not find the play.

"I gotta go back to the apartment complex," I said.

"Well," they said, "we gotta catch the plane."

Then one of the actors, Dave Hennigan, said, "I'll drive you back. We'll shift everybody in the cars and I'll drive you," because he had seen me working on it for eight weeks.

So I went back to the apartment, but I couldn't find anything. I looked in the garbage, talked to everyone, talked to the manager, looked around the units—there was nothing there. The actor said, "Look, we've got to go, or we're going to miss the second plane."

We got in the car and drove back the same way we came: one-lane highway, all prairie on the side, bramble bushes, John Wayne terrain. We went about five, six miles. We turned a bend, and floating in the air, to the right side of the car, like big yellow butterflies, were about 150 pages on yellow legal sheets.

Some were floating, some caught in the bramble bushes, some on the side of the road, but at least fifty looked like a battalion of butterflies. If I had a net, I would have plucked them out of the air. Every single one of them was there.

Obviously, when we were all helping each other pack, somebody had left it on the back of the trunk, and it had fallen off. There was a tire mark over the book, while we were at the apartment a car must have hit it just right so that it opened up, the wind caught the pages and they fluttered up. Otherwise, I never would have seen it, no one would have seen it.

There is a kind of stunning moment when something like that happens. It was probably the first spiritual experience of my life. I knew then that it would get done somewhere, that someone would do it. It was kind of blessed.

JOSEPH PAPP Jason Miller (everyone called him Jack) was in a play we were producing called *Subject to Fits*, written by Robert Montgomery, based on Dostoyevsky's *The Idiot*, and directed by A. J. Antoon, and, boy, I thought he was a good actor.

Jason was thin, his face always kind of gaunt, and there was a certain intensity to him, but he had an ingenuous smile that was very, very nice. He'd never strike you as an intellectual, there was not an ounce of affectation in him. He never changed, never turned bourgeois. He was always Scranton. He let it be known that he was a writer as well as an actor, and I finally said, "Why don't you send me the play?"

He brought it in, I read it, and I felt, "It's interesting, there's some nice things in it, but, boy, this play has a lot of problems." And I was in no mood to start to deal with a playwright's problems. It would have meant really redoing it. My whole attitude toward everything is not to do it: you've got so much to do, you'd rather not do another thing.

Jason had earlier submitted the play to some producers who were interested in doing it as a Broadway show. About a week after I'd read it, he said they wanted to go ahead and I said, "Terrific." Someone else wants to do it, my god, what a load off my mind.

"You don't mind?" he said.

"If you can get it done on Broadway, by all means. I have certain problems with the play, so if someone wants it, Jesus, go right ahead."

So he took the play. Six months went by, and he came around to the office.

"Hey, when's the play going on?" I said.

"They dropped the option."

"Why?"

"They didn't like it."

"I thought they liked it."

"They worked on it, they made some changes in it, they didn't like the changes they made, so they didn't like the play."

"Let me see the changes they made."

I took the play and I could not believe what they did with it. They'd emasculated that play, they'd actually butchered the whole thing, and then they said they didn't like it. It was so typical.

"Oh my god," I said. "They just ruined your play."

"What do you think, can you do it?"

"Jack, there's a lot of stuff in there that needs work."

"Can't we have a reading of it?"

"I don't see how I can do that."

The next thing I know, he came in with A. J. Antoon, who was one of my prime directors at that point, terrific, a marvelous disposition and a whimsical mind.

"Joe," he said, "I think this is a good play and I'd love to direct it. Can't we have a reading of it?" Jason came in again, brought his wife in, his kids were there, too, laying it heavily on me, and I'm a sucker for that. So I said okay to the reading.

GAIL MERRIFIELD PAPP Jason was very reticent, very somber, with this kind of brooding face, sunk down in the middle of the couch in Joe's office. He was squashed there. And A.J. was very supportive, really a major force in trying to retrieve this play from its manhandling. And there were still problems that needed to be worked through, but you were really hobbled until some of the grievous damage that can be done to a person about their own ability and talent had healed and confidence been recovered.

A. J. ANTOON I left the Yale Drama School in the middle of my second year—I just quit and came to New York. I did a workshop at St. Clement's Church of a Chekhov Story Theater I'd done at Yale, and an actress who saw it set up a meeting with Joe Papp.

Joe seemed very friendly, very in control, smoked a large cigar during the whole thing. I think he was impressed with the fact that I didn't like Yale. He said he didn't want to do the Chekhov, but he liked my work, and if I could come up with another project, he would give me the space.

That's when I brought him *Subject to Fits*, which a friend of mine, Robert Montgomery, had written at Yale. We had a meeting—Joe, myself, and the author—and at one point, even though I had brought him the play, Joe said to the author, with me right there, "Do you really want this guy to direct it?" I was convinced that Bob would say yes—no one else was peddling his play—but you began to realize that Joe can switch around whenever he wants to.

I saw Jason Miller walking in the corridor of the Public. He was saying, "I'm doin' it tonight. I'm doin' it—fuck! I don't fuckin' know my fuckin' lines." I wondered, "Who is that person?" It turned out he was understudying in *The Happiness Cage*, so I went to watch him and I thought, "This is the intensity that I want for Rogozhin in *Subject to Fits*." He was exactly the way I imagined Rogozhin to look and he was terrific in that part.

The coincidence around myself and Jason Miller is pretty amazing. When I had first come to New York, one of the places I stayed was at a house in Brooklyn where the husband and wife were going to Texas to do *The Odd Couple*. They invited me to a watch a run-through before they left town, and as it turned out—and only years later did I find this out—one of the cardplayers in that production was Jason Miller. And it was during that production in Texas that he almost lost the script.

When we got to work on *Subject to Fits*, Joe always left me alone. It became a big hit off Broadway, and based on that I did *Cymbeline* for him in the park, even though I'd never directed anything with more than ten people in the cast. I thought it was pretty amazing that he would trust a young director—I was twenty-six—with that job.

I ran into Jason on the street one day, and he was very, very, very depressed—and Jason can get very depressed—that these Broadway producers were turning his characters into Kennedy men and had dropped his play.

"Why don't we do this," I said. "Joe is the writer's producer. Why don't I go in and say, 'Joe, they've ruined this guy's play. What do you think?'" And that's exactly what I did.

"I used to like that play," Joe said. "That play's been on my shelf. I was thinking of doing it at one point."

Jason was acting in a play in Washington, D.C., at that time, and I suggested that I go down there. And before and after his performance we would sit down and collate the two scripts, his original and what we called the Kennedy-men script. There were a couple of good speeches in the Kennedy script, but it had lost a lot of its impact. Cutting and pasting and retyping, we put together a new script and brought that to Joe.

The next step in the process was that we would have a reading of the play. We put together a wonderful cast: Patrick McVey played the Coach, Chuck Cioffi played the businessman, and Charles Durning, Walter McGinn, and Michael McGuire played the parts they later had in the full production.

JASON MILLER I was down in Washington doing *Juno and the Paycock* with Geraldine Fitzgerald and A.J. came down with the two scripts.

"Let's cut out all the shit that you've added," he said. "Let's go back to zero. Let's go back to what it was originally, when it poured out next to a B-52 air force base in 110-degree heat in Fort Worth, Texas. Go right back. Not a period changed."

We stayed for a week in this very cold, drafty apartment in a place called Turkey Thicket and we rewrote and rewrote. At the end of that week, we came right back to the original script that was plucked out of the air, not a word changed. Not a word.

He brought it to Joe, and Joe said, "I'm not interested." Joe was into expanding the consciousness of the American theater, à la avant-garde stuff, derivative European stuff, competition against La MaMa. He was very anti-Broadway, very anticommercialism, very anti–star system. He was looking for the playwright with newness, I suppose, and this was a three-act play because these were three-act people.

But Joe had loved *Subject to Fits* and he was intrigued that A.J., who seemed to be the Ionesco director of our time, got involved in this traditional, boxed, three-act play. And he said to A.J., "Let me hear a reading of it. You cast it. You guys pick it." He gave us total artistic freedom. We knew actor's actors, no stars, no great names, but guys who were powerful and solid, whose egos would be submitted to the service of the play, to the idea of the piece.

CHARLES DURNING I had done all these Shakespearean plays for Joe, but I was playing the clowns and I wanted to play some heavy roles, something more dramatic. I told Joe, and he said, "You're here to serve our needs, we're not here to serve yours. If I cast you in one of these other roles, that means I've got to worry about you playing that role, and I've got to worry about the guy who is playing the clown because I don't know his work. But when a part comes along that I think you're right for, you'll get it."

Jason Miller said to me, "I have a play that I think you'd be good for." Now I'd heard that over and over again, so I said, "Yeah, yeah, send it to me, it would be terrific," knowing full well that it would never happen. But once Joe decided to do it, he gave it to me immediately. I was the first one cast in that show. "Remember when I said about when I had a part for you? Here it is, if you want to play it." Without reading it I said, "I want to play it. I don't give a shit. I'll play it."

JASON MILLER A.J. took the guys and rehearsed them for three days. It was a brilliant move; it wasn't reading cold. It was wonderful. I watched Papp out of the corner of my eye, lighting a cigar, leaning on the table and kind of laughing, and I knew that he was mightily impressed by this initial reading of this straight, realistic play which he had eschewed.

Joe dismissed everybody and he took A.J. and myself up to his office. He lit a cigar, walked around, had one of those long Papp pauses, and said, "I'll do it. You guys cast it, but you gotta get me a Coach. If you find me a Coach, I'll do the play." A.J. and I walked out of there exhilarated, went over to an old bar named Frank's, had a couple of beers, and said, "Well, how are we gonna find a Coach?"

A. J. ANTOON We went to Joe Papp's office, and he was about to tell us the bad news, that he was not going to produce the play, and he started off telling us all his reasons. And Jason and I just looked at each other. I started talking, dropping names like Willy Loman and King Lear, and you could see Joe visibly change. And by the end of this meeting where he was to tell us that he wasn't going to do it, he was really excited about doing it—if we could find the Coach.

JOSEPH PAPP It was an interesting reading. I saw what was nice about the play. I kind of enjoyed it, but on the other hand, there was an inconsistency that ran right through the play, there was a problem with the ending, and I thought, "I can't do this play."

I called A.J. and Jason into my office and I said, "Look, I love you guys, you're so terrific, but I just don't see myself doing this play. There are so many problems with it, I don't want to get involved. Just for example . . ."

I began to demonstrate this, I began to demonstrate that, I said, "Why does this happen in the ending?" I spoke for about an hour, and though I had been absolutely determined not to do that play, before I knew it, I said, "Okay, I'll do it." I talked myself into it just by dealing with the problems of the play. I became so involved; I surprised myself totally. You would not believe it.

CHARLES DURNING   In the meantime, I did *Look Homeward, Angel* for David Susskind, and I said to E. G. Marshall, who was in the cast, "I've got a play that you would be wonderful for. It's called *That Championship Season*, it's for Joe Papp, and they need the part of a Coach."

"I don't do off Broadway," E.G. said.

"This has the potential to go to Broadway."

"Have him call me."

Joe called him, but Joe wanted an ensemble piece, everybody the same, and E.G. wanted billing over the title, he wanted a percentage of it if it went, he wanted the world. And Joe said, "No, I can't do that."

We're still looking, and Joe called Jack Warden and Jack said, "I'm doing *Death of a Salesman* in Chicago."

"I've got *Death of a Salesman* sitting on my desk right now," Joe said, "and you can create the role."

"No, I've always wanted to play *Death of a Salesman*, so I'm going to do it."

"Just read the play."

He said no.

JASON MILLER   I believe Papp reserved the right to pick the Coach because, in essence, he identified very deeply with this role—very, very deeply. What you've got is a strong, powerful, dictatorial figure who has compassion and love as well as his own built-in cultural prejudices, his own demons. Joe Papp, beyond all the liberalism, beyond the socialism, beyond his immense social consciousness, was the Coach. I think when he heard the play read that night, it touched something very deep in him. Joe used to say to me every once in a while, "You know, I could play the Coach."

When I wrote the play, I wrote it with George C. Scott in mind. He was my prototype. A.J. sent the script to his agent, unsolicited, and we never heard a response. And Joe, in his wisdom, said, "He's a great actor, but we don't need him for this," because he didn't want to break the ensemble with a star. Then A.J. and I went to see *Little Foxes*, and there was an actor in there, Richard Dysart. A.J. and I looked at each other and I said, "That's him."

Chuck Cioffi couldn't play the businessman, so we had to find another Phil. "We've got everybody, but you lost Chuck," Joe said. "I don't want to go in without a Phil." Then A.J. went to a movie called *Made for Each Other* and Paul Sorvino was playing an old man.

"You've got to see this guy," he said.

"Are you kidding," I said. "Who's Paul Sorvino?"

Sorvino came in to read and he filled the room, I mean he filled the place. He looked at the script, threw it aside, and started improvising.

"I think that's him," Papp said.

"Isn't he a wonderful actor," A.J. said.

"Yeah, great," I said. "But let's see him read the script, though, and see what he thinks about it."

PAUL SORVINO   I was called on a Saturday while I was raking leaves at my home in New Jersey.

"You have an audition with Joe Papp at five o'clock this afternoon," someone said.

And I said, "No."

"This is the New York Shakespeare Festival and you have an audition this afternoon for a play directed by A. J. Antoon."

"It's a cartoon?" I thought. "What cartoon?"

"Who are you?" I said.

"The New York Shakespeare Festival."

"What do you mean? The Shakespeare in the Park people?" I didn't know who the hell they were, I really didn't. I had no awareness of the off-Broadway scene. I never went through that purgatory, so I knew nothing of it.

"I don't understand," I said. "I didn't ask for an audition for anyone, nor do I have one. Who are you? What do you want from me?" As yet unknown to the public, I'd already done about six movies, and between that and commercials, I was making in the six figures already, so I was getting pretty arrogant.

"Well," she said, "you've been requested."

"It's a new play, huh?" I said. "The way it works is, you call my agent, and then he and I discuss it, you send me a script, and then I'll let you know if I'm interested. But not without an offer. But, all right, I'll be there." I was very grand about the whole thing, but something told me to follow it up anyway, and I did.

I walked in and I saw this dark figure, hunched-over shoulders, with a lined, gaunt, Black Irish face and tense, coal-black eyes, eyes like eyes at the bottom of a well. His face had an extraordinarily deep look. Not to inspire fear but awe and real interest, and I said, "Who is this man?" I was absolutely fascinated by him, and I was told that that was Jason Miller. I saw into him right away, let's put it that way. There was some sort of a communication that went beyond the formalities.

I met A. J. Antoon, we talked a little bit, and he said, "I'd really like you to come and meet Mr. Papp and read for him."

"I don't know," I said. "I'll have to read the play." But something really interested me about this meeting. So I took the play, and as is my wont, I started reading it at traffic lights driving back to New Jersey. I was so fascinated that by the time I came into the house, I'd read better than half of it. I was really pulsating with excitement when I walked in. I sat down at the kitchen table and said to my wife, "I can't talk, I've got to finish reading this." I was absolutely gripped by it.

I finished reading, absolutely broken down in tears for the great tragedy of it. I looked up at my wife, and as I'm weeping, I said to her, "This is the greatest play since *Death of a Salesman*. If I do this play in New York, I'll become a star overnight." That's what I said.

I went in on Monday and auditioned for Joe Papp, A.J., and Jason. I read two speeches, got very excited, and threw the script down during one of them. I knew I was there, I just knew it.

There was never a role better written for an actor than that role was for me. It was not written for the articulate Paul Sorvino; it was written for the emotional Paul Sorvino. There was an absolute relationship, an identifiable and immediate relationship with my insides. It was as if Jason had peered into my soul, extracted it, and put it on paper. Phil Romano is very much like me without education, without sophistication, and without having married a good woman. If I had not married the woman I married, it very likely would have been me. Bitter, searching, and desperate.

Anyway, for whatever reason an actor adheres to a part, I certainly was glued to that one. It was an immediate fastening, and there was no escaping it. I knew at the audition that I had the role. I knew it immediately. They didn't say it, but they said it. It was mine.

Later, I heard that someone had said, "I wonder if he respects the material," because I had thrown the script on the ground in the emotion of the moment.

"I don't know about that," Papp said, "but he's the guy who's going to play the role."

RICHARD DYSART I had an old VW square-back and we all piled into it one day and drove up to Scranton. This was before we even got to the play, before any rehearsals or anything. I'll tell ya, that was one of the wildest times of my life; it was just a hoot. It was sort of a birthing, a coming together of various guys, actors and A.J., everyone anxious to know everyone else and to get that chemistry going. We laughed a lot—we laughed and laughed and laughed—I think because we were all aware that somehow it was going to work.

In Jason's mind, the main thing was he wanted to show us the town, he wanted us to meet a few people, and, in particular, he wanted to show us the house that he had in mind as the Coach's home. We didn't do any drinking on the way, but once we got there, we figured we better have a drink.

Right after we got there, Jason found out that there was a basketball game that evening, a high school championship game, and off we went. We left the house and the grandmothers and the aunts and what have you, who were a little awed by us, and piled in the car. Michael McGuire had a good little tape recorder with him, and when they started to play the national anthem, he turned it on and we used that for the opening of the play.

After the game, we headed downtown and went to a restaurant owned by a friend of Jason's, had some more drinks, and talked. They were closing up, so off we went to some after-hours place in Scranton or nearby and stayed there till sunup. Yeah, that was pretty wild. But, in a way, that opened us up to the experience.

THEONI ALDREDGE The rehearsal was a zoo. It was all these actors, all good actors, a lot of them with egos a little bigger than they should have been. They all had equal roles, they were all males, it was touch and go, like "Who's going to throw a fit now?"

Paul Sorvino was a little too big a head at the time, he started questioning things, and I watched Charles Durning. Don't muck around with Charles. Charles is the most patient human walking, the angel of the world. But do not step on the tenth toe. The nine don't hurt. The tenth, watch out because that is a man that has been tortured—he was in a war, it wasn't easy—so don't do that. Charlie can be violent.

I would run up to Joe and say, "I think they're killing themselves down below." And Joe would go down and say, "If anybody does any fighting here, any fighting, it's going to be me." And everybody became just calm.

Joe had authority, and authority doesn't come because you wake up one morning and decide you're Hitler. It comes because of knowledge and because of understanding. Joe knows the psyche of an actor. He knows what makes them happy or unhappy, and they know, when he screams and carries on, it's because he loves them. With as little money as we had, he said, "I don't care, Theoni, they have to be comfortable on their feet," so the shoes were always something we paid money for. It takes a caring man.

JOSEPH PAPP A crisis began to arise during the rehearsal period. The actors came to me like every day. They began to hate Paul Sorvino. He was a rather easygoing kind of character. He would fool around a lot and he never approached it seriously. He had little stage experience, but he was so right for the part. The others would say, "He's not an actor," and so forth and so on. I never saw people behave so badly. I mean, Charlie Durning was going to kill him. I saw what they were saying, but I thought he was good.

One day, Richard Dysart walked in and said to me, "Listen, it's either him or me."

"Goodbye," I said. "What the hell's the matter with you guys? You're making him the goat of the whole thing." It was a most unusual company. It went through the throes. There was a tremendous amount of turbulence, but I would not let any of those things stop the play.

RICHARD DYSART   We were a little put out, I might say, at Sorvino, because his way of getting rid of excess energy was to break into arias, which is fine, but not necessarily considerate of other people who may have wanted a little silence. I remember talking to Charlie about it, saying, "I'm pissed off about this." I didn't want to confront Sorvino with it, and I didn't want to throw it on A.J. alone, so I said, "I'll go see Joe."

I told him how difficult it was to work, how I had had a great deal of repertory experience and such, but I'd never run into anything like this before. I recall him sitting there and looking at me rather blankly, as if to say, "What's with this guy? What is he proposing to do? Is he going to pack his bags and go home?"—which certainly wasn't my intention. No, I spied that play coming early on, and I was not about to do that. Occasionally you'll pick up a play and it comes alive off the page. And that feeling grew; the whole experience took on a personality of its own.

Joe was there, and yet he wasn't there. He wasn't physically there all the time, but Joe's overall guidance, Joe's overall selectivity process, was the key to bringing everything together. He oversaw it without intruding.

CHARLES DURNING   There was a lot of dissension. It was like a family, like brothers who hate each other one day and love each other the next. One month you'd be close to one actor; the next month you'd be close to another actor. There were egos, people who thought they were better than they were at that time. The only one who was really steady and didn't give a shit about anything was the guy that nobody wanted to begin with, Walter McGinn, and he mainly held it together.

I was the first one cast in this play, and on the first day of rehearsal, Paul Sorvino came to me and said, "I'm so glad that you decided to join my show." This is the first day. That's probably something he never even remembers. I kind of went, "Who the fuck is this?" He'd get on my nerves once in a while, but I suppose I got on his nerves, too.

"This is an ensemble piece," we said. "If one person gets a Tony nomination, we turn it down. We all get the nomination, or nobody gets a nomination." We all agreed to that. Well, Paul was the only one that got the nomination, and he said, "Sure, I'll accept it." We were pissed off at him for a while.

Paul is very strong, but if he doesn't have his trailer or if somebody else has a bigger wardrobe than he does, he demands that. And he talks about himself a lot. If you can get through that, then you're all right. He is a major talent, there's no question about that, but he is also a major pain in the ass.

A.J. and I became very good friends afterward, but this was A.J.'s first major thing and he and I were having a lot of trouble. He was an unfrocked priest, a Jesuit. He was very, very, very bright, and I didn't understand any of that brightness. I was just a guy hanging around, and I thought he was condescending and wouldn't listen to other people's input.

We locked A.J. out mentally several times. The actors would get together and we wouldn't let him hear what we were saying. He'd say, "I want to hear what's going on," and we'd shut up and walk away. Not that there was any conspiracy. It was just that we didn't think he knew what he was doing.

I quit the show three times. And Joe kept saying, "What the fuck is the matter with you? You've got a play like this, and you're gonna go quit?"

"I'll stay with the play if you direct it," I said.

"I can't direct it. I've got other things to do."

"You come down once a week and direct me. I can handle everything else in between. But I don't want to talk to the director anymore."

"You've got to talk to him. He's standing there."

There was a moment after I tried to shoot Phil, Paul Sorvino's character, when I put my head through the window to holler at him. At the very end of it, I banged my head on the window, which brought a big laugh. A.J. said to me, "This is a dramatic moment. You shouldn't get a laugh there."

"The dramatic moment is over when I don't kill him," I said. "It is a legitimate laugh because it relieves tension. The only way I'm going to change it is if Joe comes down here and tells me to change it."

So Joe came down, he saw it, and he said, "Leave it in."

We had another argument about the last scene of the play, when we're all looking at the camera for a snapshot. I looked at Paul with anger, and A.J. said to me, "Don't look at Paul like that. Look out front."

"No," I said. "I think that the guy is still resentful of a guy who has fucked his best friend's wife. The only way I'm going to change it is if Joe comes down and tells me to change it."

So Joe came down, he said, "Let me see it," and then he said, "Who won the last argument?"

"I did," I said.

"You lose this one."

I had the first line in the play, and when I came onstage I was always looking at the floor. And I would see money on the stage that hadn't been there before the curtain. There'd be a quarter, a dime, pennies, strewn around the stage. I would be concentrating on "Where the hell did that money come from?" and I would go up in my line. It threw me every night.

The rest of the cast told me Dick Dysart was doing it. When I found out what he was doing, what I started to do was pick up the money. I'd just pick it up, put it in my pocket, and I wouldn't return it to him. It was a petty thing on my part and even more petty on his part. Well, he's a tight son of a bitch, and after he lost about a dollar and a half, and when he saw that it wasn't bothering me anymore, then he stopped it.

One night, off Broadway, we hadn't opened yet, we were sitting backstage, just talking and waiting to come back on again, and I turned to Dick Dysart and said, "What the hell do we have here?"

"What was your biggest hit?" he said.

I told him and he said, "This is going to run longer and we're all going to work for ten years on the success of this."

So he knew, but nobody else knew. Chuck Cioffi turned Paul Sorvino's part down. He went to do a movie for $10,000 because he didn't think it was going to go. I ran into him after we opened and I said, "Do you want me to kick you now or later?" And he bent over.

It made my career. It made all of our careers. It was like gold, like finding a pot at the end of the rainbow. Right after that I started doing movies, and I haven't stopped. I had been in a lot of plays, maybe 180 plays, but nobody was noticing it. Nobody. Including my family. The only one who took any notice was Joe.

PAUL SORVINO It was a turbulent rehearsal, boy, was it ever. It was a strange gathering of styles, because there weren't two actors who played in the same way or had the same background.

I was the Method actor. Walter McGinn was the Method and not-Method actor. Charlie Durning was the natural. I don't think he ever studied in his life, nor did he ever have to, he's so marvelous. Michael McGuire is pure Shakespearean, Guthrie Theater and all of that. Richard Dysart was very experienced, a famous regional theater actor, had been in hundreds of plays. I had very little experience onstage, and at thirty-three I was the youngest in the cast. Most of the other fellas were in their forties and fifties.

I really was the beginner, I was the upstart, I was the pain in the ass. I'm a big guy, six foot three inches tall, I have a very powerful voice, and not a quiet personality, and I know that if I don't rein that in really carefully, I can put people off, I can annoy them. And I apologize to my colleagues for this. It was all in youth, certainly not in malice. Now that I'm older, decorum has become a bigger part of my life.

It was probably my absolute assurance which rankled everybody. Not meaning to be so, and really not trying to inflict it on anyone, but because I was so melded with that role right from the start, I'm sure I had a terrible know-it-all attitude. I wasn't in doubt about anything about that role. I absolutely knew what to do, as if by instinct.

I had that arrogance of youth that thank god doesn't stay with you too long, if you have any brains at all. You think you are the answer to all questions and the last word on everything. I felt that way about my acting, and that may have bothered some who were looking for their roles.

I also have the habit of engaging the other players in solving problems. And some actors don't like that. They feel it's an invasion of their privacy, an invasion of their work process. I like to work the scenes out together. Some people can interpret that as me directing them, but it's not. If you don't know me, you can misunderstand that.

Either by inference or by direct request, I wanted us to relate to one another. I knew the value of real ensemble playing in this particular play, and I wanted that right from the start. Without even articulating it to myself, that's what I was pushing for, and that could have rankled everybody because I was ready for that much earlier than the others were.

I forced the issue every day at rehearsal, I absolutely forced it. I wouldn't let them off the hook. I regret if I put anyone off, but I certainly don't regret the results because I do think that I was instrumental. I was a good force for what became the style of the play.

McGinn and I sort of always got along. Durning didn't quite know what to make of me, he was watching me. Dysart and I were absolute polarities, total opposite ends. And we did not get along. I knew he really hated what I was doing, and I think he hated my attitude. Now that I look back, I don't blame him one bit. We never confronted one another, but I have it on good authority that he went to the power that be and said, "Me or him," and Joe said, "No way."

For some reason, Michael McGuire developed this antipathy toward me, almost in the first few days, which I did not understand. Nasty remarks, cutting remarks, noncooperation, obvious contempt for me and my work.

About the third week, it was becoming unbearable for me, so I walked up to him and said, "I can't go on with this any longer. If I have offended you, I would like to know how, and you have to give me an opportunity to make it right. But if it's not anything like that, let's go outside and duke it out right now. I'm not going five more minutes this way." We started to talk, we went outside, I don't know how the hell we did it—we probably had dinner and a drink together—but we became the very best of friends you could imagine.

A.J. was a child. He was a Jesuit who had just left the seminary, as a matter of fact. I found him an engaging fellow, you could see he was smart, and I think he has an especially wonderful visual eye. As far as performances, they were done by the actors. Our impression was that he laid back and let us do it, he allowed us to pretty much find it ourselves. He created a good climate for that, which is what a director must do.

He did not coach the actors, because he was not in a position to coach actors of such experience and ability, myself not included, because I was a young guy. Him just coming out of a seminary, he couldn't say anything to them. They'd say, "Yeah, that's nice, Fah-thah." At his age, and with this bunch of powerhouses, that was the right thing to do. You can't argue with results, because the results were phenomenal.

SANTO LOQUASTO I'm chilled at the recollection of the rehearsals. They were quarrelsome and affectionate and rough with each other, and rowdy and gentle. They were very rough with A.J., who was a gentle man and rather at odds with the world of that play. It was the kind of jocks growing up that many of us were on the outskirts of, but he was passionately drawn to it. I think his objectivity, and his fondness for it, is what gave the play the edge it had.

A. J. ANTOON Any play that deals intensely with people, which *Season* does, with the actors very close to their parts, there's bound to be some tension. Charlie Durning's own life experience very much resembled that play, with his wife leaving him. At one point, one of the actors was threatening not to come to rehearsal anymore. But it was never really severe. I don't think it ever got out of hand.

During the first two weeks of rehearsal, I thought that the animosity of the characters—not the actors, but the characters—had reached a point where the play was boring. I stopped it in the middle of the first run-through, and I started talking to them about how these people had been together for twenty years, there had to be a lot of love.

I wanted them to do it again, and the note was to postpone any confrontation, take any acting choice except confrontation. I used the example from the Jesuits, who are told, "If you see somebody doing something that looks wrong, give them the plus sign." In other words, you make a positive excuse in your head for why they are doing such a thing.

We had this one line, which is something I still use now as a director, which was, "Love one another and keep up the pace." That was the key to that one. Because if people really love each other and start hurting each other, or don't want to hurt each other and are forced into those situations, it became painful.

JASON MILLER It was like therapy, but it was beyond therapy. You'd go to rehearsal, and everybody's got their cocks out. Unbelievable. The play brought out some primordial male paranoia and competition and sense of betrayal that they could not leave on the stage.

One of the actor's wives had just left him for an Italian, and in the play, one of the character's best friends is fucking his wife. When they came to those scenes in rehearsal, we literally had to restrain the one guy, he was going to kill the other guy. I mean, there were fists thrown and bottles broken and stage managers having to tackle one guy and me having to tackle the other guy.

In the national tour, they would play the play offstage. They had fistfights at the curtain. They were punching the piss out of each other, and the audience all applauded—they thought it was the curtain call.

The stabilizing influence, the saint, the jewel of the play was Walter McGinn. His steadiness, his love of the play, his understanding of all the other actors was the example that quietly went around and started to create the ensemble feeling.

We were dealing with personality problems constantly, constantly. There was a tremendous maelstrom of, at times violent, emotional activity. Because they knew they had something, but they didn't know what they had. So, could it be lost?

Two characters would always band together against the other two characters. "What's he doing? Son of a bitch! Is he upstaging me?" And then the next week it would switch. Then—and this is just human psychology, there was nothing premeditated about it at all, they were in the grip of something that was a bit beyond them as human beings—they went after the Coach, who was the father figure. We had an arena.

Finally, Joe Papp came down. He walked onstage after a rehearsal and he said, "You've got something here, boys, and the only ones that can destroy it is yourselves." And that's all he said. I'll never forget that.

JOSEPH PAPP There were still problems with the play, and Jason would do everything I'd tell him to do. I'd say, "Look, this scene . . . ," and he'd come in the next day and he'd do it. I was getting more and more worried, because he was doing *everything* I said. I can't write the play, you know, and when the writer is as responsive as he was, it worries me.

Finally, we were about a week away from opening, and there was still a double ending to the play, things were all interwoven and confusing. "Look," I finally said to him, "you've got to make a choice about how you want to end this play, because otherwise it's going to go this way and that way and the audience will be confused. And I think you should do it this way."

"Well, Joe," he said, "I don't think so." I almost fell over with joy. With joy!

"What do you think?" I said.

He told me, and boy, he was right on. He began to change that ending, he began to fool around with that, and in a couple of days it was just right. From then on, he was his own boss. And did I love that.

JASON MILLER We played with the ending the last six or seven days, and this is where Papp and A.J. were very helpful. I had everyone leaving the house, like a slowly deflating balloon, with the Coach left alone. He put on the television set, got an old can of beer, sat down, and then the lights went down. And that was unsatisfactory to Joe and to A.J. They felt it was downbeat and very depressing, that there had to be a more poetic image.

"Don't leave the man alone, love has healed," Joe said. "It may be right in a novel, it may be right in a short story, but I don't think it's right for the theater."

I agreed with him, but I didn't know what to do. We didn't even have it during previews. We didn't come to it until about three days before we opened. A.J. and I were watching the play, and all of a sudden, when James takes the Coach's picture and says, "I got you, Coach," me and A.J. turned to one another and said, "That's the ending." And that was it. No more discussion. That was it.

PAUL SORVINO The first time we played in front of an audience, we came off after the first act and we were absolutely livid because people were roaring with laughter. We were absolutely *furious*, just terribly hurt and shocked that we had this great drama and there'd be this great laugh every minute and a half. It was too much for us to take, and it went through all three acts.

That repeated itself every time out, and we began to understand that we had a seriocomic masterpiece on our hands. As much as I like to talk about how I knew the play, I had no idea there was one laugh in it. I saw it as a great juggernaut of a tragedy. No one saw how funny the play was. We were all shocked. But once every audience did it, we began to understand what we had. We began to isolate the laughs and do it the right way.

That play made my career, absolutely made my career. That year I was offered about a TV series a week, and I was offered many movies. When George C. Scott came to see it, he was weeping at the end of the play, as so many did, and he said, "Enjoy it. You may not get this again for twenty years." And I said, "I wonder if he's right?" And he was right. The twenty years is not up yet, but I certainly haven't found it since. A play like that, with that kind of role, that is unbelievable.

JOSEPH PAPP It was a gorgeous opening, because I felt so proud of that company. I would say this was the best ensemble acting we've ever had. And I was so proud of Jack. He and his wife were so damn poor, and now they were going to get some money. The play won every prize, most highly decorated soldier in World War II.

It seemed to be the most natural thing to move to Broadway, and the set turned out to fit perfectly in the Booth Theatre. Perfectly. Ironically, Jack hasn't written a play since. Both he and Chuck Gordone. We call that the "Pulitzer curse." And I mean, those guys were *writers*.

I once went to see the Lubavitcher Rov, this great Hasidic rabbi in Brooklyn, and the place was packed, like sardines. I was way at one end of the room, and they took hold of me and kept pushing me, almost lifting me up as I went, and suddenly I'm there. Going through them, being part of that physical thing, feeling the closeness of these Jewish men in prayer, it's a form of ecstasy. It reminded me of when I was a kid in shul, constantly surrounded; it was something that was quite beautiful. And I felt that way about *Championship Season*.

We were all so close and I was in the center of the work: you feel the company say, "You are one of us." It's a funny thing, a producer needs to be accepted by the company. But you're accepted only when they feel you are with them, you are doing for them, you are looking out for them.

When that happens, it's a tremendous feeling, very strong, almost a physical thing. You've been part of that experience, you've made it happen, and you can tell by their faces and the way they look at you that there's a lot of love there. You don't get as much from your children, sometimes, because it's a different kind of relationship. It has nothing to do with long runs. With long runs, people get alienated, people move away. It's the creation of the work that's most important. You feel like you're part of something. It's just the most extraordinary thing.

JASON MILLER That play was a turning point in all our lives. One day we were going west, and the next day we were going east. We made a 180-degree turn in all our lives. It was all the clichés, an indescribable exhilaration. We conquered New York theater. A bunch of guys who were unknown, playwright unknown, actors unknown, rep guys, craftsmen, professional men who were willing, probably, to spend the rest of their lives in artistic obscurity—suddenly we had fame. Fame occurred to all of us. And how we dealt with it is another book.

I had three kids at the time, and I was living out of a Wheaties box in Queens. My mother could own a candle factory, all the candles she lit for me. I had to borrow $500 from Joe the week before the play opened.

The night it opened on Broadway, I took my wife around the block—my wife at the time—and said, "We've got to be real careful now, because poverty held us together, but this is going to be a big success. An enormous change, a solstice, is about to take place in our lives, and we've got to be careful with each other. The world loves to come between people, and I don't know how well I can handle this type of success, or you, or anyone else. It's going to be surreal." And it was. We gained a lot, but we lost a lot, too. The Lord giveth, and he taketh away, I guess.

Billy Friedkin went to see *Championship Season* and he saw my picture in the program. He had Roy Scheider already cast for *The Exorcist*. I'd never acted in a movie before in my life, but he called me up because he loved the play and he knew I'd been to Jesuit schools and he had a hunch.

"You want to play the role?" he said.

"Yeah, I'll play the role," I said.

I went down to tell Joe because he has that patriarchal sense. You sit down and you say, "Lookit, this is what I'm going to do next."

"Don't do it," he said. "It's coming too fast for you. Stay and write."

"I'm also an actor, Joe," I said. "And this fell out of the sky. I didn't campaign for it."

September 20 was my first day of filming on *The Exorcist*, and about October 10 I was on a beach loaded with people in Far Rockaway. My son Jordan, who was six, was playing by the water's edge. And a motorcycle came down the beach. I just caught it out of the corner of my eye, and I had a premonition and started running to him. I was telling him to stay there, and he thought I was telling him to come up. The motorcycle hit him and he was in a coma for ten days.

Joe came to the hospital every day, and when he didn't come, he called up. Got me the best doctors, consoled my wife, got daily reports from the doctors and called me at work with them. He brought Jordan a huge panda bear. When I had to work at night, he would go up to the hospital and sit with my wife. Joe is a man of tremendous compassion.

BERNARD GERSTEN We were really zapping them out, just like when a ball team is hitting. We had four plays on Broadway within a very, very brief span of time. First *Two Gentlemen of Verona*, then *Sticks and Bones*, *That Championship Season*, and later *Much Ado About Nothing*. I remember we hired a big sign on Forty-second Street: "New York Shakespeare Festival, the Best of Broadway" was our operating slogan. We had out-Merricked Merrick, and there was a sense of power—great, great power. Those were very heady days.

Championship Season was just a stunner because it was a triple-crown winner, which in New York theater means the New York Drama Critics' Circle, the Tony, and the Pulitzer Prize. To win any of these is quite something; to win all three is almost unheard of.

There was a wonderful quote from Lanford Wilson, who said, "Imagine what it must be like the day you sit down to write after having won the Pulitzer Prize, and the first thing you type on the typewriter is, 'This is the next play by the last Pulitzer Prize playwright.' Then try to type the next line. That's very difficult." There is a burden to being excessively rewarded for your achievements early on, before you've established all your work habits or before you've built up the hide to take it. When it happens young, it's a problem.

JASON MILLER We'd been filming the levitation scene in *The Exorcist* for two weeks because nothing worked, when I was called upstairs to take a phone call from my agent.

"Guess what?" he said.

"What?"

"You won the Pulitzer Prize."

It didn't quite register right away. I didn't do a backflip and I didn't know who to call. I was so deep in the priest's role that Jason Miller was a bit lost. And *Championship Season* was a bit lost, like something coming from another planet. Then the AD came in and said, "Come on, we have to shoot it again."

When I went downstairs, the whole crew was there, my wife and kids came in, there was champagne, and they stopped the filming for the afternoon and everybody raised a toast. But it was still somewhat removed for me, I didn't quite realize it.

Then I thought, "I'll have to get my suit and write a big speech and everything like that." I was home, working on my speech, when there was a knock on the door. There's a mailman and he's got this COD package. I gave him $2, opened it up, and there's this thing that said "The Pulitzer Prize—Jason Miller" and a check stapled to it for $1,000. And that's it. There is no ceremony; they don't bring anybody together at Sardi's. I thought there was going to at least be some kind of festivity.

When you win the Pulitzer Prize, other people go after you. It attracts them, but then they want to test you. You're always writing under a strain, you're always writing under a challenge: "How good are you, to get the Pulitzer Prize? Show me. Prove to me that you deserve this prize." Their expectations, especially if you write for movies, or if you try to do some good television work, are phenomenal.

One of the problems is, where else do you go? You gonna write another one? I mean, you can't be writing for prizes all your life. The irony of *Championship Season* is, it's against awards, it's against trophies, it's against achievement. It's a play that unequivocally says, "Life isn't about attaining awards, because that's the first vulnerability toward corruption," yet it won five of them.

Joe wants to be immortal. The theater's not so much a profession to Joe, it's a vocation, all his Hebraic spiritualism is put into this.

"The credit belongs to the man who is actually in the arena, whose face is marred by dust and sweat and blood, who knows the great devotions and the great enthusiasms, who spends himself in a worthy cause. And if he fails, at least he fails while daring greatly, so that his place shall never be with those cold and timid souls that know neither victory nor defeat." That's from *Championship Season*, and that's Joe Papp.

18

Much Ado About CBS
and Lincoln Center

Papp and Mitzi
Newhouse at Lincoln
Center
Courtesy of the New York
Public Library

For Theatrical Impresario Joseph Papp last week was like a good-news, bad-news joke. On one hand, he broadened his institutional base enough to make him the most powerful man in the American theater. On the other hand, one of his fondest dreams—to bring good drama to millions of people on nationwide TV—was given a stunning blow.

Papp's good news came from Manhattan's Lincoln Center, where he was given control of all drama production. Potentially the most prestigious and influential dramatic organization in the U.S., Lincoln Center's theater company has floundered almost since its beginning eight years ago . . .

As for the bad news, the second of a series of dramas that Papp was producing for CBS, *Sticks and Bones*, was yanked off the network schedule three days before air time. The winner of last year's Tony Award, David Rabe's play . . . was too harsh for many of CBS's affiliate stations.

Time magazine, March 19, 1973

JOSEPH PAPP I love the television medium. I think it's an important place for things to be done. The William Morris people approached me. They said, "Why don't you let us represent you? You're hot, you've just won two Tony Awards, we can get you things in film and TV." They asked me what I'd be interested in and I said, "A season of works on television, including a work by Shakespeare and a new play by a contemporary playwright." William Morris made the original contact with CBS and they were interested. They used to be called "the Tiffany network," and they were in the mood for prestige.

BERNARD GERSTEN There are periodic flirtations that take place on the part of film and television with the theater. In many television hearts and many movie souls is a yearning for a purity of purpose that perhaps is more identified with the theater. And by August of 1972, when CBS came through, we were the cat's pajamas. We had three shows on Broadway, and Joe certainly appeared to be the premier show person of New York.

It was a loss-leader for them, part of an attempt to re-create, one way or another, the golden age of television. And for us the appeal was very strong because it was expansionist. We thought it would be a source of revenue, and there was the ability to speak with a voice that addressed millions.

PHILIP CAPICE At the time I was director of special programs for the CBS television network. When I joined the company, the network was still being guided by Jim Aubrey's philosophy that you don't preempt your regular programming because it disturbs the audience's viewing patterns. So specials were few and far between, and I was asked to increase the number and try to combine, if you will, commerciality with quality and prestige. And Joe Papp seemed to be a wonderful kind of cherry on the sundae for all of this.

Joe had at that time achieved great success in his stage productions, and CBS wanted to be the network to bring him to television. They wanted to take advantage of his talents and the topspin of the publicity.

As for Joe, he'd been successful at everything else he'd tried, but it was, in terms of the audience and the mass appeal one can generate with television, small potatoes. I think he wanted more mass recognition of his talents and his work, and this was a way to do it. And having been fired by CBS, I think he was happy to be back and in a bit of a way shoving it to them, calling the shots, having the roles reversed.

JOSEPH PAPP We signed a contract with CBS to produce thirteen plays over four years for $7 million, all to be broadcast in prime time. I decided I was going to do *Romeo and Juliet* first and I was going to direct it with Ted Cornell. I bought a little camera, and I began to interview and audition people. After having been fired by CBS I'd come back in a kind of glory, where I was really in charge.

About halfway through the audition, we were just beginning to rehearse *Much Ado About Nothing* for the Delacorte. A. J. Antoon was directing Kathleen Widdoes and Sam Waterston as Beatrice and Benedick in a production set in pre–World War I America. I went to one of the rehearsals and I thought, "Gee, this is terrific. Why should I do *Romeo and Juliet* when here's this marvelous cast, a great idea about how to do it, and we can have the show in the park first anyway."

I called CBS and said, "Listen, I've decided I'm going to do something different." There was dead air for a minute. They weren't used to turning around that fast, and *Much Ado About Nothing* didn't sound like much. But I said, "This is the best thing and we're gonna do it this way," and they finally, grudgingly, accepted.

The reviews were astounding with that show, so good that I moved it to Broadway. We had a tremendous advance—we thought we were in gravy. Then CBS and IBM, the sponsor, began to advertise that the show was going to be on television, saying "Why go out when you can see the show at home?" We didn't understand the principle that if you give something away for nothing, people will say, "Why pay?" And so the whole floor went out from under this production.

The day after the television show aired, there was nobody at the box office. Not a single person showed up. Attendance fell like seventy percent, the gross just dropped, and within the week we had to close the show.

We lost money, and we also lost a very important thing. For us to have Shakespeare on Broadway is even more important than on television, because the theater needs to have classics on its main stages to stay alive. So it was devastating. But the television show was well received, CBS seemed to be pleased, and we began to talk about the second show.

I always had in mind that the second play would be socially important. I wasn't going to do Noël Coward, with all due respect to Noël Coward. I was going to do a meaningful play of the time, and I couldn't find a more important one than *Sticks and Bones*.

Except for Fred Silverman, who showed a lot of spunk, CBS was very reluctant. I don't think they could make heads or tails of this play. "You engaged me to produce these works," I said, "and this is the play I want to do. Get somebody else if you want to do this other kind of play."

PHILIP CAPICE   We knew when we entered into the arrangement with Joe Papp that he wasn't going to do nice little plays. We had all gone down to the Public to see this and there was some talk about it being a strong play and controversial. But everybody in effect said, "Yeah, but so? Let's do it. That's why we have Joe Papp."

I personally never thought it was the greatest play in the world, but I thought it was moving, as many plays can be, without being an incredible piece of writing. It had an effect. And when you hire a man like Joe Papp, you don't tell him what to do. We did not become involved. We gave him no cautions, no guidelines, nothing. We just said, "Do the play."

BERNARD GERSTEN   Freddy Silverman at CBS was a risk-taker, and he liked Joe and Joe got on with him. Freddy was a whiz kid, and when you're hot, you're hot, everybody listens, everybody underneath pulls their forelock and says, "Yes, Freddy, yes, Freddy." And Freddy had the guts to say yes to *Sticks and Bones* without regard to the controversy that was implicit in it.

Joe developed an enthusiasm for Bob Downey, who was an eccentric choice, beyond question, to direct it. Perhaps Joe should have gone for more conventionality. The mistake was not hiring the director of the stage play. We should have taken a chance with Jeff Bleckner, who had never made a movie and who has since proved to be one of the outstanding directors of television.

DAVID RABE I was happy that Joe wanted to do one of my plays as part of the CBS thing, and at the same time I didn't quite know how they would do one of these plays on television.

I remember going to a meeting in which CBS decided to do *Sticks and Bones* over *Pavlo Hummel*. I thought that they'd have been smarter doing *Pavlo Hummel* from the point of view of what the average American TV watcher might have responded to. I felt they were really making a decision on the basis of language without quite recognizing what the impact of the play was.

"They really don't know what they've done here," I said to Joe. "They've taken that one because the guy's not screaming 'shit' at the end, but they don't know what they're getting into."

Then we went to work on it, and though I had this or that quarrel, I also really felt very good about it. I liked Downey a lot, and I had been instrumental in that. We seemed very much in accord with the essential parts of *Sticks and Bones*, so I was happy with that choice.

JOSEPH PAPP I felt we should have a first-class film director. I'd seen Robert Downey's pictures, *Greaser's Palace* and *Putney Swope*, and I thought, "Boy, this guy is good." We were dealing with a stage play, and I thought it needed to be approached photographically in an interesting way. I thought Downey would be terrific. I saw something darker in him, even though you never met two more different people than David Rabe and this guy.

Downey was up all the time. I don't know why his name is Downey, it should be "Uppey." He was constantly cheerful, and he tried everything—all these weird, wild ideas. I never saw a man enjoy working more than he did; he had absolute joy in his work. He made choices that seemed far-out at first, but then they seemed to make sense. He'd work in this impulsive way, without really knowing, sometimes, whether it was good, bad, or indifferent. But I think he served the play very well.

David, by contrast, is extremely careful, everything's laid out. He liked Downey, but he was nervous about him because Downey is kind of a sensationalist. I argued to get Downey in. I was taking a chance, too. "Yes," he said, "but it's my play."

Certainly, I don't have the writer's stake, which is the greatest because he wrote it, and it's his heart, it's his soul, his blood. I know that. I make no comparison, never make any pretense that it's anything comparable to what I do. But the stakes in terms of my wanting to see him succeed are as strong as his wanting to succeed, and in that sense I felt I had as much at stake as he had.

If you hear it from him, he probably liked the film, but I think he had mixed feelings about it. On certain days he was very pleased, on other days he was very worried. He's very protective of his plays, particularly if something is being done for the first time, and this was the first time he'd had anything done on television. It was hard to tell him, "Listen, we're on the same team, we're not separate," because of his extreme caution with his work, and how *deeply* personal it was for him. During that whole period of shooting, it was never easy, there was always tension. But that was how we lived.

CBS was very cautious. They'd send their censors around all the time. Mostly it had to do with language. Rick, the younger son, had a line, "I had the greatest piece a tail tonight, Dad." And they felt, "Ah, that can't go on the air."

"Why not?"

"Well, it's prohibited."

And they came forth with another line: "I had the greatest slice of bird tonight." You'd think they'd use some human expression that we know about instead of that. There were constantly places like that where they felt words were offensive. They'd say, "What'd he say? What was that word?" It was like having the KGB watching you all the time.

ROBERT DOWNEY When I first talked to Joe, I told him, "I'm not a big fan of Shakespeare. I don't get it—too many kings and queens. It's boring to me, the language is dense. I don't enjoy it." And his answer to that was, "Well, then, you should direct *Hamlet!*"

Initially, nobody wanted me to do the film. Rabe didn't want me, Bernie didn't want me, his whole staff. He was the only one. Because of my films, they thought I was a lunatic, that I should be the last guy to do this.

"Why don't you want Bleckner to do this?" I asked.

"I've seen what he's gonna do," Joe said. "I saw it already, do you mind? You think he's gonna change?" And Bleckner could hear him say this. So Joe's a tough guy. He would say these things. He shocked me a few times, but then I looked forward to it, because it was truthful.

Joe is the *only* producer, because he talked only about the work and he encouraged me to try new things.

"Look," he said, "I've done the play and I know what I don't like about it and what I do like, but let's take it somewhere else. That's why I'm hiring you."

And he would say things like, "Keep it lean and mean" and "You're my kinda strange." But he wouldn't say much. He would just say the right thing at the right time. Maybe it was because I was a so-called film person, maybe it's because he was a little shy about me. Whereas if I'd been a theater director, maybe I'd be fucking stomped to death, I don't know.

All I'm sure of is this: of all the producers I have had on my films and other people's films and anything I've done, nine of those, there was nobody as absurd as he was, I mean really absurd.

He was doing an interview once and he made me join.

"How is *Sticks and Bones* going?" he said.

"Well," I said, "why don't we cast a horse as the POW, put blinders on him, and bring him in, since he wears shades anyway."

You know what he said? "Absolutely, let's go with it." He would go along with things like that, and he can run with language. I'm not quick enough to get his stuff, my brain damage is too deep, and he gets bored with you if you don't get them.

Joe called me up once years later and said, "How ya doin'?" I said, "Aahh—I'm all right." He said, "I think it's time the Shakespeare Festival gave you a grant."

"For what?"

"Never mind for what. Just come over here."

I went over. He handed me a check for $2,000 and threw me out the door. I couldn't believe it. It was at a time when if I hadn't gotten that, I was really in trouble. It wasn't a question of paying the rent, it was a question of eating. And he knew. I didn't call him, but somehow he knew.

David Rabe seemed creative and maybe he is, but there was something painfully lame to the point of perpetual boredom about what he was saying about the characters. "David wouldn't do this" or "Ricky wouldn't do this." Joe told me, "You'll never make him laugh." When I did, I called and told him I had, and he said, "Do it again."

At one point I suggested David direct it. And, right in front of him, Joe said, "Are you kiddin'? Look at him. He can't even talk to me or you. What do you want him to direct actors for?" Later on, Joe let him direct a play, *Goose and Tomtom*, and Joe mentioned it to me.

"Thanks a lot," he said.

"What do you mean?"

"You encouraged us to let this guy direct. That fucking cost me a lot of money."

CLIFF DE YOUNG I wanted to play Ricky, the role that I had played on Broadway, and Downey said, "No, no, you're too old to play Ricky."

"Hey, listen, fuck you," I said. "I played it on Broadway. Did you see me?" Joe and everybody are sitting there, and I'm yelling at him, getting into this whole argument.

"Okay," Downey said. "Try David. See if you can play the older guy."

I read some scenes and he said, "Okay, now play the mother."

"Well, yeah, play the mom," I said to myself. "How am I going to take this? Is this guy taking the piss out of me, or is he trying to find something realistic as a director? Is he looking for something, or is he just fucking around? Okay, I'll play his game, I'll play the mom."

So I did and he said, "Okay, now do this speech of David's as the mom." Right, fine, I did that.

"Okay, now do this speech of Ricky's as if you're blind, and then as if you're Mom with the cane."

We did a lot of those strange conjunctions, and I went with all of them. He'd say, "Do something crazy," and I got as nuts as I possibly could. That was the only way to work with Downey.

I left and I didn't hear anything for a couple of months. I forgot about *Sticks and Bones* and I got cast as the lead guy in this little low-budget horror film that was shooting down in Florida. I was going to leave in about a week, and I got a call.

"Joe Papp calling." Hey, that's a big number, right? You think, "Ah *shit*—it's Joe, it's Joe—oh, fuck."

"Cliff!" Joe said. "How ya doin', brother."

"Hey, fine, Joe, everything's cool. How are you, big guy? Love ya!" And my heart is pounding.

"Look, we want you to play David in the movie."

"Well, I hadn't heard from you, Joe, I didn't know what was going on, so I accepted this part in this little horror film."

"Tell them that you can't do it. Tell them you're doing our film."

"Gee, Joe, I really don't know the protocol or the morality of just throwing these guys over."

"Look, fuck all that. I mean, it's *Sticks and Bones*, it's your movie, I want you to play the lead guy. It's me and it's Downey, and we're gonna go. So what're you talking about?"

"Right. Okay. What am I talking about? You're right, Joe. I'll call these other guys and tell them that I've got a problem and God bless you and I'll see you at rehearsal next week."

I never thought I'd ever meet a guy like Downey, who was so uncontrolled and so bizarrely, frighteningly funny. David Rabe didn't quite know what to do with him. "Cliff," he would say, "I don't think he's getting it." The reason Downey was saying "Read the scene as the mom" was because he wanted to see if your flexibility could stretch far enough to do some weird shit.

Because David, the blind veteran, had moved out on his family, he had his little bivouac in the basement, and Downey would say, "Okay, what can we do to make the guy be weird down here?"

"What a great direction," I thought. I did a striptease to a Rolling Stones song; I did my Mick Jagger imitation and took all my clothes off. I was getting fan letters at the time, for some strange reason, addressed to

Clifty Young, so Downey would call me that, he said, "Yeah, Clifty, you get down there, man, take your clothes off, you do that shit." And I was thinking, "This is heaven with this guy. This is so freeing. Every idea that you could come up with, just these kind of bizarre conceptions, you could actually throw at this guy and he could come back and say, 'Yeah, go!' "

Joe would come out once a week and do the thing with grabbing the chin and slapping the face and saying, "Cliff, it's great, you're a good guy, I love you."

"Thank you, Joe," I said. "This is it. I'm having the most fun I could ever have."

Whatever Joe was doing, it worked with me, because I was in love with the guy.

JOSEPH PAPP   The first screening for CBS was in January of 1973, the day after Nixon announced the Vietnam cease-fire. There was very little enthusiasm for it, but I didn't care. I didn't really expect them to like it because they had been so hesitant about the piece itself. Nobody raised any objections to it at all, but the congratulations were very weak, saying "Hey, very nice . . ." instead of "*Hey! We've got something great here.*" I think it must have worried them.

PHILIP CAPICE   The play that Jeff Bleckner directed, and that we saw down at the Public Theater, was not the play that Downey delivered on film when we saw that show at CBS. It was as simple as that. There were two different interpretations by two different directors. Not just slightly different, quite different.

ROBERT DOWNEY   The first day we really met about doing the piece, and I got very excited about how I was going to do it, Joe said, "Don't get too excited. It's not going to get on the air."

"You're ridiculous," I said. "This is tame shit we're doing here."

"It's not going to get on the air. I snuck this by them. They never saw the play. They bought my Shakespeare and I put this play in, and it's going to end up not being on the air when this is over. I'm telling you, it's not going on."

"Then why are we doing it?"

"Because we gotta. We gotta do it. Let's hope we get it done well."

.   .   .

JOHN MAZZOLA   I was the president and chief executive officer of the Lincoln Center for the Performing Arts. There are ten constituent companies at Lincoln Center, including the New York City Ballet, the Metropolitan Opera, and the New York Philharmonic, all clearly the preeminent performing-arts companies of their kind in the United States.

The Vivian Beaumont Theater had opened in 1965, but the theater company had always had trouble, serious artistic and financial problems, and we, being a landlord, were responsible for finding the folks to occupy those buildings. In 1972, here we were with an empty theater on our hands and we set out on a search for a new company.

I was up in Albany, Albany being the state capital, a frigid place in the wintertime, doing some kind of lobbying for more funds from the state for the arts. While I was up there, I ran into Joe Papp and Bernie Gersten, though during the whole period of our endeavor, I always referred to them as Joseph and Bernard to make sure they understood how formal the whole activity was. I think we were in adjoining phone booths, and we went in and out of each other's booths and I said, "This is what we're doing. You can't avoid us. You have to come in and sit and talk."

Back in New York, we had a couple of discussions about what kind of institutional theater this should be, though I hate to use the word "institutional," it makes it sound like some kind of mental hospital, which is probably not far off.

We were concerned about whether or not someone who could maintain a very high-quality regional theater in some city outside of New York could survive in New York. You have a trained audience in the city of New York, and you had a built-in audience that was coming to the Vivian Beaumont Theater, and therefore the productions had to be up to the level of what those people were used to, or at least what they wanted—not necessarily both the same thing.

Joe came in, and we talked about what the theater's position should be in relation to deceased playwrights and contemporary playwrights and the playwrights yet to write. And several people on our board were quite pleased with the idea that the Public Theater would possibly come to Lincoln Center.

If you had to use one word for Joe's appeal, you'd say "quality," that is to say, what he produced was of the highest quality. Now there was a big flurry of telephone conversations, between Joe, myself, and Amyas Ames, chairman of Lincoln Center's board, and it all fell into place rather quickly, almost within a few days.

My thought, listening between the lines as to why he was interested in us, was that here was a theater that could become the preeminent theater in the United States. The Public Theater was still regarded as completely off Broadway, he had the enterprise in the park, and this would be a third and different kind of theater. It would be a national theater—we used that word an awful lot in those days. And obviously there was the element of Mount Everest in the whole activity; there it was, other guys had fallen down and that made it more interesting.

Joe had more qualms about us than we had about him, no question about that. Joe was convinced at the beginning that once he was in there, we were going to hang over his every shoulder and somehow or other exercise censorship. Amyas and I were an imposing pair—he is six feet two and so am I. We used to wear three-button suits, and if any place is an establishment operation, it's Lincoln Center. So no matter how I tried to explain to him that that just couldn't be, I don't think Joe quite believed us.

When Amyas and I were running it, the artistic level was something you just really had to keep your hands off: we certainly weren't going to tell Mr. Balanchine what to put on; we were certainly not going to tell Mr. Bing what to put on. Still, one way or another, Joe indicated his suspicion of us.

One time he asked, supposing he put on a play and the key feature of it was that all the characters were naked.

"That will never do, will it, John?" Amyas said.

"No," I said. "Joe, this is Lincoln Center. You'd really have to put on a few feathers."

We were teasing him, but Joe was just about ready to jump across the table, feeling as he did that we were going to censor his nakedness. And that remained a problem with Joe for a considerable period. It took a long time for him to get over the fact that we had no intention whatsoever of interfering with his artistic activity.

AMYAS AMES The thing that worried him was the storm he'd created in the Public Theater. I think the people who'd raised money for him, the people who had advised him, and the people who were close to him just said, "Look Joe, you're selling out on us. You're a traitor."

My impression is that they let him have it, he got a real dose of criticism from those people who had been trying and succeeding with theater at the Public. They thought for Joe Papp to go off to that great big Lincoln Center and sort of sell his soul to it was the wrong thing to do. He got that pretty heavy, but he disregarded it because he's a very independent person. He's not a man who can get pushed around, and he has a tremendous ambition.

GAIL MERRIFIELD PAPP Someone on this committee asked Joe if he would be interested in taking it over. And it had never entered his head, just never entered Joe's head at all. He was just giving himself to this purpose and trying to help them formulate their own thoughts about whom they might need. He was surprised and he said he'd have to think it over. He didn't want to just say no.

We were trying to think, why would we want to take on this big albatross with so many liabilities? It was a lousy theater and they'd had problems with the constituency. It was also a very large sitting duck for the critics, one of their favorite targets. It was more costly than trying to run a show on Broadway, you had all these upkeep surcharges, like having to pay for part of the mopping of the plaza. And how would you manage a full season downtown and another season uptown, that was incomprehensible.

But we were desperate financially, and Joe figured he could raise money, on the basis of going to Lincoln Center, that he could not raise based on the Public Theater alone, because Lincoln Center was the creation of certain foundations and other interests and they would *have* to cough up the money. So the motivation for going there was to save the Public Theater.

BERNARD GERSTEN The night after the afternoon when Joe met with the Lincoln Center search committee, Joe and Gail and my wife, Cora, and I were going to Radio City to see David Bowie. It was a midnight show and we had barely settled into our seats when Joe leaned over Gail's lap and said, "Bernie, I'm going to change your life."

"What're you going to do to change my life?"

"We're going to Lincoln Center."

And that was how we got the announcement.

KATHLEEN WIDDOES Joe has been very devoted to the people that he's worked with, and when he got the Lincoln Center Theater, you felt as if he was presenting it to you as a gift. Suddenly he had something to give to people who had been in his plays in the park. When we met in the hall and he said, "You know, now that we have this theater, now we can do this and we can do that," I felt like it was some member of my family with a present. It was lovely.

JOSEPH PAPP I had some qualms. Mostly I was worried about splitting the focus of concentration. I've always believed in a small institution doing big things: if something is good, you move it to a Broadway house. Here I would be undertaking to operate a costly theater on a year-round basis, with expenses higher than a Broadway house because of its institutional nature, and that was a great disadvantage. The physical space seemed strange, and it didn't seem to be a place where you could experiment. It had to go just like that, and I know theater doesn't work that way, no art does. And I really didn't know how I was going to run both operations at the same time.

But I said, "Okay, I'll take it on." The idea of playing in a more important kind of space always had a value to me, because it brought attention to the theater and to the work we were doing. And it was a challenge, artistically, to work on that particular stage, which had its faults, and to get into this bourgeois kind of situation and see if I could build an audience there based on the kind of plays I would do.

The basic factor, though, was economic. We were in serious debt at the Public Theater. I owed over a million dollars, and I could not raise that money. Only if the stakes were higher, if I could operate in a larger context, would I be able to raise more. I felt this was the way to do it, and I was right. And I used part of the money I raised to pay off my debts at the Public. The Public was supposed to supply the product, so as far as I was concerned there wasn't any dichotomy there.

So I told them, "I'm not going to come in here unless I have $5 million, and I expect you to help me." I went out and I raised several million dollars in a short time. I went to the Ford Foundation, which, since the days when I was a young punk, had never given us any money. I went to the Rockefeller Foundation, which was a big contributor to Lincoln Center, and I said, "I'm saving your goddamn theater now. I need money." And I got that money, close to $5 million, including the famous $1 million luncheon I had with Mitzi Newhouse.

I knew Mitzi Newhouse was a very wealthy woman. I'd met her at certain affairs, she seemed friendly and interested, so I called her and said, "I'm going into Lincoln Center and I'd like to have lunch with you to talk about a few things."

"Okay," she said. "Do you like chopped chicken liver?"

"I love chicken liver," I said. "My mother used to make it."

"Well, I make it, too, and I'm going to bring some." And she did.

She took me to this very plain restaurant and gave me the chicken liver in a little round plastic thing. While we were talking I said, "We have a theater at Lincoln Center, it's called the Forum, and I'd like to put it in your name. Give me a million dollars and we'll do that. We need this money."

I took her over to the theater, and when we got there, we showed her this hastily put-together sign that had her name in large letters and I said, "Look, this is what you could have." I don't think she was really centered on the sign, I don't know if it had to do with her height or just her concentration, but we got the money.

Overall, I felt rather ebullient about being in Lincoln Center. Starting from that small church on East Sixth Street and suddenly being in one of the major artistic institutions in the entire United States, there was something very satisfying in that. But once you get in there, it's just a lot of work, like anyplace else. You can live in a marvelous penthouse, but I don't care how fancy it is, you still have to go to the bathroom.

"To Break Down 'The Wall,' " by Joseph Papp,
New York Times, July 22, 1973

A theater in New York must respond to the reality of what is happening in the city, principally the exodus of great numbers of the white middle-class to the suburbs. It must relate to the indigenous culture and aspirations of the city's residents, whatever their previous relationship to a theater. Real estate and demography are the key factors.

The New York Shakespeare Festival's accession to Lincoln Center is both timely and reasonable. The prestige and location of this principal cultural center serve as a magnet for the people, New Yorkers and suburbanites, who are loathe to leave their homes, or will only venture out at night to well-lighted and well-populated areas of the city. Like the Delacorte Theater in Central Park, Lincoln Center holds far less fear for the average theatergoer than Broadway. The significance of this cannot be underestimated in any projection of the future of the theater in New York.

Further, the New York Shakespeare Festival, unlike most of its fellow constituents at Lincoln Center, has emerged from *popular* audience support which includes significant numbers of minority people. By bringing these sectors of our audience to Lincoln Center, we will convey to the predominantly white middle-class patrons a feeling of togetherness, rather than separateness and isolation with their accompanying fears. This psychological evaluation must be part of any consideration of long-range artistic planning.

If the principal audience we plan to play for is an amalgam of white and black middle-class—professionals, young people and the elderly, with representatives of the evolving Puerto Rican middle-class—we have then to produce a certain selection of plays in certain kinds of ways.

In our projected first season at the Beaumont, we have scheduled five plays—one a classic, Strindberg's *The Dance of Death*, one a contemporary Irish play, Hugh Leonard's *The Au Pair Man*, and the other three new American plays. Of these last three, one will be by a prominent black playwright, one will be a musical, and the other, with which we will inaugurate the season, in October, is David Rabe's new play, *In the Boom Boom Room*.

All five plays have serious themes: war, the family, man-woman relationship, the black; some deal with their themes seriously, some humorously. Any one of these plays could be produced downtown at the Public Theater, with this special difference: the productions at Lincoln Center will benefit from the luster by appearances by distinguished actors of national reputation and from all known media. Among the currently known stars for the first season are Julie Harris, who will portray a comic role in *The Au Pair Man*, and Max Von Sydow, who will make his American stage debut in *The Dance of Death*.

The Public Theater will remain the crucible of new work, new writers, new actors, new directors, new theater administrators and technicians. It is the place where primary artistic beer is brewed and it will interact with the production process at the Beaumont, the Forum and Shakespeare in the Park.

The only way for our theater to define its artistic objectives is in pragmatic terms—principally in the Shakespeare Festival's relationship to society, to the City of New York and the people living here, and, via touring, TV and films, to the rest of the country.

If there is a single driving force which characterizes the New York Shakespeare Festival, it is its continual confrontation with the wall that separates vast numbers of people from the arts. This wall—spawned by poverty, ignorance, historical conditions—is our principal opponent, and as we joust and engage with this "enemy," we distill and shape the nature and style of our theater.

The artistic style of the New York Shakespeare Festival is defined in every production that is mounted on one of our many stages: forthrightness, vigor, and the direct search for the meaning of man in his family and in society are the common characteristics. It is the social consciousness of this theater which distinguishes it from other theaters. We constantly reflect, and react to, the shifting societal scene and attempt to articulate this shift both in terms of theater workers, plays and audiences.

Our long-range artistic plans, therefore, evolve from a recognition of the need for humanity, intelligence and feeling in a fast changing world. We will address ourselves to these needs in the years ahead and welcome the thrill of that challenge.

·   ·   ·

JOSEPH PAPP   On March 6, I went to lunch at the Steak Casino, my favorite restaurant—served great martinis, I'll tell you that. I was riding high, feeling good. I'd just come from the press conference at Lincoln Center, where it was announced that this young guy from Brooklyn was taking over the Beaumont Theater. The invitation was extended by this very patrician man, Amyas Ames, two heads taller than I was, wearing a nice gray suit, and I was the kid.

Time and *Newsweek* had come out the day before with reviews that extolled *Sticks and Bones*, called it "a work of art" and all that business. We were reading those reviews and feeling the triumph of Lincoln Center, really celebrating. I was way, way up there in my feelings, couldn't have felt any higher.

We were ordering the second vodka martinis, just enjoying ourselves, when someone came to the table and said, "You're wanted on the telephone," which was near the door, right out in the open.

"Hello?" I said.

"This is Robert Wood." He was the president of CBS, the guy who'd been congratulating me all the time.

"How you doin', Bob? Great reviews, huh?"

"I have some bad news."

"What bad news?"

"We can't put that show on that night."

"You're kidding." I'd gotten a call the day before from a reporter for a Chicago newspaper who'd said, "I hear they're not going to do your show." There was some little hint here and there, but I'd brushed it out of my mind. There were ads in the papers all prepared and the whole damn business. I just couldn't believe it.

"Look," Wood said, "there have been a lot of complaints from our affiliates around the country who've seen it and feel it's inappropriate to show at this time when prisoners of war are coming back from Vietnam."

"Why does that make that inappropriate?" I said. "Under those conditions, this play is more appropriate. It was written by a veteran and is sympathetic with veterans."

"Yes, but it would be too hard on people to see this thing."

"I don't accept this at all," I said. "What's the matter with you people? You're a big corporation but you're backing out, you're letting people put pressure on you. Where's the freedom of television?"

"Joe, listen, I have the greatest respect for your point of view."

"I have none for yours," I told him. "I'm going to tell the world what a cop-out CBS is. You should be ashamed of yourself."

"I'm sorry."

"Well, goddamn it!" I said and I hung up.

GAIL MERRIFIELD PAPP When Joe came back to the table, it was unbelievable, like you were in some kind of crazy world. We had these rave reviews spread out on the table, and Joe told us he'd broken off the whole damn contract with CBS and hung up on the guy. It was *mind*-boggling.

Joe certainly had been through enough political experiences in his life, and in different eras in this country's history, to know what this kind of signal meant. It had to do with censorship. And when that happens, you need to do whatever you need to do, and Joe knew that he had to make it very public.

He spent, I would guess, at least two weeks doing almost nothing except talking and giving media interviews to every media person in the country. The phone never stopped ringing. It was just phenomenal. And you have to be prepared to lose certain things, and Joe just had no hesitation whatsoever in losing this contract.

We started doing our own research and we were astonished to find that the censorship was more insidious than we'd thought. This was not only on the part of CBS but also on the part of the Nixon administration through a man named Clay Whitehead, who had put pressure on.

We found out that Bill Paley, the one and only head of CBS, had the show screened in some tropical resort where he was and he was appalled. He just loathed it. He did not want to have it aired, and started a campaign to encourage his own affiliates to withdraw. It was the most astonishing kind of action, encouraging sabotage from within his own ranks, and he was successful: 71 of 184 stations withdrew, which gave them a plausible excuse for withdrawing the whole show.

BERNARD GERSTEN Joe said, "This is war. We're going to go to war with CBS."

I wanted to ameliorate. I said, "Listen, let's persuade them." I thought, "Oh shit, he's going to blow the contract."

"I'm canceling the contract," Joe said. "I'm walking out on the contract."

"Don't walk out on that nice contract," I said. "We've got six more shows to go. Work it out, work it out."

But Joe said, "War! We're at war!" And all of us got into a war mode. We were trying to raise money at Lincoln Center and be sufficiently reliable to be the Lincoln Center constituent, and instead we were going to have a war with CBS.

I didn't think we were two equal countries, and it could not serve us well. They were old-line Red-baiters—they weren't used to being insulted by twerps. But this was freedom of speech, and on an issue like that, Joe was not to be denied.

PHILIP CAPICE The delivery of *Sticks and Bones* dragged on, and by the time we got it and were able to consider scheduling it, veterans were beginning to come home from Vietnam. And the real drama of all of that, seeing those things on television, was greater, it seemed, than this play. The play didn't seem to be as important as it had been when we first agreed to do it.

I guess you could call it an inflammatory play, and there was some question as to whether it was the most appropriate time to show this. A lot of people were trying to ease out and forget the horror. In view of the timing they weren't as comfortable with that play as they had been before.

There was some concern at CBS, and several levels above me, I don't know how high up, looked at it. The sales department looked at it and showed it to several advertisers and nobody wanted to sponsor it. All the advertisers shared that same feeling of uneasiness. It wasn't a question of making any sort of political statement. They felt this was not the kind of program they were going to get maximum brownie points for. They didn't feel anybody would come see it.

There was also the issue, although it was probably third or fourth down the list, that this was, in our opinion, not a brilliant piece of television but a disappointing version of what we all felt had been a very powerful play.

I'm not sure if it was a question of bad taste or hard to follow, but those of us who had seen the production and had been moved by it downtown were not similarly moved by the television production. And we were all rather surprised that Joe and Bob Downey had felt that it was funny. We never looked on it as a black comedy, which they did.

So it was decided not to run the show at that time for a combination of reasons. And Joe felt that CBS was taking a political stance on the war and all that. As far as pressure from the administration, I can almost tell you with absolute certainty that that is untrue. And Mr. Paley didn't force people to do anything. I never encountered any such involvement on his part, and if that did happen, which I doubt, I was not aware of it.

Joe's feeling about CBS was not quite the same after that; there was a certain strain in the relationship. He did a lot of talking to the press about it, and CBS didn't really say very much.

I think CBS was a little bit put off by Joe's attitude about the whole First Amendment thing. They felt that that really wasn't it at all, that the facts of the matter were not what he claimed them to be. After that time, there were no more Joe Papp productions at CBS. He was disenchanted. He stopped taking this thing seriously and it just went away.

FRED SILVERMAN I knew *Sticks and Bones* was a tough play, but I also felt that this was the network of *The Defenders* and *Judgment at Nuremberg*. I thought doing *Sticks and Bones* was a good experience, a hell of a production, but I was not running the network.

There is a corporate hierarchy that gets involved in things like this. All the management types I had to report to, all those voices were heard once the picture was screened, everybody got involved in the decision. There was the head of affiliate relations and the head of sales, who couldn't give the thing away, and there were a lot of other voices that said, "My god, we can't play this."

To the best of my knowledge, the major objection was basically that a lot of soldiers were coming home and they thought it was inappropriate. When you're dealing with matters of national importance, and at that moment in time Vietnam was a very sensitive issue, you have to be cognizant of what various groups of people around the country are thinking.

The show was buried, put on at eleven at night with a disclaimer. I was disappointed, but things like that happen. Joe attacked CBS and I kind of agreed with him. He delivered what we bought. I mean, we didn't buy *Snow White*.

CLIFF DE YOUNG　It was very difficult. We were cookin', everything's goin' on all cylinders, and all of a sudden, Clay Whitehead comes in and says, "Look, the prisoners of war are coming back. Do you really want them to go home and sit down and watch this antiwar trash that makes all their efforts appear to be ridiculous and obscene?"

So three days before the show, they canceled it, and then it came on six months later with a message in front saying, "Don't watch this." It was just too late. Joe canceled his thing with CBS. It was just so upsetting all the way around.

This really taught me about politics, because who are these people that they should put down one of the highlights of my artistic life? I worked two months, living and dying on every scene, and somebody outside the artistic community said, "They can't watch this because you're too weird." It was like a personal insult from a guy who didn't know what I was doing in the first place. It hurt me very, very much and took me a long time to recover from.

DAVID RABE　When I heard about CBS's decision, probably I felt, "I knew it. I knew they didn't know what they were getting. I knew they didn't recognize what this would be like." But I was also shocked myself. I didn't like being in that position, didn't like being in the hot seat. I just didn't like it.

I realize now that I always expect a more harmonious reception for my stuff than I get. I know I'm being a little antagonistic with the writing, but at the same time I'm always a little startled by some of the reactions. I'd written the plays, they were what I felt, but as a person I didn't like being that kind of public figure.

It was more like it was all between Joe and them. They were guys of a same or similar breed, they were having their fight, and I was the troops. I was the piece of meat or the territory or whatever they were fighting over. It didn't have much to do with me anymore.

JOSEPH PAPP As I got all this anger off my chest, I finally got to Wood again on the telephone. I really didn't want to break up that relationship with CBS, even though I'd said, "I'm not going to do anything more. This is the end of our relationship." Seven million dollars over four years was a lot of money, but that wasn't the point. The arrangement was a lovely thing to get into.

I was going to try to reconstruct something, but I'd already damaged things too much. I'd called them everything I could; the relationship was really smashed. They felt they'd rather not deal with me because they couldn't control me, and there was no way, really, to get back in it. They'd wanted me for what I do, and then they hadn't wanted me to do it. It was a ridiculous kind of thing.

19

David Rabe, Act II:
The Orphan and *In the Boom Boom Room*
1973

Mariclare Costello and
Cliff De Young in
The Orphan
© Friedman-Abeles

The Orphan, despite telling moments, is an overly ambitious attempt to view man's murderous history, up to and including Vietnam and the Sharon Tate killings, in terms of Orestes, *The Orphan*, and his troubled household. Where O'Neill sought, methodically and with gathering strength, to superimpose the legend on 19th century America in his expansive *Mourning Becomes Electra*, Rabe tries, in two relatively short acts, to make it embrace the entire bloody planet.

To do so, he leans on Einstein's theory of relativity to suggest that all these events—the murders and sacrifices of the House of Atreus, My Lai, and the Tate carnage—occur simultaneously in time and space.

Douglas Watt, *New York Daily News*, April 19, 1973

⋯⋯⋯⋯⋯⋯⋯⋯⋯⋯⋯⋯⋯⋯⋯⋯⋯⋯⋯⋯⋯⋯⋯⋯⋯⋯⋯⋯⋯⋯⋯

When I read that Rabe's *The Orphan* was an Orestes play set in both past and present and featuring two Clytemnestras, I resolved to expect little; but never, never would I have expected the author of *The Basic Training of Pavlo Hummel* and *Sticks and Bones* to contrive such a strained, pretentious, muddled, clumsy and almost completely flavorless piece of claptrap. The idea, if it can be called one, is that Orestes is reincarnated in Charles Manson; that Agamemnon, Aegisthus, Calchas are the forerunners of militarism and mumbo jumbo. Clytemnestra is America herself, the traitorous mother who becomes identified with pregnant Sharon Tate. Rabe was actually seduced by his producer, Joe Papp, into spelling this out in a program note more clotted in its prose than the play itself. The notion is not only an insult to poor Miss Tate, it may even be unfair to Charlie Manson. Aeschylus I don't worry about; to his peripatetic shade, it is merely a stinkweed among the asphodel.

John Simon, *New York* magazine, April 30, 1973

⋯⋯⋯⋯⋯⋯⋯⋯⋯⋯⋯⋯⋯⋯⋯⋯⋯⋯⋯⋯⋯⋯⋯⋯⋯⋯⋯⋯⋯⋯⋯⋯

DAVID RABE I don't know what anyone else will say, but my recollection of *The Orphan* was that I was saying, "This play isn't finished," and Jeff Bleckner was saying, "I don't think I know how to direct this play." We were in the process of trying to decide whether to do it or not when CBS canceled *Sticks and Bones*, and that mobilized us, made us rally round the flag. We thought we were now obligated to slog on and do the play, to stand up and continue to make this statement. It's not martyring, because that's not what one expected, but it's along those lines.

The idea was that we as a team, having succeeded twice with the other two plays, would solve its problems in the process. Of course, that didn't happen. The production had its moments, but it wasn't working. I couldn't solve the writing, and we couldn't get in any kind of sync about it.

I'm sure there are people who'll say the play's no good, but part of the problem was that I was exhausted, worn out by the pace, which, in my view, was Joe's responsibility. When he said, "I'll do everything you write," he didn't tell me we were going to do it in the next two days.

This was an ongoing lesson, one that I couldn't learn, not to respond to Joe's call, not to answer Joe's "I only want to do it if you want to do it" with "Okay, let's do it." It was my own fault, in a sense. I can't abdicate all responsibility because I would do these things, but I was tired. It was happening so fast.

The mimeographed notes was another time when I couldn't say no to him. I would say, "Joe, it won't work. No matter how eloquently I might write these program notes, they will use them against me to show what the play didn't have in it. They'll say the play lacked this and those program notes made no sense." But I went ahead and wrote them and they were pretty much used against the play—kindly used by those reviewers that were kind and viciously used by those who weren't.

The only time reviews can be really crushing, and it's an experience I've never had, is where you feel that the play is fulfilled in the writing and is being rendered one hundred percent, and then you get bad reviews. But any time the reviews are bad, it's not pleasant—I'm not going to say it is. It makes you doubt yourself in a lot of ways. You say, "Why did I let myself get into this? I knew this, I saw this coming."

And by then I was beginning to see the world of professional theater in another light than when I wasn't in it and was looking toward it. At that time I saw it as this place where everyone was professional, and all the work was done with great concern and responsibility.

But when you're in it, you find that that's not the case, that it's frantic and slapdash, that people have more things on their minds, they're thinking about their next job, there are just a million things that concern them. When you get into professional theater, there is less the sort of complete devotion to work than there was in college or places I'd precedingly been. You run into more talent and less commitment.

At this point, I sort of felt I had no options, that Joe was my savior, the guy who'd done my play when it had been turned down everywhere else. When you're a young writer and you're inexperienced, you've never had anything done before, this is a force to reckon with. You're not prepared to deal with it. You are really, really vulnerable to that kind of onslaught and that kind of conviction, right or wrong.

It's like being the captain of the ship: he makes wrong decisions and goes on, and if people and plays are lost along the way, it's just part of the battle—from *his* point of view. If you're one of the people or plays, it's a different story.

CLIFF DE YOUNG   They asked me to come in and read for the lead guy, Orestes. Then Joe called and said, "We're going to do this; this is David's greatest." I kept reading this play, and there's great speeches in it, and there's wonderful characters, but I kept thinking, "How can this be his greatest play when it's so obviously a literary pastiche? I guess Jeff and David have a plan that I don't quite know about yet. I'll just do what I do and just kick ass and hope for the best."

Well, the best didn't turn out very well. We kept trying to get rewrites on the thing, and Joe kept saying, "Don't anybody worry about it. David's a great writer, and it's going to work." So the feeling I got was, "Look, it's a great play—don't fuck it up." That attitude was real strange to me.

JEFF BLECKNER   Cliff De Young had to climb up these poles and make a big speech that was supposed to be like he had taken acid. It was a very free-flowing, imagistic speech, sort of hallucinatory and stream of consciousness, and it was long.

There was some pretty steamy language in it also. It got into a heavy four-letter situation, and in previews, night after night, as he went through this series of words, large groups of people would get up and walk out at almost the exact same point.

Cliff desperately wanted David to cut the speech, but David wouldn't cut it. And one night, as people were walking out, Cliff, right in the middle of the speech, said, "Come on, gimme a break! I gotta stay here and *say* it, you might as well stay here and listen."

CLIFF DE YOUNG   After *Sticks* getting canceled and the failure of *Orphan*, I felt like the orphan now. I'm out on the street. Joe isn't doing any of that shit to me anymore, slapping my face, grabbing my chin. He's not even talking to me. Before, when I'd call the people at casting and say, "Hey, what's going on down there? Anything for me?," they'd go "Yeah! There's five or six things for you." But now they're saying, "No, no, Cliff, nothing for you right now."

Ray Bradbury has a story in *The Martian Chronicles* about this guy who had no kind of thing on his own. He appeared to everyone as the person they wished to see. And when I'd see Joe in all his permutations, I'd think of that.

He's talking to the actor, to the director, then he moves over to the writer, then he's going to shake some guy down for money, down with the ritzy folks downtown. He was movin' and groovin' all over town, and yet he was perfectly honest in all of those things. Those permutations were really part of his personality. He wasn't acting or bullshitting, and he wasn't a phony. That was the first time I'd ever seen anybody with the ability to be a total chameleon in all things.

JEFF BLECKNER Although no one ever said it, I knew that Joe and David felt that it was my fault that the production didn't work. Joe very much blamed me for the failure of that show, and he didn't know what to do with me. He didn't trust me as much; his whole demeanor toward me changed.

I came right out of that and into a production of *As You Like It* for the summer. I was still wounded by *The Orphan*. I knew that I was in the shithouse, and so I wasn't functioning with the strength and the energy and the assurance that I had before.

Joe asked to see a run-through after six or seven days, a ridiculously short time. How can I show him a run-through? I said, "We haven't done anything yet. I haven't staged half the play."

But Joe insisted, so I had people just sort of fake their way through. Joe called me in and said that he didn't think I had a grasp of the show, that he was going to have to come in the next day and show me how to direct Shakespeare.

"You're going to come to the rehearsal at ten o'clock in the morning and show me how to direct the play by directing the play and having me watch it?" I said.

"Yes."

"Then there's no point in my coming in tomorrow morning."

"That's fine by me. I'm going to be there tomorrow morning directing this play, if you come in or not."

That was the last time I spoke to Joe Papp for quite a few years. It took me so many years to recover from that. I spent three or four years where I could have gone out of business. I could have been crippled by the experience because I was so enamored of him, he was so important to me.

I think Joe has fascinations with people and notions and ideas, and he's unable to sustain them. He just loses interest after a while—it's really that simple. With the young directors that he gave birth to, when they came up out of the crowd and began to develop a notoriety and a degree of success of their own, when they became more of a force to be reckoned with, I don't think he cared for that.

DAVID RABE After the failure of that production in New York, I received a letter from a director named Barnett Kellman who I'd met in New Haven. He said he knew there were problems with the play but he felt there was a way to work on it.

He wanted to take it down to the North Carolina School of the Arts at Winston-Salem and do it with college students. At that point, I was thrilled that anybody thought there was value in the play. I had an idea about how to rewrite the entire second act, which I did, and then I went off to do *Boom Boom Room* at Lincoln Center.

Right after *Boom Boom Room* opened, I flew down there and they were doing a production of the play that was quite amazing. So Barnett and I decided to do it again in Philadelphia at the Manning Street Actors Theater. Joe put a little money into the production, and though some people liked it and some people didn't, they were all talking about a play, unlike in New York, where it was just a mess, gibberish, and the dramatic argument of the play was incomprehensible.

The altercation that Joe and I had came when Joe came down to see the play. The actors were all young. They were ecstatic about being in this play in front of Joe Papp—they thought this was their big break. And I at the time thought, "Gee, it's nice that Joe will see it, see what it could have been. Maybe we'll come back to New York with it."

What happened is that at intermission, I saw by the way Joe was leaving that he wasn't coming back in. I was really upset. I felt responsible for these kids and all their work and their feelings about being seen by Joe. I thought leaving like that was rude and insensitive, and that's what we had our argument about.

He could hate it, but he should go in there and act decent to these kids. I don't remember whether he went back in or not. There was nothing physical, but we'd never had an argument quite like that before. It wasn't in any real sense liberating, things weren't cleanly altered by it, but they were beginning to be frazzled. I was beginning to feel the need to do something different, to extricate myself from this.

JOSEPH PAPP We had this tremendous argument in Philadelphia when we did *The Orphan* there. We almost got into a fight outside the theater, and he would have destroyed me with one hand. I never saw him so angry. He'd made such a fuss over this production, and I thought it was not half as good as the one that was done at the Public. We got into kind of a row, yelling "You son of a bitch" at each other. We really had it out in the street.

I was just short of daring him to hit me. He was holding back, but he was purple, he had turned purple. He was clenching his fists, and if he'd hit me, I'd have been gone. I brought out this rage in him—David "Rage," I called him. But it was because we both cared a lot. I was like his father, and he would have killed his father, but he couldn't do it. Maybe we were acting out the play. It had the same conflict in it.

GAIL MERRIFIELD PAPP We saw it all the way through and then Joe and David had a fight on the doorstep outside the theater afterward. I can't remember what they were fighting about, it just broke out spontaneously, with threats of blows to each other. David was crab-red in the face, looking like the Golem and getting larger and more puffed up and red moment by moment. And I'm thinking, "Well, if these two men really come to blows, I myself will step in and do something."

There was a very strong, powerful connection that went between Joe and David. He truly responded to David's writing in a most extraordinary way. He also had an intellectual and an instinctive emotional understanding of it that was exceptional, and David knew that and appreciated it. He was able to talk to David about his work in a way that nobody did or could. Nobody.

There was also, on Joe's part, strong personal feelings toward David as a kind of son. It was mixed up with David's intractability and pigheadedness, which were, to Joe, irresistible son-like qualities. It baffled me rather continually, because Joe was so sore-provoked. He felt a lot of ingratitude and disrespect, David seemed to be so narrow-sighted and ungenerous in spirit, but there was something that obviously must have engaged Joe about that. It was like a challenge, almost.

JULIUS NOVICK
The Village Voice, November 15, 1973

With the opening of *Boom Boom Room* at the Vivian Beaumont Theater in Lincoln Center, the newest outpost of his New York Shakespeare Festival empire, Joseph Papp completes his transition from David to Goliath. He is no longer a gutsy outsider, operating on a shoestring and a dream and his own indomitable energy and persistence; he is a theatrical cartel, with no less than 10 stages and who knows how many millions of dollars under his absolute personal control. He is now probably the most powerful single figure in the American theater . . .

Joe Papp fought hard for his power and he deserves it if anybody does. But he will find his new position in some ways highly inconvenient. He has lost the privileges of the underdog: nobody will indulge him any more, or give him the benefit of the doubt. From now on he will be held very strictly to account.

CLIVE BARNES
New York Times, November 8, 1973

The first play of the season is by that Shakespeare Festival stalwart, David Rabe. This, called *Boom Boom Room*, is the fourth play of Mr. Rabe's that Mr. Papp has produced, and is the first play by Mr. Rabe that does not deal with Vietnam. The problem is to decide what it does deal with.

It is possibly intended as a portrait of a young tramp as a neurotic. Its heroine is Chrissy. Chrissy is a go-go girl in Philadelphia who dreams of—well, she seems to dream of very little really.

The trouble with the play is that we are asked to spend three hours with Chrissy, and we really know no more about her at the end than we did at the beginning.

She lives in the world of a sleazy go-go joint. She tries to get herself sexually together. She wonders whether she was ever sexually assaulted by her father or her uncles. (We never find out.) She tries to equate with men—she wants to be loved, and just not treated as "a hunk of meat." She tries to equate with an astrologically inclined square, a homosexual who works for a sperm bank, a truck driver and his mate, and has a lesbian flirtation with the dance captain back at the club. Nothing seems to work for her—and this seems quite clearly Mr. Rabe's fault.

The play is full of chic filth and a desperate Archie Bunker style of racism . . . The dialogue aspires too frequently to the comforting jargon of TV serials . . . Presumably Mr. Rabe is trying to show a simple girl fighting for individuality as a woman in a man's world. It would have been quicker if he had sent a telegram . . .

Madeline Kahn, a gifted performer, has been allowed to mug the play as if she were doing a series of blackout sketches for a revue. It is the kind of acting more suitable for Johnny Carson's *Tonight Show* than Lincoln Center.

Some of the men were better—Charles Durning was convincing as the father with prostate trouble . . . while Mary Woronov looked slinkily attractive as the bisexual dance captain. But, oh dear. Let us hope that the Shakespeare Festival will have better luck next time. There is nowhere to go but up.

. . . .

JOSEPH PAPP   Lincoln Center had been kind of a haven for safe plays, and I wanted to begin to deal with it in an entirely different way, to get some new works that were significant in there. I had to get a first play on, and I wanted to start with something from David. He was in the forefront; he was dealing with issues that I felt were the most important ones. To me he represented the theater at that time. And, coincidentally, he did have a play which happened to be around.

David was a little hesitant, as usual, and he may have been right. We rushed everything because we were opening a theater, and the play may not have been ready. You shouldn't have to worry about opening a theater when you're opening a play. It's a double-barreled problem, and I felt the split concentration did the play a disservice. We could have tested it more, but there was really no time.

BERNARD GERSTEN   Joe felt that it was essential that he open with his primo writer. He knew the symbolic value of that, but David was not keen on doing it. It was a case of the theater's interest and the playwright's interest not being perfectly meshed. I think David might have been better served, and, as it ultimately proved out, the theater might have been better served, too, had the play been tried out in a workshop rather than pushing it, ready or not, into the forefront of attention that was focused upon the first play by the Shakespeare Festival at the Beaumont Theater of Lincoln Center.

DAVID RABE   Joe did a selling job. He said that he wanted to open his regime with *Boom Boom Room*; that mine was the best play he had, that he wanted to invade the sacrosanct confines of Lincoln Center and he had no other play that he wanted to put in that position.

That's what I mean. You were always slid into the position where you were bearing the burden of his programs. It wasn't just the play that got looked at on its own merits. It was a play that was judged in terms of how it manifested or represented his program.

And, once again, I made the same kind of decision I had before, kind of talking myself into it. There's a way to look at it that says you'd be an idiot not to want your play to be the first, and I did look at it that way to some extent.

I think I was just tired. All this had happened to me in two years, and I was sort of a basket case in terms of creative energy and any kind of concentration at that point. I couldn't stop. It was like a sickness. I didn't know how to get out of it, and I just kept rolling along. It took me a long time to finally say, "No more."

BERNARD GERSTEN   Joe insisted that he had the perfect director. "I know," he said, "exactly who should direct this play."

"Who, Joe?"

"Julie Bovasso."

"Julie Bovasso? Who the hell is Julie Bovasso?"

"Only a woman can direct this play because David writes with the heart of a woman—he has a woman's understanding."

David, Joe said, had a particular ability to understand women which was manifest in his ability to write the leading woman in *Boom Boom Room*, and it took a woman's insight to be able to direct it. And so he settled on Julie Bovasso, a woman who he certainly had no direct experience with and who couldn't have been very well known to him.

Julie had a certain amount of experience in the theater, but she had worked on the fringe rather than in the center. She wasn't experienced in working with actors under so-called Broadway conditions. But somehow Joe and David convinced themselves and each other that Julie Bovasso was the ideal choice. I guess it's a lesson in the ability of theater people to persuade themselves of the most disastrous courses imaginable.

JULIE BOVASSO I started my little theater, Tempo, on St. Mark's Place in 1951. It was avant-garde and experimental, works by Genet and Ionesco were introduced there. Prior to that, I had worked with Judith Malina and Julian Beck in the Living Theatre. It was very different from what Joe was doing at the Public. We came from really opposite sides of the stick. As the wild men of Second Avenue, we used to think of Joe as very traditional, old-fashioned kind of theater.

Joe called me one day, out of the blue, and said, "I want you to come in and talk about this new David Rabe play." Rabe is not exactly a traditional writer. He's got a kinky head, sort of tilted. I loved the play, and I didn't see it as a realistic piece; my ideas were more surreal than real.

Especially since we were doing it at the Beaumont, with its huge thrust stage, I saw it as a very big play. I thought we should have things happening, simultaneous action, people appearing from catwalks way up high. Joe and David thought that was terrific. I think that's why Joe came to me, because I was known for doing these kind of wild productions.

Casting was where we got into trouble, that was the beginning of the end. Everything was fine until we had these really long casting sessions that went on for weeks and weeks. I think we must have seen every single actor in New York of any quality. I could have cast the thing in the first week. I saw the people that I wanted and they were fantastic actors. I saw two people that I felt could emotionally handle the agony Chrissy goes through, and one of them was Jill Clayburgh, who married David.

I really did not ever like Madeline Kahn. She was imposed on me. She is charming and she can be funny, but she doesn't have that kind of power. When it comes to wailing, she cannot wail. It ain't there. But this being my first-time big-shot chance to direct in a theater like that, I was not really in a position, at least in my own mind, to really put my foot down and say, "No, absolutely not. I don't want her." I really felt Joe would have said, "Take a walk."

That was strike number one, but, being something of a pragmatist and maybe having too much confidence, I started thinking to myself, "Yes, I can get it out of her." But she played everything straight out front, wouldn't relate, she was concerned with her own self-survival. This has nothing to do with acting.

I adore Robert Loggia, but I felt casting him as Al, one of the men in Chrissy's life, was clichéd. I didn't want him, either, but I got him. Then it occurred to me that all this might have had something to do with the fact that this was the first production at Lincoln Center for Joe. I think he wanted stars or names. I think that had a lot to do with it.

Myself, coming from another direction, I would just cast actors—I wouldn't care if they'd never been heard of. But, no, that was not what was wanted at the time. And that was the beginning of the end. Frankly, what did happen is I lost control as far as the actors were concerned, because I don't know how to direct stars.

MARY WORONOV   I was acting in very, very off-off-Broadway plays and my agent sent me up for the part of Susan, the dance captain. Julie Newmar was hired, and I was asked to be her understudy because she was having a terrible time learning her lines. An understudy normally sort of understudies, she never gets in the way of the star. No. I had to follow her everywhere. If she went to the bathroom, I had to be in the bathroom with her. They told me to do this, I swear to god.

One day, we're supposed to start rehearsal and I'm standing outside the bathroom, right? And the stage manager comes up to me and he goes, "Where is Julie? Where is Julie?"

"She's in the fucking bathroom."

So I go in the bathroom, and Julie's got all her clothes off—they are like in a little pile here—and she's putting on this leather bikini and this leather top and this mask. Then she puts on these really long boots—I know she didn't buy them at the Pleasure Chest because they were really fine quality—and she has like a riding crop in one hand and a bullwhip in the other.

She goes out into rehearsal. Bovasso looks at her and says, "Would you take all of those things off?" And she goes like this with the whip, WHAP! So Robert Loggia comes over and he goes, "I'm the man on the set, I think I'll handle it." And she goes WHAP!

My sense of humor's a little ripped, right, so I'm cracking up, I'm rolling on the floor. I couldn't believe it, it was just insane. Finally, they get the stage manager, who's this real beefy, good-looking guy, he's the only one who can control her. Bovasso says to me, "Take her inside and get her fucking clothes on, and let's get on with the rehearsal."

She was just an actress trying anything, but the more she would try, the more people would back away from her. No one would help her because she was strange. She scared everyone. She'd come in and David would run to the other end of the room and hide behind a chair. It was terrible.

JULIE BOVASSO   Julie Newmar was really the straw that broke the camel's back. She looked fantastic. She had every quality that you would want in that role, but she couldn't learn a line, and it was risky hiring her. Joe looked at me and said, "This is it."

"I agree," I said, "but shall we risk it?" We were aware that this lady was a problem, but we went ahead with her. The upshot was that she couldn't take direction. I would have to give her associations, have her associate lines with the blocking, otherwise she couldn't remember anything.

We were rehearsing one day, Julie went into the ladies' room and fifteen minutes later she came stomping out wearing this black leather bikini outfit, with whips and chains and a helmet. She went wild, cracking the whip around, and I said, "Oh, for Christ's sake."

I went downstairs to Joe's office and I said, "Julie Newmar's flipping out up there. Will you please come up?" He came right up and it was a big thing. He said, "You have no control of your actors. This is what your actors are doing."

"What?" I said. "I'm not a wet nurse."

He was terrible about embarrassing me in front of everybody. He's the stern father who reprimands the children in front of each other. That's part of the scene, but it's hard to take sometimes.

MARY WORONOV Little did I know that downstairs with Papp, they were rehearsing people for that role, trying to find someone. They had no intention of using me. Came back after lunch and Julie Bovasso, in the elevator says, "Well, you have the job," like "We tried everything else, you're what we're going to work with, and that's cool." It was like two days before we were supposed to go onto the stage at Lincoln Center; they weren't going to can me.

So in walks Julie Newmar, gorgeous, totally dressed again. She comes over and goes, "Mary, I really want to thank you and I wish you the best of luck." And then, opening night, she came and watched and complimented me, said I'd done a great job. Fucking class on the hill.

JULIE BOVASSO I was the one who would get all the flak, and this is also true concerning a couple of other people who had problems that had nothing to do with me. Chrissy is a bare-chested dancer, and Madeline didn't want to do that. We watched it at a dress rehearsal; she was veiled and it didn't have the impact. It was a big dog of an ending.

Joe called me up at midnight. I was asleep, and he said, "What are we going to do with the ending? The ending doesn't work, it doesn't work."

"I don't know," I said. "The girl won't take off her jacket, and I also think we need some work from the playwright here. To tell you the truth, I don't know what it is, but I think it would happen if we had that final moment."

"Is that all you can say?"

"That's it. What do you want me to do? You want me to write the ending? That's all I can say."

Furious. So he hung up.

Look, I understood exactly what was going down. He was panicked. We had a problem and someone had to take the beef. In the old days, usually they'd fire the juvenile. But now, you know, it's the director.

MADELINE KAHN I remember Julie Bovasso as being very helpful to me. She was a woman and she seemed to have a real ability to portray rage, while my fear would have been that I couldn't be really believable portraying rage. I hadn't come from a family background where everyone was really yelling at everyone else, and maybe she did, so I had courage with her leading me along a bit. She just set up an atmosphere where I felt comfortable trying out that part of myself. She's earthy and you felt very comfortable allowing those parts of yourself to come forward.

I think that experience ended unhappily for her. I really wasn't in on it. It wasn't any kind of big deal where I had a lot of notice, it just kind of happened that she was no longer the director. I was so full of what I had to do yet. I can't explain the feeling, except to say it's like you're out there in the ocean swimming, and you've got to get to shore. You can see the shore, and you just simply have to keep going. God, it's great when you're working that hard, I have to say.

I knew that I was going to be in front of an audience, and it wasn't this little off-Broadway theater—it was Lincoln Center, all white and formal-looking. That really shouldn't mean anything, but it does. And there was only so much time left, maybe a week or something, so that I felt that I simply had to jump off this one ship and jump onto the other one and just keep going.

MARY WORONOV Madeline Kahn was totally freaked out, and I don't blame her. I'm going, "Wow, man. It's three days before we're supposed to go on." She had a map in her mind of what was going on, and suddenly Joe changed everything. She had a path, a grid, about reasons and actions, and they just said, "Well, you know—do it backward." She can't.

I think she was sort of crying and Papp goes, "Where's our understudy?" He called up her understudy like that, just to keep the rehearsal going because we had no time. And the understudy did something really rude: instead of just going through and blocking it, she started really acting her ass off. In a way, I think that made Madeline so mad she said, "Fuck this shit, man. I'll just do it." She's a real trouper.

DAVID RABE   The change was made at the last minute. We were almost in previews. Everyone was floundering. It was all over the place and no one knew what the hell was going on. Joe did it just in time. It was pulled together enough that it worked up to a point, and some of it was quite good. It got close enough that I thought we might make it. Whatever sense there was to the production came when he did take over.

JOSEPH PAPP   Julie Bovasso came in and it was madness. I've never seen anything like it. She was getting more and more confused. She just didn't know what she was doing, and she couldn't make a decision. I mean, god, I could not believe it. Time was not our friend in this issue, since I was going to open a new theater as well as a new play. We were coming down the home stretch. We had maybe ten days to go, maybe less. She was paralyzed and the play was sort of falling by the wayside.

You can imagine David. His reactions are always complex, even in the best of circumstances. When things are going fantastically well, he's in a terrible mood. Just imagine when things are going very poorly. He was beyond himself, in the third state of despair. His state of mind was so ambiguous, you didn't know whether he was for you or against you. And I didn't know what to do. We were headed straight for disaster with the first show. Imagine that. "My god," I thought, "this is really the worst thing that could happen."

It was too late to get a brand-new director, so I said, "David, I've got to get rid of her, she can't move. I guess I just have to take this over and try to save it." I told Julie, "You have to go," and we had kind of a fight. "There's nothing wrong with me," she said. "I know what I'm doing." That's really madness, that she could imagine that everything was fine.

I just dropped everything, came in, and began to direct this play. I got Madeline Kahn to act. She was petulant one day and I said, "Okay, get off the stage, let the understudy go on." I waited fifteen minutes, let the understudy act, then I said, "Okay, you ready now, Madeline?" And she came back.

I did as well as I could, under the circumstances. I think the show was at least physically presentable. I changed a lot in the production. There was a very elaborate, multilevel set—it didn't need all of that. It would take hours to get up and down those things, and you wanted a more immediate experience.

There was a lot of abstraction in the actual play itself, so I thought, "Why enlarge that?" The idea was to confine it. It was really a very small play that should have been done in a very small theater. But even if it had been done splendidly, I don't think the Lincoln Center audience would have liked the play. David Rabe, per se, would not be acceptable to that audience, no matter what.

CHARLES DURNING Julie Bovasso showed up during a dress rehearsal a couple of days after they replaced her. We're all sitting there, Joe was giving us notes, and she went up and confronted him. "I want to hear an explanation," she said. "I want to know how many people are on my side and how many people want me replaced. And what about you, David?" And David just kept looking at the floor, because she's a very strong lady. I was hoping she would never ask me, because, although I liked her, I liked Joe better. And right or wrong, I'm going to go with Joe because he's the key man for me. He's the guy who put me where I am.

"Get out of my theater," Joe said to her.

"Wait a minute. Your theater? This is a public building, this belongs to the city of New York. *You're* not putting me out of *your theater.*"

It got into that kind of thing, and finally, Joe went on with his notes. She kept staring at him. It was very uncomfortable for all of us, but he gave us the notes and dismissed us. Then those two went at it privately. It must have been wonderful, because she is a tiger and he is a barracuda.

JULIE BOVASSO The day after that phone call, I went in, and there's Joe on the stage, and he was redirecting the actors.

"What are you doing?" I said.

"Don't ask me what I'm doing. This is my theater. Get out. Go sit over there. Sit over there. Go sit down."

"I'm not going to sit in the corner," I said. I got my Albanian up—there was this wild kind of eloquent anger that I'm very noted for. The language wouldn't belong in a book. The gist of it was, "What the fuck are you doing? Get the fuck off that stage, and let me work on this play."

"If you're not going to sit down," he said, "get the fuck out of the theater."

I just walked out, and my agent sent him a telegram saying that I did not want my name on the program because it wasn't my work. A lot of people just went off and let Joe redo the stuff. I was cutting loose of that kind of symbiotic relationship that happens very often with Joe and his directors. I don't think anybody sat down consciously and said, "We're going to make this woman the scapegoat for everything that is not going right," but that's what happened.

JOSEPH PAPP Ten, fifteen years ago, I used to be much more impetuous. If I'd find something going wrong, I'd fire the director and take over the show. I've done that a number of times. I know more now.

You don't get panicky. You don't do crazy things. If you do, you're in trouble, because it's almost impossible to turn a thing around that late in the game.

There are several reasons to work with the director more. One, I'll end up with a better result. Two, for myself, taking over is very disruptive of my own life. And, at the very best, you save the show from getting bad notices. If it's gone down this way, it's almost impossible to turn it into a winner. If the show is successful, it's because of the work that was done beforehand. If it's a failure, you're responsible.

GAIL MERRIFIELD PAPP There's this airless room that's off the main lobby of the Beaumont Theater, and in those days a picture of the original Mrs. Beaumont was there, with a little art light illuminating it. There was a small refrigerator and some uncomfortable butcher-block chairs for patrons to sit in when you're trying to woo them for money, which was the theoretical idea for the room.

In fact, nobody ever used it, but we were all in there after opening night and Clive Barnes's review in the *New York Times* was read to us over a speakerphone. It was just outrageous. We were so damned angry, and Joe was furious. It was something like one o'clock in the morning but he got Barnes's number, picked up the phone, and called him at home.

He woke him and really lit into him, just gave it to him. It was great, just great. He'd written a lousy, insensitive, unjust kind of review, and I thought, "Well, what are you supposed to do? Just take the poison and slink off somewhere and almost die? What are you supposed to do with this sort of stuff?" I felt it was well deserved and I was very proud of Joe.

BERNARD GERSTEN I remember the language. "Listen, Clive, you're trying to fuck me up the ass and I'm going to fuck you up the ass. You're trying to get me killed; I'm going to kill you. I'm going to get you fired." It does shine in my memory.

JOSEPH PAPP I could have killed Clive Barnes if I'd seen him in person. Every now and then you hear stories of actors killing critics, and that's not so far-fetched. There are times you feel that way. You would actually commit an atrocity because the feelings are so intense.

I called him up, twelve o'clock or one o'clock in the morning, and I called him everything I could. "What kind of review is that? If you were here, I'd kill you." I just tore this person apart. I always come out that way in support of the writer, because I feel that the playwright's been hurt and feeling like shit.

I was very much that way with David Rabe. I became so connected with his plays that I felt that I would protect them from anything. But I feel now I must have overreacted to Clive Barnes. I'm taking away from the playwright his own anger. He should be doing that, and I must have robbed him by taking that initiative.

CLIVE BARNES Everyone takes exception to criticism. How can you not? It's a very personal thing. Like most people, Joe believes that critics are very dangerous animals. He believes they are to be placated when possible, that they are fundamentally at his service, and their fundamental job is to give good notices. I'm always reminded of Sol Hurok in this context, who once told me, "The function of the critic is to sell tickets." And I said, "You're absolutely right, Sol. But you've got to let me decide which tickets I want to sell." And Joe has very much of that approach. He thinks notices should always be good.

The famous confrontation came after the first night of *Boom Boom Room*. He telephoned me at home and we had an argument. He was very insulting, and I was pretty insulting back. I think we probably gave as good as we got. But, of course, he had the advantage of knowing that it was being broadcast to his party on some kind of intercom. I had no such benefit, and when I found out, I was annoyed at that. I thought it was an invasion of my privacy. But anyway, we soon got together again, and it was nothing. We share very little in common, but one thing we do share is an inability to bear malice of any lasting nature.

DAVID RABE   That Clive Barnes business? I was staggering around, quite drunk, I'm sure, and in some bizarre costume. We had to wear tuxes, and I felt so uncomfortable with this play and these kinds of characters in Lincoln Center that I had taken half my tux off and had some leather jacket on.

I was very upset by Clive Barnes's review. I was feeling pummeled, feeling that I hadn't made good decisions myself, that I hadn't foreseen some of these things and not done the most simple things to protect the play or to create the right circumstances. Also, I felt I'd run the gamut of my entire career in two years: I'd gone from being welcomed to New York to being slapped around and told to get out. I was tired and I felt I needed a break.

I walked in as it was in progress. Professionally, it was excessive—there's no question. I always felt it was not the right thing to be doing. And I suspect Joe has felt that I've been insufficiently grateful for those kinds of warring, defending acts that he would do.

But it always seemed to me that if we'd done our work right, they wouldn't have been necessary, and there was always a part of me that was very angry about the fact that it was necessary. The right thing would have been to have done the preliminary producer work more carefully, to be more responsible in the directorial choice, to not force it. If we do our work right, we don't have to deal with this stuff.

Some of the resentment that I began to feel was that it wasn't really good producing. There were all these promises about "I'll do all your plays," there were these calls, "I'll only do it if you want to do it," all that kind of stuff, but the basic things obviously weren't being dealt with.

Joe plugged into a certain vulnerability in my character—which I guess a lot of young writers would have—as somebody who was going to take care of you. If I'd been as clear about it then as I am now, some of these things wouldn't have happened. I wouldn't have kept making the same mistake. But I did keep making the same mistake.

20

Short Eyes

1974

Tito Goya and Felipe Torres
© Friedman-Abeles

Short Eyes is unexpected even from that master of the unexpected, producer Joseph Papp. Written and mostly acted by young ex-convicts, former inmates of the Bedford Hills Correctional Facility in Westchester County, N.Y., *Short Eyes* is an astonishing work, full of electrifying exuberance and instinctive theatricality. While it won't vie with Somerset Maugham or Terence Rattigan in an anthology of "well-made" plays, *Short Eyes* needs no apology—it isn't occupational therapy and it isn't a freak show; it's an authentic, powerful theatrical piece that tells you more about the anti-universe of prison life than any play outside the work of Jean Genet.

Written bitingly by Miguel Piñero and directed like a choreographed whirlwind by Marvin Felix Camillo, *Short Eyes* portrays the tragicomedy of people festering in prison like bread being baked in a malfunctioning oven. The young convicts—heisters, muggers, druggies, whatever—act out a violent and ironic parody of straight society, complete with its racism, its conflicting codes, its moralities that are hard to tell from corruptions. For the cons the supreme sin is to be a "Short Eyes"—a sexual molester of children. On this one point everyone—black, white, Puerto Rican, Muslim fanatic and tough Irish Catholic—all come together, and the Short Eyes gets the book thrown at him, from ostracism to the indignity of being dunked in the toilet to a final act of terrible "justice."

Jack Kroll, *Newsweek*, April 8, 1974

MEL GUSSOW
From "Prison, 'Nowhere Being Nobody,' A Young Playwright Emerges to Fame," *New York Times*, March 27, 1974

The morning after Miguel Piñero's first play, *Short Eyes*, opened at the New York Shakespeare Festival Public Theater, the playwright, instead of basking in his new fame, checked in with his probation officer.

Mr. Piñero is a former convict who has spent 7 of his 27 years in prison. Before he became a playwright, he was a burglar, mugger, shoplifter, drug addict and drug seller . . .

Miguel Antonio Gomez Piñero was born in Gurabo, Puerto Rico, on Dec. 19, 1946. He came to New York at the age of 4 with his parents and his baby sister. Two children later, with his mother pregnant for the fifth time, his father abandoned the family. Mr. Piñero has not seen his father since "except when I was 12 and then only for 15 minutes."

"We were thrown out into the streets when I was 9 or 10," he recalled. "The first few nights we slept in an outdoor latrine." His mother and the younger children slept inside. He was outside guarding the door.

Finally a friendly superintendent gave them space in a basement. "I used to cover my little sister in a box to keep the rats from her," he said, describing his childhood as filled with "rats, roaches, bedbugs, flies, winos and dope fiends."

To supplement the family welfare checks, young Miguel turned to crime. "I started stealing when I was 8—milk and bread for my brother and sister. Sometimes we would go into a supermarket and I would feed my sister as we walked along. I would hustle 50 cents on the street and buy cornflakes and we would have a big dinner . . ."

The family moved back and forth between Manhattan and Brooklyn, from slums to projects. He and three friends began burglarizing apartments in Brooklyn. Over the years, he said, he participated in more than 100 burglaries. On one raid on a jewelry shop, he was caught, and sentenced to three years on Rikers Island.

It was at Rikers Island, he said, that he was introduced to drugs. "I had my first shot of dope—a big horse needle of heroin," and despite the fact that he was behind bars (often in solitary), he always managed to obtain drugs.

In and out of jail, he took drugs and sold drugs, and whenever he had money, it "went into my veins." . . . Occasionally he worked at regular jobs, "pushing a rack" in the garment district, in the Photostat department at Metro-Goldwyn-Mayer. "One time I got a job at 9 A.M. and was fired at noon. I was making guitar strings and I was strung out."

The last crime he committed was a burglary and armed robbery on an apartment house (ironically, it is two blocks from the Public Theater) . . . He received a five-year sentence and was shipped off to Sing Sing. Aged 24, he faced his longest sentence. "I was confused. I didn't know what would happen to me. I knew it was going to be hard and I would get by. I knew I was not going to die there, but I didn't care."

Mr. Piñero has always been a good talker ("My best hustle was my rap"), and he pitched into prison politics. He became an operator as well as a revolutionary—although he insisted, "I didn't consider myself a political prisoner. I was an economic prisoner."

One day he happened to stop by the prison's drama workshop, run by Clay Stevenson. He sat down and listened. Later he heard and was most impressed by Mr. Camillo, the actor and director. Mr. Piñero wondered, "Why does this guy come up here and rap as if he has convictions?"

Mr. Piñero began acting in the workshop, then announced that he had written some "dynamite poetry." For some time he had been writing—poetry, and even love letters for other inmates—but until this time he had not gone public. Acting and writing became a powerful release . . .

"When you're in prison, you're nowhere being nobody," Mr. Piñero said. "You're a number. Writing poetry and acting made me somebody in the land of nothing. I was alive and people knew I was alive. I never had so much energy. When I went to my cell, I would create something. I really got hooked on theater. It was like a shot of dope."

MARVIN FELIX CAMILLO My name is Marvin Felix Camillo, but most people know me as Pancho. In 1972 I was acting with a street theater company in Westchester, New York. I really had no interest in prisons at that time; coming from Newark I'd spent my life staying away from and out of prisons. But Polly Siwek, the president of the Westchester Arts Council, asked if I'd teach a workshop in prison.

I was very reluctant—we hemmed and hawed and fussed and fought—but I agreed to do a performance at Sing Sing and it was very emotional. I looked into the audience. It was like a mirror image—I saw myself.

During the play, one of the inmates began to laugh and heckle in Spanish, so I began to heckle him back in Spanish. It was pretty strong stuff, and the audience went wild, they stood up and they applauded and they screamed. At the end of the show, the warden came running backstage. I thought perhaps he was upset. But he said, "That was wonderful, nobody has ever come here and related to the Spanish-speaking inmates." He suggested that I return, and that was kind of the beginning of it.

I became an assistant director at Sing Sing, but the first workshop I had on my own was at the Bedford Hills Correctional Facility for Men. It started with about four people. It was a rough road. One member came to me and said, "I've been hooked on drugs all my life. I've only stayed out of prison, at most, three weeks every time I get out, and now I'm hooked on theater. What can we do?" And I said, "We can do workshops outside." So when the men were released, I'd meet them at the prison gate. Instead of them going back to the street that got them in trouble, they'd come to a theater workshop.

I thought it was important to invite the public so the actors would get some sense of what it would be like to perform for an audience of real people. We performed in schools, we performed in garages, we performed in parking lots. Many times, if the audience would arrive late, we would ask people to turn on their car lights and that was our theatrical lighting. It was beautiful, and the community became very interested. One person who became extremely interested because she felt something good was going on was Colleen Dewhurst.

COLLEEN DEWHURST "Listen," I said, "I'm really not interested in dogooding where theater is concerned. I think it's probably wonderful for people, but I can't bear amateur theater." I asked if there was a way I could see them and Marvin said there was a one-night performance of *New York, New York: The Big Apple* at a place over on the Lower East Side. A lot of it was theirs, things the actors had made up, and whoa, was it angry. It all came out, all of it, and my jaw dropped. When it came to an end, I said, "Okay, I'm interested."

Later, we were sitting in a living room in Westchester and the group was talking about a name. One of the inmates had said, "Being in and out of jail so much, I've lost the sense of what community means. For me, this is such an experience that it's like a family." And I said, "You said the name. Let's call it the Family."

MARVIN FELIX CAMILLO Miguel was one of the inmates at Sing Sing, and he became a member of our acting workshop. Oftentimes he would come and show me pieces of papers and things that he had written. He would really disturb the class when he had an idea about something he wanted to write. He would begin to whisper to me or hand me something on a napkin or a piece of paper. First it was poetry, wonderful wonderful poetry. And then he began to show me some pieces of paper where he had begun to write *Short Eyes*. I don't think he had any formal education, but you saw immediately that he was something special.

He was a great hustler, an operator. He used to say things like I was the greatest actor he knew, that I inspired one of the roles. "I'm writing this part for you," he'd say, and later, of course, I learned that he had told that to maybe nine other people. Many times you meet people in prison who promise to do well when they get out and promise to follow through on things, but it seldom occurs. They don't really have hope that society will provide them with anything.

Miguel became so interested in theater that he got a five-day furlough, a time to come out into society and look for a place, and that's when he saw the Family perform. By this time, he had the play in some shape. He went around trying to get it produced, and he made contact with the Riverside Church, which agreed to provide a place for him. For the first time, he seemed very frightened. He asked me if I would come up with him, if there was something that the Family could do to be supportive. And we said, "Fine, we can do a workshop there at the church."

We began to work on *Short Eyes*, and a great deal of the play developed in this process. We would come up with ideas and work them out, and then he would put down what we worked out. The actors in the company had known the life he'd written about so well that it was just the most exciting process imaginable.

For instance, when Clark Davis, the "short eyes," comes into the room, the way the script was originally written the prisoners jumped on him right away. We did a kind of improvisation where nobody did anything but look, and out of that a quiet, inner intensity developed.

The segment where they put his head down the toilet was developed out of each man thinking about what they wanted to do. One guy just said, "Let's put this motherfucker's head down the toilet," and it became an explosive thing where they were running back and forth and the guy was screaming.

We would always warm up together, ensemble warm-up. Reading was not a virtue with the members of the Family. Many of them had been products of inferior education, so oftentimes you'd have to trick them into reading the script and learning it.

We would sit down, we would learn the situations very well, and then just take the script out of their hands, just say, "Fuck the script." Or after the improvisations, I had them read until they were so tired and so bored with reading that they needed to get up on their feet, and then the explosions began. And once we found the life, the author would write it down and then it was locked.

MARY GOLDBERG   Colleen Dewhurst had first called Joe's attention to *Short Eyes*, but Joe didn't deal with that. As head of casting, I went to see everything; I went to the theater nine nights a week. On a Saturday afternoon, I went all the way up to the Riverside Church with David Eidenberg, the Public's production stage manager, and I flipped. I was devastated.

These guys were just out of jail three minutes and the rawness of it was unbelievable. We went straight over to Joe's house and said, "You're not going to believe this." We arranged for them to come down to the Public and do an hour of it for Joe, and he, of course, went nuts.

BERNARD GERSTEN   The extent to which Miguel Piñero was the instrument of the group experience, the annotator rather than the inventor, is not clear to me today, and I don't know that it was then. The work itself arose from the group of members who were organized by Marvin, but the agreement was that Miguel got credit as author. He had the copyright. And that was always a little bit of a sensitive spot.

Since the press needs heroes and needs sensation, it was very satisfying to take Piñero and make him the author, use him as a vehicle for publicity, give him the awards that the play won and hang the play on his shoulders. And that may not have been totally warranted.

GAIL MERRIFIELD PAPP   I always think of Miguel as being this extraordinarily physically fragile and frail person who always looks like he will disappear in the next breath. When you hug him, it's like hugging a toothpick. I think of him as being in such deep trouble it would take a miracle to extricate himself from it. His personal life is just inconceivably difficult, yet, with this kind of existence that he has, miraculously managing to be a writer.

It's a difficult relationship with him because the kind of addiction that he suffers from makes a person always manipulate anything he can to serve that particular driving need. He controverts himself constantly because of it, so it's like he's against his own personality and soul all the time. It's like being possessed by a devil. In some ways, I think being in jail may have been a relief to him and perhaps continues to be a relief to him when it happens. It takes him away from things that make his life so incredibly precarious and just profoundly agonized.

JOSEPH PAPP I was very much moved by *Short Eyes*. It was very close to me. There were several plays like that, where what I felt had nothing to do with the theater. These plays reflected exactly what was happening—the distinction between life and the theater got very blurred.

The reason I did them was that they aroused my own feelings about injustice, the terror of life, the terror of incarceration, the terror of war, the terror of being young and unprotected. I understood the feelings that went into these plays. Shakespeare, believe it or not, was comparatively a great escape for me.

When a show like that was going on, because I worked closely with the people involved, I reflected it in some way, I experienced it like it was my life. With *Short Eyes*, these were all street people. Some were shrewd and smart, and there were some that would rob me the first chance they got. But I liked them all because they were so honest in a way. They'd been through all this shit already. Since I came originally from the street, I formed a strong identification. I reverted.

The night of the opening at the Anspacher, for instance, I was in a narrow corridor and John Simon, the critic, was coming in. I stopped him and began playing with his tie as I was saying, "Hey, what's the matter with you? Why do you have to keep insulting people?" He just sort of smiled in this way he has and then, finally, before I knew it, my hand was at the top of his tie and I was holding him by the throat, suffocating him up against the wall.

"Why do you do this?" I said.

"It's only words, Joe," he said. "It's only words."

I identified so deeply with that play, with what was being said, that I felt he was insulting me just by being there as a critic who had nothing to do with the theater. I got so angry, I could have killed him.

People were shocked when I took this play to Lincoln Center. I was trying to shake the place up. It was so boring, all that red-carpet stuff, I wanted to bring the plays I loved to that arena. It was really the wrong place to put that play on, though, because audiences didn't expect it. A lot of people walked out, but I think it's one of the extraordinary plays of our time.

MARY GOLDBERG The play had achieved this incredible success at the Anspacher and then something fell out at the last minute at Lincoln Center and that's why it went up there. I was very much against it going to Lincoln Center. I didn't think the actors could handle it, and a lot of them couldn't.

You can't get out of jail and then become an immediate star and go to Lincoln Center and have people wanting your autograph. Your whole concept of reality gets warped. We were throwing them without any protection into a world that was not a world that they were going to be able to adjust to.

MARVIN FELIX CAMILLO Lincoln Center was the best of times and the worst of times. The money was nicer for the actors, but they didn't really know what Lincoln Center was. It was easy and wonderful for them; it was very hard for me. I had to take a responsibility beyond the artistic. I had to try to see to it that they weren't overly seduced.

At that point, the play was already done and it would have been wonderful for me to go off to prepare other things, but I had to go to the theater every night and make sure the actors didn't take liberties, make sure they didn't get hurt. If an actor in A Chorus Line smoked a joint, nothing would happen, but if an actor in the Family did, it became racial—it became what people expected of people in prison. Dealing with them was hard. I mean, we weren't dealing with the cast of Mary Poppins.

For me, Miguel wasn't really a criminal. He would do mischievous things, like he was Brendan Behan. I think he loved the image that the press and everybody had created. I think he began to enjoy being the bad boy. One time a taxi driver was getting drugs, and Miguel took his taxi and was driving up a one-way street. When he was arrested, he said, "I'm doing you people a favor. I'm stopping these dope deals."

I understand he's in bad straits now, but if he goes tomorrow we can say, "Here was somebody who had a ball." He really enjoyed himself during all these years—he had an extraordinary time. Even when he left the Family, there was always a very deep place in my heart for Miguel Piñero because of his talent and because of that play.

Joe Papp also has his moods. Sometimes I see him and he doesn't even know me, can't give you a moment, and other times he hugs me. Everybody thinks of Joe as their friendly enemy, but the thing I really like about him is that he really is very reachable.

Because of his background, where he started and how he started, he's willing to try things for nontraditional groups. He's closer, in a good way, to being from the ghetto than any producer I know. You see him walking, he's even got a little bop—the ghetto strut. If it's about business, either he likes it or he doesn't like it, either he's going to help you or he's not going to help you. I don't have to be so formal with Joe.

BERNARD GERSTEN   What were our middle-class expectations of what would happen to Miguel Piñero when he won the New York Drama Critics' Circle Award for *Short Eyes*? Or when his play was grossing big bucks, and suddenly he was making a couple of thousand dollars a week? He didn't put it into secure investments. He spent a good portion of it on drugs or on clothes or on whatever. He didn't suddenly get restructured as a human being in some middle-class model.

REINALDO POVOD   Miguel Piñero is a warm and real person, someone very vibrant and alive and full of joy. I never seen that man sad in my life. I always remember, we'd shoot up for many hours, then he'd get up in the morning, no money, he was sick for heroin, and he'd say, "Let's get a coffee, a newspaper, and take a walk in the park." He loves being a junkie, he loves doing heroin, and the thing is you never see him cry about it.

He is a walking genius who's only tapped in on maybe a quarter of his resources because he was consumed with killing criminal time. Willie Sutton said, "You're never more alive than when you're robbing a bank, because you could hear a pin drop," and that's what Mikey's all about, being alive. He's been at the point of the sword many, many times.

I remember one time reading something on David Mamet in the *New York Times*, saying, "Mr. Mamet knows the criminal mind." And I'm saying, "This is a fucking guy who probably never committed a crime in his life, except maybe cheat on his taxes." Miguel Piñero, he knows the criminal mind.

JOSEPH PAPP Miguel, I know, played with me to get as much as he could out of me. On the other hand, I've always loved him. He was always kind of jocular, had a marvelous sense of humor. If you'd catch him in something, he'd disarm you with his laugh. He kept going back to drugs, and he kept coming back to me.

He got picked up a lot, the "award-winning playwright arrested" stories, but there were a lot of things that happened after they stopped writing about him. I got him out of jail numbers of times. I was always down there at one of the precincts getting him out.

He was always in some kind of jam, he went out of his way to get involved in these things. It seems that he needed to do it for some reason or other. He became a homosexual in prison and he got mixed up with the wrong kid, who happened to be the brother of a gang leader here on the Lower East Side and who was out to kill him. I got him out of the city; I got him to Philadelphia and I covered for him. I took some knives away from him—he had two switchblades—because he was going to kill somebody.

He was able to capture that in-between, twilight world, to understand the nature of someone who would molest a child. It amazes me how discerning writers are who learn about human nature under the conditions he did. That's where you really learn it—you're certainly not brought up in a dream world. But you pay the price because in the process you deteriorate. Not from the knowing of it but through the kind of life you have to go through in order to know it.

I was always taking care of him when he was in the hospital, getting him some money. He'd always come for money, and finally, I put aside a special fund for him called the Piñero Fund. Now, when he calls me up and says he needs $100, I just give it to him. I don't want to put myself in a position where I begin to question him about whether he's telling the truth or not about being in this particular jam. I felt lousy about myself doing that.

He was always telling me he'd pay it back next week, that he had a picture pending, he was writing this script, he'd give me all kinds of things.

Sometimes he'd come in and he smelled like shit—he'd been through the streets and he was dirty and foul-smelling and all that, and I'd hug him—because he was destroying himself. I thought he was going to die a couple of times. I don't know where he is now.

There's an assumption with someone like Miguel, and I even had a little bit of it myself, that success will solve his problems. I was naïve about those things. I thought, "He's out of prison, he's doing so well now." But it's not true, it's not true at all.

Because that's not what he's deprived of. He's deprived of other things that have nothing to do with success. Initially, every time he got into trouble, I thought, "Why does he do that? He doesn't need to do that." It was baffling to me.

But later I began to understand that he'd gotten on a kind of track that for him seemed impossible to get off. He'd dry out several times, but he'd come right back again. He had so many things that were tearing him, so many demons, so many things that already happened that it seemed to be too late to do anything. You bring these wounds with you wherever you go. You just don't completely heal.

. . .

Miguel Piñero and Marvin Felix Camillo both died in 1988. Camillo was fifty-one years old; Piñero forty-one.

SOLILOQUY:

Meryl Streep

ROSEMARIE TICHLER In 1975, I got a call from Milton Goldman, an agent at ICM, and he said to me, "I want you to meet someone. Robert Lewis, the acting teacher at Yale, said she's one of the most extraordinary people he's ever taught." And I said, "If Robert Lewis says that, I'd be happy to meet her." It was Meryl Streep. She was twenty-four years old, just graduating from the Yale Drama School, and she hadn't done anything in New York.

When an actor comes in and auditions for me, they usually do two roles, one classical, one contemporary, to give a range. Meryl played Margaret in *Richard III*, an older and very powerful woman, then this twenty-one-year-old airheaded drinker in Terrence McNally's *Whiskey*, and I thought, "She's hot."

We were about to go into casting *Trelawny of the "Wells"* at Lincoln Center and I thought she would be wonderful in it. I brought her in for A. J. Antoon, the director, and he liked her, but he liked other people, too. I was pushing her to Joe, but before she could be cast she had to come in one night to audition for him at seven or seven thirty.

That time arrived, she's not there. A half hour passed, an hour, I'm calling, Joe's getting impatient, there's still nothing. I thought, "I'll just run into the street and see if she's coming. If not, we'll leave." And she was walking down the street, swiftly but not hurriedly. I said, "What happened?" and she said the train had been delayed for an hour and a half between New Haven and New York.

I'll never forget what happened when she walked in. I introduced her to Mr. Papp, she apologized for being late, and went right into the part. I remember sitting there thinking, "This girl is meeting Joe Papp for the first time, she's late for a callback for an important part at Lincoln Center, and she's totally unflustered."

Ninety-five percent of actresses would get hysterical, but she just . . . handled it. I thought, "She has talent and she's not neurotic, she's a very centered woman, nothing's going to stop her." Joe liked her immediately, and she's never stopped working since.

MERYL STREEP In 1975, when I graduated from drama school, Joseph Papp was undisputed lord of the theatrical realm in NYC. It was, I guess, around the beginning of the Shakespeare Festival's mid- and uptown expansion/explosion. Lincoln Center was his and he was on Broadway *and* in the park *and* on traveling stages *and* downtown and all around the town. Joe Papp's Public Theater. The tough, magic name that buzzed the halls of the drama school and drew us like a magnet into Manhattan. When I got an audition there I was wild, and when I got a *job* there I was beside myself.

At the first reading of *Trelawny of the "Wells"*—with a beautiful cast including, among others, Mary Beth Hurt, Mandy Patinkin, John Lithgow, Michael Tucker, and Walter Abel—I was so nervous I shook and trembled through the whole first act. Even my upper lip wiggled independent of the lower. All of a sudden in the middle of a sentence Joe told me to play Imogen as a Southerner. "Do a Southern accent," he said.

My Southern accent came direct to me from *The Dinah Shore Show*, "See the U.S.A. in your Chevrolet . . ." But I said, "Yessuh," and, lo and behold, the character came to some sort of life. Romulus Linney says the Bible sounds better with a Southern accent, but I think probably most anything does, and it was the hook I needed for my aging ingenue.

The curvaceous, desperately subtle flirtation in the cadences moved me toward a way of holding myself and of moving across the room, a way of sitting, and above all an awareness, because a Southern accent affords self-aware self-expression. You shape the phrase. Not to get too deep into it, it was a valuable choice and it was not mine, it was his and I still don't know where the hell he got the idea. This is the essence of his direction. *He's* direct. Do it, he says.

Joe's directness can be brutal, and I've seen that, too. Once he rounded up the heaving, exhausting tatters of a cast in workshop and took them, one by one, into a corner of the rehearsal room and fired them or kept them in the show. You're in, you're out. He has no time for weeps, because he is no weep. He has deeply felt sentiments, but he is not sentimental.

The direct and uncluttered gesture is magnificent when it moves mountains as he has done for me many times in my lifetime. He swept aside the demands of his best-beloved plays and the business of many days when my friend, actor John Cazale, was sick. He walked us through the harrowing confusion of health care in the big city—he went to tests, held hands, held his breath. I love him for that most of all. I always will.

21

A Chorus Line

1975

Manhattan phone
booth ad
Courtesy of the New York
Public Library

The conservative word for "*A Chorus Line*" might be tremendous, or perhaps terrific. Michael Bennett's new-style musical opened at the Newman Theater of the New York Shakespeare Festival Public Theater on Lafayette Street last night, and the reception was so shattering that it is surprising, if, by the time you read this, the New York Shakespeare Festival has got a Newman Theater still standing in its Public Theater complex on Lafayette Street. It was that kind of reception, and it is that kind of show . . .

The idea is bright—indeed, it glows like a beacon heavenward. Like most great ideas it is simple. It is nothing but the anatomy of a chorus line. And the gypsies themselves—those dear, tough, soft-bitten Broadway show dancers, who are the salt and the earth of the small white way—are all neatly dissected as if they were a row of chickens. Their job-hunger, their sex lives, their failures (because even the best of them never thought of themselves forever in the chorus but 99 percent of them will be there until they drop or drop out), their feeling toward dancing, why they started and what they might do when they stop—all is under coruscatingly cruel microscope.

Clive Barnes, *New York Times*, May 22, 1975

•••

The director, a fellow called Zach, runs up the aisle to the back of the house, lines everybody up, asks for stage names, real names, ages and resumes. These resumes, as sung and danced and spoken, are the show … There is a young Puerto Rican homosexual who, once the stage has been cleared, painfully reviews his painful life to Zach in a monologue that could easily have slopped over into a bleeding-heart plea but doesn't … The thin thread of plot is provided by Cassie (Donna McKechnie, a beautiful dancer and a good singer), once the lover of Zach, who pulled her out of a long-ago chorus line to almost make a star of her. She left him years before, her career has come to a dead stop, and she is determined, over his protests, to start again.

The New Yorker, June 2, 1975

•••

BOB AVIAN Michael Bennett and I met in 1960 in the European tour of *West Side Story*. I had done it on Broadway and when they got a new company together for the tour they hired a few new people, one of them being Michael. He interested me very much, and I interested him, and we instantly became best friends. He was very bright, and he was ambitious. I always saw that.

Michael was about seventeen at the time. He'd started dancing when he was three or four years old, and when he was fourteen he lied about his age and worked the strip clubs in Buffalo. He liked performing, but he really didn't want to perform; he wanted to choreograph. He used to choreograph all these high-school productions. He'd never go to class because he'd be busy putting on shows. He would finagle scenery from the local TV studios, work on these shows all semester long.

We came back from that European tour and he went on to dance in *Subways Are for Sleeping*, *Here's Love*, and *Bajour*. He needed an apartment, and he moved in with myself and my parents for a while. Then we got an apartment together that we paid $76 a month for, a walk-up on Eighth Avenue in Chelsea. I was also going from show to show at that time, going from chorus job to chorus job to chorus job, and I was tiring of dancing. I didn't see any future for myself.

Meanwhile, Michael started assisting on choreography—summer stock and a lot of television, including *Hullabaloo*. Then he got an opportunity to do *A Joyful Noise*, his first show as choreographer and the only one I did not work with him on. It was not a strong show, but Michael grabbed the bull by the horns, took the opportunity, and worked so hard, made every moment that he could work. Eventually, they did bring it to New York in December 1966. The show got killed, but his work was stupendous, and he got nominated for his first Tony Award. Even though it ran a week, he came out ahead.

Then Michael said, "Come work with me on this next show," which was *Henry, Sweet Henry*. "You'll be dance captain and assistant and all of that." I did it because we were best friends. I went into the whole job as a pal, and one of the big things about our relationship was that we always worked together that way. Being best friends is different than being paid as an assistant. You're very honest, and I think the best thing that I did with Michael was to be almost his editor; it was my taste laid upon his.

Henry, Sweet Henry was not a success, but his area came out very strong. He got nominated again for a Tony Award, and his reputation kept on growing. *Promises, Promises* was his third Tony nomination, and then we did our smash flop, *Coco*, with Katharine Hepburn. That was difficult because she was not a musical performer and she was frightened to death. I remember her one day, when she was really depressed, "I don't know what gives me the nerve to think that I can do this." But Michael is great with stars and collaborators. He gets them to believe in themselves and trust everything. He's great about protecting these people.

Then we did *Company*, followed by *Follies*, and then our first straight play, *Twigs*, by George Furth, with Sada Thompson. We opened with $28 in the box office and we ran a full season and she wound up winning the Tony Award.

The title of *Twigs* originally was *Chorus Line*. We didn't think it was right for the piece, and George Furth, agreeing with us, came up with the title *Twigs*. Later, when Michael had the idea for doing a show about dancers, he said *Chorus Line* would be great. He called up George and said, "Listen, can I have the title?," and George said, "Absolutely."

DONNA MCKECHNIE As a child, like many of the people in *Chorus Line*, I had a desire to fantasize, to go out and realize a dream. Every time I heard music, I started dancing. Really it was about approval, about feeling loved. I was sent to dance class, even though my family's religious background and beliefs—Bible Belt Baptist—held that anything pleasurable was sinful, especially dancing, where you used your body. I always felt like I was a coconspirator with my mother.

I left the Detroit area when I was fifteen and went to New York, which was always my dream. I was young and naïve and everything was sweet, very exciting, an adventure. Early on, I auditioned for Lucia Chase and the American Ballet Theatre. We started with forty-five girls and the last day there were maybe seven of us. Lucia Chase called me over and said, "I don't know you, you haven't studied here, but I'm very impressed with your work. What I would suggest is that you study with us for a year and then you can join the company next year."

If I had any sense, I would have been jumping up and down. I mean, she was offering me everything I'd ever wanted. But I was such a perfectionist, I took it as a total personal rejection. I had no education about what auditions were or what the world was, so I was crushed. I didn't take a ballet class for six months, and I didn't see a ballet for five years.

I went right to the street, saying, "Okay, I'm just going to make a living and survive." But because I'd been trained by the best and rubbed shoulders with the best in the best classes, I felt like I was an artiste. After *How to Succeed in Business Without Really Trying*, my first Broadway show, I decided that I was not going to do chorus dancing. I said, "Television's different, it's like a step up."

So I auditioned for *Hullabaloo*, a fabulous rock-and-roll variety show. That's where I met Michael, who was very attracted to my dancing style. Each of the dancers got to do their own number and I said to him, "I've always been someone who worked well off of somebody. I take a choreographer's work and add my personality to it." And he just said, very casually, "Do this and do this and do this and do this and this." I did it, and it was spectacular. It was the first inkling I had of how well we'd work together.

We always stayed in touch. Long before the *Chorus Line* process started, three years before, he had the germ of the idea. "I want to do a show about dancers," he was saying. "And I want to do something for you. I want to use you in a way that no one's ever seen you." He was excited by talent—his own and other people's.

At this point, also, the mood of the day for a lot of us was frustration and dissatisfaction. I remember going to see musicals and saying, "Is this what I dedicated my life to, seeing people with makeup on their faces moving their mouths to the music in one-dimensional things?"

Michael and Bob Avian and myself had dinner one night. I quit show business every year, but now I said, "I really mean it this time. I read that they're offering land in New Zealand, and if we got enough people together, we could get ten thousand acres, we could farm, work hard, commune, really do something good." I was kind of making a joke, but they went, "*Yeah!*"

So when the call came to do a taping session with other dancers about our lives, it sounded like Custer's Last Stand. I thought, "He's finally going to sit down and talk about that idea." I went but I really felt that my purpose there was to be his friend. Everybody was very excited to be there. Michael was a powerful figure. Even though he was a friend to many people there, we all put him on a pedestal.

We started with a class. It wasn't that intense, just to loosen us up. Once we were all kind of sweating, we went into this little room and sat down on the carpet. There were big jugs of cheap wine there, a tape recorder, and just one little lamp in the corner. We all sat around in an oval, and Michael started with the three questions that the show begins with: "Tell your name, where you were born, and why you started dancing." And that just kicked it off.

NICHOLAS DANTE I was a dancer who wanted to write. I really only had one or two Broadway credits. *Applause* with Lauren Bacall was my big claim to fame as a chorus boy. Everything else I'd done was either television or on the road and nightclubs. I'd never auditioned for Michael, but I knew him as a very talented choreographer who was coming up, the new genius on the block.

A friend of mine, a dancer named Michon Peacock, is really the one who started this entire thing. Dancers at that time were not treated very well. We were low man on the totem pole: if they needed a line spoken, they would give it to a singer because they didn't think dancers could talk.

Michon had had a very bad experience in a show. She wanted to do something about that and she didn't know what. And she and a friend named Tony Stevens went to see Michael Bennett. She didn't know what the hell she was talking about, but she just knew that something needed to be done.

Michael was feeling frustrated at the time, and he said, "Well, why don't you get a bunch of dancers together and we'll all talk?" But he didn't want to call his dancers, because he felt that they wouldn't be as honest. It was interesting that that would occur to him, but it would occur to him. That's how well he knows people. He's very shrewd, always finagling. So he left it to Michon to call people.

We met in January 1974 in a dance studio on Third Avenue in the Twenties. It was at Saturday midnight because Michael wanted to get the people that were working in shows who wouldn't be able to come any other time. About twenty-five people were there, including seven or eight who ended up in *A Chorus Line*.

We danced first, and then he had it catered; there was this big pile of sandwiches in the middle of the floor. We were all competitors—a lot of us didn't necessarily like each other, there were cliques and things—but we sat around in a big circle. And we just didn't all get in there and start rambling. There was an order to how we all talked and what ages we were covering. We talked from age one to six, and we went all around the room; then we talked from six to twelve, all the way around; then twelve to eighteen and eighteen to twenty-five.

Very early on, all guards were dropped, because the minute people started talking about their childhood or what they went through, of course you would identify with something. We were all talking about our lives and how those fantasies and desires about wanting to dance came about, and as one person would talk, it would just trigger a wealth of memories for yourself.

The session lasted until noon the next day, and at the end we all held hands, and just as we grabbed hands, the noon bells went off. It was very mystical. As I said, we did not necessarily like each other, but we had shared something extraordinary and unique and by the end of that evening, we all felt very close to one another. Ultimately, I think we captured in the show what we set out to do, because what we wanted was to recapture what we all experienced that night in that room.

I didn't know whether I was going to be able to tell my story that night in that room with all those people. But something told me that this was a very important evening and that I really had to do this. It was the story of what a tortured life I'd had as an effeminate young man; how I was forced to quit school because everybody made fun of me.

I wound up being a drag queen, a female impersonator in a show. I lied to my parents about it, and then one night they came to the theater and found me. My father said to the producer, "Take care of my son." It became Paul's story in the show, the one the whole show hangs on, so there might not have been a show if I had not told the story that night.

Originally, my story ended with the line, "My father said, 'Take care of my son.'" Then I told the story to Sue McNair, Michael's secretary, and that time I added that it was the first time he'd called me son. And Michael said, "Wait, you told this to Sue," and it was put in the show. It's a great line, and I'd never change it, but, years later, I realized that that wasn't true. My father called me his son all the time, but that was the first time it ever meant anything to me, the first time I ever *heard* it.

There was a second session, with a few new people but less powerful. Then one night I got a telephone call and it was Michael. He said to me, "I definitely think that there's a show in this material. You said you wanted to write and I want you to help me write it. If we can't get it right, then we'll hire another writer, and we'll hire another writer until we get it right. Would you be interested?" And I said, "Of course." In retrospect, what I realized

Jason Miller, winner of the Pulitzer Prize for *That Championship Season*
© Marianna Diamos/Los Angeles Times

Walter McGinn, Paul Sorvino, Richard Dysart, Michael McGuire, and Charles Durning in *That Championship Season*
© Friedman-Abeles

A confrontation in *That Championship Season*
© Friedman-Abeles

Tito Goya, Joseph Carberry, William Carden, Felipe Torres, Ken Steward, and Ben Jefferson in *Short Eyes*
© Friedman-Abeles

Miguel Piñero and Papp after *Short Eyes* won the New York Drama Critics Circle award
© Friedman-Abeles

Director Michael Bennett and composer Marvin Hamlisch in rehearsal for *A Chorus Line*
© Friedman-Abeles

The finale of *A Chorus Line*
© Martha Swope

A Chorus Line coauthor
James Kirkwood with director
Michael Bennett
© Martha Swope

Donna McKechnie and
Bob LuPone in *A Chorus Line*
© Martha Swope

Papp celebrating the success
of *A Chorus Line*
© Martha Swope

Costume designer Theoni
Aldredge
© Mary Frampton/Los Angeles Times

A scene from *The Leaf People*
© Friedman-Abeles

Dorian Harewood, Kenneth McMillan,
and Peter Evans in *Streamers*
© Martha Swope

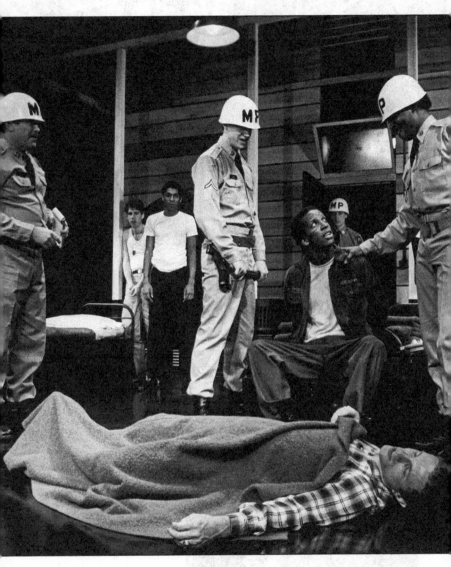

A scene from *Streamers*

© Martha Swope

(Left) *for colored girls who have considered suicide/when the rainbow is enuf* playwright Ntozake Shange
© Sy Friedman

(Right) Filmmaker Melvin Van Peebles and Ntozake Shange at *colored girls* Broadway opening
© UPI/Corbis

The cast of *for colored girls who have considered suicide/when the rainbow is enuf*
© Martha Swope

(Left) Randy Ruiz and Diane Lane in *Runaways*
© Martha Swope

(Below, left) Betty Albertin, Gretchen Cryer, and Bonnie Strickman in *I'm Getting My Act Together and Taking It on the Road*
© Susan Cook

(Below) *Runaways* playwright Elizabeth Swados
Courtesy of the New York Public Library

(Bottom) Helen Hayes celebrating Papp's birthday at the Delacorte Theater party, 1978
© Bill Stahl

Kevin Kline as the
Pirate King in *The Pirates
of Penzance*
© Martha Swope

Linda Ronstadt and Rex Smith
in *The Pirates of Penzance*
© Martha Swope

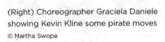

(Right) Choreographer Graciela Daniele
showing Kevin Kline some pirate moves
© Martha Swope

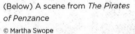

(Below) A scene from *The Pirates
of Penzance*
© Martha Swope

Linda Ronstadt and Papp at
Ronstadt's birthday party, 1980
© Martha Swope

True West playwright Sam Shepard
© Douglas H. Burroughs/Los Angeles Times

Playwright
Larry Kramer with
Brad Davis, the star of
A Normal Heart
© Martha Swope

Brad Davis in a scene from
A Normal Heart
© Martha Swope

(Right) Papp sharing a moment with
Gail Merrifield Papp
© Frederic Ohringer

(Below) Gail Merrifield Papp, director
of play development, and Papp
© Ken Regan/Camera 5

Papp and Bernard Gersten on
Ellis Island
© Benedict J. Fernandez

Advertising 1970's
all-night *The Wars
of the Roses*
© George E. Joseph

Meryl Streep and Papp
© Carol Rosegg/Martha Swope

Papp at the Delacorte,
1964
© Dan McCoy

was that Michael wanted my story. I think he lucked out in that I could write. Oh, he's very shrewd, very shrewd.

JOSEPH PAPP I wanted to do a musical about New York and I couldn't find a good enough new one. Then I thought of reviving *Knickerbocker Holiday*, because the music was by Kurt Weill and included "September Song," one of my favorite songs. The book by Maxwell Anderson seemed a little antiquated to me, but I thought, "Maybe it'll work if I get somebody good to do it." And the name that popped into my mind was Michael Bennett.

The reason it came into my mind was that I used to see him all the time at the Tonys. I had won a few Tonys, he had won a few Tonys, and we'd pass and smile at one another. And I thought his work, the tremendously theatrical choreographic ideas he had, was absolutely superb.

So I called him and said, "Michael, how would you like to do a show with me? I'd like to do *Knickerbocker Holiday*."

"Listen, would you mind if I had another idea? I want to do a show about dancers. It's been on my mind for quite a long time. I've talked to dancers over a period of many, many nights. I have some tapes. Would you mind if I brought those over and we could listen to them?"

"Fine."

He came over to the office, I think it was the very next day, and put on these tapes of dancers talking about their lives. It was the most moving story; it all had to do with parents and children. I listened for about five hours, and I'm telling you, the detail of those tapes was absolutely stunning.

It was one story after another, said in the most non-sentimental way, no self-pity, not a touch of it, which made it the more unbearable, frankly. After that I said, "Fine, let's do something with this," and I put some money into a workshop.

Michael was my first contact with a real Broadway-type professional. He was highly commercial, which means he had a marvelous sense of theatrical movement which couldn't be contained on a small stage. And he was able to be both popular and different at the same time.

He was always very down to earth; there was nothing intellectual about Michael. He was more ordinary than ordinary people, but put him in his milieu and he was extraordinary. And that had nothing to do with anything that anybody learns in school. He sees it, he feels it, he knows it, and he does it. It's pure talent, and he had it. I think he's the greatest choreographer/director I've seen on Broadway.

BERNARD GERSTEN   Michael called and said there was a project he wanted to talk about. He came down with a one-hour tape, a reduction of the original tapes the dancers had recorded on that fateful two nights of dancing and talking, and Joe responded very quickly and very much from the heart and said, "Yeah, that sounds very interesting to me. We'll do a workshop. Tell us what you need." And that's how that began.

I know that in certain quarters it's considered that but for me there would have been no *Chorus Line*. That's not really true. If I hadn't known and suggested Michael, I don't know whether Joe would have thought of him, or whether Michael would have thought of the Public Theater as a place to do something he wanted to do. I just have no idea.

But once *A Chorus Line* came into the building, because of that slight friendship over ten years, I became very custodial. And to the extent that somebody focused more on one production than another, Michael became more or less my charge. If he had special problems or needs, he would tend to come to me and I would take them to Joe and try to work them out.

Michael is an extremely talented musical-theater director and choreographer. He's not a literate person, he's not an educated theater person, but he has an extraordinary instinctual, visceral understanding, a very, very sure hand-eye-nose for the musical theater. Those are his qualities. Now, what is he like? If I were the kind of person who used the word "centered," I'd say he's a poorly centered person. As a personality, he's not well-knitted together.

I think Michael is very manipulative. Early, early on, he became aware of his power to more or less knead people into forms that served purposes that he had. Not in any unduly exploitive way, because he also believed that he was doing it for the person's own good. I hate to use a cheap phrase, but maybe he believed that what was good for Michael was good for everybody else. I like Michael, but I guess I have a residue of disappointment.

Michael and Joe are only alike, perhaps, in that there are powerful egos at work in each case. They are both very, very full of self, and they both came from essentially working-class backgrounds. But the differences are more significant than the similarities.

Joe is a thoughtful person; Michael is not a person who occupies his mind with thoughts. Michael is intellectually capable, but he is not, as Joe is, informed by a Socialist ideology or any particular ideology. Michael has a kind of wariness that is peasantlike, a sense of that which is not familiar as being threatening. To Joe, anything that is unknown is a challenge. His curiosity is limitless.

THEONI ALDREDGE I looked at this thirty-one-year-old and I said, "Here we go, I've got to babysit here." But I sat down with this man and there was another Joe Papp there. The enthusiasm of the man, and the knowledge, and the ability to put things right on the nose. They were one of a kind, both spunky, both an *enfant terrible*. They knew what they wanted, and it was great.

MARVIN HAMLISCH I had just won three Academy Awards in one night for *The Way We Were* and *The Sting*, and all of a sudden I was leaving Hollywood to come back to New York to get paid nothing, to give a year or two years of my life to a project based solely on the fact that Michael Bennett was doing it.

My movie agent was upset. He said, "Now, when the iron is hot, when the phone calls are going to be coming, *now* you're leaving?" And I said to him, "I believe in Michael Bennett enough to know that if he's got something that he thinks is that special, I want to be part of it."

You have to understand something: Michael Bennett is a powerful force. As long as he's looking at you and saying it's going somewhere, it's going somewhere. It was not like some guy with a cigar sitting and saying, "I don't know, kid." It was Michael Bennett. He's the boss man, he's the guy that you're believing in, the guy that's fueling it. He's the gas. This was a train that always had a motor, and it was always thrusting forward.

BERNARD JACOBS Michael is the ultimate director in terms of the fact that he is always manipulating people, and directing is all about manipulation. And most of the time, people were never aware of the fact that they were being manipulated, because though Michael knew where he was going, most of the time nobody else knew where Michael was going.

Michael wanted to get results out of people, and because he had the ability to motivate, he was able to get someone like Sammy Williams, who played Paul, the Puerto Rican boy, someone who'd never uttered a spoken word on the stage before, to perform as a Tony-winning professional. Michael is a remarkable talent, and anyone who argues with that is a moron.

NICHOLAS DANTE To be perfectly honest, he's the best manipulator in the world. If he really wants you to adore and love him, he will woo you. Michael is extraordinary that way, he can get anything out of you. He gets you personally caught up in him and then he pushes your buttons, which he's very good at. This small, short man with moles all over his face, he gets everybody to fall in love with him. He did it to me on *A Chorus Line*. He got me to fall in love with him.

The reason Michael called it *A Chorus Line* instead of *Chorus Line* was that when you looked up the show in the ABC directory, it would be first. I mean, he's that shrewd. It's total manipulation.

JAMES KIRKWOOD We used to work very long days on *Chorus Line*. We'd have a drink at two in the morning, and then we'd say good night. I would go home, and sometimes Michael would call me up at three, and he would say, "Jimmy, god, without you, I don't know where we'd be now. I just love the way you write and the way you work and your this and your that. We're going to go on and do other shows." He was the kind of person who really makes you feel you're the whole thing.

JOSEPH PAPP The first workshop began in August of 1974. I would just love to go in there because we'd never had a kind of show-business show before. That had never been part of my life. This was like a Broadway show, and I'd never had anything like that. We were always doing the serious plays, and it was kind of delightful and refreshing to have those dancers around. I'd come in and they would be so warm in greeting me. I'd love to see them. It was so special, and it was nice to have it in my own home, so to speak.

NICHOLAS DANTE   It was Bob Avian, Michael's right hand, who saw the show as an audition and kept saying so from the very beginning. At first, Michael thought it was this very existential, strange show in which these dancers were let in the back door and this voice was up there interviewing them. It was all very surreal and rather silly, and Bob kept saying, "It's an audition. It's an audition."

BOB AVIAN   Michael came to me and said, "We're going to be working on this project for $100 a week." We had just had a couple of shows that ran but didn't make any money. I was broke, he was broke, we were almost destitute, and I said, "Michael, $100 a week? I'm ready to become a waiter! I'm ready to teach school!"

You couldn't live on it, really, but I had a cheap apartment and some money in the bank. And we asked these dancers to do the same thing. It was tough, but if they got other jobs, we let them go do it, just so they could sustain themselves. And during the first workshop, a lot of people came and went, because they didn't know what was going on or they just didn't want to be bothered with this kind of development.

We took all the material that we liked, we just strung it together end to end, and constructed it as a play. We kept on seeing what was needed and what wasn't.

When we strung it together without any score, it ran over four hours, and it was teary and weepy and terrible. Everybody fell into the sob-story trap, each kid heard the person before them go through their story. It was mea culpa, beat yourself, they were sobbing by the time it got to them.

But what was always right about the show was that the emotion was terrific. Even with all this rambling all over the place, you were still interested in these people. There was something there.

DONNA MCKECHNIE   Those first workshops were horrible. Dancers are very rigid, and a lot of us didn't have the kind of training to improvise. And without training, we were purging as opposed to acting. Sometimes you'd be sitting there and you'd go, "*Noooo*, nooo! I don't want to talk about it." At one point, we had four hours of a semicircle of people getting up, one at a time, and, without any theatrical tension, telling their life story. We called it "The Towering Inferno."

Still, I thought the people who left during workshop were crazy. One girl said, "I want to do this other off-Broadway show, because I have two songs there and you've only given me half a song." And one guy said, "I've got to do this industrial. I need the money. I've got to leave." Sometimes I wonder how they live with themselves today.

But at the point when it would have been discouraging to a lot of people, Michael saw something. He fed certain stories with a common ground into one character. But nobody else really understood what the meaning behind anything was. It was all just forms, he was trying out forms, it was like arithmetic onstage. To get the gold, we went through every wrong road. It was like turning every corner and wrong, wrong, maybe, wrong, wrong. We tried everything. We failed entirely, and then sifted out the gold.

In the beginning, this was not Joe's cup of tea. I felt that we were kind of like the stepchild. But he is a man of vision, and he saw something, too. I think he was stretching, like he does with everything.

"This is not about Broadway," he said. "There is something else going on here. This is about the human condition. And Michael Bennett has a background of producing, not just being lip service. He's real talent." He believed in Michael. He deferred to Michael all the time. When Michael was on the scene, it was Michael's show.

BOB AVIAN   During this time, Marvin Hamlisch and Ed Kleban had agreed to work on the project. They kept coming, and we had many discussions about maybe a song here, how about this there, whatever.

Michael was amazing in getting Marvin to work on the show. He was a great friend and goes back with us a long time, but he said, "What's a workshop? And what do you mean, 'off Broadway'?" And Theoni Aldredge, who'd just won an Oscar for *The Great Gatsby*, was the in-house designer for Joe, and he suggested using her. Michael said, "Fabulous." So we had all these heavyweights on this funny, unknown project.

THEONI ALDREDGE Four months of my life we were just nitpicking the rehearsal clothes. It looks simple but it was a bastard to do, one of the most difficult shows I've ever done. He had cool lights, reality lights, which are the dancers' lights, and then show lights for when they were performing, and every color would change into ten colors. We went through hell to get the colors to light that many ways and not look crazy.

MARVIN HAMLISCH *A Chorus Line* was different than anybody's ever worked. In the old days, once you got a commitment, you were on a time-bomb schedule, because in five to six weeks you had to open somewhere. If you opened in Boston to get the kinks out, you were already reviewed, which affected the business in New York in terms of press.

The whole idea of this was getting the kinks out by rehearsing it in New York. Instead of saying, "Listen, in seven weeks we're opening," it was, "Listen, we don't know where we'll be in seven weeks. We're just doing our thing." There was no "they" involved, no "Are *they* going to like it?" It was about if we liked it. If Michael felt good about it, it was going to go ahead. There was no "Uh-oh, who's looking over our shoulder?" I never felt that anybody was looking over our shoulder.

It started out as not a musical. We just kept watching the rehearsals, and they were very, very slow and tedious because there was no book. As we slowly but surely inserted the music, the shape of it started to come. It was just a process of trial and error. "What would happen if . . ." Try something and see what that was like. It was amorphous, truly the ultimate work in progress.

The way the songs were written is this. Ed Kleban loved to interview. He used yellow pads and got as much information about each person as he could. For instance, for the song about Diana, the Puerto Rican girl from the Bronx, he talked to Priscilla Lopez, the girl who played her. He could talk to her for five hours; he would come back with these thousands of pages. I mean he would just get this ton of material about *the* actual person, and we would start picking up what was interesting. One thing would lead to another and he'd say, "Nothing, I have nothing," and I would go away and start writing a melody.

DONNA MCKECHNIE   I'll never forget the first time we heard the music because it was too perfect. Marvin Hamlisch, who'd won all these awards in Hollywood, had I think quit about three times, and Michael was fighting him every step of the way. He kept saying to him, "What do you want? You want to be an artist or you want to be famous?" He'd always appeal to him that way, and Marvin would go, "Oh, this is awful."

But Marvin came in with Ed Kleban's lyrics, he sat down at the piano, very serious. He went into "Everything Is Beautiful at the Ballet," and I don't know how they wrote that. It was everything we discussed, and it epitomized our show. That moment was a turning point for me, when I thought for the first time, "This is really great."

BERNARD GERSTEN   We saw a run-through, and Theoni and I were profoundly moved, and Joe said, "I'm going to talk to Michael and I'm going to decide whether we're going to go on or not." Theoni and I sat there and decided what we were going to do if Joe decided not to go on, whether we'd take over the show or persuade him or threaten to quit or kill him—whatever was necessary.

Because those of us who knew and loved him best knew that the very popularity that we perceived in the show, its ability to address itself to such a broad audience, might make it unacceptable to Joe. Or the very thing that had drawn him, as part of his omnivorous curiosity, to it in the first place, which in part was the extent to which it examined homosexuality as a dominant sexual preference among male dancers, he would now feel was dealt with too fliply or too superficially.

JOSEPH PAPP   Michael had taken time out to direct Neil Simon's *God's Favorite*, and then he began a second *Chorus Line* workshop at the end of December. We had put a considerable amount of money into the show, $350,000, and we weren't sure how it was going to work out because there were problems with the story. It was nowhere, sort of muddling along, and it had always been a very delicate matter: in the original, Zach had a gay relationship as well as one with Cassie.

Michael and I sat in my living room one night and I said, "Make a choice about what this play is going to be about. I think you could get one of those men out of the picture, some way, because it's screwing up the whole thing." I sat with him and he began to tell me his life story. Spent hours, told me how he started, when he first felt he was gay, how he became a dancer. It was the most intriguing story.

Finally, by the end of the evening, it was very late. I said, "Do you think you can pull this off?"

"Yes, I can."

I looked in his eye and I believed him. I knew he'd do it.

"Okay," I said. "We're going to go ahead with it."

A few days before, people had come to me and said they wanted to put some money into the show. I was considering that, because I thought, "I'm a nonprofit organization, I can't afford to put any more money in this."

After I met with Michael, I met with those money people again, and I thought, "What am I doing in the same room with these people? I have nothing in common with them." I just could not get into any partnership with people like that. I never have and I never will. It was the smartest move I ever made, and it had nothing to do with my being smart. I just couldn't stand them.

BERNARD GERSTEN   We were concerned about what the cost of the production would be. We certainly wanted to go forward with it—there was no question of abandoning it for lack of money. Maybe it was Michael who suggested that if we were having a problem coming up with the money that his agent might be able to help us.

So I had a meeting in my office that Joe did not attend with Michael's agent, Jack Lenny, an entrepreneurial type. And they said if we needed money in order to complete the production, they were prepared to put up the sum of money that was required. In other words, what they were offering to do was buy half of A Chorus Line for $150,000.

I went back to Joe and he said, "What do you think?" And my feeling was definitely that, one way or another, we should manage to do it without taking that money. I recommended that to Joe, and he agreed. And gross box-office receipts from the stage production of *A Chorus Line* are somewhere between $180 and $225 million. So didn't we all do well not to give it away and sell it off?

BOB AVIAN We had gone with Nick Dante as writer because Nick's story in the show was very strong, he articulated it so well, and he had an ambition to be a writer—so Michael said, "Go ahead and try." And Nick really did good work, but it got to a point where, as we got closer and closer to being a real show, we needed a professional in terms of craft and the knowledge of how to write a dramatic scenario. And we needed to create a plot with a love interest, which was not really in the show.

We had gotten friendly with Jim Kirkwood and Michael thought he would be the perfect person to collaborate on this. He *theatricalized* the Cassie-Zach situation; he worked a lot on that aspect. It was hard on Nick in the beginning. He thought, "Oh, I'm going to lose my show," but then he embraced the situation.

NICHOLAS DANTE Before the second workshop started, Michael called me and said, "I'm bringing in another writer. It's Jimmy Kirkwood, and I want you to come by the house on Monday and meet him." Click. I wasn't thrilled about the way Michael did that, but I knew Jimmy and I would get along because he had written my favorite book. And actually, when I went in to meet Jimmy, and for the first few days afterward, I realized that these two men didn't know how to make the situation work. They felt awkward, and I had to put them at ease about it, which I found very ironic.

Actually, I think I was sort of relieved that they had brought in Jimmy. It did me a big favor because it took all the pressure off me. In the whole month's hiatus, I was so stuck, I didn't write a word, and I was just terrified that I had let Michael down.

JAMES KIRKWOOD I wrote a play called *P.S. Your Cat Is Dead*. Of course, it always goes to Mike Nichols first: I think if an Eskimo wrote a play, he'd put it on an ice floe and push it toward Mike Nichols. We went through that and then I thought, "What about Michael Bennett? He's very talented." He was very much intrigued with it, we had many talks, but at the end, he decided not to do it, and I was very disappointed and a little annoyed. It's almost like a tease, one day he's going to do it, and the next day, "No." So I had a little chip on my shoulder about that.

One night I went to the theater and I bumped into Jack Lenny, Michael's agent, at intermission.

"Oh, Michael's here tonight," he said.

"Say hello to the little bastard for me."

"Oh, Jim, don't be like that. Go over and say hello."

So I went over and said, "Hello, you little bastard."

"Jim! My god!"

"What?"

"I've been trying to get a hold of you the last few days. You've been on my mind. Have you ever thought of writing a musical?"

"I've thought of it, but I don't know how."

"Nobody does, really. If everybody knew how, there'd be all these musicals coming out. But I have an idea, and I think it might appeal to you because you were an actor in musicals. Why don't we have lunch tomorrow?"

So we had lunch and he said, "It's going to be about chorus dancers, and its going to be about auditions, and it's going to be about competition," and right away I was hooked because I think the audition system, especially for musicals, is the closest thing to the Romans throwing the Christians to the lions. It really is brutal.

He didn't talk much about the first workshop, maybe because he didn't want to throw up any warning signs that the project was really on its way and I was just kind of coming in at the last moment. And it wasn't until another meeting that he said to me, "Oh, by the way, there's a fellow named Nick Dante who I've been working with. And he will be your co-author."

That always spells trouble to me because collaboration is so difficult. But Michael set up a meeting at his apartment, and when I came in Nick Dante got up, and as he crossed the room to shake my hand he said, "You wrote one of my favorite novels of all time, *Good Times, Bad Times*." And I turned to Michael and I said, "There'll be no problem here." And there wasn't.

It was a very, very happy collaboration, the happiest I've ever been involved in. Michael was very strong throughout and never allowed anything to really erupt. If there was a problem, he would get us all together and we would solve it.

The one thing that I think has been highly overwritten and spoken about are the tapes. I never heard the tapes. No matter how much you talk to how many dancers, they're not going to write a show for you. They can certainly give you the background and the richness of the material, but then it has to be written, it has to be edited and cut and trimmed.

I was given a transcript at one point, in a huge box, but it was continuous. Whoever did the transcribing didn't ever say who was talking. You didn't even know whether it was a man or a woman. So I just gave up, though I do remember taking one line.

It was obviously a man and he said, "The first time I realized I was gay, I was so depressed because I was very much into clothes and I thought, 'Gee, now I'll never get to wear nice clothes.'" And I thought, "That's such a wild line, it's so non sequitur. If anyone's gay, you think you would wear nice clothes." So we put that line in the play.

BOB AVIAN The original Zach was Barry Bostwick. He was good, but he thought that the character was not sympathetic and that he didn't have enough onstage scenes. And with musical material coming in, there seemed to be nothing for him. His career was on a good rush then, and from an actor's point of view, I understood totally what he was thinking. What happened was that we pushed Bob LuPone, the guy who was playing Al, into the role of the director, and he did very well.

NICHOLAS DANTE The Zach-Cassie relationship was a problem partly because nobody knew how much was Donna and Michael or wasn't Donna and Michael. The show did need that sort of plot hook to make it work, but because it was so honest and so true overall, in a way I think it was the least important and least fascinating part.

At one point, the Cassie character was not working and we had this meeting to figure out why. And I told them it was because her scenes were reversed. In her first scene, she did a lot of yelling at Zach, berating him, and she did the "I Can't Act" material in her second scene.

"She's got sixteen kids coming out before her and being fabulous and vulnerable, and she comes out and she's this bitch," I said. "We have to change that, she has to be *more* vulnerable than them." So we went in and switched it and she started working with the audience.

DONNA MCKECHNIE Cassie's story was based on truth, but it was the most fictionalized character because it had to serve the play in a way that no other character had to serve the play. I got *so* tired of defending that. I finally gave up and said, "Yeah, it's me, it's me, it's me." If I was just myself, it would have been much easier.

Michael was always trying to find the dramatic tension of the play. So we sat around and went, "Maybe they should be in love" or "Maybe they were married" or "Isn't it more interesting if they used to go together and then they're not." I used to get very defensive about it. I wanted people to acknowledge that this was real work and thought and imagination. This wasn't my life story. I was acting.

BOB AVIAN Toward the end of the play, Paul falls down and hurts his knee, and the kids go, "Oh, my god, he can't dance." And Michael said one day, "I have to do the accident scene today and I don't want to just start blocking it. How do I get these kids to play this? How do I get them to understand?" Then he said, "I'm going to take a dive today. Bob, you take the phone, stage managers go to the doors. We'll fake it, pretend we're making the calls that are necessary."

So Michael was teaching them a combination, they were all up there, and he fell so hard to the floor, like he had broken his ankle. He played it for about five minutes, and we all watched the kids to see their reactions: the strong ones went right to him, the confused ones backed out, some of them were crying by the sides of the room.

When he pulled out of it, they were so angry at him, they were furious. And he said, "Do you remember everything you just did?" And of course they did, and the root of the scene was there and acted incredibly well. Michael did a lot of experiments like that when he needed to get them places in a hurry.

NICHOLAS DANTE   Michael said to me one night, "We don't have time to talk to everybody on the line, but I want to get the feeling of talking to everybody, and I don't know how to make that happen."

"Remember the night of the session?" I said. "Somebody would say something and it would trigger something in your brain and you would go off on a tangent."

"Yes, but people don't think the way they talk."

"I know how to write thoughts."

I went home and I turned my papers sideways, listed the interviewees, and then I started writing just thoughts, random thoughts, not who said them. I came in two days later and I'd written a whole section. People started to be interviewed individually, but then we went into this montage, you grow up with everybody. That was "Hello Twelve, Hello Thirteen, Hello Love," and it's my favorite contribution to the show.

MARVIN HAMLISCH   Very early in the process, we realized that it could get scary for an audience to see sixteen people up there. They'd go, "Oh, my god, they're going to have sixteen songs in a row." So we came up with the thought that we would have to do a major montage in order to meet the other characters. And writing that was the monumental chore.

I was given mostly dialogue, and even before I gave it to Ed Kleban, I was the one who took it over. I remember putting it all on the floor at my apartment and practically doing a gluing and pasting job, just to see which dialogue I thought was important enough to put to music. We called it "Hello Twelve, Hello Thirteen, Hello Love."

JAMES KIRKWOOD   There were times when Marvin and Ed would get stuck. The one instance I remember specifically was the "Hello Twelve, Hello Thirteen, Hello Love" montage. Marvin and Ed just had one hell of a time with that. Finally, we had a meeting and everyone said, "Jimmy, you and Nick write a little one-act play about childhood and adolescence, write everything that you can think of, that anybody ever thought of." And Marvin said, "Then we'll take that and raid it."

"Raid it?"

"Yeah. We'll take what we want and make a musical number out of it."

Nick and I had a sublet down in the Village, and we worked maybe five days, just writing this thing. We put in everything we ever remembered about being a kid or being in high school. They built the musical number on that, which is why, when you listen to it, so many of the lines don't rhyme: "If Troy Donahue could be a movie star, I could be a movie star"; "One little fart, and they call me 'Stinky' for three years." That was an example of us all working together.

JOSEPH PAPP Marvin Hamlisch wrote some very fine songs, but there was one that I didn't care for, and I told him that. It was "What I Did for Love" and I thought it was a cop-out of the show. He'd written this gorgeous score, it reminded me of Puccini, and the integrity of it was so great, because no song stood out for its own sake except this one.

Also, I felt this song was not really an answer to the question of what would you do if you couldn't dance anymore. It was a kind of pseudo-romantic/sentimental setup, and I never liked that. It worked very well, and everybody cried and so forth, but it was the only song that wasn't inherent, that wasn't tied into the story of the play.

BOB AVIAN One of the ideas we had was that each of the members of the company would come out and be staged in a number, as a star would be staged. One would sit on a piano, another character would come down a stairway, but we never got to it. Then we thought of doing it with an empty spotlight, as if there was a star there. Then we thought of taking someone out of the audience every night.

We had all these ideas, and all of a sudden it was the end of our last workshop, we had maybe two or three days to go until our dress rehearsal, and we still didn't have a finale. So after taking a year to stage the show, Michael and I threw the finale together in four hours. I mean, when you're out of time, you have to do it.

JOSEPH PAPP Michael came to me at the end and he said, "I have a great finale. It's not a finale, it's a curtain call."

"Fine," I said.

"But I have to get some costumes for it."

"Well, what do you need for a curtain call?" I thought it would cost $5,000 or $10,000 at the most.

"It will cost about $50,000."

"Jesus, that's a lot of money for a curtain call." It would probably be about half a million dollars today.

"But it's going to be terrific, it's going to be remarkable." And he began to describe these costumes and these top hats.

"Listen," I said, "I've gone along with you on everything so far," and I said okay. It was the best $50,000 I ever spent.

THEONI ALDREDGE Comes the finale, and Michael sees red.

"No," I said.

"What do you mean, no?"

"No. I'm not going to do red clothes."

"Why not?"

"Because you are telling me this is a fantasy. They've all made it, even the ones that flunked are in that final line. Red is too definite a color. I'm going to do champagne, to look like bubbles."

"Okay," he said. "If it doesn't work, it comes out of your salary."

"What salary? You don't seem to understand. What's $75 a week? I have no salary to give you."

Comes the day of the dress rehearsal and he said, "I better not have made a mistake—your stupid champagne-colored garments." There is this dead silence, there is this beat, and one at a time they come on. First kid came, the second kid, the third. Michael turned around and said, "You are right." And that was it. I decided this man is the man of my life, there's nothing this man will ask I won't do because he had the manliness to say, "You are right."

JAMES KIRKWOOD After a while, the cast was getting a little punchy from over-rehearsing. There would just be the six of us—Michael, Bob

Avian, Marvin, Ed, Nick, and me—sitting in chairs this far from them. After a while, they don't know what they have. They don't know what's touching, they don't know what's funny, and then they start going crazy. I remember saying to Michael one day, "I think we have to throw them to the lions soon. We just have to."

So on one Sunday afternoon, we went down to the Public Theater. We were each allowed to ask five or six people, and there were maybe seventy people there. No sets, no mirrors, no hats. And it just took off immediately. We could feel it. It was a very sunny day and I remember people coming out into the light, with tears in their eyes, saying, "Jesus Christ. What is that? That's amazing!"

BOB AVIAN The true ending of *A Chorus Line* was Cassie not getting the job. In the first preview, she didn't. Neil Simon and Marsha Mason came and saw that performance. Neil suggested some line fixes to Michael, to help the humor, and Michael spoke to Marsha on the phone. "She has to get the job," she said. "She might not in real life, but the audience needs her to get the job. She has to make that step." We agreed, and by the second or third preview, Cassie got the job.

DONNA MCKECHNIE I started feeling like Cassie, and I felt terrible when I didn't get the job. One time, I said, "I've had it." I just left at the end of the second scene and I didn't come back. That lasted one night, and Michael said, "Well, that's the end of the show. You can't leave. Even though the relationship is secondary, you can't leave." Then I realized how much of a catalyst the part was for saying certain things that the play needed to say.

Michael was trying to be very true, but he said, "I have to take the license to make it hopeful. Because if you don't get the job, you're a loser, and the audience worries about you, whether you're going to go home and kill yourself. And Zach is a loser because he can't forgive and forget. Everybody's a loser. So even if they just do lip service to it, everybody has to go on and get bigger."

JOSEPH PAPP I objected to the fact that they sweetened the ending by giving Cassie the job. They had played it with Cassie walking out instead of Sheila, Kelly Bishop's character, and that was much more truthful to the play and true to life. With Sheila doing it, it became less important.

But the feeling was that it was too sad with Cassie. People would find it too cruel. This was the writers' decision, and I thought, "Well, if they want to do that . . ." I could have made a big fuss about it, but I didn't want to at that point. I expressed myself on it, but I didn't force it.

JAMES KIRKWOOD When we first started to preview, there were those people who said, "Oh, it's a great show, but it's really for people in the business. You get the average audience in there, especially an older audience that doesn't know about dancers, are they going to care?" And we all thought, "Oh," because you never really know.

But in one of the earliest previews, they had a special performance for the Golden Age Club. There were four very old people behind me; they were almost ready to take their naps. Early on, Cassie says, "Zach, can I talk to you?" And he says, "Sure, go ahead." And she says, "No, I mean in private." And he says, "I'm sorry. I don't have time now. We're running behind." And one of the old women said, "Why is he talking so mean to her? Shame on him." And I thought, "Ah—they care. They care."

GAIL MERRIFIELD PAPP The audience went absolutely bananas at every performance downtown. It was so emotional, just crazy, like a carnival. Every single night at the Newman they leapt to their feet, they cheered, they cried, they screamed. It was a small theater, so it was very, very intimate, a personal discovery for every person. I've never experienced anything like it since then.

JOSEPH PAPP From the very first preview, it was already a smasheroo. We kept it at the Public for a long while. We lost a lot of money there, but quite deliberately, because we were creating a tremendous pressure while we planned the advertising campaign and everything else about the move to Broadway. And LuEsther Mertz put up the $250,000 to make that move to the Shubert Theatre possible.

MERLE DEBUSKEY If *Chorus Line* had never been under the Shakespeare Festival's imprimatur, the Shakespeare Festival would never have been the Shakespeare Festival it's become, and Joe Papp would never be what Joe Papp became. It was his single biggest financial source. It gave him his independence and his platform to a great degree. Other than himself, it was his single most significant factor.

JOSEPH PAPP From the beginning, I gave Michael Bennett a big chunk of the thing, without any kind of question, and I never regretted doing it, because he was so terrific. Our relationship has always been good. I never put him down; he never put me down. Which is what often happens when a lot of money passes in people's hands. Where before it was done for love, it suddenly becomes very commercial, which I despise.

In fact, we made a written agreement, in sort of highfalutin' Elizabethan English, shortly after the play opened on Broadway. We promised to "perform all the duties, obligations, expectations, as they are construed and understood to apply to the term 'friendship' such as loyalty, fealty, mutual assistance, honesty, truthfulness and trust in all dealings."

We pledged to "set a shining example of integrity in human affairs, in contradistinction and toward the obliteration of backbiting, undermining, innuendo, opportunism, greed, the devil's larder of subtle seductions preying on man's weakness for aggrandizement at the expense and over the corpus of his fellow." We signed it, Gail witnessed it, and we've kept that ever since.

JAMES KIRKWOOD I think when you talk to Nick Dante you will find the same emotion I'm going to tell you about, which was that I was quite hurt after the show opened and Michael and I began to drift apart.

He was suddenly doing *Ballroom*. I heard they were in trouble, and I thought, "Why doesn't Michael call me?" And then I saw him doing what he'd done with me with other people, seducing them in that way creative people have. I saw him do it with Dorothy Loudon, and then, snap, when *Ballroom* closed, that was the end of that relationship.

NICHOLAS DANTE Everybody, in some way or another, got a little bent after the show opened. Michael was a very difficult man. He woos everybody, and then he drops you—you're just dropped cold. He did it to Dorothy Loudon in *Ballroom*, he did it to Swoosie Kurtz in *Scandal*, he did it to me. Michael said to me, "I'm going to take care of you. Don't worry about it." And then he deserted.

A lot of ugliness came out of all this love, out of this fabulous show. People got greedy, they wanted money. The people from the original taping, I wouldn't say hello to almost any of them if I saw them on the street today. Because ultimately what happened is that because they contributed material they all thought they wrote *A Chorus Line*. There was such little regard, really, for what went on, they just got greedy and nasty and ugly. Everybody thought that they were really being cheated, and I thought that was extraordinary. Not giving credit, not even to Michael.

Because the one thing I will say is, I will always appreciate and give credit to Michael. He absolutely led us all there, there's no question. But I will also tell you, if he had a different group of collaborators, he would not have had *A Chorus Line*. It was magic because all the cogs were right. Change one and it would not have been.

. . .

On September 29, 1983, A Chorus Line *became the longest-running show in Broadway history with its 3,389th performance. It closed on April 28, 1990, after its 6,137th performance. Proceeds to the New York Shakespeare Festival are estimated at $30 million.*

22

The Leaf People and
New American Playwrights
1975

A scene from
The Leaf People
© Friedman-Abeles

Joseph Papp had hoped that *The Leaf People* would be the first of five new plays by young playwrights to be brought to the Booth this season; for financial reasons, the program has had to be abandoned, and the young play-wrights will be manifesting their gifts at the Public Theater, in the cool off Broadway precincts where the Pappacy flourishes . . .

The New Yorker, October 1975

JOSEPH PAPP There were no really modern plays being done on Broadway at that time, there were just none. Broadway was bereft, and not only did I want it to have real writers of drama, I wanted to give these writers Broadway recognition. They were first-class, serious writers and they'd never had that.

I wanted to do it in a big way, so I made an arrangement with the Shuberts to take over the Booth Theatre, which I'd always liked, and in May I announced a low-priced series of new American plays by Dennis Reardon (who'd written *The Happiness Cage*), Thomas Babe, John Ford Noonan, Miguel Piñero, and Michael Weller. The first one to go into production was Dennis's *The Leaf People*.

BERNARD GERSTEN Joe had this bone in his throat, as it were, a discontent about not having succeeded in finding a better platform for American writers than was afforded by the Public Theater.

"What we should do is take the theater on Broadway," he said. "Broadway is the natural and historic habitat of living American writers, that's where they've had their successes. We will be fulfilling a mission that is in abject neglect at the moment, because all Broadway does is musicals." In other words, transfer the impulse that for two years we had tried to impose upon Lincoln Center to Broadway.

And, indeed, the need that Joe perceived was very true and real. The only thing that was less than true and less than real was the answer that we came up with. The ideology and his own conviction was leaping ahead of the plays he wanted to produce. There was a disparity, a gap, between Joe's announcement of a reality and the reality.

DENNIS REARDON It's about the first contact a tribe of Amazon Indians has with white men, and the consequences of that initial contact. Thematically, I suppose you could restate it as "the road to hell is paved with good intentions."

There's a saintlike figure in the form of an anthropologist who goes into the rain forest and waits for four years to make contact with this extremely reclusive and ferocious tribe. He succeeds, finally, in being accepted by them, and in the course of so doing, inadvertently causes a civil war to break out within the tribe, which results in the more benevolent chief being overthrown by a despot who promptly leads the tribe to catastrophic aggressiveness toward the intruding whites. It's really a meditation on the ruthlessness of history and the inevitability of the tragic destiny of these dying people in the Amazon. And to tell it, I had to invent a foreign language.

I wanted to find some way of conveying these people's thoughts in a manner authentically alienated from what we know to be speech. I could have made them speak some kind of extemporized gibberish, I could have had subtitles flashed from the back of the theater, I could have had them not speak at all. I didn't want any of that, and I didn't want them to learn any authentic dialect, because most of the true Brazilian Indian words are highly polysyllabic and very hard for actors to say.

Having considered the alternatives, I wanted to create a language that actors could speak trippingly on the tongue, and one that still didn't sound anything like any human speech.

It took me about four months to actually do the language part. I wrote it in English first, and then I went back and, at the rate of about seven new words a day, created about a 450-word vocabulary and tried to bump the words into each other as pleasantly as possible.

Initially, we tried to have the actors learn it as you would learn a foreign language, with lessons for a couple of hours in the morning. But ultimately they memorized it phonetically, and in the process I acquired immense respect for what actors can do. Because the show got heavily rewritten during production, the most awesome aspect was that the actors were memorizing the rewritten Leafish with as short as six hours' notice before going onto the stage to spew this gibberish out. And they did it.

Two years ago, I ran into Ray Berry, the guy who played Gitaucho. This is ten years after the play, and Ray said, "I can *still* do that role!," and he rattled off this long monologue in inimitable Leafish. He remembered it syllable for syllable a decade after that—what can you say about actors? They can do any fucking thing you ask them to do.

GAIL MERRIFIELD PAPP Dennis has an amazing sense of what is effective dramatically, with a most original turn of mind. He invented this fictional language that had not only words, it had sentence structure, whether a noun would come before a verb, what the verb endings would be for different tenses, everything like that. He'd worked all this out. It was a complete language that you could study and speak like Esperanto. I began to learn it in the office, and I could speak a few sentences in it. It was just amazing.

DENNIS REARDON The play was nothing if not ambitious, and I think the audacity of it appealed to Joe. It was unique. It will probably be a long time in the history of the American theater before somebody tries to write another play in a foreign language, and they certainly won't be taking it to Broadway if they do. So it had a certain exotic quality about it that appealed to him.

Also, it made a social comment. One should never underestimate Joe's social consciousness. Let's face it, he comes out of a leftist-Jewish humanist tradition, very much concerned with the individual, the downtrodden, the oppressed, and this play was very much a part of that whole spectrum of thought.

We went out and got a director and cast it, and then we had a reading. We assembled about thirty theater professionals, about a fifth of whom—David Rabe, Michael Weller, a few of that ilk—were prominent playwrights. The language was in by that time, and it was being translated by two interpreters in the interstices between the spoken Leafish.

I expected it to be a disaster because it was so untried and experimental, but this reading was a stunning success, beyond what I dreamt it would be. Everybody followed it completely, all the nuances, and this despite the fact we were fifteen actors sitting around in a semicircle in chairs. It was, because it was so unexpected, probably one of the happiest moments I've had in the theater.

DAVID RABE There was a little reading of *The Leaf People* in one of the upstairs theaters, and it was really one of the most exquisite things I'd ever seen. But again, what happened was that Joe had a policy of putting five new plays on Broadway, and I saw a play that I thought had been delicate and really beautiful just go into this machine for Broadway.

I'm not blaming Broadway, but once the play was put in the vanguard of this new program being manifested on Broadway, it then carried all that pressure, the burden of being a test case, rather than just having its own burden of trying to manifest itself, which is problem enough for any play that's complex.

DENNIS REARDON   Joe immediately sequestered himself and started scheming about what to do with this, and I went back upstate to my little farm and pruned apple trees and kind of forgot about it. I had specifically written this thing with the notion of filling the stage of the Vivian Beaumont at Lincoln Center, which had never been fully utilized before. It was at some point during the summer that I discovered that that's not what Joe had in mind. Joe wanted to take it to Broadway.

I was up in an apple tree with a chain saw, chopping away, and my wife came out and said Bernie Gersten was on the line. And Bernie told me to come down to Shubert Alley, to meet him there at one o'clock the next afternoon. In the course of the conversation he said something about Broadway and *The Leaf People*, and I said, "What are you telling me? Are you saying that *The Leaf People* is going to be done on Broadway?"

He like swallowed his tongue; he couldn't believe I hadn't been told this before. "Joe didn't mention this? Oh—I—hm—well—I gotta go now." And he kind of hung up on me. Joe frequently does not advise you and seek your opinion on these things. I guess he just assumed that any playwright in the world would be thrilled at the prospect of going to Broadway. In point of fact, I had always abhorred Broadway, had never perceived myself in any way, shape, or form as a Broadway playwright. I admit it—I was a real prick about Broadway. *I Didn't Like Broadway.*

So I went down to Shubert Alley the next day. Four other playwrights were there: Tom Babe and Miguel Piñero and John Ford Noonan and Michael Weller. John—the guy's about six foot eight and 280 pounds—he was wearing his pirate's turban and bib overalls. Miguel was wearing a dashiki and a beret. Weller was dressed in a peacoat. And I was wearing a headband, a T-shirt, and blue jeans and had hair halfway down my back.

Our picture was taken—we looked very countercultural—and people presumed, when they saw that photograph endlessly reproduced in the

New York Times, that we consciously decided to show up in the most offensive garments that we could pick out of our wardrobe in an effort to astonish the Broadway establishment.

But in point of fact, there was no premeditation involved. It's just what we would have been wearing any day of the week. We didn't know why we were going to be there. Nobody had told us our pictures were going to be taken. Bernie had been very mysterious and said, "Just be there."

That picture became the focal point for a very controversial ad campaign, which centered around the idea of us as insurrectionists, assaulting the bastions of the establishment as personified by Broadway.

"Wanted!" read the headline. "The five desperados pictured above are living American playwrights. And they've been MISSING from the Broadway scene too long." Tactically, that probably was not wise. It tended to make the critics very antagonistic before you ever put a thing on the boards.

JOHN FORD NOONAN Everybody in that picture was half my size, so I felt odd; it reminded me of grammar school. I didn't like the tone of it—it was cheap, there was something bullshit about it. If you ain't got a gun, you can't confront the police. PR-wise, it was wrong. To say we're a bunch of street urchins who are invading Broadway in clothes that look like they aren't washed is really tacky. We should have gotten suits and been fun and charming. But that's the way Joe is. He's like a Joe Frazier. He goes out and bang-bang-bang.

JOSEPH PAPP I loved *Leaf People* because it had to do with trying to preserve a culture. But it was not just the theme of it, because if it's only the issues you might as well put it in the newspaper. It's how the playwright wrote it, his perception of it, his particular creative genius. This whole piece was so alive, so original, so unusual.

Dennis always reminded me of Strindberg a little bit, in terms of the pain. I love writers that put their bodies on the line, because that's the way I feel. And Dennis is one of those writers. He never tells a lie. It's all truth, painful, dug out of his bowels.

I thought Tom O'Horgan was a very good director, someone with a lot of imagination who was used to doing things that were unorthodox. This was not the normal kind of show with a normal form or structure. It had an offbeat quality, and I thought he would be ideal for that.

But with all due respect to O'Horgan as a creative talent—and he's a very good director and a smart guy—I don't think he really understood the play. With all its strangeness and weirdness, there was an essential humanity in the play that I don't think Tom had a grasp of. The play wasn't reflecting itself onstage—it didn't come across as well as it read. And if that play isn't done well, it becomes a little ludicrous.

Tom is very much his own person. Instead of just trying to understand what was going on in the writer's mind when he wrote this thing, he felt he needed to put his stamp on the production. And he didn't get on too well with the writer. I don't think he got the best out of him. I found myself very much involved in that relationship—too much so, I thought. Once I get too deeply involved, then there's something wrong.

TOM O'HORGAN I loved the idea and I loved the play. It was the only play I ever saw that had a dictionary in the back. It just sprawled and it needed to be looked at, so you knew what was important and how to focus it.

But getting it up there and focusing it in front of an audience is not necessarily the best trip. We've learned a few things about that process since then, but at that time we were brave enough to just plop them up there and hope we could make them float. And people who came to see the first gasps of that play really saw some of the most horrendous things.

I always thought the show had three parts, only one of which the audience was part of. The first part was the lineup: instead of wardrobe people, there were painters and everybody had to come an hour early to be painted with elaborate body paint. We really researched to find out the least toxic of all paints, and it turned out that green and red are like monsters, they're just very difficult to find in a paint that isn't going to kill you.

Then we did the show, and the third part was the showers. It wasn't so much the paint as the washing it off that caused the skin to dry and flake, and then it cracked and they'd get infections. Let me tell you, it got to be a real scene, all those people in the showers every night.

Most people say, "You take a script and put it up there and make a few minor changes." It doesn't work that way. It's my experience that it takes about eight scripts to get a piece on, particularly if the idea's complex, and god knows, this was a complex idea and a very big subject. It just took forever to focus that, to find how to make it really work onstage.

How do you communicate, how do you really understand what these people are saying? We had these two actors up in two little glass things, they were the interpreters, which was a wonderful conceit but it works for two seconds, then you've had it. The play was written so cleverly, in a way, that the audience could get what was happening, but it just took time to make that happen.

It's easy in hindsight to say, "We should have done some workshops and worked it out and then got it up there," but we didn't know that then. And lord knows, we were all there working. What happened was not for lack of effort. There was endless rewriting and cutting and fixing. Joe came down, and we all rolled up our sleeves and tried to help make the thing happen.

Dennis is a very fixed person in what he wants to do, and Joe's being there made him make the necessary changes. But he's only human, he can only make so many changes, the mind only works so fast. Things were flying very fast and furious at that point, and poor Dennis was like, "Whew!" It's a tough row to hoe, being a writer under those circumstances.

DENNIS REARDON I knew what I was getting when I agreed to O'Horgan: I was getting a visual hauteur. For instance, when the Indians attacked, they would drop from one tier of shot cord down to the next in rapid succession. You had these waves of bodies hurtling some thirty vertical feet to the floor. It was a very evocative idea, but it took up a lot of rehearsal time, which I would have preferred having them spend on running lines.

Frankly, O'Horgan is not a terribly literal-minded director. He did not come highly promoted as a man who was interested in the text; he started with it as a springboard and went from there. I would come up to him and say, "Tom, how do you think this reads?" and he'd fish around like he's checking his pockets and say, "Well, I can't find my glasses. Why don't you just put it up on the stage and we'll see how it looks?"

It's very hard to know, in rehearsal, how long a show's going to run.

Because you don't have the rhythms down, because people are falling all over their lines and doing exorbitant business which eventually is going to be cut. You can't get a good, solid fix on a running time. This was particularly so in *Leaf People* because I had weird pagination that was no help: half of every page would be Leafish and half English, and you didn't know how they were going to overlap.

Still, I had a suspicion it was running long. I kept asking people, "Don't you think this is running kind of long? I mean, it looks to me like it's going to go about three hours." Nobody, and I mean nobody, from top to bottom in that show, told me that they thought there was a line that should be cut. When you're dealing with thirty actors who are busting their ass to memorize these words, you don't want to get people uneasy and insecure. Because the first thing that happens when you start cutting and slicing and writing is that people panic. They think, "The playwright's not sure of what we're doing. The director's not sure of what we're doing." It spreads like an epidemic through the company. So a lot of times, things didn't get done on *Leaf People* for fear of an imagined negative response.

It wasn't until after the first preview on Broadway that O'Horgan came up to me and said, "We got to lose an hour, babe." Maybe it's an excess of self-abnegation, but I somehow feel I should have known before that point that I had to do this.

My reaction was, "Argh, my god, why didn't you tell me this two months ago? Now I have to rewrite this thing in full view of the public, with paying audiences coming in while I chop up four scenes, hoping to get to the next four scenes sometime in the middle of next week. And I'm rewriting in two languages—English and this made-up monstrosity called Leafish."

Joe very much stayed away, and though at the time we very much appreciated it, in retrospect it appears to have been a bad idea. I think Joe was staying away because he knew how temperamental O'Horgan was and how O'Horgan would recoil from any kind of producer looking over his shoulder. I mean, this is the guy who did *Hair* on Broadway and *Jesus Christ Superstar*. He knew his way around the block. He'd been to Broadway and back and lived to tell the tale.

Joe was very good at fending off the press and giving me time to work this thing out. He canceled the opening on two occasions. I was working twenty hours a day, averaging four hours sleep a night, seven days a week, and just holding it together. I had a three-hour show, and I was being asked to cut a third of it out, which meant writing a new play.

I had to completely replot the thing. I was throwing characters out right and left, and trying not to show where the lost scenes were in the re-stitching. It was a major amputation, and it took a long time for the actors to get back in the groove of this thing. If I had seen the show fresh as a paying customer back in September of that year, I would have been appalled myself.

It became a real test of my survival capacity, and when I was done, Joe said something that made me feel very good. He slapped me on the shoulder and said, "You're a real pro. You rewrote this like a musical," meaning musicals out of town with songs getting tossed out and written in. You have to be a very skilled play doctor to do that before a show gets to Broadway.

Unfortunately, we were already on Broadway.

I truly wish that we had been given the option of trying this out of town, in Philadelphia or Baltimore or Boston or New Haven or somewhere. Because while all this was going on, we were generating horrible word of mouth, absolutely poisonous word of mouth.

We took about a month and three weeks to get the thing to the point where we had the guts to open it, and then came the final blow. It was the night we were to finally open and I was in a state of terminal exhaustion. It was very much the way I imagine battle fatigue to be: I didn't really care whether the show was a hit or a flop, I just wanted it to be over with as quickly and expeditiously as possible. I wanted to get on with my life before this thing killed me.

About four in the afternoon on October 20, 1975, I was hanging around in front of the Booth Theatre when somebody came up and gave me a press release. It was a press release that was at that precise moment being distributed to the New York journalistic theater corps announcing the cancellation of the Booth's New American Play season, effective after mine. And this was like two hours before these tuxedoed and cummerbunded critics waltzed into the theater to review my show.

Needless to say, I was rather taken aback by this turn of events. I couldn't at the time conceive of why Joe was doing this. In the press release he made it very clear that in the absence of revenue from *A Chorus Line*—because of a musicians' union strike—he didn't have the wherewithal to fund the Booth season, which may very well have been entirely true.

But I also knew that it would not wash with the critics, that they would come up with their own reasons as to why this season was being canceled, and that I would figure prominently in their speculation—which is, in fact, exactly what happened.

I've never really harbored any animosity toward Joe for the timing. He tends to act impulsively, and this seemed to have been a decision made on an ad hoc basis. I think what he was trying to do was to spare me that kind of vindictive personal attack by deflecting the cancellation away from me and onto the musicians' union, and doing it before they could get a shot at me. The net result of it, of course, was to tell the critics that they were to get only one shot at the whole concept of the New American Play series, and that it was to be my show.

It was like the Broadway critics' first shot at the whole hippie subculture, and I have believed all along that those reviews were essentially written before they ever saw the show.

Nobody had really gone to Broadway that fit that description before. It had been all these tweedy bastards in turtlenecks with lisping British accents, and suddenly there was not one but five people looking like escapees from a heavy metal band and being presented as radicals.

Papp was trying to send a message to the Broadway establishment that their territorial imperative was being encroached upon, and that's certainly the way they perceived it. He didn't ask their permission first, you know what I mean? He went out and he rented an entire goddamn theater for the entire season and he said, "I got the money, I got the theater, here are my playwrights. What are you going to do about it?" And they showed him. I was first at bat, and they went after me like mad dogs.

They let us run a week after that. I'll always wonder how things would have gone had that show been done at the Vivian Beaumont. It would have stripped it from this challenge to the commercial interests to control the industry. It would have automatically entered into a more artistic setting and just said to people, "This is a work of art. This is not intended to replace

Hello, Dolly!" I think it would have gotten a nicer reception and I think it would have been stunning on that stage. But we'll never know.

JOSEPH PAPP I was hoping that one play would pay for the others, but that theory failed because we got lousy reviews and we went down right after the first play. Boy, I hated the critics. I could have killed each and every one of them.

Dennis was destroyed by those reviews; they murdered him with that play. Poor son of a bitch, he couldn't recover for years. I think one of the greatest injustices, one of the greatest losses to the theater, was Dennis. Next to David Rabe, I think he was the most powerful writer we've had.

I pulled out of the Booth; later I pulled out of Lincoln Center. I can pull out of a lot of things. I've canceled plays, I've had disasters, I've had to close shows I loved after a lot of money was put in them. Those are disasters, bang, bang, bang, bang, and they don't make you feel good.

It's certainly discouraging when you get into a thing like the Booth series, because you plan, you build up so many hopes, you come into the ring and after one punch you're down and the fight is over. But I've never said I couldn't go on. I've never felt, "This is the end." I've always thought I'd come back to fight another day.

THOMAS BABE When Dennis Reardon's *Leaf People* opened on Broadway to less than favorable notices, that self-same morning Joe called up all the other writers involved and said, "Get your asses in here. We're all going to sit down with Dennis." And, in Joe's office, that's what we did.

I shall never forget that morning. It was grimly affirmative, or affirmatively grim, however you want to look at it. What it was, though, was an expression of solidarity the likes of which I'd never seen before.

Everybody looked terribly hungover, but everybody was there, and I think everybody thought two things at once: "What a great thing you've done, Dennis" and "We're all in the same boat." It was not something anybody concocted. For one brief moment, we were all in the same boat. It was a real emotion that doesn't happen often. That was a genius thing to have done.

DENNIS REARDON After those reviews, I know that I really didn't want to have anything to do with the theater for about two years. I didn't even want to see anyone else's plays, and the last thing I wanted to do is write another one of these things.

Most people are not capable of surviving one such trashing, and playwrights routinely get them. I don't know of any other art form where you are made to feel like a war criminal if somebody doesn't like what you create. It's like you've exposed yourself in public, you've been caught doing something really dirty. All you've tried to do is entertain people and make them think, but if they don't like what you're asking them to think about, they'll kill you. It's a strange profession.

The feeling I always got from Joe when I got bad reviews was one of chagrin. I always felt like I had let him down, that I had in some way failed him personally. It was not like, "Oh, I've been subject to public ridicule" but "What will Joe think of me?"

He incontrovertibly created a paternalistic relationship with his young male writers. Even when you were aware of it, you fell into it and tried to work within it. It was not a conspiratorial kind of thing on his part. It was natural to want somebody to take your hand and say, "It's going to be okay. Just do what I tell you to do, and they won't hurt you." And then, when it doesn't work out like that, you think, "Oh, my god! What have I done? I've really failed this wonderful man." It's psychically hard.

After *The Leaf People*, Joe and his wife, Gail, both came by one night, completely unannounced, to my little flea trap on MacDougal Street. The bell rings, I go down, and here's the number-one producer in America standing in my roach-ridden hallway. He came up and allowed me to be maudlin for about an hour and a half, which was certainly above and beyond the call of duty.

Joe said, "I want to see your next play," and that's a very important thing for a writer to hear. It's like, "You haven't failed me. I still want you. You still have a patron. There's a place to go with your work." The fact that he wants to *see* your next play does not mean he wants to *do* your next play. But the mere fact that he'll look at it is a nice gesture, and his coming over is a gesture that meant a great deal to me at the time, and one I continued to appreciate over the years.

TOM ALDREDGE Joe was devoted to this playwright; this playwright had to work it out, and you can't work it out on paper. You've got to work it out in front of an audience, and that's what Joe's all about. When he comes across some kind of voice, he knows you've got to let the voice talk. You can't shut it up and say, "Don't say that, that isn't right what you're saying now." You've got to let him say it all. Thank god, Joe will let him have that experience of failing, which is so rare.

But although Joe will champion a certain person, like Rabe or Dennis Reardon, Joe champions them for his reasons, which is the theater. They're not interested in the theater. They're interested in their play, in furthering their next work. David Rabe's interested in what he has to say; he's not interested in the history of the theater. So there eventually comes a time when their two goals go different ways.

DENNIS REARDON When he talks, you listen. You absolutely hang on every syllable. He has a great way with actors. He walks among them like Henry V the night before the battle at Agincourt, a little touch of Harry in the night. And the actors love it, love it, eat it up.

He's a good play doctor, and an immensely powerful man. He'll have about fifteen things you should think about fixing. And maybe six of them will be right. And you never know what six. I don't know how else to say this, but he'll always make me feel like a little boy. Even at age fifty, I'll never feel quite grown up around him.

23

David Rabe, Act III:
Streamers
1976

Peter Evans and
Dorian Harewood
© Martha Swope

NEW HAVEN, Feb. 7—A man plummeting through space. On his back is a parachute. He pulls the cord, and the white silk billows out, twisting upward, but fails to open. It remains a streamer, a white unopened tulip, and the man, struggling like a marionette, plunges to his inevitable, but earlier than expected, death. That is the theme of David Rabe's play *Streamers*, which, directed by Mike Nichols, had its world premier at the Long Wharf Theater here last night.

Clive Barnes, *New York Times*, February 8, 1976

The locale is a Virginia army camp in 1965. Carlyle is black, and he has been assigned to a company of "untouchables," i.e., men on perpetual KP and other menial duties. He is desperately afraid that he will be shipped off to Vietnam.

As an outcast in search of attention, affection and "a home," as he puts it, he begins frequenting the quarters of three technical sergeants, two white, one black. They are men of caste status in an army hutment, an odd lot indeed. Richie (Peter Evans) is an avowed homosexual. The college-bred Billy (Paul Rudd) may be a latent homosexual, but won't admit it. And Roger is a black who has bridged the racial gap through competence and an equable temper.

The action proceeds mainly as a kind of extended barracks-room bull session, but eventually, sexual desire between Richie and Carlyle triggers a racist diatribe from Billy. Suddenly Carlyle flips out his switchblade, slashes Billy (apparently mortally) and then carves up a fat intruding master sergeant, killing him. Physically and dramatically, this seems like an arbitrarily gory denouement, but the logic of inevitable violence has governed the play all along.

T. E. Kalem, *Time* magazine, May 3, 1976

. . . .

Streamers is the great play that has been trying—in several guises and with several degrees of success—to burst out of David Rabe in the five or so years he has been on the scene. It is at the Mitzi Newhouse now, in a stunning production directed by Mike Nichols; neither the author nor director has come close to this level of accomplishment in the past, and I urge you to share with me the keen pleasure of having your faith restored in the power of American drama to make important and worthwhile sense.

Alan Rich, *New York* magazine, May 10, 1976

. . . .

GAIL MERRIFIELD PAPP   We had *Streamers*. My recollection is we intended to do it—it was certainly going to be the play of David's that we would do next. I never heard anything else, nor did I ever dream of anything else. I don't know how it ended up at the Long Wharf. It was something that came out of a relationship problem. A misunderstanding, possibly. It was very strange and I was really shocked. I didn't understand it at all, and I still don't to this day.

MIKE NICHOLS I had talked to David about screenplays, and he gave me a play, which I didn't get a chance to read right away. I was working on a movie, *Bogart Slept Here*, which I shut down after five days of shooting because I didn't think it was any good. I came back after having decided not to go on with it, read *Streamers*, which was on my desk, and wanted to do it.

David wasn't sure he wanted to do this play, and he wasn't sure he wanted to do it in New York. He felt that he'd fared badly with something not long before. I said, "Let's do it at Long Wharf. It's not New York." What I wanted was that theater, that smaller theater in which the play would be right in the audience's lap.

DAVID RABE I had gotten to the point where I said, "I've got to get out of here," meaning both New York and the Public Theater. Joe was saying, "I want to do this play right away," and, finally, I said, "No, I can't." I wanted a break. My marriage was falling apart, I just wanted something else. I needed money. I wanted to try and see what I could get to write a movie, so I went to Los Angeles.

I was out there looking for work when I saw Mike Nichols. I'd met him at the Tonys, we'd just said hello, but it was enough so that I could phone him and say I'd like to talk. We had these meetings where I would try to find out what I could write for him in movies, and *he* would try to talk about the theater. He was sick of movies; he was in a cycle where he wanted to come back to the theater, so we'd have these cross-purposes conversations.

Finally, Mike said, "What kinds of plays do you have?"

"I have this play that I did, but I don't want to do it."

"Well, can I read it?"

"Sure."

So he read it and he started on me about doing the play, phoning me from London and all kinds of places where he'd gone to buy horses and do

Mike Nichols things. I would go home to visit my wife and he would call. It was weird; there I was again with another guy who I was saying no to. Finally, I said, "Well, okay, we'll do it."

I asked him where he wanted to do it and he said the Long Wharf in New Haven. I said, "Joe was interested in the play," and he said, "I don't want to do that." He wanted to do it out of town, and he didn't want to be involved with Joe.

JOSEPH PAPP I was aware of the fact that it was going to the Long Wharf and I was very unhappy about it. I felt it was kind of an act of disloyalty. I would always feel that way, particularly when you put all your energies, your money, and your feelings into a writer and he goes elsewhere. I wouldn't like that at all.

MIKE NICHOLS The Long Wharf was really hard. It had this sort of cuddly, middle-class audience that they'd built over the years by doing a certain repertoire, and the audience was quite appalled. It took us a long time to understand and control the play, and we lost a lot of people every night: twenty, thirty, sometimes as many as sixty people. They would walk across the stage in the middle of the play, throwing their programs down and calling to each other, "Come on, Joe. Come on, Ed. We're going out this way!"

One of our happiest nights came in January when an entire busload of senior citizens left in this manner, crossing the stage and talking to each other. They got outside, and found that the bus driver had elected to stay and watch the rest of the show. They couldn't get back in the theater, and there were these little pathetic scratches on the outside doors while the bus driver calmly sat and enjoyed the rest of the play.

DAVID RABE I'd said to Joe, "Let's do it up there, and if it comes to New York, you can bring it in," and he said he didn't want to do that. It was the break, so to speak. Joe was angry, there was some rancor expressed, he was emotionally vindictive.

We went up and did it in New Haven, and once again Joe was given the opportunity to be the rescuer, because in fact the play couldn't come to

New York. A lot of producers saw it at the Long Wharf, movie people had come, and no one would fucking bring it.

Joe could have said, "See what you got now? The hell with you." On the other hand, he loved the play and the production, and being who he is, it was nothing he could turn away from. It was totally to his credit, although we could have had it all arranged ahead of time, gracefully, rather than going through all this.

MIKE NICHOLS   I worked for eight months on *Streamers*, counting the Long Wharf and New York, and after eight months I thought, "This is as close to right as anything I've ever worked on. This is the thing I'm proudest of that I've been connected with." It was a terrific experience.

David Rabe is painful and rewarding to work with, because everything means so much to him. When he feels you've taken something from him, his anger is terrible, he wants to kill you, and that's hard in work.

But because he brings all of his considerable person to every decision and to every thought and to every line and word and idea, it's always worth it. It's never time wasted. It has weight in the true sense of the word. He is a passionate, engaged man, and he and Joe have something similar that's very rare in the theater, a powerful moral sense.

It was the first day of rehearsal and I was really down because the company was tired, they had done it already, under very different circumstances, at Long Wharf. Three of them, in my view, were not ideal for what I had by this time learned about the play, but they had invested all this time and there was nothing I could do.

So I'm in the middle of this sort of dispirited rehearsal in which I'm trying to start fresh, and the actors are just looking at me with glazed eyes, when Joe called and said, "I'm sorry to interrupt your rehearsal, but I need to talk to you."

I went over and he said, "We can't make the arrangement with Long Wharf. They want coproduction credit, and I don't give that. I must be alone up there. It's just the way I've always done it, that's the way the Public does it. If we can't work it out, I'm going to have to call it off."

And I amazed myself by saying, "I think you're being amazingly foolish about this." I didn't really know him, I just found myself saying that.

"Be that as it may," he said. "How are you feeling about the play?"

"I'm pretty discouraged on my own, because I think three of the actors are no longer right for what my new understanding of the play is, but I owe them the investment that they made in our painful work in New Haven."

"I'll tell you what—I'll make a deal with you. If I can work out my problem, I will pay the actors you want to replace for the length of the run. You won't have to feel guilty about them. You can replace them without feeling that you've harmed them in any way." And that's how it turned out.

And from that moment in which something about him freed me to say I thought he was being a fool, we've always told each other everything, and he has been easily the most helpful and supportive and practical producer that I've ever worked with.

PAUL RUDD Out of the original quartet, only one actor remained. I think Mike wanted new, fresh players and I think Joe wanted new, fresh players. I happened to be in Joe's favor then. Joe wanted me to play Billy Wilson, so he got me.

I had seen the play at Long Wharf, and I said to Mike one day, "I want to talk about my death in this play. I thought that it was far too bloody in New Haven, and I would like to contribute something here. Is it possible that we could tone it down and make the death mean something? I don't want to make it spiritual; I want to make the death an awful void. Somebody who was alive is now dead."

I said I wanted Billy to ease out of life. And Mike told me this story, he said, "This is what death is like." He talked about somebody getting stabbed in the subway. He said the man wanted to just crawl to a corner. The man didn't want anybody to notice that he was dying, so he put his raincoat over his wound and just sat there until the medics came to get him. That's how people die, they don't scream, "Blood! Oh my god!"

Mike's open and flexible. He seals you off in a psychological space, this wonderful cocoon, a bubble that protects you and allows you to explore things that you never thought were possible before—the kind of ugly side of ourselves, the kind of veins that run through all of us that we never knew until somebody was able to open a door.

Mike always reminded me of Joe in a lot of ways. Joe can be very peremptory about things. If he wants to get something fixed, he, by Christ, fixes it, and if something's not pleasing him, he'll do whatever it takes to get it to work.

Mike would suddenly get bored and say, "I want him fired." It could be the box-office manager. One time he said, "I'm so fucking bored with directing this play. Will somebody direct this scene? I don't know what to do anymore." Dolph Sweet, who played one of the sergeants, had a couple of suggestions and Mike put them in.

Streamers was a unique piece of theater that made the theater a pressure cooker. It was a remarkable experience, nothing like it. In fact, I have friends that could not come back to say what they thought about the play. They were literally so profoundly upset they had to wait two, three days, while I'm going, "Fuck, I got these people nice seats. What's the problem? They hated it?" Then they'd call up and say, "When you died, I thought you literally had died. I was afraid to go backstage, because I didn't want to ruin that kind of wonderful horror at the end." You don't hear that very often about plays.

ROSEMARIE TICHLER   Mike wanted Dorian Harewood for Carlyle, and I wanted him, and Joe wanted him, and David did not want him. It was clear that he was wonderful, but David couldn't see it.

It was a wonderful way to cast it, because it was not casting it as a bad guy. It's so easy to cast the bad guy as the killer, and it's boring. If you cast this nice guy, you see the possibilities of how his life was fucked up, you feel something for him, you don't write him off.

David wanted a heavier, more obvious kind of actor, he was afraid Dorian couldn't do it. Mike never wanted to do something that David didn't agree with—any director in casting wants to please his playwright. I remember getting a call from Mike in the middle of the night asking me whether I was sure it was right.

When someone as close to it as the writer, who you respect enormously, is so against it, you start questioning yourself. And Dorian did it, and, of course, it worked out beautifully and everyone was happy.

DORIAN HAREWOOD   Originally, I'd read for and got the role of Roger in the Long Wharf production. That was the more calm role, the guy that's pretty much close to myself. But I got a pilot for a TV series and they did it without me. Mike Nichols called me later on to see if I was available to do the New York production. He talked me into doing Carlyle, which was the wild-man part.

He said the problem they'd had in Long Wharf was not that the actor who'd played it wasn't good but that he was so different physically and age-wise from the other three characters, the effect of the play was lost. This whole story was belonging, group belonging, and it was obvious he didn't quite belong.

"Think about it, Dorian," Mike said. "Obviously, you can play Roger, because it's like you. But think about playing Carlyle, this wild, on-the-edge-of-insanity kind of street guy, a street animal. It would be a great stretch for you, and I know you can do it." He gave me the confidence to do it. He brings out the best in his performers. Rather than saying, "This is the way it's got to be done, fit what I want," he allows actors to search their own instincts and then fine-tunes what they do.

I had a six-month contract, and they wanted me to continue with the play after it was up, but there was no way I was going to renew; it was that depressing. My character hated himself, and the only way I could get into the role was to become the role and feel what he was feeling. My whole demeanor was different. I was so depressed every night from that character that I said, "When this thing is up, I'm out of here." It was very draining, very draining.

JOSEPH PAPP   I always had to turn my head away every time that guy went on a rampage and stabbed this boy. I knew it was staged, but it was hard for me to bear. I still feel that way in certain plays that I see. I can't watch: even though the act is on the stage doesn't necessarily mean it doesn't have any reality about it. And the play itself was so true, just full of sadness and horror. David is horror, always horror and sadness and violence.

24

for colored girls who have considered suicide/when the rainbow is enuf
1976

A scene from
colored girls
© Sy Friedman

These pieces are tremendously effective mini-dramas that explode onstage, showering shrapnel of significance. Shange's poems aren't war cries—they're outcries filled with a controlled passion against the brutality that blasts the lives of "colored girls"—a phrase that in her hands vibrates with social irony and poetic beauty. These poems are political in the deepest sense, but there's no dogma, no sentimentality, no grinding of false mythic axes. "Being alive, being a woman and being colored is a metaphysical dilemma I haven't solved yet," says the poet. Your scalp prickles at the stunning truth of her characters: the high-school girl ponders whether or not to surrender her virginity in "the deep black Buick smelling of Thunderbird and ladies in heat," the dancer who has all the earth-force of the Mississippi, the sexpot who turns men on with a Babylonian arsenal of seductive machinery but then emerges from her post-coital bathtub with the soul sadness of a "regular colored girl."

A young director named Oz Scott has staged the work with power and grace, and the women—Shange herself, Trazana Beverley, Rise Collins, Janet League, Aku Kadago, Laurie Carlos and dancer-choreographer Paula Moss—are unforgettable. Beverley is devastating in her hilarious put-down of a vacillating suitor and in her depiction of a girl whose children are killed by her lover. What I said about *The Belle of Amherst*—that it should be seen by the whole country—applies, perhaps even more strongly, to this thrilling and poignant show.

Jack Kroll, *Newsweek*, June 14, 1976

NTOZAKE SHANGE I was driving from Oakland to Sonoma early in the morning on a fairly mountainous section of Highway 101. As I came around a bend, I saw half of a gigantic rainbow, and when I finally got around the curve, I realized that I was going to drive underneath it. Seeing this whole huge rainbow, I was able to feel a sense of beauty, the fragility of nature, and the dignity of being alive. I felt absolutely ecstatic, I thought I had been blessed, and that's why, say since 1973, I used the image in the title of my shows.

I used to do poetry readings, working with a lot of dancers and musicians and essentially creating a cabaret with my friend Paula Moss. I would sometimes watch her dance and make up the words, or sometimes she would hear me and choreograph something herself. It was never as if the dance part of it was minimal; we were very much peers.

There are poetry bars in San Francisco, in much greater numbers than in Manhattan. There's a fairly resilient and committed audience for poetry, and that was our audience. And when we called it *for colored girls*, we meant the women of color straight across the board, not just the black, English-speaking women.

There's an art to making a poetry reading work as something other than something sort of stiff. I designed readings the same way people would design a play: you have a peak moment, you have happiness, you have sadness, you deal with all these different elements, and you keep the thing going emotionally. I was working much more as a performance artist than as a theater person. I felt much more relaxed in an improvisational environment. The adventure to me was that it kept changing all the time.

There was an alternative jazz festival called the Summer Music Festival in New York, and I wrote to ask if we could be part of it, because I did have a band, and they said yes. So Paula and I drove across country and appeared at the Studio Rivbea. Then we started working every Monday night at the Old Reliable Nightclub on Third Street. People would just come by to see us and then they'd get up and perform themselves, or we might draw them into it ourselves, so it got to be an entire night of surprise.

My sister, Ifa Iyaun, was working on a children's play at the Henry Street Settlement, and she brought this guy, Oz Scott, to see us. He was a stage manager at that point, but he wanted to be a director. After he saw us do what we do, he talked to me about not just doing all the poems myself but including actresses in it. Because up until that point, Paula didn't talk. I read all the words.

OZ SCOTT I'd once asked somebody, "How do I become a director?" and they said, "Oz, go around telling everybody you're a director. You will eventually get a job. At which point, you will have to prove that you can direct."

I had directed two one-acts, not much of anything, though I was very confident. I got into NYU's Theater Department as a director, and while I was there I started working with the Public Theater as a stage manager.

I met Ifa in 1975, and she said to me, "Oz, my sister has all these poems. Why don't you come and see what you can do with them?" And Zake said, "Why don't you do this for me, put it together in a production." I said, "Give me some poems and let me read them."

The poems were in no particular order; she'd change them however she felt. She would read, she'd get whatever improvisational avant-garde jazz group was there to back her up, and they'd improvise the dancing. It was a performance piece, not a play, but I thought there was potential and possibilities. I said, "You give me a time and a date and a place to do this, and I will have the production ready for you."

We took the poems (they weren't all in there at that point), we talked about them, we juggled them around, and we gave them a crude outline, basically from birth on. I went out and I got Trazana Beverley, who I'd gone to NYU with, and Laurie Carlos, who I'd done some work with, four or five actresses besides Zake and Paula. I told them, "In the way I work, you have to do more than just dance. You have to talk, also." I'd just disburse the lines and make the poems into dialogue between people. Each one of them got poems to do.

TRAZANA BEVERLEY   I was an out-of-work actress when I met Oz in a local restaurant and he said, "Oh, I've been trying to reach you, Trazana." And I figured, "Ah! Must be a job." So I sat right down.

He proceeded to tell me about this black writer, woman, whose material he had been reading. He said it was very, very beautiful. He thought it would be just the kind of thing I would be interested in, and I asked him, "Is there any money in it?"—which has to be one of the first questions that you ask. And he said, "Well, I don't think . . ." and I went, "Oh, how could you *do* this to me. You give me this great big buildup and now you tell me that there's no money in it. Man, I gotta eat." And he said, "Oh, come on, Traz, just try it." So shortly after I agreed to meet with the rest of the ladies and have a reading of it.

Zake carried a mystique. She was from the Bay Area, and in those days a black girl from there carried herself a certain way, read certain books, and dressed in certain colors. Zake brought a kind of exoticism with her, and it was something that was somewhat new to the city. You eventually grow to emulate the leader, and that's what happened to each of us in lesser or greater degrees. So that if we were coming out of the theater, going to have some lunch or some dinner, they would say of us, "There go the Colored Girls."

Once you had the opportunity to hear her do the material herself, it was just mind-blowing. It was her material, so she was most passionate about it. I mean, when you were in her presence and you heard her do it, it just ran through you, it just welled up such emotions inside. We would pause, we would cry, we would sit and say nothing, stare at each other, and then get up and work on it. It was the kind of piece for women that would automatically bomb the ladies who were participating in it, and that's what happened to us.

We worked on the material for roughly a year. Most of the poems as such remained intact. It was the arrangement in the play that got changed. We went through a very tedious process of putting all of that in order. We started at a Latin club over on the Lower East Side called DeMonte's. We were in a back room, sharing this two-by-four stage with a big Christmas tree and a bowling-ball machine, so we had some competition. But we took the roof off that place, and it wasn't about a lot of screaming and venting of anger. It was just the sheer emotional power of the play.

We would also do a couple of spots at some colleges. The director would call us up and say, "Let's go over here and do this." And we'd get up early in the morning, very little argument, just go pile in the car, do the piece, talk about it, disperse, and get together two days later and continue to work.

Another time we had to rehearse from eleven or twelve o'clock at night until six o'clock the following morning, because that was the only time the studio space was free. It was certainly difficult to juggle making money, getting some other jobs—professional jobs if you could—and keeping your schedule in order. But we were having just a wonderful love affair with the material and we didn't mind.

NTOZAKE SHANGE It was very unnerving to me to hear actresses read my words. I was always the only voice, I had never heard anybody read my things before, and while it was enlightening it was also very frightening because they found things in the poetry that I didn't know were in the poetry. It was quite a growing period for me, until I got used to being sort of pulled apart by other artists. I had to deal with the implications of working in theater as opposed to the implications of always being an experimental artist.

Oz and I tried to place the poems in an order that made sense. We cut some things, and I put a lot of things in first person that had originally been in a second- or third-person voice, to make it more intimate for the actors.

The four love poems that are in the show that everybody got so upset about were just a letter that I had sent somebody. At that point in time I kept copies of everything I wrote—grocery lists, anything, I kept copies of it. And Oz read this letter I had written to this crazy man I thought I was in love with and he said, "This is perfect. We must use this. This is wonderful!"

OZ SCOTT Zake was completely bewildered by why she was even giving me any control. She said to me, "I've never given any man any control over my life, period. And now you're coming in and you're just . . ." But really, I think our biggest success was because Zake, who at that point was not a playwright, did give me a lot of control and I would say, "This is what we have to do and this is what we have to do and this is what we have to do," and she would sort of say, "Uh—okay. Okay."

I'm not a choreographer, and Paula Moss would do the choreography. She would choreograph it pretty, make it fluid and beautiful, and I would always have to come and bastardize it so that the majority of the audience would understand what it was I was trying to do. At one point I remember getting behind Paula, taking her arms, and saying, "This is what I want," and she would go nuts with me. I really bastardized what she would do to give it some sort of much more hard-hitting form.

TRAZANA BEVERLEY I have a profound respect for Oz Scott and I personally think he did a most extraordinary job as a director. The obvious trap to fall into with this is to play it for the anger, and one of the critical insights that Oz had in bringing the essence of this material alive was when he told us, "You have to remember that you *loved* these men. You cannot get on a stage and splatter it with anger. You must show these people how much you loved them, through the material." You don't have great hurt unless you have great love: that is the truth that he said.

With seven women, you can imagine Oz had his hands full. I give him credit, not any man could have pulled that group together. His spirit is very laid-back, and while I know from time to time we frustrated the dickens out of him, he never talked down to us. Some men are just more sensitive to women, they don't feel intimidated by them, and I don't think Oz felt intimidated by us.

The "Beau Willie" piece, the large piece where my children are thrown out of the window, that was a true collaboration between Oz and me. Our heads were constantly together on that piece, talking about it, improvising on it, and what came to pass was my getting a Tony for it. That play changed my career, it absolutely changed my career.

OZ SCOTT   Joe was very much a part of the beginnings of *colored girls* without knowing anything about it. I'd started working as stage manager at the Anspacher Theater on Miguel Piñero's *The Sun Always Shines for the Cool*, and as soon as Marvin Camillo would finish his rehearsals, I'd have the *colored girls* come into the theater. Nobody let me use the Anspacher, I just snuck everybody in.

Woodie King of the New Federal Theater came to see us at DeMonte's. He said he was interested, but he was vacillating. So we performed it for Joe and Gail in the little space that is now the movie theater at the Public.

GAIL MERRIFIELD PAPP   It arrived at my desk in the play department, brought in by a young man named Oz Scott who'd been a stage manager on some shows for us. I always remember the strangeness of titles when I first encounter them, like *Hair* and *Pavlo Hummel*, and here was this *for colored girls who've considered suicide/when the rainbow is enuf*. And I thought, "Well . . ."

I couldn't comprehend it. Then I looked at it and I saw it was all poetry, so I was all the more puzzled. I heard it was being done a few times at midnight at a bar that I'd been to way, way over on the Lower East Side. I told Oz, "There's no way I can get to either one of these performances. What do you suggest?" He said, "We'll come and do it for you."

Something like eight or ten of us were in the audience, and I remember just being absolutely overwhelmed. It didn't seem like something being acted in front of you that you were observing, it just spoke to you and drew you in. There was something very startling about having performers onstage speaking to you so personally and so directly and having such eloquent language at their disposal. You felt like you'd been singled out to be talked to in this extraordinary fashion, so it sunk in very deep.

I really couldn't speak afterward, I was so moved by it. I was crying, and I was kind of ashamed of crying, of people seeing me crying. It was so original and fresh, so powerful and beautiful. I thought it was brilliant, absolutely brilliant. It really knocked me out. And afterward I sort of gulped and dried my eyes and told Joe, "We have to do this. We *have* to do this."

TRAZANA BEVERLEY Gail was tremendously moved by the production. Even though she was a white woman, she was reacting very, very strongly to it. It was a woman's piece and she was a certain barometer or gauge for him. It's a wise man who listens to his wife.

JOSEPH PAPP God, the writing was superb. It was all poetry, exquisite writing, very rich and full of black vernacular, plus a certain kind of literary departure from black common speech. So I said, "I'd like to meet the writer," and out comes this funny, kind of tough-looking person. She had an earring in her nose, a red bandana on her head, and didn't even look me in the eye: a real picture of a young black revolutionary-type woman. "Boy," I thought, "she's a tough one."

I was much more active within plays at that time than I am today, particularly when there are new people involved who have never done that kind of work before. I was influential in selecting how the material ran from place to place, the order of it, how things built. I thought she was hostile at the beginning, but it proved not to be so. She was very responsive to almost everything I said. She wanted it to work, to be successful. But Oz was at the center, he was the director, and he was key in the fact that she trusted him.

OZ SCOTT Joe loves his playwrights, but he likes having control. Once Zake said something to Joe that really hurt him. He told her everything that he wanted to do with the play, what he thought, and Zake turned to him and said, "Oz and I have to go and talk about what you said because we don't air our dirty laundry in front of other people." For Joe to be termed "other people" really hurt.

I always thank Jack Hofsiss for the success of *colored girls*. He was directing *Rebel Women* and Joe thought that play was going to go farther than *colored girls*. I would say, "Joe, would you come and see the show?" and he'd say, "I've got to go down and deal with Jack. I've got to deal with Jack." So that gave me a lot of space.

One weekend, when we were getting ready to go into previews, Joe went away and I realized I had to go back to what we had originally planned. "Okay," I said, "I'm going to get fired now, I know for sure." But I went to him and I said, "Joe, I want you to know that I tried what you asked, but it didn't work. So I put it back to what we had and gave it some other changes."

"Well, is it working now?"

"Yeah."

"Then get out of here. Stop bothering me." And he walked away.

TRAZANA BEVERLEY The audience response was always intense. Very, very, very intense. But I don't think any of us thought that the show would ever go to Broadway. This show? I very clearly remember turning to Laurie Carlos, who was one of the actresses who went to Broadway with the show, when we were down at DeMonte's and saying, "Laurie, what do you think they're going to do with this?" And she said, "Well, it's probably too way-out for them," and I said, "Yeah, I think so."

JOSEPH PAPP Zake called it a "choreopoem" and I thought, "That's what closes in Boston." But, totally unexpectedly, surprising everybody, the audiences loved it. It was thought to be a marvelous off-Broadway show, but I thought, "Can a choreopoem work on Broadway?" I weighed it in my mind and I said, "I think it can." Everybody said, "Oh, come on, they're not going to take this. This is all poetry," but I said, "I think it'll work there."

I took a chance, invested some money, and moved it to the Booth Theatre where it became a Broadway commercial success. It ran for a year, it began to reach all kinds of audiences, a rare kind of bird to be performing on Forty-fifth Street.

NTOZAKE SHANGE I knew who Joe was, but I think I was frightened when I met him. And I was very suspicious because I was entering big business. But Joe helped us refine *colored girls*, we got rid of all kinds of extraneous things. He gave us incredible support in terms of public relations and he gave us enormous support in just saying, "I want this thing heard." And he used to listen to me.

I would ask him all kinds of strange questions because I wanted to know. And he never acted like I was stupid, and he also never tried to undo my politics, as much opposed to some of them as he was. If I could change myself, and feel good about it, fine. But he wasn't going to insist that I get some other persona.

When Joe said he was going to move it to Broadway, I thought he was going to move the show up there and leave me alone. My political and aesthetic aims in life were, I thought, contrary to everything Broadway represented. If you live in California long enough, and you're part of an underground poetic experience like I was, you don't even have dreams of going to Broadway. I never even thought about it, it was totally outside all the realms that I knew about.

So I knew he wasn't talking about me, I was absolutely certain he wasn't talking about me. So I said, "Who's going to take my part?" And he said, "No, no, you have to open in the show. *You're* going to take your part." It was me. I had to go take my part. There wasn't any big discussion about it. He just said I had to do it.

I left the show after three weeks at the Booth. It was just too much attention. I didn't want to be famous, I wanted to do my work. It was a horrible, horrible time. You do three or four interviews a day and then go do a show. I wouldn't even be out of the shower and they'd start. It was just awful. It got to the point where I threw a brush at somebody who walked into my dressing room without knocking and tried to interview me. He just opened the door and said, "Hi, I'm here to—" and *Boom!*

They did all these meddlesome things, asking you about your personal life, stuff that was none of their business. But I didn't know it wasn't any of their business, so it was my own ignorance and naïveté that got me in a lot of situations. I was just stunned. I was suffering from a really severe reaction to a lot of press and applause, and I just wanted to get away from it all. I went away to Europe and stayed for eight weeks.

I have no regrets, though, because it forced me to see beyond my very leftist, radical-feminist perspective, made me see that I could relate to the rest of the population in a way I hadn't been relating. And over the years, Joe and I have developed a different kind of relationship. I have a really great daddy of my own, but it got to the point where I used to call Joe my "art father," because it was through him that I got ushered into a new way of looking at my work.

25

The End of Lincoln Center:
Postmortem

Papp at Lincoln Center
Alix Jeffrey Photograph Archive, The
Harvard Theatre Collection, Houghton
Library

The theater policy at Lincoln Center will be altered radically next season by Joseph Papp to emphasize classical dramas with international stars and traditionally styled contemporary plays with established American performers and directors . . .

"We engendered a great deal of anger and frustration on the part of the audience; outright hostility," Mr. Papp said in explaining why he was abandoning at Lincoln Center the sort of experimental approaches that made him famous at the Public Theater and in Central Park.

"We began losing audiences. They could not bear endless obscenities. I did not want to alienate the audiences. But I couldn't help but alienate them."

From "Papp Will Go Traditional; Cites Audience 'Hostility,' "
by Murray Schumach, *New York Times*, March 8, 1975

. . . .

Joseph Papp is leaving Lincoln Center. In a surprise move, the impresario announced yesterday that his New York Shakespeare Festival, which has operated the Vivian Beaumont and the Mitzi E. Newhouse theaters since 1973, would vacate the theater complex at the conclusion of a return engagement of Chekhov's *The Cherry Orchard*, which will begin June 28.

Mr. Papp, who said at a news conference that he had been "trapped in an institutional structure both artistically and fiscally," said he would now be free to focus his energies and his assets on developing new plays for his Public Theater . . . He also said it was his belief that no theater company could operate at Lincoln Center and make a profit.

From the *New York Times*, June 10, 1977

. . . .

JOHN MAZZOLA Our financial director came to me one day. He'd been going through the annual reports of the Shakespeare Festival, especially its operation at the Beaumont, and he said, "They're in financial trouble."

"That's the trouble with you damn accountants," I said, "you don't understand people like this. Joe's not saying he's in trouble. He's got all this other income you haven't been counting right. What the hell is the matter with you?"

And within two weeks, Joe came to my office and said, "I have to leave the Beaumont because of my financial problems."

At the closing ceremony, which was a press conference at the Public Theater, Joe gave various reasons for his departure, and only once did Amyas Ames and I really call him seriously, and that was when he said that his was the only creative organization at Lincoln Center doing new things.

"I think Mr. Balanchine would be very surprised to hear you say that," I said. I mean, the Metropolitan Opera is basically more museum in nature, but the Chamber Music Society does a lot of new works every year, as does the Philharmonic, and the ballet company depends on new works and new creativity.

I think losing his audience at the beginning, those blowups with the critics not liking the stuff, the audience not showing up in a very expensive house, that just made the difference. Our understanding from Joe was that the Beaumont stage with its thousand seats would be an extremely good place to put on Shakespeare and the classics, and the small three-hundred-seat theater downstairs would be an ideal place for experimental theater.

Having said that, Joe pretty much did the opposite, and with *Boom Boom Room* and *Mert and Phil* substantially decimated his enormous subscription: in two years' time, it went to less than fifty percent. It's interesting to note that at the end, he was doing *Threepenny Opera* and *Cherry Orchard* upstairs and *Streamers* downstairs. So he eventually got around to where he said he was going to start off.

Joe is the master of a process of theater that he didn't follow at the Beaumont. Joe starts a new project in a closet, and then if it's reasonably good, he puts it into a small room, and then he works on it and develops it until it gets into a larger room, and finally into a small theater, and then a big one, and so forth. I mean, just think of all the levels that *Chorus Line* probably went through.

Yet what he was doing was taking a new product and just *bang!*—opening it in New York in the most public locale, where the critics jump you on the first day they see the play. There's a certain amount of perversity in each of us, and when you're known as someone who's antiestablishment, you have to live up to your role every once in a while.

MARTIN ARONSTEIN A very low point for everyone involved in the New York Shakespeare Festival was the taking on of the Vivian Beaumont. Joe did a number of plays at the Beaumont that I thought were too strong, too controversial. They were terrible. *Mert and Phil* was one of the worst things I've ever experienced in my entire life. It made absolutely no sense doing those plays in that theater.

I don't know if Joe was trying to force his will on an audience, but that doesn't work. If you go to the theater and you don't enjoy it, the next time they do a production, unless it's something tried and true, you're not going to go back. Why go back?

ESTELLE PARSONS *Mert and Phil* was a play about mastectomies. From the moment I read it, I just thought, "This play is really, really stark and bold and hard to take." It very much had to do with women and what their options were and how much their identity and self-respect was connected with their being sex objects, and their confusions about that.

I think it was an extraordinary play, but the language was very rough, the truthfulness of it about lower-class Americans was rough, a little too honest for your upper-middle-class white Lincoln Center audiences. I thought it was much too strong and too stark to do in a subsidized theater.

Joe, of course, liked to shake those people up. Somebody has to be first with that stuff, and Joe very often is first with it. He knows that it's important to be first, and he knows that you take your lumps when you are. If he sees something that he knows should be done, he does it. He doesn't think, "How will this be?" or "Will this go with this audience?" If you second-guess all those things, pretty soon you're not an artist anymore.

SANTO LOQUASTO The saddest part of *Mert and Phil*, in terms of my involvement in it, was Bernie Gersten's phone call to me. We had been out of town with *Mert and Phil*. We dragged all these productions to Philadelphia and they limped back to New York, and Bernie called me and said, "We're working on this project downtown with Michael Bennett. He needs to have someone put some mirrors together for him, and I wondered if you could possibly give him a hand."

I said, "I really couldn't possibly. I'm up here with Joe, he's adding all these dream sequences and things, you should really get someone Michael works with regularly." The rest, as they say, is history.

JOSEPH PAPP The Lincoln Center audiences hated me. Listen, people were yelling for my neck. People were saying, "Kill Papp!" You had these kind of conservative audiences that would never raise their voices about anything, never protest anything, and suddenly they became vehement. They felt I was affronting them in some way.

In Philadelphia, there was a theater where we tried our shows before coming to Lincoln Center, and people there were absolutely vicious about *Mert and Phil*. "Okay, here I am," I said. "Any questions from the audience?" Guy says, "Mr. Papp, why do you bring this shit to Philadelphia?" "Well," I said, "*that's* a point of view."

It was the same thing at Lincoln Center, and I used to fight back all the time, get furious at them. "I wish you people would get angry at the war in Vietnam before you get angry at me and this play. I've never seen you get angry at that. Where does all this emotion come from suddenly? Why the fuck don't you lift your hand or do a damn thing to stop injustice?"

I never did any plays to piss people off. I did plays because I thought they were good plays. I didn't go into Lincoln Center and say, if the audience doesn't like it, let them go someplace else. I was hoping to get an audience that would like these plays, and I didn't entirely succeed with that.

In addition, it was costing us money to work in Lincoln Center: no matter how successful we were in terms of selling tickets, we still had a huge deficit. One year we were averaging ninety percent capacity and still lost $3.7 million. It's too costly to operate there, you couldn't possibly pay your way. You were maintaining a very expensive institution year-round, whereas in a Broadway house, you were maintaining it only for the time you're running a play.

So I said, "Why am *I* supporting this goddamn Lincoln Center? Why should *I* have to be worried about getting another couple of million dollars?" Also, I began to miss my concentration down at the Public Theater, my home turf.

PAUL RUDD Somebody said that the Beaumont is a place that never should have been built. They should have filled the lobby with water and made it into an aquarium. It just doesn't have a spiritual focus, a reason to be. To just say, "Okay, we've got an opera house, we've got a dance theater, let's put in a theater, too," you just can't supermarket stuff like that. It's a temple that was built before the religion was begun.

ROBERT KAMLOT Joe loves challenges, and Lincoln Center was an enormous challenge. Everybody that had been there had failed. To him it was also visibility, which he needed at that time. He considered being one of the constituents at Lincoln Center very important to the New York Shakespeare Festival. He's a risk-taker and it was an enormous risk.

Joe, being the kind of iconoclast he was, was determined to bring what he would call "hunchback" plays, plays which were usually not accepted in the mainstream, into the established bourgeois theater. He was going to bombard the audience with those things that they really didn't want to see, like sticking a person's head in the toilet in *Short Eyes*.

They used to attack Joe physically in the lobby of the theater, saying, "God, how could you do this to us? Why are you giving us this garbage?" I think one of Joe's failings was his obdurateness in trying to cram things down people's throats. He was going to do it, no matter what. It was stubbornness, that's all it was, total stubbornness.

Oddly enough, our last season we did three productions that were extraordinary: the Richard Foreman production of *Threepenny Opera* with Raul Julia, Andrei Serban's *Cherry Orchard* with Irene Worth and Meryl Streep, and Liz Swados's production of *Agamemnon*. And that was the year that Joe said, "Okay, enough." Joe always did the unexpected. That's endemic to our business—people are very volatile, they say one thing and an hour later they've changed their minds. Joe had it honed to a science.

GAIL MERRIFIELD PAPP   It was, I must say, a very interesting kind of experience, but it was very troublesome and difficult. We lost them in the first season because we were doing things they'd never heard of or seen before, and it outraged their cultural sensibilities.

Then we started doing a mix of classics like *Threepenny Opera*, *The Cherry Orchard*, and *A Doll's House* with new works, and got some of them back. We started building a different kind of audience that was really quite extraordinary and unprecedented. And with *What the Wine-Sellers Buy* and *Black Picture Show*, it was the first time that the theater had ever had a primarily black box-office audience.

But we were there about long enough. It's a stodgy place, kind of oppressive, you don't create anything there. And trying to keep it afloat was really incredibly difficult. That place costs a fortune to operate, just a fortune. There was no significant money raised after an initial $5 million, so what ended up happening was that we were floating Lincoln Center to the tune of millions of dollars with income from *A Chorus Line*. It was the kind of support the federal government should have been giving. The reason we finally pulled out was not because of any kind of artistic failure but because we just didn't want to put another $2 or $3 million a year into that place without any kind of return or greater support.

CLIVE BARNES This was his Bay of Pigs, and it was his Bay of Pigs because he was pigheaded. It was a total miscalculation from beginning to end. He thought that he could run Lincoln Center like the New York Shakespeare Festival. He thought he could merely use it as a rather classy auditorium for his existing organization and do much the same kind of plays.

He didn't understand the geographic place that Lincoln Center has in the intellectual life of the country. He didn't realize that any theater at the Vivian Beaumont, by virtue of its geography, by virtue of its juxtaposition with the Met, the New York City Ballet, the New York Philharmonic, will, whether it wants to or not, be considered a national theater. He didn't understand that the need there was for some kind of classic repertory company, didn't understand that his brief, whether he knew it or not, was not to reproduce the New York Shakespeare Festival but to reproduce the Royal Shakespeare Company in an American version.

BERNARD GERSTEN Joe was much more at home in Central Park, with a theater such as the Delacorte which is exposed to the sky. Joe was more comfortable with his theater with no roof, or in a theater that was geographically sited down between the East and West Village. That was far more interesting than the marble halls of Lincoln Center and peer status with the Met and the Philharmonic and others who he wasn't interested in rubbing shoulders with. In Elizabethan terms, Joe would have been much happier with the people who were standing in the pit than the lords and ladies who were elegantly dressed and were sitting in the rings above. Joe would choose groundlings rather than the bourgeoisie.

AMYAS AMES The last year he was there, he was a harried man. I got the impression of a human being who was running too fast. The truth is, he exceeded his own physical and nervous capacity. He was doing so many things. He would not give up one single thing about the Public Theater but he would add the Beaumont. I guess with Joe Papp and his ambitious mind, it was a perfectly logical thing to do, but I think it was too much for him.

His heart was never in Lincoln Center. He thought of it as a symbol of money and power and bigness, and he didn't believe in those things. He had an antagonist to fight, and he fought it. But I think that was in Joe Papp's personality and character and not inherent in Lincoln Center.

He was a man of the present, and the people that were going to Lincoln Center, who were listening to these beautiful treasures of humanity, as I would call them, they weren't his game. He violently disagreed with what he considered playing the dusty records of the past. He was going to show them.

And the thing about it is, it would have worked. There isn't any question at all that if he'd concentrated on Lincoln Center, if his heart had been in it, he would have been a great success. But that was not the case. It was a second priority, and when he found out that he just was doing too many things at once, the second priority got his second attention. As it would have mine or any man's. Which was why the Lincoln Center thing didn't work.

26

Elizabeth Swados and *Runaways*

1978

Carlo Imperato (right)
in a scene from
Runaways
© Martha Swope

Elizabeth Swados's *Runaways*, which opened last night at Joseph Papp's Public Theater Cabaret, is an inspired musical collage about the hopes, dreams, fears, frustrations, loneliness, humor and, perhaps most of all, the anger, of young people who are estranged from their families and are searching for themselves. There are moments of joyfulness and youthful exuberance, but basically this is a serious contemplative musical with something important to say about society today.

This is a rare case in which a show was organically created. Ten months ago, Miss Swados decided to write a musical about runaways and to do research for the project at the same time that she was gathering a cast. As composer, lyricist and author, Miss Swados has transformed the material. As director, she has transformed her cast. Some of the youths were actual runaways, a few were experienced professionals; now they were all actors. One of the pleasures of *Runaways* is that the company retains its rough edges and its freshness.

The structure of the show seems simple. On a playground the company gathers and, in a mosaic of songs, monologues, scenes, poems and dances, gives us a complete portrait of urban children on the run. We see what prods youngsters to leave home and what disturbs—and nurtures—them in their escapes. The musical takes a harsh and uncompromising look at the world of runaways, but it is written and performed with great compassion.

Mel Gussow, *New York Times*, March 10, 1974

ELIZABETH SWADOS I had been working at La MaMa, with a good deal of notoriety in the avant-garde, but I didn't want any more work with other people's directing or other people's concepts. I was still practically just a baby, but I wanted to do my own thing. And I wrote to Joe and said, "I like your theater," because he combined politics with theater. I was longing to connect with America and its issues, and as far as I was concerned there was no place for that but the Public Theater.

Gail Merrifield was the person who really hooked into me at first. She came over to where I was working and listened to about two hours of music. I guess she went back to Joe and said, "This is not a phony person. This is obviously someone who is searching for a voice." He came up to me after a performance of Brecht's *The Good Woman of Szechuan* and said, "You want to work for me?" And I said, "Yeah." He said, "Okay." And that was it.

GAIL MERRIFIELD PAPP Liz wrote to Joe, presented herself, said she would like to have a meeting and so forth. Joe was very tied up at that time, so he marked the letter for me. I tried to get in touch with Liz, didn't succeed, and then I was out of the office for a couple of weeks. When Liz did not hear anything in proper response to her letter, she wrote a second letter which was just spitfire and hellcat stuff, a sense of outraged, self-righteous indignation which really made your hair stand on end.

I read it and I felt a little sick. I realized what it must seem like to her. You could say that the gigantic passion of this letter was uncalled for without one more exploratory phone call, but I can't argue those things.

I acted and I got in touch with her and explained why she hadn't heard more promptly. She understood that, because, if anything, Liz has a very profound understanding of human frailties. I went over the next week to hear some of her material and I could not believe this woman. I wrote a memo to Joe. I said, "I think she's a genius."

ELIZABETH SWADOS Joe was talking to Andrei Serban, who was my close collaborator, and because I was the little one of the group, it seemed that there had to be some dues for me to pay before I could have my own show. And those were to continue the Serban-Swados collaboration, but move it over to Lincoln Center, where I did the music for *The Cherry Orchard* and *Agamemnon*.

Ever since I was in college, I thought I was going to be doing *Alice in Wonderland* as my first independent show. And then this thing with these kids all over New York started to happen in my heart. When I came back from Africa with Peter Brook, I just kept seeing kids in the street, and I kept thinking, "New York, Minneapolis, Detroit, Buffalo, what's happening?"

I began to notice that a lot of the illness of the nation, from the time of Vietnam and the civil rights struggle, had moved down to the youth. It wasn't an ABC Movie of the Week, "My father's got Alzheimer's, my mother's on crack, and we all go to AA together and try to deal with it." There was something deeply wrong.

So when Joe and I were supposed to have our meeting about *Alice in Wonderland*—and this is typical of our relationship—I went in and said, "I know I said I wanted to do *Alice*, but I have another idea."

He kind of blinked at me, because I'd been pushing *Alice, Alice, Alice, Alice,* and suddenly here I was saying, "No, it's not time to be doing that right now." I told him we should be getting these kids off the streets and from schools, interviewing them, and just doing it. And he switched gears in twenty-two seconds. He responded by saying, "Go ahead." Period. "Just do it."

Never in a zillion, trillion years could that happen again. But this, of course, was at a time when Michael Bennett had not only set the precedent for a commercially oriented workshop, but the Shakespeare Festival had the funds from the initial rush of *A Chorus Line* to take risks. And Joe, whatever else he does, comes back to a political or a humanitarian wish; he's always been rooted in that. Even if he doesn't achieve it, the wish is in him.

That was the beginning of my real relationship with Joe, even though he must have woken up about a week later and gone, "What the fuck have I done? Who is this twenty-six-year-old girl?" And I'd come in and say, "Man, I just saw this skateboarder. I don't know if he can speak, but he can do the most amazing things on his skateboard." Or "I just went to this place called the Theater for the Forgotten, I met this professional graffiti artist, and he was telling me how they steal bicycles and stuff." Joe was very excited by this, but I imagine he had a few moments of sweaty palms.

JOSEPH PAPP She was very strong in what she wanted to do and I liked her immediately. I had faith in her ability and I trusted her, so I said, "Why not?"

It wasn't just somebody walking in from off the street. She'd already shown she had this kind of vitality and talent. I didn't know if it would work or not, but I never think of that, I never say, "Will this succeed, will this make it?" That's not in my mind. I set something going because I think it has possibilities, not because I expect it to happen.

She was, again, a new force, as all of these people were in my life. They brought something else, something new to me. My fundamental interest in the theater is this connection with life outside the theater. It's where I get my strength from. We're not just putting on a show; society is present at all times. And what I was interested in was that she was dealing with a real social problem of the time and trying to put it on the stage. She was like a runaway kid herself.

GAIL MERRIFIELD PAPP *Runaways* was hatched-from-the-egg stuff—it was created from scratch. The first problem was, we're sitting in this office, wanting to do this work about runaways—where do you go from there? What's next?

What she wanted was to go around and find talented young people in different places around the city. She wanted to have children performing from different sources, using their material that she would adapt, musically, and create with them. And she also wanted to learn who had the capability of sustaining a certain kind of discipline, who had natural ability, and so forth. We found her a crackerjack assistant, Neva Peterson, and they put together a staggering schedule, going to three or four places a day all over the five boroughs for two and a half months.

ELIZABETH SWADOS I had a seventeen-year-old assistant and I said to her, "Go and hang out, find out where everybody is these days." Because for eight-to-nineteen-year-olds, a twenty-six-year-old is an elder. I went around to basketball courts, to open festivals at high schools, to the Brooklyn Museum, to a special school in Suffolk County for troubled children. I had a Hispanic boy who walked me through Alphabet City. I went up to Harlem and worked with a community-action theater group. It's not really auditions; it becomes research.

What I understood was to make them want to do this—not because they'd be rich or because they'd be famous but just so they'd want to do it, so they'd get off on it. That became the number-one audition thing: Did they care about at least a little something? Was there a spark? So I developed all these bizarre and wonderful exercises to find out if they could be precise, if they had energy and concentration enough to get through two hours, or if they'd be goofballs with me.

For instance, I had them run in place until they were dying and then start with the voice, saying, "I am running away from . . ." What that did was help the voice be free of the body's movement, and I could see whether they would be willing to keep up a maniacal form of energy.

We had what I called the "belief exercise," which was to take one thing and pretend that it was something else completely. My demonstration of it would be to take a piece of paper and say, "This is the most delicious slice of pizza," and I would proceed to eat the piece of paper as the kids looked at me like "What have we gotten into?"

Then I had them tell me a lie, like "This is not my body, I borrowed it for today." The more imaginative the lie, the more that told me that there was an inner life that had not been tapped.

I remember being above a grocery store in the Bronx for a community organization that was helping with kids. We were having them jump up and down and tell us stories. I wasn't seeing any kids I thought were right when this little blond Italian kid, about four foot four, comes in and goes, "I've never done nothin', but I know I'm gonna be an actor." I looked at him and I just fell in love with him, and he ended up in the cast.

CARLO IMPERATO I grew up in the Bronx. When I watched TV, I used to see the kids who were my age and I'd say, "Mom, they're nothing. I'm his age. Why is he doing it and not me?" But every kid says that when they watch TV. I got started when I was thirteen and Liz Swados came to my high school, Christopher Columbus, and gave out the word that whoever wanted to audition for a show that she was doing should go to a couple of offices they'd rented over Key Foods on Morris Park Avenue, right where I lived.

I went down to the audition and there were twenty-five kids from my school there. My audition called for dribbling a basketball and singing "Happy Birthday," a lot of improv, a lot of just talking to me and finding out my background. Liz said she wanted real street kids, and she mentioned Joseph Papp's name, and at that time I had no idea who he was. I was very naïve, I didn't understand. It was over in twenty minutes and I went about my business like nothing ever happened.

The next day I came home from school, and my father and my grandmother and my grandfather were sitting in the kitchen, and I said to my father, "Dad, did that lady Liz Swados call up?" And my father said, "Yeah, you got a callback." So my parents took me down to the Shakespeare Theater and I wound up getting the part.

Liz is a very, very strong individual. When I goofed off, she got on me. It was like my big sister reprimanding me. She never did it like a boss, like

"You're gonna get fired," it was like family with her. She would get on me in a loving way, which was a lot worse than if she was my boss, because if she was my boss and yelled at me, I would say, "Hell with you! If you don't like what I'm doing, then I quit."

She would scream, but it wasn't just yelling, it wasn't just screaming to be heard. She was making a point. The lady never opened her mouth when she didn't have anything important to say. You might turn around and say, "This lady's hard," but when I got to know her, she was like a guardian to me. But if you weren't in there and putting out, you were gone. She would say, "How are you going to even know if you can do it unless you try it? You haven't even tried it!" She would hate that. Hey, she's been called a tyrant, but she's a great lady.

I'll tell ya, there were a couple of kids in the show, real street kids. You didn't play around with them. These kids did not take nothing from nobody. They were rough, and Liz would get right in their face. She'd say, "If you don't want to listen to me, you can get the hell outta here. You want to run your own show? You want to do whatever you want? Then you leave!"

She would stand right up—she'd come up to like their chest and have her chin straight up in the air. These were some bad dudes, and she was ready to slug it out with them. She's not afraid of anybody, that's one of her great qualities.

DIANE LANE My dad, Bert Lane, was a teacher of acting in the fifties with John Cassavetes; they had a workshop together. I first met Liz when I was six years old and answered an ad in *The Village Voice* for her and Andrei Serban's La MaMa production of *Medea* that a friend of my mother's gave me as kind of a joke Christmas present. Then my dad asked me if I really wanted to audition for this thing and I said, "Sure."

I got the role of the little girl who gets killed in the play, and that just blossomed into *Electra* and *The Trojan Women*, a trilogy of Greek plays. Every summer we would tour Europe and some of the Eastern countries, interesting places like Iran and Lebanon. That was basically how I grew up.

When I met Liz, I thought she was a little bit introverted. She didn't share a whole lot of herself. She didn't smile unless she wanted you to feel like she was happy with you. I felt she was just vulnerable and protecting herself, and I could understand that.

Originally, I did not want to do *Runaways*. I had given up on being an actress. I said, "That was a nice time of my development." I was perching on adulthood, looking forward eagerly to Hunter College High, an incredibly competitive school.

Then I got a phone call from Ellen Stewart, like "Baby, I want you to know that Liz wants you to do a production." So I said to my dad, "There's no way I can do that schedule and go to school." It was rehearsing from noon till six every day for five months. And Dad said, "You either do the play, or you leave and go to your mom." He felt that creatively it was going to be the most important thing that I'd done so far in my career. But I said, "Okay, I'm going to Mom." That didn't work out, so I said, "Guess I'm doing the play, huh?"

We made the play from scratch, together, out of the kids sitting around telling their personal stories. Liz would make songs either out of our stories or out of her own head from what she'd seen in the world. It was almost like therapy in certain ways, because the things that came out were very revealing. You were talking about violations that had happened to you. You had to bare your soul a little bit to the group, and it required trust. It was a wonderfully creative process, different from anything I'd ever seen or heard of or done.

Liz was very much the orchestrator of that, making sure that everybody was coming from the same place. She was vocal, but she was vocal on your side. She never said anything about you she didn't believe just to hurt you. She let me know what she thought, but she never violated anything about me.

I felt under a lot of pressure, I felt I had to set the damn example, because I had known her since I was six years old. If I began a remote form of mutiny, it would be hell to pay. When I say mutiny, I mean being five minutes late from lunch. I didn't want to push my luck with her. She was very—tough love, you know.

CRAIG ZADAN It was a difficult process because Liz at that time—how do I say this—was a bit strident. She felt a need to be a disciplinarian with the kids. It was run a little militaristically. When the kids were all gathered, they were so undisciplined, they were all over the place.

The only way to get them to come through was for her to really let them know that she was in charge and that they were going to have to work their asses off. It was a process that I thought was quite effective, because by the time the show opened, they were tight as a drum: she'd whipped them into shape.

ELIZABETH SWADOS I'm not a person who believes that you have to go live with a whale for six years to write whale songs, but I really am an old-time experimental theater person. I believe that the audience will get something more if the process has been true. I can't stand that we grow up confusing intense theatrical experience with real life. So I felt it was necessary to expose all of the company to what they were really talking about, so that they wouldn't get all hoity-toity about the fact that they were really down and out.

We took a trip to the Kennedy Home for runaways in the Bronx. It was a dangerous thing to do because we had kids who were very sensitive and scared. It was a frightening experience because some of them were afraid of the kids, afraid on some unconscious level that they were going to end up back there.

There was a girl who talked about wanting to put her fist through a window because she was tired of being moved from home to home. There was another kid who talked about how people took kids into bathrooms and raped them. They talked about never knowing how long they were going to be someplace.

It was a scary day. It equalized the group, it humbled them, and it also informed their improvisational work and their sympathy for one another. After that the kids never again could be so hoity-toity about what they thought they knew about angst.

I wasn't looking to be their hero. It's a disservice to young people to presuppose that you can cure what is already something that is deeper than anything you know by being sweet or talking superficially about how to feel better. The most important healing that anybody can do is to let people be powerful in themselves. And that's what I did. I built their chops. And sometimes at the expense of my own popularity.

CARLO IMPERATO   I remember the day Vinnie Spano left. He got a *movie!* Liz was upset. She'd cast everybody because of the chemistry, she felt a real camaraderie, and she didn't want anybody to leave. She was hurt.

Liz takes everything very personal. She don't take it business. "You're my friend, and I'm doing this for you, you're supposed to do something for me." She is not into agents, managers, publicity people at all. She hated getting involved with that side of the business. She wants her company, she wants her work, and she wants it one-on-one. A friendship. This is us and we're going to make it happen. No one else is going to come in and mess this up, and no one else is going to come in and help it out.

DIANE LANE   Vinnie said to me, "Listen, Diane, I don't think I'm gonna be in the play."

"You gotta be kidding," I said. "Make it work. What are you doing? Don't have an ego problem with the director. You nuts? You're fifteen, give it a chance. You got nerve, boy. You are gonna go places."

And, of course, he has and will, but there was an ego conflict there. I remember Liz saying, "We lost a member of the company today," and it was almost like a funeral day. Very quiet, very odd.

ELIZABETH SWADOS   I was at that point outraged that anybody would not see the incredible value of what I was doing. What I really mean is that my ego was burned, because I was young and impetuous and arrogant and just morally outraged. Also, I was scared, afraid that we were going to start to be raided, because my training is exceptional with kids. Sometimes I have a lot of problems with adult actors. They say, "What the fuck are you doing? I'm a grown-up!" But with kids I'm tremendously successful.

I didn't know what Vincent Spano's leaving meant. I didn't know if people were going to start using me and then leaving. And I took it out a lot on this one kid. I was vitriolic, I was vicious. I think my motivations were genuine, but I was very wrong. I don't feel badly about it anymore—how long can you kick yourself—but I wasn't a good girl that time.

JOSEPH PAPP She was a stern disciplinarian, like a firm mother, but with very little sentimentality. Her biggest problem was structure, and I played a role all the time with that. I used to come in and say, "No, that can't be, this has to move this way, it's just aimless here." She always knew that, and she would accept me and even want me to be there.

ELIZABETH SWADOS All human experience of real devastating quality has now been serialized to the point where any single incident sounds like episode four of *St. Elsewhere*, but the fact is that some very real things happened at the opening. The mother of one of the kids came in and said, "I have to talk to you."

"Oh, god," I thought, "an hour before and no understudy."

"Da-da-da's father has just been arrested," she said very plainly. "Shall I tell him now, or after the show? Because I want the show to go well for him."

"What's he been arrested for?"

"He's not going to see him again for a long time."

It turned out the guy had been arrested for murder. So I said, "I think you should tell him after the show."

When finally they got up on that stage, forgive me for sounding like a proud mother, but they did perform like no other kids ever had in America. There was a natural quality and an energy that was very rare, and a generosity that was not forced. In the first months, there was nothing like it; it became the *Star Wars* of off Broadway.

Later on, it became not so good. They got real tired, and so did I. It's a well-known fact that applause and praise do not fill the fundamental wound which makes you need. Sometimes, the more applause and the more praise, the more it opens the wound, because whoever it is who isn't loving you isn't there. It's everybody else but them. We had a lot of that, a lot of psychological trauma that began to happen as there was more and more success. It's the old story: success can kill perhaps easier than failure, because they were used to failure.

CRAIG ZADAN   We moved *Runaways* to Broadway, but it didn't work there because the subject matter was a very hard pill to swallow. It wasn't sugar-coated, it wasn't sweet, it was uncompromising, with a real hard-edged documentary feel. I think that Broadway has become Las Vegas to some extent; the audiences are not so open to seeing work that makes them feel not good about themselves.

ELIZABETH SWADOS   When Joe first brought Broadway up, we felt, "Wow! This is the most amazing thing in the world." It was like a fucking miracle. This man was a magician. And to this day I have to say that, politically, I was sure glad to be there on Broadway scaring the shit out of people while everybody else was namby-pambying around. The work of the theater, to me, continues to be to find out what is the most courageous thing to do at the right time to move consciousness and sensibility and the language of the theater forward, to break through barriers and prejudices and fears. And I think we did that, but at an enormous cost.

I don't like exploiting children for the sake of putting on a play which says "Don't exploit children," and I wish we had had another company so the kids didn't get tired and didn't get flippy. We should have had a complete alternate cast, so they could have played opposite nights and gotten sleep. They could have gotten into their lives, they could have been brought down to earth by the parents who were good, and we could have intervened with the parents who were misspending the money. We could have dealt with the kids who were buying cars and forging Joe's name, the kids who were carrying around guns—I mean, we had a lot of problems.

The first time I took the kids into the Plymouth Theatre, I said, "I want you to just take over, do whatever you want, and enjoy this space. It's yours. I don't care that it's bigger. Do what you must do." And one of the kids went up in one of the box seats, jumped off onto the stage, and smashed his heel. And that told me we were too high, too soon, and that we didn't have a good pilot—me.

I hadn't been trained for jet flying, I didn't have the equipment. Broadway isn't what *Runaways* was about, and the fact that we ended up there is totally due to the charisma and incredible courage of Joe. I didn't meet his courage at that point. I just didn't know how.

DIANE LANE   I'm convinced that I would not have gotten the part in *A Little Romance* unless George Roy Hill had come to see my work in *Runaways*. Then came the news that we were going to Broadway. It was a peak that I'd never even fantasized about because it is as far as you can go. But that was the exact time I got offered *A Little Romance* and I never got to go to Broadway.

My leaving the play was a very awkward situation between Joe and myself. Because I had three months' time, I could have done all of the rehearsal and had almost two months onstage, but Joe said, "No, Diane. Either you stick with the play all the way or you get out now." And I was very hurt by that. I felt like I was betrayed. I took it personally because I didn't think that he would take it personally.

But he was very possessive of his pupils, as it were. There's a respect that he expected from the people working for him. If this was La MaMa, I could feel he was justified in what he was saying, but we weren't a theater company. I thought he'd be happy as heck for me that I was going to do a movie in Paris with Laurence Olivier. Give me a break, what could possibly be better?

On opening night at the Public, he'd given me a gorgeous Cartier bracelet. I was crying. I was moved that he would be that generous. And the card said, "Some day, Juliet." I was dating Tim Hutton and we were going to pursue doing *Romeo and Juliet* together, for Joe, in the park. It never happened. It was such an awkward cut-off point for me. I haven't spoken to or had any communication whatsoever with Joe since I left.

Years later, I went down and auditioned for a play. It didn't go well; I didn't feel like anyone there was on my side. I just felt awful, I practically ran out of the room. I just wanted to do it to see if I could survive the experience, and I did. I never spoke to him.

ELIZABETH SWADOS   Joe's very Talmudic in needing to find what resonates. He'll look at everything until he exhausts you, he's so tortured for the truth. He and I share the wish to make trouble, to be on the edge. On the other hand, like a vaudevillian, he loves to ham it up, he's just tap-dancin' like everybody else. This is a dead culture we're in now, a culture that doesn't claim its passions, and he dares to be alive.

Joe's a Jew, and Jews arouse terrible hatred and extreme love. They deserve whatever they get because they're out there. He puts himself out there, he gets what he asks for, and he knows it. Joe's a heavy-duty soldier, he comes out and he takes in fire. He doesn't always enjoy it, and he carries many scars. But at least he does it. I'm so tired of these intellectual, safe, equivocating, nice-nice-nice-nice scumbags who'll stab you in the back the second that your profits are dropping.

He's never cheated me out of any money in my life, which a lot of people have. He's never cheated me out of credit in my life, which a lot of people have. He's never, to my knowledge, said a shitty word behind my back, which *lots* of people have. Maybe other people have valid complaints, but aside from the fact that he is a human being with deep needs, what's his crime?

27

I'm Getting My Act Together and Taking It on the Road

1978

Gretchen Cryer
© Susan Cook

I'm Getting My Act Together and Taking It on the Road is a musical entertainment about a 39-year-old woman finding herself.

For once, the standard disclaimer must be reversed: The subject does not do justice to this summary description.

There is some freshness of aspiration but none of achievement in this collection of songs and skits about the troubles of a pop singer trying to find a new image for herself.

There is a touch of wit here and there. Gretchen Cryer, who wrote the book and lyrics and plays the leading character, is trying to say something about aging and feminine identity. Her perception fails her; she falls into platitude after platitude and comes up with a show that is both insubstantial and very heavy.

Self-celebration is the affliction of *I'm Getting My Act*. Its songs and skits spell out the conflicts—the little girl who has to smile for her daddy; the wife who has to pick up her husband's socks and talk baby talk to him; the liberated women who find that men don't much like them—with little individual perception, imagination or rigor. The lyrics, and the music, are effortless and not in the best sense of the word.

Richard Eder, *New York Times*, June 19, 1978

....

The critics have had their say about the musical *I'm Getting My Act Together and Taking It on the Road*. Now the audiences are getting into the act.

Men and women are remaining in the Anspacher at the Public Theater after Wednesday night performances to talk about the show and its message with the cast headed by Gretchen Cryer, who stars in it and wrote the book and lyrics (to the music of her collaborator Nancy Ford). They're manifesting a depth of feeling about the musical that creators of more critically admired shows might well envy. The intensity is surprising for a show that takes a comic approach to its subject—the changing relationship between men and women—and doubly surprising for a show that was unfavorably received by most critics. As a result of such involvement, *I'm Getting My Act Together* has become an unexpected hit, its run extended indefinitely by producer Joseph Papp beyond the originally scheduled six weeks.

Allan Wallach, *Newsday*

....

GRETCHEN CRYER Nancy Ford and I met when we were eighteen-year-old freshmen at DePauw University. We started writing together that year. We did two original shows there and we got a lot of early encouragement at that amateur level. Having that period where we were nurtured in an academic environment was just great: to try to jump straight into the mainstream in New York, it's awful.

Both of us got married to men who were going to be ministers. Both of our husbands went to Yale Divinity School, and Nancy and I were both secretaries supporting them. Both of them decided to leave divinity school and go to Boston to graduate school, and Nancy and I wrote another show in Boston, which my husband, who was now in graduate school in theater, did as a project at Boston University.

We came to New York to seek our fortunes, not knowing anybody or knowing the ropes. We had to read *Back Stage*, *Show Business*, and *Variety* to even see how the business worked. We had *no* idea whatsoever. Nancy started playing piano off Broadway and I started being a chorus girl in Broadway musicals. It took us five years to get our first professional production on, *Now Is the Time for All Good Men*, in 1967. Then, three years later, we had *The Last Sweet Days of Isaac*, which was a very good critical hit.

NANCY FORD In 1972, we did another musical, *Shelter*, and after that we started writing individual songs. Our publisher thought the way for us to get them out was to make a record album and sing them ourselves, so we made two albums for RCA. We went out on the road with those songs, performing in cabarets where we would be the opening for some very famous act, and a lot of the experiences were less than satisfying and rewarding. We often felt as though we were put in a package and sold, and that cabaret and performing experience went into *Getting My Act Together*.

GRETCHEN CRYER The main impetus for the show had to do with feeling so deeply the changes that I had personally gone through in my life. I came out of the fifties with one set of expectations for my life, having to do with marriage, family, what place women had in men's lives. When I got married, I thought it was forever. I didn't think in terms of what I wanted to do with my life. I thought in terms of finding a man whose teammate I could be, and then I would decide what I was going to do. As soon as I found the man that I wanted to marry, then I would figure out what I could do to fit into *his* life.

It turned out that by trying to fit into the cracks of the man's life, I ultimately found what was very satisfying to me, but that was a lucky chance. And I thought, "It's such a long journey from back when I was eighteen and had one whole set of ideas about what life was going to be like to what it's like now."

For five years, Nancy and I wanted to write about this subject because so many women that we knew had gone through the same trip. It was a deeply emotional, very personally felt thing. Mostly my thoughts were rather mundane, about a woman who goes through a marriage and all that. I couldn't find a theatrical metaphor for it.

Then one night, while Nancy and I were performing, I just thought of that phrase—I'm getting my act together and taking it on the road—because she and I were always moving around and packing and unpacking our equipment. And suddenly, within a flash, an instant, I thought, "Ah, this show could be about a woman who's getting her act together, and her act has songs about her life in it, and she's decided to make her act about her life. She's having to say, 'I have to define myself now. I can't be who I was to please everybody else.'" So it became a complete metaphor for what was going on personally with me. And the minute I had that idea, it just seemed to write itself.

CRAIG ZADAN During the Broadway at the Ballroom series, one of the composer-lyricist teams that performed was Gretchen Cryer and Nancy Ford. They sang one song, "Natural High," which they said was the opening number from this new musical they'd written, *I'm Getting My Act Together and Taking It on the Road.*

It sounded like a terrific show, and when I ended up at the Public Theater, the first thing I did was call Gretchen and Nancy and say, "Remember when you sang that song?"

"Yeah."

"Can I hear the show?"

"We haven't really written it yet. We have a couple of numbers and we have it worked out, but it's not done."

"Look," I said, "I really think I want to do this show. Would you finish it?" I kept calling them and saying, "Where is it? Where is it?" We auditioned it for Joe, he loved it immediately, and said, "Let's do it."

NANCY FORD We did sort of a backer's audition, just Gretchen and me doing it for Joe. He sat there and said, "I want to do it." I remember how impressed we were with the fact that he was so decisive because we'd dealt with a lot of people who would say, "Mmm, yeah, well, we'll get back to you."

We had a completely different ending on it at the time, a rapprochement between Gretchen's character, Heather, and her parents. And Joe thought that that got sentimental. He suggested we scratch that, that we needed a statement. As a result we wrote the Happy Birthday song that comes at the end of the show.

JOSEPH PAPP I listened to it, and I had mixed feelings about it. I didn't say, "God! We're going to have to do this thing!" I very seldom do that. I do everything rather reluctantly. It's a sort of resistance I've developed over the years. But once I say I'm doing it, I'm the biggest booster for it.

I did love the music, but I had a problem with the show's balance. For one thing, I thought the male was not male enough. I felt everybody should have his say in court. I mean, Shakespeare lets his villains have it—Richard III has his say, Iago has, certainly Shylock has.

Also, I felt it was too nice. It was like milk compared to the strong, powerful brew of *Mod Donna*, Myrna Lamb's women's liberation musical I'd put on in 1970. It was like *Ms.* magazine to me, more than anything. And it was veering toward sentimentality in certain places, which I can't stand. There's nothing worse than sentimentality on the stage—or anyplace, for that matter.

But Gretchen Cryer sings quite beautifully, and I said, "Okay, I'll do it."

"Well," she said, "let's see if we can cast this."

"We're not going to cast this. You're going to play the part."

"Oh, I can't."

"I won't do it without you," I said. "You're exactly the woman for the part."

GRETCHEN CRYER We did the audition, and immediately afterward Joe said, "I'll do it." Instantly. He got up with this group of people, they walked to the elevator, the elevator doors closed, and Nancy and I were jumping up and down with joy. Moments later, the doors opened again and Joe, with his entourage, came back in.

"Wait just a minute," he said to me. "I've got to have something understood here. You are going to be in it, aren't you?"

Now up to that point, I had no thought of being in it. I was the writer; I hadn't had my primary focus toward being an actress. "I'll have to think about it," I said, "because I think it's very difficult, as a writer, to maintain your perspective when you are in a piece that you've written."

"I think that the piece is enough written that you're not going to be having to do that many rewrites," Joe said. "Go home and think about it."

I thought about it, talked to Nancy, who was all for it, and called Joe and said, "Yes, I will be in it." The funny thing is, people thought that I'd written the thing for myself, which I didn't at all. I got cast in it by Joe, unexpectedly.

About two or three weeks into the rehearsal, Joe came in one day, unannounced, sat down in the audience, watched a little bit, and said he was dropping the project. He'd seen only bits and pieces, but he thought it was a mess, it wasn't going to work. Craig Zadan talked to us and said, "What you've got to do is go in, talk to Joe, and convince him." So we went in and said to him, "Give us two or three more days. At the end of three days we'll do the whole show for you."

So for three days we rehearsed like crazy, got the whole show together, and invited a hundred friends to be an audience. Now, we hadn't told him we were going to do that. We phoned everybody we knew, we said, "Please come over, he's got to see that it's not a diatribe, that it's going to be funny." He'd seen it on a deadly day; it didn't look funny to him at all.

Joe was late for the performance, so in order to keep everybody's spirits up, we had our band start playing. The audience was loving the band, and when, a half hour later, Joe walked in, we just started the show straight out of this excitement of our band playing. Joe loved it, the audience loved it, they laughed like crazy. The minute it was over, Joe said, "We're going ahead." Never questioned that he was going to do it from that moment on. And, ultimately, having the band out there was the way we started the show, the same way that it happened for Joe.

CRAIG ZADAN From the moment we started previewing, we knew we had a big hit, because I had never seen an audience react the way they reacted to this show. They were screaming and applauding during the show, yelling things out. There were nights when it was like you were at a football game. The show did touch a nerve, and word got out about it very quickly. The house was packed with women, and it was their show. When Gretchen would give her speeches about "I'd rather be alone than be with you and not be myself," the audience went berserk. It didn't feel like a play, it felt like an event.

GRETCHEN CRYER On opening night, right before we were about to go on, Joe came back and wanted me to change something, change my attack on the first scene or something. I got very upset because we'd had a whole month of previews to change things, to say something, and he didn't. I think he was trying to keep me on my toes, but my personality is not such that I respond to that kind of thing positively. Now some people rise to the challenge, but for me it was bad. It threw me, and I had to go onstage unsure of what I was doing.

The opening night was deadly. For some reason, a theater party had been booked, a group from Long Island that was studying the theater. So a third to a half of the audience were students who had their notebooks out. They weren't there as an audience; they were there to study the piece and make notes on it. And the rest of the house was filled with critics who had *their* notebooks out. We gave a very good performance, but people weren't laughing, they weren't responding. And we did not get very good reviews.

CRAIG ZADAN I knew the reviews would be bad because the opening-night performance was dire. It was really a matter of opening-night jitters, and the audience was just dire. There's a danger with filling a house that small with all press. The night before, the audience was in pandemonium. The night after the critics came, there was pandemonium again. That one night was death. There were no laughs, there was no applause, it was like, "What happened?" So therefore we got terrible reviews, but it didn't matter because we got past the reviews and the audiences just loved it.

NANCY FORD There were a lot of people who looked upon it as a feminist tract. They thought that Heather was an angry woman who was blaming men for her predicament. Gretchen and I did not. We thought that it was about relationships between men and women. That it was specifically about a woman, from her standpoint, shouldn't necessarily make it a feminist tract. I don't know if a show correspondingly about a man would be considered somehow chauvinistic. I kind of doubt it.

GRETCHEN CRYER There was a lot of hostility toward the subject matter; a lot of the reviewers were irritated by it. Male chauvinism was a very sensitive issue at the time. A lot of people were very hostile about those macho qualities being laughed at. In 1978, to reduce that to laughter was threatening and insulting.

It got labeled feminist, which was really crazy, because before I had written this show, I hadn't even noticed the feminist movement very much. I wasn't active politically in any feminist issues, I had never joined any feminist groups, but I wrote this show and suddenly everybody was inviting us to come and sing for every gathering of feminists around the country. I've carried that label ever since. Indeed I am a feminist, but that wasn't my initial idea in writing that.

NANCY FORD Even with the bad notices, Joe was so supportive. He kept it open, and that was a real act of faith. A lot of producers might have closed it based on the reviews. But he saw that there was an audience for it, and that the audience was building. He saw it as being especially appealing to women who were alone, and he knew there were a lot of those in New York. So he nurtured it. Thank goodness.

I often saw arguments between people in the audience. One time a man told Gretchen that it was a good thing he didn't have a gun because he would have shot her if he had. There was a line in the show where the manager says, "Linda Ronstadt doesn't have wrinkles," and someone in the audience said, "She will!"

There was a lot of connection from the audience. It was very life-affirming for a lot of women who were trying to be independent. They felt good when they left the theater because the play was saying, "You can do it. Go on. We know it's tough, and there's a lot of pain involved. But ultimately, there's a triumph, too."

GRETCHEN CRYER At first, we were probably going to close at the end of the six-week run that had been planned for the show. But I was in it every night, and I could see the audience response: they were going crazy about it, coming back in droves to talk to me after the performance, sending so many letters, fan mail and stuff.

Joe called me up excited one day and said, "I think we've got an audience." There was an article in the *New York Times* that there were fifty thousand single women in the city of New York. "We ought to be able to tap into that audience," he said, so he got the idea of continuing to run the thing. I will always be thankful to Joe for hanging in there with it, for responding to the public response to it, for having faith in it.

We were trying to figure out how to pull people in on Wednesday nights, because Wednesday was very sparse. We always had people coming backstage after the show, sitting around in the greenroom and having discussions, so we thought, "Why don't we just invite the audience to stay in their seats and talk to the cast?" We had some incredible discussions on Wednesday nights. People got to air their hostilities; they got into fights in the audience, terrible fights.

There was a tender moment at one point in the show, and I remember one man in the audience moved over to put his arm around his wife and she went, "Don't *touch* me!" so loud we all could hear it onstage. Often wives wanted to stay for the discussion and husbands would want to leave, so we would have things going on like, "All right, you just stay, I'll be in a bar across the street." Or "If you wait too long, I'll be at home, just get home however you can."

During the discussion, often we would just sit there in the middle of it, while the audience was battling it out around us. It would be about sexual politics, relationships between men and women. Quite often, the women had some kind of bone to pick with the men. They had seen something in the play which they identified with, and having heard it talked about onstage, they felt like they, too, could talk about it, that they would have some kind of an ally.

For instance, a wife could suddenly say something which she'd been aching to say to her husband for a long time. Knowing she'd be backed up, she wouldn't have to make her little case all alone. And then he would say something, and he'd be backed up by other males in the audience. It became a public forum for very personal issues. I never ceased to be amazed and stimulated by every one of those Wednesday-night sessions. It never got boring.

ROBERT KAMLOT The women are the theatergoers in this country, and they drag their husbands. And they loved it. The timing was absolutely right. It was a gentle, soft-rock musical that had something to say about the women's lib movement. We moved it to the Circle in the Square downtown, and it took off and ran down there for quite some time. Between the Public Theater and the Circle in the Square, it probably ran about three years. And we licensed it to a number of other producers throughout the country, which was the first time we did that. And we made a lot of money. That show probably made about $600,000 for the festival.

GRETCHEN CRYER The Public Theater is the one place that gives a piece a chance to find its own audience. If I had done *I'm Getting My Act Together* in any other arena, with any other producer, it would never have gotten out there. It would have closed within a week.

28

The Brotherhood,
the Birthday Party, and *Ballroom*

1978

Bernard Gersten, Mayor
Ed Koch, Mike Nichols
© Bill Stahl

JOE: Why do you suddenly turn against me? After all these years together?
BERNIE: I haven't turned against. I'm stunned.

—From *Take a Dream*, by John Guare, written for
and performed at Joseph Papp's surprise fifty-seventh
birthday party, Delacorte Theater, June 22, 1978

One: The Brotherhood

PEGGY BENNION PAPP   Bernie was one of the first of Joe's friends from
the Actors' Lab that I met. It was an extremely close relationship. They had
an enormous amount of fun together, and they were very funny together.

They were almost like a comedy team, because they would start punning at each other and puns would go on and on. Bernie was a very effusive, warm, wonderful guy, extremely admiring of Joe.

MEIR ZVI RIBALOW We'd have these meetings, and Joe would come in and say, "This is what we're gonna do," and start talking in characteristically visionary terms about what was going to happen. And then leave. We'd all watch him go and turn around and Bernie would be sitting there, waiting till he'd gone. And Bernie would say, "Okay, now, you do this, and you do that, and this is how we're gonna do it."

Joe didn't even want to deal with that because it would distract him from thinking about the big picture. And no matter what abstractions Joe was tossing out, Bernie could translate them into what we actually had to do. Bernie had a great gift to field what Joe was saying anywhere it was hit to him and make a perfect, seemingly effortless throw to first base. He was like Brooks Robinson out there.

MEL SHAPIRO Joe was Warner Brothers, dark, moody, and probing; and Bernie was MGM, sunshine and Technicolor and tap dancing and vivaciousness.

MARY GOLDBERG The two of them made one person. Even though Joe's always coming out with funny one-liners, he's more tormented as a person, more in touch with a certain seriousness and angst, with the not-so-sunny side of the human condition than Bernie. Where they complemented each other very well was that Bernie was able to bring a lighter side to things. Bernie, for instance, was the one who would organize the parties. And he organized great parties. I mean, if it was up to Joe, I don't know that we ever would've had parties.

Two: The Birthday Party

BERNARD GERSTEN It started as a result of two funerals. Walter McGinn, an actor who had been in *That Championship Season*, died, as did

John Cazale, Meryl Streep's friend. After each death there was a memorial gathering at the Newman Theater, and at the end of the second, I recall saying to Irene Worth, "How awful it is to have these things, these memorializations of someone when they're dead. If you're going to celebrate somebody's life, you ought to do it while they're alive." And I resolved to do a celebration of Joe while he was still alive.

What was the occasion? The most obvious one was his birthday, and the one that was coming up was his fifty-seventh, the same as Heinz's 57 Varieties. "That's no celebratory birthday," I thought. "There's fifty, there's sixty, but fifty-seven?" But I felt it didn't matter, the thing to do was to do it now. There seemed to be a kind of urgency to it for me. I convened a small group, the preliminary planning group, and said, "I have this idea to create an event that will celebrate Joe's life and the festival's life simultaneously."

I think from the first we said it would be a surprise party, because Joe would have disapproved of it. It was a two-level thing: to surprise him, because that's fun, and, though I don't think I ever thought of it consciously, because if he had agreed to doing it, then he would have taken it over. "There's nothing lost if the surprise is blown," I said. "If he knows, so what? But let's try to do it."

We decided on a ruse, a decoy act. Joe was in his country house in Katonah, New York, so we said, "LuEsther Mertz wants to give a small surprise birthday party for you for six or eight people, so please come." That was laid on in advance. LuEsther was in on the gag as well, and he accepted that.

GAIL MERRIFIELD PAPP Joe and I were spending a few days at Katonah. We'd been able to stake out the time to get away and we were enjoying it very much, kind of unwinding and planning to spend his birthday up there.

Then I got a phone call from Bernie saying there was this surprise birthday event that required Joe to arrive at the Delacorte Theater at a certain time on the night of his birthday, without any suspicion. I was kind of startled to hear this, but obviously it was a fait accompli. It sounded vast and glorious, with mayors and stars and prominent people in the audience and a whole program especially arranged. It was amazing that it had been kept secret from Joe, but he had no inkling of this and neither did I.

I think the main reason I hadn't been involved in the preparations for this party was that they'd think I would bring up the question of the propriety of it, which, indeed, I would have. There's no question I would have brought it up and I'm surprised nobody else did. Because our board of trustees was involved, and expenditures of money, it struck me as being completely cockeyed and improper, period. It's like something had gone a little crazy in the works.

What was being asked of me was to tell Joe a cockeyed story about having a surprise dinner. I was really just trapped. Here were mayors, all kinds of important people, plans made over a period of months and months. It was just something I didn't want to do, but I had to do it. And doing it put me in just an absolutely terrible state. I didn't want to lie to Joe.

BERNARD GERSTEN We knew that Joe was going to go home to Ninth Street first, so we planned to phone him there with a ruse to get him from the restaurant where he thought the dinner was going to be to the Delacorte.

There was a rehearsal in the park that night of *All's Well That Ends Well* that Wilford Leach was conducting, and we had Wilford say that he was having trouble with an actress, Pamela Reed. Wilford was very reluctant to do it because he was going to have to lie to Joe and act a part.

WILFORD LEACH I've never been one for surprise parties and the whole event was a nightmare for me. They were going to have this thing and they said, "You have to get Joe to come to the theater."

So we went to the office, and they had all these cameras going, they were making a film of the whole thing. They're dialing the phone and I'm still saying, "Look, this is not right. It's immoral. I know it's well intended but you can't do this to people." Not to Joe. It just didn't feel right, calling up Joe and lying to him. As a matter of fact, Joe later said, "You're the only one that came out of this all right because I saw you protesting on film."

BERNARD GERSTEN We had it timed out to a fare-thee-well. We all gathered at seven or seven fifteen and had supper. Everybody as they arrived at the theater got a picnic basket for two from Zabar's. We had recorded Wilford Leach's telephone conversation, and we played it to the audience, and we said, "The trap has been baited."

We had people along the roads with radios who were going to signal Joe's arrival. We darkened the house, so when Joe's car drove up to his usual parking space, he was coming into a really blackened theater. We had somebody with a flare gun who sent a red flare up as a signal that Joe had crossed the gate. Moments later he walked up onto the stage, and when he got there, the lights in the house were switched on, we released a thousand balloons, and everybody yelled "Surprise" and sang "Happy Birthday." It was beautiful, beautiful.

He was conducted to a seat and then the program began. We passed a microphone around the house and had testimonials. People spoke for one or two minutes. It brings tears to my eyes to remember it. It was a brilliant evening, the flow of entertainment beautifully planned. There were four fucking mayors of the city of New York in that room that day. The world was there. And the congratulations. I have never been so congratulated, I just had never received that.

CHRISTOPHER DIXON Bernie Gersten asked me to put together a crew to film the evening. The format was live acts interspersed with slides or a piece of video, all celebrating twenty-five years of the Shakespeare Festival. For instance, the original cast of *Hair* came out and did "Aquarius," then we'd cut to a clip of James Earl Jones doing Lear. George C. Scott called live from California. He said, "There's nobody alive who could have done what you've done," and Joe said, "I'll accept that." Helen Hayes sang "Happy Birthday" and the kids from *A Chorus Line*, having just done the show downtown, were bused up and re-created the last kick line.

At the end, Joe spoke for about thirty minutes: we kept running out of film. "This is the most overwhelming thing I've ever seen," he said. "I don't know how Bernie did this. I thought I was pretty good. Bernie, you're a genius."

BERNARD GERSTEN The party gave me satisfaction on a great number of counts, but not the least of them was that indeed I had caused to take place what I had so much wanted to take place. Joe had been ill at one time or another, and certainly he had felt his life threatened. I don't know that I ever really thought he would or might die, but I thought, not unreasonably, that anybody can die.

If I had to declare today what this was, it was a very pure act. I wanted Joe to be witness to a celebration of the esteem for what he had achieved, and let that celebration roll out in front of him, not after he was dead. It had no purpose other than that. It wasn't any seeking of his approval or seeking of anything. I just did it because I thought it should be done. It was that simple, it was that pure.

JOSEPH PAPP   I walked up these wooden steps that lead into the theater, and as soon as I got to the top step, I was flabbergasted. Sparklers started going off, music started playing, kids came running to me, photographers and cameramen were shooting this thing, and I was absolutely *stunned*. I couldn't have been more surprised in my life, but I was delighted. I felt, "What a beautiful, beautiful event." I don't think anybody in his own lifetime has had that kind of recognition and love and attention.

There was a whole show put on, and there was an original play that John Guare had written. I took it in the spirit of the evening, as a satirical thing, a caricature, even though it did say that I was the coward and Bernie was the one protecting me, which was hardly the fact. It didn't bother me, but Gail was a little more offended by it; she felt more about it than I did.

BERNARD GERSTEN   There was one significant area that did indeed prove to be a very heavy-duty problem. We asked John Guare to write a sketch, a very gay, very witty send-up. The only thing was that it rode roughshod over certain aspects of Gail. It was risky, it ran the risk of somebody taking offense, but it seemed very funny to me and good-humored. I thought it was okay.

I was played by John Guare and portrayed very sympathetically. Barnard Hughes played an irate subscriber who came into Joe's office waving a gun and complaining about the plays being put on. "I just want to go to the theater and have the lights go down and the curtain come up," he said. "I can't take any more guilt." Then he asked, "Which one of you is Joe Papp?" and Joe asked Bernie to come in and said, "There's Joe Papp." And

Barney Hughes shot John Guare as me. That kind of summed up John Guare's view of our relationship.

Joe responded very well, as I recall. But he was torn between his feelings about what he was seeing, which was a tribute to him, and his concern about his wife. That was the unplanned part, something we just had not calculated.

WILFORD LEACH The skit was, without a doubt, one of the more horrifying things. It was in such poor taste, I can't describe it—it was just awful. It was one of those things where you wanted to crawl under the seats because it was so horrible a presentation of two wonderful people. Joe can take it, he's used to it, but Gail, who couldn't be further from the person who was caricatured, isn't used to it. Satire's one thing, but this wasn't satire, it was just character assassination. I hated it, I was just physically ill. Joe's two kids, Tony and Miranda, got up and left, bless 'em, but Gail just wouldn't move. It was not a good evening.

GAIL MERRIFIELD PAPP Did I enjoy John Guare's skit? Yes and no. It was terribly funny, but I'll tell you, I was having a hell of a time. Because the human complexity of this event was that Joe's two youngest children, Tony and Miranda, had also been roped into this to sit with us. They had been kind of bumped around and were both in a very foul state of mind on Joe's birthday, and I was trying to deal with them not being in such a great state of mind.

It was sort of a brilliant producing feat that Bernie accomplished— he's a very skillful producer in his own right—and I must say, it was organized like a military campaign. I think he did it because of his feeling of devotion to Joe, to give Joe a whopping birthday party.

But you know, when you hear so many tributes to Joe, and you hear "legend" and "national treasure," you tend to think that people are trying to bury a person with adulation while they're still alive, and that aspect of it struck me personally.

BERNARD GERSTEN I was very gratified, but I suffered some pain afterward. I was aware of Gail, I felt badly, certainly, and I had to apologize. I sent her a plant, and I said I was not sensitive. And we made up and we kissed and we hugged and so on.

It was a hurt in the relationship, but I thought it would heal, that we would recover. I was a Communist Party guy from a long time ago, and if you did something wrong and somebody criticized you, you said, "Yes, I accept the criticism." What else were you supposed to do? We're a Western culture, we don't commit hara-kiri. You say, "I'm sorry. I was insensitive, and that was wrong." We were all insensitive. Nobody said, "Bernie, you really shouldn't do that." Nobody thought it was that terrible. It was a send-up.

My relationship with Joe in part was based on my never having been a threat to him, my never having been ambitious, my never having a need to push him off center and to take center for myself. That is not my role in life; one of the things that has given me my value is that I'm a very good second. And perhaps this altered it in some way for him, so that Joe's rationale, in part, about my departure was, "Maybe Bernie needed to be on his own."

JOSEPH PAPP I felt it was a beautiful, beautiful event, but as the evening wore on, I began to think, "Wait a second—I wonder how much this cost? And how come I didn't know about it at all?" I mean, after all, I'm running an organization. I slowly began to realize that the thing had been done under my nose, without me knowing it, and money—some $40,000, which was substantial at that time—had been spent without my approval.

Bernie was like my chief executive officer, a good guy with a warm, generous nature who knew his stuff. He had been in a position to quote/unquote "protect" me from anything that would be annoying or disturbing, things he felt I didn't have to hear about. You know, when you get too protected, suddenly you are protected from things that you should know about. And this party became to me an amazing display of that.

How could something on this enormous scale have been perpetrated—I'll use that word; policemen always say "the perpetrator"—without me knowing? How could it have used the resources of the Shakespeare Festival without my having the slightest inkling about it? I thought, "That's the way revolutions are made or governments are overthrown."

So there was something that was not kosher in this whole thing, even though I certainly will say it was an extraordinary event, and I didn't let any of my negative feelings about how it came about take away from my enjoyment and appreciation of it. But the incident stayed with me and it was, I think, the harbinger of what would happen between Bernie and I later on.

Three: *Ballroom*

JEROME KASS I was working with Michael Bennett on a film project called *Road Show* when Bob Avian, who used to tape musicals for Michael, told me that the one made-for-television movie that he had ever taped was *Queen of the Stardust Ballroom*, which I had written.

One night we decided to watch it together, and Michael said, "This would make a great musical. Furthermore, it would be the perfect musical to do after *A Chorus Line*, because instead of its being about young people who are dancers, its about *old* people who dance." In some way he saw the story, which was about a woman in her late fifties whose husband dies and who falls in love at the Stardust Ballroom, as a geriatric *Chorus Line*.

Michael anticipated that *Ballroom* would cost a million dollars and it seemed like the most obvious thing that Joe would provide backing. I don't think anybody sat down and said, "Now, who are we going to get to produce this?" *A Chorus Line* had been such a huge success and so important for the Public Theater that I don't think there was ever any question that Joe would do whatever Michael wanted to do.

MERLE DEBUSKEY Michael came to Joe and said, "Look, let's do this together." There was no question Michael was doing it for Broadway; he could not, he felt, do it at the Public Theater, in an institutional environment.

Joe didn't immediately say no, but he had some second thoughts about whether it would be proper for him to become involved. "I don't think I ought to put the Shakespeare Festival's finances at risk for a Broadway production," he said. "I think it would be improper for me to do that." One may differ with that feeling, but you can't say he's wrong.

Some of us—Bernie principally, and myself as well—felt, "Look, if this is Michael, someone who has given us our greatest good fortune, and he says, 'I want you to participate with me on another project and it won't fit down here,' even if it is going to Broadway, why not? Joe, we owe it to the guy. He's an artist, and we owe it to him as an artist."

BERNARD GERSTEN *Ballroom* started independently of the festival, and Michael had had one workshop prior to Joe's birthday party. Joe had his usual mixed feelings about things, but finally, he said yes, we would do it.

Then, about two or three days later, Joe said, "No, I don't want to do it. I really don't like the material." And what I felt at the time, and nothing that has happened subsequently has persuaded me otherwise, was that Joe had a grudge against Michael, and the grudge was that Michael did not behave like a good son.

He did not come to Joe and say, "Joe, I have a wonderful idea for a musical, *Queen of the Stardust Ballroom*, and will you help me do a workshop of it?" Michael had a yearning for independence, he wanted to be free of Joe, he wanted to produce the work and be free of everybody.

There were three separate instances in which Joe said yes and Michael said yes and then it would come unglued. Nothing objective would have happened, except that change of opinion. At one point Joe said, "No, I just won't do a show straight on Broadway. That's a violation of what we're supposed to do." I said, "Why?" When he turned it down the third time, I was so disappointed I said, "Joe, do something for me. Michael wants me to work on it, and I want to work on it, and I can do that and still do all my festival work as well."

"No, you can't do that," Joe said.

"Joe, I'm going to work on the show whether you let me or not."

"You can't do that. You're not accepting my decision. You're not obeying my order."

"Joe, I'm gonna do it."

"Then you'll have to quit," or words to that effect.

"I won't quit. You'll have to fire me."

"Then I fire you."

And he gave me a letter the next day, saying, "In consideration of your insubordination, I herewith give you notice." I was going to stay for a couple of weeks, but Joe said, "I want you to leave today. I want you to just get out." And so I had to get out.

JOSEPH PAPP Michael was always trying to emulate my work. He built that theater over on 890 Broadway just to emulate what I'd done. He developed *Ballroom* himself, but he wasn't the one that pushed me about investing in it. It was Bernie.

I told him I wasn't going to invest in that show. First of all, we can't invest in a commercial show—it's illegal for us to do so. Secondly, my evaluation was that even if we could invest in it, I wouldn't think it would be a good investment.

But Bernie felt he wanted to make the major decision about *Ballroom* despite my objection to it. There are always people that have been in the shadow of someone else and then feel, for some reason or other, that they want to come out front. It had to be made clear that Bernie couldn't be the decision maker in this instance.

Bernie's a very rare kind of person in terms of his value in an organization. I was very grateful to Bernie for, really, being very gentle and helpful and supportive of me in every possible way. He was a highly capable executive with a very good mind. He had all these virtues which made quite an outstanding person, but he was the person who brought this situation to a head.

He seemed to be in a psychological state of mind that was testing to see how far he could go; he seemed determined for me to fire him. I gave him every possible option. I said, "Don't insist on this, Bernie, because you're making it impossible for me." I thought it was just madness. But he wanted to make the decision. It reached the point where he said he would go there and work himself even if I said no. "You can't work for the festival if you're going to work there," I said. "You can't do both things."

It seemed to me he was determined to lose his job. "He really wants me to fire him," I thought. "He wants me to say, '*You are fired.*'" I couldn't believe what I was watching, but I couldn't see any other way. "Well," I thought, "if that's what he wants me to say, I'm going to say it," and I did say it. It was the most amazing display of someone saying to me, "Here, cut my throat."

It was very painful for me to make that move, particularly given people's reactions to it, but on the other hand, I felt it was absolutely the right thing to do. One of Bernie's favorite quotes from Shakespeare was "When two men ride a horse, one must ride behind." It has nothing to do with being superior; someone has to be responsible. There's a single leader in an institution who has to be in a position to make decisions and bear the brunt of it.

I was getting a lot of negative flak from people. Bernie's such a nice guy, and I was always the bad cop, so everybody said, "Oh, isn't it terrible, after all these years." But I'll tell you, Michael Bennett was the only guy that not only called but came over to me. "I understand what you're going through," he said. "People are blaming you; people think you're the shit. But I know exactly that you were not the villain of this piece."

MERLE DEBUSKEY I thought this was one of the most horrendous events in the lives of these people with whom I was intimate. These two guys went all the way back to just post–World War II, they literally cut their eye teeth together. So I went down and spoke to Joe. It was exceedingly emotional; we were both kind of teary, but my argument didn't get anywhere.

Joe reminds me of an imperial palm. They grow very tall and narrow, the fronds fall off as they grow, and the growth is only at the top. Joe is like that. Very majestic, all of his growth has fallen away, and the only thing that's left is that which is current. It stands there—tall, majestic, and lonely.

BERNARD GERSTEN My pain and anguish and despair when Joe and I were separated made that the most profound trauma of my life. My parents died at an old age, I haven't separated from a wife or lost a child, which I take for granted must be the most complex traumas in the world. So maybe I'm lucky that the worst thing that ever happened to me was getting fired by Joe.

Why did Joe let me go? Why did he do that? It's hard for me to understand it today. I think he made a mistake, by the way. Never mind for me, I think for him. He was always happier when I was there—it just made him happy.

In the course of the years since, what we've agreed on was that it was wrongheaded on both our parts and, unfortunately, there was no one who was able to alter our wrongheadedness. I said, "Joe, why couldn't you have just allowed me to do something wrong? Say I was wrongheaded in wanting to help Michael. Why couldn't you let me be wrongheaded? And it was Michael. It wasn't an alien; it was a friend. What would have been so terrible?"

There was no answer. It was unfortunate that neither one of us would budge from our positions. But on the other hand, why did I have to give in? Why couldn't he have given in? What was so terrible on that side?

I did bring a spirit to the festival, which just is my spirit. I supported Joe, and I could rationalize supporting him in almost any course of action that was not deadly immoral or deadly illegal or deadly wrongheaded. And in the course of doing that, I would whisper in his ear or push him this way or push him that way or interpose in whatever fashion seemed appropriate.

There's a word that I like to use to describe someone who behaves with someone else, and it is "handler," like a boxer's handler. The boxer comes to the corner, and the handler rubs his stomach and takes the mouthpiece out and pours water on his head and puts a Band-Aid on the cut and says, "Watch out for the left." That role with another human being is a vital role, and guys who work publicly are lucky when they have a handler.

29

The Pirates of Penzance
1980

Kevin Kline, Linda
Ronstadt, Rex Smith
© Martha Swope

A Pappadox, a Pappadox, a most ingenious Pappadox is *The Pirates of Penzance* at the Delacorte. Ingenious and inspired and—be warned, all rip-off entrepreneurs with visions of Fame via Xerox—absolutely inimitable. The 100-years-later sound and manner that director Wilford Leach, conductor-orchestrator William Elliott, actor-singers Linda Ronstadt, Rex Smith, Patricia Routledge, George Rose, Kevin Kline, and a crowd of other onstage and back-stage talents have devised for *Pirates* fit the operetta like a second, Day-Glo skin . . .

The show opens with 21-year-old Frederic being released from his apprenticeship to a band of pirates. He soon encounters the daughters of Major-General Stanley and is snubbed by all of them except Mabel. The pirates return to the scene and are about to carry off the girls to the nearest clergy-man, this being G&S, but are dissuaded when Stanley arrives and tells them he is an orphan. (Everyone knows the pirates never harm orphans, a fact that has kept the gang in rather straitened circumstances.) Later, however, the Pirate King and Ruth, former nursemaid to Fred and present "piratical-maid-of-all-work," tell the lad that since he was born on February 29, he is a long way from his 21st birthday and is still one of them. Frederic, being the operetta-subtitle's "slave of duty," tells them Stanley is not an orphan. The pirates attack Stanley's estate and overcome the frightened police, but Ruth reveals that the pirates are all "noblemen who have gone wrong," so everything is put right with rousing prenuptial chorus.

Leighton Kerner, *The Village Voice*, July 30, 1980

Yes, the New York Shakespeare Festival's production of *The Pirates of Penzance* does sound crazy. One needn't be an orthodox Savoyard to wonder what two American rock singers, Linda Ronstadt and Rex Smith, are doing smack in the middle of one of Gilbert and Sullivan's most beguiling operettas. Or to wonder why they are surrounded by an eclectic crew of Broadway and West End actors, all belting to the electronic strains of a small, stringless pit band. But if this *Pirates of Penzance* at first seems like a misbegotten ship of fools, I'll be damned if it doesn't sail. If I were you, I'd run to Central Park's Delacorte Theater on your first free moonlit night and save any doubting questions for the morning after . . .

Kevin Kline, cast as the clumsily swashbuckling Pirate King, is a musical actor of extraordinary gifts. A deft pratfall artist with an ability to convey deadpan innocence, narcissism and self-deprecating irony at the same time, the handsome, big-voiced Mr. Kline is blessed with the best qualities of Ben Turpin, Errol Flynn, Chevy Chase and Alfred Drake . . .

Maybe the New York Shakespeare Festival has forsaken Shakespeare this season, but it has nonetheless given us a rhapsodic midsummer night's dream.

Frank Rich, *New York Times*, July 30, 1980

WILFORD LEACH   You want to know how *Pirates* happened? Everybody wants to know how *Pirates* happened. Well, it is interesting. In the summer of 1980, the city did not give any money to Joe for Shakespeare in the Park, and he was very upset. We were at Katonah, where his summer house is, and Gail and Joe and I were driving along through the country.

Joe had just complained about the fact that he wasn't going to do Shakespeare: if they wouldn't give him money, he wasn't going to do it. Joe has a habit of sort of half whistling, and the thing that's interesting about it is that the lyrics are always relevant. We'd be in an elevator, for instance, having come from a meeting or something, and I'd say, "I know what's on your mind," because he always finds a song that relates to this.

So this time he's driving along and singing and I said, "Why are you singing 'Three Little Maids from School'?"

"I was in that when I was in school," he said. "I played one of the three little maids."

He's still singing away, and he said, "*The Mikado*'s a great production. You should do *The Mikado* in Central Park."

"Gosh, Joe," I said, "I don't think I have a thought on what you could do. First, I don't like Gilbert and Sullivan. When I was in high school, they always did a Gilbert and Sullivan every year, and I hated it. Secondly, I can't imagine a bunch of Americans dressed up, doing Englishmen playing Japanese. It's too many times removed."

"Gilbert and Sullivan's terrific," he said.

"Oh Joe, I just don't—"

"*Mikado*'s the best one. You should find out about it."

"All right," I said. "I'll go to Barnes & Noble, I'll get *Mikado* and some other things, I'll see what I can do."

So I went to Barnes & Noble, which had only two or three Gilbert and Sullivan two-record sets. I had money enough to buy only one pair of records, and I thought, "The jacket of *Pirates of Penzance* is terrific, and the other ones look so boring." And that's the truth of it.

I took *Pirates* home and stared at it. I'd read the Gilbert and Sullivan libretti and thought they were terrific, but when I went to see the D'Oyly Carte productions, I was just bored, so my assumption was that somehow the material didn't play, that the music wasn't any good.

At any rate, after staring at the record, I said, "Well, I've just gotta play it. I'll see what this is, and later I'll go get *The Mikado*." I put on side four, because that usually ties together all the music, and it was just wonderful. So I called Bill Elliott, the composer I'd worked with, and I said, "Bill, we're doing *Pirates of Penzance*," even though I had only heard side four.

The problem with doing classics is that they're classics. Everybody has an attitude and an image they want fulfilled. Clive Barnes has read twelve prefaces and he wants it to be like his favorite preface. The tradition of Gilbert and Sullivan is that you do it according to a set of stage directions which the D'Oyly Carte people will happily supply you with. Well, that doesn't interest me. I'm interested in it before it was a classic, thinking about how people experienced it when it was a new play.

In the nineteenth century, *Pirates* was pop music, it was sung on the street corner. And the vocal style was the popular style of the period. My interest was to say, "How can I get a contemporary audience to experience something like that first night when it was fresh, when it was not this thing distanced by a vocal style that is no longer appropriate? How do you eliminate the distancing?"

That's why I decided to use pop singers. The revitalization came from casting it very carefully, and then calling on the actors to treat it as a new work. My job was more than half done once it was cast.

Every morning when I woke up, I put on the television and watched *The Today Show*. A few days after this, John Rockwell of the *New York Times* was on, talking about new records. He said something about Linda Ronstadt, and I said, "Oh, god, yeah, that's the voice that I love. It's so pure and so beautiful, it's the real thing."

Joe was sitting in his office and I said, "I think we should ask Linda Ronstadt." And he said, "Oh, yeah, I've met her." And he said to his assistant, "Get me Linda Ronstadt on the phone."

LINDA RONSTADT It all started with Colette. I was sitting in my dressing room in one of those awful coliseums that you do rock-and-roll shows in and it just wasn't happening for me. I don't like the architecture in those big places and I was miserable. I'd bought this new kind of blue kohl for my eyes, and I was sitting there looking at it when there was a knock on the door.

A backstage official type came in and said, "A fan left this book for you." It was *The Vagabond*, by Colette. I had never heard of this writer before, but I had twenty minutes to kill, so I thought, "Oh, a book! Great, I'll read." I opened up the book and it starts with, "The girl is sitting in front of her dressing table. She just put blue kohl on her eyes, and she has twenty minutes to kill. There's a knock on the door." And I went, "What is this?"

I was just delighted with the book. This girl was so much like me; she had a dog and a weird boyfriend she called the Big Doodle. And I thought, "Well, this is really what I want to do. I want to play in a beautiful little theater with people there that are not all wearing T-shirts." Right after that, we went to Europe and played concerts in small, exquisite proscenium theaters, and I thought again, "I want to do shows in these kinds of theaters." So really, it was architecture that led me to Joe Papp.

I talked to my friend John Rockwell and I said, "I'd like to put a show together that is more theatrical."

"Oh, you really have to talk to Joe Papp," he said. "He's the most exciting guy in this whole field. You really must meet him." And he called up and made the arrangements.

I had no idea who Joe Papp was. I had no idea that he's the busiest man in New York, and that a million people, of infinitely greater magnitude than I, with much clearer ideas of what they would like to do, had been pounding on his door and standing in line, trying to get in to see him. I don't know why he saw me, but when we met, we had instant rapport. We just adored each other. Or at least, I just adored him. He acted like he liked me.

We talked, and I said, "I'd like to do something in a theater with a curtain." Looking back on it, I realize how completely ridiculous this was. He asked me if I could act, and I said that I thought that it might be similar to singing, but I wasn't sure. He listened very politely and said, "It's good to know that you're interested. If something comes up, I'll give you a call."

So when Wilford Leach saw Rockwell on television talking about me and said to Joe, "The person we really ought to get for *Pirates* is Linda Ronstadt," he said, "Oh—I know her already." So he called me up and the message I got was that Joe Papp wanted me to be in *H.M.S. Pinafore*.

My sister had been in that when she was twelve or thirteen and I thought it was the most wonderful thing ever. So I called up and said, "Oh, I'd love to do *Pinafore*." It turned out it wasn't *Pinafore*, it was *Pirates*, but Joe said I could have the part; I didn't have to try out for it or anything. "Hang on there," I said. "You don't even know if I can sing it. And neither do I." I insisted on flying back and auditioning for him, just to make sure they wouldn't throw up their hands.

WILFORD LEACH   George Rose was my first choice for the Major-General, and he was the first choice of the casting office. He came around and said, "I've never done Gilbert and Sullivan, but I'd like to." And George you leave alone. He comes prepared with a full and total character worked out and it's always terrific.

GEORGE ROSE   I think probably at this point in my career I am almost undirectable in the theater. The text becomes the point of my performance; ever since I worked with Noël Coward in 1953, I have come to the first rehearsal word-perfect. This was always his way of working. He said, "I cannot go home in the evenings after a hard day's rehearsal and learn lines. My mind isn't fresh."

I'd never done Gilbert and Sullivan. I came from a generation that was really very turned off by everything Edwardian/Victorian. That was mother and father and grandfather's standards, and extremely repressive. The only production I ever saw was *H.M.S. Pinafore* done by the local grammar school when I was a kid, and that didn't make me want to explore any further.

But when I was asked to do the Major-General, I'd just come off playing twenty-two weeks of a three-handed drawing-room comedy with Rex Harrison and Claudette Colbert, and I was raring to go at something that was slightly more meaty.

Also, I'm an inveterate record collector and I'd just bought a reissue of cylinders by a singer called Workman, a second-generation Savoyard who'd heard the original Gilbert and Sullivan cast and was considered probably the greatest interpreter of the patter songs. I listened to him, and I realized that the speed was absolutely incredible, and the precision was quite incredible as well. So I based the performance on that.

I was fortunate that I had some remarkable diction training from the Central School of Speech and Drama. It was founded by a lady called Elsie Fogerty who was the doyenne of English speech teaching. In fact, when Edward VIII, who had a very bad stutter, abdicated for Mrs. Simpson, it was to Elsie Fogerty that the king was sent before his radio speech.

She was a remarkable old lady and she had very, very set and precise ways of dealing with speech. We spent the first fifteen minutes of every day doing nothing but breathing exercises. We would then go to phonetics. We would have a piece of chicken bone placed between our teeth and attached to a string that went round our necks so we didn't swallow it. It was shaped like a Y at each end so that it would fit over the teeth and keep the jaw propped open, and we would do consonant exercises for many a half an hour with the jaws open that way. This sounds very Victorian, but it actually worked. It's technique, like playing scales on an instrument. It's got nothing to do with "How am I feeling today?"

I knew of Linda Ronstadt, but I must say her work I didn't know. I think it was Arnold Bax, the British composer, who said, "There are two things that I'm not interested in—incest and folk dancing." You can say the same about rock and roll as far as I'm concerned. I know it sounds very snippy of me, but you have to draw the line somewhere.

When we were introduced I said, "Where are you from?" She said, "Rock and roll," and I said, "Where's that? Arkansas?" I thought it was something like Little Rock or Painted Tree. But she turned out to be a wonderful natural musician and she looked absolutely right.

ROSEMARIE TICHLER   I remember Kevin Kline being very glad that George Rose was in it because he didn't know what kind of a production would have Linda Ronstadt. Kevin was a theater man, and initially you hear Linda Ronstadt and you think, "What is this?" I told him George Rose and he said, "Oh wonderful, wonderful." And then he was very interested.

KEVIN KLINE   At some point Raul Julia was set to play the Pirate King, and the role of Frederic was open. That's a tenor role, and though I'm not a tenor, no one thought Linda had it in her range to sing the role of Mabel in the original keys. So they said, "Maybe we can go with a high baritone," and I came in.

Then they got word that Linda wanted to sing in the original keys, so they did need a tenor, and around the same time Raul signed a movie deal with Francis Ford Coppola. So he dropped out and they said, "What about the Pirate King?" That's when I sat down and heard the record all the way through for the first time, and I thought, "This is the Marx Brothers, really silly, funny, wonderful stuff."

But then I thought, "Oh god, I don't want to do another musical with a lot of physical comedy in it." I've always been sort of wary about musicals. The acting there is usually embarrassing to me, because you've either got great singers who are not really actors or actor/singers who have to act in such a way that if they suddenly launch into "Oh, what a beautiful morning" it seems perfectly natural. It's a fairly overstated form and it *can* induce bad acting. So I thought, "Naahh, I've done this," and I kind of passed on it.

But my agent kept saying, "I think you should do it. It's good to work, it's work that gets work." Then a play I was going to do in Los Angeles got put off and my agent again said, "Why don't you do the Pirate King?" I just happened to have bicycled through the park to get to his office, it was spring and it looked great, and I thought it was a sign or something. "What the hell," I said. "This using rock stars is another Joe Papp–Wilford Leach goofy idea, but it'll be over quick." Little did I know.

WILFORD LEACH   Kevin wanted to play Frederic, and I said, "Kevin, you're just too old. It should be a boy. But you should be the Pirate King." And he said, "No, no."

A month went by, and one day I looked out of the window of my office and there, just sitting on the steps of the festival's administrative entrance, was Kevin. So I knocked on the window and said, "Stay there. I'm coming down."

I sat beside him on the steps and I said, "Kevin, are you going to do it?" And he said, "No. I didn't want to come in. I just wanted to think about it one more time out here." And I said, "Well, think about it one more time, and tell me you're going to do it." And he sat there a minute and said, "All right. I'm going to do it," having just said he wasn't going to do it. So that's how Kevin came into it.

Meanwhile, I couldn't find a Frederic. We auditioned maybe fifty tenors, and they were all tenors, you know what I mean. They all sounded the same, and they couldn't do it. Then we went into the rock/pop world. We saw every possible rock singer, because they all wanted to sing opposite Linda. But they simply couldn't do it; they did okay down below, but they couldn't sing the top stuff. Also, they didn't have that purity. Gilbert and Sullivan is so airy and transparent. You can't have these sort of jaded guys in it, especially opposite Linda, who was so pure and sweet.

So we came right up to Saturday, and we were rehearsing Monday, and I still didn't have anybody. The week before, checking out of a supermarket, I'd seen all these teen magazines on the stands. I called the casting office and said, "What about these boys? I mean, they *are* Frederic." Rex Smith was on one cover, and one of the casting women said, "Oh, yeah, I met Rex Smith, I'll find out." She called, he was interested, and he flew to New York and arrived Saturday night.

"What is this thing?" he said.

"Gilbert and Sullivan," I said.

"What's that?"

"Well, I can just tell you about the role. It's like Errol Flynn."

"Oh! Good! I can do that."

"What makes you think you can do that?"

"I have Errol Flynn's picture in my wallet." And he took out his wallet and, be damned, he had a picture of Errol Flynn.

"Why are you carrying that?" I said.

"Because I intend to swash until I buckle."

"You are Frederic," I said. "Anybody who would say that with a straight face and mean it is him." It was so naïve and utterly correct because it was sincerely felt. Then I asked, "Can you hit a B flat?"—which is the top note.

"Sure, I can hit a B flat," he said, and he did. Just out of nowhere, he hit this B flat.

"That's amazing," I said, and he did it again.

"Stop!" I said. "You only get to do one a day." It's a physical thing, nobody can do it five times in a row, unless you're trained for the opera, and none of them would ever do five in a row. But I couldn't stop him from hitting the B flat.

I called Joe right then and said, "I've got a Frederic."

"What makes you think you've got a Frederic," he said.

"He just told me he intends to swash until he buckles. And he can hit a B flat."

"Let me hear the B flat."

So I took the telephone, gave it to Rex, and said, "Sing a B flat." He did and Joe said, "Okay, you got the job."

REX SMITH I started out doing hard rock and roll. A lead singer in a band was what I always wanted to be, and at that point I'd signed with Columbia Records and done two six-month tours opening for Ted Nugent, which was as rock and roll as you can get.

I'd never acted before, but someone asked me to do a TV movie and this successful single, "You Take My Breath Away," came out of it and I became a teen idol around the world. And suddenly I also became like a no-talent, teen-idol bum. I was not some guy lying on the beach at Malibu. I'd paid as much dues as Bruce Springsteen, but suddenly I was sitting in radio stations with people giving me a hard time because I was a teen idol.

I played like the eighth generation of Danny Zuko in *Grease* on Broadway, and then I moved out to California. I felt it was time for me to come to Hollywood, but maybe I was a little premature in the thought, because I spent six months out here trying to convince my dog, Pal-o-mine, to go to the bathroom on the other side of the front door. That was my career at the time.

I went to New York to promote another TV movie and my manager said, "They want to see you at the Shakespeare Festival." I walked in and I sang a few notes and Bill Elliott went, "My god—you can get up there." I was just very cocky at that time in my life, and I kept going higher and higher.

Bill got really excited about my voice, and Wilford said, "What makes you think you could play a pirate?" I said, "I've got a picture of Errol Flynn in my wallet and I intend to swash until I buckle." I still have the picture, it's a beat-up old thing that says, "Flynn's third and last wedding reception was interrupted when he was handed a warrant for raping a seventeen-year-old." That was a little much. Will laughed and said, "Anyone who can come up with a line like that deserves the part." So they called Joe and they pretty much asked me to take the job.

GRACIELA DANIELE   The first day of rehearsal came, and when Rex came in, I must confess I thought Wilford was crazy. Here comes this gorgeous California beach boy. I mean, to die. To die. The beauty is like, you just want to jump on him. The suntan and the physique and the little shorts and the wonderful body.

He had a tennis racket, he was playing with a ball, and I looked at him and thought, "Boy, is he gorgeous" and "My god, that is not Frederic." And I turned to Will and said, "I don't know what you saw in him." But what Wilford saw was his naïveté, his innocence. He can play macho and all that, but inside him is a child. And Wilford knew exactly how to draw this out of him.

WILFORD LEACH   The rest of the cast, which was New York actors, were very skeptical about him because his background was the teenybopper world. For the opening rehearsal, one of them somewhere got a hold of this big poster taken by Richard Avedon of Rex, nude except for this little thing, and they put it up on the wall.

So in came Rex, and he walks by the poster and looks at it as if it were the most normal thing in the world to have this big picture of himself on the wall. They were all waiting for him to be embarrassed and humiliated, and he didn't react to it at all. It was the most normal thing in the world to him, which was Frederic. He was just so open.

REX SMITH   I got a lot of razzing because of the teen-idol stuff—Mister Sexy Rexy—but I hardly noticed. I was handed the music on Monday morning and found out I had to sing thirteen songs per show.

I used to come offstage and listen to everybody else complain: "The spotlight's not following me" or "My mike's not up." And I'd go, "Guys, I wish I could hang around and complain, but I gotta go back to work." Everybody's back there drinking tea or whatever and complaining about it's too hot in the theater, and I've got two seconds to try and get some spit back.

That B flat in "One Maiden Breast" was like Moby Dick for me. It was the bane of my existence. My day was made or broken by that one note. I reached a point where I started literally choking on that note. I was thinking too hard about it and my throat was really getting tight.

I couldn't figure out a way to beat it until I read Jim Bouton's *Ball Four*. Then I just thought of my B flat as my fastball, and going for that breath as my windup. I started calling matinees doubleheaders and getting really sick about the whole thing, but it worked and psychologically I was able to beat it.

First day of rehearsal, I see Linda Ronstadt and I'm going, "Mmmm-hmmm." Then I meet Kevin, and by lunch time I'm feeling pretty conspiratorial with the guy, at least enough to say, "I'm gonna ask her out." And Kevin goes, "Let me give you a little Broadway advice: don't date your leading lady." Next week, he's taking her out. So that was the first lesson in theater I learned from Kevin.

Kevin's the most charming guy I ever knew. He was like my John Houseman. My Southern accent was driving him crazy, and he would have me in the stairwell on breaks going, "Get, not git. Consequently. Henceforth." Working center stage with him is like two years' worth of Juilliard right there. Because that guy is like a black hole. Everything implodes around him and if you're not keeping up, then you're left way behind.

But Kevin learned a few things from me, in terms of just sort of ripping it up. One night we were back at my place, we were going to have some dinner, and I got him on the actor's idea of having a few drinks.

"Listen," I said, "it seems like the Pirate King would have taken Frederic back to the grog one night as sort of a rite of passage." And he said, "Yeah, yeah. Now wait a minute, characterization, I can see that, I can see that." As long as you justify it with Kevin, you can get him to do about anything.

"Let's just have a little snort of this vodka here," I said. We never did get out to dinner; we just sat at the grog table drinking vodka. We ended up just juiced out of our minds and ran out into the streets of New York, Kevin singing "Pirate King," jumping on trash cans and swinging on poles. Little did people know that they were getting for free what they were going to be paying for in about six months. The last I saw of him, he was in the middle of the street, on his knees, going, "I didn't know life could be so fun." That was the last statement out of his mouth.

KEVIN KLINE Frederic is the Pirate King's apprentice, and Rex and I had a parallel relationship running offstage. Here was a guy who was all eagerness and earnestness and energy and youthfulness and handsomeness and virility—he made me feel so old. We hung out together and got roaring drunk one night. We started drinking vodka and apple juice, in character, which means you don't do sips, you do draughts. Rex claims I was in a gutter, spouting Shakespeare, about two o'clock in the morning.

The night was still young then, but the next day we had to rehearse and I have never been so sick in my life. We had to rehearse this patter song, all this "ha-ha-ha" and I could barely move. We were so hungover that it forced a kind of economy of action. We were bleary-eyed and in tremendous physical pain, but what came out of it was so funny. Our physical condition gave it an edge, and I began to understand why so many great actors were drunks.

Wilford Leach had said, "I want to do this as if it were written for us, today, to do. Let's just make it our own, and find our way of doing it." Wilford and I talked, and we decided the Pirate King is just like an Errol Flynn who misses, or someone who's carried away with the romantic image of being a pirate and kind of overdoes it a bit. Because you find out at the end that they're not pirates, they're all noblemen. The essential comedic ingredient was they're all people trying to do something they're not, which is always funny.

All of my misgivings or doubts about these rock singers proved to be unfounded. They were completely dedicated and hardworking, and their freshness, their naïveté about stagecraft—not knowing upstage from downstage or offstage—provided a freshness which was crucial to the spirit which infused the production.

There was a wonderful honesty and lack of pretension about Linda that gave her a presence and an undisputed charm. She would do what was required, but she was not interested in becoming an actress. She was learning as she went along, but she was smart enough to know she wasn't going to learn to act in four weeks. I think she made it apparent that she was there to sing the songs. It was like, "Look, I'm not going to try to fool you all out there into believing I'm an actress. I'm not. I'm a singer. And I'll do what I can."

LINDA RONSTADT We never slept that summer. We had too much fun to sleep. In terms of just great camaraderie and artistic exhilaration, that was the most fun I've had.

Will was always teasing me; he was being like the busy bee, saying, "I got you somebody really cute for Frederic." The first I saw of Rex was this giant life-size cardboard thing of him and I went, "Are you kidding? Who is this beach boy?" I was afraid that he would have kind of a rock-and-roll attitude and turn out to be one of those people I was trying to flee from.

But as soon as I met him, I just adored him. He is like a giant puppy dog, a huge golden retriever. When we walked into the rehearsal room, he took my hand and said, "Do you know what this is? This is like going into church." And I thought, "This is it, the Colette book. Here I am."

I modeled Mabel after Snow White, because she was just my favorite girl. The great thing about Snow White is that she was so earnest and pure and sweet, and she had the most beautiful, exquisite tiny soprano voice. Now Mabel took herself a lot more seriously than Snow White did—Snow White was a lot better at laughing at herself—but basically Snow White has a real good heart and so does Mabel.

But when I really learned about her character, I used my dog Molly as a model. Wilford doesn't do a lot of telling you what to do, which is great for a seasoned actor but I didn't know anything. I didn't know not to turn my back on the audience; I didn't know that I couldn't talk in a natural voice. And I was asking everybody, "What do I do?"

One of the pirates, Keith David, said, "Look, here's what it is: Mabel wants Frederic, and that's all she thinks about." And my dog Molly can concentrate on things like that. When she sees a squirrel or something and she wants it, she has a way of cocking her head.

So I started being Molly onstage, I even used to imagine that my bonnet had little ears. The funniest thing was, one of the chorus girls came up and said, "They say dogs and their owners resemble each other, and sometimes you do the things that Molly does." It was so ridiculous, but I didn't know anything about acting, it was all I had. A canine soprano I was.

Directors are accused of being control freaks, but Wilford was not competitive and ridiculously egotistical in that way. When he saw that somebody was getting ready to cause trouble, a difficult spot where someone's ego might be bruised or where someone wasn't seeing things clearly, he would always be able to step back and wait until that person could find their way.

If they still couldn't after a long time, he'd enlighten them, but he would do it so gently and so sweetly, he never did it in a way that was devastating or destructive. That really knocked me out, because I'd seen too many other people who just love to throw their weight around just because they can do it. And he never did that.

JOSEPH PAPP Being of a kind of gentle nature, Wilford is always amused by people who are tempestuous. I guess that's why he likes me. He came from an academic background, teaching at Sarah Lawrence, and he started with me as my assistant on a production of *Henry V*. He likes what I do in my way, but he's an entirely different director than I am.

His greatest skill, aside from having a very strong conceptualization of things, is that he doesn't go after it with obvious intensity. He creates lots of room for the actors, encouraging them to create themselves. He never imposes on them. You'd see him walking around with his hands in his pockets and you'd think he was just an innocent bystander observing what was going on, but actually he has set certain things into motion and they're working, self-generating. I admire that. I learned a lot just by watching him.

WILFORD LEACH Anything that I'm enthusiastic about or have a deep interest in, Joe is always so supportive of. He does come up with thousands of ideas for everybody and everything, but he would never force it. Besides that, *he* wouldn't even do it the next day. What he says on Monday isn't what he does on Tuesday. Consistency is not his problem.

At one point, Joe came rushing in with some lyrics that placed *Pirates* in the Civil War and made it about the *Monitor* and the *Merrimack*. And then another time he thought it should be about street gangs in New York. He kept coming up with these ideas and finally one day he said, "You know what it is? I don't like pirates. I hate pirates. I don't like the way they dress. I don't like them as characters." This was one week before first rehearsal, and I said, "Joe, I can't think of any way that I'm really happy to do *Pirates of Penzance* without any pirates." He said, "All right, all right," and that was all that was ever said.

KEVIN KLINE It was like a celebration in the park. We were getting these prolonged standing ovations every night, and then people started saying, "Well, this is going to move to Broadway." And I said, "What? This? Come on, it's just a romp. We're just having fun here."

Because there were no matinees in the park, I'd developed a performance that was horribly draining and physically grueling. It was the most athletic thing I'd ever dreamed of, like I'd taken all the sports things I'd done in high school and added them all up for one evening's performance. The guy was a maniac, completely carried away with his own physicality. He would never walk when he could run; he would never step up on something if he could leap. A lot of Gatorade was consumed—a lot.

Then they said, "We're doing it eight times a week on Broadway," and it was like, "Oh, my god, I've created a monster here. I'm gonna die." And there certainly were nights when I wasn't sure I really felt up to this, but once you got the shirt and the boots on, that helped a lot.

I also used to play Beethoven in the dressing room. I would conduct it and that was a great kind of warm-up, it got your whole being into this kind of heightened state. I would conduct the chorale finale of Beethoven's Ninth Symphony, and ironically, when I went to meet Alan Pakula to talk about *Sophie's Choice*, he said, "I've added this scene which isn't in the book where Nathan's conducting the finale of Beethoven's Ninth," and I said, "I do that every night! That's part of my warm-up." It was like, "I'm your guy."

WILFORD LEACH Once the thing had opened on Broadway, there were so many articles saying how clever it was of Joe, just when *A Chorus Line* was going down, to put on *Pirates*. Well what's fascinating is that nobody in their right mind would put on Gilbert and Sullivan as a way to make money. Certainly there was never even the remotest thought that it was commercial. He didn't think to do it. None of us thought to do it. We thought it was going to be on for a few weeks and that was it.

REX SMITH One night I was going across the hall to see George. I was just in a towel, and here comes Marcello Mastroianni and Fellini, with the coats over their shoulders, going, "Bravo! Bravo!" Fellini's pinching my cheek, he's going, "In Italy, we have no actors like you," and I go, "Well, they don't have many in America like me."

Before I left New York and moved out to California, I took a walk down to the Public Theater and just stood across the street for about an hour. I was too shy to go in. I have this thing where if I'm not actively involved with people, I begin to feel like it would be kind of embarrassing for me to impose.

That was my school, and what a great education. Not just learning the craft. I'm talking about enjoyment and fulfillment. I've gotten a good paycheck out here, but I've never had the sense of fulfillment on a soundstage that could compare with the camaraderie, the sense of family, everything I had there. When you see *Pirates* as sort of a milepost or a reference, a lot of things pale next to it. Fellini never went to see Joan Collins; you could do *Dynasty* for eight years and Fellini's not gonna stop by with Marcello in tow.

30

Sam Shepard and *True West*

1980

Tommy Lee Jones and
Peter Boyle
© Martha Swope

True West is a tale of two brothers. Austin is a college-educated, modestly successful screenwriter ... desperately trying to finish a contemporary
Western love story in his mother's tract home 40 miles east of Los Angeles.
He is distracted by the arrival of his older brother Lee, a cat burglar and drifter
returning from self-imposed exile in the Mojave Desert. The two men struggle
against their shared parental demon, enacting finally the ritualized exchange
of identities Shepard has explored in earlier plays: Lee steals Austin's movie
deal with a dumb, old-fashioned story of his own, and Austin reduces himself
to stealing the neighborhood's toasters. Locked in their common yet irrecon-

cilable natures, each with a radically different vision of the *True West*, both are portrayed as victims of a new kind of Western brutality.

From "Saga of Sam Shepard," by Robert Coe, *New York Times*, November 23, 1980

....

"If I ever do another Sam Shepard play," said Joseph Papp, "Sam will have to be here. I won't let what happened stop me from producing him, but he'd have to be here."

"He'll never see another play of mine," said Sam Shepard.

Friction between the playwright and the producer over casting, a not unfamiliar theatrical ingredient, has erupted into a rancorous quarrel at the Public Theater over the production of Mr. Shepard's new play *True West*, which will have its official opening on Tuesday. It has also caused the play's director, Robert Woodruff, to resign and to dissociate himself from the production.

From "Joseph Papp: A 'Divisive Force' or a 'Healing' One," by Fred Ferretti, *New York Times*, December 20, 1980

....

Some day, when the warring parties get around to writing their memoirs, we may actually discover who killed *True West*, the Sam Shepard play that finally opened at the Public Theater last night. As the press has already reported, this failure is an orphan. Robert Woodruff, the nominal director, left the play in previews and disowned the production. Mr. Shepard has also disowned the production, although he has not ventured from California to see it. The producer Joseph Papp, meanwhile, has been left holding the bag. New Year's will be here shortly, and one can only hope that these talented men will forgive and forget.

At least their battle has been fought for a worthwhile cause. *True West* seems to be a very good Shepard play—which means that it's one of the American theater's most precious natural resources. But no play can hold the stage all by itself. Except for odd moments, when Mr. Shepard's fantastic language rips through the theater on its own sinuous strength, the *True West* at the Public amounts to little more than a stand-up run-through of a text that remains to be explored. This play hasn't been misdirected; it really looks as if it hasn't been directed at all.

Frank Rich, *New York Times*, December 24, 1980

. . . .

GAIL MERRIFIELD PAPP Joe and Sam Shepard met only once, in Joe's office. It was just the three of us. Joe felt there was something very powerful in Shepard's writing that had not been fully expressed yet in a play, and he said, "Why don't you write a family play?" I felt it was an amazing thing to suggest to Shepard. I thought, "Ay, I don't know how he's going to like that." But it was something he responded to, and at this point, he was also in need of money.

So what Joe did was to say, "I will commission your plays for the next five years. Anything at all that you wish to write." It didn't have to be a family play—that was just an idea, not a restriction. We sat around in Joe's office and though it was friendly and it was cordial, it was also a typical first meeting with polite-edged behavior because you don't know the person too well and you don't know what to make of him. And the first of the series was *Curse of the Starving Class* in 1978.

JOSEPH PAPP I've only seen him one time, and he came to me. I didn't know him that well, but even in our brief meeting, I was as warm to him as I could be to a young writer. He was kind of broke, and he said he'd heard that I was interested in plays about fathers and sons.

Well, I had that reputation. It's not entirely untrue, but it's not entirely true, either.

I may have indirectly played a role in encouraging him by saying, "Yes, I'm interested," but I can't claim any influence over his choice of theme. He already wanted to do that. "I have a play here that's a family play," he said, "but I'd like to make some arrangement with you because I need money. I'll promise you my plays for the next few years."

He was very protective of himself, and didn't hesitate to tell me that. He was very straightforward about it. We spent just a half hour, maybe forty-five minutes together. I let him know that I'd support him, that if he needed money, I would help him. I didn't ask him for plays. He volunteered. I might have just let him have the money. But he was so very proud, he didn't want money for nothing.

He had a certain slightly uptight bearing about him, his face was a little tight, and I thought, "That's the way writers get, being in the position of having to beg for money and all that shit." Certainly, my heart goes out to writers who can't make it, and I thought, "Well, give him a break and give him some money." I asked what he wanted, and we started to talk about $5,000, which I gave him.

At the time, not everybody was rushing to do Sam Shepard's plays. I respected him, but he wasn't exactly my kind of writer. He wasn't somebody of whom I would immediately say, "Gee, I would love to do his plays."

For one thing, it wasn't like with David Rabe or Elizabeth Swados, where the roots were set with me: he had started with another theater in San Francisco. And as happened earlier with David, I just didn't understand him that well. It took me awhile to comprehend how he thought and how he presented things. Remember, I was not of this generation, so I have to be given credit for adjusting to people from another generation and reaching a point where not only do I understand them but I become their strong advocate. So I was going through a learning process.

Sam said he had this one play to start with, *Curse of the Starving Class*. I even liked the title. I thought it sounded very socialistic, and also melodramatic, like "Papa, come out from behind the bar, Mama's been waiting for you all night." For the director, he was interested in someone he had worked with in San Francisco, Bob Woodruff.

ROBERT WOODRUFF I was working in a church basement in San Francisco when, totally out of the blue, I received a call from Sam saying he wanted me to do *Starving Class* in New York. The whole idea of going with the Shakespeare Festival, with Mr. Papp, who at that point was some Olympian myth whose path I never thought I'd cross, was staggering at that moment.

I flew to New York to meet Joe, and he was really quite wonderful. It was an exciting time for me, a whirlwind of events. I loved the material. I had a great ensemble of actors, and the audiences were agog. Joe was very supportive to the company, and working at the Public at that time was really the most exciting thing you could do in American theater. The energy around the building was just contagious. There was no other place you wanted to be.

Sam and I talked about the play just once, for a half hour. Basically, he gave me total license, total freedom, an unbelievable amount of trust to just go and do it. That's what he said, "Just do it." He'd never seen it performed, so he said, "If you don't want something, cut it." He doesn't fly, so he wasn't going to travel out to see it. He has a lot of friends in New York, and the reports that he had were wonderful, so he was not concerned about the work.

JOSEPH PAPP Sam's next play, *Buried Child*, was produced in New York by Theater for the New City. He said he'd promised them a play before we'd made our agreement, and would I mind if he let them do it even though he'd promised me his next five plays. What can I say—"No, this is part of the agreement. I want to do that play"? So though I found it interesting, I said, "If you made a promise to them, it's okay with me." And that play won the Pulitzer Prize.

The next play he gave me was *True West*. Again, this reminded me of David Rabe. It had elements of *Goose and Tomtom*, where the author splits himself into two brothers and examines the internal violence that's inherent in that situation. I felt it was a good play, and I said to Sam on the phone, "I would like another director to work on this play. Let me speak to some other people and let them speak to you." I suggested JoAnne Akalaitis, who was with Mabou Mines. Sam called her but he said, "No, no, a woman can't understand this play." He wanted Bob Woodruff again.

I tried everything I could to change that particular relationship. I felt it wasn't good for the play, because Woody was so tied into him—he was pale with his subjugation to this man that he stood in awe of. That's not healthy, I don't think, in real life or in stage relationships.

But Sam was very flat out about it. I could have said, "Well, fuck you. I don't want to do your play, then. Forget it." But he was out there, I was here, and I said, "Okay, I'll do his play this way if that's what he wants." That began the nightmare.

ROBERT WOODRUFF   I read the first draft of *True West* and I thought, "This is a bit odd. There's no ending, it kind of wanders around." The next draft was infinitely more concise and it started to feel brilliant. We were to do the first production in San Francisco, at the Magic Theatre, and that was the height of any collaboration I had with Sam. Peter Coyote played Austin, the writer, and Jim Haynie was Lee. It was riveting theater. These two actors, although they didn't see eye to eye on a lot of things, were brilliant together.

I've never known Sam to attend a production as much as this. He would come every night because he was just fascinated by it. He would sit in the back on one side of the theater, me in the back on the other side, and we'd just keep turning to each other and laughing.

During the course of the piece, we went to see the Sugar Ray Leonard–Roberto Duran fight, and we said, "This is exactly the play. Duran is Lee and Leonard is Austin." It was just an exciting time, and it was right. The production closed sometime in August, and I had to come to New York in September to cast it.

· ·

Fred Ferretti
From "Joseph Papp: A 'Divisive Force' or a 'Healing' One,"
New York Times, December 20, 1980

It was in the first production that the seeds of the battle were sown. Two unknown actors, Peter Coyote and Jim Haynie, were cast as the brothers. They were eventually replaced in the Public Theater production by Tommy Lee Jones and Peter Boyle, over the objections of Mr. Shepard and Mr. Woodruff...

"He convinced Woody to accept them," said Mr. Shepard.

· ·

ROBERT WOODRUFF   We knew from the get-go that we were going to do it in San Francisco and then New York, and there was some talk that we would bring the cast from San Francisco to New York. Both Sam and I felt that Jim's performance was worth repeating and showing to a New York audience, so I brought Jim out and he auditioned for Joe.

Since he'd already done the piece onstage, and was doing it this time with a reader, he was caught in that netherworld between auditioning and performing. "What exactly am I doing? I've done this role." So it was awkward, kind of a strange situation, and Joe just said, "No, I don't want this." I think he wanted a new production. He wanted to start from scratch.

ROSEMARIE TICHLER   Jim Haynie came in and he auditioned terribly. He was very nervous, he was anticipating things, he wasn't alive in the moment. It was terrible, and Woody knew it. We gave him another chance, and it was better, it was okay. And Joe said that if that's what Woody wanted, he could do it.

But I was working on it. I felt these were two fabulous roles and we could get two major actors to do it. Why get an okay actor to do it at that point? So we finally cast Tommy Lee Jones and Peter Boyle. And Woody approved them. In the twelve years I've been here, Joe has never and I have never forced the director to take any actor. It just doesn't work that way. The director and playwright have approval of actors. Obviously, Sam didn't see them, but Woody, as Sam's representative, spoke to Sam and it was approved.

GAIL MERRIFIELD PAPP   The casting of *True West* was not done against anybody's wishes, it was not done in violation of anybody's consent, and nobody ever sued us for breach of contract or understanding. That was very clear. The major problem I had was that the writer was not there to cast what is essentially a two-character play.

The way we cast is always a three-way affair, with the writer, the director, and Joe as the producer, and agreement has to be very strong. If the writer says, "No, I absolutely do not want this person," that is it. That's also true if the director or Joe happen to feel that strongly, but usually it's the writer that will take that kind of position.

It has never happened that we've cast against the wishes of the writer, even against our own better judgment, which has been several times. We just don't do it. So it was very difficult to go about all this without Sam being there. Not to have the writer as a force in the casting was truly incomprehensible.

JOSEPH PAPP   We ended up with two marvelous actors. Woody went along with it. He was playing both sides to stay alive. Sam was against it, but I convinced him. I said, "No, they'll be very, very good." There was a little pressure, a kind of resistance and fighting, and I finally got my way. I wanted those two guys. I kept saying, "I just don't like this other actor, and I'm producing the play here. If you're in New York, come here and we can talk about it. But I can't do this thing on the telephone."

ROBERT WOODRUFF   I'd done a reading with Peter Boyle before, and I'd found him to be an infinitely charming man and an interesting actor. I was introduced to Tommy Lee Jones, an actor who I'd seen on television doing an amazing Howard Hughes piece. I put them together, and there wasn't a lot of chemistry there, but Tommy had been off the stage for a while, and Peter hadn't done much stage recently, either.

So I said, "Okay, I want to go with this." I cast the play, with whatever Joe's influence was in steering me in that direction. I listened to him, I considered what he had to say, and then I cast the play. I don't remember any dogmatic response to the situation. He didn't cast the play. I try to get that very clear. I cast the play. Nobody twisted my arm. It was fine.

GAIL MERRIFIELD PAPP   My first bafflement came when I realized that there seemed to be a dark concept that was enveloping this production. I started asking people in my own department who'd read the script, "Did you find it funny? Or was it just me?" And I was not the only one. So I thought, "What on earth is going on?"

The next thing I heard was that there were problems with the actors. First I heard that they didn't get along with each other, then it was crazy things like they were scared of each other in a physical way and might come to blows. I thought, "My god, what's going on here?"

Woody was having endless difficulties with the actors. He would call Sam Shepard every night on the pay phones in the lobby outside the Anspacher. He was always at those phones, or at some other phones, calling and calling, talking and getting feedback, reporting what went on. It was all disturbed and he was unhappy. The actors weren't doing the things that he wanted them to do. He was not satisfied with what he was getting. But what they were doing was specifically what he'd asked them to do.

One evening, Woody looked very drawn and pale and really "sore besought" to me, and I felt, "Jesus, I wonder what the hell could be wrong?" So I said, "Why don't we talk a little bit after the show? Just you and me, just totally private, off the record and everything." Anything at all I might have to offer to him to try and understand what was going on, I was willing to do, because it was going wrong. We all knew it was going wrong.

He came into my office, it was very late at night, and I saw he was very overwrought. "Listen," I said, "is there anything at all that I can do? What do you need?" I meant what I said, but he really was not willing to talk straightforwardly to me. Or he couldn't. Somehow he couldn't. He was too caught up in certain kinds of relationships at that time, primarily his one with Shepard, to be able to have a conversation of that sort with me.

The next day I heard that he just left the show. With a few previews to go before press opening, he had simply left the show. We were all just shocked. Absolutely shocked. It's never happened before or since that the director left a show that way. I'd heard of people getting angry, resigning with a lot of hullabaloo, but I never heard of someone just disappearing overnight. If you're a professional, you really don't abandon people like that.

ROSEMARIE TICHLER Tommy was having problems with the role of Austin, which was a problem role. Even in the very successful production that was done by the Steppenwolf Theatre, it was Lee that John Malkovich played. Lee is the motor in the engine of the play. And Peter Boyle was a little bit of the movie actor and not learning his lines as he should. He doesn't like to memorize lines early, he likes to wait on that.

Both of them were strong men, and here was Woody, who was new. They were more experienced actors than he was a director. He's a very laid-back guy; he's not about being assertive and showing his power. I think they probably weren't listening to him. I don't think it was the play this time; it was the dynamic between the director and the actors.

And Woody was doubly worried because he had a great respect for and love of Sam. And since Sam wasn't there to see anything, he was functioning in two capacities and worried he was failing Sam. It was a terrible burden to fail Sam and, believe me, that is the truth of this production. Most directors just have, "There's a problem, the play's not working," but he had that burden on him, too.

Woody was panicking and didn't know what to do, and Sam, sensing his panic, was taking over for him and giving orders from the West Coast, telling Joe that Woody wanted to fire the actors. A week before previews he wanted to fire the actors! Sam was looking to get a scapegoat. There's an old saying in the theater: When the play isn't working, change the costumes. Blame had to go somewhere.

Joe respects Sam enormously, and though Joe is a yeller, he was conciliatory; he never yelled. I was in that office when Joe was saying, "Come in and see it. Come in right now. See what we're doing. I don't think we should fire these actors." Then Woody just lost it, he just disappeared. Then I started reading that Sam and Woody said the actors were forced on them. That's a total lie. I felt betrayed by Woody, and I didn't speak to him for five years. He's gone past it now, he's a better director, but it was a very bad time.

TOMMY LEE JONES Of all the versions of that play that were done at that time, around New York and around the country, ours was distinguished by being the worst. It had moments of brilliance, but I wasn't really delicate enough to play Austin, and Peter wasn't insidious enough to play Lee.

Woodruff didn't have the cast that he wanted, and many of the first steps were faltering ones. There was a certain amount of acrimony going on there. I think part of it had to do with language. Bob's directing methods were somewhat different than what Peter Boyle was accustomed to. Suppose one guy says, "A-B-C-D" and the other guy thinks he's said, "1-2-3-4"—it was like ships passing in the night.

Half the time, I couldn't understand what the director was saying. Couldn't understand him, couldn't tell what he wanted. I don't say that that was his fault or mine; it was like a dog and a monkey. There were very fundamental problems with the process, with the most basic aspects of rehearsal, like blocking. It was like trying to build a barn and you have a rubber hammer and glass nails.

I would have liked to have had Sam there. I guess he was in New Mexico at the time. I understand Sam doesn't like to ride airplanes, but hell, you can get to New York City in a pickup truck in two days if you don't waste a lot of time. He could have gotten his truck and come to town. But he had his own reasons not to, and that's none of my business. He might have been busy or something, I don't know. As I say, it's none of my business.

On the other hand, I've been a professional actor for almost twenty years, and for consistently high quality of the life of the mind, the only place other than the Public where I've been completely satisfied, where every dawn rose on a brave new world, was when I was a schoolboy actor, and that's the truth.

You felt proud to be an actor at the Public, happy to be an actor, privileged to be an actor, and that's not very common in my profession. The only way to avoid what happened on *True West* was if Joe would quit doing plays. If nobody would act or produce or direct, well, then, there would never be any such thing as an unhappy production.

ROBERT WOODRUFF What happens between brothers is one of the truly complex human relationships in our society. The hate and the love and the anxiety and the jealousies were the fundamentals which made the play rich and alive and surprising at every turn. Ultimately, the play's switch of roles and identities, which had to go on, had to come from the two actors being tuned into each other and exchanging these things. Not pretending to, but really doing it live and in the space.

So we began the work, and it was the most difficult experience I've had in the theater. There was a lot of pressure coming off of *Buried Child*, and the Sunday *Times* ran this huge story that Robert Coe wrote about Sam and the San Francisco production.

Peter was going through a hard time personally, and Tommy hadn't been on the stage in, I think, six or seven years. I had difficulty creating a situation in which they were going to grow, in which they were going to learn to trust each other and delve into the material.

They very much treated it on the top. Whatever chemistry was developing between them had a lot of bile in it, and it was not a healthy relationship. Ultimately, I think the production broke down because these two actors could not communicate on a level to make the work fruitful, and I couldn't provide that atmosphere. Wherever you want to lay it, that's where it falls.

These are two giant men, strong, physical presences, and yet there was nothing happening, there was nothing going on, no energy was being exchanged; it was kind of stopping two feet in front of each man, which I'd never seen before. Peter would call the stage manager, and I'd hear messages on her machine: "I'm not going to perform with Tommy tomorrow night because I don't trust . . ." There was no trust in this room.

I tried everything. At one point I just threw out the entire staging. I said, "Tonight there's no blocking." This was petrifying to them, but I had to shake up what was going on. As a director you pride yourself on being resourceful in order to get what you want in the performance. And this was an amazing test of that, because I was drawing on things I didn't even know I had to draw on.

I spoke to Sam constantly in Austin as this was going on. We talked about approaches of how to make it work with these two actors. We began a very long preview period, and about two weeks into it, I found myself waking up at night in the proverbial cold sweat and screaming, because this was the most frustrating situation I'd ever come up against.

It had worked in such a brilliant way the first time, the frustration of not being able to make something work this time was becoming devastating to me. I took two days off and went to the end of Long Island. It was already turning cold, nobody was there, and I walked along the beach for a while. At this point I decided I wanted to close the show.

I was convinced this was not going to work. I communicated this to Sam and Sam communicated it to Joe. I knew the possibilities of this play, and it was the dissatisfaction of falling short of that that made us want to close it.

A friend of mine came over to my house Wednesday of the third week of previews. We just talked for a while, and at that point I decided I had to leave the production. It didn't look like there was any help on the horizon and my mental health at this point was really not doing well.

I went up to Joe and I said, "I'm going to leave the production. Sam has already disowned it—through dialogue with me, he says it's not what he wants on the stage." The quote that I remember was, "You can't go around being a messenger boy for a playwright all your life." Then Joe took the production over.

I wanted my name taken off, but they wouldn't do that. I'm not sure what he did to the play. I didn't go back to that theater, and it took me a few years just to walk into that building again. It was a bit difficult, but I don't want to come off as a victim. I dealt with something there and it just didn't work. That's the theater.

JOSEPH PAPP You'd be amazed at how weird rehearsals can become. In a healthy situation, you find the actors are relaxed, talking directly to each other, everything that's said makes sense. There's hard work and there's good rapport.

But in an unhealthy situation, people are knitting their brows, there are arguments going on, people are fighting one another, you find everything in a state of disarray. It always reminds me of *The War of the Roses*, the same kind of situation, and that's what *True West* was like.

Tommy and Peter are marvelous actors, but they're also tough people to deal with, I'm telling you. Woody had a problem handling them. He didn't have the kind of maturity necessary to deal with the eccentricities and the charisma of certain actors, with all their moves. As in Shakespeare, it was "Woe to the country that has a child for a king." People start to fight, they blame themselves, then they blame each other, everything goes wrong. Because of the lack of leadership, some of the feelings that were in the parts were coming out and the actors were turning against each other.

I finally got Sam on the phone, and he was angry as hell. He'd been getting calls from Woodruff saying that these actors really can't do it—they don't have the ability and so forth. When a director starts to blame actors, watch out. Sam was furious that he didn't have his own people in it and was making some kind of threats to withdraw the play. I said, "You can't withdraw the play. It's on. Why the hell don't you come to goddamn New York and see what's going on? You're getting reports, you're not seeing it."

"I'm not coming to New York," he said. "I don't want to fly." I thought, "Why doesn't he walk or something," but he didn't want to come.

Peter was like crazy. He threatened to quit every day; those two guys were almost going to fight on the stage. I got Sam on the phone again and I said, "Sam, you better come here." And he started to shout at me, "I'm not gonna come!" I never heard a more hysterical voice in my life. High-pitched, completely out of character with Sam's public image as this close-lipped, taciturn Westerner. They don't know he's a screamer, a hysteric of the first water. Finally, two or three days before the critics were scheduled to come, Woody resigned. Sam Shepard told him to disappear, to quit, and he disappeared.

GAIL MERRIFIELD PAPP   We had a rudderless production. The actors came every day and sort of rehearsed themselves onstage, but they needed some help. Both Peter and Tommy asked Joe if there was anything he could do to help, and Joe, who was completely over his ears directing another show in another part of the building, said, "Well, not much." He spent about three hours over a period of maybe two days discussing the play with them, but he never took over the direction because he couldn't. There was nothing that deviated from Woody's production, nothing.

. . . .

FRED FERRETTI
From "Joseph Papp: A 'Divisive Force' or a 'Healing' One,"
New York Times, December 20, 1980

Mr. Shepard, in an interview from his northern California home, insisted that Mr. Papp had been a divisive force rather than one for healing and that "artistic control of the play was taken out of the hands of the playwright and the director by the producer, and by a producer who keeps saying how much he is doing to help new, young playwrights. He just has no respect for the relationship that exists between Woodruff and me, no idea of how we work together."

Mr. Shepard added, "His judgments are out to lunch." . . . He acknowledged that Mr. Papp gave him $5,000 for five plays in 1978 "when I was broke, but I'm going to refund the money and terminate the whole thing. I just can't have a relationship where I have to beg. He's not the only game in town."

. . . .

ROSEMARIE TICHLER   Sam disowned it and said he'd never do anything here again and Joe was taking over. I remember thinking, "It's one thing when it's true, but when it's fucking not true, it's infuriating." There was no way we could bring someone else in then, it was too late. Woody didn't ask that. It was just Sam, from afar, saying all this. He had no right to do that when he hadn't seen it. He acted very badly—I think that's the fact.

JOSEPH PAPP   Sam had said that he didn't want this production to go on, that it didn't represent his play, and I said, "I'm sorry, the play is going to go on." He said, "I'm going to deny this production," and I said, "You do what you have to do."

Sam destroyed his own play. It wasn't great, a lot of things were wrong, but it was a very interesting evening in the theater. But the critics had already been told that it was lousy work and they turned against it. I went ahead, but I expected the worst. I thought, "Okay, I'm gonna get it." Because once Sam Shepard says his play has been mauled by this King Kong producer who has no sensitivity and so forth, what chance did I have?

ROBERT WOODRUFF   I wasn't leaving the house; this whole thing just was not going too well with me. I don't know why I didn't get out of New York, but I didn't. Then I decided to get out of the house and I picked up the Saturday *Times* and there were one, two, three, four columns, and two columns of photographs, Joe and Sam talking about me, and the scribe did not talk to me at all. Sam said, "This isn't mine, this isn't Robert's, this is Joe's." I think he hyperbolized the situation, because I don't think he was privy to a lot that went on here. He was at a great disadvantage, being at that distance.

The last thing I wanted to see is these two guys talking about me. I mean, fuck, you two have some problem here, argue it between yourselves, I don't want to be the middle guy. This was devastating, and I remember the thought occurring to me, "This is history, this is how it's going down."

Because four columns in the *New York Times* is history; it could be "Lincoln Gets Shot at *Our American Cousin*." This gave me a whole new insight into the way the world works, the way history is written and who writes it. Because I realized that Joe was writing it and Sam was writing it and, if anything, I was going to be a footnote.

GAIL MERRIFIELD PAPP Tommy and Peter felt abandoned, and they said they were not going to perform unless either Joe or I were there at every performance. That was the condition. Well, Joe was directing, so I had to be there for them. I went to every performance we ever gave of *True West* for the whole goddamn run, going backstage before and after, two shows on Saturdays and Sundays. I was there every single time. I saw *True West* until it was coming out of my ears. I thought I'd go crazy if I saw the show again.

Also, it was painful to me because this is a show I'd howled over when I read it, and it had been given this dark, Pinteresque kind of portentous production. I was pleased in an excruciating way years later when it was done on Broadway by other people and was funny. I went to see it and I thought, "This is the show I thought we had that we should have done, and I don't know why the hell it didn't happen."

ROBERT WOODRUFF Sam was a writer of major stature by the time Joe took his work on. Joe's reputation was built on helping writers like Tom Babe to begin, and I think perhaps he misconceivingly treated Sam in the same fashion rather than dealing with a mature artist who knew what statement he wanted to make and how he wanted to make it.

THOMAS BABE When Joe invited Sam Shepard into his theater, what ought to have been an ideal match turned out to be the mismatch of the century. On his own as a writer, Sam had been doing the same thing that Joe had been doing as a producer. Sam had been saying, "The American theater is bigger than melodrama," and Joe had been saying, "The American theater is bigger than melodrama." Maybe it was destined that they would never get along, because there are titanic ambitions there about altering the face of the world.

JOSEPH PAPP I've said about David Rabe, if he weren't a writer, he'd be a murderer because there's so much there, so much anger. I don't think Sam would be a murderer. I don't think he has the guts to murder anybody.

31

David Rabe, Act IV: *Goose and Tomtom*

1982

David Rabe
Courtesy of the New
York Public Library

David Rabe, whose *Goose and Tomtom* opened Thursday night at the Public Theater, said yesterday that he had thought the play was closing, at his own request, last weekend. "If I hadn't looked at the newspaper," he said, "I wouldn't have known that my own play was opening."

Mr. Rabe, who sent messages to theater critics on Thursday disavowing the production, said he had asked Joseph Papp, the producer, to close *Goose and Tomtom*, and he thought Mr. Papp had agreed to do so. "When I didn't hear from Joe all week," Mr. Rabe said, "I assumed the play had closed. I've never had a dialogue, the way we would have in the old days." . . .

Mr. Rabe, who wrote *Goose and Tomtom* four years ago, financed two productions himself at the off-off Broadway Cubiculo Theater, but did not invite critics to review it. Subsequently, the New York Shakespeare Festival, which Mr. Papp heads, twice attempted to mount productions. One production closed in rehearsal; the other had a few preview performances and then closed.

"Admittedly, it's a difficult play," Mr. Rabe said. "I tried to nurture it at the Cubiculo. I gave Joe permission to make cuts and rearrangements in the new production, but with the understanding that it wouldn't officially open. If the critics write about it, by necessity they'll write about the play's point of view, but the production now just doesn't express that point of view."

On Friday, Mr. Papp had said that he and Mr. Rabe were still friends, and that Mr. Rabe, in fact, had offered him his next play.

"That was earlier," Mr. Rabe said. "Talking to Joe is like the *Perils of Pauline*, and I think this is the final chapter. I doubt very much that he'll do my next play."

From "Rabe Disavows the 'Goose' He Thought He Had Closed," by John Corry, *New York Times*, May 8, 1982

David Rabe has disavowed the production of his play, *Goose and Tomtom*, which opened Thursday night at the Public Theater. Perhaps it would have been more judicious of him to disclaim the play. It is difficult to believe that the author of the searing *Basic Training of Pavlo Hummel* and *Streamers* could have created such an impecunious caper comedy . . .

Goose and Tomtom (no explanation for their names) are a pair of jewel thieves, a couple of wrong guys, who in collaboration with a lady named Lorraine have amassed a swag of gems, only to have the booty ripped off by a rival gang. The play is a whodunit that leaves the theatergoer thinking, who cares?

The evening begins in the dark, with Tomtom (Jerry Mayer) suffering horror-movie hallucinations: the stage is filled with spectral, hooded figures, who arbitrarily return individually or in groups. The crowded nightmare is followed by the arrival of Goose (Frederick Neumann). Baited by their sensual moll (Gail Garnett), the two partners engage in a contest to see which one is the tougher mug. She pushes pins into their arms as they suppress groans of agony. Pins and crayons are among the show's unproductive running gags.

In the background there is a cut-throat mobster named Bingo, and lurking offstage are hoods with animal names like Joey the Rabbit and Monkey

Murphy. To complicate the anthropomorphy, Goose is convinced that he is a frog and Bingo is sure he is a puppy . . . The play is so formless that it could float right off the stage, and that is approximately what happens.

Mel Gussow, *New York Times*, May 8, 1982

DAVID RABE   I knew the play was difficult to figure out, and I funded my own little productions at the Cubiculo a couple of times to keep control of it and avoid problems. I guess I was being overly protective, but we couldn't figure out how to do it.

I thought, "I'm not going back with Joe," but then he had a meeting with my wife, Jill Clayburgh, about acting at his theater, and in the course of the meeting he asked about me. She came home feeling that there was a real sense of affection from Joe, kind of nostalgia and genuine interest. So I thought, "Well, I don't want to hold a grudge forever. Maybe we can handle it. Maybe we'll go down and work together and avoid those kinds of pitfalls that had really undermined the work." It's that father-son thing that is so strong in Joe's history with a lot of people, not just me. Sooner or later, the son stands up, and it's trouble for the father if he's not ready for it.

GAIL MERRIFIELD PAPP   Joe had been reading the script one night at home, and I said, "Wait a second. Don't read that script all by yourself. I haven't had a chance to even look at it; I want to hear it, too." So Joe went back to page one and he started to read it aloud to me in bed. He read the whole play out loud to me that night, and I thought, "My god, this is amazing. It's an absolutely extraordinary play. But what is it? Where are we? Who are these people?" But I just loved it, I thought it was wonderful, and so did Joe.

JOSEPH PAPP   David called me in the middle of the night and he said, "I've written this extraordinary play." I read it and it was hallucinatory, never below the surface of dreams, and that's why it was so scary, so nightmarish. There was a tremendous kind of mystery there, it was more a dream than a play; if it had been a play, it could have been the most powerful of all of his plays. It was so much him—he was without any skin at all. You can't do a play that exposes that much; it's too raw. Every play needs an artistic coating to give it a kind of protective structure. This was like raw horror.

He said he wanted to direct the play and I said, "Okay, if you want to." He'd never directed before, and he was too close to the play, but he got very excited about directing it and I went along with him even though I knew it was going to be a disaster. You have to be objective as a director, and he was thoroughly incapable of that here. I could tell by the way he was talking to the actors. I saw it happening, but I didn't stop it, I let it go.

I was indulging him, in a sense, but I didn't want to hurt him. I gave him everything he wanted. I in no way stood in his way. It was like Lear saying, "I gave you all." I gave David all.

DAVID RABE It was a mess, but I still had this love for the play. Whatever the reasons, whatever the explanation, I felt we just weren't learning how to do it. Psychologically, I pretty much said, "I'm never going to know how to do this play. I don't want any more to do with it, but maybe we'll find somebody that can do it."

JOHN PYNCHON HOLMS I worked closely with Lee Breuer on several projects with Mabou Mines, and Joe approached Lee and I to take a look at this play. *Goose and Tomtom* was much more personal than David's previous work, much more about David's fears, David's obsessions. The language in the piece is wonderful, seductive, but extremely difficult. And Joe, I think, wanted David to have an opportunity to have the play done, to show another facet of his writing.

Lee was called away to do another show, and I did the workshop. Joe and David both liked the workshop very, very much; you could see that there was real potential. So Joe decided to go with it and we moved toward production.

DAVID RABE Some Mabou Mines people were going to do a little reading of the first scene. Jerry Mayer and Fred Neumann were doing it in these chairs with wheels, rolling around the stage, and it was hysterically funny. My agent was there, we were both giddy laughing at it. So I thought, "Well, shit, maybe this is the answer, maybe some Mabou Mines thing that isn't rational or logical will reveal this play. I don't know *what* this means, or why it works, but it's very funny."

JOHN PYNCHON HOLMS   I approached the play as really kind of a thirties gangster fantasy. I decided that the equivalent to an automobile would be the rolling chair, so I had Goose and Tomtom spending a lot of time moving around their office on their wheeled chairs. Everything on the set was on wheels.

Initially, David was very present all the way through the process. He was there from the very beginning, at rehearsal almost every day, at every design meeting. It was my choice to involve him all the way through, so that everything we did was clear, so that when we came to the moment of getting it in front of an audience, he wouldn't be flying in from the coast and saying, "This is not what I saw."

David told me in the first meeting that we had about the play that he had written it very, very quickly, that it seemed to really pour out of the typewriter. He implied that while he understood a lot about where he was going with other material, he didn't know with this one. It was very mysterious to him. I was reminded at times of *Long Day's Journey into Night*, a play that was so personal, so much about O'Neill's life that he didn't want to see it and didn't want people involved with it until he was gone. I don't want to make a literal comparison, but I think this play is as personal.

In the first week of previews, for whatever reason, whether he suddenly just didn't like what he was seeing or whether it was his turn and he didn't know what really to do next, David began to withdraw. He stopped looking at rewrites, or looking for rewrites, and wouldn't work on cuts. He stopped dealing with the play. He and I'd become relatively close, we had gotten to know each other a little bit, and it was difficult when he withdrew the way he did.

DAVID RABE   They set it up and they went into rehearsal. I wasn't too involved in it at all. But about midway or three-quarters of the way through, I started coming by and it was beginning to make less and less sense and have less and less vitality than what it had had when it started. I was ready, at that point, to fight on, but I was also ready to totally give up and admit that the fucking play was no good.

Then we had a meeting, John and Joe and myself. John and I were talking about some moment in the play, what it should be, and Joe is sitting there with the script on his lap. And Joe said, "No! Tomtom hates Goose."

"What?" I said.

"He hates Goose."

And then he started to read the scene, he started to read other scenes, both characters, and I said, "Oh my god. That's why I haven't been able to do the play. I haven't understood the most fundamental thing." I began to understand what the whole play was about in my own life, where it came from, and what it meant to me.

It was Joe who illuminated this and I began to try and talk to him, still thinking we're a team. "That's not down there and it'll never be there," I said. "Let's just stop this agony now and do it again. You understood it, you made it clear, you should direct this play." This big production, with a lot of special effects, seemed misguided to me, and I wanted Joe to do it.

JOSEPH PAPP   I think I understood that play better than anybody because it was so much David, and I was as close to him as I could possibly have been to any man. David said to me, "There's only one person who can direct this play."

"Who?"

"You."

"David, I will *never* direct this play. *Never*. It's too personal a play for you."

"But you're the only one who understands it."

"Yes, but I wouldn't do it."

And David started to get slowly unhappy. I didn't feel the mystery of this play had been plumbed by any means, but I thought it was a very good production. If I thought the play was a disaster, I wouldn't have put it on. But nobody could have satisfied David with that play.

I was going crazy with him, giving him every opportunity, but he could not decide. Finally I said, "I'll open it for the press if you want me to. If you don't want me to, I won't open it." And the last word I had from him was,

"You decide." So I thought it was my decision. I'd sort of had enough with it, and I said, "Well, I'm going to open the play." We had gone through so many things by that time that I felt the play had to go on, and I'd understood that we were both agreed on that.

But when he heard the play was in fact going to open, David denounced it the night before, said this was not his production and he was disassociating himself from it—just like Sam Shepard. Some of the best writers in this country have denounced me.

That whole thing was such a nightmare for me, as well as for all concerned. He undermined the play, his own work, which I felt was a mistake, and that began the alienation between us. But one thing David was not was clear-minded and reasonable and even-tempered. He was a powerhouse of mixed emotions, going from the most infantile kind of reactions to things to the profoundest, most extraordinary perceptions. Remember that huge baby in *2001*? He reminded me of that a lot.

DAVID RABE Joe said, "I feel I have to continue with this, I have my subscribers and da-da-da," and I said, "Whatever." The issue then became him saying, "I don't want to open it unless you say so" and me saying, "I don't want to." After a period of time, he'd call me again and say, "But don't you think we should?" We'd go round and round and round, and this time I kept saying no, I didn't want it opened.

Finally, after a lot of phone calls, it did reach a point where perhaps I gave in by saying, "Joe, you obviously can't live with this decision this way. I don't want to open it, but you decide what you want and you let me know. Call me back."

At this point in time he could interpret that, I suppose, as giving him permission to open it, but it wasn't what I meant and there was no permission to give. He had a legal right to put it on. I didn't hear from him and the following Wednesday, I happened to look at the theatrical ABC listings, which I really don't do very often, and I saw that the play was opening.

At that point, I decided to run around and send those telegrams. You do that because you still believe in the play, still believe that it has a future and can be done well, some way, somehow. You do that ahead of time because you don't want the critics thinking that you think it's good this way.

If you say "I didn't like it anyway" later on, they don't believe you, but if you do it up front, they have to know that you mean it.

It is a little nasty, I suppose, to those people that are in the play and to Joe—they can't appreciate it—but it isn't done for that purpose. It's done to create the possibility of space for the play at a later date. And the irony was that, had he not told me those things that day and opened the heart of the play up to me, I would have said, "Fuck it. Open it."

JOHN PYNCHON HOLMS David disavowed the production and I felt like I was in the middle of a real family crisis, the disintegration of the relationship between Joe and David. David felt betrayed and Joe was in a great deal of pain about all this. I'm sure that the easiest thing for him to do would have been to just put the play aside. But I think he had a sense as a good producer that this was something David had to deal with in order to move on.

A lot of writers get into the position of being fixed on a piece of material to the degree that it's hard for them to move to the next piece of work, and Joe wanted to resolve this question so that David could continue to write. I think he was thinking about David more than David was thinking about him.

DAVID RABE As a playwright, the play is predominant for you. And Joe, for all his interest in new plays and interest in any given playwright, Joe is building an institution, and his primary interest was and always is the institution. Sometimes those things are in conflict, and that's where it's confusing.

When you have someone who's telling you that he'll do whatever you want, he'll do all your plays, all those kind of grand promises don't admit that there can be a built-in conflict underneath between this sort of personal connection and the fact that it's finally a business. And there is no question where his loyalty will fall when that conflict comes. Once you see it, you say, "Well, of course, what else is he supposed to do?"

Nor is there any question about where the playwright's loyalty will fall, unless he's totally bamboozled. A lot of successful and failed plays are the mortar for that place; there are fulfilled things and a lot of bones and dead people in there. In some cases, one is as good as the other to build an institution. The dead soldier and the live one, it takes both. He's built the institution, and it's great to have it, but along the way you realize certain things.

JOSEPH PAPP   I appreciate talent. I appreciate people who really are great in their work. When I see an extraordinary actor or director, I'll give him everything. I gave David Rabe everything because he was an extraordinary writer, and I'll still do it, because my heart goes out to those people. I feel, even if they fail, it's worth it because they're so marvelous.

David's departure is a loss. I regret we're not together here. I think he is a great writer. I would put him in a very high position in terms of writers who have existed since O'Neill. He hasn't been a big commercial success because his subject matter and his way of looking at things are hardly conventional. There's too much bitterness and feelings that go way beyond the range in which most people who go to the theater want to feel.

I have nothing but the most positive thoughts about David. I don't feel any wounds from him. I saw him just a few months ago, sitting with his wife in a restaurant. I always feel good when I see him, and I went over, put my arm around him, and said, "How you doin', David?" I'll never let him continue being angry, and nothing would give me greater pleasure than to be friends with him again. And the greatest pleasure I could have would be producing another one of his plays.

DAVID RABE   Joe's combination of tremendous ambition and power and desire for control is in conflict with an equally strong artistic, human, and compassionate side. Both sides exist, and they are really in huge and unresolved conflict. When you encounter him at a certain moment, the side that's on top is what you get.

I was very angry at Joe at one point, felt disappointed and so on, but I don't carry along an ongoing sense of ill will toward him. I suppose I could fall into the same trap again and say, "Well, now we're all older . . ." I never want to say never in this business.

I wrote a play called *Slag* in 1970, and the director went away to New York with it in his pocket and called me up and said that Joe Papp wanted to do it. I'd never heard of him. And then Joe rang me up and said, "Are you coming over?"

"I'd be delighted to," I said. "Are you paying?"

"No." And so I never came.

He rang me once again during the run. He said, "I'm closing your play."

"But I understand it got very good reviews," I said.

"It did get very good reviews, but not the kind you can quote."

"What do you mean?"

"The most commercial line in Clive Barnes's review in the *New York Times* is, 'He pushes out lilacs through the dead land.' You can hardly put that in neon, can you?" Obviously, I thought he was rather mean, an impression that has since been corrected.

In 1982, after four years of relentless lobbying, mostly from Gail, Joe finally agreed to do *Plenty*. He did it with maybe not the best grace, in the sense that he had been talked into it. He felt prickly and resentful about having to resort to the English for social and political plays, and I think I was a symbol of everything the English theater represented and therefore he was deeply suspicious of me. Also, I brought my own leading lady, Kate Nelligan, who had played it in London, so not unnaturally he felt less of a producer than usual.

But once he commits himself to something, then he's a wonderful producer. He understood a great deal about how to present it, that's to say he managed its Broadway run very brilliantly. And he managed everything to do with the publicity brilliantly.

The balance he produced in the play, both by things that he said to me and how certain of the parts were strongly cast and strongly played, made it a much better balanced play than it had been in London and spectacularly more successful. I think he himself would say that the show itself was largely our work. He didn't take a very active part in that.

You have to understand, I have a slightly unusual relationship among the writers in Joe's theater, in the sense that he himself says that he doesn't really understand my plays on the page. He always says, "But I trust you. Go ahead and do what you want."

That seems to me is what makes him a great producer, that his primary loyalty is to people. When he senses that somebody has something interesting to say or an interesting way of doing things, then he will back them to the hilt. If you say to Joe, "I don't know, it's just an instinct," he'll always accept it, because that's how he works.

Joe's supreme gift is for understanding what is happening in the auditorium between the audience and the play. When he sits in the auditorium, he will tell you where you lost the audience and why you lost them. He can see the story of a play and what it is that's attractive about it or what repels people about it. He makes you confront what you don't want to confront. Joe is like an almost uncanny navigator of the emotional currents of the evening.

Also, Joe has got some political grasp, and so few American producers have. He is not leftist in the way that the English understand, but his politics are radical on behalf of people who get a raw deal. When you look at the state of the New York theater, you have to say, "Here is a man whose criteria are not success and failure, and, basically, everybody else's criteria are commercial."

I remember going to the Tony Awards for *Plenty*. I'd never seen the American theater, and when all these people walked out, I turned to Joe and said, "I didn't realize this is what you were protecting me from." And he said, "Yes, it's hell out there. Don't you realize it's hell out there?"

Now Joe's genius, if you like, was for understanding that if you want to set up an institution to fight the crappiness of values, the crappiness of the failure-success syndrome, it can't be on the fringe. He understood that you had to fight with an institution which was as large and as powerful as the commercial institutions.

So Joe is never trying to raise $10,000, he's always trying to raise $10 million. He's never trying to work one little theater, he tries to work six theaters. He understands that in New York, anything which is alternative dies. You've got to be in the mainstream, even if your values aren't mainstream.

Joe has very strange bouts of life. One day I met him at a party at seven thirty in the evening, and he said, "I like that suit very much. Where did you get it?"

"I can't remember where I got it."

The next day, his secretary said, "God almighty, you got us into trouble last night."

"What do you mean?"

"We spent the whole evening, till ten thirty at night, going round to Barney's, Bloomingdale's, three other big department stores, with Joe standing in the middle of the floor saying, 'I want a suit like David Hare wears,' and describing it in detail to all these assistants." At whim, he will set off on expeditions like this, usually dragging his staff around with him.

Joe has an artist's temperament, and he has a tremendous frustration about the fact that, although he can burst into song, try to act, run six plays at once, ride his exercise bike, be the world's official spokesman on AIDS, do five hundred things, finally, he's never written a play.

When we did *A Map of the World*, there was a certain point when I suddenly thought, "The relationships are reversed." The director and writer is meant to be the person with the artistic temperament, and the producer is meant to be the man who's calm, looking after you, taking an overview. And I was dealing with Joe's artistic temperament, which seemed infinitely more feverish and volatile than my own. And I thought, "Hold on, hold on, he's meant to be the one comforting me, not me looking after him."

32

The Normal Heart

1985

Brad Davis (left)
in a scene from
The Normal Heart
© Martha Swope

The blood that is coursing through *The Normal Heart*, the new play by
Larry Kramer at the Public Theater, is boiling hot. In this fiercely polemical
drama about the private and public fall-out of the AIDS epidemic, the playwright starts off angry, soon gets furious and then skyrockets into sheer rage.
Although Mr. Kramer's theatrical talents are not always as highly developed as
his conscience, there can be little doubt that *The Normal Heart* is the most
outspoken play around—or that it speaks up about a subject that justifies its
author's unflagging, at times even hysterical, sense of urgency.

What gets Mr. Kramer mad is his conviction that neither the hetero- nor
homosexual community has fully met the ever-expanding crisis posed by
Acquired Immunity Deficiency Syndrome. He accuses the governmental,
medical and press establishments of foot-dragging in combating the dis-

ease—especially in the early days of the outbreak, when much of the play is set—and he is even tougher on homosexual leaders who, in his view, were either too cowardly or too mesmerized by the ideology of sexual liberation to get the story out. "There's not a good word to be said about anyone's behavior in this whole mess," claims one character—and certainly Mr. Kramer has few good words to say about Mayor Koch, various prominent medical organizations, *The New York Times* or, for that matter, most of the leadership of an unnamed organization apparently patterned after the Gay Men's Health Crisis.

Frank Rich, *New York Times*, April 22, 1985

It concerns, first, the troubled involvement of Ned Weeks, a writer, with an AIDS-crisis organization that he helped found but that eschews his confrontational tactics and eventually dumps him. It concerns, second, Ned's love affair with Felix, a *New York Times* fashion reporter, who comes out of the closet for Ned even as Ned comes out of emotional lethargy for him. There is, third, Ned's tricky relationship with his heterosexual lawyer brother, made trickier by their Jewishness. Fourth, there are the efforts of Dr. Emma Brookner—a smart, tough, tireless doctor confined to a wheelchair by polio—to combat AIDS, succor the victims, and mobilize the purblind or adversary medical powers that be. Lastly, there is the complex interaction—or inaction—of city and federal governments; the vagaries of the heterosexual and homosexual press; public opinion or apathy or hostility; and violently conflicting views and plans of action in the crisis center.

The play's most original contribution is its examination of the relationship between promiscuity and AIDS, a certain swinging homosexual life-style and the spread of the disease. Although the author's preference is for loving monogamy, persuasive spokesmen for a whole spectrum from abstinent celibacy to extreme indulgence as a supposed homosexual hallmark are given hearing. As a result, what could have been a mere staged tract—and, in its lesser moments, is just that—transcends often enough into a fleshed-out, generously dramatized struggle, in which warring ideologies do not fail to breathe, sweat, weep, bleed—be human. Despite some awesome self-importance, there is also a leaven of humor and self-criticism, and language that can rouse itself out of a tendency to creak into moving arias and duets of passion.

John Simon, *New York* magazine, May 6, 1985

....

LARRY KRAMER In July 1981, there was an article in the *New York Times* that said, "Rare Cancer Found in 41 Homosexuals." A friend who wrote about medical stuff for *The Native*, the gay newspaper, suggested I go and speak to Dr. Alvin Friedman-Kein of NYU, the doctor who had reported this. While I was there, I ran into two people I knew, one who'd just been diagnosed and one who had been diagnosed earlier. That sort of hit home, brought a personal immediacy to bear much more than just reading about it in the newspaper had.

Over the next six months, there were various attempts to get an organization going to deal with this, none of them terribly successful, and in January of 1982 six of us decided to regroup and refocus and we gave ourselves the name Gay Men's Health Crisis. We grew and grew, but in 1983, there was a fight that led to my expulsion. I went abroad, sort of bummed around a bit, and in July or August of 1983, I went to Cape Cod and started writing what became the play, which is, to an extraordinary degree, autobiographical.

During the two years I was involved with AIDS and GMHC, I was very much aware that I was a witness to an extraordinary time in history, and that very few writers had been given this opportunity. So I knew I had to write about it eventually. My closest friend, Rodger McFarlane, GMHC's executive director, has the theory that I unconsciously promoted my expulsion in order to free myself *to* write about it. I don't think that was the case, but one doesn't know what one's unconscious is capable of.

I began to cast around for ways to write about it. I'd had one earlier experience in the theater, a play called *Sissies' Scrapbook*, that was a success at Playwrights Horizons but a huge flop as a commercial venture. We closed on opening night, which was exceedingly painful to me, needless to say, so my experience with the theater had not been one that I wanted to repeat. I tried to write this as a novel, called *City of Death*, but it didn't seem to have the kind of immediacy I needed—it didn't, what I call, yield.

But when I was abroad I saw David Hare's *A Map of the World*, which fused theater and politics, and I said, "Wow, let me think about this as a play again." So I rented this little sea shack on Cape Cod and it just poured out. The first draft for me is always what I call the vomit-out. Then a friend lent me what she calls her Jewish log cabin, a place in the Virginia wilderness but with all the conveniences, and I wrote the second draft.

While I was there I remembered a line from an Auden poem, "We must love one another or die," and I called my friend Richard Howard, who is a Pulitzer Prize–winning poet, and he identified the poem and read it to me. And as soon as he got to the phrase "the normal heart," I said, "That's it."

I submitted that draft to the Public, where I knew no one but which always seemed to be the logical place. I gave it to a guy named Emmett Foster who was a volunteer at GMHC. Emmett, who was Joe's assistant, said it had to go through the process at the Public, and I started sending it to agents, and every agent turned it down. I'm talking about *every* agent—I mean, you name 'em. But if you believe in what you're doing, you've got to fight very tenaciously for it, try every possible avenue, and you don't take no for an answer.

I sent the script to Tommy Tune, because he had been generous to GMHC and I thought he would be a good director. I dropped it off on a Wednesday and literally that weekend his associate called me, and then Tommy called me two days later, and they were both in tears. But Tommy said he couldn't direct it; it was too moving for him, he didn't know how to handle all of that. He was going to send it to Mike Nichols, but I already had, and a week later Mike Nichols called and said, "I think Tommy should direct it," and I said, "Well, Tom said he thinks you should direct it." And they both hemmed and hawed.

Meanwhile, I kept writing these letters to Joe, who I didn't know at all, saying, "Mike Nichols said my script is good, and Tommy Tune said my script is good, where are you? Why am I not hearing from you?" I still didn't hear, and at one point I wrote a very nasty letter, saying, "How dare you not pay more attention to all of this?" But Emmett didn't put the letter through; he saved me on that one. Then, in April of 1984, I got a call to come over and meet Gail.

GAIL MERRIFIELD PAPP When very long first drafts of plays come into the office, I say, "Get out the scales! How much does it weigh? Is it a four-pounder or an eight-pounder?" And what came into the office from Larry, though I didn't know this at first, was something in the vicinity of a seven-pounder. It looked like it could have been a novel, it was that thick, it was perhaps a seven-hour experience in the theater.

Larry, who was in a combative mood because of his recent experiences, had written a covering letter to Joe with his submission of the manuscript that was considered, to use a mild word, inappropriate, actually offensive in tone. For some reason, he assumed that the play was not going to be read, and he overcompensated, shall we say, in this letter, trying to crash through the barriers that he foresaw. Someone who knew Larry read the letter and decided not to show it to Joe or me. We never saw the damn letter; we just heard reports of it. Probably just as well.

After I heard about the submission, I said, "Well, who has the script?" I'm head of the play department and it's one of the questions I ask when something comes in. And, to my astonishment, I heard that four people in the office had already read the play and just loathed it. This was before my assigning the script or even knowing its goddamn title.

Everybody was kind of hot to read it because of Larry's reputation, which was that he can get hysterically angry to the point where he does in the very cause he's trying to put forth, that he makes outrageous claims and is untrustworthy in his reportage, and that his propensity to deliver insults to a person's face in order to get their blood boiling in the proper way is counterproductive and out of line. Now all of this is true and not true, and that's all I'm going to say on that subject.

"Give the script to me and I'll read it," I said. The play indeed was sprawling all over the place, but here and there, there were parts of it that I found quite remarkably written. And when I finished, something happened that has almost never happened to me, perhaps once or twice in my whole memory: I just broke down and cried. I was so damn moved, despite the fact that it was just one hell of a mess of a play. And I thought, "Jesus, this is something to work on."

Meantime, what had happened was that there had been horrendous yelling matches going on between Larry and various people on the staff. People were saying, "I won't talk to that man again; I won't talk to that man." I wasn't there when all this happened, but then I saw huge bowers of flowers arriving for my secretary and other people with notes of apology from Larry. "What the hell's going on?" I said. I was quite astonished, and I said, "Okay, get him on the phone." I called him up and said, "Listen, I liked your play very much. I was extraordinarily moved by it. It needs some work. Let's get together."

His play began as a play about himself and his brother, who is straight and a lawyer. The first draft was very, very long, with a great deal of flashback scenes having to do with him and his brother and their upbringing. When Larry came in, I started talking with him, asking him a lot of questions, first just to find out what he was trying to do with the play. Anything I didn't understand, I'd ask him, a process that went on for about eight or nine months. He'd come in every week, and we'd spend a few hours sitting around the office talking.

I asked him about a speech in the play which equates the burying of the news of this kind of public health crisis with what went on in Hitler's Germany. And he told me of a trip he'd made to the concentration camp at Dachau, and what he'd read about the role of American Jews during the war. He'd made a very deep connection in his soul about what it's possible for people to ignore, to do nothing about. And the more we talked about it, we were getting less and less into the whole brother relationship, and I said, "Why do you have the childhood flashback here? What do you want that to accomplish?" He was very, very tied to the whole story, he was adamant about having that in the play, but I saw it as two plays vying for the same space.

Larry's a marvelous rewriter, fast and smart. And he had a tremendous sense of urgency and passion and commitment to write this play and get it on as fast as possible. Not just because of wanting to have his own creative expression out there in the open; he felt the news had to get out. So he would start explaining certain things to me, and in the process of his own explanations, Larry would clarify certain things for himself. He worked and worked and worked on that play, and finally, he did the most terribly hard, painful thing a writer can do: he took out the stuff he loved best, which was almost all the brother stuff.

I was also very concerned that all of the statements of supposed fact, with respect to the city administration and with respect to the *New York Times*, were completely supported and true. I told Larry I needed to have documentation for each and every thing. He brought in a sheaf this thick, and it all checked out. There was not one misstatement of fact in the whole play, so I respected him a lot. And in the course of all these months, he was so nice. Maybe because he got shouted down a lot, he was grateful that somebody was willing to listen to him.

LARRY KRAMER Working with that woman was for me one of the most moving, creative, fertile, productive, challenging, positive experiences of my entire life. As I look back on it, knowing my temperament, I'm amazed at my patience. I'm not in any way that malleable; if I don't agree with you, I will fight you tenaciously. But something inside me must have just said, "This woman can teach you." Because I had no commitment from the Public, no contract, no promises, nothing. And to do all this work on spec was very unlike me. I don't know that I will ever be able to really put it in any kind of words, but we had something very special.

A good editor doesn't tell you what to do; he or she has the ability to bring out of you, pull out of you, your very best. And Gail never, ever told me what to do, but somehow, in our interaction in our meetings, she made me so aware of yet further possibilities within the script that I couldn't wait to get home to dramatize them. At the end of a meeting, she would say goodbye to me, not expecting to see me for a month, and I would literally be back there in a week or ten days with the new stuff. She had known all along that she wanted to do the play; it was just a question of how hard I was willing to work. It was an awesome experience.

GAIL MERRIFIELD PAPP Now you have to realize that everybody around the office hated this play. They were astounded that I was spending so much time with Larry. God knows what they thought I was doing. Joe knew

I was meeting with this guy, but he didn't know what it was all about, either. He would pass by the desk and say, "Whatever it is, it better be good."

We put in months and months of very hard, good work, and though it wasn't completed yet, I felt the play was incredibly moving and important. There was a sense of urgency about getting it on, and since getting a play on or not is Joe's decision, not mine, I decided it was time he read the script.

I brought it home one night, and it turned out to be one of life's most inopportune moments. It was after supper, when one gets sleepy, and Joe had many important and urgent programs and plans on his mind that he wanted to discuss with me. He was lying on the sofa, and in the midst of all this, I interjected the thought that I had a play with me that I'd like him to read that very night. It was the last thing in the world he wanted to hear.

"Why should I read this play tonight of all nights?" he said.

"Because I think it is a potentially very powerful play, and I need your advice about how we should go about it. I've had no support on it, and perhaps I'm mad, perhaps I've lost all judgment and all my faculties have gone out the window. I need you to tell me if I'm just plain crazy."

So Joe magnanimously said, "I don't want to."

"Oh, please, please," I said. "Just start."

"Can I read just a few pages?"

"No, you can't read just a few pages of this one. It's not that kind of play. You must read it from start to finish. You're going to like some parts more than other parts, but just keep going, have faith, and then tell me if I'm crazy."

So he started reading, read the first few pages, and put it down. "I don't like this at all," he said. "It's terrible. Why are you having me read this play?"

"Yes, I know you're not going to like the first ten pages, but please read on. You've got to read on."

He was good enough to do that, and then he was silent for an hour, he never put it down. And when he finished it, he had the same reaction I did: he was in tears. He was so goddamned moved he could hardly talk. "No," he said, "you're not crazy. Let's work on it. Let's try to do it."

JOSEPH PAPP Gail told me she'd found an interesting play about AIDS. "It's a monster, it's huge," she said, "but I think it has great possibilities."

"I don't want to do a play about AIDS," I said. "I hate to do plays about cancer, I hate to do plays about illness, I just don't want to do the play—and I have no time to read it."

She let it go for a few days and then came back and said, "Would you just try to read it?"

"I don't want to read it," I said. "First of all, it's too fat, I can't get through the damn thing, and secondly it'll just depress me."

After about a week, she said, "Just begin it."

"All right," I said. "But I'm not going to like it. I'll tell you right now, I'm not going to like it."

I read the first twenty pages, put it down, and said, "Gail, there's so much junk in this thing, I can't get through it. It's overwritten, overblown, and who cares about this guy's brother?"

She didn't say a word, and a day or so later I picked it up again and began to plow my way and plow my way through it. At several points I put it down and said, "I can't get any further with this," but I finally plowed my way through the whole thing. I put the damn thing down, I said, "This is one of the worst things I've ever read," and I was crying. Can you believe that? I was crying. There was so much feeling in the play, I was moved. It was cluttered with all this junk, but the heart of *The Normal Heart* was beating. And that's the way it began.

GAIL MERRIFIELD PAPP   Joe and I were going away, and I didn't want Larry to lose any kind of continuity in his work on it. So I asked Larry if while we were away Bill Hart, our dramaturge, could be his man. And Bill did some excellent work with Larry, really excellent. The scene near the end, where Ned and Felix have a terrible argument and Ned breaks a carton of milk when he throws it to the floor, that really came out of his work with Bill Hart.

LARRY KRAMER   Gail and I worked on the overall, mammoth, granite-like structure, and Bill and I worked on the nose and the eyes and the detailing. We used to sit around playing the parts back and forth to each other. I learned a lot from him: how to shape a scene, what was extraneous, where a beat was needed. And I would keep rewriting things; I must have easily done a dozen drafts.

BILL HART *The Normal Heart* came in. It seemed to have such a courageous and powerful core, but it was overdone, excessive, Larry was putting everything into it. Gail worked at removing a lot of the excess, but it still didn't kick through all the way, and that's when I came in. Because Larry was so concerned with information about this phenomenon, he felt he had to put a great deal of it into the play, and I kept thinking that it was interfering with the flow of the drama. You deaden people's heads with all this data, so we had to work out how much to put in.

Larry would often just throw all my ideas right out the window, but every once in a while something would catch fire. If I thought he wasn't giving one character a fair shake, I would try to show how this guy could be more interesting. Also, Larry needed to get even wilder.

Late in the play there is a very loving scene between Ned Weeks and his dying lover, and I felt it was too sweet. Larry might have been afraid there was no love in the play, but I said, "You've got to make this thing more gutsy. Stop being so nice." So we turned it into this slam-bang, milk-throwing, "If you want to die, die!" scene. Mostly, it was just finding what was already there, encouraging Larry to put himself even more on the spot.

LARRY KRAMER I had always been terrified of Joe. He was this big eminence, and since I knew he had a bad temper, and I knew I had a bad temper, I said to Gail, "Please keep us apart. I don't want to have a fight." But he agreed to do the play, even though it attacked two of his meal tickets: the *New York Times*, which reviews all his plays, and the mayor, who's his landlord. For him to take on a play of this nature was enormously courageous. So from being frightened of him, it slowly grew into what I can only call a love affair.

Joe became like Daddy. We would always go to Daddy when we wanted things. And he gave in, it became his pet project. Joe is out of the thirties, he's out of political anger and fury and passion. He loves it when people get up and scream at each other, make noise and confront an audience. Theater should be angry, theater should be dangerous, and he loved all of that, that's basically what he responded to.

JOSEPH PAPP   Everybody told me about Larry. They said, "He's an impossible man. He'll threaten, cajole, wheedle, he'll do anything to get to you." He's a fighter, he goes after things, and I wouldn't want to have him for an enemy. But I never found him to be troublesome.

I told Larry, "Listen, I don't want anything here that you cannot actually prove, because you've not only written a play, you're making very clear statements about people." He gave me all this data and I corroborated everything.

I was determined to do the play, so I called Mayor Koch. I said, "Mr. Mayor, I have a play here about AIDS that I'm going to put on. The playwright criticizes you and your administration. I'm not going to be a censor. I just wanted to let you know." And he said, "Fine, thank you for telling me."

Then I called Arthur Gelb, and I said, "Artie, listen, I'm doing a play here and it's critical of the *Times*."

"What do you mean?" he said. "We were the first ones to put that thing in the paper. How can you say that?"

"Mind you, Artie, I didn't write the play. I'm putting it on because it's an important theme. If you think the guy who wrote it is wrong, sue him."

LARRY KRAMER   It was really hard finding a director. I tried to find a guy called Michael Lindsay-Hogg whom I had known briefly when I lived in London. He was in New York, I sent him the script, and he called back that night and said, "I like it very much. Where do we stand?"

He had never worked at the Public, and Joe doesn't like taking on new directors. I had everything going against me. The only plus was that his mother was Geraldine Fitzgerald, whom Joe adores. So I sat down and wrote Joe this note. I said we had this chance with Michael who was so excited about it, and would he meet with him. Joe met with him, and everything was fine.

MICHAEL LINDSAY-HOGG   Larry said he'd written this play about AIDS and could I read it. I read it, and I thought it was sort of a mess in standard play terms, but it had the potential of being extremely powerful, sort of like *An Enemy of the People*. It was unwieldy, but unwieldy like a heavyweight boxer who misses sometimes, but if he connected, it would really snap your head back.

We started trying to cast it, and it proved endless. The whole thing was difficult because it was a period when if you drank water out of the same glass as someone who had AIDS, or if you ate something off a fork that hadn't been properly washed, you were frightened.

I remember being introduced at a party by someone who said, "This is Michael, he's doing a play about AIDS," and coincidental with the word AIDS the person removed his hand from mine and just rubbed it down the side of his leg. A lot of people said, "I don't want to see the play, because will I get AIDS by being in the room with people who have it?" There was a whole period of fear, and all of us felt it was an act of necessary courage that we did this play.

LARRY KRAMER We had a hard time casting Ned. We waited a long time for Al Pacino, who said he was interested, and it really looked like a possibility that he was going to do it. Joe had it sent to Martin Sheen, who subsequently did it in London, but it turned out that Martin's agent at the time, CAA, had never even passed the script on to him when they turned it down. An offer was made to Judd Hirsch, and the minute it was made to him, we regretted it, but in any event, he turned it down. If one were going after big stars, Dustin Hoffman was the one I certainly would have wanted the most. But he was not available to play the part on the stage, nor would he. He never tells you no; you just sort of get strung along.

MICHAEL LINDSAY-HOGG One night I was watching television, sort of out of half my eye, and I saw one of those TV miniseries about Bobby Kennedy. I had no particular interest in watching yet another Kennedy piece, but I found my attention going more and more to the screen because I thought Brad Davis was sensational in it. So the next day I came in and said to Larry, "I think we might have it."

"Who?"

"Brad Davis."

Larry first of all said, "He's too young," and then laughed, because Brad had been in Larry's first play. I kind of persisted, Brad came to New York to read for us, and we all thought he was right for it because he was brave and he found the jokes.

LARRY KRAMER   I laughed because Brad was like my little protégé. I had really been instrumental in his career, giving him a kick in the ass and shaping him up early on, and the thought, somehow, that this little kid would come back, in essence playing me, made me laugh. I found it hard to make the leap or whatever, but I said, "Sure, why not?" Brad is very dear and very special and very personal, and I can't be very objective about him.

BRAD DAVIS   Larry sent me the play not to be in it but because I'm an old friend of his. I read it and I was so moved I called him up when I finished it, which was like two thirty or three in the morning L.A. time, six o'clock his time. I was just going on and on about how impressed I was, how rich and moving and upsetting and angry the whole thing was.

I'd spoken with Larry every now and then and he'd told me he was trying to get stuff done about this disease, but it was so removed from me and far away, maybe that's why I was so blown away when I read the play. It was like BC and AD, like there was no consciousness of AIDS before *The Normal Heart*.

I was so effusive that he said, "Well, would you be interested in playing it?" At the time, a play was the last thing I wanted to do, the last thing I could really even afford to do. But the more I talked with him, the more the idea of my playing it appealed to him. And right in there, Michael Lindsay-Hogg saw *Kennedy* on TV and I flew to New York to read for him and Joe Papp. They were having trouble getting a really name actor to play Ned, because you read this play, and it could look like really big trouble. I didn't see it that way. I only listened to my heart. I was just so moved.

Feeling somewhat quote/unquote "safe" coming into this, I freaked out in the middle of rehearsals. I mean, I got terrified. You start learning the facts about this virus and it was clear that it was no "This will never come into my life" kind of thing. The insidiousness of it was pretty overpowering when it really hit. So I cut off all my hair.

I used to do that all the time when I was younger, any time I was going through any kind of catharsis. If somebody looked cross-eyed at me at a stoplight, I'd go get the scissors and chop all my hair off. There have been some real Auschwitz looks, but I stopped short of that this time because something said, "Brad, you have to go to rehearsal tomorrow, and in three weeks you open in this play." The next day, Larry saw me at the gym, called Michael, and said, "Our middle-aged leading man looks like a West Point prep boy."

I've never had a rehearsal period like that. It was like we were all going on this journey into our own consciousnesses as people as well as creating a play as actors. The reality of the life that this play represented came into the play, and everybody just banded together so tightly. We had no guarantee that we weren't going to get creamed, but everyone was so committed with their hearts that they dropped the ego that came with their particular station. The experience we had chosen to have was so powerful that it overshadowed everybody's act. Everybody laid down their guns. Their sole purpose was just to take care of this child called *The Normal Heart*.

LARRY KRAMER   As an actor, Brad is exceptionally good at telling you what you don't need. And there were things we had tenacious fights over that I would not give in on. At one point Brad just exploded and said, "You know, he is not the Information, Please Almanac." After we opened, when I continued to try and put stuff in, he did rebel and we had quite a bad fight over it.

Brad saw Geraldine Page having dinner with Michael in a restaurant, and he ran up to her and said, "Did Tennessee Williams rewrite plays after they opened? He didn't do that, did he? Of course he didn't." And Geraldine said, "Are you crazy? He would send rewrites from the other side of the moon when we only had one week left to run." And he just said, "Oh."

JOSEPH PAPP   Michael Lindsay-Hogg was a very positive force. I felt his greatest value as a director was that he created a very pleasant ambience for people to work in, but I was hoping that he'd have more control over the structure of the play. I felt there was not enough sense of organization, so the play rambled a lot, and I let him know that. And I did come in there a number of times to try to get some kind of form to this.

MICHAEL LINDSAY-HOGG   Whatever the bad bits were, the play wouldn't have been done without Joe. And because it was done at the Public under Joe's aegis, it made the whole thing seem even more solid. Joe, in quotes, "legitimized" the project, helped you read the political nature of the play rather than just the gay nature of the play. And that was a very good way to use the weight of a powerful theatrical institution. I don't mean he's the most lovable man of all time, but you do have a sense of moral commitment from Joe, his sense of right and wrong is very powerful, and that's rare.

The downside of Joe is that to get where he's got and to even get the theater working, it's necessary to bully city institutions and financial people. That filters down to running a system where a lot of people are afraid of him. Joe is, by nature, confrontational. I don't think it worries him that people are intimidated by him. But the upside is that at least he bullies in the right causes. The Public's the only place in New York you can do a play with bite, the only place to do something which has great risks.

And on opening night Joe was the one who got us all in a room and read the *New York Times* notice. It was kind of like your father, or for the younger members of the cast, your grandfather, reading this important thing. He said, "It's okay. It's not great, but I think we'll be okay." And then the play took on its own life.

LARRY KRAMER   Joe said to us on opening night, "I'm going to keep this play running. I don't care if nobody comes. I'm going to keep it running." And every time it came to close, Joe literally would say, "I can't bring myself to close this play." And then we'd have to run it for two more weeks with nobody in there, because there was no advance, until word got out and it built up again. It ended up being the longest-running play that's ever run there.

JOSEPH PAPP   Just like David Rabe's plays and all the plays about women and blacks and their struggles, here was a play that I felt was dealing with a major crisis, putting us in touch with the world again, and I was very proud to do it. I told the cast, "Once in every ten years or so, a play comes along that fulfills my original idea of what role theater must play in society," and I meant it.

At the same time as *The Normal Heart*, we were running a play about Vietnam called *Tracers*, and it was, again, a very moving portrayal of young people dying. And I had the thought, "I could easily do both these plays with the same cast," because the audience reactions at the end were so close. Every night after the curtain, ten, twelve, or fifteen young men would sit in their chairs and be unable to move, absolutely stunned. And several other people in the audience, mostly men, would go over and sit with that person, put an arm around him. The same after both plays.

Blacks, Latinos, women, Vietnam veterans, people in the AIDS situation—in a way these are all victims of society, victims of whatever is going on. And our theater has reflected the problems and needs, the dilemma of these people. I feel like they're my people, as they should be everybody's people.

33

The Mystery of Edwin Drood

1985

George Rose
© Martha Swope

While it may be possible to imagine a more exciting show than *The Mystery of Edwin Drood*, the jolly new musical at Central Park's Delacorte Theater, it's hard to picture a more democratic one. The audience not only gets to see this New York Shakespeare Festival extravaganza for free, but it also gets to help write the script's ending. *Edwin Drood* is a very loose adaptation of the half-finished novel Dickens left at his death in 1870. When Dickens's plot runs out in mid-Act II of the musical version, the audience "solves, resolves and concludes the mystery" by voting by voice and hand to a series of multiple-choice propositions.

This rollicking plebiscite, which shapes the musical's final half-hour, is both delightful and ingenious. Much of the delight comes from watching the evening's waspish emcee, the convivial George Rose, lead the voting with a tongue so far up his cheek that one half-expects it to emerge from his ear. The ingenuity belongs to Rupert Holmes, the author of the show's book, music and lyrics. Mr. Holmes has written an ending, songs included, that can flexibly accommodate any balloting results. Since there are seven suspects who might have murdered Drood—not to mention two other plot questions adding more variables to the mix—Mr. Holmes' all-purpose conclusion must cope with nearly as many statistical possibilities as a Lotto contestant.

The voting is such a tonic that one sometimes wishes the procedure might be extended throughout *Edwin Drood*. This is a charming, attractively cast musical that allows both veteran musical performers (Mr. Rose, Betty Buckley, Cleo Laine) and relative newcomers (Howard McGillin, Patti Cohenour) the opportunities to shine in some fetching moonlight. It is also a diffuse show that would benefit from being a shade tighter, zippier, wittier and more melodic than it is. If only its creators had made firmer choices in editing and focusing their material, *Edwin Drood* might offer as much pizzazz as it does sweet spirits and cheering interludes. Too bad the audience can't vote along the way to decide which extraneous songs, scenes and gags might be weeded out.

The roots of the show's big promise and uneven follow-through all stem from its imaginative premise. Mr. Holmes has not merely written a straight-forward musical version of the Dickens novel, but has instead made *Edwin Drood* a play-within-the-play. The musical is set in a provincial town, Greater Dorping-on-Sea, where a motley London music-hall troupe is performing its own hammy *Drood* adaptation—"a musicale with dramatic interludes," as the company's impresario, Mr. Rose, puts it. In other words, we are watching a parody—a Dickens dramatization as it might be done by the Victorian acting troupe satirized by Dickens in *Nicholas Nickleby*.

Frank Rich, *New York Times*, August 23, 1985

RUPERT HOLMES   My father was an American GI and bandleader who was stationed in England where I was born in a town in the county of Cheshire. We moved to the United States when I was three, but my mother never really allowed myself to be absorbed into American culture. I had this strange hybrid upbringing. I was brought up to believe, essentially, that the American Revolution was a diplomatic blunder on George Washington's part that would all be set straight someday.

I wanted desperately to be in the recording business, and I found out that the one great way to get into a business is to say yes to everything and to work for nothing. By the time I was twenty, I was arranging some of the last recordings done by the classic acts of the fifties like the Drifters and the Platters and also supplying the voices for an infinite number of non-existent bubblegum studio groups.

I really wanted to sing my own songs, though. I mean, if you're writing songs for *The Partridge Family*, you are not going to really explore the depths of your philosophical beliefs. I went out and made an album called *Widescreen*, which became a cult classic, and one of the copies found its way into the hands of Barbra Streisand and the next thing I knew I was producing her album called *Lazy Afternoon*.

I was continuing to release my own albums, so my songs were being recorded by people like Dolly Parton, Dionne Warwick, Barry Manilow, and the Manhattan Transfer. I had the first number-one record of the eighties, a song called "Escape," which the world came to call "The Piña Colada Song." One of the people who had been an ardent supporter of my work was a fellow named Craig Zadan, who was working for the Shakespeare Festival, and he started touting my albums to both Gail Merrifield and Joe Papp.

CRAIG ZADAN   Joe made me director of musical theater projects, and a great deal of my time was spent having people come in and audition musicals. We were going to every source, looking for stuff. I had been over at Barry Manilow's house and he said, "You know Rupert Holmes?" I said, "No." He played me his records, and I flipped out.

I got all his records, and I made Joe and Gail listen to them and they fell in love with the work. At one point, Rupert came up with an idea about a show about a recording studio, but it ultimately didn't jell. But I told him, "I believe you're a great theatrical writer and you should write for here."

GAIL MERRIFIELD PAPP   Craig left, a couple of years went by, and I had no idea how you got in touch with Rupert. Then I saw his name in the paper, appearing at a club named Dangerfield's, singing his own songs.

"Joe," I said, "would you mind very much if I went to an eleven o'clock show?"

"What!" he said. "What time are you going to be home?"

"I don't know. I think the show's about two hours."

"That's too late already. Don't wake me up when you come back."

Rupert Holmes came on and he was a most engaging performer. And I wondered, who the hell knew, if after all these years he might still be interested. I thought I'd try to go backstage, but it was terribly crowded, I could not wedge my way through any of that.

Fortunately, I had one crumpled business card in my wallet, so I stood against a wall and wrote a little note: "I wonder if you are interested in writing for musical theater. If so, I'd love to have a chat with you." I saw a doorman in a livery suit and I said, "Listen, Mr. Holmes is expecting this note and I wonder if you'd be very certain to get it to him tonight," and he said, "Oh yes, definitely."

Rupert called me the next day, he came down, and I just found him delightful, a witty, wonderful person. God knows how he survived so many years in the record business, which is just awful. He was like a kindred soul, and I thought, "My god, a kindred soul of the theater with this talent? I can't believe my luck."

I asked him if he had something in mind and he said, "I have a lot of things in mind. I'll distill my thoughts a little bit and come down again." And in the middle of the second meeting he mentioned *The Mystery of Edwin Drood*, which, frankly, I had never heard of before.

RUPERT HOLMES   The first time I encountered the book of *Edwin Drood*, I was in my very early teens or maybe even a little younger. I loved mystery stories, and when I saw it among the complete set of Dickens we had I thought, "Oh, good."

But my father said, "That's not a mystery the way you think of mysteries. It's like a Gothic novel, and also, the problem with it is, there's no finish to it. Dickens died while he was writing it." That intrigued me, and I immediately lunged to the last page of the book.

This particular edition ended with an incomplete segment called "The Sapsie Fragment," and so on the last page there were three ominous dots in the middle of a sentence and it just said, "The End." And I truly pictured Dickens gasping and keeling over with ink staining the entire page. It was a very bold image.

The next real encounter I had with the book was when I was taking the train from L.A. to New York, which I used to do because I hate flying. I wanted to grab a book to take on the trip with me from a display rack at Union Station in Los Angeles. I saw one of them was *The Mystery of Edwin Drood*, and I thought, "Here's a chance to really read it."

Since I was now active in the record business, I couldn't help but notice that there were a lot of musical leitmotifs in the book itself. John Jasper, the villain, was a choirmaster, a composer, and a superb pianist. The object of his obsession, Rosa Bud, was his music student. And in describing Jasper's opium hallucinations, Dickens talked about this strange Eastern music. And another of the characters, Deputy, a typical Dickensian street urchin, sang songs of his own composition. So I thought, "You know, somewhere in this is a possible musical."

This was in the early seventies, and when I got back to New York, I tried to write that musical. And it came out very somber—a dark, weighty, gloomy thing. And a bit self-indulgent. It just wasn't what I wanted to create, so I set it aside.

When I talked to Gail, I mentioned the book very, very vaguely. And then I did something that was a lot of fun for me and I think helped the idea set: I decided I'd write a term paper on the book that had no deadline and was not going to be graded by a teacher.

I went to all the libraries one goes to, read all the cross-references and speculative theories and quotes like Mark Twain saying, "A great number of researchers have already thrown a tremendous amount of darkness on the subject, and if they continue their work, we shall soon know nothing about it at all." I wondered what I could do with this premise that I hadn't done when I first attempted to write it, something that would make it light and fun and entertaining. And on the last two pages of this forty-five-page paper, these two ideas popped up.

The first was Victorian vaudeville. I had always enjoyed the English music hall, and I thought what if, instead of writing a musical *Mystery of Edwin Drood*, I wrote a musical about a hammy, perhaps a little seedy, certainly shamelessly eager-to-please Victorian music-hall company.

I especially liked the convention of a Chairman, who serves as narrator and not only interacts with the audience, but overtly insults them when he feels their applause isn't strenuous enough. I thought this might allow me to make cuts and leaps within the Dickensian plot, and also, when the story collapsed, the audience was not abandoned; it left us with a shell that the audience could still deal with.

The second idea was, how would one end it? I had never written for theater before, but sometimes when you're blundering into a new area, in your own naïve way you see the forest better than the individual trees.

As an audience member, I have always delighted when something unplanned happens, a prop falls, someone goes up in their lines. You sit there shivering in your seat from the joy of realizing that what you've just seen is a one-time event.

I thought, "Why create something for theater that could be done better either on a record or in a movie or on TV? Why not take the essence of theater, which is that what I saw I would not see if I went again tomorrow night, and build it into the structure of the show, so the audience literally comes away every night saying, 'I affected the outcome of the show.'" And that was how I came to the idea of having the audience vote on the outcome.

Gail was my initial coconspirator on this thing. I was writing it with the notion of "I'd better get these pages done and read them to Gail." I felt such a sympathetic ear from her, she got so caught up in all levels of the fun that could be had, that it never really dawned on me to question what the world at large would think. I was writing this thing so that I would have something to read for Gail.

JOSEPH PAPP   I have to give Gail all the credit for *Drood* coming into being. In the same way she worked with Larry Kramer, she got Rupert into her office, encouraged him to write this work, and really saw it through.

I was very much influenced by Gail in this particular area, but it isn't a question of having a wife that's trying to influence a producer to do something that he doesn't want to do.

I have my own judgment, and if I really dislike something, I don't do it. Naturally, when she's involved, I become more interested because not only is she my wife, she's my co-worker and the head of the literary department. She's crucial to the organization in an artistic way. I don't exist in a vacuum in some kind of high place. I exist in terms of relationships like that.

GAIL MERRIFIELD PAPP All I had to offer was endless enthusiasm for Rupert's ideas, and he responded to the fact that I really just loved what he did so much. I work with writers in the early stages, when Joe didn't know who they are. He sees them in my office, comes by, and says, "Well, it better be good." Strikes the terror of God in their hearts! They turn pale, they nearly faint. I have to rush out and get bouillon soup for them. It undoes two weeks of good work.

Then I have to think, "What next?" I mean, I'm not doing this to be kind. I'm doing a job so we can produce very good work. When act one was all finished, Rupert said, "What should we do now? Should we tell Mr. Papp about it and show it to him and so forth?" And I said, "He already knows about you. I mention you every morning over breakfast. Let's do a reading of that one act only, to see what you've got and perhaps help you with act two."

The kinds of people we wanted to get were the very best. We wanted George Rose for the Chairman, because the conceit of the music-hall form means you have to keep the whole show energized through that character. We wanted Cleo Laine for Princess Puffer, who runs the opium den, and so forth. And these people said yes immediately, because they saw that it had gorgeous music to sing. George Rose said to me, "This is the best musical I've come across in fifteen years. I'll do it if he finishes it." I mean, you very seldom have people saying things like that to you—ever.

RUPERT HOLMES I finished act one and performed that first. I said, "I'm not even going to mess with act two and the multiple endings if what I've written here is unacceptable." I made up a tape with the songs' accompaniments, so I wouldn't have to keep running to the piano, and I performed it by myself for Joe and Gail. It took me an amazing three hours just to do act one, and I immediately volunteered to cut one number.

Then it was decided to do a reading of it. I didn't know about those things. I didn't expect that we would have famous people. I remember a casting person saying, "And I sent a copy of the script to George Rose." And Gail, who was with me, looked a little ashen and said, "Does he understand that it's not anything like a finished work?"

In fact, George instantly understood all the conventions of the character, understood everything there was to know about the Chairman. "I love the work," he said, "and I'll be glad to work on it anytime." So I was able to write act two with that wonderful voice in mind. George made things work.

GEORGE ROSE After I reached the "breakdown scene," when I said, "Ladies and gentlemen, it was at this point in our story that Mr. Charles Dickens laid down his pen forever," then I would play very freely with the audience. I would get responses from them that had to be dealt with, and I was very surprised at my ability to ad-lib and handle an audience like that.

There were old music-hall/pub gags that I used which seemed to work very well. There was a line that I got from an old comic who I'd once heard work in a pub in London. When he was interrupted by a woman, he said, "Madame, please don't interrupt me. Do I come round to your house and blow out the red light?" I used that a great deal.

There was another I'd heard used by an old stripper in a London show thirty years ago or more, I never thought I'd have a chance to use and then one night somebody blew a raspberry. I stopped the show and said, "I can't believe my ears, sir. Would you mind doing that again?" He did it again and I said, "Just once more, sir, it's a beautiful sound." He did it once more and I said, "Now, do one with your mouth!"

WILFORD LEACH Joe, who kept saying, "I gotta have musicals, I need the money," one day said to me, "I want you to meet Rupert Holmes." I went to Joe's office, Rupert came in, and Joe said, "If you're interested, I want you to do this thing." Rupert sang just part of one song and I said, "I'll do it."

The song was so original, and there was something about Rupert's spirit—I just knew it was for me. It's like casting: you develop an instinct, between the time they come in the door and get over here and start talking about what they're going to do, I pretty much know what I think.

Rupert had so much material, it was hours. I cut it and rearranged it, he ran it through his computer, it was reworked and reworked and reworked and reworked. And I'd say maybe half of the material he had was eventually eliminated.

Most people cling to their petty little ideas, but to Rupert, ideas are like Kleenex. You say to him, just in passing, "Gosh, Rupert, that line isn't very funny," and he'll come back with ten lines. Rupert is a menace only in one area: anybody can say anything to him and he'll try to do something about it. One of the actors will pass him in the hall and say something, and Rupert will come in having written all this material for him. "Rupert," I'd say, "you've got to stay away from these people."

RUPERT HOLMES I think everyone had in their mind from the outset that if we were received kindly by the critics and the audience enthusiasm was real, that this was something that could go to Broadway. It was conceived that way.

But when you got a script on *Drood*, it was so huge it looked terrifying. The last fifteen minutes occupied more pages than everything that had preceded it because it allowed for every possibility in the voting. There were finally five possible choices for who Dick Datchery really is, seven possible choices for who the murderer is, and twenty-one possible combinations of lovers to sing a duet, which makes for something like seven hundred different permutations of endings.

At first, the actors may have thought, "There's no way this can work, there's no way I can learn all these options." Then they seem to get into the challenge of it. It is an unusual show in that when an actor sets off for work, he or she really has no idea if, come the end of the show, they will have a featured extra solo that night.

I did the orchestrations for all of this as well, which meant six hundred pages for twenty-six musicians. Even now, I have a hard time looking at the full orchestrations without getting, actually, a little ill. I never got the joy of watching the early rehearsals because I was just entrenched with the orchestrations. I made a total of 120 million notes. If you ever said to yourself, "I think I'll get blank paper and just make 120 million little dots on it," not even saying that the dots have to mean anything or be in the right places, you'd then say, "I can't do this."

Two of the votes are applause and one is actually counted, and that evolved from our experience with the audience. The vote for Datchery could be by applause, which was simpler, because it was a good way to start easing people into this voting notion and it wouldn't kill the suspense if people knew who the winner of that was.

But we did feel that if the audience immediately knew who the murderer was, if they all raised their hands at the same time to vote, then that's it, they're sitting out the next fifteen minutes with an outcome they already know. So we tried to figure a way that the vote could be done honestly, and yet at the same time keep the audience in suspense as to who done it. What we came up with was the idea of dividing the audience into districts, like an electoral college. That way, you could see how the people within a few rows of you were voting, but it would be very hard to monitor who all the other districts were voting for.

Still, I was worried that the audiences would always vote for the same people, so I wrote an option, which we never had to use, in which the Chairman says that certain cast members have been bringing in relatives to rig the voting, and to override this, we would be employing a wheel of fortune to determine the murderer.

Picking the lovers for the duet was applause again, because by that time it's just a kind of silly popularity contest. I don't know any choice of lovers that was ever sensible; in the entire run of the show in New York, I don't think we ever had Jasper and Rosa as the lovers, and that was the duet I always wanted to hear.

But by time, the audience is in an aren't-we-rascals mood— they're trying to see whether they can throw us a curve and choose the most oddball combination. We had some very perverse ones. One time they actually did choose the brother and sister, thinking that there would be no way to cover that. But I'd written some lines just in case incest occurred on Broadway. It was not Tennessee Williams–level incest, though.

When I first proposed the voting to Joe, he grilled me on the idea in an amicable way: Did I really think it could work? I was blithely unaware that anyone was worried. Then, the first night at Central Park, he turned to me and said, "It works." And I looked at him in absolute shock. Suddenly the horror hit me that maybe no one had believed that it would. And it had never occurred to me that it wouldn't. And I said, "You mean you had doubts?"

WILFORD LEACH I thought the multiple endings was a great idea, the thing that was going to sell the show. Joe thought it was not a good idea. He said one day, "You have to have one." But it was like not liking pirates in *Pirates of Penzance*, he didn't hold to it.

The only problem we ever had with the endings was that people wouldn't believe it was true. People were absolutely convinced it was rigged. And we spent a lot of time trying to dispel that because, like the critics, people are basically very skeptical and distrustful.

Just saying it doesn't convince anybody. No matter how much you say it, they look for an angle that they will believe. They really felt they were supposed to vote a certain way or that there was a correct answer. We'd say over and over, "It's not a guessing game, it's not like Agatha Christie, your guess is as good as anybody's." But they found it hard to accept that fact.

JOSEPH PAPP The idea of moving a show to Broadway is very important for me. We have no income, outside of money we try to raise, other than money coming in from shows that have some degree of success. We have to have a hit now and then, we have to have a show that brings in revenue, and it's very seldom you get close enough to even be in the game.

I took a chance taking *The Mystery of Edwin Drood* to Broadway because the reviews were not great, they were mixed. There was a lot of money involved in that move, $1.2 million, so I made the decision with great hesitancy.

I thought we had a chance because there were very few musicals on

Broadway at the time, and I was proven right, thank god, but I was worried as shit. We at least returned our investment, barely made a little money, and we won five Tonys, including Best Musical. All my prognostications happened to work out, but I was walking on a tightrope. It was an awfully risky thing.

34

Aunt Dan and Lemon
1985

Kathryn Pogson and
Linda Hunt
© Donald Cooper

Not merely the most important play of the current New York theater season, *Aunt Dan and Lemon* is destined to become a classic. It's a profound reflection of the age and style we live in, the most important American play of the Reagan era.

Aunt Dan and Lemon may also become our decade's most controversial play. Audiences exit enraged, cursing, perplexed, in shock and—most significantly—full of self-doubt and self-analysis.

And yet initially those same audiences are greeted with a charming Old World grace. From the stage, a lovely young woman nicknamed "Lemon" welcomes all: "Hello, dear audience, dear good people who have taken yourselves out for a special treat, a night at the theater . . . If everyone were just like you, perhaps the world would be nice again, perhaps we would all be happy again."

What a charming invitation!

Lemon informs all how ill she is, surviving on strange juices, forced into a reclusive existence. But Lemon is so matter-of-fact, so full of courage and empty of self-pity, so tender and shy that our sympathies go out to her. She tells how her deceased parents left a small inheritance. Now she rarely ventures outside except for visits to doctors.

"Lately I've been reading about the Nazi killing of the Jews," Lemon says, somewhat shyly, as if embarrassed at having so little in her life worth discussing. So she talks about what she read, describing the style of death at the Treblinka concentration camp . . .

Lemon continues—sanely, logically, sweetly—to recite how the Nazis' treatment of Jews resembles our society's treatment of criminals, communists, cockroaches. We are not so very different from Nazis, she points out, except that "they observed themselves extremely frankly in the act of killing."

We, on the other hand, prefer that our killing be done in secret. Let the Contras do it. Or the CIA. Or the Marines.

"It's easy to say we should all be loving and sweet," concludes Lemon, "but meanwhile we're enjoying a certain way of life—and we're actually *living*—due to the existence of certain other people who are willing to take the job of killing on their own backs."

Richard Stayton, *Los Angeles Herald Examiner*, March 16, 1986

Along with the discomfort, there is a lot of mordant laughter. Much of it is provided by the character known as Aunt Dan (Linda Hunt), a friend of Lemon's parents who, during the Vietnam 60s, was the principal influence on the youthful heroine. A brilliant, American-born Oxford don, Dan (for Danielle) is obsessed with defending the honor of Henry Kissinger. As she explains to Lemon at bedtime each night, Mr. Kissinger was a "prayerful" man offering "the entire world the hope of a safe and decent future" even as he was thwarted by "filthy, slimy" journalists and "young intellectuals who studied economics at the Sorbonne or Berkeley." . . .

In this play's case, Dan's pro-Kissinger arguments are warped and expanded in her acolyte's subsequent rationalizations of Nazi Germany. But Mr. Shawn goes further still, refusing to settle for blaming Lemon's callous convictions entirely on the political ideology she inherits from Aunt Dan. As we gradually learn, Dan instructed the young Lemon not just in public policy but also in private morality, regaling her with reminiscences of her wild salad days as an Oxford student. Most of these reminiscences center on Mindy—a high-priced prostitute who gleefully murders a client and whom Dan regarded as "the most exciting person she ever met."

Mindy's amoral escapades—approvingly recounted by Dan and presented voyeuristically on stage in sexually graphic, hallucinatory fragments—are the ultimate dramatizations of what Mr. Shawn regards as the rot eating away at a supposedly civilized world.

Frank Rich, *New York Times*, October 29, 1985

....

WALLACE SHAWN In the 1974–75 season, the Manhattan Project was more or less in residence at the Public Theater, and it came to pass, after three years of rehearsal, they were actually going to do a play of mine in January of 1975. Shortly after *Our Late Night* opened, I met Joe on the corner of Lafayette Street and Astor Place. He asked me what I was doing, and I said I'd been working in the garment district as a shipping clerk, which I had been for the previous six months. He asked what they paid me, and I believe it was $125 a week. He said, "I will pay you that to work on another play."

This was a thrilling act on Joe's part, and one that was enormously important to me at that moment. I started writing plays in 1967, and during those eight years until that play opened in 1975, I had had the fantasy that the theater was this real world that you could enter and be part of. And if you were to be so lucky as to succeed in breaking into the real professional theater, that was comparable in some way to passing the bar and becoming a lawyer, in the sense that you would then be a member of a profession that would have its own dignity and would actually pay you some kind of living.

It was really only when my play opened that I think I actually understood that there was no theater, that theater is a hobby and an amateur activity, something that certain people who have a certain character defect enjoy doing together, for pleasure. It isn't really an institution in American society, as I had imagined it to be.

I was very downcast by that realization, and Joe's offering me money at that very moment sort of renewed my hopes in a certain way. It was very flattering and delightful that this sort of optimistic man would meet me on the street and show his enthusiasm in that way.

JOSEPH PAPP   I ran into Wally walking down the street and I said to him, "Wally Shawn—what do you do for a living?"

"I'm working in the garment center, carrying things."

"How much are you making a week?"

"A hundred dollars."

"Quit your job," I said. "I'm giving you $100 a week. You just write. You have no obligation to me. Write for yourself."

"Are you serious?" he said.

"*Quit your job,*" I said. "*Quit—your—job!*"

What I figured was, here's an interesting writer, and $100 a week is nothing to get this guy to write. It would be great if he wrote a play, and if he did, in all likelihood he'd ask me to produce it. But even if he didn't, even if he never wrote a play, I thought, "This is what I do." And he gave up his job.

Wally is one of a kind. When he has to write a play, he groans, but he has an extraordinary mind and a high moral sense. He writes with powerful, inexorable logic, and he's devastatingly truthful without saying, "I'm going to be truthful." I don't think it's a conscious thing on his part, that's just the way he is, he has that morality in his being.

WALLACE SHAWN   In *Aunt Dan and Lemon*, the author's point of view is hidden, and that means that, inevitably, there are going to be a certain percentage of people in the audience who are not going to get it. *Aunt Dan* ends with a monologue from the narrator which defends Nazism and fascistic ideas, and many people were afraid that perhaps some of the less quick-witted members of the audience would take this to be the author's own opinion—perhaps people would think that the man who wrote the play was a fascist, or even that Joe Papp himself had put on this play in order to defend Hitlerism. A lot of people are not used to the idea that the narrator of a play should be looked upon with suspicion.

Obviously, the way the last scene was acted, and presented by the director, could have provided the audience with a number of clues to elucidate unmistakably that the person saying these things was intended to represent someone that the writer, director, and producer all despised. There are many ways that it could have crudely pointed out that they didn't share the ideas she was espousing. And that would have saved Joe from some headaches, conceivably.

But that also would have been harmful to the intention of the play, which is to confront the audience rather brutally with these ideas, to raise the possibility that in fact this girl is speaking for them, to raise the very definite question in each person's mind of whether or not they themselves actually share some of these thoughts.

The intention of the play is to leave the audience unsatisfied rather than satisfied, to create an anxiety and an uncertainty which is dispelled if you just look at Lemon as a nutcase. And Joe absolutely encouraged us to be fearless and take this as far as it would go, to the effect that the actress did sell her message to the audience as convincingly as possible. All his advice was in the direction of making the play more alarming and dangerous and disturbing.

Of course, I myself believe that the things she's saying are actually things that America lives by, whether the members of the audience like to face it or not. The play, to put it crudely, alludes to the fact that even though we as nice American liberals don't believe in brutal ideas, we still live off of brutal actions, and our high standard of living is defended by us and was acquired by us through brutal actions stretching all the way back to the massacre of the Indians. What is the poor liberal supposed to do? The play provides these disturbing questions, and it would not raise them very successfully if the author leapt in and provided the answers.

JOSEPH PAPP When I first read that play, I thought, "That son of a bitch Wally Shawn has turned Fascist. This sounds like one of the most anti-Semitic plays I've ever read." And I was furious at him. I said, "How can he say those things?"

But when I reread the play, I said, "Oh." This young woman is so interesting, so attractive, that the natural tendency was to accept her as someone you're supposed to like. And this other woman, Aunt Dan, was so impressive and Lemon's mother was so weak in her arguments. I felt, "The liberal argument is so weak—where is it? You're giving all the other people all the big words to say and all the power." But I realized that Wally was saying that the liberal argument is weak. It's more hypothetical, more intellectual, it doesn't have any real strength in it. To believe in it, you really have to think for yourself.

WALLACE SHAWN The play was done first in England, at the Royal Court Theatre under Max Stafford-Clark's direction, mainly because I wanted it done in England first. I had never had a good experience with an American audience up until that point. In every case, the audience had hated the play; enormous numbers of people had walked out of all my plays as they had been performed at the Public Theater. People had booed, and so on.

In contrast to that, I'd had some wonderful experiences having my plays done in England. The audiences understood them and seemed to like them very much. So I thought, "Why don't we begin in England? People will probably respond better and the actors will feel confident and then we can take on New York."

LINDA HUNT Wally came to see a production of *Mother Courage* that I was in up at the Boston Shakespeare Company. We saw each other briefly afterward—because I was too exhausted to see anybody for long after four hours of Brecht's finest—and Wally said, "Well, Linda, I have something I really want to talk to you about, but I don't feel that I can yet. I just hope that you're going to be around long enough to talk to you about this at some point."

So there was this mystery. Spring came, and Wally called me up and said, "Well, Linda, I'm ready to talk to you now, and what I have to say to you is that I've been working on this play, for years, really, and even though I haven't been able to talk to you about it, I really have written it for you. It's finished now, and I can talk to you about it."

We met and he gave me a copy of *Aunt Dan and Lemon* and told me that Joe had already made the arrangements with Max Stafford-Clark in London to have it be part of the play exchange between their two theaters. I was a little overwhelmed. You never know you *are* being overwhelmed by Wally until ten minutes later. Then you fall down on the sidewalk and you realize that he's gotten you right between the eyes.

I read the play and I was very confused by it—it seemed like a very mysterious, disturbing piece. I was in a state for having read it, but I couldn't put my finger on why, exactly. Nor could I, after having read it for the first time, have told you the story. I couldn't say, "The play begins and this happens and that happens." I realized that some kind of normal way of reasoning and retaining information had been suspended in the course of reading it, and I thought that was great.

Then Wally turned out to be the most persistent human being, certainly in New York City, I suspect on the face of the earth. A new side of Wally came bounding out, this man who does not take no for an answer. He started to hound me, day in and day out, about when I was going to do it.

There was no doubt in my mind but that I would, but it was a question of many new things happening in my life and how we would fit all of this in. And finally, a year later I suppose it was, we figured out how and when to do it. How to do it not in any large sense, mind you. I'm not sure we ever figured out how to do the play.

It was a very difficult process, working on the play, and it was a very difficult time for me. I had just had my fortieth birthday, I had just bought my own first home in Connecticut and moved into it, my father died, totally unexpectedly, seven weeks later, and three weeks after that I flew off to London to start rehearsals for *Aunt Dan*.

I don't think I ever understood the play. I'm not sure that I do now on all the levels that one would normally feel comfortable understanding a play if one were going to work on it. The territory isn't staked out at all, because there's no character in the play representing the playwright. This is an extraordinary thing that's so seldom done by writers of any sort. Also, the play is so dense in its rigorous moral stance and the amount of language that just comes at you, that it's like trying to swim through a pool of the thickest seaweed you can imagine without anyone saying, "Look, there might be an opening here, or the hint of a path there."

When you're playing to an audience that's deeply confused that way, in a real predicament, an actor's first response is to want to help them. Because they are, for that moment in time, your partner and you're going to sink or swim according to how well they're doing.

But Wally's given you no way to do that; he's given you no recourse at all. He's set the direction and said, "Walk," but there are no maps. You know where you need to wind up at the end, but you have no idea of how you're going to get there. And trying to bring it to life for the first time, there was a great deal of doubt in our minds that it could be done.

In playing Aunt Dan, I felt as though I was turning myself inside out to get at something that I knew had to be in me because I believe that each of us contains everything, that's why it's possible for actors to do the magic that they do. The work of an actor is to find what you have in common with a character, even if you find it through opposites, by saying, "We don't touch here and we don't touch there."

But I kept turning myself inside out to find the corners of Dan in me, and not really knowing where to look for them because I didn't understand the very parameters of Dan. Dan was so complex, and the play so easily can exist on an intellectual and cerebral level, that you fail to make very deep, practical, just simple emotional connections. I feel that I suffered from that inability throughout, and that the production as a whole did. Something on a profound level failed, because I remained feeling that Dan stood there in that corner and I stood in this corner.

For me, personally, it had a lot to do with how many profound calamities and changes I'd been through in my life at that moment, and how in control, or not in control, of my powers I was. I was psychically exhausted and holding off grief with one arm.

Wally was in this kind of Alice in Wonderland position of having written an extraordinary piece, understanding what he had written, but having no idea how to make it into a living, breathing play. In terms of these problems which were so immediate to us, he would have given anything, he would have just chopped off limbs or had rabies shots every day, anything he could think of, to have been of service to us, but in fact, he couldn't.

Max Stafford-Clark is, I still think, probably the greatest theatrical director I've ever worked with. Max invents rehearsals out of the guts of a play. He is wonderful at inventing the tiniest, most specific exercises to put you right on the pulse of something terribly important. You spend two hours like little scientists, drilling right into the center of something in the play, and you come up with pay dirt.

But Max, for one reason or another, was never able to do this with *Aunt Dan and Lemon*, so we kept tapping, tapping, the way you do to see where the studs are in a wall. We were so much like moles in a hole during that rehearsal process. Darkness all around us and so little grasp, seemingly, of how to find the light.

MAX STAFFORD-CLARK That particular production was a strain. Some of the material is quite unpleasant. Embracing that and finding a way through it was a fascinating challenge, but to describe the working method that I use would be a two-hour lecture.

Because there are monologues, the danger of the play is that it would be dramatically inert. And part of the problem in rehearsal that we addressed ourselves to was moving it forward and making direct address to the audience. Direct address to the audience is always tricky to rehearse because no matter how much you rehearse it, you can only really rehearse it for the first time in front of an audience.

LINDA HUNT In New York, you'd have the feeling, instinctively and from the beginning, that people couldn't distance the play from themselves as they had in London. In London you could say, "Really, it's not ours. There are these English characters in it, and there are parallels being drawn to imperialism around the world, but it's basically an American play, isn't it?" So the outrage in London was slightly more self-righteous in tone, while here you just knew from the very beginning that you'd come into the belly of the beast.

Aunt Dan's ravings about Kissinger seemed to elicit extraordinary responses from people, always abusive. People would say, "Oh yeah? You wanna bet?" Sometimes when I launched into the press, there would be a response, too. People would go, "Oh, my god," as though this was just going to be one step too many. How far could this woman go? Too far. And it was as if people had to release some sound. They couldn't just sit there anymore, making faces, whispering to their partner, something had to be released in order for them to just get room to breathe. It was terrifying.

What people most commonly did was just to get up and walk out, loudly, loudly. Or they would start to move around in their seats a lot. They'd make noise with programs, attention-getting devices. When Eli Wallach and Anne Jackson came to see the play, Joe told them, "This is a very difficult play, very controversial. People get up and leave all the time. So much so that the actors were complaining how distracting it is. And they asked me to carpet the stairs, and I did, so now the audience can leave in silence."

WALLACE SHAWN I don't want to exaggerate the extent of this, but in New York the play did meet with a certain amount of misunderstanding, particularly from some of Joe's faithful subscribers, who in many cases wrote grief-stricken letters to Joe accusing him of defending Hitler. Some of the people who were in the audience were themselves refugees from Hitler, people who'd lost their families to Hitler, and here they thought that history was repeating itself and forty years later they were once again hearing praise of Hitler.

That was a situation that was very painful for me, and it was very painful for Joe, and it was a mean and awful thing to do to those people. I wish that they would have somehow known that they shouldn't come to this play.

Because if you don't quite get the play, if you don't understand how the whole thing fits together, and you only see a series of bizarre fragments, then the last speech defending Hitler stands alone and you might well think that it represents the author's viewpoint or the producer's. But Joe wrote some very eloquent statements on my behalf and was very supportive to me all through that.

BILL HART Joe's wanting to be open to the new—to disenfranchised people and dislocated groups and unpopular issues—creates countless misunderstandings. When we were doing *Aunt Dan and Lemon*, some woman came up to him at the opening party and said, "Mr. Papp, why are you producing this anti-Semitic play?" And Papp, who was probably exhausted by such misunderstandings, turned to her and said, "Oh, I'm always looking for good anti-Semitic plays."

LINDA RONSTADT I was enjoying myself watching *Aunt Dan and Lemon* and at some point somebody got up and stalked out, hitting his heels, and afterward I asked Joe, "God, what was that all about?" And he said, "I always like it better if it gets them mad." If it was just so bland that it couldn't even make anyone angry, then it wouldn't be communicating, it wouldn't be having any effect on people. Joe feels that if it gets a person angry, if it's gotten under his skin, then he's succeeded.

LINDA HUNT If you had to point at one person who's kept theater alive in this country in the past quarter of a century, it's Joe. No hesitation, it's Joe. He's been the central person in keeping any sense of purpose, of voyage, of something new yet to be explored.

Joe has been the entrepreneur par excellence, the voodoo man, the magic man, the medicine man who went and found all the people, who played the drum and brought all the folks in from the wilderness and gave them a fire to gather around. He kept bringing people in, bringing people into the circle, and that's his great gift.

Afterword

When Joe Papp died of prostate cancer in 1991 at the age of seventy, it could have been predicted that finding a successor to lead the New York Shakespeare Festival and the Public Theater would have been difficult, and so it proved to be. As Bernard Gersten, Papp's longtime associate and executive producer of Lincoln Center Theater, told the *New York Times*, "It was a near impossible spot to move into. The New York Shakespeare Festival was made in Joe's image. The festival was Joe; Joe was the festival."

Adding to the problem was the particular kind of theater Papp had run for thirty-seven years. Playwright Tony Kushner explained: "People don't get the radicalism of Joe's mission. There was an absolute commitment to a revolutionary relationship between life and art, and a mistrust of anything that compromised that."

Two months before he died, in August 1991, Papp named JoAnne Akalaitis, a highly regarded director and one of the founders of the avant-garde Mabou Mines company, to take his place. While Papp's title remained producer, Akalaitis was appointed artistic director.

Less than two years later, in March 1993, the executive committee of the festival's board asked Akalaitis to resign. She had directed two well-received productions in her tenure, Georg Buchner's *Woyzeck* and John Ford's *'Tis Pity She's a Whore*, but she had not created the kind of atmosphere the board wanted.

Akalaitis's successor was writer/director George C. Wolfe, whose landmark *The Colored Museum* had opened at the Public in 1986. He was one of the New York theater's most highly regarded directors, responsible for staging the Broadway opening of Kushner's *Angels in America*, and the playwright himself said, "If anyone could fill Joseph Papp's shoes, he can."

Wolfe took Papp's title of producer and successfully ran the Public for a decade as he attempted to, in his own words, get the theater to "vibrate with this city's energy and be inclusive in a healthy, non-token way."

Wolfe's accomplishments included the remunerative decision to have the theater itself produce the touring production of Savion Glover's tap-dance extravaganza *Bring in 'Da Noise, Bring in 'Da Funk*. And though his Broadway productions of *The Wild Party* and *On the Town* did not do well, Wolfe brought a wide variety of plays there, including Kushner's *Caroline, or Change*; *Elaine Stritch at Liberty*; Richard Greenberg's *Take Me Out*; and *Topdog/Underdog*, which won a Pulitzer Prize for playwright Suzan-Lori Parks. He also oversaw the 1998 opening of Joe's Pub, an intimate cabaret space at the Public that has been highly successful.

Finally, though, the conflict between running an institution and wanting to return to full-time writing and directing proved insoluble for Wolfe. "The one thing I haven't been able to figure out," he said in announcing his departure, "is how to be a writer and a producer. The Public Theater requires one to be very public, and writing requires one to be very private. You have to be available to the invisible voices that are swirling around you."

In the spring of 2005, Oskar Eustis, a man with considerable connection to and affection for the Public, took over the top spot and the title of artistic director.

The person who had commissioned *Angels in America* when he ran the Eureka Theatre Company in San Francisco, Eustis had auditioned for Papp when he was a young actor. The artistic director of the Trinity Repertory Company in Providence, Rhode Island, since 1993, Eustis had been courted by both the Yale Repertory Theatre and the Mark Taper Forum in Los Angeles, but he told reporters Trinity was the only theater he wanted to be associated with, "with the possible exception of the Public Theater in New York."

"The thing I care about most in the world is new work, particularly new American writing that is socially engaged and represents the diversity of America, and that's what the Public Theater stands for," Eustis said on taking over. "How could I say no?"

One of Eustis's early successes at the Public was Stew's *Passing*

Strange. It had been commissioned by Wolfe but developed by Eustis over a three-year period. The eventual Broadway production was nominated for seven Tonys and won for Best Book of a Musical.

"When this place works best," Eustis said in announcing the theater's fiftieth anniversary season in 2005, "is when as many artists as possible feel they can call it home." So it has been from the beginning and so it continues to be.

Cast of Characters

THEONI ALDREDGE. Costume designer. Fifteen Tony nominations; Tony Award for *Annie, Barnum, La Cage Aux Folles.* Oscar for *The Great Gatsby.*

TOM ALDREDGE. Actor. Five Tony nominations. Films include *Cold Mountain, The Assassination of Jesse James by the Coward Robert Ford.* Television roles include *The Sopranos, Damages.*

JONELLE ALLEN. Actress. Tony nomination for *Two Gentlemen of Verona.* Television roles include *Dr. Quinn, Medicine Woman; ER; Generations.*

AMYAS AMES. Honorary chairman of Lincoln Center for the Performing Arts. Chairman emeritus of New York Philharmonic. Died in 2000.

DAVID AMRAM. Composer, musician, writer. Composer of more than one hundred orchestral and chamber-music works. Film scores include *Splendor in the Grass, The Manchurian Candidate.*

FLORENCE ANGLIN. Actress. Films include *Trading Places, Falling in Love.* Television roles include *Law & Order.*

A. J. ANTOON. Director. First person to be nominated for two Tonys for Best Direction in the same year: *That Championship Season* and *Much Ado About Nothing.* Died in 1992.

MARTIN ARONSTEIN. Lighting designer. Five Tony nominations. Died in 2002.

WILLIAM ATHERTON. Actor. Films include *Ghostbusters, Die Hard, Pelican Brief.* Television roles include *Desperate Housewives; Law & Order; Murder, She Wrote.*

BOB AVIAN. Choreographer. Six Tony nominations; Tony Awards for *A Chorus Line*, *Ballroom*.

THOMAS BABE. Playwright, director. Plays produced in England, Ireland, Canada, Germany, and Holland. Died in 2000.

CLIVE BARNES. Senior drama and dance critic for *New York Post*. Senior consulting editor for *Dance Magazine*. Died in 2008.

RICHARD BENJAMIN. Actor, director. Films include *Deconstructing Harry*, *The Sunshine Boys*, *Portnoy's Complaint*.

TRAZANA BEVERLEY. Actress. Tony Award for *for colored girls who have considered suicide/when the rainbow is enuf*.

DAVID BLACK. Former general manager of New York Shakespeare Festival.

JEFF BLECKNER. Director. Tony nomination for *Sticks and Bones*. Six Emmy nominations; Emmys for *Hill Street Blues*, *Concealed Enemies*. Directors Guild of America Award for *Hill Street Blues*.

JULIE BOVASSO. Actress, director. Films include *Moonstruck*, *Saturday Night Fever*. Died in 1991.

PHOEBE BRAND. Actress. Member of the Group Theatre. Films include *Vanya on 42nd Street*. Died in 2004.

ROSCOE LEE BROWNE. Actor. Tony nomination for *Two Trains Running*. Films include *Babe*, *Super Fly*, *The Liberation of L. B. Jones*. Emmy for *The Cosby Show*. Died in 2007.

MARVIN FELIX CAMILLO. Director. Founder and director of theater group the Family. Died in 1988.

J. D. CANNON. Actor. Films include *Cool Hand Luke*. Television roles include *McCloud*; *Law & Order*; *Murder, She Wrote*. Died in 2005.

PHILIP CAPICE. Producer. Television credits include *Dallas*, *Eight Is Enough*.

MORRIS CARNOVSKY. Actor. Member of the Group Theatre. Films include *The Life of Emile Zola, Rhapsody in Blue, Cyrano de Bergerac.* Died in 1992.

LAMAR CASELLI. Director. TV credits include *Death Valley Days, General Electric College Bowl.* On the emeritus faculty at Loyola Marymount College.

TED CORNELL. Director.

GRETCHEN CRYER. Actress, playwright, lyricist. Collaborations with Nancy Ford include *Anne of Green Gables, The American Girls Revue.*

GRACIELA DANIELE. Choreographer, director, lyricist. Ten Tony nominations, including *Ragtime, Once on This Island, The Pirates of Penzance.*

HERTA DANIS. Fund-raiser.

NICHOLAS DANTE. Playwright. Tony Award for *A Chorus Line.* Died in 1991.

BRAD DAVIS. Actor. Films include *Midnight Express.* Died in 1991.

MERLE DEBUSKEY. Press agent. Retired in 1996 after forty-eight years and more than five hundred shows.

GEORGE DELACORTE. Founder and publisher of Dell Publishing. Died in 1991.

COLLEEN DEWHURST. Actress. President of Actors' Equity. Eight Tony nominations; Tony Awards for *All the Way Home, A Moon for the Misbegotten.* Twelve Emmy nominations; Emmys for *Murphy Brown* (twice), *Those He Left Behind, Between Two Women.* Died in 1991.

CLIFF DE YOUNG. Actor. Television roles include *Sunshine, Alias, Jack and Bobby.* Films include *Suicide Kings.*

CHRISTOPHER DIXON. Filmmaker. Independent consultant in media and entertainment.

ROBERT DOWNEY. Director. Film credits include *Putney Swope, Greaser's Palace, Rittenhouse Square.*

CHARLES DURNING. Actor. Tony Award for *Cat on a Hot Tin Roof*. Screen Actors Guild 2008 Lifetime Achievement Award. Two Oscar nominations. Eight Emmy nominations.

RICHARD DYSART. Actor. Four Emmy nominations and Emmy for *L.A. Law*.

ELDON ELDER. Scenic designer, theatrical consultant. Died in 2000.

NANCY FORD. Composer, playwright. Collaborations with Gretchen Cryer include *Anne of Green Gables*, *The American Girls Revue*.

BOB FOSSE. Director, choreographer. Nine Tony Awards. Three Emmys. Oscar for *Cabaret*. Died in 1987.

GERALD FREEDMAN. Director. Dean of Drama Department at North Carolina School of the Arts.

JOEL FRIEDMAN. Actor and director for more than sixty years.

SYLVIA GASSELL. Actress. Films include *Cruising*. Television roles include *Third Watch*.

ARTHUR GELB. Author, former managing editor of the *New York Times*. Books include *O'Neill* and *City Room*.

BERNARD GERSTEN. Executive producer at Lincoln Center Theater since 1985.

MARY GOLDBERG. Casting director. Film credits include *Amadeus*, *Ragtime*.

CHARLES GORDONE. Playwright. Pulitzer Prize for *No Place to Be Somebody*. Taught at Texas A&M. Died in 1995.

LEE GRANT. Actress, director. Seven Emmy nominations; Emmys for *The Neon Ceiling*, *Peyton Place*. Four Oscar nominations; Oscar for *Shampoo*.

JOHN GUARE. Playwright, lyricist, composer. Works include *Six Degrees of Separation*, *House of Blue Leaves*, *Landscape of the Body*. Six Tony nominations; Tony Award for *Two Gentlemen of Verona*.

CAST OF CHARACTERS

T. EDWARD HAMBLETON. Producer, cofounder of Phoenix Theatre. Tony Award for Lifetime Achievement in 2000. Died in 2005.

MARVIN HAMLISCH. Composer. One of two people (the other is Richard Rodgers) to have won a Tony, Oscar, Emmy, Grammy, and Pulitzer Prize.

DAVID HARE. Playwright, director. Three Tony nominations. Works include *Plenty, Stuff Happens, Via Dolorosa.* Knighted in 1998.

DORIAN HAREWOOD. Actor. Films include *Full Metal Jacket.* Television roles include *Roots: The Next Generations, The Jesse Owens Story.*

BILL HART. Dramaturge, director. Died in 2008.

AUGUST HECKSCHER. Philanthropist; former New York City commissioner of cultural affairs. Six Central Park baseball fields named in his honor. Died in 1997.

RALPH K. HOLMES. Lighting designer. Died in 2005.

RUPERT HOLMES. Author, composer, lyricist. Six Tony nominations; three Tony Awards for *The Mystery of Edwin Drood.*

JOHN PYNCHON HOLMS. Director. Co-author of *Terrorism: Today's Biggest Threat to Freedom.*

LINDA HUNT. Actress. Tony nomination for *End of the World.* Oscar for *The Year of Living Dangerously.* Television roles include *The Practice.*

CARLO IMPERATO. Actor. Television roles include *Fame.*

ANNE JACKSON. Actress. One Tony nomination. Films include *The Shining.* Television roles include *Law & Order, ER.*

BERNARD JACOBS. President of Shubert Organization. Broadway's Royale Theatre renamed in his honor in 2005. Died in 1996.

JAMES EARL JONES. Actor. Tony Awards for *The Great White Hope, Fences.* One Oscar nomination. Eight Emmy nominations; Emmys for *Gabriel's Fire, Heat Wave.*

TOMMY LEE JONES. Actor. Three Oscar nominations; Oscar for *The Fugitive*. Two Emmy nominations; Emmy for *The Executioner's Song*.

WALTER JONES. Actor, director, playwright.

RAUL JULIA. Actor. Four Tony nominations. Posthumous Emmy and Screen Actors Guild Award for *The Burning Season*. Died in 1994.

MADELINE KAHN. Actress. Four Tony nominations; Tony Award for *The Sisters Rosensweig*. Two Oscar nominations. Died in 1999.

ROBERT KAMLOT. Former general manager of New York Shakespeare Festival. General manager of more than forty Broadway shows.

JEROME KASS. Playwright, screenwriter. Tony nomination for *Ballroom*. Emmy nomination for *The Queen of the Stardust Ballroom*.

JAMES KIRKWOOD. Playwright, author. Tony Award for *A Chorus Line*. Novels include *P.S. Your Cat Is Dead*. Died in 1989.

KEVIN KLINE. Actor. Tony Awards for *On the Twentieth Century*, *The Pirates of Penzance*. Films include *A Prairie Home Companion*, *The Pink Panther*, *My Life as a House*. Oscar for *A Fish Called Wanda*.

LARRY KRAMER. Playwright. American Academy of Arts and Letters Award in Literature.

DIANE LANE. Actress. Films include *Unfaithful*, *A Walk on the Moon*, *Must Love Dogs*, *Under the Tuscan Sun*.

WILFORD LEACH. Director, set designer. Former artistic director of New York Shakespeare Festival. Tony Awards for *The Pirates of Penzance*, *The Mystery of Edwin Drood*. Died in 1988.

MING CHO LEE. Scenic designer. Tony Award for *K2*. Co-chair of Design Department at Yale School of Drama.

RHODA LIFSCHUTZ. Joseph Papp's sister.

JOHN LINDSAY. Former mayor of New York City. Died in 2000.

MICHAEL LINDSAY-HOGG. Director. Films include *Object of Beauty, Frankie Starlight*.

SANTO LOQUASTO. Scenic designer, costume designer. Fifteen Tony nominations; Tony Awards for *Grand Hotel, Café Crown, The Cherry Orchard*. Three Oscar nominations.

STANLEY LOWELL. Former deputy mayor of New York City. Trustee of New York Shakespeare Festival. Died in 2005.

GALT MACDERMOT. Composer. Tony Award for *Hair*. Records with the New Pulse Band.

PHILLIP MARTEL. Joseph Papp's brother.

JOHN MAZZOLA. Consultant. Former president and CEO of Lincoln Center for the Performing Arts.

DONNA MCKECHNIE. Actress, dancer. Tony Award for *A Chorus Line*. Cabaret shows include *My Musical Comedy Life, Gypsy in My Soul*.

LuESTHER T. MERTZ. Philanthropist. Died in 1991.

JASON MILLER. Playwright, actor. Pulitzer Prize for *That Championship Season*. Films include *The Exorcist*. Died in 2001.

DAVID MITCHELL. Scenic designer. Seven Tony nominations; Tony Awards for *Annie, Barnum*.

ROBERT MONTGOMERY. Attorney; partner in Paul, Weiss, Rifkind, Wharton & Garrison. Died in 2000.

MICHAEL MORIARTY. Actor. Tony Award for *Find Your Way Home*. Three Emmy nominations for *Law & Order*.

MIKE NICHOLS. Director. Nine Tonys, four Emmys, an Oscar, and a Grammy.

JOHN FORD NOONAN. Playwright, actor. Films include *Flirting with Disaster*, *Adventures in Babysitting*.

TOM O'HORGAN. Director. One Tony nomination. Three Drama Desk Awards for Best Director. Died in 2009.

GAIL MERRIFIELD PAPP. Director of play development for New York Shakespeare Festival; secretary of the board of trustees of the Public Theater.

PEGGY BENNION PAPP. Senior supervising faculty member at Ackerman Institute for the Family. Founder and director of Ackerman's Depression and Gender Project.

ESTELLE PARSONS. Actress. Four Tony nominations. Oscar for *Bonnie and Clyde*.

DANIEL PETRIE. Director. Television credits include *Wild Iris*, *Walter and Henry*. Died in 2004.

SHELLEY PLIMPTON. Actress. Films include *Alice's Restaurant*.

REINALDO POVOD. Playwright. Works include *Cuba and His Teddy Bear*. Died in 1994.

ANTHONY QUINN. Actor. Oscars for *Lust for Life*, *Viva Zapata!* Died in 2001.

DAVID RABE. Playwright, screenwriter. Four Tony nominations; Tony Award for *Sticks and Bones*.

JAMES RADO. Playwright, lyricist, performer. Tony nomination for *Hair*.

GEROME RAGNI. Playwright, lyricist, performer. Tony nomination for *Hair*. Died in 1991.

ELSA RAVEN. Actress. Films include *Titanic*. Television roles include *Wiseguy*.

DENNIS REARDON. Playwright. Head of playwriting program at Indiana University.

ANN KINGSBURY RESCH. Former assistant at New York Shakespeare Festival.

MEIR ZVI RIBALOW. Artistic director of New River Dramatists.

LINDA RONSTADT. Actress, singer. One Tony nomination. Emmy for *Canciones di mi Padre*. Eleven Grammys. Recent albums include *Adieu False Heart*.

GEORGE ROSE. Actor. Five Tony nominations; Tony Awards for *My Fair Lady*, *The Mystery of Edwin Drood*. Died in 1988.

PAUL RUDD. Actor. Associate director of MFA drama program at the New School for Drama.

GERALD SCHOENFELD. Chairman of the Shubert Organization. Broadway's Plymouth Theatre renamed after him in 2005. Died in 2008.

GEORGE C. SCOTT. Actor. Five Tony nominations. Four Oscar nominations; Oscar for *Patton*. Died in 1999.

OZ SCOTT. Director. Extensive work in theater, motion pictures, and television.

NTOZAKE SHANGE. Playwright, author. Tony nomination for *for colored girls who have considered suicide/when the rainbow is enuf*.

MEL SHAPIRO. Director. Distinguished Professor of Theater at UCLA.

APRIL SHAWHAN. Actress, director. Adjunct assistant professor of theater at UCLA.

WALLACE SHAWN. Playwright, actor. Plays include *The Fever*, *The Designated Mourner*. Films include *The Princess Bride*, *Vanya on 42nd Street*, *Kit Kittredge: An American Girl*.

MARTIN SHEEN. Actor. One Tony nomination. Films include *Apocalypse Now*. Nine Emmy nominations; Emmy for *Murphy Brown*.

ED SHERIN. Director, actor. Recipient of the Robert B. Aldrich Award from the Directors Guild of America.

FRED SILVERMAN. Former vice president of programming at CBS. Independent producer, the Fred Silverman Company.

SAMUEL J. SILVERMAN. Attorney at Paul, Weiss, Rifkind, Wharton & Garrison; judge. Died in 2001.

REX SMITH. Actor, singer. Television roles include *Solid Gold*, *Street Hawk*.

PAUL SORVINO. Actor. One Tony nomination. Films include *Mr. 3000*, *Bulworth*, *The Cooler*, *William Shakespeare's Romeo & Juliet*.

JOE SPINELL. Actor. Films include *The Godfather*, *The Godfather II*, *Rocky*, *Maniac*. Died in 1989.

MAX STAFFORD-CLARK. Director. Longest-serving artistic director of the Royal Court Theatre.

JERRY STILLER. Actor. Television roles include *Seinfeld*, *King of Queens*.

MERYL STREEP. Actress. One Tony nomination. Fifteen Oscar nominations, the most for any actor or actress; Oscars for *Kramer vs. Kramer*, *Sophie's Choice*.

ELIZABETH SWADOS. Playwright, director, composer, musician, author of three novels, two nonfiction books, and nine children's books. Five Tony nominations.

ROSEMARIE TICHLER. Casting director. Teaches at Juilliard and Tisch Institute of Performing Arts. Co-author of *Actors at Work*.

GLADYS VAUGHAN. Director. Died in 1988.

STUART VAUGHAN. Director of more than forty New York productions. Author of *Directing Plays: A Working Pro's Method*.

ROBERT F. WAGNER. Former mayor of New York City. Died in 1991.

CHRISTOPHER WALKEN.   Actor. Tony nomination for *James Joyce's The Dead*. Oscar for *The Deer Hunter*.

SAM WATERSTON.   Actor. One Tony nomination. One Oscar nomination. Eight Emmy nominations. Television roles include *Law & Order*.

ROBERT WHITEHEAD.   Producer. Tony Awards for *A Man for All Seasons*, *Death of a Salesman*, *Master Class*. Tony for Special Lifetime Achievement in 2002. Died in 2002.

KATHLEEN WIDDOES.   Actress. Four daytime Emmy nominations for *As the World Turns*.

ROBERT WOODRUFF.   Director. Artistic director of the American Repertory Theatre.

MARY WORONOV.   Actress. Films include *Rock 'n' Roll High School*, *Eating Raoul*, *Scenes from the Class Struggle in Beverly Hills*.

CRAIG ZADAN.   Director, producer. Credits include *Chicago*, *Hairspray*. Cofounder of Storyline Entertainment.

Acknowledgments

The story is told of an old man sitting on the curb on a busy street corner and crying. When asked by a passerby what the trouble was, the man replied through tears, "I have a beautiful young wife, she loves me very much, and our house is a stunning showplace." Somewhat perplexed, the passerby asked what there was to cry about. The answer: "I can't remember where I live."

That old man is not me, but I sympathize with his predicament. I owe serious thanks to numerous individuals, but because most of the research and writing of this book took place more than twenty years ago, I no longer remember the names of many of the people—the assistants, the go-betweens, the facilitators, the intrepid woman who turned hundreds of hours of tape recordings into thousands of pages of transcript—who were essential in setting up the interviews and making this book happen. You know who you are, and you have my gratitude.

Easier to remember are the more than 160 people who agreed to be interviewed for the book and who invariably told their stories with candor and verve. Not all of them made it into the final draft, but their contributions were invaluable. Without them, it doesn't need to be said, there would be no book.

I am especially grateful to Joe Papp, who had the idea for this project and was zealous about contacting the people in his life and encouraging them to participate. For someone who cared more about the future than the past, he was extremely generous with his time and his thoughts. The same holds true for the people closest to Joe, especially his wife, Gail, the Shakespeare Festival's director of play development. A special shout-out has to go to Joe's long-time personal assistant, Emmett Foster, and to Serge Mogilat, the festival's indefatigable and impeccably organized archivist, who made the research trains run on time.

The one part of the project that was put together recently was collecting the book's numerous photographs, which had to be first located and then reproduced and licensed—no small tasks. Special thanks go to Louise Martzinek, my guide to the photography at the Billy Rose Theatre Collection at the New York Public Library for the Performing Arts, where the Shakespeare Festival/Public Theater archives are held. Without the patient assistance of Louise and the library staff, I would have been lost. Thanks also go to Thomas Lisanti, the NYPL's manager of photographic services and permissions, who oversaw the creation of digital copies of many of the images.

Speaking of images, I'm especially grateful to the photographers who took these present-at-the-creation pictures and gracefully allowed their work to be used.

These (and their associates) include Martha Swope, George E. Joseph (Loretta Joseph), Ken Regan (Kelly Clark), Frederick Ohringer, Dan McCoy (Coco McCoy), Donald Cooper, Benedict J. Fernandez (Siiri Fernandez), and Susan Cook and Carol Rosegg. I should also acknowledge Leo Friedman, Joseph Abeles, and Sy Friedman of Friedman/Abeles, whose work is the core of the NYPL collection.

Also essential were the organizations that controlled rights to images. Thanks go to Nancy Matherson and Marcia Hoffman at Getty Images, Dilcia Johnson at Corbis, Cornelia Schnall at Landov, David Lombard at the CBS Photo Archives, Pamela Madsen and Frederick Woodbridge Wilson at the Houghton Library's Harvard Theater Collection, and, at my own *Los Angeles Times*, Robin Mayper and Erica Varela.

Other people involved with illustrations were Frank Vlastnik, who pointed me in the right direction, Lisa Bagley and Lindsay Galin of the Hearst Corporation, and Richard Workman of the University of Texas' Harry Ransom Center, all of whom helped with *New York Journal-American* issues; Anh Stack of Black Star; and Dennis Reardon, who came up with crucial last minute help on *"The Happiness Cage."*

Not all photo research led to a picture being in the book, but the work of trying to make things happen in a losing cause was just as daunting. Among those helpful in that way were Carla Pinza, Shelley Wanger, Berta Serrano, Duane Michals, Keith Stern, Ralph Blumenthal, Leo Friedman, and Christina Benson.

Two people whose influence on this book is invisible but essential need to be mentioned. Peter Osnos, founder and editor at large of Public-Affairs, was a champion of *Free for All* during its years in the wilderness when few others cared, and that will always be appreciated.

Then there was Stephen Rubin, now executive vice president and publisher-at-large at Random House. He was the editor who helped get my book career started decades ago when he purchased *Call Me Anna: The Autobiography of Patty Duke* at Bantam, and he purchased this one as well when he was president and publisher of the Doubleday Broadway Group. Without his energy and passion, who knows what would have happened?

Far from invisible, and in fact the key person in molding the final book, was my peerless editor at Doubleday, Gerald Howard, whose ability to see both the forest and the trees deftly maneuvered this manuscript to safe waters. Also invaluable for taking care of all matters great and small was assistant editor Katie Halleron.

I also want to say a word about the friends associated with the places the book came together. Delia Ephron and Jerome Kass were the ears that took it all in during the years of trips to New York to try and get it done. Robin Swicord and Nick Kazan own the house in Vashon where key parts of the work was done, and Elizabeth Freeman and her house in Kauai had a more crucial part in the book coming back to life than she realizes.

Special thanks must go to the MacDowell Colony, and to the individuals—Michael Chabon, Ayelet Waldman, and A. Scott Berg—who not only convinced me to go there but helped me gain admittance. Without the luxury of the solitude MacDowell provided at a key juncture, without the gift of this very special place to work, my thoughts about the book and the book itself would have had a very different shape.

Three people have stuck with *Free for All* from the very beginning, surviving all its labyrinthine twists and turns. My agent Kathy Robbins made the original deal and stuck by it, never making me feel foolish for persevering. And Gail Merrifield Papp proved to be an invaluable reader and sounding board, the person whose passion for the project was invaluable.

As for my wife, Patty Williams, the source of all that's good in my life, she helped at all times and in all ways. Even after all these years, words fail me.

Index

(Page numbers in italics indicate photographs)